Food Theory and Applications

Food Theory and Applications

Edited by
PAULINE C. PAUL
and
HELEN H. PALMER

John Wiley & Sons, Inc.
New York · London · Sydney · Toronto

The Contributors

Marion Bennion
Department of Food Science and Nutrition
Brigham Young University
Provo, Utah

Jane Bowers
Department of Foods and Nutrition
Kansas State University
Manhattan, Kansas

Ada Marie Campbell
Department of Food Science and Institution Administration
University of Tennessee
Knoxville, Tennessee

Helen Charley
School of Home Economics
Oregon State University
Corvallis, Oregon

Dorothy L. Harrison
Department of Foods and Nutrition
Kansas State University
Manhattan, Kansas

Marion Jacobson
College of Home Economics
Washington State University
Pullman, Washington

Elizabeth M. Osman
Department of Home Economics
The University of Iowa
Iowa City, Iowa

Helen H. Palmer
Western Regional Research Laboratory
Albany, California

Mary S. Palumbo
Wyndmoor, Pennsylvania

Pauline C. Paul
Department of Food and Nutrition
University of Nebraska
Lincoln, Nebraska

To the memory of the late Miss Belle Lowe, a pioneer in the application of scientific principles to experimental food studies.

Preface

For many years *Experimental Cookery* by the late Belle Lowe has made a unique contribution as a college textbook and as a reference for students, research workers, and food processors who need to understand the properties of basic food materials and the processes by which these materials are prepared for consumption. The uniqueness derived partly from the breadth of coverage and the level of presentation of the subject matter, and partly from the emphasis on the properties and processes of importance to persons concerned with the preparation of the final product for consumption.

The need for a revision of the last edition of Belle Lowe's book has been widely recognized. Since 1955, fundamental knowledge of the important components of food materials, and of the physical and chemical systems characteristic of food products, has expanded greatly. Changes in production and processing practices, in many instances, have altered the properties of food materials commonly used in food preparation.

As the present volume developed, it became obvious that the necessary changes went far beyond those usually envisioned in the preparation of a new edition. Thus this new book is called *Food Theory and Applications*. However, the aims of this volume remain essentially the same as the ones Belle Lowe listed in her fourth edition: to present the chemical and physical basis of food preparation in a form suitable for use as a textbook in college and university courses, to provide a reference source for research studies on food materials and processes, and to introduce the student to the literature related to food-preparation problems.

Recently, much better understanding of the structure and properties of basic food materials has developed from studies in many scientific fields. These studies underline the necessity for a greatly increased understanding of the chemistry, physics, and physical chemistry of food materials and the processes used in preparing them for consumption. Toward this end, brief resumes are included on the role of energy in food preparation, the current theories of the structure and organization of the protein macromolecule, the unique properties of water, and similar factors that influence the properties and reactions of food materials.

Multiple authorship brings to each subject area a wealth of specialized knowledge and experience. It also gives a concrete demonstration of the wide variety of orientations and approaches to food-preparation problems. These differing approaches illustrate the many viewpoints possible and usually desirable in a scientific study of complex food materials and the alterations they undergo during preparation for consumption. The reader is also challenged to select the ideas and procedures appropriate to a given situation.

The previous book, *Experimental Cookery*, recognized the significance of practices in agricultural production and commercial processing but considered them in less detail than we do here. Since there is a constant trend toward more prepreparation of food materials, we give more attention to these phases. The term "food preparation" is used in a general sense to include all the steps between production of raw material and consumption of the finished product. Parts of the total process may occur in the field, in storage, during transportation, or in the food-processing factory, as well as in the institutional or home kitchen. However, it is impossible for us to give adequate coverage to all these phases. Therefore, the major emphasis is on final preparation steps. Some areas —for example, microbiological problems—have been omitted entirely.

Furthermore, it is impossible for one volume to summarize (or even refer to) all the literature relating to food preparation. Review articles or books are available for many individual topics. References to the topics that are most pertinent have been included. Journal article citations were selected to illustrate particular issues, to offer a starting point for further literature search on a given topic, and to give some concept of the wide range of materials available as to both fields of study and geographical location of workers engaged in these studies. We hope that students will be encouraged to study and evaluate original papers, including the ones cited and many others referred to in the literature.

It seemed wise to discontinue the detailed instructions for laboratory procedures. Variations in laboratory facilities and equipment available, and in the research interests of the departments where advanced foods courses are given, cause great differences in the types of laboratory work appropriate in given situations.

We thank the many people who have helped in the preparation of the manuscript. Also we thank our colleagues, students, and teachers for their generous assistance and understanding. But, most of all, we acknowledge the inspiration provided by Belle Lowe.

Contents

Food Theory and Applications

CHAPTER 1

Basic Scientific Principles, Sugars, and Browning Reactions

PAULINE C. PAUL

All foods are chemical compounds and undergo various chemical reactions in progress from production to consumption. In order to understand these reactions and their effects on the final outcome, it is necessary to utilize the basic laws of chemistry. Many of the processes employed in preparing foods involve physical changes, so knowledge of some of the laws of physics is also necessary. In order to properly orient those who study the science of food preparation, a brief review of those principles of physics and chemistry of most importance in food preparation is advisable. This is not intended to be exhaustive, so texts in these fields should be consulted as necessary for fuller treatment.

MATTER

Matter can exist in three states—*gas, liquid,* or *solid.* In general, as the temperature is raised, a pure substance will change from solid to a liquid, and then to a gas, without change in chemical composition. However, many organic compounds will decompose, undergoing various chemical reactions rather than a change of state, with increasing temperature. Thus ethyl alcohol, C_2H_5OH, is liquid at room temperature, changes to a solid at $-117.6°$ C, and becomes a gas at $77.8°$ C. Glucose, $C_6H_{12}O_6$, a polyhydric alcohol, is solid at room temperature, changes to a liquid (melts) at $148–150°$ C, and decomposes at slightly higher temperatures. Starch, $(C_6H_{10}O_5)n$, a polymer of glucose, is also solid at room temperature, but decomposes rather than liquefying when heated.

1

Properties of Matter

All matter has certain properties of importance in food studies. *Density* is the mass per unit volume. More frequently used in food research is *specific gravity,* the ratio of the weight of a given volume to the weight of an equal volume of water at the same temperature and pressure. *Adhesion* is the attractive force between unlike molecules, and *cohesion* is the force of attraction between molecules of the same kind. All foods are made up of molecules, and the molecules of atoms. These molecules often undergo chemical change in food preparation, and the reactions obey the laws of thermodynamics. Where the appropriate data can be obtained, energy changes and reaction rates can be calculated. However, due to the complexity of food materials and the fact that usually they are undergoing physical as well as chemical changes, the identification of the specific compounds involved, the reactions occurring, and the energy changes involved has not been possible to date. In this respect there is a great deal to learn about food materials.

Gases

In a gas, the molecules are free and in a constant state of motion. The gas laws are summarized in the equation

$$PV = nRT$$

where P, V, and T represent *pressure, volume,* and absolute *temperature* on the Kelvin scale, n is Avogadro's number, and R is the gas constant. This equation indicates the relationship among pressure, volume, and temperature, since n and R are constants. Thus, as temperature is changed, either (or both) volume and pressure will change also.

The equation above is for a so-called perfect or ideal gas. However, real gases show deviations from this law. A Dutch chemist, van der Waals, attributed these deviations to two factors: (1) the volume occupied by the molecules making up the gas and (2) the attractive forces between these molecules. Although the volume of the gas molecules is negligible in relation to the total volume of the gas at ordinary temperatures and pressures, at high pressure the total volume is small, so the volume of the molecules will form an appreciable part of the whole. The attraction of the molecules for each other is demonstrated by the tendency of all gases to condense at temperatures sufficiently low to allow these forces to overcome the kinetic energy of the molecules. These forces (called *van der Waals forces*) are considered to arise from nonspecific attractions between two atoms as they approach each other, due to induced dipoles caused by this nearness. In very close proximity, the attractions change to repulsive forces due to the overlapping of the outer electron shells of the atoms. These attraction and repulsion forces are balanced at a distance specific for each size of atom, and at the balance point can act as a weak bond between atoms. The van der Waals bonding force varies with the size of the atom, but for average size atoms is about 1 kcal/mol (Watson, 1965). This is just slightly more than the average thermal energy of molecules at room temperature (0.6 kcal/mol), so it takes several van der Waals bonds between atoms within 2 molecules to supply enough energy to overcome the dissociating tendency of random thermal motion.

Liquids

As a gas is cooled, the motion of the molecules decreases, and the gas condenses to a smaller volume and changes to the liquid state. The molecules of a liquid are still in motion, but at a much slower rate than in the gaseous state. Since the molecules are closer together, they are attracted to each other by van der Waals forces, but also repelled by compression of the molecules. The balance between these forces gives a liquid a degree of structure not found in a gas.

Liquids have a distinct bounding surface. Since the molecules of the liquid are in motion, there is a tendency for molecules to escape from the surface and to return to it. Increasing the temperature increases the rate of motion, and therefore increases the rate of escape and return. At any given temperature, in a closed system, the two tendencies will be in balance, and the pressure in the vapor phase is the *vapor pressure* at the temperature.

The molecules of a liquid are attracted to one another by cohesive forces. Within the body of the liquid, these forces will be in balance, any given molecule being equally attracted in all directions. But at the surface, the attractive forces will be unequal, as illustrated in Figure 1, since the molecules in the vapor phase are much farther apart than in the liquid. In general, the magnitude of attractive or repulsive forces

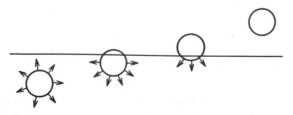

FIGURE 1. A diagrammatic representation of attraction of liquid molecules for other molecules in the liquid. From B. Lowe, *Experimental Cookery*, 4th ed., Wiley, New York, p. 11.

varies with the square of the distance between the molecules, so increasing the distance decreases the force rapidly. This inequality of forces in the surface produces the *surface tension,* a measurable quantity characteristic for each liquid under a given set of conditions. To increase the area of the surface by bringing more molecules into it requires work to overcome the unequal attraction, so the minimum surface area represents the minimum potential energy. Surface tension is the term used for the energy of the interface between a gas and a liquid, while *interfacial tension* is used when the boundary is between two immiscible liquids.

The *viscosity* of a liquid is often of great importance in determining the characteristics of a food product. Viscosity is a measure of the internal friction between adjacent layers of a liquid, and can be considered to be the resistance of the liquid to flow. Viscosity is usually measured by flow rate through a circular tube, and the equation for the coefficient of viscosity is

$$\eta = \frac{\pi P R^4}{8l} x \text{ (time/unit volume of flow)}$$

where η is the coefficient of viscosity, R is the radius of the tube, and l is its length. In practice, viscosity of a liquid is often measured by comparison to a standard or reference liquid. In this case, the equation becomes

$$\frac{\eta_1}{\eta_2} = \frac{\varrho_1 t_1}{\varrho_2 t_2}$$

where η_1, ϱ_1, and t_1 are the coefficient of viscosity, density, and time of flow for the test liquid, and η_2, ϱ_2, and t_2 are the corresponding quantities for the reference liquid. Values for η and ϱ of a number of reference liquids are given in handbooks of chemical data; t_1, t_2, and ϱ_1 are measured, and these data permit the calculation of η_1.

Solids

Cooling a liquid decreases the motion of the molecules still further. When the temperature is reduced sufficiently, another change of state occurs, and the liquid becomes a solid. The characteristic feature of a solid is structure. In a *crystalline* solid, the molecules are arranged in an orderly fashion characteristic of the compound. Solids may also be *amorphous,* the arrangement of the molecules being random. In very large molecules such as starches or proteins, parts of the molecule may be in an orderly crystalline arrangement, and other parts in a random, amorphous distribution. In the solid state the molecules are closely packed and confined to a definite space, although each molecule is still in motion within this space.

In ionic compounds such as NaCl, the sodium and chloride exist as ions, with each positive ion surrounded by negative ones, and each negative ion by positive ones. The ions are held together by the attraction of opposite charges. Nonionic compounds such as glucose are held together in the crystalline state by van der Waals forces and hydrogen bonds. The atoms in such molecules are held together by covalent bonds, and the type of packing of the molecules into the space lattice of the crystal depends on the shape and size of the molecules. In general, in solids as in liquids, all molecules tend to assume the order corresponding to occupation of the smallest possible space consistent with the energy balance between the forces of attraction and repulsion, so as to minimize the total free energy of the system.

Some numerical values for properties of gases, liquids, and solids of importance in foods are given in Table 1.

ENERGY

All matter contains *energy,* and any change in a given quantity of matter includes a change in the energy balance of the system. Therefore, study of the energy relations in food materials, and the changes in the energy of the system during preparation, is fundamental to an understanding of why the processes used in food preparation produce the results obtained. Present knowledge in this area is very incomplete, but progress in the basic science of food requires much more attention to the energy aspects.

Forms of Energy

Heat and *mechanical* energy are familiar concepts in food studies. As the temperature of a food material is raised by heating or lowered by cooling, the energy content of the system is being changed. Stirring, beating, whipping, grinding, or otherwise manipulating a food supplies mechanical energy to the system.

Heat Transfer

Methods of heat transfer into and within a food material include *conduction, convection,* and *radiation.* Transfer of heat from the energy source to the food material usually involves some intermediary agency (or agencies) such as the air in the oven; the metal, glass, or ceramic of which the food container is composed; or the water, steam, or oil that may surround the food and/or container. It should be kept in mind that

TABLE 1. Constants for Some Important Food Chemicals

Chemical	Formula	State at Room Temperature (20° C)	Melting Point (°C)	Boiling Point (°C)	Surface Tension (Dynes/cm)	Viscosity (Centipoise)	Solubility in Water (g/100 ml)	Vapor Pressure (20° C)	Density or Specific Gravity
Carbon dioxide	CO_2	Gas	−56.6 at 5.2 atmospheres	−78.5 sublimes			0.355^0 0.145^{25} 0.097^{40} 0.058^{60}		
Water	H_2O	Liquid	0	100	72.75^{20} 75.6^0 58.9^{100}	1.0050^{20} 0.2838^{100}		17.54 mm Hg	1.000^4 liquid 0.999^0 solid 0.917^0
Sodium chloride (common salt)	$NaCl$	Solid	801	1413			35.7^0 39.12^{100}		2.165
Sucrose (sugar)	$C_{12}C_{22}O_{11}$	Solid	186^a	[a]			179^0 487^{100}		1.588^{15}
Sodium bicarbonate (baking soda)	$NaHCO_3$	Solid	$-CO_2$, 270	—			6.9^0 16.4^{60}		2.159– 2.22

TABLE 1. (*continued*)

Chemical	Formula	State at Room Temperature (20° C)	Melting Point (°C)	Boiling Point (°C)	Surface Tension (Dynes/cm)	Viscosity (Centipoise)	Solubility in Water (g/100 ml)	Vapor Pressure (20° C)	Density or Specific Gravity
Acetic acid	CH_3COOH	Liquid	16.6	118.1	27.6^{20}	1.30^{18} 0.43^{100}	∞		$1.049^{20/4}$
Cream of tartar (potassium acid tartrate)	$KHC_4H_4O_6$	Solid	—	—			0.42^{25}		1.954
Starch	$(C_6H_{10}O_5)_n$	Solid	[a]						1.50^{21}
Cottonseed oil		Liquid	+12 to −13						0.917– $0.918^{25/25}$

[a] Decomposes.

both the transfer agent(s) and the food materials themselves vary widely in ability to transfer heat energy. Woodams and Nowrey (1968) give data and sources for thermal conductivity of a wide variety of food materials.

Temperature

While heat is a form of energy, temperature is a measure of the rapidity of motion of the molecules in a system. As the temperature increases, the molecules are moving more vigorously and eventually can separate.

Temperature is a relative quantity, and expresses the intensity or amount of heat energy present. Absolute temperature is proportional to the average kinetic energy of the molecules of which the material is composed, and the zero point of the absolute scale is the point at which molecular motion ceases. It is customary in scientific work to use the centigrade scale, where zero is the transition point of water from solid to liquid, and 100° is the transition point of liquid water to the vapor phase, at standard pressure. The zero point on the centigrade scale corresponds to 273° on the absolute, or Kelvin, scale. The centigrade system is related to the popularly used Fahrenheit scale by the equations

$$C = 5/9(F - 32)$$

and

$$F = 9/5\,C + 32$$

Because of the complexity of many food systems, the changes produced by alteration of temperature frequently vary with the rate of temperature change and/or the differential between the external and internal temperature, as well as the final internal temperature attained. For example, two pieces of meat of the same size and composition, heated to the same internal temperature, will differ widely if one is heated rapidly, the other slowly.

Surface Energy

There are several other forms of energy that are also important in foods. Thus all solid and liquid foods possess surfaces, and surfaces possess energy. Subdividing a solid (as in grinding) or a liquid (as in making an emulsion) increases the surface, thereby increasing the energy content of the system. This additional energy may be supplied by the muscle power of the arm, or by electrical power running a mixer or grinder. Beating a fluid such as egg white to a foam also increases the surface, the necessary energy coming from the beating process.

Electrical Energy

In food preparation, electricity may supply power to operate a mixer, to heat a stove element, or to compress the refrigerant gas in a refrigerator. However, there is another very important aspect of electrical energy. All atoms are made up of equal numbers of *positive* and *negative charges,* the positively charged protons in the nucleus and the negatively charged electrons in various orbital positions around the nucleus. So the molecules of a food can be considered distributions of charged particles in space. Overall, the charge on a molecule is neutral, since there are equal numbers of positive and negative charges. However, in the molecules of which foods are made up, these charges are seldom symmetrically distributed, so there are localized areas with a charge. Each charge generates an *electric field,* and the intensity of this field at any point is the force per unit charge exerted on another charge placed at that point. The electric *potential* of a charged body is the work per unit positive charge done in carrying any charge from the ground (zero potential) up to the charged body, and the *potential difference* between two bodies is the work per unit positive charge done in carrying any charge from one body to the other. While the magnitude of each charge, electric field, and potential from a molecule or segment of molecule is very small, the sum of all charges in a given food material may be of considerable magnitude and may have a significant influence on the reactions and changes that take place in the food during preparation.

Thermodynamics

In studying chemical reactions, energy is usually dealt with in terms of the laws of *thermodynamics,* the study of the flow of energy. The *first law* of thermodynamics is given in general terms as the law of conservation of energy—that energy cannot be created or destroyed. In other words, to increase the energy content of a given system, energy must be supplied from outside the system; while to decrease the total energy, some energy must be given off to the surroundings. In chemical systems, this leads to the two quantities, the *internal energy, E,* and the *enthalpy, H.* The internal energy is the energy stored in a given system, and depends only on the temperature in an ideal case. The enthalpy is the sum of the internal energy plus the product of pressure and volume.

$$H = E + PV$$

In solids and liquids, as the energy of the system is increased or decreased, the changes in enthalpy and internal energy are almost equal, since the volume changes are small. For gases, increasing the temperature increases not only the energy of the individual molecules but also the volume and/or pressure.

The first law of thermodynamics is utilized in the measurement or calculation of the energy (heat) absorbed or given off in chemical reactions. It is also used in the calculation of the energies of chemical bonds, which will be discussed later. However, it does not indicate in which direction a chemical reaction will proceed, that is, it gives no information as to the equilibrium position of the reaction.

The general statement of the *second law* of thermodynamics—that natural processes tend to go to a state of equilibrium at the lowest energy level—can be developed to provide information as to the direction and equilibrium position of chemical reactions. From this law is derived the separation of the enthalpy of a system into *entropy, S,* and *free energy, G,* related to enthalpy by the equation

$$G = H - TS$$

T being absolute temperature. The free energy of a system can be regarded as the part of the total energy that, theoretically, can be used to obtain some useful work or result, while entropy is a probability function of the energy levels available for the arrangement of the atoms within a molecule. For the latter, at equal total energy, the state with more available energy levels has the higher probability and therefore the higher entropy.

Changes in energy may be positive, negative, or zero. Calculations based on these changes can predict the direction of a chemical reaction, and the energy that must be supplied to, or absorbed from, the system in order to produce the desired change.

The *third law* of thermodynamics, that the entropy of all materials at absolute zero is zero, permits the calculation of entropy changes, thus making it possible to determine changes in free energy and in entropy in chemical processes.

Energy Values

Treatment of data gained from experiments, using the equations derived from the laws of thermodynamics, provides the values for the energy that must be supplied to, or dissipated from, a system undergoing a given change. In this context, the *heat of vaporization* is the energy required to change a liquid to a gas, and the *heat of condensation* is the energy evolved when a gas condenses to a liquid. Similarly, the *heat of crystallization* indicates the energy change when a material goes from the liquid to the solid state. Energy changes are also involved in the solution of one substance in another, the *heat of solution,* while *heat of reaction* denotes the energy change in a chemical reaction. Also, by using the laws of thermodynamics it has been possible, with some simple compounds, to calculate the energy values for the bonds holding the atoms together in the molecule.

Bonding Forces

The bonding forces that hold atoms together in molecules, and molecules together in solids and liquids, are of great importance in determining the characteristics of food materials and the changes these materials undergo during preparation. These bonds include the ionic and covalent bonds that join atoms to make up molecules, and the various bonding forces that give structure to liquids and solids. Of the latter, hydrogen bonding and van der Waals forces are especially important in food materials.

Ionic bonds occur where an actual transfer of one or possibly two electrons from one atom to another will give each atom an inert gas configuration (outer electron shell complete). This causes each atom to become an ion, and the ions are held together in the molecule by the coulombic attraction of opposite charges. Purely ionic bonds occur principally among atoms that have one electron in the outer shell, or require one electron to complete the outer shell—for example, sodium and chlorine, to form NaCl.

Covalent bonds involve the sharing of a pair of electrons between two atoms, rather than the transfer of an electron from one to the other, to give all the participating atoms stable configurations. The simplest example of this is the shared pair of electrons in the formation of a molecule of hydrogen, H_2, each hydrogen atom furnishing one electron of the pair. In homonuclear molecules, such as H_2, the electrons are shared equally between two identical nuclei, so the bond is entirely covalent. However, in molecules where the atoms involved are different, the bonding electrons are apt to be more closely associated with one nucleus than with the other, leading to some degree of imbalance in the distribution of the charges, so the bond is partly covalent and partly ionic. Strictly ionic or strictly covalent bonds are the extreme types, the bonds in most molecules being intermediate between these extremes. A continuous series of intermediate types is possible. In considering the unequal sharing of bonding electron pairs between nuclei, the *electronegativity* is used as an index to represent the tendency of bonding electrons to be drawn toward a particular atom. Pauling (1960) gives a table of electronegativities for various elements.

Bonds at the first, or *s* orbital, level have no specific directional properties, since the orbitals project equally in all directions. But the next (*p* orbital) levels are directed in space, leading, for example, to the tetrahedral arrangement of bonds around the carbon atom. This leads to molecular structures with definite configurational properties of great importance in foods work. An example is found in the comparison of such compounds as glucose and galactose, two hexose sugars of identical atomic makeup but differing structural arrangements that result in differences in solubility, sweetness, ease of fermentation, and other characteristics that affect the results obtained in food preparation.

The chemical bonds require energies of the order of tens of kilocalories to break or to cause major rearrangements. Van der Waals forces, described previously, require energies in the range of a few tenths of a kilocalorie for rupture, so they are readily reversible. Between these two extremes in bond energies, there are interactions of intermediate energy value, which tend to produce clusters of molecules, or complexes, by association. A very important interaction of this type in food material is the *hydrogen bond* (H-bond). Sandorfy (1965) states that "Hydrogen bonds are as common in nature as ordinary chemical bonds. . . . There are billions of them in every living organism . . . and they are most important for the basic mechanisms of life."

Pimentel and McClellan (1960) define the H-bond as the bond existing between a proton-donating group (A-H) and an electron donor (B) when (1) there is evidence of association and (2) there is evidence that the new bond linking A-H and B specifically involves the hydrogen atom already bonded to A. Hydrogen bonding may occur between groups within the same molecule, as in proteins, or between different molecules, as in water. The acidic group (proton donor) is usually a carboxyl, hydroxyl, amine, or amide group, all common in food materials. The usual electron donors in foods are oxygen in carbonyls, ethers, and hydroxyls, and nitrogen in amines. The presence of H-bonding may alter the size, shape, and mass of molecules, as well as the electronic configuration of functional groups, since H-bonds are highly directional in nature (Watson, 1965). Hence, H-bonds may have a pronounced effect on physical and chemical properties such as freezing and boiling points, solubility, electrical conductivity, liquid and vapor density, viscosity, structure of crystals and of macromolecules, adsorption, and enzyme activity. Water is strongly H-bonded, intermolecularly. This is of major importance in the scientific study of foods, since almost all foods contain relatively large amounts of water. Murrell (1969) has reviewed current thinking on the hydrogen bond.

WATER

Water is such a common ingredient that its influence on foods and their properties is often neglected. However, an understanding of water and its behavior is essential to any scientific study of food materials. Water is the most nearly universal solvent, and it occurs in large quantities in most food materials. For example, fresh meats, fruits, and vegetables range from about 70 percent to nearly 100 percent water.

Water has a number of unusual properties, and its behavior is quite unlike that of any other liquid, or of compounds of approximately similar composition. Similar compounds from the same class in the periodic table are expected to show a certain degree of regularity in their properties. But Figure 2 shows that the melting and boiling points of hydrogen oxide (water) are quite different from those of the hydrogen compounds of the other members of the oxygen class. On the basis of these data, water should be a gas at room temperature and have a freezing point of around $-100°$ C. Table 2 gives some physical constants for water and for a few other compounds of similar molecular weight.

The unusual characteristics of water are due to the shape of the water

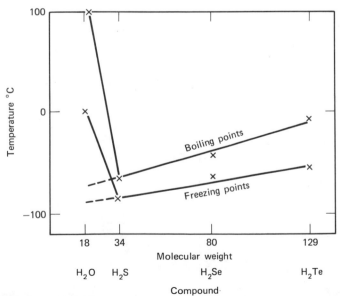

FIGURE 2. Freezing and boiling points of hydrogen compounds in the oxygen class of the periodic table.

TABLE 2. Some Physical Constants of Water and Other Compounds of Similar Molecular Weight

Compound	Formula	Molecular Weight	Melting Point (°C)	Boiling Point (°C)	Density (Liquid) (g/cc)	Viscosity, 20° C	Surface Tension, 20° C	Specific Heat, 15° C
Water	H_2O	18	0	100	0.999^0 1.00^4	1.005	72.75	1.00
Hydrogen sulfide	H_2S	34.08	−82.9	−61.80				0.253
Ammonia	NH_3	17	−78	−33				0.52
Methane	CH_4	16	−184	−160				0.59
Methyl alcohol	CH_3OH	32.04	−97.8	64.7	0.796^{15}	0.596	22.6	0.60

molecule, and its high capacity for forming hydrogen bonds. In the water molecule, the bonds between hydrogen and oxygen lie at an angle, somewhat similar to the tetrahedral bonds of the carbon atom. The angle between the two O-H bonds is calculated to be about 105°, as illustrated in Figure 3. Also shown in Figure 3 is a diagrammatic

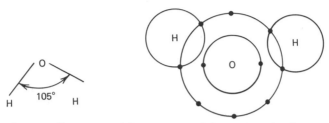

FIGURE 3. Schematic illustrations of the structure of the water molecule.

representation of the equilibrium position of the electrons in a molecule of water. The concentration of the electrons of oxygen on one side of the molecule, and the relatively bare positive nuclei of the hydrogens on the other side, produce an unbalanced distribution of the electric charges, making water a highly polar molecule. H-bonds form between the hydrogens of one molecule and the oxygens of other molecules. Similarly, H-bonds can be formed between water molecules and appropriate groupings in other types of molecules. A more detailed discussion of the characteristics of water will be found in Davis and Day (1961).

Properties

Among the unusual properties of water that influence the character and reactions of food materials are density, freezing point, melting point, specific heat, surface tension, dipole moment, and dielectric constant.

As was indicated earlier, the freezing and boiling points of water are much higher than those of similar compounds. Water exists in all three states of matter (solid, liquid, or gas) within the range of normal environmental temperatures and pressures. These high freezing and boiling points are due to the strength of the H-bonds, since it is necessary to add energy as heat to break these bonds. Water is most dense not in the solid state, but at 4° C. This is why ice floats in cold water. The volume increase as water solidifies is one source of damage to foods preserved by freezing.

The highly polar nature of the water molecule gives it a large *dipole moment.* The dipole moment is a measure of the tendency of a molecule to orient in an electric field with the negative portion of the molecule toward the positive pole, and the positive portion toward the negative pole. The magnitude of the dipole moment is a function of the charge and the distance separating the charges. A compound such as water is a *permanent dipole,* since the polar character is built into the molecule. In a symmetrical molecule that is nonpolar, an *induced dipole* can be produced by the close approach of a strong positive or negative charge that will distort the even distribution of the charges on the nonpolar molecule. These dipoles, both permanent and induced, are another source of attraction between molecules, and can have a considerable influence on the structural organization of molecules in food materials.

Since water has a high dipole moment, the molecules tend to orient themselves so as to neutralize an electric field, giving water an unusually high *dielectric constant.* The dielectric constant is a measure of a substance's ability to neutralize the attraction between electric charges. This high dielectric constant helps to account for the solvent power of water, especially for compounds held together by ionic bonding. For example, when the ionic bond of NaCl is broken in water, the water reduces the attraction between the charges on the Na^+ and Cl^- ions. The tendency of these ions to reassociate is further discouraged by the tendency of water to aggregate around the ions, with the hydrogens of the water oriented toward the negative Cl ion, and the oxygens toward the positive Na ion.

Water also has an unusually high *specific heat.* This is the amount of heat required to raise the temperature of one gram of a substance one degree centigrade. So a material such as dry flour, if heated, will soon start to char, while the same amount of heat energy applied to a mixture of flour and water will raise the temperature of the system only a few degrees. This high specific heat of water is due to the ionic character of the oxygen and hydrogen of the molecule, so that much of the energy is absorbed as increased ionic vibration rather than as increased temperature.

Along with high specific heat, water also has unusually high *latent heats of fusion* and *of vaporization.* These are measures of the energy requirement at the change of state, without any increase in temperature. Thus, while one calorie per gram is required to raise the temperature of water 1° C, 79.7 calories are required to change one gram from solid to liquid at 0° C, and 539.4 calories from liquid to gas at 100° C. Since energy cannot be destroyed or created, but only stored or changed in form, these latent heats represent a storage of energy. Therefore, when steam is used to heat food, if conditions are such that during the heating process the steam condenses to liquid, the energy released by the change of state will also be available to increase the temperature of food material.

With the exception of mercury, water has the highest *surface tension* of any of the commonly occurring liquids. This is due to the strong attraction between water molecules, giving water a high degree of cohesion. Water also exhibits strong adhesion with many other compounds. These forces of surface tension, cohesion, and adhesion have many applications in food problems—in the rate at which water will "wet" a given material, the amount of energy needed to break up and disperse oil droplets to form an oil-in-water emulsion, the role of surface-active agents in lowering the surface tension of water or of salt in raising it, and so on.

Purity

Pure water in the chemical sense is difficult to obtain and to store. Water is such a good solvent that it usually contains some other chemical compounds or ions. Tap water varies widely in its composition, depending on the locality and the source of the water.

Hard water contains the salts of calcium, magnesium, and sometimes iron. Hardness of water may be temporary or permanent. Water containing calcium and magnesium hydrogen carbonates is termed temporary hard water since heating decomposes these salts, forming carbonates that deposit as crusts on the inside of the cooking utensil. Such waters become less hard when boiled. Permanent hard water contains the sulfates of magnesium and calcium, which cannot be removed by boiling. Some water is both temporarily and permanently hard.

Softened water, which is used a great deal at the present time, has the calcium and magnesium replaced by sodium. Distilled water has had most of the chemical impurities removed by boiling the water and condensing the steam. Impurities can also be reduced by the use of ion-exchange resins, yielding deionized water.

One must investigate carefully the type of water being used in food studies, since small amounts of impurities can often materially alter the results obtained. For example, hard water is usually alkaline and may have a significant influence on the color and texture of cooked vegetables. Divalent ions such as Ca^{2+} and Mg^{2+} may react with pectic substances in plant materials, altering the texture. Smardžić et al. (1969) reported that water hardness, especially that due to magnesium, influenced the absorption, extensibility, and viscosity of doughs. Many waters have distinctive flavors that can alter results obtained when solutions are tasted. The term potable water means that the water is safe to drink, not that it is chemically pure.

Roles

Water has a number of very important roles in food studies. It is widely distributed in the food materials themselves. Only a few, such as salt, sugar, and baking powder, can be regarded as practically free of water. Even such concentrated foods as hard candies and dehydrated products contain a small amount of moisture, while a material such as flour usually is 12–14 percent water. Some fresh fruits and vegetables are as high as 97–98 percent water.

Water acts as a heat-transfer medium in many food-preparation procedures, ranging from the use of an ice-salt mixture for freezing ice cream to that of steam under pressure to attain boiling points above 100° C. Water is a very important reaction medium. Physical processes include solution of chemicals such as sugar, baking powder, salt, and hydration of starch, gelatin or gluten. Water is frequently an essential ingredient in chemical reactions such as hydrolysis.

Water often has a major influence on texture, as in maintaining cell turgor in fresh fruits and vegetables or muscle tissue. It is an important factor in the stability of many foods, influencing the storage stability of dehydrated foods, the growth of microorganisms, and the possibility of enzyme activity.

For many years food scientists have searched for a relationship between total moisture content and the juiciness or moistness sensation when a food is eaten. More recently, the theory has been advanced that juiciness or moistness may be related to the activity or availability of the water, rather than to the total amount of water present. Rockland (1957) presents one of the earlier discussions of the methods of determining water activity and the roles this may have in determining food quality, and Labuza (1968) gives some of the later data.

Bound Water

Part of the water in biological materials can be removed fairly readily by pressure or by heat, but some cannot. These two forms are generally referred to as free and bound water.

Bound water is so closely associated with the molecule with which it is combined that it no longer has the characteristics of ordinary water. Some of these changed characteristics are: (a) it no longer acts as a solvent for solutes such as sugar; (b) it has no appreciable vapor pressure; (c) it cannot be frozen except at very low temperatures; (d) it cannot be pressed from the tissue except by use of very high pressure; and (e) it is very dense.

Early studies on bound water utilized techniques of very low temperature and/or very high pressure. More recent studies report use of high-frequency spectroscopy (Hopkins, 1960) and nuclear magnetic resonance (Bratton et al., 1965). Toledo et al. (1968) refer to the difficulty of defining "bound water" because there is no standard method of measurement.

Many food products, such as meat, eggs, custards, gels, and baked products, have some part of the total water present in the bound form. Under certain conditions, part of the water may shift from one form to the other, thereby influencing the characteristics of the food. For example, Bratton et al. (1965) suggest that the amount of bound water decreases during contraction of muscle. So the relative state of contracture may influence the amount of free water and the juiciness of meat.

ACIDS, BASES, BUFFERS, pH

The relative acidity or alkalinity of the system can have a major influence on the changes that occur in foods during preparation. A brief review of the concepts involved in the consideration of acidity and alkalinity follows.

Acids and Bases

An acid is a substance that has a measurable tendency to release protons (H^+ ions). The strength of the acid depends on the extent of this tendency, a strong acid having a marked tendency and a weak acid a weak one. For any given acid substance, the strength will vary with the solvent and with the experimental conditions. In the same sense, bases are substances that have a measurable tendency to capture protons, or are formed from acids by the loss of protons.

An uncharged acid does not of itself dissociate into a positive proton and a negative ion. Some source of energy must be available to produce this change. This energy is often supplied by a chemical reaction between the proton and the solvent.

$$H_2SO_4 + H_2O \leftrightarrows H_3O^+ + HSO_4^-$$

While the proton involved is H^+, water acts as a base to form the hydrated ion, H_3O^+, the hydronium ion. By long custom, this hydrated proton is usually referred to as the hydrogen ion, and this terminology will be used hereafter.

Water itself has only a slight tendency to dissociate into ions.

$$HOH + HOH \leftrightarrows H_3O^+ + OH^-$$

The extent of this dissociation is expressed by the ionization constant, K_a,

$$K_a = \frac{a_{H_3O^+} \times a_{OH^-}}{a_{H_2O}}$$

where $a_{H^3O^+}$, a_{OH^-}, and a_{H^2O} are the activities of the hydrogen ions, hydroxyl ions, and undissociated water, respectively. Since the amounts of the ions present are very much smaller than the amount of undissociated water, the water can be considered a constant, and the ionization constant of water expressed as

$$K_w = a_{H_3O^+} \times a_{OH^-}$$

The approximate value of K_w at $25°$ C is 1×10^{-14}. In all aqueous solutions, the product of the hydrogen and hydroxyl ions is a constant, K_w. So if an acidic substance is dissolved in water, the protons liberated increase the hydrogen ion concentration, and the hydroxyl ion concentration must decrease, so that their product remains constant.

pH

In food materials, the concentrations of hydrogen and hydroxyl ions are usually low. For example, in fresh milk the hydrogen ion activity is usually about 2×10^{-7} equivalent per liter, or 0.0000002. Either of these modes of expression is rather awkward. In 1909, Sorenson suggested the term pH, which is now defined as

$$\text{pH} = -\log a_{H_3O^+} = \log \frac{1}{a_{H_3O^+}}$$

So the expression for the hydrogen ion activity of milk becomes

$$\text{pH} = \log \frac{1}{0.0000002} = 6.70$$

A similar expression can be written for hydroxyl ion activity

$$\text{pOH} = \log \frac{1}{a_{OH^-}}$$

and

$$\text{pH} + \text{pOH} = \text{p}K_w = 14$$

Since the sum of pH and pOH is constant, either pH or pOH can be used to define the system in this respect. pH is used much more commonly than pOH.

pH is a logarithmic function, and the change of sign makes the pH scale inverse to the actual hydrogen ion activity. Thus, a shift from pH 1 to 2 means a *tenfold decrease* in the hydrogen ion activity of the system.

The pH is influenced by the temperature at which the measurement is made. This is due to the increase in degree of dissociation as the temperature increases, as shown in Table 3. So the temperature is usually specified, or if not specified, is assumed to be around 25° C.

TABLE 3. Ionization Constants and pH of Water at Various Temperatures

Temperature (°C)	$K_w \times 10^{14}$	pH
0	0.114	7.47
10	0.292	7.27
25	1.008	7.00
40	2.919	6.77
60	9.614	6.55

pH is well-known to influence a wide variety of food characteristics. Examples include the influences of pH on the color of fruits, vegetables, meat, angel food cake, and chocolate cake; the texture of meats, vegetables, and candies; the flavor of many items; the susceptibility of microorganisms to heat inactivation; and enzyme activity. Anon. (1962) lists pH values for a number of food products, ranging from a pH of 1.8 for limes to 9.5 for frozen egg white.

Titratable Acidity

Hydrogen ion activity is a measure of the ionized acid or base present. Total acid (or base) includes both the ionized and unionized forms. The total acidity or alkalinity is measured by titration, and gives the titratable acidity (alkalinity). Kefford (1957) discusses various methods of determining both pH and titratable acidity in food products, where the use of indicators is often vitiated by the presence of pigments that interfere with visual determination of color changes.

Buffers

A small amount of strong acid or strong base added to pure water will cause a large change in the hydrogen ion activity, or pH, since water alone cannot neutralize even traces of acids or bases. However, a solution containing a weak acid plus one of its salts, or a weak base with one of its salts, can neutralize both acids and bases. Such solutions are known as *buffers,* since they tend to resist change in pH when acid or base is added. Buffers are very important in food study, since most foods are altered radically by any appreciable change in pH. Many food materials contain quite effective natural buffer systems.

The mechanism of buffer action can perhaps best be understood by comparing titration curves for strong and weak acids and bases. Titration curves show the alteration in pH as acid is added to base, or vice versa. The curves on the left side of Figure 4 show that as NaOH is added, the change in pH is much more gradual with a weak acid, such as acetic acid, than with a strong acid, such as HCl. The right side of

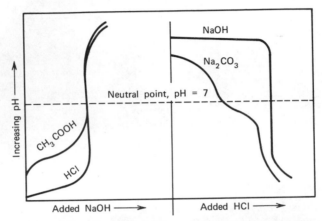

FIGURE 4. Titration curves for strong and weak acids and bases.

Figure 4 illustrates the same difference between the strong base, NaOH, and the weak base, Na_2CO_3, when HCl is added. In addition, the curve for Na_2CO_3 shows two points of inflection, the first for the change from Na_2CO_3 to $NaHCO_3$, the second from $NaHCO_3$ to NaCl. Many detailed investigations of food systems need to be carried out in appropriately selected buffer solutions, to avoid complicating alterations that might be induced by marked shifts in pH.

SOLUTIONS

Solutions and solubility are important in food studies. There are many compounds in food that are truly soluble, such as salt, sugar, and baking powder. In addition, most natural foods contain substances in solution, since water is an excellent solvent. In this chapter only true solutions will be considered. Other types, such as colloidal solutions, which have rather different properties, will be discussed in later chapters.

A true solution is composed of two parts. The *solute* is the dissolved substance and the *solvent* is the substance in which the solute is dissolved. It is customary to call the component present in larger proportion the solvent. A solution is homogeneous, alike in all parts. Any sample of a solution will have the same composition as any other sample of the same solution. This is in contrast to a mixture, where the distribution of one material in another is nonuniform. It is possible to have solutions of each of the three states of matter in one of the other states, or the solute and solvent may both be in the same state. However, in foods the primary interest is in solutions of gases, liquids, or solids in liquid water.

Solubility

The *solubility* of a substance is expressed as the amount of that substance that will dissolve in a given volume of a specified solvent at a given temperature and pressure. If the solvent is not mentioned it is understood to be water. Solubility is generally expressed as the number of grams of solute that will dissolve in 100 ml of solvent. If the temperature is not stated it is usually understood to be 20° C.

The term *miscible* is often used in speaking of degree of solubility. Liquids that are miscible will form solutions of any degree of relative concentration of each component. Those that are nonmiscible are insoluble in each other. When two liquids (such as alcohol and water) are miscible in all proportions, either one can be regarded as the solvent.

Temperature, the fineness of division and nature of the solute, and the nature of the solvent influence the degree and/or rate of solubility. Some substances are highly, others only slightly, soluble in water, and still others are insoluble in this solvent. Some substances dissolve best in alcohol, chloroform, ether, or benzene. Some liquids are mutually soluble in all proportions, but there is a limit to the solubility of all crystalline substances.

Fineness of Division of the Solute

A very finely divided or powdered crystalline solute is more quickly dissolved than the same substance in large crystals, as the increased surface of the small particles gives them more total surface energy.

Temperature

Sugars and most salts have negative heats of solution; that is, they absorb heat when dissolved, and are more soluble at higher temperatures (see Table 1, p. 6). If a salt evolves heat upon solution, its solubility is decreased with elevation of temperature. Calcium hydroxide is only half as soluble at 100° C as at 20° C. Sodium chloride absorbs little heat on solution, so its solubility changes little with temperature. The solubility of gases in liquid usually decreases as the temperature is increased.

Nature of Solute(s)

Two forms of the same compound may have different solubilities. Thus anhydrous lactose has one solubility and the hydrated form another. In addition, different crystal forms of the same compound are fairly common. This is known as polymorphism, and the polymorphic forms often have different solubilities. The alpha and beta crystal forms of lactose, mutarotation forms of the same compound, differ in solubility. Often the addition of another substance will alter the solubility of the solute. If, after all the sucrose possible is dissolved, some potassium acetate, sodium chloride, or other salt is added to the solution, more sucrose can be dissolved. This may affect the solubility of sugar in candy making, for it is known that different waters, with different proportions and kinds of minerals, do not always give identical results.

Saturated Solutions

A saturated solution is one that contains all the dissolved solute that the solvent can take up at a given temperature when in contact with undissolved solute. In other words, it is a solution that, when placed with excess of the solute at a definite temperature, is in equilibrium.

Supersaturated Solutions

If water is heated to 70° C and all the sucrose added that can be dissolved by the water at this temperature, the solution is saturated. If this solution is cooled carefully to avoid initiating crystallization, more sucrose will be in solution than if the water had not been heated, and the solution is supersaturated. This excess beyond saturation remains in solution as the temperature drops, until crystallization is initiated by treatments such as seeding or agitation. Some substances, such as the sugars, require more time than do others for crystallization to commence. This will be discussed in more detail in the section on crystallization.

Solvent Properties

A solute dissolved in a solvent affects the properties of the system, altering certain of its characteristics: (a) the vapor pressure of the solvent is lowered, although the vapor pressure of the solution may be increased, since the latter is the sum of the partial pressures of the solvent and solute; (b) the boiling point is usually elevated, although it will be lowered if the solute is more volatile than the solvent; (c) the freezing point is lowered, since this depends on the vapor pressure of the pure solvent; and (d) the osmotic pressure is increased. These characteristics all depend on the number of solute particles present, and so are termed *colligative properties*. The solute particles may be ions, molecules, or aggregates of ions or molecules.

Vapor Pressure

Vapor pressure is the gaseous pressure of a liquid; it depends on the tendency of the molecules to escape from the liquid surface into the space above the liquid. This gaseous pressure soon reaches a maximum in a closed container at any given temperature, the rate of escape and the rate of return of molecules to the liquid being equal. The maximum pressure at a definite temperature represents the vapor pressure of the liquid. Some liquids, like alcohol, evaporate rapidly and have high vapor pressure. Others, like water, evaporate more slowly.

Effect of the Solute

When a substance is dissolved in a liquid the vapor pressure of the solvent is lowered, that is, there is less tendency to pass into the vapor state; hence the gaseous pressure is decreased.

In highly concentrated water solutions of some substances, there is a tendency for water to be absorbed from the air. Such systems are called *hygroscopic*. This is particularly true of sugar solutions, when the humidity of the air is high. On damp, rainy days, fondant and similar candies have to be beaten for a longer time to crystallize, unless they are cooked to a little higher temperature so as to obtain a greater concentration.

The fact that solutes lower the vapor pressure, making it harder for the vapor to leave the surface of the liquid, is utilized in the following ways, or similar ones, to keep food moist. A covered vessel containing food loses moisture from the food until the air space is saturated with vapor. If the vessel is tight enough, the food does not dry out to an appreciable extent. If two foods are placed in the same container, the one with more sugar will gradually absorb moisture from the other, since sucrose has a very high affinity for water. This is why an apple, put in a box with a fruit cake, dries and keeps the cake moist. Cake and unwrapped bread should not be stored together, as the bread will become dry quickly.

Water standing in an open vessel gradually evaporates. Evaporation takes place more rapidly on warm days than on cool ones, because the molecules are in more rapid motion due to the higher temperature, and more rapidly from a wide shallow vessel than from a narrow deep one, since more surface area is exposed.

The Boiling Point

When heat is applied at the bottom of a pan of water, the vapor forms as bubbles at the bottom of the liquid. The bubbles, being less dense than the liquid, rise toward the surface, but cannot reach it until the pressure within each bubble is just slightly greater than the pressure exerted on it by the weight of the liquid above it and by the atmospheric pressure on the surface of the liquid. With increasing temperature, the formation of vapor is more rapid, the speed of the molecules increases, and greater pressure is generated, so the vapor can escape from the liquid. When the loss of heat from the escaping vapor is equal to the heat received by the liquid, the temperature is constant. This is the boiling point. Another way to define the boiling point is to say that it is the temperature at which the pressure of the saturated vapor within the liquid is just greater than the outside pressure on the surface of the liquid.

The Bureau of Standards defines the boiling point of water as the point at which ebullition is violent. Slowly bubbling water does not register quite as high a temperature as rapidly bubbling water, but in cooking food in water there is no great advantage to having the water boiling violently, unless it is desirable to evaporate the liquid quickly. Violent boiling may lead to disintegration of pieces of food such as vegetables or fruits, producing an unattractive, mushy texture.

The conversion of water from a liquid to a gaseous state requires a certain amount of energy, the heat of vaporization (see p. 10). If the heat applied to boiling water is increased, the quantity of water changed to vapor in a given time is increased. The temperature of the water cannot be increased, because the heat lost by evaporation is equal to the heat received.

Lowering the Boiling Point

The boiling point of a liquid may be lowered by reducing the pressure on the liquid. This may be done by boiling the liquid in a partial vacuum. The boiling point is also lowered with increased elevation above sea level. The atmospheric pressure is not as great at high altitudes because of the lessened depth of air. At sea level the boiling point of water is 100° C. For each 960 feet above sea level the boiling point is decreased 1° C.

Elevation of the Boiling Point

The boiling point of a liquid can be elevated by increasing the pressure on it. The pressure of a gas increases as the temperature increases (see p. 2). When vapor is confined, as in a pressure cooker, the boiling point of a liquid in the cooker is elevated. As the temperature is increased, the pressure of the confined vapor on the surface of the liquid is increased. Therefore a higher temperature is required to form great enough pressure in the vapor bubbles within the liquid for them to reach the surface of the liquid. Thus the boiling point is elevated.

The Boiling Point of Solutions

If a nonvolatile soluble substance is added to a liquid, the resulting solution will have a higher boiling point than the liquid itself. Each gram-molecular weight (mole) of a nonionized substance in a liter of water elevates the boiling point 0.52° C. The boiling point of a liter of water containing 342 grams of sucrose (1 mole) is elevated 0.52° C. Two moles of sucrose would elevate the boiling point 1.04° C. The boiling point can be elevated as long as the substance added is soluble. When the solution becomes saturated, the boiling point is constant for substances that behave normally in solution. If boiling is continued so that the solvent is vaporized, the excess solute beyond saturation is crystallized.

Effect of Ionized Substances on the Boiling Point

Some substances ionize when dissolved in water. In a solution of sodium chloride, for example, rather than NaCl molecules, one has Na^+ and Cl^- ions. If 58 grams of sodium chloride (a mole) are added to a liter of water, and the sodium chloride is completely ionized, the boiling point will be elevated 1.04° C. The mole of sodium will elevate it 0.52°, and the mole of chlorine will elevate it 0.52°.

Some compounds produce more than two ions per molecule, increasing the effect on the boiling point. Other substances, when dissolved, ionize partially rather than completely. When this happens, the boiling point is elevated according to the degree of ionization.

At high altitudes it is possible to cook foods more rapidly by adding salt to the cooking water to raise the boiling point. However, it is not practical to use NaCl to raise the boiling point more than about 1° C, since the use of larger amounts of salt would make the food unpalatable.

Boiling Point of Sucrose Solutions

Browne (1912) lists the boiling point of sucrose solutions as shown in Table 4.

Sucrose behaves abnormally with respect to its effect on the boiling point, since it raises the boiling point more than the molecular concentration would predict. This is attributed to the very strong attractive forces that exist between sucrose and water, the theory being that some

TABLE 4. Boiling Point of Sucrose Solutions (Browne, 1912)[a]

Percent sucrose[b]	10	20	30	40	50	60	70	80	90.8
Boiling point, °C	100.4	100.6	101.0	101.5	102.0	103.0	106.5	112.0	130.0

[a] From B. Lowe, *Experimental Cookery*, 4th ed. 1955. Wiley, New York, p. 63.

[b] A 10 percent solution of sugar is one that contains 10 grams of sugar and 90 grams of water or one having these proportions.

of the water is actually immobilized, with the effect of lessening the amount of water available to act as solvent so that the solution is more concentrated than the amounts of sugar and water used in preparing the solution would indicate. Temperatures considerably above the melting point of the sugar can be obtained, but at these temperatures caramelization and decomposition of the sucrose occur quite rapidly.

Heat of Solution

Some substances may liberate heat when they go into solution. The example of mixing water and sulfuric acid is well known. Other substances, instead of giving off heat, cause the temperature to drop as they go into solution. They are said to have a negative heat of solution, since heat is absorbed.

If sugar and water of the same temperature are mixed, the temperature of the solution drops as the sugar is dissolving. Salt and many other substances also absorb heat as they go into solution. When such substances are crystallized from solution, heat is liberated and the temperature is elevated slightly.

Surface Tension of Solutions

When a substance is dissolved in water, the surface tension of the solution may not be changed, it may be raised, or it may be lowered. The substances that scarcely change the surface tension or elevate it slightly include most electrolytes and some organic compounds. Sugar increases the surface tension of water. These substances are called capillary-inactive or surface-inactive. The substances that lower surface tension include organic compounds such as aldehydes, fatty acids, fats, acetone, amines, alcohols, tannins, saponins, and proteins. This group of substances is called capillary-active or surface-active. They often markedly influence the properties of food systems.

If a substance lowers the surface tension, its concentration is greater in the boundary layer than in the bulk of the liquid; conversely, if the substance raises the surface tension, the concentration is less in the boundary layer. Surface tension can be lowered tremendously, but it can be raised to only a slight extent.

Substances like the fatty acids, formic, acetic, propionic, and butyric, that belong to a homologous series, show an increased lowering of the surface tension as the series is ascended, if they are kept at the same concentration. This regularity of increase with such a series is known as Traube's rule.

CRYSTAL GROWTH AND STRUCTURE

The size, shape, and solidity of crystals influence the speed of solution of materials such as salt, sugar, baking powder, soda, and cream of tartar. Crystal characteristics also markedly alter the textural qualities of candies, frostings, frozen desserts, fats, and foods preserved by freezing or combinations of freezing with other processes such as dehydration. In cases such as the crystallization of sugars in fruit jellies, or tartrates in grape juice, or of struvite in canned fish, the formation of crystals is undesirable and lessens the acceptability of the food.

Crystallization

As a pure liquid is cooled, a temperature will be reached at which the material undergoes a change of state from liquid to solid. Solids may be of two types—either crystalline or amorphous. If the molecules fit together into a regular geometric arrangement (crystal lattice), the material is crystalline. If, however, the molecules agglomerate in a random, disordered fashion, an amorphous solid will be produced.

In discussing crystallization, not only the properties of individual atoms and molecules but also the interactions between particles must be considered. A number of different types of bonds may be active in holding a substance in the ordered arrangement of a crystal. The molecules of ionizable compounds such as NaCl are held together in a crystal by the ionic attractions between Na^+ and Cl^-. Covalently bonded molecules are held in the crystal lattice primarily by the relatively weak van der Waals forces. Other types of forces that may be involved in the maintenance of crystal structure include covalent bonds in one, two, or three dimensions, hydrogen bonds, and metallic bonding between the atoms of metal crystals.

Crystallization may be considered from the standpoint of the change of state of a pure material, as in the case of the solidification of pure liquid water into ice. However, food systems frequently deal with the crystallization of a dissolved solute from a solution. In both cases, the development of crystals requires the formation of nuclei and the continued deposition of molecules on these nuclei to form perceptible crystals. The formation and growth of crystals are influenced by the nature of the crystallizing substance, the concentration, temperature, rate of cooling, degree of agitation, impurities in the solution, nature of the container walls, and the size and previous history of the sample.

Eutectic Point

In food systems there are two aspects of crystallization, with quite different results. In cases such as the crystallization of sugars in candy making, the solute is changing to the solid state, so that the remaining solution becomes more and more dilute, although it is still saturated, since the temperature is decreasing. In freezing, however, the solvent is solidifying, so the remaining solution is becoming more concentrated. In the latter case, with continued cooling, a temperature is eventually reached at which the entire system solidifies. This is known as the eutectic point, the temperature at which the solute(s) and solvent crystallize together. This point is important in determining such things as ratios of ice and salt to use for freezing, and storage temperatures for frozen beverage concentrates.

Formation and Growth of Crystals

Nucleation

Some degree of supersaturation of a solution, or supercooling of a liquid, is required before crystal formation can proceed. This is due to the high energy requirement for the formation of crystal nuclei of sufficient size to be stable. As the first few molecules come together to form what Van Hook (1961) terms the "germ" of the nucleus, there is an increase in free energy until the critical size is reached. At this point, further increase in size leads to a decrease in free energy, so the nucleus is stable and will continue to grow. A system that is supersaturated or supercooled, but not sufficiently to generate nuclei, is called *metastable*. Figure 5 illustrates these zones schematically.

Within the metastable range, treatments such as seeding or agitation will lead to instant crystallization. Seeding may be deliberate, as by the addition of crystals of the compound to be crystallized, or accidental from dust in the air. If crystals are floating in the air, they may serve to seed solutions and thus start crystallization (Tutton, 1924).

Rate of Growth

After stable nuclei have formed, the crystals grow by addition of particles properly oriented to fit into the crystal lattice. Van Hook (1961) lists the five steps involved in this process as (1) transport from the medium to the growing environment; (2) adsorption on the crystal

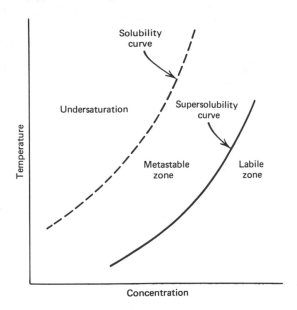

FIGURE 5. Saturation zones. (From *Crystallization: Theory and Practice*, Andrew Van Hook. Copyright © 1961 by Litton Educational Publishing, Inc., Published by Reinhold Publishing Corporation.)

surface; (3) orientation in the surface; (4) desorption of the products; and (5) dissipation of the products. The product of crystallization is the heat of transition from liquid to solid, so steps 4 and 5 are concerned with removal of heat energy. The amount of heat may be considerable if crystallization is rapid. This can be seen in the thinning and slight temperature rise of a viscous candy sirup as crystallization is initiated. Any one or a combination of the five steps may be the rate-limiting factor in crystal growth.

Nature of the Crystallizing Substance

Some substances crystallize readily from water solution, while others do not. Salt requires only a very slight supersaturation to start nuclear formation, and all excess salt in the solution beyond the saturation point is precipitated as crystals. With sucrose it is often necessary to have a considerable degree of supersaturation before crystallization commences. Sucrose, in turn, crystallizes more readily than fructose.

Concentration of the Solution

Supersaturation favors the development of small crystals. Nuclei form more readily in a more concentrated solution. A fondant sirup cooked to 114° C contains less water and is more concentrated than one cooked to 112° C. When cooled to the temperature recommended for beating a fondant, the 114° C sirup will contain a greater excess of solute, and so a larger number of nuclei will form when crystallization is initiated. The viscosity of a very supersaturated sirup delays crystal growth, since the thickness of the system hinders the transport of the solute particles from the medium to the surface of the growing crystal.

Temperature and Rate of Cooling

Other things being equal, the higher the temperature at which crystal formation is initiated, the coarser the crystals (Bancroft, 1920). Higher temperatures give more regular and larger crystals, since the solvent is more fluid and the solute usually more soluble. Fewer nuclei are formed, as the thermal agitation at the higher temperature tends to prevent the attainment of stable size. The most favorable temperature for crystal growth in a saturated sucrose solution boiled to 112° C is between 70 and 90° C. Although crystallization occurs in a very short time when the sirup is stirred at these temperatures, the crystals formed are larger than when the sirup is cooled to a lower temperature. Compare the crystal sizes in Figures 6 and 7.

If a system such as a concentrated sucrose sirup is cooled very rapidly, it may set to an amorphous "glass" without ever crystallizing. The viscosity increases rapidly, and slows up the motion of the solute molecules so that they are prevented from forming stable nuclei. This can be seen in the "cold-water test" for the various stages of sirup cookery.

Agitation

Stirring a solution favors the formation of nuclei and hinders the depositing of the material of the solution on the nuclei already formed. Hence, crystals in solutions that are stirred do not develop to the size that they do in spontaneous crystallization. If small crystals are desired, the conditions should be such that many nuclei are formed. Small crystals are obtained in sirups of proper concentration and temperature, if the sirup is stirred until the mass is kneadable. However, if the sirup is stirred for only a short time, some nuclei are formed, but after agitation is stopped, crystal growth is favored. Figure 8 shows crystals from fondant stirred for only a few seconds. The crystals are much larger than those in Figure 6, which shows crystals from fondant that was stirred until the mass could be kneaded. Fondant with small crystals is very smooth and velvety on the palate. This emphasizes the importance of stirring candy and icing sirups until practically all the material is crystallized, if small crystals are desired.

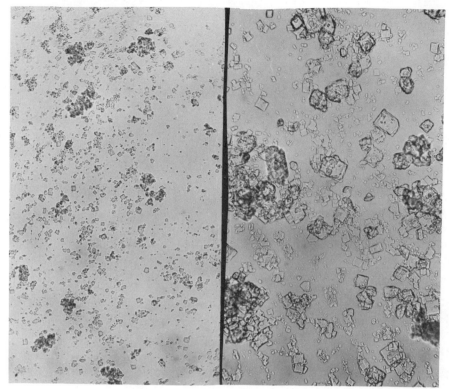

FIGURE 6. Crystals from fondant. Sirup cooked to 112° C, cooled to 40° C, beaten until the mass stiffened. Magnification 50x.
FIGURE 7. Crystals from fondant. A portion of the same sirup as Figure 6, beaten without cooling. Magnification 50x.

Stirring also helps to prevent formation of aggregates of crystals. In a system crystallizing without agitation, neighbor crystals may touch and grow together, forming perceptible masses. Stirring keeps the crystals in motion through the solution, producing more individual crystals.

Storage of crystalline candies may lead to increased crystal size. The small crystals have more surface area, and therefore greater total surface energy than large crystals. Hence small crystals tend to dissolve gradually in the sirup surrounding the crystals, the solute then reprecipitating on the larger crystals in the mass.

Impurities

Booth and Buckley (1955) point out that even small amounts of impurities may slow or stop crystal growth. The rate of crystal growth is

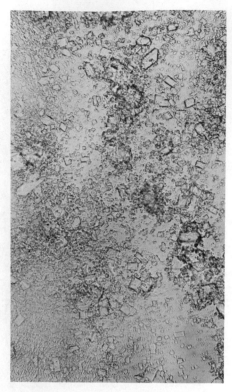

FIGURE 8. Crystals from fondant. A portion of the same sirup as Figure 6, cooled to 40° C, stirred a few times to initiate crystallization, and then allowed to stand without further agitation until crystallization was complete. Magnification 50x.

retarded because of adsorption of the foreign substance by the crystals. The crystal grows by adsorption of solute particles on the crystal face, followed by orientation of the particle into the crystal lattice. Foreign particles that are adsorbed fill the adsorbed layer but cannot be incorporated into the crystal lattice. If the substance is strongly adsorbed, crystallization may be practically abolished, even though the solution is very supersaturated with the crystallizing substance. Since the adsorption prevents crystal growth, if a precipitate is formed in the presence of a substance strongly adsorbed by the precipitate, it will crystallize in a much finer state of subdivision. Sometimes the substance is more strongly adsorbed at one crystal face than at another, so that this face grows more slowly than is customary and thus becomes comparatively large in relation to other faces. This explains why crystals from pure solutions may have different shapes from those obtained from impure solutions. Impurities may also influence degree and rate of crystallization by either increasing or decreasing the solubility of the principal solute, by altering the viscosity of the system, or by altering the degree of solvation of the compound to be crystallized. The latter, in turn, would change the concentration of the system by increasing or decreasing the amount of free solvent.

The degree of surface activity of the impurity will influence crystallization. The interfacial tension of the system is a power term in the equations dealing with nucleation and growth of crystals. Surface-active materials reduce the interfacial tension, so they should favor crystallization, provided they are not adsorbed onto the surface of the crystal.

Condition of Sample

The size of sample influences the rate of crystallization, small samples tending to crystallize more slowly than large ones. Also, the previous history of the sample apparently has an influence, since varying results may be obtained from one sample to another seemingly treated in the same way. The container is also important, as flaws in the surface can act as centers for nuclei formation.

Crystal Forms

Although the shapes of crystals seem endlessly variable, crystallographers recognize certain fundamental principles dealing with axes, angles, and symmetry, which permit classification. Seven crystal systems are listed, based on axial length and angles. Of common crystalline food materials, sucrose crystals are monoclinic; NaCl, cubic; and ice, hexagonal. The hexagonal ice crystals account for the lessened density of ice from that of liquid water at $0°$ C, since the hexagonal arrangement is more open.

The external form, or habit, of crystals of the same material may vary depending on the conditions under which the crystals are grown. One axis or face may grow more rapidly than another. Crystals may grow together, or extend variously in different directions. Crystals may continue to grow or change in shape, even when the entire system appears solid. A soft crystallized mass such as fondant still contains a small proportion of solvent, or hygroscopic materials may absorb water from the surrounding atmosphere. This permits formation of a film of saturated solution on the surface of the crystal. This solution will concentrate at points of contact between crystals, due to capillary forces, and on cooling or evaporation will crystallize to form solid connections between the crystals.

Polymorphism is another source of variation in crystal form. A given substance may yield crystals belonging to different crystal systems, or different forms within a system, depending on conditions. For example, crystallization from a supersaturated solution of lactose below $93.5°$ C yields α-lactose monohydrate. Above 93.5° C, β-lactose is obtained. The α- and β-forms differ in a number of properties such as degree of solubility, melting point, and specific gravity. In general, the polymorphic forms that a given compound can assume are relatively limited, one or two being most usual. However, fats and oils may show a wide variety of different crystal forms.

Crystallization in Food Preparation

The most important cases of crystallization in food products involve the freezing of water in frozen desserts and in food preservation, the crystallization of fats as it influences texture of shortenings and chocolate products, and the crystallization of sugars in a wide variety of food products. Freezing of water and crystallization of fats will be discussed in later chapters. The structure and properties of the sugars influence their crystallization and the roles they have in food materials.

MONO- AND DISACCHARIDES

The commonly occurring crystallizable sugars in food materials belong to the classes of mono- and disaccharides. Some of the monosaccharides and their derivatives also form the basic monomers from which carbohydrate polymers such as starch, pectin, and cellulose are built up. These polymers are discussed in Chapters 4 and 6.

Following is a brief outline of the structure and some of the properties of the most important mono- and disaccharides. For a more extended coverage, see Pigman (1957), the yearly issues of "Advances in Carbohydrate Chemistry," or an organic chemistry text. A review of many of the properties and roles of sugars will be found in Schultz et al. (1969).

Classification and Structure

Carbohydrates are polyhydroxy aldehydes, polyhydroxy ketones, or substances that yield these on hydrolysis. Monosaccharides are carbohydrates that cannot be hydrolyzed to simpler molecules.

Monosaccharides

Monosaccharides are classified according to the length of the carbon chain and whether there is an aldehyde or a ketone group present. Trioses contain 3, tetroses 4, pentoses 5, and hexoses 6 carbon atoms in the chain. If the molecule contains an aldehyde group, it is an aldose, while one with a ketone group is a ketose. Glucose (dextrose), fructose (levulose), and galactose are the commonest food monosaccharides. These are all hexoses with the same molecular formula, $C_6H_{12}O_6$. Their

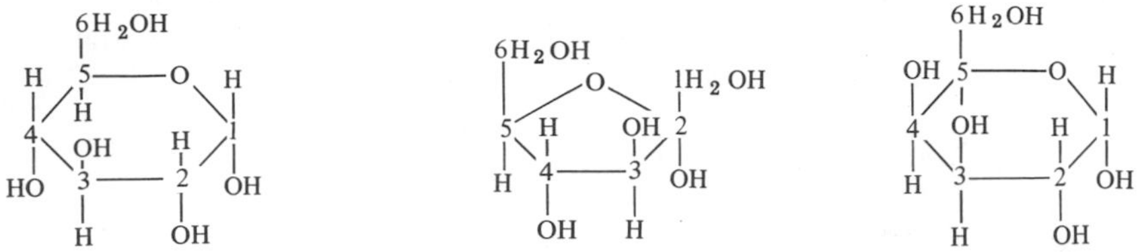

FIGURE 9. Structural formulas for glucose, fructose and galactose. Numbers refer to the carbon atoms.

structural formulas are shown in Figure 9, in the Haworth perspective formula. The "plane" of the Haworth ring is a conventionalized presentation, since the actual molecules are three-dimensional. The numbers refer to the carbon atoms. The attachments at the top of the vertical lines are considered to be above the plane of the ring; those at the bottom, below the ring. It can be seen that glucose and galactose, for example, differ only in the arrangement of the hydrogen and hydroxyl attachments on carbon atom 4. Glucose and galactose are shown in the pyranose, or 6-membered, ring form, while fructose has the furanose, or 5-membered, ring.

These rings can open, breaking between the oxygen and C_5. This gives the reducing-sugar characteristic to these compounds, since glucose and galactose become aldehydes, and fructose a ketone, in the straight-chain form. When the rings are re-formed, the hydroxyl groups on C_1 of glucose and galactose, or C_2 of fructose, may go either above or below the plane of the ring. The α-form has the hydroxyl groups below, the β-form above, the ring plane. In solution the α- and β-rings and the straight-chain form exist in equilibrium. Holum (1962) gives the proportions for glucose at room temperature as approximately 36 percent α, 0.02 percent open chain, and 64 percent β.

These differences in structural arrangement may seem small. But α-D-glucose has a melting point of 146°, while that of β-D-glucose is 148–150° C. The α-form of glucose is the basic unit of starch, while the β-ring is the monomer of cellulose. Fructose is the sweetest of all sugars, as well as the most water-soluble, while galactose is less sweet than glucose.

Disaccharides

Carbohydrates that yield two monosaccharide units on hydrolysis are known as disaccharides. The commonest ones in foods are sucrose, lactose, and maltose. Their structural formulas are illustrated in Figure 10.

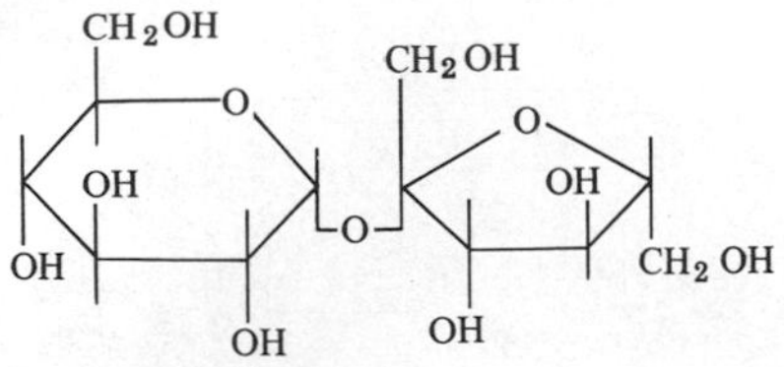

Sucrose
(α-D-glucose, β-D-fructose)

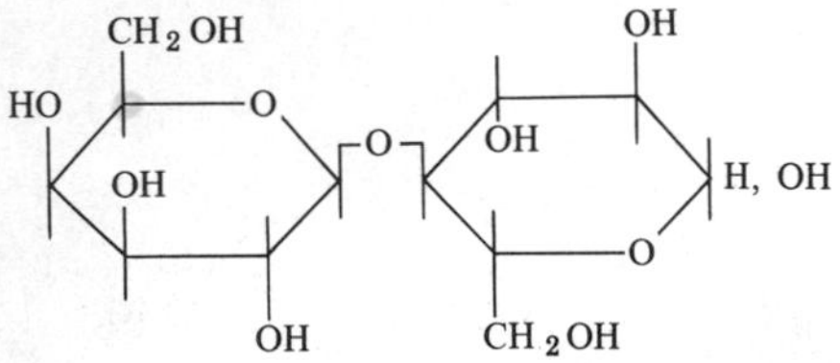

Lactose
(D-galactose, D-glucose, β-linked)

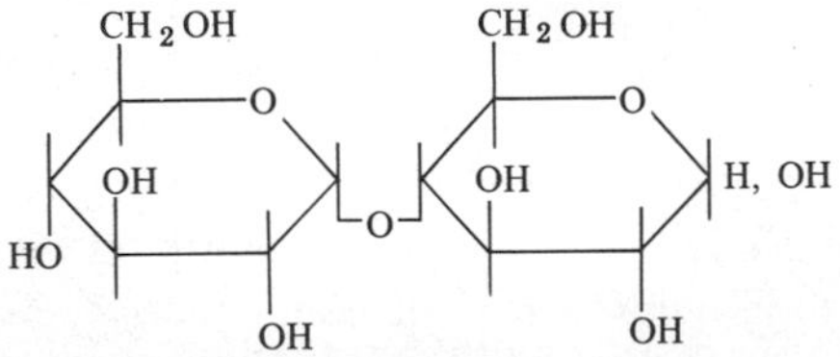

Maltose
(2 D-glucose units, α-linked)

FIGURE 10. Structural formulas for sucrose, lactose and maltose. Formulas abbreviated by omitting carbon and hydrogen atoms.

These show the customary method of abbreviating the formulas by omitting the carbon and hydrogen designations on the ring. Oligosaccharide is the general term used for carbohydrates that contain several monosaccharide units (usually 2 to 9), and polysaccharide for molecules containing many monomer units (usually 10 or more).

Sources

Glucose occurs free in nature in many plant materials. One of its early names was "grape sugar" because it could be obtained from grapes. It also occurs in combined form in sucrose, lactose, maltose, and polysaccharides such as starch, cellulose, and glycogen. Glucose is widely distributed in animals as the principal transport form of carbohydrate in the bloodstream.

Free fructose is found primarily in the plants. Probably the most familiar food source is honey. Fructose is one of the two monomers in sucrose, and the basic monomer of the polysaccharide inulin. Galactose does not usually occur free. It is one of the monomers of lactose, and its derivative, galacturonic acid, is the monomer of the pectic substances.

Sucrose is widely distributed in plants, and occurs in sufficient concentration in sugar cane and sugar beets to justify commercial extraction and concentration, to yield the familiar sugar of commerce. Johnson (1969) lists analytical data for sorghumcane and sugarcane sirups. Lactose is primarily a product of mammalian metabolism, although there have been a few reports of its occurrence in plants. It occurs primarily in milk, the concentration varying between species as well as within species. Maltose is a disaccharide produced by hydrolysis of starch.

The restriction of this discussion to three monosaccharides and three disaccharides should not be taken to indicate that these are the only ones that occur naturally or are produced by hydrolysis of polysaccharides. These are the ones that are most often present in appreciable amounts in, or are added to, food products.

Reactions in Food Materials

Acids

Strong concentrated acids decompose all the sugars, producing humic substances. The effect of weak acids depends on the size of the carbohydrate molecule, the kind and strength of acid, and the temperature and duration of heating. As an example, Shaw et al. (1967) list products obtained by heating fructose in citric acid solutions of pH 3.5 and 2.15, and in HCl at pH 1.0. Of the disaccharides, sucrose is hydrolyzed very easily, maltose less easily, and lactose only slowly. Starch is readily hydrolyzed by dilute mineral acids.

Enzymes

Enzymes also bring about hydrolysis of oligo- and polysaccharides. Since heat inactivates enzymes, the reaction must occur at a relatively low temperature. The enzyme invertase causes hydrolysis of sucrose, maltase hydrolyzes maltose, and lactase hydrolyzes lactose.

Inversion and Invert Sugar

The hydrolysis of sucrose is often referred to as inversion, because of the change in rotatory power of the solution. If a beam of light is passed through a solution of sucrose in a polariscope, the light will be rotated to the right, and so sucrose is dextrorotatory. Glucose is also dextrorotatory, but fructose is levorotatory (rotates light to the left). Fructose has a stronger rotatory power than glucose, so that the mixture resulting from hydrolysis of sucrose is levorotatory, the rotation has been inverted, and the mixture is called invert sugar.

Alkalis

Carbohydrates are readily attacked by alkalis. Even a weakly alkaline salt such as $NaHCO_3$, or the alkaline salts in hard water, may cause considerable decomposition. The reactions promoted by alkaline pH are very complex and poorly understood, but they result in changes in color and in flavor. Shaw et al. (1968, 1969) list some of the compounds produced by base-catalyzed degradation of fructose and sucrose.

An alkali acting on glucose first produces a yellow tinge, which becomes deeper and finally brown. This decomposition is called caramelization. With only slight caramelization of glucose the flavor change may not be very noticeable, but as the reactions proceed, the flavor becomes stronger and more bitter, being characterized by a pungent, acrid aftertaste. In sections of the country where the water is very hard, enough decomposition to affect the flavor may be brought about in ordinary cooking.

Thermal Degradation

Carbohydrates are readily broken up by temperatures reached in certain preparation procedures, such as the external surface temperature in baking or frying, or the heating of dry sugar to caramelize it. Many of the products formed influence the color and/or flavor of the food. Fagerson (1969) lists products that have been identified.

Moisture Absorption

Sugars are hygroscopic; that is, they tend to absorb moisture from the atmosphere. This may lead to the formation of lumps or the caking of the entire mass. Nelson (1949) states that white sugars are best stored at relative humidities below 60 percent and at temperatures below 38° C. Since brown sugars contain about 4 percent moisture, they are better if stored under damper conditions than white sugar. Nelson suggests a humidity between 60 percent and 70 percent and a temperature below 24° C.

Browne (1922) reports that the sugars having the highest absorptive power from a saturated atmosphere are the fructose-containing substances: invert sugar, honey, and molasses. Honey and molasses are used in many products to be stored, since they remain moist; in many instances the moisture content seems to increase during storage. Invert sugar may be added to foods, or may be formed from sucrose during cooking.

Solubility

The difference in the solubilities of the sugars is one of the factors that influences use in food products. It is obvious that a sugar of low solubility could not be used successfully for concentrated sugar products such as jellies, jam, candies, or frostings.

At room temperature, fructose has the highest solubility of the sugars used in foods, followed by sucrose, glucose, maltose, and lactose, in order of decreasing solubility. The relative solubilities and influence of temperature are shown in Figure 11.

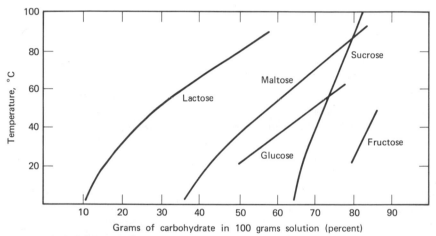

FIGURE 11. Solubilities of some mono- and disaccharides.

Sugars vary in their water-binding capacity and, therefore, in solubility. Schliepake (1963) points out that water may be held as compressed water of hydration, or trapped in clusters of associated molecules. Water of hydration is held by hydrogen bonding. The mechanical binding of water by capillary attraction is usually significant only in more concentrated solutions. Taylor and Rowlinson (1955) state that the thermodynamic properties of sucrose solutions indicate stronger or more abundant hydrogen bonding between sucrose and water molecules than between the water molecules themselves. Schneider et al. (1963) measured the viscosities of sucrose solutions and concluded that the sucrose molecules form associated clusters at concentrations above 30 to 40 percent. Fincke (1952) states that the volume of free water is less than the solution volume in concentrated sucrose solution, since the dissolved particles take up part of the volume and some of the water is bound to the sucrose. These help to account for the variation from predicted colligative properties in concentrated sucrose solutions. Barrow (1961) points out that in concentrated solutions the withdrawal of water by hydration of the solute may have an appreciable effect on all colligative properties.

The solubility of a given sugar will vary with the presence of added solutes. For example, Segur and Miner (1954) state that in a mixture of sucrose and glucose the presence of one will decrease the solubility of the other in water, although the combined solubilities will exceed that of either one alone. Also, they found that the addition of glycerol reduced the solubility of the sucrose-glucose mixture.

Relative Sweetness

Sweetness is a quality that is detected by taste. Much depends on how the test is conducted. Bollenback (1969) points out that sweetness scales are based on dilute solutions of pure sugars. Foods often contain mixtures of sugars along with other materials, and the sugars are frequently present in fairly high concentration. Cameron (1947), Pangborn (1963), and Wick (1963) all reported that the relative sweetness ratings were materially influenced by concentration of the sugars. Pangborn (1963) also found that fructose was less sweet than sucrose when compared in pear nectar rather than water solutions. Stone and Oliver (1969) noted synergistic effects in several sugar combinations, and a shift in the relative sweetness values for a particular sugar when the reference sugar or reference concentration was altered.

Cameron (1947) and Tsuzubi and Yamazaki (1953) pointed out the influence of temperature on the sweetness sensation. The optimum temperature for detection of the sweet taste is said to be 35–50° C, although this varies with individuals.

Steinhardt et al. (1962) and Boyd and Matsubara (1962) found that the isomeric form of the particular sugar influenced sweetness, but Shallenberger et al. (1969) reported that their panel could not distinguish significantly between the sweet taste intensity of a given D-sugar and its L-enantiomorph. Other factors that have been reported to influence relative sweetness ratings include viscosity of the solution (Pariser, 1961) and the presence of other solutes (Pariser, 1961; Pangborn et al., 1960).

Nieman (1958) reviewed the sweetening capacity of various sugars. In comparing the relative sweetness of sugars in dilute solutions, it is customary to use sucrose as the standard. Sugars sweeter than sucrose are ranked higher and those less sweet lower than the standard. Some typical values are listed in Table 5.

TABLE 5.   Relative Sweetness of Various Substances in Solutions of Moderate Intensity

Substance	Sweetness Rating (Citation Numbers in Parentheses)
Saccharin	675 (3), 306.0 (6)
Dulcin	265 (3), 90.7 (6)
Calcium cyclamate	33.8 (6)
Fructose	1.16 (1), 1.15 (2,6)
Sucrose	1.00
Glycerol	0.84 (6), 0.77 (1)
α-Glucose	0.64 (6)
α-, β-Glucose (equilibrium mixture)	0.79 (2), 0.76 (5), 0.68 (1), 0.65 (4), 0.61 (6)
Galactose	0.67 (1), 0.59 (6)
D-mannose	0.59 (6)
Maltose	0.47 (2), 0.46 (6)
Lactose	0.38 (1), 0.30 (6)

(1) Cameron (1947); (2) Dahlberg and Penczek (1941); (3) Gilman and Hewlett (1929); (4) Lichtenstein (1948); (5) MacLeod (1952); and (6) Schutz and Pilgrim (1957).

MATERIALS HAVING A SWEET TASTE

There are a number of commercial forms in which the simple sugars may be obtained, and also some other compounds that can be used to give a sweet taste. Ballinger and Larkin (1964) list the principal sweetening agents used in the United States as sugar (sucrose), corn sirup, glucose, and the noncaloric sweeteners such as saccharin and the cyclamates.

A number of types of plant materials are used in various parts of the world as sources of sugar, including cane, sugar beet, sorghum, potatoes, corn, various other grains, maple sap, and the sap of certain varieties of palm trees. In selecting a sugar for experimental purposes, the source and the degree of refinement must be considered, since even small amounts of impurities can alter the effects obtained.

Commercial Sources of Sucrose

The commonest sources of sucrose in the United States are sugar cane and sugar beets. In the unrefined state these differ somewhat in the types of impurities (nonsucrose) that they contain. However, white sugar as sold in the market is about 99.9 percent pure sucrose, and can be used interchangeably whether produced from cane or beet.

White sugar can be purchased in either the granulated or powdered form. The granulation may range from ultrafine to coarse. The usual consumer form of granulated sugar is fine granulation, while powdered sugar may be labeled 6X (ultrafine) or 4X (very fine). For commercial use sucrose may also be obtained in liquid form—a clear solution of highly purified sugar. Liquid sugars are available in varying concentration of total solids and various percentages of sucrose, invert sugar, or both.

White sugar is produced by concentrating cane or beet juice, centrifuging out the crystals that form, and purifying these crystals. Details are given in Honig (1963) and Van Hook (1961). Raw sugar is an intermediate product containing crystals of sucrose covered with a film of sirup containing nonsugar impurities.

Brown sugar consists of sucrose crystals covered with a film of dark-colored sirup that gives the characteristic color and flavor. The color varies from almost white to dark brown, depending on the level of refinement. The sucrose content varies from 91 percent for dark brown to 96 percent for yellow, and the moisture content from 2 to 4 percent.

Molasses is the sirup or "mother liquor" separated from the crystals in the production of sucrose. The usual industrial process involves three concentrations, yielding three grades of molasses, the last one giving the product known as "blackstrap." Refiners' sirups are strongly flavored, dark-colored sirups containing 70 to 80 percent solids, 50 to 75 percent being sucrose plus invert sugar.

Invert sugar is usually produced commercially by heating sucrose in dilute acid. Invert sugar is more soluble than sucrose, and has higher moisture-retaining properties, due to the fructose content. Quinlan (1954) discusses the various grades and uses of a variety of commercial sugar products. A number of papers on uses of carbohydrates are published in *Advances in Chemistry*, No. 12 (1955), and in Schultz et al. (1969).

Corn Sirup and Sugar

Corn sirup is produced by hydrolysis of corn starch to produce a mixture of glucose, maltose, and a mixture of higher polymers of glucose. Hydrolysis may be induced by acid or enzymes, or both. The term "starch sirup" is sometimes used rather than corn sirup, since similar sirups can be produced from other starches such as potato, rice or barley (Nieman, 1960; Houle and Goering, 1961).

The degree of conversion to glucose and maltose is expressed as dextrose equivalent (D.E.). It is based on the amount of reducing sugars present, calculated as glucose (dextrose) and expressed as percent of total dry material. Corn sirup solids are essentially dehydrated corn sirup, and contain about 5 percent water. Corn sirup and corn sirup solids are available in the range of 28 to as high as 88 D.E., depending on the point at which hydrolysis is stopped. The usual classifications are: low conversion, 28–37 D.E.; regular conversion, 38–49 D.E.; intermediate conversion, 50–57 D.E.; and high conversion, 58 D.E. or higher. As D.E. increases, sweetness and hygroscopicity increase, and the viscosity decreases. The approximate percentage of various saccharides in corn sirups of differing D.E. is given in Table 6. Birch (1968) has pointed out that D.E. is of more value in characterizing acid-hydrolyzed corn

TABLE 6. Approximate Distribution of Saccharides in Various Corn Sirups, Percent

Type	D.E.	Monosac-charides	Disac-charides	Trisac-charides and Higher
Regular conversion	38–49	19	14	67
Intermediate conversion	50–57	30	18	52
High conversion	58 and higher	39	33	28
Dual conversion	43	5	36	59

sirup than for enzyme or dual-conversion types, since the acid process is more nearly a random degradation than are the other two.

Lewis (1956) and Gehman et al. (1957) have reviewed the use of corn sweeteners in food products. Dual-conversion corn sirup is processed to produce a higher percentage of maltose and less glucose than regular conversion, so the dual-conversion sirup is considered to give better resistance to nonenzymatic browning (Stevens, 1962; Saussele and Fruin, 1962), due to the lower glucose content. Cantor (1969) mentions the use of glucose isomerase to produce a sirup in which approximately $\frac{1}{3}$ of the glucose has been isomerized to fructose.

Honey

Honey is a natural sirup varying in composition and flavor with the plant source of the nectar, and with processing and/or storage. The principal carbohydrates are glucose and fructose. A typical analysis is given as glucose, 34 percent; fructose, 41 percent; sucrose, 2.4 percent; and water, 18.3 percent. Honey is slightly acid, White et al. (1964) listing the pH as 3.84–4.22. White et al. (1962), Subers et al. (1966),

White and Kushnir (1967), Aso et al. (1960), and Watanabe and Aso (1960) give data on composition of honey.

Honey has a sweetness that is difficult to compare with that of sucrose. Its sweetness varies with concentration and degree of crystallization (Helvey, 1954). Lucas (1945) states that the majority of investigators find honey to be 70 to 75 percent as sweet as sucrose, although individual results ranged from 57 to 122 percent.

White et al. (1964) discuss the gradual color and flavor change that occurs during storage of honey, and the parallel development of hydroxymethylfurfural. It is frequently necessary to heat honey before storage, to prevent both fermentation by yeast and crystallization. Dyce (1931) showed that crystallization was caused by formation of glucose monohydrate. If the honey is heated to dissolve any crystals present, the high viscosity tends to prevent granulation, provided that the honey is protected from seeding. Glabe et al. (1963) describe the preparation of honey solids and their use in baked products.

An interesting extension of the information concerning granulation of honey is found in the work of Nury et al. (1964) on the problem of hardening of raisin paste during storage. Since the raisins have much the same sugar and water composition as honey, they theorized that the difficulty with raisin paste might be due to formation of glucose monohydrate. They obtained data to confirm this, and showed that heating to dissolve the crystals prevented hardening, as the re-formation of crystals was inhibited by the difficulty of nuclei formation in the viscous paste.

Maple Sugar and Syrup

Maple sirup and sugar are made from the sap of the hard maple (*Acer saccharum*). The sap contains about 2 percent solids, mostly sucrose, with trace amounts of a number of other compounds. The maple sap is concentrated to sirup by boiling at atmospheric pressure. The characteristic color and flavor of maple sirup are developed by heating above 100° C, as concentration at reduced pressures or by freeze-drying gives a flavorless (except sweet), colorless sirup. Soon after the start of evaporation at atmospheric pressure, the sap becomes sufficiently alkaline to induce fragmentation and polymerization of the hexose sugars, with resultant browning. Underwood and Willits (1963) reviewed research on maple sirup. Filipic et al. (1969) list compounds identified as contributing to the flavor.

Noncaloric Sweetening Agents

The commonly-used noncaloric sweeteners are saccharin and Na- or Ca-cyclamate. Sodium cyclamate is the common form, while calcium cyclamate is used in products for low-sodium diets or where the calcium ion is necessary, as in the gelling of low methoxyl pectin systems. Beck and Nelson (1963) have reviewed the properties of cyclamate and its role as a sweetening agent. The cyclamates are usually considered to be about 30 times, and saccharin about 375 times, as sweet as sucrose (Anon, 1963). Kamen (1959) points out that the cyclamates also have a bitter component, as does saccharin. The current (1971) concern as to the safety of use of cyclamates is prompting a search for alternate noncaloric sweetening agents.

ROLES

The sugars influence many properties of foods in addition to flavor. They alter the degree of hydration of many substances, influencing the viscosity of starch pastes, the firmness of gelatin and pectin gels, and the formation and strength of gluten strands. They increase the gelation temperature of gluten and of egg proteins. In many cases, they alter the color and texture of fruit products. They increase the moisture-retaining ability of many foods. And the size of sugar crystals influences markedly the textural characteristics of candies and frostings. One of the problems in substituting noncaloric sweetening agents is to identify acceptable sources to supply these other roles of sugars.

CANDY

Sugar cane is believed to have first developed into a field crop in India. The term "candy" is thought to come from the Sanskrit word, Kanda, meaning solidified or dried sugar (Artschwager and Brandes, 1958). While sucrose is usually the principal sugar used as an ingredient in candy formulas, an acid system will cause partial hydrolysis of sucrose to glucose and fructose; use of corn sirup means inclusion of glucose, maltose and other glucose polymers; honey contributes fructose and glucose; and milk as the liquid means the addition of some lactose, while the use of nonfat dry milk solids can contribute a considerable amount of lactose. So the "sugar" in the final candy is apt to be a mixture of sugars, rather than sucrose only. In addition, the high cooking temperatures needed to attain the low final moisture content may lead to chemical breakdown of the sugar molecules. Martin (1955) states that ". . . reactions which may occur in the production of even the simplest types of candies are extremely complex. . . ."

Types

Lewis (1955) classifies candies as (1) hard, (2) chewy, (3) aerated, and (4) crystalline. Martin (1955) groups them as (1) those made

Ingredients

The primary ingredients of candy formulas are sucrose and water. A wide variety of other ingredients may be used to influence the degree and type of crystallization, and to alter the textural characteristics of the resulting product. In addition, various coloring and flavoring materials may be added. These latter will not be discussed, except in cases where they also influence the texture and consistency.

White sugar is very nearly pure sucrose. Water, however, may vary widely from place to place, depending on the type and degree of hardness, and the particular salts dissolved in it. Many hard waters are slightly alkaline. Wodtcke (1962) gives the following rankings for effects of ions on the inversion of sucrose by acid: cations, $Mg^{++} > Ca^{++} > Sr^{++} > Ba^{++} > Li^+ > Na^+ > K^+ > NH_4^+$; anions, $ClO_4^- > Br^- > Cl^- > NO_3^- > SO_4^=$. He suggests that there also may be an influence due to direct interaction of neutral salts with sucrose. Lindemann (1953) found that the presence of $CaCl_2$, $MgCl_2$, or Fe or Cu salts produced discoloration of boiled candy.

Weak acids used in food preparation, such as lemon juice, vinegar, fruit juices, or the acid salt cream of tartar, all cause inversion of sucrose. If the sirup is boiled slowly for a long time, more inversion takes place than if it is boiled quickly. Hydrolysis may also occur during storage. The extent of hydrolysis will depend on the amount of acid present, and the time and temperature of storage.

Alkalis will cause structural alteration and degradation of most carbohydrates. Whistler and BeMiller (1958) state that in the presence of oxygen, both oxidation and alkaline degradation occur, leading to very complex mixtures of products. One familiar example of an alkaline candy is the addition of $NaHCO_3$ in making peanut brittle. Alkaline water may also give a candy mixture with a pH greater than 7.

The presence of sugars other than sucrose alters the crystallization characteristics of the candy mixture. Niedzielski (1963) found that increasing concentrations of invert sugar from 0.01 to 10 percent increased the time interval for appearance of crystals from about 100 to about 700 minutes in a sucrose solution with a supersaturation of 1.4 at 25° C. Milk products contribute lactose, which is much less soluble than sucrose. The various impurities in brown sugar or molasses will also influence crystallization. Goodwin (1958) has reviewed the functions and uses of sugars in the confectionery industry. Volker (1966) discussed the preparation and use of dextrose fondant.

A number of substances may be added to delay or prevent the formation of crystals. These include proteins of milk, gelatin, or egg; carbohydrates of starch, pectin, or dextrin; and fats. The use of cream, chocolate, or cocoa will contribute a considerable quantity of fat, while cocoa also contains dextrin. Depending on the amount used, these materials may reduce the rate of crystal growth or prevent crystallization by hindering the formation of nuclei. Surface-active agents such as glycerol mono-esters, lecithin, and polyhydroxy alcohols also influence the properties of candy products. Knightly (1961) has reviewed the roles of these materials. Gordon (1966) studies the effects of replacing milk solids with soy flour in caramels and nut pastes.

One of the interesting applications of inversion of sucrose is the addition of the enzyme invertase to fondant before encasing in a chocolate coating. The invertase is added to the fondant when it is melted for molding. The chocolate coating prevents water loss. During storage, as some sucrose is inverted, the liquid can dissolve more sugar; that is, a given amount of liquid will dissolve a greater quantity of three sugars, fructose, glucose, and sucrose, than of sucrose alone. With the dissolving of the sugars, the centers soften and may liquefy. Jansen (1960) has reviewed the mechanism of inversion and the necessity for control of pH, cooking time, sugar, sirup and water content, and casting temperature, in order to obtain the desired endpoint. Invertase is also used for bonbons, which dry out more rapidly than chocolate-coated candies, although a small amount of egg white added to fondant lessens the evaporation.

Fondant

Fondant is made when sucrose is cooked with water to a definite temperature, the sirup cooled and beaten, and the mass crystallized. According to accepted standards, fondant should be snowy white, the crystals so small that they are imperceptible, not gritty on the palate, and the fondant soft enough to be plastic and velvety, not dry and crumbly.

Cooking of Fondant

All the sucrose must be dissolved during the cooking period, as undissolved crystals will seed the mass and cause premature crystallization. A damp cloth may be used to remove crystals formed on the side of the pan during cooking. Figures 12 and 6 show the comparison between the crystal size in the original sugar and the crystal sizes in fondant prepared from this sugar.

The mixture should be stirred to aid in dissolving the sugar. Because boiling sugar solutions are not saturated solutions, they may be stirred as much as desired during boiling without causing crystallization, provided that no sirup is splashed on the sides of the pan. However, after the sirup stops boiling, it cools quickly and soon reaches the supersaturation point. If the sirup is poured for cooling from the pan in which it is cooked, this should be done quickly. The portion clinging to the side of the pan should not be scraped with the spoon, for this may cause crystals that seed the entire mass. Neither should the thermometer be allowed to roll around in the sirup, for this agitation of the sirup may start premature crystallization. The container into which the fondant is poured to cool should have a smooth surface, as rough surfaces may induce crystallization.

Concentration and Temperature

A sucrose solution contains 80 percent sucrose, that is, 80 grams of sucrose and 20 grams of water, boils at 112° C, is saturated at 90°, and is supersaturated below 90° C. Hence no crystals are formed in such a sucrose sirup until the temperature drops below 90° C. The higher the temperature to which the sirup is cooked, the less the percentage of water in the fondant. With too small a proportion of water, the fondant is dry and crumbly; with too much it is sirupy and runny. Sirups cooked to 109–111° C give a fondant too fluid to knead or mold unless beaten when hot. Fondant sirup for ordinary home use may be cooked to 113–115° C. Lower temperatures give a softer fondant for remelting; higher temperatures give a drier fondant for molding. Evaporation is proportionally greater from a small quantity of fondant, during stirring and kneading, than from a larger quantity. Jordan (1926) states that commercially the amount of moisture in fondant is controlled carefully according to the use for which it is intended, as a difference of one percent of moisture results in a fondant too soft to handle or too dry to knead.

Crystallization

Factors affecting the growth of crystals have been discussed previously. These principles apply to crystallization of sugar in candy making. Smaller crystals are obtained if the syrup is cooled before beating to increase the viscosity, then beaten until crystallization is complete to prevent aggregation of crystals. Compare the size of crystals in Figures 6, 7 and 8. Appelboom (1956) gives details of a method of preparing fondant to obtain crystal grain size of about 10 microns (μ).

Just as crystallization starts, the temperature of the mass rises slightly, and the mixture softens because of decreased viscosity. The temperature change is due to the release of energy at the change of state from liquid to solid. The decrease in viscosity is caused in part by the increased temperature, and in part by the decreased concentration of the remaining solution as part of the sugar solidifies.

Crystals in fondant grow in size during storage (Halliday and Noble, 1946). This can be seen by comparing Figures 6 and 13. Substances such as fats may be added to interfere with crystal growth; see Figures 14 and 15. Comparison of Figures 13 and 15 show the reduction in crystal growth during storage brought about by the addition of 5 percent butter to the fondant.

Addition of Egg

The addition of beaten egg white to fondant retards the rate of crystal growth during storage. Swanson (1929) found that not more than 6 percent beaten egg white could be added to fondant without making it too fluid. She found 3 percent added egg white as effective as 6 percent in preventing growth of crystals during storage.

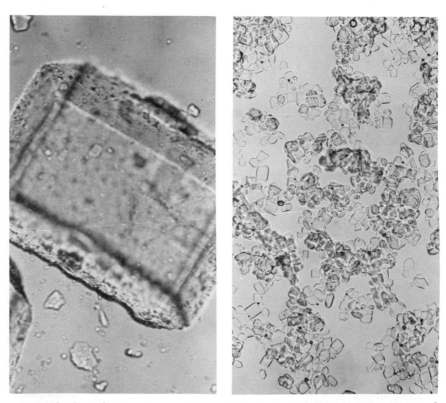

FIGURE 12. Crystal size of sugar from which fondant in Figure 6 was prepared. Magnification 50x.
FIGURE 13. Same fondant as Figure 6, after 2 months' storage at room temperature. Magnification 50x.

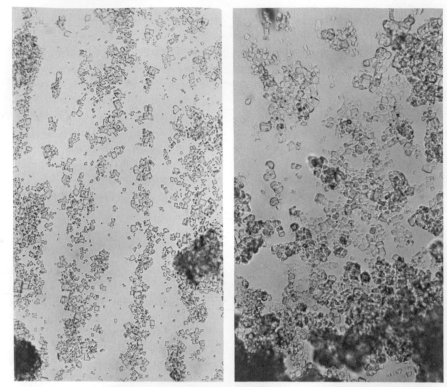

FIGURE 14. Fondant similar to Figure 6, with 5 percent butter added. Magnification 50x.

FIGURE 15. Same fondant as figure 14, after 2 months' storage at room temperature. Magnification 50x.

The addition of up to 2.5 percent dried egg yolk to fondant before cooking has been reported to permit usable fondant with a higher moisture content, giving a tender but readily moldable product (Maczelka, 1956).

Addition of Glucose, Fructose, or Invert Sugar

Glucose, fructose, or invert sirup may be added directly to sucrose solutions to aid in regulating the size of the crystals, or invert sugar may be formed during cooking of the sucrose solution by adding citric, tartaric, or acetic acid, or cream of tartar. It is difficult to regulate conditions, such as the time of cooking, to obtain a definite percentage of invert sugar in the cooked product, for sucrose is inverted more rapidly with higher temperatures, longer time, and greater acidity. Hence it is sometimes preferable to add a definite quantity of glucose, fructose, or invert sugar. Hamaguti et al. (1939) give the following ranking for increasing hydrolytic power of organic acids on 60 percent sucrose solution at 50° C: acetic < malic < fumaric < formic < tartaric < citric < malonic < maleic < oxalic. Woodruff and van Gilder (1931) found that cream of tartar inverted the sucrose more slowly than citric, tartaric, or hydrochloric acids at the same pH. If too large a quantity of acid is added, too much invert sugar is formed, the fondant is too fluid, and the flavor of the fondant is quite acid.

Woodruff and van Gilder (1931) state that sirups containing concentrations of 43 percent or more invert sugar will not crystallize; those containing 16–23 percent form a semifluid mass of crystals; and those with 6–15 percent give a plastic, moldable product. Crystals in candies of observed coarse texture measure 45 μ or more. Differences in crystal size of 6 to 10 μ could be detected by the tactile sense. DuRoss and Knightly (1963) state that crystal size should be in the range of 2 to 5 μ for good gloss, texture, and keeping quality of fondant.

The addition of corn sirup (Halliday and Noble, 1946) tends to prevent the growth of crystals in fondant. Maczelka (1956) found that additions of carbohydrates such as invert sugar, starch, and corn sirup retarded crystallization of sucrose, and also retarded drying out of the mass during storage.

Color

Fondant crystallized without stirring is translucent rather than snowy white. The snow-white appearance is due to the small crystal size and the tiny air bubbles incorporated during agitation. Paine (1924) states that the addition of a small quantity of egg white prevents the aggregation of the air particles, aiding in keeping the fondant white. The beaten egg white also incorporates additional air.

Fondant made with hard water, pH 7.2 to 7.8, has a creamy tint. If, to some of the same sugar and water, a little cream of tartar is added, a snowy white fondant is obtained. If, however, corn sirup is added to the sugar to make fondant with the above water, a gray color develops. If distilled water is used with the corn sirup and sucrose, the gray color does not develop.

Ripening

When fondant stands 12–24 hours it seems moister, is more plastic, and kneads more easily than when it was first made. In the candy trade this is known as "ripening." Fondants that contain substances that cause slow hydrolysis of the sucrose become softer because of the formation of invert sugar, but "ripening" is an additional process. Carrick (1919) suggests that the reason for this "ripening" is that the small crystals in the mass are dissolved, letting the large crystals move more easily, and the candy is thus more plastic.

Honey Fondant

Candies made from pure honey usually become very sticky a few hours after they are made, due to the high fructose content and its moisture-absorbing property. Phillips (1935) reports Stratton's (1932) combination of honey, whole milk, and lactose sugar to make fondant. Fondant usually contains some crystals of each of the sugars that enter into its composition, but in this instance the crystal phase is entirely lactose, the crystals being particularly minute. The lactose crystals have a tendency to grow so that the fondant becomes somewhat grainy.

Fudge

The same factors control the size of the crystals in fondant making and in fudge. Fudge may be made with brown sugar, giving a product that crystallizes less readily than if made with white sugar, due to the slight acidity of brown sugar. Fudge also ripens with storage, and if placed in a container with a tight-fitting lid, it becomes softer and more velvety after 24 hours' storage. Very fine crystal size is desirable not only for the immediate textural sensation, but also to prevent migration of fat and water to the surface of the candy mass. Grainy fudge allows this migration with consequent decrease in desirability of texture (Woodroof, 1960).

When cocoa is substituted for the chocolate in fudge, if other conditions are standardized, the final temperature to which the sirup should be cooked depends on the proportion of cocoa used. It is probably the dextrin in cocoa that affects the consistency of the sirup; with increasing amounts of cocoa, the temperature to which the sirup is cooked should be lower. Fat, such as butter, added to replace the fat of chocolate increases the temperature to which the sirup should be cooked.

Caramels

Caramels, taffy, and brittles are types of candy that are firm but amorphous. To prevent crystallization, larger quantities of glucose, fructose, corn sirup, or other substances are added than when making fondant or fudge. If these substances are not added directly, larger quantities of substances that produce inversion of sucrose are used, thus giving a higher percentage of invert sugar. These types of candy are cooked to higher temperatures than are crystalline ones. The greater concentration increases the viscosity of the mass, hindering crystallization.

The temperature to which caramels are cooked depends on the ingredients and their proportion. With increasing amounts of corn sirup, because of its dextrin content, this temperature is lowered. But with molasses or honey the temperature to which the caramels are cooked is higher than when corn sirup is used.

Amount of Milk

A large quantity of milk in caramels produces a characteristic flavor. Slow cooking develops more of the brown color and flavor than does rapid cooking. The color comes from lactose-protein compounds and the caramelization of the lactose with high temperatures and long cooking. If all the milk is added when cooking is first started, the milk may curdle. If most of the milk is added slowly after the sirup is thick it seldom curdles. The protein of the milk will tend to prevent crystallization. Duck (1959) found that increased milk protein increased the viscosity but decreased the elasticity of caramel, and that viscosity was more important than elasticity in determining the consistency and chewy texture of caramels. Large quantities of fat increase the richness of caramels.

Caramels are stirred or handled as little as possible after the sirup stops boiling. Stirring the sirup or scraping the pan during cooling tends to produce crystals.

Taffy

Taffies or pulled candies have vinegar, lemon juice, or cream of tartar added during cooking. These substances cause inversion of the sucrose, preventing crystallization. Glucose, corn sirup, or molasses may be added to the sucrose to prevent crystallization. Pulled taffies become white, or if made with molasses become much lighter in color, due to the air bubbles incorporated during pulling.

The cooking temperatures of pulled candies vary according to the ingredients and their proportions, but follow the same general rules as for caramels. Those containing large quantities of corn sirup are cooked to lower temperatures. Taffies are firmer than caramels and are therefore cooked to higher temperatures.

Brittles

Brittles are much harder than caramels or taffies and are cooked to high temperatures. At the temperatures to which they are cooked, caramelization of the sugar may take place, and this as well as added substances tends to prevent crystallization. If caramelization is very extensive, a number of decomposition products of sugar may develop, among which are some acid substances. The greater the amount of caramelization, the stronger the flavor developed. Soda is often added to brittles. It not only neutralizes the acidity developed and lessens the bitter flavor but, owing to gas formed, also gives a porous texture to the brittle.

Storage of Candy

Woodroof (1960) has reviewed a number of factors affecting the storage life of candies, including humidity, temperature, odor-free atmosphere, ingredients such as hydrogenated shortenings, emulsifiers and antioxidants, and types of coatings or packaging. The high sugar content of candies tends to make them quite hygroscopic. Heiss and Schachinger (1953) state that water may diffuse into the surface of candy, forming a saturated sugar solution. At 35–40 percent relative humidity (RH) this may form a continuous sticky surface film, while if the RH is as high as 65–72 percent, the candy may soften. Heiss (1959) found that in hard candies, formation of a sticky surface film may lead to graining, the rate of graining increasing with increasing RH. Makower and Dye (1956) found that amorphous sucrose gained water at appropriate RH conditions and then lost it on crystallization, since the crystallized form is anhydrous. The liberated water lowered the viscosity of the amorphous sugar, promoted cementation, and increased the rate of crystallization. They also found that glucose acts in the same way as sucrose, only more rapidly.

Instrumentation

In common with many areas of food research, there is increasing interest in the development of instrumental methods of measuring the characteristics of candies. This lessens the dependence on human evaluation, and increases the validity of comparisons of results obtained at different times and/or in different laboratories.

Microscopic observation is widely used in the study and recording of crystal sizes and shapes in crystalline candies. Measurements of viscosity and/or consistency of sirups and candy masses often yield valuable data. For example, Lipscomb (1956) has discussed viscosity as related to behavior of fondant sirups, toffee, and boiled bonbons. Martin et al. (1957) describe an instrument for measuring the consistency of fudge, while Duck (1959) discusses an instrument designed to measure stress relaxation in caramels. Nury et al. (1964) describe a modification of the L.E.E.–Kramer press· that they used to follow changes in consistency.

BROWNING REACTIONS

Browning reactions occur very widely in food materials. The colors produced range from pale yellow to dark brown or black, depending on the type of product and the extent of the reaction. In many foods the colors produced are considered desirable, for example, the brown crust of baked products and the color of caramel, maple sirup, or peanut brittle. In other foods browning is detrimental, as in darkening of dehydrated fruits, vegetables, eggs, and canned or dried milk. Even in foods where browning is desired, an excess produces an undesirable product.

Changes in odor and flavor often accompany the development of brown colors. Again, these may produce the characteristic flavors associated with a food or undesirable bitter flavors that make the food unpalatable. Hodge (1967) has reviewed the role of browning reactions as a source of flavor in food materials.

Types

Browning reactions may be either enzymatic or nonenzymatic. Many of the enzymatic type are recognized in fruits and vegetables, and involve the oxidation of polyphenolic compounds mediated by oxidative enzymes in plant cells. These are discussed in more detail in Chapter 6.

The nonenzymatic browning reactions frequently involve sugars or sugar-related compounds. The process of caramelizing to produce a brown sirup with a characteristic flavor is one of the traditional techniques in food preparation. More recently, the role of the reactions between amine groups of amino acids or proteins and the carbonyl groups of sugars in the production of brown color and altered flavor was recognized. In the past few years, it has been determined that browning reactions can also occur in lipids and in such compounds as ascorbic acid and other organic acids.

The chemistry of these reactions is exceedingly complex, and much of it is not well understood. However, there has been and continues to be a wide variety of studies, both with model systems in an attempt to elucidate the reactions, and in various food materials to determine the conditions necessary to produce and/or control the development of browning.

Sugar-Amine Reactions

Maillard (1912) was the first to describe the development of a brown color in mixtures containing amino acids and reducing sugars. Later it was shown that proteins as well as amino acids may react with the reducing sugars (Ramsey et al., 1933). Hodge (1953) summarized studies on model systems and proposed a general scheme for the reactions. Cole (1967) gave a simplified picture, and discussed the production of carbon dioxide, pigment, and conjugated unsaturated carbonyl compounds. Reynolds (1963, 1965, 1969) has reviewed the information available on the chemistry of these reactions.

The first step in the chain is the reaction between the carbonyl group of the sugar and the amine group of amino acids or proteins to form an aldosylamine. This then undergoes the Amadori rearrangement to produce a ketoseamine.

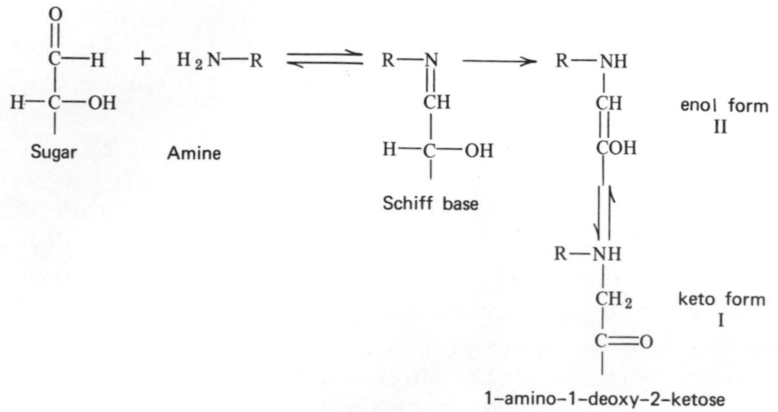

FIGURE 16. Proposed type reactions involved in initiation of nonenzymatic browning.

Compound I in Figure 16 is regarded as the critical intermediary for the formation of the autocatalytic system. Both I and II readily undergo fragmentation, dehydration, and condensation reactions. A wide variety of reactions can occur, the products eventually condensing to form brown polymers and copolymers known as melanoidins. The reaction system does not require oxygen. Hodge (1968) and Reynolds (1965) list a wide variety of compounds that may participate in these reactions.

A number of factors are known to influence the rate and degree of sugar-amine browning in foods. A few examples from the voluminous literature on model systems are cited below as an indication of the variety of work being done.

Burton and McWeeny (1963) indicate the importance of the initial configuration of the aldose on the rate of production of potential chromophore-developing compounds. Heynes and Paulsen (1960) list the reactivity of sugars in model systems, in order of decreasing reactivity: xylose, arabinose, galactose, mannose, glucose, lactose, and maltose. Reynolds (1963) points out that pentoses react more rapidly than hexoses to produce ketoseamines and brown pigments. Markuse (1960) studied the browning of glucose with 17 amino acids. The maximum effect was obtained with lysine, followed by tryptophane and arginine. The least change was shown with glutamic acid or proline. Glucose reacted more strongly with lysine than did lactose or fructose, while lactose reacted most readily with tryptophane. Since sucrose is a non-reducing sugar (no potential aldehyde group), it does not seem to fit the current conception of this reaction scheme. But Schoebel et al. (1969) and Karel and Labuza (1968) have shown that hydrolysis of sucrose can proceed even at very low water levels, with the hydrolysis products then participating in browning reactions.

The rate of browning increases rapidly with a rise in temperature. Reynolds (1963) states that studies on both foods and model systems show activation energy values in the range of 21 to 42 kcal. Täufel et al. (1958) studied browning produced by grinding mixtures of glycine with various sugars in a ball mill. For glucose, arabinose, or xylose, they found the effect of grinding to be more pronounced than that of heating to 100° C, although the temperature of the mass being ground did not rise. Ionizing radiations have also been shown to promote browning in sugar-amino acid systems (McCabe, 1960).

The pH of the system is another important factor in determining the rate and degree of browning. Underwood et al. (1959) found that the color development increased with increasing pH above 6.8 for glucose-α-amino acid solutions, and above pH 6.0 with glucose-ω-amino acids. Saunders and Jervis (1966) found that the presence of phosphate, citrate, and/or acetate buffer salts accelerated the rate of browning in their model system. Burton et al. (1962a) reported on the influence of pH on the effectiveness of sulfite in suppressing color development.

Ellis (1959) points out the importance of concentration, the reaction rate usually being decreased at low or very high water levels, although the dry materials will react. The reaction is also generally catalyzed by the presence of metals such as Fe and Cu, and by phosphate ions.

The reaction process produces a wide variety of compounds, both as intermediaries and as end products. Burton et al. (1962b), Hodge et al. (1963), and Kato and Fujimaki (1968) discuss some of the intermediate compounds formed. Ferretti et al. (1970) list 40 products isolated from a lactose-casein browning system, and Koehler et al. (1969) studied the reaction routes by which pyrazine compounds are formed.

Sugar-Browning Reactions

Many browning reactions occur with sugar alone, without the presence of compounds containing amine groups. Perhaps the most familiar of these is the browning of sugar when heated to produce caramel.

Hodge (1953) refers to the chemistry of the caramelization reactions as "astonishingly underdeveloped." Two basic types of reactions, dehydration and oxidation-reduction, can occur. Dehydration reactions produce furfural derivatives. Oxidation-reduction leads to fragmentation of the sugar molecule with the formation of reductones and other enediols. In both cases the number of end products can be very large, and these condense to form brown-colored polymers or copolymers.

Many foods are exposed to high temperatures in such procedures as roasting, baking, or frying, with resulting flavor change or development. Fagerson (1969) has reviewed the thermal degradation of carbohydrates. He lists 96 compounds that have been identified from heated glucose, including aldehydes, ketones, aromatics, furans, alcohols, acids, lactones, and other carbohydrates, and indicates a number of these which have been identified in various food products. Walter and Fagerson (1968) found that the distillate from heating anhydrous glucose in air at 250° C for 30 minutes contained at least 100 compounds. Johnson et al. (1969) give a list of products obtained by the pyrolysis of sucrose. Their results supported the hypothesis that many hexose pyrolysis products are formed by reactions similar to those occurring in strongly reducing aqueous acid media, but also suggested that other reactions must be occurring to explain many of the compounds formed.

Jenness and Patton (1959) list the possible dehydration and fragmentation products of lactose heated in buffered solutions near neutrality, including hydroxymethylfurfural, furfuryl alcohol, acetol, lactic, formic and acetic acids, levulinic, pyruvic and saccharinic acids, methyl glyoxal, acetaldehyde, and formaldehyde. Compounds other than sugars that will form brown pigments when heated in the absence of amine groups include polysaccharides, polyhydroxycarboxylic acids, reductones, α-dicarbonyl compounds, and quinones.

The rate and extent of browning in carbohydrate solutions are influenced by many of the same factors that influence the Maillard-type browning; heat, pH, type of sugar, irradiation, and the presence of catalysts. In general, the caramelization reactions have high energy requirements, so that they usually occur only at elevated temperatures. However, the energy requirement can be lowered by the presence of such catalysts as alkalis, carboxylic acids and their salts, phosphate ions, and metallic ions—especially Fe and Cu. Liggett et al. (1959) found that heating dry sugars or sugar solutions produced ultraviolet spectra characteristic of furfural derivatives, while irradiation of these systems yielded spectra characteristic of reductones, enediols, or enols.

Acids and bases both increase the browning of sugar solutions, with alkalis being particularly effective. Acids generally promote dehydration reactions, with the production of furfural derivatives, while alkalis induce isomerization and fragmentation of the sugar molecules (Lindemann, 1955; Berl and Feazel, 1954). Ramaiah and Agarwohl (1960) concluded that alkali acts as a catalyst in the caramelization of sugar, and is eventually neutralized by some of the reaction products, rather than reacting directly with the sugar. Kapur et al. (1957) studied the rate of browning of solutions of various sugars with organic acids. Under the conditions they used, fructose usually showed the greatest degree of browning, followed closely, or sometimes exceeded, by sucrose. Galactose solutions showed much less browning, and glucose least of all.

Other Nonenzymatic Browning Reactions

Reynolds (1965) discusses the browning reactions in lipid materials. The amino groups of phospholipids and lipoproteins can react with aldehydes and reducing sugars. Or carbonyl groups formed in the lipid material may initiate browning. Reynolds also mentions the roles of sugars containing nitrogen in the ring, uronic acids, and ascorbic acid. Burton and McWeeny (1963) review the role of phosphatides. Involvement of these types of compounds in browning reactions has been recognized only in the past few years, so there has been much less study of the mechanisms.

Browning Reactions in Foods

The study of browning reactions involving sugars is complicated in food materials not only by the complexity of the chemical makeup of the foods, but also by the fact that several different types may be occurring simultaneously. In addition, foods may contain compounds other than sugars that can undergo browning reactions. The browning reaction contributes to the aroma, flavor, and color of many foods such as ready-to-serve cereals, toffees, roasted coffee, malted barley, and baked goods (Lea, 1950). Peck (1955) has reviewed the production of caramel color and its use to color and flavor foods such as soft drinks, alcoholic beverages, bakery products, soups, gravies, sauces, condiments, cake mixes, canned meat products, coffee products, and bouillon cubes. Studies on the role of browning reactions in producing desirable colors and flavors in foods have been reported for potato chips (Shallenberger et al. 1959), maple sirup (Underwood et al., 1961), bread (Kiely et al., 1960; Linko and Johnson, 1963; Rothe and Thomas, 1959; Rubenthaler et al., 1963), baked products (Nordin and Johnson, 1957; Kováts and Rajky, 1958; Johnson and Miller, 1961), fresh pork (Pearson et al., 1962), and cookies (Pomeranz et al., 1962). Pomeranz et al. (1962) point out that cereals contain pentoses as well as hexoses, especially if the wheat embryo is present or if rye flour is used. As has been indicated, the pentoses are generally even more chromogenic than the hexoses. One of the familiar examples of desirable color and flavor change is that produced by deep-fat frying thin potato slices for chips. Talley and Porter (1968) have outlined a more quantitative approach to this problem by using discs of filter paper soaked in solutions of sugars and amino acids, rather than the vegetable tissue. The discs can then be applied directly to resin columns for ion-exchange separation of the browning intermediates and residues.

The undesirable effects of the browning reaction have been known in the sugar, beer, and malting industries. Many other food products may be affected. These include dried foods such as milk, eggs, fruits, fruit juices, meat, fish, coconut, and vegetables (Barnes and Kaufman, 1947); canned products such as milk, fruits, fruit juices, and juice concentrates; and other foods such as molasses. The color may vary from light cream to nearly black. Coconut develops a saffron color.

Studies on deleterious browning reactions have been reported for such varied products as wheat germ (Pomeranz and Shellenberger, 1961), fish (Jones, 1959 a, b), dehydrated meat (Sharp, 1957), milk and milk products (Patton, 1955; Dutra et al., 1958), processed potatoes (Schwimmer et al., 1957), orange juice (Lalikainen et al., 1958; Tatum et al., 1967), lemon juice (Clegg, 1964), dried peaches (Huang and Draudt, 1964), and dried cabbage (Ranganna and Setty, 1968).

Control of Browning Reactions in Foods

The same factors that are important in browning reactions in model systems also influence the browning of foods. High temperatures promote the browning of the crust on baked products and meats, while low storage temperatures delay the development of brown colors in dehydrated products. The types and concentrations of amino compounds and/or sugars influence the degree and rate of browning. The water content of the food is also important, although the relationship is a complex one. For example, reducing the water content of dehydrated foods will reduce browning until relatively low levels are reached. However, if the water content is reduced further, the rate of browning will increase. The critical water level varies with the food product under consideration.

The pH of the food is very important in influencing the browning. In general, increasing pH enhances browning. Many foods increase in pH during cooking. In addition, certain formulas are designed to produce an alkaline system, as in the use of soda in a devil's food cake or in peanut brittle. However, many of the organic acids also promote browning, and can contribute to the browning of materials such as canned fruit juices.

Yu et al. (1969) studied the prevention of browning in radiation-sterilized seafood products. They reported that the only samples that remained white were those in which the reducing sugar content of the fish tissue had been decreased by leaching, and antioxidants, binders, SO_2, and $CaCl_2$ had been added in formulating the fish product.

Sulfur dioxide is widely used to prevent or lessen browning in a great variety of food products. Joslyn and Braverman (1954) have reviewed the use of SO_2 and sulfites especially with reference to foods of plant origin, while Gehman and Osman (1954) considered the chemistry of the sugar-sulfite interactions in relation to food products. Ellis (1959) suggested that the effectiveness of SO_2 may be due to the ease with which it combines with furfuraldehyde, while Ingles (1960) proposed an oxidative mechanism involving the conversion of part of the reducing sugar to acids and related compounds. Burton and co-workers state that sulfites act in a complex manner, and believe that their effectiveness may be enhanced by this diversity. In varying model systems, they found that bisulfite appeared to add to unsaturated aldehydes (McWeeny and Burton, 1963), may block a necessary configurational change in the structure of the sugar (Burton et al., 1963a), or may combine both with the carbonyl group and with unsaturated centers (Burton et al., 1963b). Song and Chichester (1967) suggest that the sulfite inhibitor forms free radicals that then interact with chromophoric intermediates and melanoidin precursors to prevent pigment formation.

Kapur et al. (1959) found that the addition of β-carotene delayed the formation of brown precursors in a glucose-glycine solution stored at 55° C. In a few cases, browning can be controlled by removal of sugar. Egg white is treated with glucose oxidase to oxidize the glucose to gluconic acid before dehydration, to prevent browning of the dried egg white.

References

SCIENTIFIC PRINCIPLES

Anon. 1962. Plant Handbook Data. Table 2. pH values of food products. *Food Eng. 34*, No. 3: 98.

Bancroft, W. D. 1920. Supersaturation and crystal size. *J. Phys. Chem. 24*: 100.

Bratton, C. B., A. L. Hopkins, and J. W. Weinberg. 1965. Nuclear magnetic resonance studies of living muscle. *Science 147*: 738.

Booth, A. H., and H. E. Buckley. 1955. The effect of boric acid on the growth of ethylene diamine tartrate crystals. *Can. J. Chem. 33*: 1162.

Browne, C. A. 1912. *A Handbook of Sugar Analysis*, 2nd ed., John Wiley & Sons, New York.

Davis, K. S., and J. A. Day. 1961. *Water the Mirror of Science*. Anchor Books, Doubleday & Co., Inc., Garden City, N.Y.

Hopkins, A. L. 1960. Radio-frequency spectroscopy of frozen biological material: dielectric heating and the study of bound water. *Ann. N.Y. Acad. Sciences 85;* Art. 2: 714.

Kefford, J. F. 1957. Acidity and pH values. *Food Pres. Quart. 17*: 30.

Murrell, J. N. 1969. Current awareness No. 13. The hydrogen bond. *Chem. in Britain 5*, No. 3 (March).

Pauling, L. 1960. *The Nature of the Chemical Bond and the Structure of Molecules and Crystals*. Cornell U. Press, Ithaca, N.Y., 3rd. ed.

Pimentel, G. C., and A. L. McClellan. 1960. *The Hydrogen Bond*. W. H. Freeman and Co., San Francisco.

Samardžić, V., Z. Šljivarić, Z. Kovač, and B. Mikas. 1969. Influence of water hardness on rheological properties of dough. *Kemija Ind. 18*: 164; Abstr., *J. Sci. Food Agric. 20*: ii–147.

Sandorfy, C. 1965. Reports of symposiums: hydrogen bonding. *Science 147*: 910.

Toledo, R., M. P. Steinberg, and A. I. Nelson. 1968. Quantitative determination of bound water by NMR. *J. Food Sci. 33*: 315.

Tutton, A. E. H. 1924. *The Natural History of Crystals*, Chapter VI. E. P. Dutton & Co., New York.

Van Hook, A. 1961. *Crystallization: Theory and Practice*. Reinhold Publ. Corp., New York.

Watson, J. D. 1965. *Molecular Biology of the Gene*, p. 112. W. A. Benjamin, Inc., New York.

Woodams, E. E., and J. E. Nowrey. 1968. Literature values of thermal conductivities of foods. *Food Technol. 22*: 494.

SUGARS AND CANDIES

Advances in Carbohydrate Chemistry. Yearly volumes. Academic Press, Inc., New York.

Advances in Chemistry Series No. 12. 1955. *Uses of Sugars and Other Carbohydrates in the Food Industry.* Amer. Chem. Soc., Washington, D.C.

Anon. 1963. Boom in dietetic products boosts sweeteners. *Chem. and Eng. News. 41*, No. 19: 30.

Appleboom, A. F. J., Jr. 1956. Fondant graining—a micro-grain for low-grade massecuite seeding. *Int. Sugar J. 58:* 99.

Artschwager, E., and E. W. Brandes. 1958. Sugarcane: origin, classification, characteristics and descriptions of representative clones. *U.S.D.A. Handbook No. 122*, Washington, D.C.

Aso, K., T. Watanabe, and K. Yamao. 1960. Studies on honey. I. On the sugar composition of honey. *Tohoku J. Agr. Res. 11:* 101.

Ballinger, R. A., and L. C. Larkin. 1964. Sweeteners used by food processing industries; their competitive position in the United States. *Agr. Econ. Rep. No. 48*, Econ. Res. Serv., U.S. Dept. Agr.

Barrow, G. M. 1961. *Physical Chemistry*, p. 61. McGraw-Hill Book Co., Inc., New York.

Beck, K. M., and A. S. Nelson. 1963. Latest uses of synthetic sweeteners. *Food Eng. 35*, No. 5: 96.

Birch, G. G. 1968. The characterization of acid-hydrolyzed corn sirups: A theoretical appraisal. *J. Food Technol. 3:* 159.

Bollenback, G. N. 1969. Sugars. In *Symposium on Foods: Carbohydrates and Their Roles*, H. W. Schultz, R. F. Cain, and R. W. Wrolstad, eds., Avi Publ. Co., Westport, Conn., p. 373.

Boyd, W. C., and S. Matsubara. 1962. Different tastes of enantiomorphic hexoses. *Science 137:* 669.

Browne, C. A. 1922. Moisture absorptive power of different sugars and carbohydrates under varying conditions of atmospheric humidity. *Ind. Eng. Chem. 14:* 712.

Cameron, A. T. 1947. The taste sense and the relative sweetness of sugars and other sweet substances. *Sugar Res. Found., Sci. Rep. Ser.* No. 9, N.Y.

Cantor, S. M. 1969. Introduction to the symposium. In *Symposium on Foods: Carbohydrates and Their Roles*, H. W. Schultz, R. F. Cain, and R. W. Wrolstad, eds. Avi. Publ. Co., Westport, Conn., p. 1.

Carrick, M. S. 1919. Some studies in fondant making. *J. Phys. Chem. 23:* 589.

Dahlberg, A. C., and E. S. Penczek. 1941. The relative sweetness of sugars as affected by concentration. *N.Y. Agr. Exp. Sta. Tech. Bull.* No. 258.

Duck, W. 1959. A study of the consistency of caramel. *Mfg. Confect. 39*, No. 6: 29.

DuRoss, J. W., and W. H. Knightly. 1963. Key to fine candy grain extends shelf life. *Candy Ind. Confectioner J. 121*, No. 2: 5.

Dyce, E. J. 1931. Fermentation and crystallization of honey. *Cornell Univ. Agr. Exp. Sta. Bull.* No. 528.

Fagerson, I. S. 1969. Thermal degradation of carbohydrates, a review. *J. Agr. Food Chem. 17*: 747.

Filipic, V. J., J. C. Underwood, and C. J. Dooley. 1969. Trace components of the flavor fraction of maple syrup. *J. Food Sci. 34*: 105.

Fincke, A. 1952. Bemerkunge zur Berechnung und Messung des pH-Wertes Konzentrierten Zuckerlösungen. *Zucker-Suesswarenwirt. 5*: 81.

Gehman, H. G., M. Moffet, and C. R. Keim. 1957. Usages alimentaires des amidons et de leurs sirops. *Ind. Aliment. Agr. 74*: 553.

Gilman, H., and A. P. Hewlett. 1929. Some correlations in constitution with sweet taste in the furan series. *Iowa State Coll. J. Sci. 4*: 27.

Glabe, E. F., P. F. Goldman, and P. W. Anderson. 1963. Honey solids—a new functional sweetener for baking. *Baker's Dig. 37*, No. 5: 49.

Goodwin, R. W. L. 1958. Sugars and starches. *Confect. Prod. 24*: 141; 417; 774.

Gordon, A. 1966. Effects of full fat soy flour in caramel and nut paste confectionery. *Food Process. Market. 35*: 429.

Gunther E. 1959. Protein in candy. *Mfg. Confect. 39*, No. 9: 27.

Halliday, E. G., and I. T. Noble. 1946. *Hows and Whys of Cooking*, 3rd ed., University of Chicago Press.

Hamaguti, E., T. Simizu, and T. Niinuma. 1939. Inversion of sucrose by various organic acids. *J. Soc. Trop. Agr., Taihoku Imp. Univ. 11*: 300; *Chem. Abstr. 34*: 7131 (1940).

Heiss, R. 1959. Prevention of stickiness and graining in stored hard candies. *Food Technol. 13*, No. 8: 433.

Heiss, R., and L. Schachinger. 1953. Untersuchungen über die Haltbarkeit von Hartkaramellen. I. Vorgänge in der Randschicht. *Stärke 5*: 152.

Helvey, T. C. 1954. Study on some physical properties of honey. *Food Res. 19*: 282.

Holum, J. R. 1962. *Elements of General and Biological Chemistry*, p. 251. John Wiley and Sons, Inc., New York.

Honig, P. 1963. *Principles of Sugar Technology*. Vol. III. American Elsevier Pub. Co., Inc., New York.

Houle, M. J., and K. J. Goering. 1961. Enzymatic conversion of barley carbohydrate into syrup. *Food Technol. 15*: 25.

Jansen, F. 1960. Invertase and cast cream centers. *Mfg. Confect. 40*, No. 4: 41.

Johnson, A. R. 1969. Analytical profiles of sorghum cane and sugar cane sirups. *J. Assoc. Offic. Anal. Chemists 52*: 1.

Jordan, S. 1926. Chemistry and confectionery. *Ind. Eng. Chem. 16*: 336.

Kamen, J. 1959. Interaction of sucrose and calcium cyclamate on perceived intensity of sweetness. *Food Res. 24*: 279.

Knightly, W. H. 1961. Surface active agents: Their functions and application in confections. *Mfg. Confect. 41*, No. 2: 29.

Lewis, F. A. 1955. Corn syrup is more than a sweetener. *Food Eng. 27*, No. 5: 75.

Lewis, F. A. 1956. Corn sweeteners in food-products manufacture. *West. Canner and Packer 48*, No. 11: 26.

Lichtenstein, P. E. 1948. The relative sweetness of sugars; sucrose and dextrose. *J. Exp. Psychol. 38*: 578.

Lindemann, E. 1953. Der Einfluss von Salzen im Stärkesirup auf die Inversion der Saccharose beim Bonbonkochen und die Verfärbung der Bonbonmassen. *Stärke 5*: 175.

Lipscomb, A. G. 1956. Die Rheologie von Süsswaren-Sirupen und gekochten Bonbons. *Fette, Seifen, Anstrichm. 58*: 875.

Lucas, P. S. 1945. Honey in ice cream. *Mich. Agr. Exp. Sta. Quart. Bull. 27*: 377.

MacLeod, S. 1952. A construction and attempted validation of sensory sweetness scales. *J. Exp. Psychol. 44*: 316.

Maczelka, L. 1956. The properties of and changes in sucrose-water systems containing additives and a crystalline solid phase. I. *Elelmez. Ipar, Budapest 10*: 231; *Food Sci. Abstr. 29*: 621 (1957).

Makower, B., W. B. Dye. 1956. Equilibrium moisture content and crystallization of amorphous sucrose and glucose. *J. Agr. Food Chem. 4*: 72.

Martin, L. F. 1955. Applications of research to problems of candy manufacture. *Advan. Food Res. 6*: 1.

Martin, L. F., C. H. Mack, A. G. Smith, and F. J. Fahs. 1957. Progress in Candy. Res. Rep. No. 31, Nat. Conf. Assoc. and Southern Utilization Res. and Dev. Div., June, Agr. Res. Serv., U.S.D.A.

Nelson, T. J. 1949. Hygroscopicity of sugar and other factors affecting retention of quality. *Food Technol. 3*: 347.

Niedzielski, Z. 1963. Inhibiting effect of invert sugar on the formation of crystal nuclei in a supersaturated sucrose solution. *Gaz. Cukr. 71*: 156; *Sugar Ind. Abstr. 26*: 64 (1964).

Nieman, C. 1958. Relative sweetening capacity of different sugars. *Zucker-Suesswarenwirt. 11*: 420; 465; 505; 632; 634; 670; 752; 791; 878; 933; 974; 1012; 1051; 1088.

Nieman, C. 1960. Sweetness of glucose, dextrose and sucrose. *Mfg. Confect. 40*, No. 8: 19.

Nury, F. S., J. E. Brekke, and H. R. Bolin. 1964. Raisin paste: measurement and control of consistency. *Food Technol. 18*: 377.

Paine, H. S. 1924. Constructive chemistry in relation to confectionery manufacture. *Ind. Eng. Chem. 16*: 513.

Pangborn, R. M. 1963. Relative taste intensities of selected sugars and organic acids. *J. Food Sci. 28*: 726.

Pangborn, R. M., G. L. Marsh, W. R. Channell, and H. Campbell. 1960. Consumer opinion of sweeteners in frozen concentrated lemonade and orange juice drink. *Food Technol. 14*: 515.

Pariser, E. R. 1961. How physical properties of candy affect taste. *Mfg. Confect. 41*, No. 5: 47.

Phillips, E. F. 1935. Overcoming difficulties in the use of honey. *Food Ind. 7*: 61.

Pigman, W., ed. 1957. *The Carbohydrates: Chemistry, Biochemistry, Physiology.* Academic Press, Inc., New York.

Quinlan, D. 1954. Sugar types and uses. *Food Eng. 26*, No. 6: 85.

Saussele, H., Jr., and J. C. Fruin. 1962. 71 D. E. Corn syrup. *Mfg. Confect. 62*, No. 47.

Schliepake, D. 1963. Structure of aqueous sucrose solutions. *Zücker 16*: 523.

Schneider, F., D. Schliepake, and A. Klimmek. 1963. Über die Viskosität von Reinen Saccharoselösungen. *Zücker 16*: 465.

Schultz, H. W., R. F. Cain, and R. W. Wrolstad, eds. 1969. *Symposium on Foods: Carbohydrates and Their Roles.* Avi Publ. Co., Westport, Conn.

Schutz, H. G., and F. J. Pilgrim. 1957. Sweetness of various compounds and its measurement. *Food Res. 22*: 206.

Segur, J. B., and C. S. Miner, Jr. 1954. Sugar solubility: sugar mixtures in aqueous glycerol. *J. Agr. Food Chem. 2*: 132.

Shallenberger, R. S., T. E. Acree, and C. Y. Lee. 1969. Sweet taste of D- and L-sugars and amino acids and the steric nature of their chemo-receptor sites. *Nature 221*: 555.

Shaw, P. E., J. H. Tatum, and R. E. Berry. 1967. Acid-catalyzed degradation of D-fructose. *Carbohyd. Res. 5*: 266.

―――, ―――, ―――. 1968. Base-catalyzed fructose degradation and its relation to nonenzymic browning. *J. Agr. Food Chem. 16*: 979.

―――, ―――, ――― -. 1969. Base-catalyzed sucrose degradation studies. *J. Agr. Food Chem. 17*: 907.

Steinhardt, R. G., Jr., A. D. Calvin, and E. A. Dodd. 1962. Taste: structure correlation with α-D-mannose and β-D-mannose. *Science 135*: 367.

Stevens, G. 1962. High-maltose syrup aids quality. *Food Eng. 34*, No. 9: 97.

Stone, H., and S. M. Oliver. 1969. Measurement of the relative sweetness of selected sweeteners and sweetener mixtures. *J. Food Sci. 34*: 215.

Stratton, N. J. April 19, 1932. U.S. Patent 1,854,430.

Subers, M. H., A. I. Schepartz, and R. P. Koob. 1966. Separation and identification of some organic phosphates in honey by column and paper chromatography. *J. Apicultural Res. 5*: 49.

Swanson, E. L. 1929. The effect of egg albumen on the crystallization of sugars from sirups. M.S. thesis, unpublished, Iowa State College Library.

Taylor, J. B., and J. S. Rowlinson. 1955. The thermodynamic properties of aqueous solutions of glucose. *Trans. Faraday Soc. 51:* 1183.

Tsuzubi, Y., and J. Yamazaki. 1953. On the sweetness of fructose and some other sugars, especially its variation with temperature. *Biochem. Z. 323:* 525.

Underwood, J. C., and C. O. Willits. 1963. Research modernizes the maple-sirup industry. *Food Technol. 17:* 1380.

Van Hook, A. 1961. *Crystallization: Theory and Practice.* Reinhold Publ. Co., New York.

Volker, H. H. 1966. Problems in the preparation and use of dextrose fondant. *Stärke 18:* 354.

Watanabe, T., and K. Aso. 1960. Honey. II. Isolation of kojibiose, nigerose, maltose and isomaltose from honey. *Tohoku J. Agr. Res. 11:* 109.

Whistler, R. L., and J. N. BeMiller. 1958. Alkaline degradation of polysaccharides. *Advan. Carbohyd. Chem. 13:* 289.

White, J. W., Jr., and I. Kushnir. 1967. Composition of honey. VII. Proteins. *J. Apicultural Res. 6:* 163.

White, J. W., Jr., I. Kushnir, and M. H. Subers. 1964. Effect of storage and processing temperatures on honey quality. *Food Technol. 18:* 555.

White, J. W., Jr., M. L. Riethof, M. H. Subers, and I. Kushnir. 1962. Composition of American honeys. *U.S.D.A. Tech. Bull. No. 1261.*

Wick, E. L. 1963. Sweetness in fondants. *Mfg. Confect. 43,* No. 5: 59.

Woodroof, J. G. 1960. Recent developments affecting the storage of confectionery. *Zucker Suesswarenwirt. 13:* 286.

Woodruff, S., and H. van Gilder. 1931. Photomicrographic studies of sucrose crystals. *J. Phys. Chem. 35:* 1355.

BROWNING REACTIONS

Barnes, H. M., and C. W. Kaufman. 1947. Industrial aspects of browning reaction. *Ind. Eng. Chem. 39:* 1167.

Berl, W. G., and C. E. Feazel. 1954. Ultraviolet spectra in alkaline solutions. *J. Ag. Food Chem. 2:* 37.

Burton, H. S., and D. J. McWeeny. 1963a. Non-enzymatic browning reactions: consideration of sugar stability. *Nature 197:* 266.

Burton, H. S., and D. J. McWeeny. 1963b. Role of phosphatides in nonenzymatic browning. *Nature 197:* 1086.

Burton, H. S., D. J. McWeeny, and D. O. Biltcliffe. 1962a. The influence of pH on SO_2-aldose-amino-reactions. *Chem. and Indus. 16:* 1682.

Burton, H. S., D. J. McWeeny, and D. O. Biltcliffe. 1962b. Development of chromophores. *Nature 196:* 40.

Burton, H. S., D. J. McWeeny, and D. O. Biltcliffe. 1963a. Sulphur dioxide and ketoseamino reactions. *Chem. and Indus. 17:* 693.

———, ———, ———. 1963b. Non-enzymic browning: the role of unsaturated carboxyl compounds as intermediates and of SO_2 as an inhibitor of browning. *J. Sci. Food Agr.* 14: 911.

Clegg, K. M. 1964. Non-enzymic browning of lemon juice. *J. Sci. Food Agr.* 15: 878.

Cole, S. J. 1967. The Maillard reaction in food products: carbon dioxide production. *J. Food Sci.* 32: 245.

Dutra, R. C., N. P. Tarassuk, and M. Kleiber. 1958. Origin of the carbon dioxide produced in the browning reaction of evaporated milk. *J. Dairy Sci. 41*: 1017.

Ellis, G. P. 1959. The Maillard reaction. *Advan. Carbohyd. Chem. 14*: 63.

Fagerson, I. S. 1969. Thermal degradation of carbohydrates: a review. *J. Agr. Food Chem. 17*: 747.

Ferretti, A., V. P. Flanagan, and J. M. Ruth. 1970. Non-enzymatic browning in a lactose-casein model system. *J. Agr. Food Chem. 18*: 13.

Gehman, H., and E. M. Osman. 1954. The chemistry of the sugar-sulfite reaction, and its relationship to food problems. *Advan. Food Res. 5*: 53.

Heynes, K., and Paulsen, H. 1960. Uber die chemischen Grundlagen der Maillard-Reaktion. *Wissenschaftliche Veröffentlichungen der Deutschen Gesellschaft für Ernährung. 5*: 15.

Hodge, J. E. 1953. Chemistry of browning reactions in model systems. *J. Agr. Food Chem. 1*: 928.

Hodge, J. E. 1967. Origin of flavor in foods: non-enzymatic browning reactions. In *Chemistry and Physiology of Flavors*, H. W. Schultz, E. A. Day, and L. M. Libbey, eds., p. 465. Avi Publ. Co., Westport, Conn.

Hodge, J. E. 1968. Enzymatic browning of foods. *Proc., Current Topics in Food and Nutrition*, p. 127. Dept. Home Econ., Univ. of Iowa, Iowa City, Iowa.

Hodge, J. E., B. E. Fisher, and E. C. Nelson. 1963. Dicarbonyls, reductones, and heterocyclics produced by reactions of reducing sugars with secondary amine salts. *Proc. Amer. Soc. Brewing Chemists*, p. 84.

Huang, I-Y., and H. N. Draudt. 1964. Effect of moisture on the accumulation of carbonyl-amine browning intermediates in freeze-dried peaches during storage. *Food Technol. 18*, No. 8: 124.

Ingles, D. L. 1960. Chemistry of non-enzymic browning. XI. The reactions of bisulphite with reducing sugars. *Aust. J. Chem. 13*: 404.

Jenness, R., and S. Patton. 1959. *Principles of Dairy Chemistry*. John Wiley and Sons, Inc., New York.

Johnson, J. A., and B. S. Miller. 1961. Browning of baked products. *Baker's Dig. 35* (Oct.): 52.

Johnson, R. R., E. D. Alford, and G. W. Kinzer. 1969. Formation of sucrose pyrolysis products. *J. Agr. Food Chem. 17*: 22.

Jones, N. R. 1959a. "Browning" reactions and the loss of free amino acid and sugar from lyophilized muscle extractives of fresh and chill-stored codling (*Gadus Callarias*). *Food Res. 24*: 704.

————. 1959b. Kinetics of phosphate-buffered, ribose-amino reactions at 40° and 70% relative humidity: systems related to the "browning" of dehydrated and salt cod. *J. Sci. Food Agr. 10*: 615.

Joslyn, M. A., and J. B. S. Braverman. 1954. The chemistry and technology of the pretreatment and preservation of fruit and vegetable products with sulfur dioxide and sulfites. *Advan. Food Res. 5*: 97.

Kapur, N. S., B. S. Bhatia, D. S. Bhatia, and G. Lal. 1957. Non-enzymic browning of food products: sugar-organic acid model systems. *Food Sci., Mysore, 7*: 181.

Kapur, N. S., B. S. Bhatia, D. S. Bhatia, and G. Lal. 1959. Non-enzymic browning of foods: effect of β-carotene on glucose-glycine model systems. *Indian J. Appl. Chem. 22*: 103.

Karel, M., and T. P. Labuza. 1968. Nonenzymatic browning in model systems containing sucrose. *J. Agr. Food Chem. 16*: 717.

Kato, H., and M. Fujimaki. 1968. Formation of *N*-substituted pyrrole-2-aldehydes in the browning reaction between D-xylose and amino compounds. *J. Food Sci. 33*: 445.

Kiely, P. J., A. C. Nowlin, and J. H. Moriarty. 1960. Bread aromatics from browning systems. *Cereal Sci. Today 5*: 273.

Koehler, P. E., M. E. Mason, and J. A. Newell. 1969. Formation of pyrazine compounds in sugar-amino acid model systems. *J. Agr. Food Chem. 17*: 393.

Kováts, L. T., and A. Rajky. 1958. Zur Frage der nicht-enzymatischen Bräunung. *Nahrung 2*: 893.

Lalikainen, T., M. A. Joslyn, and C. O. Chichester. 1958. Mechanism of browning of ascorbic acid-citric acid-glycine systems. *J. Agr. Food Chem. 6*: 135.

Lea, C. H. 1950. The role of amino acids in the deterioration of food: the browning reaction. *Chem. & Ind.*, p. 155.

Liggett, R. W., C. E. Feazel, and J. Y. Ellenberg. 1959. Browning reactions initiated by gamma irradiation. *J. Agr. Food Chem. 7*: 277.

Lindemann, E. 1955. Die Spektralphotometrische Bestimmung von Furfurol und 5-oxymethylfurfurol in Kohlenhydrathydrolysaten. *Stärke 7*: 280.

Linko, Y. Y., and J. A. Johnson. 1963. Changes in amino acids and formation of carbonyl compounds during baking. *J. Agr. Food Chem. 11*: 150.

Maillard, L. C. 1912. Action des acides amines sur les sucres: formation des mélanoidines par vois méthodique, *Compt. rend. 154*: 66.

Markuse, Z. 1960. Browning and reducing power of sugar solutions heated with amino acids. *Acta Chem. Acad. Sci. Hung. 23*: 247.

McCabe, L. J. 1960. Effects of ionizing radiations on carbohydrates and related substances. *Diss. Abstr. 20*: 3957.

McWeeny, D. J., and H. S. Burton. 1963. Some possible glucose/glycine browning intermediates and their reactions with sulphites. *J. Sci. Food Agr. 14:* 291.

Nordin, P., and J. A. Johnson. 1957. Browning reaction products of cake crumb. *Cereal Chem. 34:* 170.

Patton, S. 1955. Browning and associated changes in milk and its products: a review. *J. Dairy Sci. 38:* 457.

Pearson, A. M., G. Harrington, R. G. West, and M. E. Spooner. 1962. The browning produced by heating fresh pork. I. The relation of browning intensity to chemical constituents and pH. *J. Food Sci. 27:* 177.

Peck, F. W. 1955. Caramel color, its properties and its uses. *Food Eng.* 27, No. 3: 94.

Pomeranz, Y., J. C. Johnson, and J. A. Shellenberger. 1962. Effect of various sugars on browning. *J. Food Sci. 27:* 350.

Pomeranz, Y., and J. A. Shellenberger. 1961. Changes in dye absorption capacity of wheat embryos undergoing a browning reaction. *J. Agr. Food Chem.* 9: 428.

Ramaiah, N. A., and S. K. D. Agarwohl. 1960. On studies on the kinetics of caramelization of sugars. Further studies on the kinetics of caramelization of sugars. *Proc. 28th Ann. Conv. Sugar Technol. Assoc. India,* pp. 101.

Ramsey, R. J., P. H. Tracy, and H. A. Ruehe. 1933. The use of corn sugar in the manufacture of sweetened condensed milk. *J. Dairy Sci. 16:* 17.

Ranganna, S., and L. Setty. 1968. Nonenzymatic discoloration in dried cabbage. Ascorbic acid-amino acid interactions. *J. Agr. Food Chem. 16:* 529.

Reynolds, T. M. 1963. Chemistry of nonenzymic browning. I. The reaction between aldoses and amines. *Advan. Food Res. 12:* 1.

Reynolds, T. M. 1965. Chemistry of nonenzymic browning. II. *Advan. Food Res. 14:* 167.

Reynolds, T. M. 1969. Nonenzymic browning: sugar-amine interactions. In *Symposium on Foods: Carbohydrates and their Roles,* H. W. Schultz, R. F. Cain, and R. W. Wrolstad, eds., p. 219. Avi Publ. Co., Westport, Conn.

Rothe, M., and B. Thomas. 1959. Über Bildung, Zusammensetzung und Bestimmung von Aromastoffen des Brotes. *Nahrung 3:* 1.

Rubenthaler, G., Y. Pomeranz, and K. F. Finney. 1963. Effects of sugars and certain free amino acids on bread characteristics. *Cereal Chem. 40:* 658.

Saunders, J., and F. Jervis. 1966. The role of buffer salts in non-enzymic browning. *J. Sci. Food Agr. 17:* 245.

Schoebel, T., S. R. Tannenbaum, and T. P. Labuza. 1969. Reaction at limited water concentration. 1. Sucrose hydrolysis. *J. Food Sci.* 34, 324.

Schwimmer, S., L. E. Hendel, W. O. Harrington, and R. L. Olson. 1957. Interrelationships among measurements of browning of processed potatoes and sugar components. *Amer. Potato J. 34:* 119.

Shallenberger, R. S., O. Smith, and R. H. Treadway. 1959. Role of the sugars in the browning reactions in potato chips. *J. Agr. Food Chem. 7:* 274.

Sharp, J. G. 1957. Deterioration of dehydrated meat during storage. II. Effect of pH and temperature on browning changes in dehydrated aqueous extracts. *J. Sci. Food Agr.* 8: 21.

Song, P.-S., and C. O. Chichester. 1967. Kinetic behavior and mechanism of inhibition in the Maillard reaction. IV. Mechanism of the inhibition. *J. Food Sci.* 32: 107.

Talley, E. A., and W. L. Porter. 1968. New quantitative approach to the study of non-enzymatic browning. *J. Agr. Food Chem.* 16: 262.

Tatum, J. H., P. E. Shaw, and R. E. Berry. 1967. Some compounds formed during nonenzymic browning of orange powder. *J. Agr. Food Chem.* 15: 773.

Täufel, K., H. Ruttloff, and R. Friese. 1958. Non-enzymic browning reactions under the influence of kinetic and thermal energy. *Ernährungsforsch.* 3: 536.

Underwood, J. C., H. G. Lento, Jr., and C. O. Willits. 1959. Browning of sugar solutions. 3. Effect of pH on the color produced in dilute glucose solutions containing amino acids with the amino group in different positions in the molecule. *Food Res.* 24: 181.

Underwood, J. C., C. O. Willits, and H. G. Lento. 1961. Browning of sugar solutions. VI. Isolation and characterization of the brown pigment in maple sirup. *J. Food Sci.* 26: 397.

Walter, R. H., and I. S. Fagerson. 1968. Volatile compounds from heated glucose. *J. Food Sci.* 33: 294.

Yu, T. C., M. K. Landers, and R. O. Sinnhuber. 1969. Browning reaction in radiation-sterilized seafood products. *Food Technol.* 23: 224.

CHAPTER 2

Colloidal Systems and Emulsions[1]

PAULINE C. PAUL and HELEN H. PALMER

COLLOIDAL SYSTEMS

A number of properties of *true solutions*, and their roles in certain types of food products, were discussed in the previous chapter. *Suspensions* are typically dispersions of coarse particles in a liquid, the particles being large enough so that continuous agitation is required to keep them dispersed. When agitation ceases, these particles settle out by force of gravity, and the system separates into two phases.

Between the particle sizes represented in true solutions and those of suspensions lies the area of *colloidal systems*. Here the particles are large enough to impart to the system some properties different from those usually found in true solutions, but small enough so that the particles do not settle out on standing. The continuous bombardment from molecules of the dispersions medium gives the colloidal particles a random movement known as *Brownian motion*. In the size range of colloidal particles, the total surface area of the particles is very large in proportion to the mass, so the properties of these surfaces are very important in governing the behavior of colloidal systems.

Thomas Graham's contributions constitute the first firm foundations of colloid chemistry (1862, 1864). But it is only since the first publications of von Weimarn and of Ostwald in 1906 and 1907 that rapid development has been made in this field of chemistry. It is a very much shorter time that applications of colloid chemistry have been made to food preparation.

---

[1] Pauline C. Paul wrote the section on colloidal systems and Helen H. Palmer wrote the one on emulsions.

The great progress made in recent years in understanding of colloidal systems stems from four major areas of advancement. First is the greatly increased understanding of the structure of matter and the ways in which atoms are linked together to form molecules, based on the development of the quantum theory and the application of X-ray diffraction techniques to the study of molecular architecture. Second is the development of sophisticated techniques for the study of the size and shape of particles—electron microscopy, ultracentrifugation, density gradient centrifugation, adsorption chromatography, electrophoresis, and liquid-liquid and liquid-gas partition systems. Third is the production of synthetic high polymers that resemble in properties many naturally occurring colloidal materials, but can be obtained and studied in relatively pure preparations rather than the complex mixtures of native biological materials. And fourth is the greatly increased knowledge of the properties of the dividing surfaces between solids, liquids, and gases.

The material presented in this chapter is too brief to take the place of courses in colloid chemistry or biochemistry. At best it can only serve as an indication of the importance of colloidal systems in food preparation. The topics covered are those common to many food products. For additional information the student may wish to explore books and articles such as Osipow (1962), Davies and Rideal (1963), Danielli et al. (1964), Derjaguin et al. (1964), Hansen and Smolders (1962), Van Wazer et al. (1963), S.C.I. Monograph No. 7 (1960), Mould (1962), Debye (1957), Sievers (1963), Casey (1962), West (1963), Tanford (1961), yearly volumes of Transactions of the Society of Rheology, Advances in Chemistry Series No. 25 (1960), Barrow (1961), and Wallwork (1960).

COLLOID CHEMISTRY

Colloid chemistry deals with dispersed systems of a definite size, since it is the *size of particles* in the colloidal range or zone that imparts the specific and characteristic properties that are not explained by the laws governing solid, liquid, or gaseous states of matter.

Size of Particles

The lower limit for the size of colloidal particles is usually given as 1 mμ, the upper limit as 0.1μ (10^{-6} to 10^{-4} cm). However, there is no distinct line of demarcation. Instead, there is a gradation in properties as well as in size. Particles approaching the limits of the size of one zone may show properties of two zones. For example, sugar may exhibit both crystalloidal and colloidal properties in food systems. Even the particles within the colloidal range do not behave alike. The properties of colloidal particles around 1 mμ in size are different from those of particles approaching 0.1μ. The gluten particles of hydrated flour proteins have colloidal dimensions, but the gluten particles formed from cake and pastry flours are more dispersed or of smaller size than those from bread flours. This is one reason for the different results obtained in cakes when bread flour is used instead of cake flour.

Some of the characteristic differences of true solutions, colloidal dispersions, and suspensions are listed in Table 1.

TABLE 1. Characteristic Differences Among Systems

True Solutions	Colloidal Dispersions	Suspensions
In molecular or ionic subdivision	In colloidal subdivision	Too large to remain dispersed throughout the system
Particles are not visible with ultramicroscope	Refracted light of particles is visible with ultramicroscope	Particles visible with ordinary microscope or naked eye
Particles less than 1 mμ	Particles from 1 mμ to 0.1μ	Particles greater than 0.1μ
Formation of gels is not characteristic	Formation of gels is characteristic	Formation of gels is not characteristic
Transparent	Transparent to translucent	Generally opaque
Particles pass through parchment membranes	Particles pass through high-grade filter paper, but not parchment	Particles do not pass through high-grade filter paper
Intense kinetic movement	Less kinetic movement; more Brownian movement	Little movement
Systems show high osmotic pressure	Systems show low osmotic pressure[a]	Systems show no measureable osmotic pressure
Can be reproduced when temperature, pressure, and concentration are known	In addition to temperature, pressure, and concentration, size of dispersed particles and hysteresis of system are needed	

[a] Because of their large size, colloidal particles will usually be relatively few in number for a given concentration, and so have only a small effect on colligative properties such as osmotic pressure, boiling point, or freezing point.

The more obvious of these differences can be illustrated by considering dispersions of glucose, starch, or shredded filter paper (cellulose) in water. Each of these has approximately the same elementary composition [glucose, $C_6H_{12}O_6$; starch and cellulose, $(C_6H_{10}O_5)_n$], but the size of the particles differs. If 1 gram of each is mixed with 100 ml of cold water, glucose gives a true solution, while both starch and cellulose yield suspensions. If each system is heated rapidly to 100° C and then cooled to room temperature, the glucose system remains a true solution and the cellulose one a suspension, but the starch suspension has changed to a colloidal dispersion, is translucent, and has become thicker. The influence of heating and cooling on the starch-water system illustrates the importance of *hysteresis* (the previous history), since the system has been altered by the addition of a heat treatment to its past history. Another illustration of hysteresis is found in the work of Choate et al. (1959) with casein. They treated calcium caseinate fractions of various sizes to produce identical solutions of Na caseinate. When these were dialyzed against skim milk, the particles reaggregated to size ranges dependent on those of the original systems from which they were prepared.

Altering the Degree of Dispersion

Many of the functional properties of food materials and the changes that occur during food preparation stem from the properties of the colloidal state of matter. Since the colloidal state depends on particle size, it is important to look at the methods and the ingredients used in food preparation that influence degree of dispersion.

Although breakdown of the particle may occur, its state of subdivision as indicated in Table 1 may not change. Sucrose is in molecular subdivision in solution. Hydrolysis of sucrose gives products (glucose and fructose) still in molecular dispersion. Peptides and proteoses from protein hydrolysis are of colloidal dimensions. Starch, when acted on by enzymes, may pass from the suspension into the colloidal (dextrins), and then into true solution (maltose and glucose).

Heat

Increasing the temperature may bring about a greater or a lesser degree of dispersion. The heating of water increases its dispersion by breaking H-bonds between water molecules. The dispersion of fat globules in milk is increased by the application of heat to the milk, but heat coagulation decreases the dispersion of proteins.

Mechanical

The grinding of meat, nuts, and cereals is a mechanical means of dispersion. Beating and stirring also come under this means of bringing about dispersion. Stirring may prevent lumping or clumping, as in white sauce. Beating a curdled custard may reduce the size of the particles, although neither the beating nor the processes mentioned above may reduce the size of the particles enough to change the systems from suspension to colloidal systems. Homogenization of milk or cream is a mechanical means of increasing the dispersion of fat particles. Beating an egg white is a mechanical means of lessening the degree of dispersion, as it brings about partial coagulation of the egg white in the cell walls surrounding the air bubbles.

By Acids

The addition of or the development of acid in food preparation may bring about a greater or lesser degree of dispersion. The development of acid during the fermentation of bread dough induces dispersion of the gluten. The addition of acid to milk causes the casein to form a clot. If enough acid is added, the casein clot may be dispersed. The effect of acid on many proteins depends on the resulting pH in relation to the isoelectric point of the protein. This will be considered later.

By Alkalis

The addition of alkalis also may tend to produce a greater or a lesser degree of dispersion. In quick breads and cakes, the addition of soda in excess of the amount required to neutralize the acidity of the mixture may bring about increased dispersion of the gluten particles, altering the grain or crumb of the final product.

The different methods of increasing or decreasing the degree of dispersion are applicable to all food products. Sometimes the effect may be modified by other factors. It is interesting to trace these through different classes of food products. If alkali is taken as an example, its effects on some foods may be cited. The alkalis, hydroxides of ammonia, sodium, and potassium or their basic salts, are the ones considered. Calcium and magnesium salts may have different effects.

When alkalis are added to the monosaccharide sugar, they bring about decomposition. The sweetness is partially or wholly lost, depending on the extent of breakdown of the monosaccharide. A brown color may also develop.

Vegetables and fruits are softened by the addition of alkalis during cooking, and may become mushy and disintegrate. This is probably due to the greater dispersion of the cellulose and pectic substances. In dried legumes, alkalis may also increase the disintegration of some of the protein.

Milk is prevented from curdling or coagulating by the addition of alkali. Curdling is a lessened dispersion of the milk protein, casein. The addition of alkalis to eggs elevates the temperature for coagulation. Alkalis added to doughs cause a greater degree of dispersion of the gluten, which may result in a dough that is runny and sticky to handle. In larger quantities the baking quality of the flour is partially destroyed. Alkalis added to gelatin tend to prevent its setting, and they may cause greater dispersion in emulsions.

By Enzymes

Enzymes may also cause an increased or lessened degree of dispersion in foods. The clotting of milk upon the addition of rennin is an example of lessened dispersion, but the proteinase enzyme in flour increases the dispersion of the gluten.

Surface Area

Many of the properties peculiar to the colloidal state result from the very large ratio of surface area to weight or volume of the particles. The enormous surface areas involved may be illustrated by considering what happens when a large particle is divided into ones of colloidal size. A cube 1 centimeter (cm) on each edge has a surface area of 6 square cm. If this is divided into cubes 1 mμ on each edge (the lower limit given for the colloidal range), the total surface area of the cubes increases to 6000 square meters, or approximately 1.5 acres.

The most important surfaces in food materials include gas/liquid (foams), liquid/liquid (emulsions), and solid/liquid (sols). Many food systems are three-phase systems of air/liquid/solid, as for example in a cake batter or bread dough.

Matter at a surface boundary possesses properties that are different from those of the same substance freely extended in either of the continuous phases separated by the interface. For example, the free energy, entropy, and volume of molecules forming a layer between a liquid and the saturated vapor above it differ from those of the same molecules in the liquid or the vapor phases. In true solutions, the contribution of free surface energy to the total free energy is small. But in colloidal systems, where the ratio of surface to volume is large, the free surface energy modifies, or largely determines, the characteristics of the system.

TERMINOLOGY

The term *colloid* is generally used for materials that usually exist as small molecules, but become colloidal due to aggregation. *Micelle* is frequently used to denote aggregations of surface active materials, as in

Rosano et al. (1969). Micelle may also be used in referring to crystal-loidal areas in starch or cellulose, or in discussing casein particles. Many of the biological molecules such as starch and proteins are of such high molecular weight that they can form colloidal dispersions without aggregation. These are designated as *macromolecules*.

A number of other special terms are used in describing colloidal systems. A *sol* is a fluid colloidal dispersion, usually noticeably viscous, while a *gel* is a semirigid system containing some degree of continuous structure. In this, as in the following groupings, the classification is not always satisfactory, for there is no distinct line of demarcation between the different subdivisions.

Hydrophilic and Hydrophobic Colloids

The terms lyophilic and lyophobic include all dispersing media, whereas hydrophilic and hydrophobic indicate that the dispersing medium is water. Hydrophilic means "water loving," and hydrophilic colloids have an affinity for or are soluble in water. Hydrophobic means "water hating," and hydrophobic substances or groups are characterized by low solubility in water. Two of the chief differences between hydrophilic and hydrophobic colloids are their degree of hydration or solvation and their reaction to electrolytes. The hydrophilic colloids are characterized by a high degree of hydration and require a large quantity of an electrolyte to bring about flocculation.

There is no distinct line between hydrophilic colloids and hydrophobic ones. Often slight modification may change a given colloid from one group to the other. For example, egg albumin, with a high affinity for water, is a hydrophilic colloid. But when coagulated by heat it becomes insoluble in water and therefore hydrophobic. Denatured proteins are more or less hydrophobic. The hydrophilic colloids are not hydrated to the same extent; hence their stabilities vary. Typical hydrophilic colloids are gelatin, agar-agar, starch, pectin, and native proteins.

Since the dispersion medium of food is usually water, the terms hydrophilic and hydrophobic will be used hereafter, rather than the more general terms lyophilic and lyophobic.

Reversible and Irreversible Colloids

If, after a colloidal solution is concentrated to dryness, a sol is reformed upon the addition of water, the colloid is classified as a reversible one. Gelatin and dried egg white are examples of this type. An irreversible colloid does not spontaneously form a sol with the addition of water, after water has been evaporated. Reversible colloids are generally hydrophilic, while irreversible ones are usually hydrophobic.

Protective and Denaturing Colloids

A substance in the colloidal state that prevents the aggregation of particles is called a protective colloid. Hydrophilic systems (Hauser and Lynn, 1940) are particularly efficient in protecting hydrophobic systems. The ratio of the protective colloid to that being protected is important. If too little is used, it may sensitize instead of protect. The colloid bringing about sensitization is known as a denaturing colloid.

Many protective colloids are utilized in the formulation of modern prepared and partially prepared food products. An example is the use of gums such as carrageenan in pudding and pie filling mixes. These protective colloids may influence many of the properties of the finished product, including appearance, feel, stability, viscosity, odor, and taste.

Sorption

Sorption is a general term implying that some substance is moving from one phase of the system to another, especially when one of the phases is solid. *Adsorption* indicates that the material is held or bound on the surface, while *absorption* refers to penetration and holding in the interior of the particle or phase.

STABILIZATION OF COLLOIDAL SYSTEMS

The dispersed state of colloidal particles is maintained by either or both of two factors, (1) the charge on the surface of the particle and (2) a layer of oriented water molecules around the particle. In any given system, the charges on the surface of the colloidal particles will all have the same sign, and since like charges repel each other, this tends to keep the particles from clumping and precipitating. The charged surface is regarded as the chief stabilizing agent in hydrophobic colloidal systems, although Derjaguin et al. (1964) have found evidence for the existence of additional repulsive forces that are nonelectrostatic in nature.

In hydrophilic colloids, a shell of oriented water molecules around each particle helps to keep the particles from aggregating. This is in addition to the potential barrier to flocculation imparted by the charged surface of the particles.

Charge

All matter is made up of positively charged protons and negatively charged electrons. Normally, the protons are embedded in the nuclei of atoms, so only the electrons are free to move. An uncharged body has an equal number of protons and electrons; an excess of protons (deficit of electrons) gives a positive charge, and an excess of electrons, a negative charge. The two kinds of charges, + and −, are always produced simultaneously and are always equal, but not necessarily at the same place. So with colloidal systems, the charge may be unequally distributed, with the surface of the particles having an excess of one sign, and the dispersions medium an excess of the opposite sign.

In any given colloidal dispersion, the system as a whole must be electrically neutral, with equal numbers of + and − charges. No large spatial separation of these charges is possible, because of the large attractive forces between oppositely charged ions. But very small separations can and do occur, and these can produce important electrical and mechanical effects in the system. Separation of the charges is encouraged by thermal motion.

Source of Charge

There are a number of possible sources for the charge on a colloidal particle. In macromolecules such as proteins, ionization of carboxyl or amine groups not involved in peptide bonding will produce surface charges. Unequal charge distribution in macromolecules may also be produced by the type of winding or coiling of the backbone chain so that certain groups tend to be on the surface while others are "buried" in the interior of the particle. When micelles of surface-active materials such as soaps or detergents are formed in a water medium, the polar heads on the exterior may ionize, giving a charged surface. It is assumed that such materials selectively adsorb either H^+ or OH^- ions from the aqueous phase, the choice depending on the relative capillary activity of the different ions in a particular solution.

Polar Groups and Molecules

Molecules such as water are called polar molecules because the charges are not uniformly distributed. The separation of the charges gives + and − poles, and the molecules have a dipole moment. Symmetrical organic molecules such as CH_4 have no noticeable charge separations, so are nonpolar. The charge distribution can also be influenced by the charges on nearby molecules, to give an induced dipole.

Groups within organic molecules may also be polar or nonpolar. A polar group in an organic compound confers on it a degree of solubility in water. Some of the polar or hydrophilic groups are those containing oxygen, nitrogen, sulfur, iodine, bromine, phosphorus, and double and triple bonds, such as COOH, CHO, $C=O$, $C\equiv C$, OH, NH, NH_2, SH, S—S, SO_4H, PO_4H_2, and NCS. Some of the nonpolar groups are the CH_3, the straight hydrocarbon chains, the branched hydrocarbon chains, and the ring compounds. Many substances like the proteins and fatty acids contain both hydrophilic and hydrophobic groups; that is, they are neither completely hydrophilic nor completely hydrophobic. The efficiency of emulsifiers and stabilizers in foods depends on a balance between polar and nonpolar groups.

Double Layer

Even pure water exhibits a small degree of ionization or separation into positive and negative ions. The addition of ionizable substances such as salts will materially increase the total number of ions present. These will be distributed at random throughout the body of the liquid. When particles of colloidal dimensions are introduced into, or formed in water, their charged surfaces tend to collect a concentration of ions of the opposite charge around the particles, so the ions are no longer distributed completely randomly. The distribution of ions will be determined by the balance between the attractive forces between opposite charges and the dispersing forces of thermal agitation that tend to redistribute the ions at random throughout the solution. The ions closest to the charged surface are held tightly, and form a fixed layer. This layer will remain with the particle as it moves through the solution. Surrounding this, at a slightly greater distance from the charged particle surface, is a more diffuse layer of opposite charges that will move with the liquid rather than with the particle. Thus a double layer of charges surrounds each particle, the fixed layer and the diffuse layer.

The presence of these charged layers generates an electric potential, ε_b, between the particle and the body of the solution. This can be measured, for example, by inserting one electrode in a block of gelatin immersed in water and the other electrode in the water. A part of the total boundary potential ε_b is known as the electrokinetic or zeta (ζ) potential, the potential that exists at the plane of shear between the fixed layer that moves with the particle, and the diffuse layer that moves with the liquid.

The zeta potential is of major importance in determining certain properties of colloidal systems. If this potential is lowered by the addition of electrolytes, at the "critical potential," the double layers collapse, and the particles may aggregate and precipitate. The zeta potential can be measured on the basis of electrical and mechanical phenomena arising from relative motion of the particles and the bulk solution—streaming potential, sedimentation potential, electroosmosis, or electrophoresis.

Isoelectric Point

The charge distribution within a system can be altered by shifting the pH, or by adding salts with varying degrees of ionization potential.

For each colloidal system there exists a point of overall particle neutrality, where the positive and negative charges on the particle are equal. This is known as the *isoelectric point* (IEP). This does not necessarily mean that there is no charge on the particle, just that the charges are in balance in that particular system. At this point, the particles will no longer migrate in an electric field. Hydrophobic colloids that are stabilized only by the charge will flocculate at the isoelectric point. With hydrophilic colloids, although the hydration is at a minimum, there is usually sufficient attraction to maintain an appreciable water layer that prevents precipitation. In this case, a dehydrating influence such as heat, or the addition of salts having a high affinity for water, is necessary to flocculate the colloidal particles.

Hydration

The other chief source of stability for colloidal particles is the extent or degree of hydration. In discussing systems where water is the dispersion medium, it is customary to use the term "hydration," although "solvation" is the more general term applicable to any solvent medium. Many of the macromolecules found in food materials have a high degree of affinity for water. This water tends to form a surface layer or shell around the particles, helping to prevent their coalescence and flocculation. Part of the water is held by hydrogen bonding, part by capillary attraction within the interstices of the intricately folded macromolecules, and part by the interaction between the surface charges of the particles and the dipole moment of water molecules. Other as yet undetermined forces may also be operating to assist in holding this oriented shell of water around the particles.

Brownian Motion

A secondary contributor to stability of colloidal dispersions is the Brownian movement of the dispersed particles. This tends to keep the particles dispersed throughout the system, and helps prevent sedimentation. Brownian motion can be decreased by increasing the effective viscosity of the system (Gillespie, 1960). Changes in the charge on the particle and/or in the degree of hydration can influence the effective viscosity by changing the size and shape of the particles, or altering the amount of water available to act as a dispersing medium, or both.

Flocculation

Of Hydrophobic Colloids

Since the hydrophobic sol is not hydrated, its stabilization depends only on its electric charge. The particle is rendered isoelectric and flocculated by the ion of the electrolyte having the opposite charge from that of the particle, that is, the cation, if the particle is negatively charged, and the anion, if positively charged. If more of the electrolyte is added than is required for precipitation, a sol may reform that possesses an electric charge opposite to that of the initial sol. In general, the amount of the salt required to produce flocculation varies with the valence of the ions bringing about the flocculation. Monovalent ions are less effective than divalent ones, and in turn divalent ions are not nearly as powerful as trivalent ions. The effect of valence and of the addition of electrolytes may be illustrated by substituting distilled water for milk in custard. Heating renders the egg proteins hydrophobic, but added salts are necessary to bring about "setting" of the custard. The amount of salt required varies with the valence of the cation. There are some exceptions to the effect of valence in that some monovalent ions have greater flocculating power than polyvalent ones.

The concentration of the colloid also affects the amount of electrolyte required. If the electrolyte is added in small portions, more is required than if it is added all at once. Presumably this might mean that the addition of salt to cream of tomato soup in small portions would be less likely to cause it to curdle (flocculate) than if all the salt were added in one portion. If the large quantity of milk in a caramel recipe is not added in small portions, it nearly always curdles. A definite time may be required before flocculation occurs.

Casein of milk is a good example of a food colloid that is little hydrated and is stabilized chiefly by electric charge. It can remain in the sol form when negatively or positively charged. However, when the charge is neutralized, the casein flocculates. The charge is neutralized in natural souring, and when the isoelectric point of the protein is reached, the casein clots.

Of Hydrophilic Colloids

Hydrophilic colloids can be reversibly precipitated by high concentrations of ammonium sulfate and magnesium sulfate. The reason for this "salting-out" effect is that both stabilizing factors are removed—that is, the hydration and the electrical charge. Dehydration of the hydrophilic colloid may be brought about by different means, such as heating, the use of tannin, and alcohol. The colloid is then sensitive to the effect of small amounts of electrolytes. If small quantities (Kruyt, 1927) of electrolytes are added to a starch or agar-agar sol, the electrical charge is removed but the particles do not precipitate. If alcohol is then added, flocculation occurs. It is immaterial in which order the two stability factors are removed. The removal of one has no evident effect, but the removal of both factors causes precipitation.

PROPERTIES OF COLLOIDAL SYSTEMS

Because of the size of the dispersed particles, surface phenomena assume an important place in colloidal reactions. Surface tension, interfacial tension, adsorption, formation of surface skins, orientation of molecules, cohesion, and adhesion all have application in food preparation.

The importance of surface reactions in food preparation cannot be overemphasized. They occur in emulsions, foams, and throughout food systems when such substances as fat, sugar, salt, baking powder, flour, and egg are combined in batters and doughs.

Surface Tension

A brief discussion of surface tension as a property of liquids is given in Chapter 1. Surface tension is defined as the amount of work necessary to produce a new surface of unit area at a constant temperature. To enlarge the surface, work must be expended. The amount of work required is greater the higher the surface tension of the liquid and the more the area is to be increased. The amount of work expended to enlarge a surface multiplied by the area increased is known as the free surface energy. This energy tends to be a minimum quantity, since the area of the surface also tends to be minimum as a result of surface tension. The free surface energy is decreased (a) by reducing the surface area or (b) by reducing the surface tension. Hence, small drops of liquid will unite with large drops if they are within the same space so that they are connected by their vapor, thus reducing the surface area.

Surface tension decreases with increase in temperature, becoming zero at the critical temperature.

Interfacial Tension

Interfacial tension refers to the tension at liquid/liquid or liquid/solid interfaces. When two nonmiscible liquids are combined, one liquid forms a layer on top of the other, thus making a liquid/liquid boundary. The less the solubility of two liquids in each other, the greater the interfacial tension. Added substances that decrease surface or interfacial tension tend to concentrate at the interface.

Surface-Active Agents

Surface-active materials are those that lower surface or interfacial tension. They are known as dispersing agents and emulsifiers. A surface-active agent usually possesses a polar or hydrophilic group and a nonpolar or hydrophobic (organophilic) group. In general, the most effective agents are those whose hydrophilic groups exhibit a strong affinity for water, whereas the hydrophobic groups have a strong affinity for the organic liquid or organophilic phase. A surface-active agent with both strong hydrophilic and hydrophobic groups is oriented at the interface and lowers the surface tension (and free energy) at the interface. A more extended discussion of surface-active agents as emulsifiers will be found in the section on emulsions.

Adsorption

Adsorption has been defined as the concentration of a substance at an interface. As has been noted, free surface energy tends to a minimum. Substances that lower the surface tension concentrate in the surface, thereby decreasing the free surface energy. Positive adsorption is defined as the concentration of the solute in the interfacial layer; negative adsorption, as its concentration in the interior, or conversely, the concentration of the solvent in the interfacial layer. The amount adsorbed depends on the nature and concentration of the material being adsorbed and the extent of the surface at which it can be adsorbed.

Foam Formation

A foam is a system with a dispersed gaseous phase, the dispersing medium often being a liquid. Mickevic (1955) speaks of the use of foams to "engineer structure into foods." The solutions of substances that lower surface tension tend to froth, particularly if the liquid is not so volatile or so mobile that the foam collapses readily. Freundlich (1922, 1924) states that the formation of a foam is a complicated phenomenon. "Whilst in most other colloidal structures the particles of the disperse phase are of colloidal minuteness, this is by no means essential or even usual, in the case of foams. On the other hand the dispersion medium is often of colloidal fineness, that is, the gas bubbles are separated from one another by liquid films, having a thickness of only a few mμ. Hence in a foam the surface of a liquid has been enormously extended, which is in opposition to the tendency of surface tension to make the surface a minimum. For this reason a liquid must fulfill a number of special conditions. In the first place the surface tension of the liquid must be small, for otherwise its tendency to reduce the surface would be too powerful." A second condition for the production of stable foams is that the vapor pressure be small, for substances with high vapor pressure evaporate rapidly. The surface films must not coalesce readily. These conditions are fulfilled by aqueous solutions of surface-active substances, and especially by sols of many colloids such as soaps, saponins, tannins, and proteins. Freundlich states that in protein solutions a third influence plays a part, for many proteins have the property of forming thin "pellicles" or surface skins on the boundary layer, which tend to prevent evaporation. At least part of these pellicles are the layers of adsorbed, surface-denatured proteins. Hansen and Smolders (1962) point out the inadequacy of our knowledge of the mechanical properties of surface films, and list this and the nature of foams as two of the areas of surface chemistry that need much more work. Mysels et al. (1959) discuss film formation and thinning, and extend these concepts to foam formation and stability. In food systems, alteration of pH and heating or chilling the material may also be used to alter stability of foams.

Since the substance that lowers surface tension of the liquid is found in greater concentration in the foam, if the foam is continually removed as it is formed, the greater portion of the surface-active material is removed. This finds application, for example, in the removal of foam by skimming fruit jelly solutions. This removes much of the tannins and other substances that might adversely affect the flavor of the jelly.

Rahn (1932) states that "If protein is concentrated on the surface it has a tendency to become solid, but all proteins do not behave alike. Some solidify rapidly, others slowly, and some do not solidify at all. Quite often, this solidification is irreversible, and the protein, when put back into the solution, will not dissolve again." In milk foams, protein films form around the air bubbles and, when the foam settles, these films of protein can be seen with the aid of a microscope.

Recent research has led to the development and use of many different foam-forming or promoting substances in foods. Examples of these are the use of sodium lauryl sulfate in angel food cake mixes, and the foam forming characteristics of soybean protein (Eldridge et al., 1963).

Rheology of Colloidal Systems

The basic principles of viscosity, and of viscosity of true solutions, were mentioned in the first chapter. Viscosity is also an important property of colloidal systems. As a general rule, the lyophobic colloids show viscosities little greater than that of the dispersion medium. But lyophilic colloids may show very high viscosities or even plasticity.

Recognition of the wide variety and importance of viscous behavior in many types of systems has led to the development of the branch of science known as *rheology*, the study of flow and deformation. Three basic concepts are involved (Scott-Blair and Reiner, 1957): the force applied, the deformation (flow), and time. Another important factor is temperature, since viscosity generally decreases rapidly with increasing temperature, provided that other reactions are not occurring.

The viscosity equations given in the first chapter apply to true, or Newtonian, viscosity. In fluids that exhibit Newtonian viscosity, as the force applied (shear stress) increases, the rate at which the material shears increases in direct proportion to the increase in stress, giving a straight-line relationship. Most food materials, however, exhibit non-Newtonian viscosity; that is, the shear rate does not change in a straight-line relationship with changing stress. Or the shear rate may change with time, even though the stress remains constant.

A number of different types of viscous behavior are illustrated in Figure 1. The Newtonian system shows a straight-line relationship of constant increase in rate of shear with increasing stress. In a *dilatant*

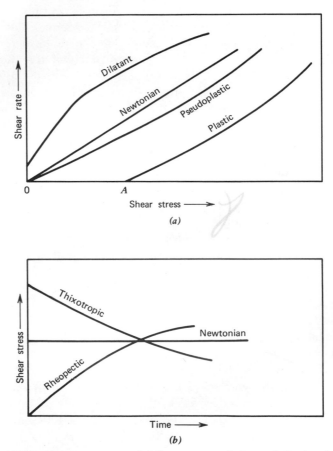

FIGURE 1. Schematic representation of different types of viscous behavior. (*a*) Change in rate at which various systems shear as the force applied increases. (*b*) Alteration of force required to shear with increase in length of time that shear stress is applied.

system, the shear rate increases more rapidly, while in a *pseudoplastic* one it increases more slowly than proportionally to the increase in force. A plastic system shows a yield value (OA); that is, a certain amount of stress must be applied before any deformation or flow occurs. A *thixotropic* system is one in which the viscosity decreases with continued application of stress, while a *rheopectic* system shows increased viscosity with time.

Figure 2 shows some possible effects of hysteresis in non-Newtonian systems. Some systems show a different path for the change in shear rate as the force is increased from zero to maximum and then returned to zero. In others, the path by which the equilibrium value with time

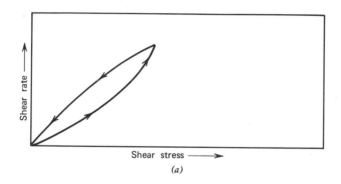

(a)

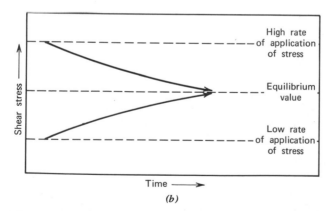

(b)

FIGURE 2. Schematic representations of role of hysteresis in viscosity measurements on non-Newtonian systems. (a) Different path of change of shear rate as force is first increased, then decreased. (b) Different path to equilibrium value, depending on whether shear is applied rapidly or slowly.

is reached will vary depending on whether the stress is applied rapidly or slowly.

The rheological behavior is an important characteristic of many food materials. The thickening of a starch-liquid mixture as it is heated, or of cake batter as it is mixed, are examples of changing viscosity. Also, many food systems, such as gelatin, egg, or pectin mixtures, will form gels, and exhibit plastic behavior. Plasticity is also an important property of fats used for cakes, biscuits, and pastry. A plastic fat has a consistency such that it will form a thin sheet or layer in a batter, or will retain air bubbles when "creamed." Many instruments have been devised for measuring the viscosity of such non-Newtonian systems. A wide variety of these are described by Van Wazer et al. (1963). Measurements on a number of different food materials are described in S.C.I. Monograph No. 7 (1960). Kovac and Ziemba (1965) discuss the applications of rheological information to food production processes. Yang (1961) reviews the theoretical and experimental aspects of Newtonian and non-Newtonian viscosities as applied to polymer solutions, and their application to the determination of the shape and size of protein molecules.

Viscosity of Hydrophilic Systems

Ostwald (1922) lists ten factors causing variation in viscosity of hydrophilic systems: (1) concentration, (2) temperature, (3) degree of dispersion, (4) solvation, (5) electrical charge, (6) previous thermal treatment, (7) previous mechanical treatment, (8) the presence or absence of other lyophilic colloids, (9) the age of the lyophilic sol, and (10) the presence of both electrolytes and nonelectrolytes.

Viscosity is closely related to the consistency of the finished product in food preparation. So close is this relation in many cases that the ten factors listed by Ostwald may nearly be taken as ten commandments of food preparation. Thus the consistency of a custard is influenced by the concentration of egg or protein; the temperature to which it is cooked; the degree of dispersion of the colloidal particles, which is influenced by the reaction, the kind and concentration of salts present, and the like; the beating of the egg; the use of milk or water; how long the custard has aged in addition to the age of the eggs and milk when used; the kinds and concentration of salts in the egg and milk as well as the addition of sodium chloride and the nonelectrolyte sugar.

Since the line of demarcation between sols and gels is not a definite one, fruit jellies, gelatin, milk, and cream, as well as egg dishes, may be included in the group of foods in which the consistency of the finished product is related to viscosity. The structure or type of product in baked goods is closely related to the viscosity of the batter or dough, which in turn is influenced by all the factors listed by Ostwald. Of course, these factors or nearly the same ones affect other properties as well as viscosity of food materials. Thus the extensibility of gluten and the heat coagulation of proteins are influenced by many or all of these factors.

Osmosis and Dialysis

The phenomenon of *osmosis* depends on the existence of a *semipermeable membrane* that will allow one component of a solution to pass through while preventing the passage of another component. Cell walls in plant and animal tissues act as semipermeable membranes, permitting the passage of water and of small molecules in and out of the cells, but preventing the movement of large molecules or particles.

Osmotic pressure can be demonstrated and measured by separating a colloidal dispersion from additional pure dispersions medium by a membrane permeable to the solvent but not to the dispersed particles. In such a system, there is a tendency for additional solvent to migrate through the membrane into the colloidal system. The pressure that must be applied to the colloidal solution to prevent this migration is known as the osmotic pressure. This is a colligative property, dependent on the number of particles present. Kupke (1960) discusses the theory and measurement of osmotic pressure, with applications to the study of proteins and other macromolecules.

Semipermeable membranes can also be used to alter the concentration of colloidal solutions. This process is known as *dialysis*. If a colloidal dispersion enclosed in a semipermeable membrane is immersed in a solution of higher concentration, water will be drawn out of the colloidal system. If the external solution is of lower concentration, small molecules such as salts or sugars will migrate through the membranes. *Reverse osmosis* (Morgan et al., 1965) is the process of removal of water from food by forcing water by pressure through a membrane that does not pass most other molecules. This process is now being applied in the food industry to concentrate materials such as whey proteins.

Gel Formation

Many colloidal dispersions will form gels under the proper conditions. Gels are fluid-containing systems of various compositions and varying degrees of dispersion. They are distinguished from colloidal sols by differences in mechanical properties. They have much in common with the solid state of aggregation—high viscosity, elasticity and/or plasticity, and yield value. *Elastic* materials show deformation due to stress with complete recovery of the original shape when the stress is removed.

Plastic materials are those that do not return to the original shape when the stress is removed. The *yield value* is the point at which the material ceases to be elastic and the change becomes plastic. The actual size of the yield value is influenced not only by the characteristics of the material but also by the conditions of measurement—for example, the rate of application and removal of the stressing force. An approximation of yield value often applied to food gels is the percent *sag* or *slump*. This is the change in height of a gel from that measured in the mold in which it was made to that of the free-standing gel on a flat surface. Sag may be of two types: (a) the initial sag due to relaxation of elastic forces, or plastic deformation and (b) thermal sag or melting due to change in temperature.

Food gels range in consistency from that of the thick part of raw egg white to that of the rigid structure of hard-cooked egg white. There is no distinct dividing line between a thick sol and a thin gel, but rather a continuous gradation of change in physical properties. Food materials that can produce gels under the proper conditions include starch, pectin, egg proteins, gelatin, and various plant gums such as agar or carrageenan. The contractile proteins of muscle tissue exist naturally in the gel state. The gluten of flour forms a gel as it is developed, and milk proteins will gel on long heating or by action of acid or certain enzymes.

Mayonnaise resembles a gel in being semirigid. However, it is not a true gel, since the rigidity is due to the high concentration and packing of the emulsified oil droplets. It is an example of a *thixotropic* food system—one that tends to liquify when stirred, then stiffen up again on standing.

Gel Structure

A gel is defined as a two-phase system with a high degree of interface between a continuous (or at least intermeshed) system of solid material that holds a finely dispersed liquid phase. In order to form the continuous phase of a gel, very large molecules with a long, thin shape are required. These are usually long-chain polymers. They must have some degree of cohesion to form the necessary cross-links between chains, and for permanence, must also have a considerable degree of attraction for water. The liquid phase (water in food materials) is held on the solid molecules mainly by hydrogen bonding, and between the chains by capillary attraction.

In the sol, before the gel is formed, the solid chains are randomly distributed. As the system approaches the gel state, these chains become oriented at various points and to different degrees, to give "crystalline"

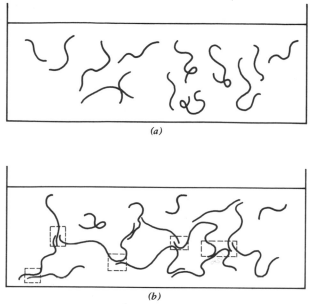

(a)

(b)

FIGURE 3. Schematic representation of chain orientation in gel formation. (a) Random distribution of long, thin molecules in sol. (b) Development of "crystalline" or organized areas (indicated by dotted enclosures) in gel formation.

or organized areas interspersed in the random distribution. This is illustrated diagrammatically in Figure 3. The number of "connecting points" in a gel is thought to be relatively small. Ferry (1948) estimates that as few as 5 to 6 loci of crystallization per gelatin chain would be sufficient to form a rigid network, while Harvey (S.C.I. Monograph No. 7, 1960) speaks of "interlocking of molecules in a few places along their length to form a three-dimensional network." The flexibility of the polymer chains and the small number of connections between them, contribute to the elastic-plastic nature of the gel structure, while the type and strength of the connections influence the response of the gel to such things as mechanical agitation or temperature change. Reversible elastic deformation involves only a stretching of interatomic bonds. Permanent plastic deformation results when these bonds are broken, and new bonds form.

Gel Strength and Permanence

The forces linking the polymer chains together in a gel may be covalent in nature, like the disulfide links in gluten, but are usually weaker bonds such as hydrogen bonding.

The bonds holding the chains in the gel structure can usually be broken by mild forces. When the force is removed, these links may be reestablished in the same location or at other locations on the same or different molecules. The bonds are often quite susceptible to changes in temperature, becoming more labile as the temperature rises. In a reversible gel, which breaks down on heating and re-forms on cooling, the melting temperature is usually higher than the setting temperature. A gelatin gel is a good example of this. Gel structure may also be influenced by mechanical agitation such as stirring, and the gel may or may not be reestablished when allowed to rest.

The rigidity or strength of a gel may be influenced by a number of factors in addition to temperature and agitation. Concentration of each phase of the system is important. Most gel-forming food materials have a high affinity for water and so can form gels with a relatively small amount of solid phase. Other substances present or added may influence gel strength by (a) competing with water for binding loci (sugar softening a starch gel); (b) interacting chemically with either or both phases (ions that can form cross-bridges, such as Ca^{++} with pectin); (c) altering the pH (acid in pectin gels); (d) altering the charge distribution on the polymer molecules and thereby changing the cross-bonding pattern (salt in flour batter); or (e) competing with the solid phase for liquid (dehydrating agents such as sugar or alcohol). The actual affinity of the solid phase for the liquid may be altered by heating, to either increase or decrease the number of available bonding loci, as for example the swelling of starch granules or the coagulation of meat or egg proteins.

After the gel has formed, part of the liquid may be squeezed out by external pressure, or by internal pressure generated by the formation of additional intermolecular bonds on standing. The latter decreases both the number of loci available for liquid binding and the amount of intermolecular space available to hold liquid by capillary attraction. This loss of fluid is known as *syneresis*. This is often seen in milk, pectin, or starch gel systems.

Swelling of Gels

The ability of proteins and starches to imbibe water is very great. The extent of swelling is influenced by many factors, including the previous history of the material. The addition of such substances as acids, alkalis, mineral salts, and sugar may increase or inhibit the degree of swelling. Many such combinations are made in food preparation. Lemon juice and vinegar may be added for flavor. Soda, salt, and baking powder may be added to foods. Different proportions of mineral salts are found in foods, and the proportion may vary in the same food from different sources. In general, the addition of acids or alkalis increases the swelling of colloidal gels. With acids, this usually continues until a maximum is reached at pH 3.0 to 2.5, when imbibition is decreased with greater acidity. With alkalis the maximum swelling is about pH 10.5, although gluten gels are likely to disintegrate when they become as alkaline as this. Sometimes the addition of acids or alkalis lessens hydration. This depends on the pH of the substance when the acid or alkali is added. In general, salts lessen the degree of swelling even in the presence of acids or alkalis.

EMULSIONS

Food emulsions exhibit the characteristics of colloidal systems, although the droplet diameters in emulsions generally exceed the upper limit of colloidal particle size.

An emulsion has been defined as "a heterogeneous system, consisting of at least one immiscible liquid intimately dispersed in another in the form of droplets whose diameters, in general, exceed 0.1μ. Such emulsions possess a minimal stability, which may be accentuated by such additives as surface-active agents, finely-divided solids, etc." (Becher, 1965). The dispersed-droplet phase of an emulsion is known as the internal or disperse phase; the phase in which the droplets are suspended is the external or continuous phase. The additives employed to keep the droplets from coalescing are known as emulsifying agents or emulsifiers.

Various theories have been developed to account for the development of an emulsion structure. The theory of micelle development accounts for many of the characteristics of emulsions. According to this theory, colloidal particles tend to become organized in a structure with their nonpolar groups in contact and their polar groups exposed to the liquid. Such an aggregation is termed a micelle. The point at which the micellar concentration becomes appreciable and its properties abruptly change is termed the critical micelle concentration (Becher, 1965). The shapes of micelles have been studied, but conclusive data have not been obtained. A spherical grouping has been suggested, since such a shape best satisfies geometric and thermodynamic requirements.

Preparation of emulsions usually requires energy in the form of work to reduce the size, increase the surface area, and separate the particles of the internal phase. The emulsification process results in a large increase in interfacial surface, the surface between the disperse and continuous phases. A liquid tends to contract to a condition of minimum surface, a condition of lowest energy. A stable boundary or interface between the phases counteracts the tendency for the dispersed phase to coalesce. Thus the properties of interfaces are important in the study of emulsion stability. The tendency for the phases of an emulsion to coalesce is manifested by the interfacial tension, the tension at the boundary between the phases. The magnitude of the interfacial tension depends on the difference between the attractive forces acting on molecules within the two liquids and the attractive forces at the interface. The molecules in the body of a liquid are generally subjected to balanced attractive forces, while the molecules on the surface are subjected to unbalanced attractive forces with the main force directed inward.

A high interfacial tension contributes to emulsion instability. The addition of certain types of solutes causes a lowering of the interfacial tension. These substances concentrate at the interface. The molecules that produce this effect are generally "amphiphilic" molecules; they are oriented at the interface, with the lipophilic portion extending into the nonaqueous phase and the lyophilic portion extending into the aqueous phase. The interfacial film thus created exerts a stabilizing influence. The phase in which the emulsifying agent is more soluble will be the external phase, and the dispersed phase will be on the side of the film with higher interfacial tension.

The consistency of an emulsion or its resistance to flow is of commercial importance, since the value of many emulsions depends on a particular consistency. The consistency of emulsions may range from liquid to plastic solid. Consistency depends on the viscosity of the external phase, the concentration of the internal phase, and attractive forces between the particles. Viscosity increases with increasing concentration of the dispersed phase; generally emulsions remain liquid until the concentration of the dispersed phase approaches close packing. The droplets of oil-in-water emulsions may be deformed, and in such systems the viscosity of the internal phase as well as the viscosity of the external phase can be significant. The droplets in water-in-oil emulsions behave as rigid spheres, and their chemical nature may be more important than their viscosity (Sumner, 1960; Becher, 1965).

Emulsions composed of oil and water phases are of two types, depending on whether the water or the oil is the dispersed phase. The water-in-oil type is abbreviated W/O; the oil-in-water type is abbreviated O/W. The same designations are used to describe food emulsions, although the phases are not strictly water and oil. The water phase of a food emulsion may contain, in addition to water, the water-soluble constituents of milk, vinegar or citric acid, fruit juice, a cooked starch paste, whole egg, and proteins, as well as salts and other water-soluble compounds. The oil phase may contain any edible oil or fat-soluble compound. Oil/water emulsions are more common in foods than water/oil emulsions.

Several methods may be used to determine the type of emulsion. (1) Emulsions in which water is the continuous phase may be expected to show high conductivity; since most oils are poor conductors, a W/O emulsion does not readily conduct an electric current. (2) An emulsion can be readily diluted by the type of liquid that constitutes the continuous phase. A drop of the emulsion is placed on a microscope slide, and while it is observed through the microscope, a small drop of water is added and stirred with a pin point. If the water blends with the emulsion, it is an O/W emulsion. If oil added similarly to a drop of an emulsion blends with the emulsion, it is a W/O emulsion. (3) Another method of determining the type of emulsion is through the use of a dye that is soluble in one phase but not in the other. Sudan III or Sharlach R red dyes are soluble in the oil but not in water. A small portion of the finely powdered dye is dusted over the surface of the emulsion. If oil is the external phase, the color gradually spreads throughout the emulsion; if water is the external phase the color does not spread but is confined to the oil with which it comes in contact on the surface. The microscope is used to determine the type of emulsion formed. If the oil is dyed red, a red field with clear globules indicates a W/O emulsion; red globules in a clear field show an O/W emulsion. (4) Emulsions containing oils that fluoresce under ultraviolet light may be examined under the light to determine emulsion type. Fluorescence of the whole field indicates a W/O emulsion; fluorescence of droplets indicates an O/W emulsion.

MECHANICAL AIDS TO EMULSIFICATION

Mechanical devices are used to provide the energy needed to reduce the size and separate the particles of the internal phase of an emulsion. They include stirrers, beaters, homogenizers, and colloid mills. Becher (1965) suggests use of the terms emulsator or emulsor to describe mechanical aids to emulsification to distinguish them from the surface-active or other substances known as emulsifiers or emulsifying agents.

For a temporary emulsion such as French dressing, the work required may be no more than vigorous shaking before each use. Mayonnaise may be prepared in small batches with an egg beater or whip or in large quantities using commercial equipment. Machines of different types are used for making commercial emulsions (Joffe, 1954; Finberg, 1955; Smith and Rees, 1959). In some, agitation is accomplished by stirring or beating; in others, centrifugal force is utilized, one liquid is pre-atomized, or pressure is applied. Mixers may be used to pre-mix the emulsion before it is put through a colloid mill or homogenizer. In a homogenizer, dispersion is accomplished by forcing the mixture through a small orifice under very high pressure. In a colloid mill emulsification is accomplished by the shearing action as the mixture passes through a gap between a stator and a rotor revolving at speeds of 1000 to 20,000 rpm. The clearance may be as small as 0.001 inch. If mayonnaise is homogenized, the particle size of the dispersed phase must not be too small, or the interfacial area may become too large to be stabilized by the quantity of emulsifier present.

EMULSIFIERS OR EMULSIFYING AGENTS

Emulsifiers or emulsifying agents are surface-active or other agents that are added to an emulsion to increase its stability by interfacial action (Becher, 1965). Particles of the dispersed phase of an emulsion are prevented from coalescing by adsorption of molecules of the surface-active emulsifier on the surface of the dispersed phase. The most stable emulsifiers have both strong polar and nonpolar groups, but one group must be slightly dominant. If the polar group is dominant, it is adsorbed more strongly in the water than in the oil phase and thus lowers the surface tension of the water, so that water becomes the continuous phase. The nonpolar groups may be partially adsorbed in the oil phase. Thus the emulsifier can be likened to a film between the two phases of the emulsion. Hydrogen bonding is also important in solutions of surface-active agents (Becher, 1965).

Emulsifying agents have been classified in categories that are not mutually exclusive: surface-active materials, naturally occurring materials, and finely divided solids. Some naturally occurring materials are also surface-active; some substances added primarily to increase viscosity of the mix may also indirectly increase the stability of the emulsion.

The additives available for use as emulsifiers in foods are limited by both federal and state legislation. The Food and Drug Administration should be consulted regarding questions of approved additives or tolerance limits, since these may change on the basis of new information. Tables are available listing emulsifiers that are generally recognized as safe (the GRAS list), those approved with tolerance limits, and those that have been proposed for use (Brokaw, 1960; Meyer, 1960). Emulsifying agents that have been approved by the Food and Drug Administration for addition to foods include the following: diacetyl tartaric acid esters of mono- and diglycerides from the glycerolysis of edible fats or oils, mono- and diglycerides from the glycerolysis of edible fats or oils, monosodium phosphate derivatives of mono- and diglycerides from the glycerolysis of edible fats and oils, and propylene glycol.

Egg yolk is the outstanding natural food emulsifying agent; yolk lecithoproteins, lipoproteins containing lecithin, are responsible for its emulsifying ability. Other natural emulsifiers and stabilizers in foods are proteins of milk, flour, and gelatin, and starches. Egg yolk is the only emulsifying agent permitted in mayonnaise. According to Brokaw (1960), the oil-to-water ratio in mayonnaise borders on the limit of, or appears to defy, some rules of emulsion theory. Emulsifier usage and technique makes a good product possible.

The standards of identity for salad dressing and French dressing permit, in addition to egg yolk, the inclusion of gum acacia (gum arabic), carob bean gum (locust bean gum), guar gum, gum karaya, gum tragacanth, extract of Irish moss, pectin, propylene glycol ester of alginic acid, sodium carboxymethyl cellulose (cellulose gum), methyl cellulose U.S.P., hydroxypropyl methylcellulose, or any mixtures of two or more of these (Anon., 1964). The quantity of any such emulsifying ingredient or mixture used amounts to not more than 0.75 percent by weight of the finished dressing. Both types of dressings may also contain other stabilizing ingredients. These include seasonings, such as mustard, paprika, and other spices; and, in the case of salad dressing, a cooked starchy paste. The latter stabilizers, however, are not sufficient to keep the dressing stable without the use of one or more of the permitted emulsifiers.

Water-soluble gums, such as gum arabic, gum tragacanth, gum karaya, and guar gum, stabilize oil-in-water emulsions principally by increasing viscosity and gelling characteristics (Becher, 1965; Glicksman, 1962). They often concentrate at the interface to form strong interfacial films (Serallach and Jones, 1931). They are generally complex polysaccharides. Alginates and carageenan are similar products. Two cellulose derivatives, methyl cellulose and carboxymethyl cellulose (CMC) are also principally useful in increasing viscosity of the aqueous phase of oil-in-water emulsions (Becher, 1965). The composition of these products is discussed in Chapter 4.

"Emulsifying agents" in baked goods serve two purposes: in the preparation of a dough they improve the intimate mixing of the components and the quality of the final product, and in the final product they retard staling, possibly by inhibiting the formation of hydrogen bonds between adjacent starch chains in bread or cake (Becher, 1965). Mono- and diglycerides are used in shortenings to improve cake-making quality. They permit baking of cakes with a higher ratio of sugar to flour, giving sweeter flavor with no loss in volume. Partial ester non-ionic emulsifiers such as sorbitan partial esters of fatty acids and poly-oxyethylene derivatives of fatty acids improve the texture and prolong the keeping quality of yeast-raised breads, rolls, and doughnuts (Pratt, 1952).

Consumer salad oils usually do not contain added emulsifiers as do plastic shortenings, since such emulsifiers reduce the smoke point. Emulsifiers are used in margarine to prevent "weep" and to control spatter and foam. The finely dispersed water droplets evaporate quietly during heating instead of spattering (Harris et al., 1941). Lecithin or mono- or diglycerides are optional ingredients in margarine.

Emulsifiers control the "bloom" or change in surface color of chocolate coatings by keeping the fat in a more stable emulsion within the chocolate. Lecithin and monosodium phosphate derivatives of mono- and diglycerides are used. They decrease the chewiness of caramels and prevent their sticking to the wrapper. Emulsifiers also help to disperse essential oils and flavors, which are not water-soluble, in candy and beverages.

STABILITY, INVERSION, AND BREAKING OF EMULSIONS

Emulsions have been classified according to their stability. *Temporary* emulsions need vigorous shaking before each use. French dressing composed of oil, vinegar, and dry seasonings is such an emulsion. Temporary emulsions are typically of a low viscosity. *Semipermanent* emulsions have the viscosity of thick cream, and this increased viscosity retards separation. Salad dressings containing syrups, honey, condensed soup, or commercial stabilizers such as gums or pectin are in this class. *Permanent* emulsions have high viscosity, which helps retard the coalescence of the internal phase. Maintenance of this emulsion structure during storage and transportation is dependent on both internal and external factors.

Creaming, inversion, and demulsification or breaking are terms denoting emulsion instability. Creaming, applied to the separation of cream in unhomogenized milk, also indicates the separation of an emulsion into two emulsions. One (the cream) has a higher concentration of the disperse phase, and the other has a lower concentration than the original emulsion. In creaming, the emulsion does not break, but since creaming occurs when the droplet size is large, it may eventually lead to breaking of the emulsion.

A change from an O/W to a W/O emulsion or vice versa is known as inversion. This is a function of several factors, including the type and concentration of the emulsifier, the concentration of the disperse phase, the previous history of the emulsion, and possibly the temperature. Corran (1946) described a multiple emulsion of oil and water with two emulsifying agents, lecithin and cholesterol. Lecithin favors an O/W emulsion, cholesterol a W/O emulsion.

Demulsification or breaking of an emulsion may be accompanied by creaming or inversion. The droplets of the disperse phase usually aggregate, and the aggregates combine to form drops that combine and separate completely from the continuous phase.

Emulsion stability is affected by the same factors that influence its preparation; stability depends largely on emulsion composition and the method of preparation. Internal factors affecting stability of emulsions include the type and concentration of emulsifier, the kind and concentration of components of the disperse and continuous phases, the viscosity of the continuous phase, the ratio of the dispersed to the continuous phase, and the particle size. The charge on the emulsion droplets promotes stability by repulsion of particles of similar charge. External factors affecting stability include agitation or shaking, evaporation (which causes coalescence of oil on the surface of O/W emulsions), and temperature.

The extent to which the emulsifier lowers interfacial tension affects stability of the emulsion, since an emulsion with a high interfacial tension is relatively unstable. The concentration of the emulsifier and the strength of the interfacial film are important in the stability of emulsions. Cream puffs and mayonnaise exemplify foods in which concentration of the emulsifier is critical. The stability of salad dressing to frozen storage also increases as the concentration of egg yolk emulsifier is increased (Hanson and Fletcher, 1961). The increased stability is probably due to the resistance of the thicker film of egg around the oil globules to puncturing by crystallized oil fractions.

The composition of dispersed and continuous phases affects stability. The concentration of oil in food emulsions varies from a very low percentage to about 85 percent. Mayonnaise by definition contains at least 65 percent oil and often ranges to 75 percent. Mayonnaise with over 90% oil is very stiff and separates readily. The characteristics of both oil and thickening agent are important in the stability of salad dressings to frozen storage (Chapter 13 and Hanson and Fletcher, 1961).

The addition of an electrolyte generally results in a decrease in interfacial tension in solutions containing amphiphilic compounds (Becher, 1965). E. D. Gilbert, in a discussion of a paper by Sumner (1960), reported that electrolytes (NaCl) can improve stability of an emulsion.

This may explain the increase in stability to frozen storage resulting from an increase in salt level from 0.5 to 1.7 percent in salad dressing (Hanson and Fletcher, 1961). In salad dressings prepared with safflower or peanut oil and held at 20° to —10° F, oil separation was least in those with the highest salt concentration, whether all of the salt was added in the emulsion phase or part was added in the starch paste.

A sufficiently viscous continuous phase is generally recognized as important in the production of stable emulsions. The proteins and gums that produce viscous sols or gels with low concentration inhibit coalescence by this means.

The ratio of the dispersed to the continuous phase affects emulsion stability. A mayonnaise emulsion breaks if the oil concentration becomes too high. A broken mayonnaise emulsion can be re-formed by adding the broken emulsion gradually, with beating, to additional egg yolk or to a small amount of water or vinegar. It will not reemulsify if the egg, water, or vinegar is added to the mass of broken emulsion. Salad dressings with a high proportion of emulsion to starch paste usually show oil separation; dressings of low oil content show water separation when held at low temperature (Joffe, 1942; Hanson and Fletcher, 1961).

The size distribution of the dispersed particles affects emulsion stability. A condition of maximum stability is represented by a large percentage of low-diameter droplets and a very limited number of larger-diameter droplets of limited maximum diameter. A change in size distribution during storage and an increase in percentage of larger-diameter droplets indicates an unstable emulsion. Homogenization of milk illustrates the effect of droplet size; the fat in the milk does not coalesce after homogenization. Too small a droplet size may be a cause of instability in some emulsions, however, since small droplets have a large interfacial area and thus require an increase in emulsifying agent. There is some evidence that after mechanical dispersion of the oil during emulsification, depending on the diameter of the globules, an equilibrium in diameter is reached (Heublum and Forrest, 1939). This equilibrium may require days or weeks to attain. Thus mayonnaise, properly prepared, may be more stable some time afterwards than on the day of manufacture.

A reflectance technique for determining surface-average particle diameters in oil-in-water emulsions has been described (Lloyd, 1959). The technique was applied to studies of the stabilities of paraffin oil emulsions containing starches, starch derivatives, water-soluble gums, and surfactants. The technique is applicable to evaluation of emulsion stabilizers and to studies of the kinetics of emulsion coalescence.

Heating, resulting in too much evaporation of water, may cause separation of fat in emulsions such as gravies, sauces, and cream puffs. Gravies and sauces, therefore, may be made smooth again if this inbalance of ingredients is corrected by adding water and stirring while heating. Heat may cause curdling and separation if it coagulates emulsifiers. For example, if the temperature of the vegetable, fish, or meat on which Hollandaise sauce is served is higher than about 74° C, curdling may occur. In cooked salad dressings thickened by both starch and egg, maximum thickening is obtained from both if the starch and liquid are heated above 90° C before the egg is added. Heating after the egg is added should continue only until thickening from the egg occurs. Heating beyond this stage may result in subsequent separation, thinning, and curdling of the salad dressing.

The spattering of margarine when heated to frying temperature is the result of breaking of the emulsion that contains partially hydrogenated oils, cultured skim milk, NaCl, and mono- and diglycerides of fatty acids. The aqueous phase drops by gravity to the bottom of the pan, heats, and breaks through the fat layer with violence. Low levels of specific surface-active agents are used to eliminate the difficulty (Harris, 1960).

Chilling causes separation of oil-in-water emulsions (Rochow and Mason, 1936; Joffe, 1942; Harris, 1960; Hanson and Fletcher, 1961). On the basis of microscopical observations, the mechanism of breaking of emulsions by freezing was attributed by Rochow and Mason (1936) to destruction of the film surrounding each globule, rather than to the freezing of the continuous phase. An increase in yolk content, changes in ingredient composition, and the incorporation of stabilizers are required to improve the stability of mayonnaise and salad dressing at low temperatures (Hanson and Fletcher, 1961; Joffe, 1942).

FOOD EMULSIONS

Emulsions have several important functions in foods: some foods exist in nature as emulsions; some foods are, themselves, emulsifying agents; some prepared foods depend for their consistency or structure on the development and maintenance of an emulsion. Emulsions are also used as vehicles to add flavors, to dilute ingredients, and to hide objectionable odors or tastes.

Milk and *cream* (Chapter 10) are natural emulsions consisting of a dispersed fat phase in a liquid continuous phase. The dispersed fat phase is approximately 3.7 percent of cow's milk, 11.7 percent of half-and-half, 31.3 percent of light whipping cream, and 37.6 percent of heavy whipping cream (Watt and Merrill, 1963). The fat globules of milk and cream are stabilized to a considerable extent by phospholipids and to some extent by casein, albumin, globulin, and salts. Evaporated milk is a more concentrated emulsion; water is removed by evaporation and the emulsion is homogenized to promote stability. In ice cream the milk proteins are involved in the development of a rigid layer at the oil-water interface, probably through lipoprotein complex formation (Sherman, 1961).

Butter and *oleomargarine* are emulsions of water in oil with a plastic continuous phase. They contain about 80 percent fat, and the remainder consists of salt, protein, and water. The fat phase in butter is milk fat; in margarine it may be a variety of fats or oils of animal or vegetable origin. Flavor in margarine is provided by the addition of pasteurized milk, inoculated with selected microorganisms that promote, by fermentation, a flavor resembling butter (Sutheim, 1946). Stability of butter and margarine emulsions is maintained by the semisolid consistency of the continuous phase rather than by perfect emulsification.

Egg yolk (Chapter 9) is a natural emulsion with a dispersed-fat phase; it is also an efficient emulsifying agent. Lecithoproteins, lipoproteins containing the phospholipid lecithin, are responsible for the emulsifying ability of yolk. Yolk consists of about 49 percent water, 16 percent protein, and 32 percent fat. Egg lipids comprise about 70 percent of the yolk solids and are composed of triglyceride fat (65 percent), phospholipids (30 percent), cholesterol (4 percent), and carotenoids, vitamins, and the like. Lecithin and lysolecithin comprise about 79 percent of the phospholipid fraction (Lea, 1962).

Hollandaise sauce is an emulsion containing 40 to 50 percent oil, emulsified and thickened by egg yolk. The liquid in the emulsion is water and lemon juice or vinegar. The emulsion thickens during cooking to a temperature of 66 to 74° C.

Gravies, sauces, and *cream soups* are emulsions stabilized with flour. Since flour does not have the emulsifying ability of egg yolk, these products must have a higher percentage of water and a lower percentage of oil for stability.

Chou or *cream-puff* paste is an emulsion composed of water, shortening, salt, flour, and eggs. Heat is used to boil the water and melt the shortening before the flour is added. After slight cooling of the thick paste thus formed, eggs are added gradually with stirring to complete emulsification of the fat. If an insufficient quantity of egg is used, the emulsion will not form properly, and the baked puffs will have low volume. Their centers will not be sufficiently hollow.

Some of the fat is emulsified in other batters and doughs. *Griddle cakes, waffles,* and *muffins* are prepared from batter that is an oil-in-water emulsion. The fat in *cake batter* may be wholly or partly emulsified.

Products labeled as mayonnaise, salad dressing, or French dressing must conform to the definitions and standards of identity published by the U.S. Food and Drug Administration (Anon., 1964). There are many dressings used for salad and foods for which no standards of identity have been promulgated. These include cooked dressings containing butter and fruit juices thickened with starch and/or egg, and dressings such as Thousand Island and Russian, which may have mayonnaise or French dressings as a base. These were called salad dressings before the present definition of salad dressing was promulgated. Mineral oil is no longer permitted in dressings for which definitions have been promulgated because of its adverse effect on absorption of fat-soluble vitamins from the digestive tract.

Salad dressing contains oil, egg yolk, acidifying ingredients, and a cooked or partly cooked starchy paste. The paste may be prepared with a food starch, tapioca flour, wheat flour, rye flour, or any two or more of these. Water may be added in preparation of the paste. Salad dressing contains not less than 30 percent by weight of vegetable oil and "not less egg-yolk-containing ingredient than is equivalent in egg-yolk solids content to 4% by weight of liquid egg yolks." It may contain, in addition to egg yolk, specified optional emulsifying ingredients or mixtures of not more than 0.75 percent by weight of the finished salad dressing, and EDTA as in mayonnaise.

French dressing is a separable liquid food or the emulsified viscous fluid food prepared from edible vegetable oil and an acidifying ingredient. It may include salt, sweetening ingredients, suitable food seasonings, flavoring ingredients, tomato paste, tomato puree, catsup, or sherry wine. It may also include eggs or other specified emulsifying agents in amounts no more than 0.75 percent by weight of the finished dressing, and EDTA as in mayonnaise.

Mayonnaise is a semisolid emulsified food prepared from edible vegetable oil, acidifying ingredients, and yolk-containing ingredients. It contains not less than 65 percent by weight of oil. It may contain salt, sweetening ingredients, and suitable harmless food seasonings or flavorings that do not impart color simulating the color of egg yolk. The acidifying ingredients may include vinegar, lemon juice, or lime juice diluted with water to not less than a specified acidity. The egg-yolk-containing ingredients may be liquid, frozen or dried egg yolks, or whole eggs or any of the foregoing mixed with liquid or frozen egg white. It may contain calcium disodium EDTA or disodium EDTA or both, not more than 75 parts per million by weight of the finished food, with the label statement indicating their use . . . "to protect flavor" or "as a preservative." It may be packed in an atmosphere in which air is replaced in whole or in part by carbon dioxide or nitrogen.

THE PREPARATION OF MAYONNAISE

The rational explanation for the mixing method used for mayonnaise is the need for a product of high consistency early in the process; otherwise the mixing efficiency will be low and satisfactory emulsification will not be obtained (Becher, 1965). The order in which mayonnaise ingredients are added and the quantities added at various times during the mixing depend on the equipment and mixing conditions. The salt, mustard, and other dry ingredients are usually mixed with the egg yolks. Enough of the acidifying ingredient is added to make a viscous paste, followed by alternate addition of small amounts of oil and vinegar. The first oil particles emulsified are quite large. With each subsequent increment of oil, the dispersed particles become smaller, and the mayonnaise becomes stiffer (Figs. 4, 5, 6, and 7). The addition of vinegar at any stage of emulsification causes some of the dispersed particles to coalesce, and the mayonnaise temporarily becomes thinner. After an emulsion is started, emulsification of additional oil is readily accomplished. Addition of previously prepared mayonnaise to the egg yolk and vinegar before addition of the oil facilitates emulsification of added oil in a way that is analogous to seeding in crystal formation and the addition of a gel to gelatin to hasten gelation.

Mayonnaise may be formed by either continuous or intermittent mixing. The size of the container for batch-type mixing should be appropriate for the quantity of mix. If the container is too large for the mix, the ingredients will not come into contact sufficiently for an emulsion to form. There is an optimum temperature range for emulsification. For mayonnaise and salad dressing manufacture this range is reported to be 45 to 50° F (Finberg, 1955). With most liquids the surface tension is lowered with rise in temperature. Oils becomes less viscous and more mobile. To a certain point this increases ease of emulsification; but a rise in temperature also decreases viscosity of the mix, and an adequately viscous mix is also essential.

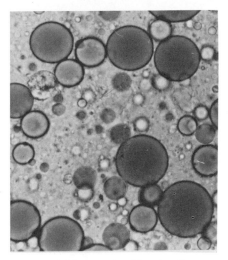

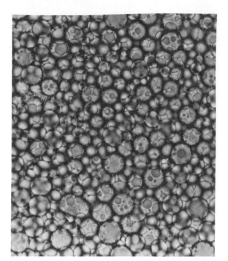

FIGURE 4. Mayonnaise. Showing the coarse emulsion formed after the addition of 1 tablespoon of oil. The vinegar and seasonings were added to the egg yolk before the oil was added. Magnification approximately 200x.

FIGURE 5. Mayonnaise. Same as Figure 4 but after adding ¼ cup of oil. Magnification approximately 200x.

FIGURE 6. Mayonnaise. Same as Figure 4 but after adding ⅜ cup of oil. As the oil spheres become smaller with the addition of more oil the mayonnaise becomes stiffer. Magnification approximately 200x.

FIGURE 7. Mayonnaise. Same as Figure 4 but after the addition of ½ cup of oil. Magnification approximately 200x.

References

COLLOIDAL SYSTEMS

Advances in Chemistry Series No. 25. 1960. *Physical Functions of Hydrocolloids.* Am. Chem. Soc., Washington, D.C.

Barrow, G. M. 1961. *Physical Chemistry.* McGraw-Hill Book Co., Inc., New York.

Casey, E. J. 1962. *Biophysics: Concepts and Mechanisms.* Reinhold Publ. Corp., New York.

Choate, W. L., F. A. Heckman, and T. F. Ford. 1959. Size memory of casein colloid particles. *J. Dairy Sci. 42:* 761.

Danielli, J. F., K. A. G. Pankhurst, and A. C. Riddiford, eds. 1964. *Recent Progress in Surface Science,* vol. 1. Academic Press, New York.

Davies, J. T., and E. K. Rideal. 1963. *Interfacial Phenomena.* Academic Press, New York.

Debye, P. J. W. 1957. How giant molecules are measured. *Sci. Amer. 197* No. 3: 90.

Derjaguin, B. V., T. N. Voropayeva, B. N. Kabanov, and A. S. Titiyevskaya. 1964. Surface forces and the stability of colloids and disperse systems. *J. Colloid Sci. 19:* 113.

Eldridge, A. C., P. K. Hall, and W. J. Wolfe. 1963. Stable foams from unhydrolyzed soybean protein. *Food Technol. 17:* 1592.

Ferry, J. D. 1948. Protein gels. *Advan. Protein Chem. 4:* 1.

Freundlich, H. 1922. *Colloid and Capillary Chemistry,* translation by H. S. Hatfield, E. P. Dutton & Co., New York.

Freundlich, H. 1924. *The Elements of Colloidal Chemistry,* translation by G. Barger, E. P. Dutton & Co., New York.

Gillespie, T. 1960. The limited flocculation of colloidal systems. *J. Colloid Sci. 15:* 313.

Graham, T. 1862. Liquid diffusion applied to analysis. *Phil. Trans. 151:* 183.

Graham, T. 1864. On the properties of silicic acid and other analogous colloidal substances. *J. Chem. Soc. (London) 17:* 318.

Hansen, R. S., and C. A. Smolders. 1962. Colloid and surface chemistry in the mainstream of modern chemistry. *J. Chem. Educ. 39:* 167.

Hauser, E. A., and J. E. Lynn. 1940. *Experiments in Colloid Chemistry.* McGraw-Hill Book Co., New York.

Kovac, G. M., and J. V. Ziemba. 1965. Rheology can help you. *Food Eng. 37* No. 2: 81.

Kruyt, H. R. 1927. *Colloids,* translation by H. S. van Klooster. John Wiley & Sons, New York.

Kupke, D. W. 1960. Osmotic pressure. *Advan. Protein Chem. 15:* 57.

Mickevic, M. 1955. Engineering structure into foods. *Food Eng.* 27 No. 5: 66.

Morgan, A. I., Jr., E. Lowe, R. L. Merson, and E. L. Durkee. 1965. Reverse osmosis. *Food Technol. 19*: 1790.

Mould, D. L. 1962. Application of methods of physical chemistry for the isolation of virus and subcellular particles from biological tissue. *Arch. Biochem. Biophys.*, Suppl. *1*: 30.

Mysels, K. J., K. Shinoda, and S. Frankel. 1959. *Soap films: studies of their thinning.* Pergamon Press, N.Y.

Osipow, L. I. 1962. *Surface Chemistry: Theory and Industrial Applications.* A.C.S. Monograph, Reinhold Publ. Co., New York.

Ostwald, Wo. 1922. *An Introduction to Theoretical and Applied Colloid Chemistry,* translation by M. H. Fischer. John Wiley & Sons, New York.

Rahn, O. 1932. Why cream or egg white whips. *Food Ind. 4*: 400.

Rosano, H. L., A. P. Christodoulou, and M. E. Feinstein. 1969. Competition of cations at charged micelle and monolayer interfaces. *J. Colloid Interface Sci. 29*: 335.

S.C.I. Monograph No. 7. 1960. *Texture in Foods.* Soc. Chem. Ind., London.

Scott-Blair, G. W., and M. Reiner. 1957. *Agricultural Rheology.* Routledge and Kegan Paul, Ltd., London.

Sievers, E. T. 1963. *Rheology of Polymers.* Reinhold Publ. Corp., New York.

Tanford, C. 1961. *Physical Chemistry of Macromolecules.* John Wiley and Sons, Inc., New York.

Transactions of the Society of Rheology. Yearly volumes. Interscience Publ., Inc., New York.

Van Wazer, J. R., J. W. Lyons, K. Y. Kim, and R. E. Colwell. 1963. *Viscosity and Flow Measurement.* Interscience Publ., Inc., New York.

Wallwork, S. C. 1960. *Physical Chemistry for Students of Pharmacy and Biology,* 2nd ed. John Wiley and Sons, Inc., New York.

West, E. S. 1963. *Textbook of Biophysical Chemistry,* 3rd ed. Macmillan Co., New York.

Yang, J. T. 1961. The viscosity of macromolecules in relation to molecular conformation. *Advan. Protein Chem. 16*: 323.

EMULSIONS

Anon., *Dressings for Foods,* U.S. Food and Drug Administration, Federal Register, Sec. 25 (Feb. 12, 1964).

Becher, P. 1965. *Emulsions: Theory and Practice,* 2nd ed. Am. Chem. Soc. Monograph No. 162, Reinhold Publ. Co., New York.

Brokaw, G. Y. 1960. Status of emulsifiers, *J. Am. Oil Chemists' Soc. 37*: 523.

Corran, J. W. 1946. In *Emulsion Technology,* Chemical Publ. Co., Brooklyn, 176.

Finberg, A. J. 1955. Advanced techniques for making mayonnaise and salad dressing, *Food Eng. 27* (Feb.): 83.

Glicksman, M. 1962. Utilization of natural polysaccharide gums in the food industry, *Advances in Food Research 11*: 109.

Hanson, H. L., and L. R. Fletcher. 1961. Salad dressings stable to frozen storage, *Food Technol. 15*: 256.

Harris, B. R. 1960. Some lesser known aspects of stability in commercial emulsions, Advances in Chemistry Series, 25, *Physical Functions of Hydrocolloids*, Amer. Chem. Soc., Wash., D.C.: 64.

Harris, B. R., A. K. Epstein, and F. J. Cahn. 1941. Fatty interface modifiers. Composition, properties and uses in the food industries, *Oil and Soap 18* (9): 179.

Heublum, R., and J. E. Forrest. 1939. Mayonnaise, its nature and manufacture, *Food 8*: 161.

Joffe, M. H., ed. 1942. *Mayonnaise and Salad Dressing Products,* The Emulsol Corp., Chicago.

Joffe, M. H., and M. Lipschultz. 1954. Salad dressings, *Encyclopedia Chem. Technol. 12*: 37.

Lea, C. H. 1962. Adipose tissue and animal lipids, In *Recent Advances in Food Science* (London, eds. J. B. Hawthorn and R. M. Leitch), Vol. 1: 92.

Lloyd, N. E. 1959. Determination of surface-active particle diameter of colored emulsions by reflectance, and application to emulsion stability studies, *J. Colloid Sci. 14*: 441.

Meyer, L. H. 1960. *Food Chemistry,* p. 357. Reinhold Publ. Co., New York.

Pratt, C. D. 1952. Certain partial ester emulsifier levels in food, *Food Technol. 6*: 425.

Rochow, T. G., and C. W. Mason. 1936. Breaking emulsions by freezing, *Ind. and Eng. Chem. 28*: 1296.

Serallach, J. A., and G. Jones. 1931. Formation of films at liquid-liquid interfaces, *Ind. Eng. Chem. 23*: 1016.

Sherman, P. 1961. Rheological methods for studying the physical properties of emulsifier films at the oil-water interface in ice cream, *Food Technol. 15*: 394.

Smith, F., and L. H. Rees. 1959. A study of the continuous production of mayonnaise, *J. Am. Oil Chem. Soc. 36*: 217.

Sumner, C. G. 1960. Emulsions in theory and practice, *Chem. and Ind.* (March), p. 333.

Sutheim, G. M. 1946. *Introduction to Emulsions.* Chem. Publ. Co., Inc., Brooklyn.

Watt, B. K., and A. L. Merrill. 1963. Composition of foods, U.S. Dept. Agric., Agriculture Handbook No. 8, 190 pp.

CHAPTER 3

Proteins, Enzymes, Collagen, and Gelatin

PAULINE C. PAUL

PROTEINS

Proteins frequently are of major significance in determining the organoleptic characteristics and nutritional value of a food. Because proteins may be surface-active they can serve as foaming and emulsifying agents; because of their water binding properties, they form viscous sols and gels under appropriate conditions; they may act as protective colloids; their molecules may aggregate to form viscoelastic systems; and some are important for their enzymatic activity.

The protein group is large and includes materials of widely differing properties. Since these are compounds of high molecular weight, determination of the details of their chemical and physical nature is difficult. Mahler and Cordes (1966) refer to the chemistry of proteins as "not completely manageable." However, development of new methods for isolating and studying proteins has greatly increased the information available, although there is still much to learn.

Much helpful information is now coming from chemical and physical studies of isolated proteins. In attempting to apply this knowledge to an understanding of reactions in food materials, it must be remembered that the presence of the other components of food often alters the reactions of proteins. Also, it is well recognized that each level of structural organization imposes restraints. Food proteins frequently occur in complex cellular or tissue organizations, and so are different in this respect from isolated protein in a test tube.

Roles in Foods

The major roles of proteins in food preparation include the ability to form foams or gels, water-binding capacity, coagulation by heat, emulsi-

115

fying properties, and enzymatic activity. No one protein, of course, has all of these abilities. The particular reactions involved are complex, and much influenced by the other constituents of the food system. But understanding of these processes in food materials will be improved by application and integration of the information gained by study of the properties and reactions of individual proteins. Feeney and Hill (1960) review many of the roles and problems of proteins in food processing.

Composition

Proteins are polymers of amino acids. The types of amino acids and the order in which they are arranged determine the three-dimensional design of the protein molecule, and thereby many of the properties important in food preparation. Therefore it seems worthwhile to review briefly the types of amino acids and some of their chemical characteristics.

Amino Acids

About 20 different amino acids make up the bulk of the monomer units in proteins. With the exception of proline and hydroxyproline, which contain imino nitrogen, all these have an amine group on the carbon atom alpha to the carboxyl group. The remainder of the molecule is collectively labeled the R group. This gives the type formula

$$\underset{\underset{NH_2}{|}}{\overset{\overset{H}{|}}{R-C}}-COOH$$

The carboxyl group ionizes as an acid, while the amine group ionizes as a base. Therefore, these amino acids are *amphoteric*, that is, they have both acidic and basic characteristics.

The tendency of any group to ionize is indicated by its pK_a, the pH at which the group is half dissociated and half associated. The α-carboxyl group has a pK_a in the range of pH 2 to 3, while that of the α-amine group is around pH 10. So in the pH range of approximately 4 to 9, amino acids exist as dipolar ions (zwitterions) with both the carboxyl and the amine group ionized.

pH ca. 2–3	pH 4 to 9	pH ca. 10
$\underset{\underset{NH_3^+}{|}}{\overset{\overset{H}{|}}{R-C}}-COOH$	$\underset{\underset{NH_3^+}{|}}{\overset{\overset{H}{|}}{R-C}}-COO^-$	$\underset{\underset{NH_2}{|}}{\overset{\overset{H}{|}}{R-C}}-COO^-$
	(zwitterion)	

Some of the amino acids have side chains with appreciable acidic or basic characteristics, which alter the extent of ionization at a given pH.

In the formation of a protein, the basic linkage in the backbone of the polymer is the peptide bond formed by the reaction between the amine (or imine) group of one amino acid and the carboxyl group of another.

$$
\underset{\underset{NH_2}{|}}{\overset{\overset{H}{|}}{R-C-COOH}} + \underset{\underset{NH_2}{|}}{\overset{\overset{H}{|}}{R-C-COOH}} \longrightarrow \underset{\underset{NH_2}{|}}{\overset{\overset{H\ \ O\ \ H\ \ H}{|\ \ ||\ \ |\ \ |}}{R-C-C-N-C-COOH}} + H_2O
$$

R Groups

The R groups vary widely in their nature, and are now considered to be the major determinants of the type of coiling or other arrangement in space that exists in the native protein. They also are the groups which are available to interact with other parts of the same protein chain, with other protein chains, or with other compounds in the environment.

The R groups can be classified in several ways. One of the most important characteristics from the food standpoint is whether the group is polar or nonpolar. The nonpolar groups are essentially hydrocarbon in nature, and have little or no affinity for water. The polar groups vary, but all have some degree of attraction for water, so are hydrophilic. The R groups are illustrated in Table 1. In addition to the amino acids, the amide derivatives of glutamic and aspartic acids are also widely distributed in food materials, either free or as components of proteins. These also are shown in Table 1.

Several of these R groups are recognized as making specific contributions to various reactions important in food, in addition to the influence all of them have on the spatial arrangement of the protein molecule. A very important one is the ease with which cysteine can be oxidized to cystine and cystine reduced to cysteine.

$$
2\ HS-CH_2-\underset{\underset{H}{|}}{\overset{\overset{NH_2}{|}}{C}}-COOH \underset{\text{reduction}}{\overset{\text{oxidation}}{\rightleftharpoons}} \underset{\underset{COOH}{|}}{\overset{\overset{CH_2-S-S-CH_2}{|\ \ \ \ \ \ \ \ \ \ \ \ \ |}}{H-C-NH_2}} \quad \underset{\underset{COOH}{|}}{H-C-NH_2}
$$

Others include the role of proline and hydroxyproline in determining the structure of collagen, of histidine as the connecting link between protein and the prosthetic group in the muscle pigment myoglobin, and of glutamine as a flavoring material. Other specific roles will undoubtedly be recognized as our detailed knowledge of proteins increases.

TABLE 1.   The Principal Amino Acids That Occur in Proteins

Type formula	$HOOC—C—R$ (with H above and H_2N below the central C)
Hydrophobic (nonpolar)	
Glycine	$—H$
Alanine	$—CH_3$
Valine	$—C(H)(CH_3)—CH_3$
Leucine	$—CH_2—C(H)(CH_3)—CH_3$
Isoleucine	$—C(H)(CH_3)—CH_2—CH_3$
Phenylalanine	$—CH_2—C_6H_5$
Proline	$HOOC—CH—CH_2$; $HN—CH_2$ with CH_2 bridge
Hydrophilic (polar)	
Sulphur-containing	
Cysteine	$—CH_2—SH$
Cystine	$—CH_2—S—S—CH_2—$
Methionine	$—CH_2—CH_2—S—CH_3$

TABLE 1. (*Continued*)

Hydroxyl–containing	
Serine	—CH$_2$—OH

Threonine	—CH—CH$_3$
	     $\mid$
	     OH

Hydroxproline	HOOC—CH—CH$_2$
	       $\mid$ $\rangle$CH—OH
	    HN—CH$_2$

Basic	
Lysine	—CH$_2$—CH$_2$—CH$_2$—CH$_2$—HN$_2$
Arginine	—CH$_2$—CH$_2$—CH$_2$—NH—C$\begin{smallmatrix} \nearrow NH_2 \\ \searrow NH \end{smallmatrix}$

Histidine	—CH$_2$—C=CH
	      HN N
	        C
	        H

Acidic	
Aspartic acid	—CH$_2$—COOH
Glutamic acid	—CH$_2$—CH$_2$—COOH
Tyrosine	—CH$_2$⟨benzene ring⟩—OH
Heterocyclic	

Tryptophan	—CH$_2$—C⟨indole ring⟩
	    HC—N
	        H

Amide derivatives	
Asparagine	—CH$_2$—C—NH$_2$, (C=O)
Glutamine	—CH$_2$—CH$_2$—C—NH$_2$, (C=O)

Sequence

Until relatively recently, although the amounts of the various amino acids in a given protein could be determined with reasonable accuracy, little information was available as to the order in which they occurred in the protein chain. In 1954, Sanger and coworkers published the complete amino acid sequence for insulin—the first protein so defined. Since then, the amino acid sequences for a number of other proteins have been published, and more are being determined. Tristram (1963) gives details on many of these, as do Dayhoff and Eck (1967–1968). Abelson (1968) refers to the determination of amino acid sequences of proteins as "one of the most important research activities today."

Structure

As with investigations on amino acid sequences, the three-dimensional arrangement of the atoms and groups making up a protein structure is a very active area of study. The application of X-ray diffraction techniques initiated marked advances in knowledge of details of these large and complicated molecules. At the present time, four levels or classes of structural organization are considered in studying the architecture of isolated proteins.

Primary

The primary structure of a protein is determined by the number and sequence of amino acids in the chain. These are held together by the covalent forces of the peptide bond, to give the basic backbone chain of

$$-C-C-N-C-C-N-C-C-N-$$

Each —C—C—N— group represents one amino acid residue. Since the carbon-carbon and carbon-nitrogen bonds are directed essentially tetrahedrally rather than in a straight line, the backbone chain is better represented as a zigzag, with the R groups alternately above and below the chain.

The amide group is essentially planar (see Figure 1*a*), with no rotation possible around the N—C bond because of the partial double bond nature of the peptide bonds (Figure 1*b*). However, rotation is possible around the remaining two bonds that make up the backbone unit of the polypeptide.

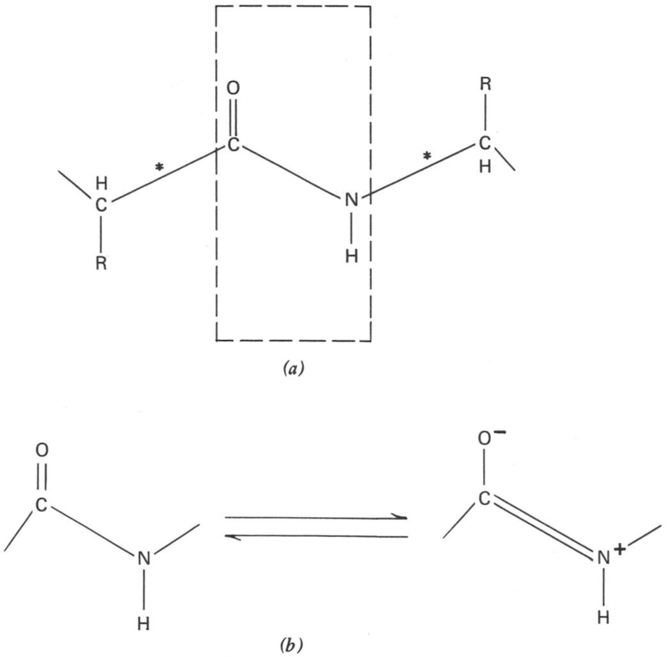

(a)

(b)

FIGURE 1. Planar nature of the peptide bond. (a) Planar amide group; rotation can occur around bonds marked *, but not around the bond in the planar group. (b) Partial double bond nature of the planar amide group.

Secondary

The rotation that can occur around some of the bonds in the peptide chain allows the chain to assume a number of shapes. The shape for any given chain usually depends on the number of weak bonds that can be formed either intrachain or interchain, to give a configuration having significantly less free energy than any of the other shapes that are theoretically possible.

This ordering of the peptide chain depends primarily on the formation of hydrogen bonds between the carboxyl oxygen and the amide nitrogen of the backbone chain. Such formation may yield either helical or sheet structures, depending on whether the hydrogen bond formation is intrachain or interchain, respectively. Intrachain bonding may cause the chain to fold back on itself, producing a compact, globular shape.

Proteins that contain the α-helix of Pauling and Corey may be either globular or fibrous, but the sheet structures are found only in fibrous proteins. The latter are usually insoluble in water or aqueous solvents. The protein portion of myoglobin is considered to be about 80 percent α-helix, while lysozyme of egg white is about 35 percent in the α-helical form, and β-lactoglobulin of milk probably contains no α-helical structure.

Another helical form found in food materials is that of the collagen molecule. The presence of relatively large amounts of proline and hydroxyproline in the molecule alters the shape of the backbone chain so that it does not fit into the α-helix. The collagen molecule is thought to consist of three chains wound together in a helix, to form a coiled coil. Figure 2 illustrates diagrammatically a simple helix, the α-helix, and the coiled coil of collagen.

Tertiary and Quaternary

Most proteins are now considered to exist in their native state in compact structures, either globular or rodlike. Ovalbumin, β-lactoglobulin, and myoglobin are examples of globular structures, while collagen and ovomucin are rodlike in character. The tertiary level of structure is considered to be caused by folding or twining of the polypeptide chain, due to interactions of the side chains of the various amino acid residues. The overall shape of the molecule is a compromise between the tendency of the backbone to form a regular helix with H-bonds between $>C=O$ and $>N-H$, and the tendency of the R groups to twist the backbone so as to maximize the strength of the secondary bonds between side groups. By reference to Table 1, it will be seen that almost half the R groups are nonpolar. These will tend to be turned toward the interior of the chain where they can form hydrophobic bonds with one another. Polar groups may be directed either internally or externally, since they can H-bond with water as well as with one another.

Quaternary structure is induced by aggregations of individual protein chains, due to interactions between side chains and also between exposed portions of the peptide backbones. One of the best-known examples of quaternary structure is that of hemoglobin, where the association of four polypeptide chains is necessary to produce the physiologically active protein particle. It appears that most proteins having a molecular weight greater than about 50,000 are composed of subunits held together by bonds other than the covalent peptide linkage. Klotz (1967) has published a summary of subunits in proteins. Ramachandran and Sasisekharan (1968) have reviewed the conformation of proteins, with special reference to stereochemical aspects.

The four levels of structure reviewed briefly above are those used by research workers studying isolated proteins. When one considers proteins in food materials, there are additional levels of organization in the assemblage of proteins into the intracellular and intercellular units in which they occur in plant and animal products. As indicated previously,

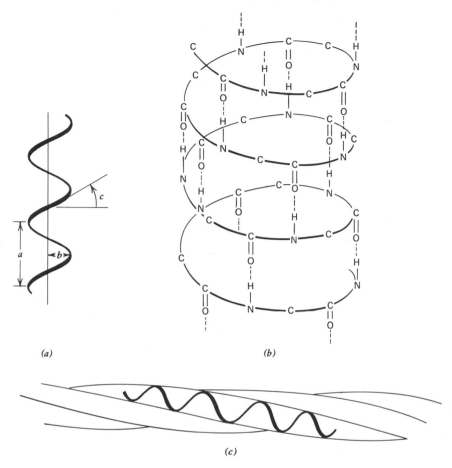

(a)

(b)

(c)

FIGURE 2. Diagrammatic representation of a simple helix and of helical structures believed to occur in food proteins. (*a*) Simple, right-handed helix (*a* = pitch, *b* = radius, *c* = pitch angle). (*b*) The α-helix, left-handed form, showing the H-bonds (dotted lines) between adjacent turns. R groups of amino acids are omitted for clarity. (*c*) The coiled-coil of collagen. Detail shown in one strand only. Each strand is a helix.

each level of organization imposes restraints and may alter the properties and reactions of the component molecules.

Bonds in Proteins

Most molecular shapes are determined by weak bonds, which are relatively easily broken to permit shape changes. The bonds that maintain the structure of proteins include the peptide bond, hydrogen bond, covalent disulfide bond, electrostatic attractions between ionized groups, van der Waals interactions, and hydrophobic bonding. These have been discussed (see Chapter 1), with the exception of hydrophobic bonding.

Proteins are formed in an aqueous medium in plant and animal cells. Water is a highly structured substance, due to its tendency to form hydrogen bonds. Water has a strong tendency to exclude groups or compounds that cannot form H-bonds. The hydrocarbon side chains on amino acids have no affinity for water, so they tend to interrupt or break up the normal structure of water. The tendency of water to maintain its normal structure forces the hydrocarbon residues closer to one another, to reduce the surface and thereby the free energy of the system. This brings the hydrocarbon groups close enough for van der Waals forces to hold the R groups together in a state now designated as hydrophobic or apolar bonding. Examples of hydrophobic bonding are shown schematically in Figure 3.

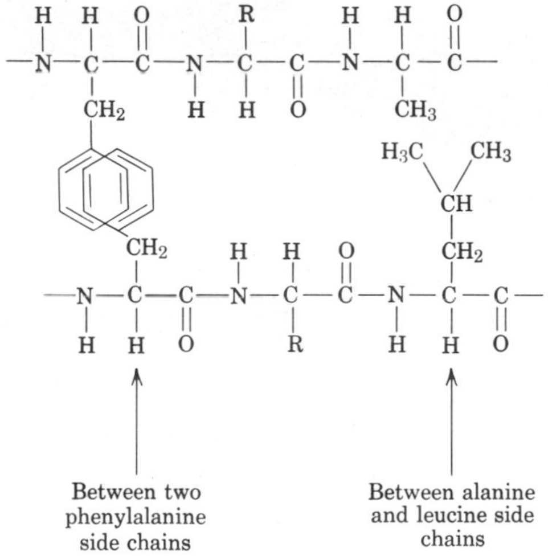

FIGURE 3. Schematic representation of hydrophobic bonding between apolar amino acid side chains.

Evidence now available indicates that these apolar bonds are a very important factor in maintaining the higher orders of structure in proteins. The native folding of the chain(s) is thought to orient the hydrophobic R groups into the interior of the macromolecule, with the polar groups exposed on the surface (Edelman and McClure, 1968). In this way, the structure of the protein can influence the relative reactivity of the various side chains, by altering their accessibility to reagents.

Evidence is accumulating that at the quaternary, cellular and tissue organization levels, nonprotein materials may participate in linkages within and between proteins. Thus, casein and ovalbumin contain small amounts of phosphorus, while polysaccharide derivations are found in connective tissue.

Properties and Reactions of Proteins

Proteins can be hydrolyzed into the component amino acids of which they are made. However, unless catalyzed by enzymes, this is a relatively difficult procedure involving long heating in strong acid or strong base. Hill (1965) reviewed studies on hydrolysis of proteins especially as used in determination of amino acid sequence. Of more relevance to food studies are many of the alterations that occur with much milder treatments.

Charge

Like the amino acids, proteins are amphoteric. Depending on the pH and ion concentration of the system, they may be either positively or negatively charged. As with other colloidal particles, the charge contributes materially to the stability of the dispersion. The charge also is the basis for electrophoresis, a widely used technique for separating and purifying proteins, based on their ability to migrate in an electric field.

At the isoelectric point (IEP), the protein particle will not migrate in an electric field. Most proteins have isoelectric points near neutrality on the pH scale, but pepsin has an IEP around 1, while lysozyme's IEP is around 11. The IEP of proteins is influenced by the salt concentration of the solution in which the measurement is made, due to the capacity of proteins to bind ions.

Ability to Interact with Small Ions and Molecules

As just indicated, proteins have considerable capacity to bind ions. The extent of binding is a function of the nature of the protein itself, the pH of the system, and the size, charge, and concentration of the ions. Multivalent ions usually bind more readily than monovalent, as can be seen in the relative effectiveness of Na^+, Ca^{++}, and Fe^{+++} in influencing the gelation of egg proteins. Proteins can also bind many smaller uncharged molecules, such as steroids or long-chain alcohols.

Solubility

The solubility, or stability of dispersion, of proteins is influenced by pH and by the ionic strength of the system. All proteins show marked minima in solubility at or near their IEP.

Ionic strength, $\Gamma/2$, is defined as

$$\Gamma/2 = \frac{1}{2} C z^2$$

where C is the concentration and z the charge on the ions present. Inclusion of ionic strength specification in food studies offers possibilities for improving understanding of the influence of various salts in food systems. At low ionic strengths, many proteins tend to be more soluble than at higher ones.

Steinhardt and Beychok (1964) review in some detail the effects of ions on proteins, pointing out that practically every property of solutions is influenced by hydrogen ion activity. For food systems, these properties include solubility, osmotic pressure, viscosity, stability of the native form (resistance to denaturation), enzymatic activity, and binding of other ions. In turn, these properties may also be influenced by parameters such as temperature, ionic strength, and presence of other dissolved substances (for example, sugar).

Water-Binding Capacity

Proteins vary widely in their ability to bind water, and therefore in their degree of hydration. As with the charge, hydration is a source of stability to the protein macromolecule in an aqueous system. Thus ovalbumin, with a high degree of hydration, forms stable dispersions, while casein, with a much lower degree of hydration, is readily precipitated by alteration of the pH to its isoelectric point.

Water is held on proteins by hydrogen bonding to backbone structures and by hydration of polar side chains. Lauffer (1964) suggested that ions on the protein surface may bind water by electrostriction, and/or water may be organized in "iceberg" form around hydrophobic groups. Berendsen and Migchelsen (1965) review the effects of various groups in proteins on water and water structure. The first part of the absorbed water is believed to be held intramolecularly, the next part on the surface of the molecule (Eley and Leslie, 1964). Thus, the degree of binding and the mobility of the water varies. This influences the plane of motion of the protein particle in a dispersion, and so plays a role in the measurement of the zeta potential. Schwann (1965) suggests that the general range of bound water varies from 0.2 to 0.5 gram water per gram of protein. Even crystallized proteins, such as ovalbumin, contain a considerable amount of water.

In the living cell, there are soluble proteins that are probably dispersed as individual molecules, for example the soluble proteins of the sarcoplasm of muscle. There are also insoluble proteins organized into fibers, membranes, and other structures, as in the contractile and connective tissue fibers of muscle. But even these insoluble proteins will adsorb, and possibly absorb, water, changing the degree of hydration with consequent alteration in their physical and chemical properties. An example of this can be seen when milk or tomato juice is mixed with ground raw meat—the meat will take up a considerable quantity of fluid.

Viscosity

The viscosity of protein solutions varies greatly, depending primarily on the size and shape of the macromolecule and the charge on it. Thus lysozyme, myoglobin, β-lactoglobulin, and ovalbumin, all globular particles, have intrinsic viscosities ranging from 3.0 to 4.0, while the rodlike particle of collagen has an intrinsic viscosity of 1150. Since protein particles have considerable electrostatic charge at most pHs, each particle has an ionic atmosphere that tends to increase the viscosity of the system. The viscosity will vary with the factors that influence size, shape, and charge, such as temperature, degree of hydration, pH, and ionic strength.

Aggregation and Dissociation

In many cases the degree of aggregation of proteins is relatively easily influenced by changes in temperature, pressure, pH, and type and concentration of other molecules or ions present. This may alter the aggregation or dissociation of the subunits making up a protein, or may involve protein-protein interactions. Precipitation occurs in protein mixtures when the pH is such that the proteins have net charges of opposite sign. There may also be interactions between proteins of the same sign, as in the combination of α- and β-casein to form casein. Then, proteins of the same type can interact, as in the polymerization of globular (G) actin to form fibrous (F) actin. Lauffer (1964) has reviewed some of these interactions. The formation of the gluten structure in bread dough is an example of aggregation on the macroscale, while the action of certain salts in softening a dough is due to the increased dispersion of the protein.

Denaturation

There have been a number of definitions proposed for denaturation. Perhaps most widely accepted is Kauzmann's definition (1959): "a process (or sequence of processes) in which the spatial arrangements of the polypeptide chains within the molecule is changed from that typical of the native protein to a more disordered arrangement." Scheraga (1961) has suggested that denaturation might be considered as a phase transition from the crystalline to the amorphous state. A native protein is a highly ordered structure, and as it is denatured, the arrangement of the chains becomes more nearly random, similar to the amorphous state. Tanford (1968) defines denaturation as a major change from the original native structure, without alteration of the amino acid sequence.

Denaturation is considered to involve breaking of part or all of the bonds that make up the ordered structure of the native molecule, with the exception of the peptide bonds linking the amino acid residues into the backbone chain. The process appears to be a continuous one, rather than "all-or-nothing," with various segments of the molecule changing at different rates and possibly in different ways, depending on the method being used to denature the material.

Methods of Study

Mahler and Cordes (1966) indicate one of the major difficulties in the study of denaturation is how to measure it. A large number of experimental techniques have been used (Kauzmann, 1959) and the results obtained usually are a function of the method of measurement employed. In the earlier investigations, the endpoint was taken as loss of some biological function of the protein, such as enzymatic activity. In food, the processes that initially produce denaturation are often carried far beyond this stage to give some desired endpoint in terms of the functional properties of the system.

Denaturation was originally considered to be irreversible. Cole (1964) points out that with better understanding of the basic process, and better control of experimental conditions, many cases of reversible denaturation are now known. Reithel (1963) lists 2 types of reversible denaturation studies, those involving disulfide-sulfhydryl transformations and those involving non-covalent bonding. However, in food preparation procedures, the systems are usually too complex and the processes carried too far for the changes to be reversible.

Causative Factors

A wide variety of treatments and reagents are known to cause denaturation of proteins. Of these, the ones relevant to food preparation processes include heat, surface changes, alteration of pH, and changing concentrations of salts or detergents. Many of these can interact, as in the close connection between the denaturing effects of pH and temperature. Also, added substances used in foods may either protect or disrupt the protein structure. Von Hipple and Wong (1964) reviewed the effects of a wide variety of neutral salts on macromolecular conformations. $CaCl_2$ acts as a denaturant, while K_2HPO_4 strongly stabilizes the native conformation. Sucrose and glucose have long been recognized as exerting a protective influence on protein structure, diminishing the rate of denaturation by heat (for example, Hardt, Huddleson, and Ball, 1943), and altering foam-forming ability (MacRitchie and Alexander, 1961).

Different denaturing agents may lead to different configurational changes, so any given protein may be subject to several different denaturation reactions. Also, a given agent may lead to two or more successive reactions, since as various bonds are broken in the unfolding of the molecule, they may recombine with other parts of the chain, with other chains, or with other nonprotein materials in the system. In addition, different proteins give different types of results with the same denaturing agent. With so many variables involved, it becomes very difficult to predict or explain precisely the results obtained in studies of denaturation.

Results of Denaturation

Denaturation influences many properties of proteins that are important in food. The protein usually becomes less soluble, and the viscosity of the system usually increases, probably due to changes in shape and/or water-binding ability and also to secondary association reactions. Denaturation also usually increases the reactivity of side chain groups. This has been studied especially with relation to the sulfhydryl-disulfide groups and their interchange. It is thought that some of the sulfur-containing groups are fixed in the interior of the native protein and only become exposed to reactants when the structural organization is disrupted. Proteins that function as enzymes usually lose this ability when denatured. Most proteins are more susceptible to attack by proteolytic enzymes when denatured, so this process usually increases digestibility.

Terminology

Colvin (1964) has suggested that since the term denaturation is used for a wide variety of processes on a wide variety of substrates with a wide variety of results, the word itself should be deleted, substituting more explicit terms. However, this word is still widely used in scientific literature.

Another source of confusion in terminology in food preparation studies is the set of terms used to designate later stages of processes that start with denaturation. Thus when an egg and milk mixture is heated to produce a custard, the first stage undoubtedly involves structural alterations in the egg protein (denaturation). These are followed by secondary association reactions, which lead to gelation or coagulation, and eventually to curdling or flocculation. But Jenness and Patton (1959) use clotting to refer to formation of a milk gel, and coagulation for the precipitation of casein as loose separate flocs. Surface denaturation of proteins is involved in the formation of egg white foams, but here the term flocculation is used to refer to the dry stage at which the protein films break into fragments, rather than the wet stage of a flocculated custard undergoing syneresis. It is necessary to read carefully and thoughtfully to be clear as to the meaning being employed by different authors.

Roles of —SH and —S—S— Groups

One of the interesting possibilities in food studies is investigation of the many roles of the residues of cysteine and cystine. As indicated previously, they have an important part in establishing and maintaining the native architecture of many protein molecules. Cystine bridges have been found forming loops and cross-links within a polypeptide chain (for example, in ribonuclease), and as cross-links between different chains forming a protein (for instance, in the insulin molecule). Some of the —SH groups are reactive in the native molecule; others become reactive only after denaturation. Cecil (1963) suggests that the unreactive —SH groups are involved in apolar bonding in the interior of the native protein, since the sulfhydryl group is generally a hydrophobic group.

Sulfhydryl-disulfide interchanges have been shown to be involved in many reactions important in food preparation. They occur during thermal denaturation of proteins, being involved in the aggregation of chains to produce a coagulum (Jensen, 1959). Gawronski et al. (1967) point out their implication in the pre- and post-rigor reactions important in the ultimate tenderization of muscle. Dimler (1965) has reviewed their role in the formation of the gluten structure of bread dough. Poglazov (1966) reviews the role of —SH groups in the polymerization of actin and in the ATP-ase activity of myosin, both of which are important in the structure and function of muscle tissue. Kice (1968) emphasizes the relative ease with which the disulfide bond can be made or broken as contributing to the biochemical importance of this group.

The sulfhydryl group appears to have an essential role in the activity of many enzymes. The active site of many enzymes contains either an —SH group or a bivalent metal ion. In the latter case, the ion is frequently bound to the protein through the S atom of a cysteine residue. In a number of cases, prosthetic groups essential to enzymatic activity are known to be bound to the protein chain through the —SH group.

ENZYMES

Enzymes are macromolecular catalysts of biological origin. All known ones are largely or entirely proteins, mostly of molecular weight of 50,000 or more. Many contain prosthetic groups, which are smaller, nonprotein units linked to the protein chain. Some require activators. These are small molecules, frequently an inorganic ion, required for, or stimulatory to, enzyme activity. The role of Cu^+ and Fe^{++} in stimulating enzymatic activity is well known in food processes. There are also many materials that can act as inhibitors, decreasing the rate of the enzyme-catalyzed reaction. Avidin is a naturally occurring inhibitor, while other inhibitors may be present or added to the food system. The latter materials include such things as Ag^+, metal chelating agents such as EDTA, pyrophosphates, and sulfonamide.

The study of enzymes is another of the very active fields of biochemical investigation. Neurath et al. (1967) state that "the past few years have seen spectacular advances in the characterization of the structure and function of several . . . proteolytic enzymes." But Bradley (1966) points out that in considering the role of enzymes in biological processes, the organization of the total system must be regarded, since "a cell is not a bag of enzymes and substrates interacting at random."

Importance in Food Materials

Since enzymes are of biological origin, most food substances contain them. Under the appropriate conditions, enzymes can catalyze a wide variety of reactions, with either desirable or undesirable results. Among the many enzyme-catalyzed reactions that influence palatability of foods are pectin hydrolysis, enzymatic rancidification of fats, enzymatic browning of cut fruits, changes in anthocyanin or chlorophyll pigments, hydrolytic changes influencing texture of muscle tissue, starch-sugar changes in potato storage, flavor changes in fruits and vegetables, yeast leavening of doughs, and changes in frozen products. Schultz (1960), S.C.I. Monograph No. 11 (1961), Acker (1962), Reed (1966), and Lund et al. (1969) review various aspects of enzyme activity in food materials.

Nomenclature

With the exception of a few historical names such as pepsin and trypsin, enzymes are named for the substrates on which they work, or the type of reaction they catalyze. The suffix -ase indicates an enzyme. The Commission on Enzymes of the International Union of Biochemistry (see Florkin and Stotz, 1964) adopted the following classification:

1. Oxidoreductases, which catalyze oxidation-reduction reactions.
2. Transferases, which catalyze transfer of groups.
3. Hydrolases, which catalyze hydrolytic reactions.
4. Lyases, which catalyze addition of groups to double bonds or vice versa.
5. Isomerases, which catalyze isomerizations.
6. Ligases or synthetases, which catalyze condensation of 2 mole-

cules with cleavage of the pyrophosphate bond of ATP or a similar triphosphate.

Within each of these large classes, a wide variety of enzymes and substrates is represented.

Mode of Action

Enzymes, like all catalysts, function by altering reaction rates without themselves being changed. Enzymes are exceptional catalysts in several respects. (1) They are highly efficient. Reactions may proceed at rates 10^8 to 10^{11} times as fast as the corresponding nonenzymatic ones. Hammes (1968) comments that "enzymes are innately fascinating because of the extreme efficiency with which they catalyze chemical reactions. . . ." (2) Most enzymes are specific for the reaction catalyzed and the substrate utilized, some to the extent of attacking only one type of bond within a macromolecule. (3) Enzymes are versatile in that within the entire class they catalyze a very wide variety of reactions, as is shown by the classification above.

As discussed in Chapter 1, chemical reactions involve energy changes. In general, reactions of biological importance have high activation energies—the energy needed to get the reaction started. Reactions that absorb energy are called endothermic; those that release energy are termed exothermic. See Figure 4.

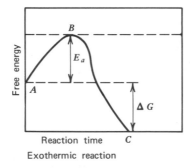
Exothermic reaction

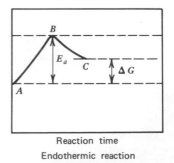
Endothermic reaction

FIGURE 4. Energy changes in exothermic and endothermic reactions. A = energy level of starting compounds, B = energy level of activated state, C = energy level of reaction products, E_a = Energy of activation, and ΔG = Change in free energy between starting compounds and reaction products.

Enzymes function as catalysts in reactions involving breaking covalent bonds, as the other types of bonds are much more easily broken. In order to break a covalent bond, the atoms involved must be partially separated (activated) to allow them to recombine with other atoms. The energy required for activation is generally much above the amount that can be supplied by thermal motion except at high temperatures. Enzymes act by lowering the activation energy to levels that can be supplied by heat of motion at physiological temperatures, and so allow the reaction to proceed more rapidly.

For example, in the reaction $H_2O_2 \rightarrow H_2O + O$, the activation energy, E_a, is about 18 kcal/mole if no catalyst is present. With a platinum catalyst E_a decreases to about 12 kcal/mole, but with the enzyme catalase, E_a drops to 2 kcal/mole, a ninefold decrease from the uncatalyzed reaction.

Factors Affecting Activity

A wide variety of conditions and materials influences the effectiveness of enzyme catalysis.

1. As with any chemical reaction, the appropriate reactants (substrate) must be available and the products of the reaction must be removed for the reaction to continue. In many foods, the enzyme and substrate are separated by cellular barriers. These are broken when the cell is ruptured as in peeling or cutting fruit. In other cases the enzymes may be immobilized by removal of water in dehydration or by freezing. However, in fatty materials, fluid lipids may provide the means for enzyme and substrate to come together, even though no water is available. In many commercial processes, enzymes are deliberately added, with thorough mixing, to achieve some desired result, as in the addition of glucose oxidase to desugar egg white before dehydration.

2. Temperature has a very important, twofold influence on enzyme-catalyzed reactions. These reactions follow the general rule that the reaction rate approximately doubles for each 10° C rise in temperature, that is, Q_{10} = approximately 2. But enzymes are proteins and so may be denatured or disorganized by heat, destroying their catalytic activity. Therefore, rising temperature may first increase the reaction rate, and then decrease it. Thus each enzyme has an optimum temperature for a given period of time. In many food systems, an additional factor is the rate of heat transfer in the food. Thus, in large amounts of food or other cases where heating is slow, there may be a significant amount of enzyme activity before the enzyme is denatured.

Most studies have utilized enzymes having activity optima in the range of 30–40° C. Many enzymes are destroyed by 5 minutes' exposure to 75° C, but some are inactivated at 40° C, while a few can resist temperatures as high as 100° C (Dixon, 1961). Microorganisms are known that can grow and reproduce at temperatures as high as 92° C (Brock, 1967). Tappel et al. (1956) showed that papain exerted the maximum hydrolytic effect on muscle proteins in the range of 60 to 80° C. At the other extreme, studies on cold-water fish and shellfish suggest that enzymes from these organisms can operate at much lower temperatures, so these reaction rates are not slowed up to the same extent by refrigeration or freezing. Thus there is wide variation in the effects of altered temperature on enzyme catalysis.

3. pH, like temperature, has a 2-part effect on enzyme activity. An enzyme-catalyzed reaction usually has an optimum pH at which maximum reaction velocity is attained. But enzymes are stable only in a limited pH range, and are inactivated by denaturation at pHs above or below this range. In some cases, enzyme systems show a double pH optimum. Schwimmer (1962) attributes this to (1) the presence of two isoenzymes with different pH optima, (2) the formation of active enzyme-substrate complexes by two ionic species of the enzyme, or (3) the presence of an ampholyte inhibitor. McLaren (1957) gives evidence that the pH optimum for an enzyme on the surface of a cell or cellular particle may not be the same as for the enzyme in solution.

4. Other materials present will influence enzyme activity. The roles of activators and inhibitors have already been discussed. Wilder (1962) found that the ionic strength of the buffer solution influenced the heat inactivation of peroxidase. In fact, all the substances that promote or delay denaturation of proteins could be expected to influence enzyme activity.

COLLAGEN, GELATIN

The influence of the chemical and physical nature of a protein on characteristics of a food may be illustrated by a review of the properties and uses of gelatin. Gelatin is used extensively in food formulas as a gelling agent; as a whipping agent in foams; as a clearing agent in fruit juices, wines, and beer; to increase viscosity; and to prevent ice-crystal growth in frozen desserts. Historically, it is the only relatively pure protein widely used in food. It is a derived protein, prepared from collagen, so some explanation of the chemical and physical nature of collagen is necessary to understand the current theory as to the structure and mode of action of gelatin.

Collagen

The collagens are widely distributed in the animal kingdom, forming the principal supporting structural elements of most tissues. They serve this essential role through their ordered fibrous structure. Although collagens from different species and from different tissues in a given animal vary in many details, the general character of most vertebrate collagens appears to be quite similar. However, certain invertebrate collagens may differ substantially from vertebrate collagens.

In vertebrates, collagen forms a substantial portion of such structures as skin, tendons, and inter- and intramuscular sheaths. It also is the principal matrix material of mineralized tissues such as bones and teeth. It is found in the vitreous humor of the eye, and in swim bladders and fins of fishes. The principal sources of edible gelatin are mammalian bones and hides.

Characteristics that appear to be common to most collagen fibers include: they tend to swell in acid, alkali or concentrated solutions of certain neutral salts or nonelectrolytes; they are relatively inelastic; in the native state they are resistant to the action of most proteolytic enzymes, but are readily attacked by collagenase; when denatured they are susceptible to attack by a number of proteolytic enzymes; under standard conditions, at a temperature characteristic for each species, but differing among species, they exhibit thermal shrinkage to a fraction of their original length; and they are substantially converted to soluble gelatin by high temperature treatment, or a combination of exposure to acid or alkali followed by hot-water extraction.

Collagen is believed to be elaborated by the cells as tropocollagen, a triple-stranded coiled coil (Figure 2c). The tropocollagen molecule, the monomer of collagen fibrils, is a rodlike molecule approximately 2800 Å long and 15 Å in diameter. It is soluble in cold dilute acid (Veis, 1964).

The tropocollagen molecules are released into the ground substance and are then cross-linked to form collagen fibrils. Piez (1966) states that noncovalent bonds such as H-bonds are probably sufficient to explain the first stage of fibril formation, but not the long-term stability of collagen fibers. So collagen tissues are thought to have variable amounts of covalent interchain cross-links, probably formed through lysyl-derived aldehyde groups at the amino terminal end of the single chains of the tropocollagen molecule (Bornstein, 1968; Page and Benditt, 1969). Recent studies relating degree of solubilization to age of connective tissue suggest that the degree of cross-linking increases progressively with age. For example, McClain et al. (1969) studied the cross-linking in the epimysium of the longissimus dorsi muscle, and estimated the number of cross-links per molecule as 4.09 in the 1-week old pig, 7.73 in the 5-month old pig, and 21.31 in commercial-grade cow.

Since collagen varies in degree of cross-linking, it also is variable in the ease with which it can be solubilized. A small amount is extractable with cold neutral salt solutions. This is believed to be largely newly synthesized tropocollagen. Other small portions can be extracted with dilute alkali buffers and dilute acid buffers. Klein et al. (1969) suggest that citrate-soluble collagen is derived from fibrous collagen that is not yet cross-linked intermolecularly, but that acetic acid probably solubilizes "insoluble" collagen. Mature collagen fibers require autoclaving or treatment with acids or alkalis to solubilize them.

Collagen appears to be quite different from any other protein in its amino acid makeup. Approximately one third of the residues are glycyl, and about one fourth contain the pyrrolidine ring (proline, hydroxyproline). It is the only protein known to contain hydroxyproline, with the exception of elastin, which has a much smaller amount. It also contains hydroxylysine. It has no cysteine, and only a very small amount of methionine, its only sulfur-containing amino acid. Veis (1964), Harrington and Von Hippel (1961) and Hall (1961) list amino acid analyses for collagens from various tissues.

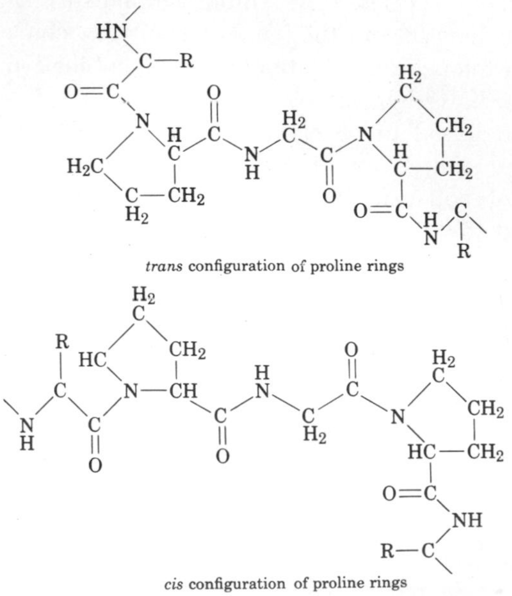

trans configuration of proline rings

cis configuration of proline rings

FIGURE 5. Protein backbone chain containing proline.

The presence of the pyrrolidine rings in proline and hydroxyproline influences the shape of the helix of the collagen chains, since these introduce a bend in the primary backbone chain as illustrated in Figure 5. This figure should be compared with the backbone chain figure, page 120 and Figure 2. The tropocollagen molecule is stabilized by intra- and interchain H-bonds, plus the stereochemical restrictions imposed by the pyrrolidine rings. It is calculated that every third residue must be glycine because of the space restrictions that leave little room for side chain groups. The core of the chain is believed to be very compact, with all the side chains directed externally where they are easily accessible for intermolecular reactions.

A variety of sugars have been found to be associated with collagens in various tissues. However, the amounts remaining in highly purified collagen preparations are small, generally less than 2 percent of the total weight. Melcher (1969) has found evidence suggesting the presence of bound lipid on mature collagen fibers.

The stable helical configuration of the protein chain that is characteristic of collagen occurs in the nonpolar regions of the chain which are high in proline and hydroxyproline. These configurations are heat labile, so heat denaturation of collagen produces first the collapse of the ordered structure at the shrink temperature, T_s. This is analogous to the melting of a crystal structure. With more drastic treatment, the chains dissociate, eventually to the gelatin stage. These changes are accompanied by marked changes in viscosity, molecular (or particle) weight, volume of the particles, ease of proteolysis, and tendency to form gels.

As indicated previously, the T_s of purified collagen fibers varies among species. For example, the T_s for calfskin collagen is 65° C, but that for codskin is 40° C. However, the T_s obtained depends on rate of heating, pH of the system, and any treatment the tissue may have undergone. The thermal denaturation temperature, T_D, for soluble collagen derived from collagen fibers is considerably lower than the T_s of the fiber itself, the T_D for calfskin being 36° C and for codskin 16° C.

Conversion of Collagen to Gelatin

The conversion of collagen to gelatin involves the collapse of the ordered structure of the collagen backbone chain, plus rupture of a considerable number of the cross-links that hold the chains together. The ordered structure is eliminated by heat treatment, but breaking the cross-links requires more drastic treatment.

The "parent gelatin" employed in studies of molecular properties is usually prepared by isolating the soluble tropocollagen from collagenous tissues. This is then converted to gelatin by heating or treating with denaturing chemicals. This gives quite uniform material, with a molecular weight of about 1.35×10^5, but it is still not homogeneous. The three intertwined chains of the tropocollagen molecule may still be cross-linked, or the cross-links may have been partially or completely broken. In addition, the three chains are not of identical composition, and probably not of equal molecular weight. And the number and distribution of cross-links is probably not uniform from molecule to molecule within a given sample, nor between samples from different sources.

The degree of inhomogeneity in gelatin is increased by the methods used for preparation of the gelatin used in food materials. In general, the commercial processes of conversion involve three steps: (1) the removal of noncollagenous materials from the stock; (2) conversion of the purified collagen to gelatin; and (3) recovery of the gelatin in dried form. There are several different processing schemes in use, producing gelatins of different chemical and physical properties.

The acid-treatment process is usually applied to pig or rabbit skin, and to ossein, the collagenous matrix of bone. The stock is soaked in an approximately 5 percent solution of inorganic acid for 10 to 30 hours. It is then washed thoroughly, the pH adjusted to about 4, and the material subjected to a series of hot-water extractions, starting with about 60° C and increasing the temperature 5–10° for each successive treatment. This process gives gelatin with an alkaline IEP (about pH 8.9), and the gelatin will bind small ions in the pH 6–9 range. The gelatin molecules are believed to be network structures, very similar to intact collagen fibrils but with the secondary structure disorganized and some peptide bond hydrolysis.

The alkali treatment is the most widely used commercial process. It can be used on any collagen stock. The stock material is soaked in a saturated solution of CaO (lime) for 3 to 10 months. Then the lime is washed out, the pH adjusted to 5–8, and the material subjected to a series of hot-water extractions as in the acid-precursor process. The alkali soak causes some peptide bond hydrolysis, and also disrupts the intermolecular forces, permitting extensive swelling of the stock, and producing less compact molecules of a lower order of cross-linking than the acid process. The IEP of a high grade alkali-precursor gelatin is around pH 5. Increased duration of lime soak increases the rate of conversion to gelatin on heating, decreases the nitrogen content and the number of amide groups, increases the number of amino terminal groups, decreases the chain weight, decreases the IEP, and increases the gel strength of the derived gelatin. So variations in the soaking time contribute to the heterogeneity of commercial gelatin.

Bogue (1923) studied the effect of time, temperature, and pH on the conversion of alkali-precursor collagen to gelatin. The rate of conversion increased with temperature, that at 95° C being least affected by pH (Figure 6). At 80° C, the extent of conversion increased with time, except for the 168-hour treatments at pH > 10 (Figure 7). In the latter samples, the decrease in nitrogen recovery was attributed to secondary hydrolysis, and loss of nitrogen as ammonia. In all the trials,

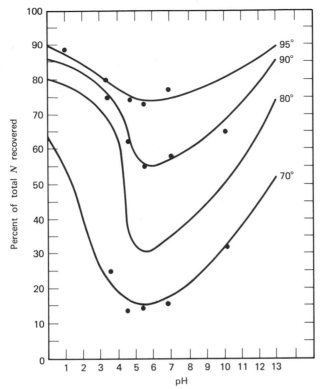

FIGURE 6. Hydrolysis of collagen to gelatin: Influence of temperature on total N recovered in the solution at varying pH. (Courtesy of Dr. R. H. Bogue and *Industrial Engineering Chemistry*.)

secondary hydrolysis tended to increase at pH $>$ 8, especially at pH 11 and 12. The conversion of collagen to gelatin was minimal at pH 5–6.

In both the acid and alkali treatments, each extract is dried separately, and the resulting gelatin graded for gel strength and viscosity. Each successive extract varies in its properties. For example, Marks et al. (1968) list the following data on gelatins from limed ossein.

	First Extraction	Third Extraction
Gel strength, Bloom, g	256	82
Viscosity, mp	52.3	21.1

So it is customary to blend gelatins from several different extractions to obtain the properties desired in the final product. This also contributes to the heterogeneity of commercial gelatin.

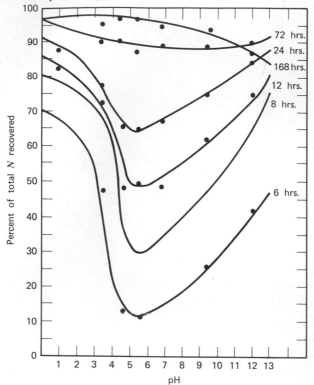

FIGURE 7. Hydrolysis of collagen to gelatin. Effect of period of heating at 80° C on total N recovered in the solution at varying pH. (Courtesy of Dr. R. H. Bogue and *Industrial Engineering Chemistry.*)

A third process used in some commercial gelatin preparation is high-pressure steam extraction of crushed bone. No pretreatment of the stock is required, the high temperature hydrolyzing the bonds that make the collagen insoluble. The extraction of the gelatin is completed at a lower temperature to minimize degradation of the gelatin.

Microcrystalline collagen (Battista, 1967) is prepared by a process that first loosens the chain network by chemical treatment, then separates the microcrystalline particles by violent agitation. This gelatinlike material, prepared from bovine-hide collagen, is said to hold 10 times as much water as conventional gelatin (Anon., 1967).

The source of the collagen influences the properties of the gelatin prepared from it, since the different tissues vary in structure and organization, and in the other materials present. Fish collagens are usually more readily solubilized than mammalian ones. This suggests a lower degree of bridging between the collagen chains in the structural tissues of fish.

Gelatin

Gelatin has a long history of use in food materials. Veis (1964) refers to it as "among the most poorly understood manufacturing substances of commercial importance" due to the diversity and complexity of the collagenous tissues used as extraction stock.

The peptide chains in the gelatin molecules have random configurations in aqueous solutions at higher temperatures. A given sample of gelatin will contain a variety of peptide-chain species, usually differing in molecular weight, in the number of acidic and basic groups in the side chains, and possibly in amino acid sequence. These factors influence interactions between gelatin molecules, and between gelatin and solvent, and so affect the viscosity, gelling power, and other properties. The variation in IEP due to the method of preparation has already been indicated.

Gelatin tends to deteriorate, either in the dry form or in solution. Dried gelatin tends to lose solubility in storage, especially at higher temperatures (35–40° C) and high humidity. Gelatins from limed stock are more apt to insolubilize than those from acid-treated collagens. Marks et al. (1968) state that loss of solubility appears to be due to polymerization of gelatin molecules, probably involving cross-linking and H-bonds. Extent of insolubilization was increased by higher moisture content, by prolonged heating during drying of the gelatin extract, and by the presence of Na^+ or glucose.

In aqueous solution, gelatin appears to undergo slow but progressive hydrolysis to smaller-molecular-weight compounds, with decrease in viscosity and loss of gelling power. The rate of hydrolysis is influenced by temperature, pH, pressure, and nature of other solutes present. Acid-precursor gelatins are more stable in acid systems than in alkaline, while alkaline-precursor gelatins are more stable in alkaline systems. Tiemstra (1968) gives nomographs that may be used to estimate the loss of gelling power under given conditions of pH, temperature, and time.

Gelatin molecules are also susceptible to enzymatic hydrolysis, being readily attacked by almost all proteolytic enzymes. Incorporation of raw fruit that contains naturally occurring proteolytic enzymes into gelatin solutions causes rapid loss of gelling ability. Examples are fresh pineapple (containing bromelin), papaya (papain), or figs (ficin).

Veis (1964) states that gelatin may also be degraded by oxidative chain cleavage, when treated with oxidizing agents such as hydrogen peroxide.

Swelling

The extent to which gelatin swells in water is modified by the surface area, the initial pH, the presence or addition of acids, alkalies, and inorganic salts, and the previous history of the gelatin. In swelling, gelatin changes from a hard, brittle substance to a soft, flexible one.

The mechanism of swelling has been the basis for many investigations. Although many different suggestions for the structure of gelatin in gels have been advanced, the evidence indicates that it is fibrillar. Long-chain molecules such as cellulose, starch, pectins, gelatins, and many other proteins have the ability to absorb large amounts of water. Moran (1926, 1932) stated that this water exists in two states, the bound water associated with certain groups in the molecule and the free water held in the interstices between the molecules. According to Sponsler et al. (1940), with 0.2, 15, and 33 percent of water, the number of water molecules bound per molecule of gelatin are 4, 260, and 750, respectively.

In general, with increase of hydrogen-ion concentration, absorption of water increases until a maximum is reached. This maximum varies with different gelatins and their preparation. With still further decrease in pH, swelling decreases. As the alkalinity is increased, swelling is also increased, the maximum being reached at pH 9. With further increase in alkalinity, hydrolysis of the gelatin to amino acids and other products occurs.

Salts affect the swelling of gelatin, some inhibiting and others increasing water absorption. Lloyd et al. (1933) found that gelatin gels at or near the IEP swell more in salt solutions than in water.

In food preparation utilizing dry gelatin, the gelatin is allowed to swell in a small amount of cold water. The cross-links between the chains prevent solution of gelatin in the cold water, and confine the swelling to a definite limit. When the temperature is increased, either by heating or by addition of hot water, the weak intermolecular bonds are broken and the gelatin disperses. The prior swelling increases the ease with which the gelatin can be dispersed to form a sol when hot water is added.

Gel Formation

The ability of a gelatin solution to form an elastic, semirigid gel on cooling is an example of the general process of gelation. Many substances besides gelatin have the ability to gel under the proper concentration and temperature conditions—for example, cooked starch pastes and pectin gels.

On cooling to temperatures less than about 35° C, an aqueous solution of a reasonably high molecular weight gelatin will increase in viscosity. Depending on the concentration of gelatin, the solution may become more turbid, or may set to a gel. The first step in gel formation in gelatin is thought to be the return of the nonpolar regions of the chain which are high in imino acid residues to the ordered collagen-fold configuration. These structured areas are connected by flexible, unstructured individual peptide chains. At concentrations high enough for the effective areas of the molecules to overlap, aggregation and/or gelation will follow. At the gel point, a continuous network forms throughout the system, probably due to nonspecific bond formation between the ordered segments of the chains. Hydrophobic, hydrogen, and electrostatic bonds may be involved in this cross-bonding. The formation of the collagen-fold is considered a rapid process as the correct temperature is reached, but the formation of cross-bonds is a slower process. So under the correct conditions, the strength of the gel will increase with time as more cross-bonds are formed.

The formation and stability of a gelatin gel is influenced by a number of factors, most of which are interrelated. The concentration of the gelatin must be high enough for the molecular domains to overlap—a concentration of approximately 0.5 percent for single-chain gelatins at neutral pH and moderate ionic strength. Rigidity of the gel increases with increasing concentration, the increase being nearly proportional to the square of the concentration up to about 6 percent. However, deviations from this relationship often occur, probably due to type of gelatin, extent of degradation, previous thermal history, pH, and ionic strength.

The temperature must be below 35–40° C, but the actual gelling temperature, T_g, varies with rate of cooling, aging or tempering of the gel, molecular weight and degree of cross-linking of the gelatin, pH, and type and concentration of other solutes that may be present. A gelatin sol cooled at 15° C has a higher T_g than one cooled at 0° C (Eldridge and Ferry, 1954). Apparently the slower gel formation at the higher temperature allows for the formation of more stable cross-bonds. Aging or tempering at temperatures below the melting point will allow the formation of stronger junction points in a gel that is weak due to rapid gelation, increasing the rigidity of the gel. Dahlberg et al. (1928) reported that, for the weak gelatin solutions used in ice cream, gel formation requires a long time. They allowed 18 hours for gel formation and aging in most of their tests. However, they found that the gumminess in ice cream with too much gelatin increased during 4–5 weeks' storage.

Solutes such as neutral salts or organic acids may either increase or decrease T_g. The effect of anions at equal concentrations is given as follows. The first of the series elevates the gelation temperature, and it is slightly lower for each succeeding anion, until the iodide may lower T_g below 0° C. The order above the IEP is SO_4 > citrate > tartrate > acetate > Cl > ClO_3 > NO_3 > Br > I. When enough acid has been added so that the system is below the IEP, the cations may have more effect than the anions.

Dahlberg et al. (1928) found that the gel strength was greater in milk than in water, even when the proportion of gelatin added to the milk was based on the water content of the milk and not its total volume or weight.

The rigidity of the gel increases rapidly with increasing molecular weight of the gelatin, up to a certain point. The molecular weight for maximum rigidity varies from sample to sample of gelatin. High-molecular-weight gelatins are already cross-linked, so have a lessened tendency to form network junctions. The presence of covalent cross-links appears to favor intrachain folding rather than interchain junctions.

The pH of the system influences gel strength to a small extent, with the highest rigidity values usually in the range of pH 5 to 10. Idson and Braswell (1957) suggest that the pH of a gelatin dessert should be about 3.0–3.5 for proper tart flavor. The rigidity at a given pH also varies with ionic strength, and with the presence of nonelectrolytes such as sugars. Friedman and Shearer (1939) found that small concentrations of sucrose or fructose increased setting time, the maximum being reached at 0.02–0.03 M. Concentrations exceeding 0.1 M caused the gel to set more rapidly. They also found the diffusion velocity varied directly with the time of setting and concluded that the slower-setting gels had a more open structure.

Reversibility of Gelation

When a gel melts the processes for development of rigidity are reversed, but the change occurs more slowly than that produced by cooling (Ferry, 1948). The melting and gelling temperatures usually differ, but the size of the difference varies with the rate of heating or cooling. The gel may be remelted and solidified many times. A gelatin sol that has solidified and then remelted will form a gel in a shorter time for the succeeding gelations. If some gelatin that has solidified is added to a freshly made gelatin sol, setting takes place more rapidly.

Gelatin possesses the ability to reform a gel structure at low temperature after the gel has been destroyed by agitation. This property is not exhibited by agar-agar gels.

Foam Formation

Gelatins are often beaten when they have become thick but not firmly set. The beating incorporates air, forming a foam, and the gelatin mixture increases in volume. Bogue (1922) states that the ability to form a foam is greatest at the IEP. At this point the gelatin particles have a strong tendency to adhere to each other, and this favors foam formation. If the beating is done at the time when the gelatin has cooled enough to be quite viscous, but not brittle so that the edges break apart, the volume may be increased two or three times over that of the original unbeaten gelatin. The gelatin at this stage is elastic and stretches to surround the air bubbles. If the gel becomes too firm before the beating is started, the gel breaks and air is not readily incorporated. The foamed gel will be less rigid than the original, due to the incorporation of air into the structure.

Methods of Study

The preceding discussion has indicated the wide range of variables that can influence the performance of a given sample of gelatin in a food product. These emphasize the necessity for a complete history of the gelatin utilized, and for careful control of all experimental conditions, if reliable results are to be obtained.

Standard methods for evaluation of gelatin samples have been published by Gelatin Manufacturers Institute (1964) and by A.O.A.C. (1965). The gel strength is usually determined by the use of the Bloom gelometer. The rigidity of a gelatin gel may be measured by bending or stretching strips of gel, measuring the torque produced by various rotating devices, measuring the distortion of the meniscus or displacement of volume produced by air pressure, or determining the velocity of propagation of transverse vibrations (Idson and Braswell, 1957). Viscosity of a gelatin sol is usually measured by flow time at 60° C, using a special pipette.

References

PROTEINS

Abelson, P. H. 1968. Amino acid sequences in proteins. *Science 160*: 951.
Berendsen, H. J. C., and C. Migchelsen. 1965. Hydration structure of fibrous macromolecules. *Ann. N.Y. Acad. Sci. 125*, Art. 2: 365.

Cecil, R. 1963. Intramolecular bonds in proteins. I. The role of sulfur in proteins. In *The Proteins: Composition, Structure, and Function,* H. Neurath, ed., 2nd ed., Vol. 1, p. 379. Academic Press, New York.

Cole, R. D. 1964. Personal perspectives in the practice of protein chemistry. In *Symposium on Foods: Proteins and their Reactions,* H. W. Schultz and A. F. Anglemier, eds., p. 3. Avi Publ. Co., Inc., Westport, Conn.

Colvin, J. R. 1964. Denaturation: a requiem. In *Symposium on Foods: Proteins and their Reactions,* H. W. Schultz and A. F. Anglemier, eds., p. 69. Avi Publ. Co., Inc., Westport, Conn.

Dayhoff, M. O., and R. V. Eck. 1967–1968. *Atlas of Protein Sequence and Structure, 1966.* National Biomedical Research Foundation, Silver Spring, Md.

Dimler, R. J. 1965. Exploring the structure of proteins in wheat gluten. *Baker's Digest* 39 (Oct.): 35.

Edelman, G. M., and W. O. McClure. 1968. Fluorescent probes and the conformation of proteins. *Accounts Chem. Res. 1*: 65.

Eley, D. C., and R. B. Leslie. 1964. Adsorption of water on solid proteins with special reference to haemoglobin. In *The Structure and Properties of Biomolecules and Biological Systems,* J. Duschesne, ed. *Advan. Chem. Phys.,* Vol. VII, Interscience Publ., p. 238.

Feeney, R. E., and R. M. Hill. 1960. Protein chemistry and food research. *Advan. Food Res. 10*: 22.

Gawronski, T. H., J. V. Spencer, and M. H. Pubols. 1967. Changes in sulfhydryl and disulfide content of chicken muscle and the effect of N-ethylmaleimide. *J. Agr. Food Chem. 15*: 781.

Hardt, C. R., I. F. Huddleson, and C. D. Ball. 1943. The protective action of glucose in bovine plasma against heat coagulation. *Science 98*: 309.

Hill, R. L. 1965. Hydrolysis of proteins. *Advan. Protein Chem. 20*: 37.

Jenness, R., and S. Patton. 1959. *Principles of Dairy Chemistry.* John Wiley and Sons, Inc., N.Y.

Jensen, E. V. 1959. Sulfhydryl-disulfide interchange. *Science 130*: 1319.

Kauzmann, W. 1959. Some factors in the interpretation of protein denaturation. *Advan. Protein Chem. 14*: 1.

Kice, J. L. 1968. Electrophilic and nucleophilic catalysis of the scission of the sulfur-sulfur bond. *Accounts Chem. Res. 1*: 58.

Klotz, I. M. 1967. Protein subunits: a table. *Science 155*: 697.

Lauffer, M. A. 1964. Protein-protein interaction: endothermic polymerization and biological processes. In *Symposium on Foods: Proteins and their Reactions,* H. W. Schultz, A. F. Anglemier, eds., p. 87. Avi Publ. Co., Inc., Westport, Conn.

MacRitchie, F., and A. E. Alexander. 1961. The effect of sucrose on protein films. II. Adsorbed films. *J. Colloid Sci. 16*: 61.

Mahler, H. R., and E. H. Cordes. 1966. *Biological Chemistry.* Harper and Row, New York.

Poglazov, B. F. 1966. *Structure and Function of Contractile Proteins.* Academic Press, New York.

Ramachandran, G. N., and V. Sasisekharan. 1968. Conformation of polypeptides and proteins. *Advan. Protein Chem. 23:* 283.

Reithel, F. J. 1963. The dissociation and association of protein structures. *Advan. Protein Chem. 18:* 123.

Scheraga, H. A. 1961. *Protein Structure.* Academic Press, New York.

Schwan, H. P. 1965. Electrical properties of bound water. *Ann. N.Y. Acad. Sci. 125,* Art. 2: 344.

Steinhardt, J., and S. Beychok. 1964. Interaction of proteins with hydrogen ions and other small ions and molecules. In *The Proteins: Composition, Structure, and Function,* H. Neurath, ed., 2nd ed., Vol. II, p. 139. Academic Press, New York.

Tanford, C. 1968. Protein denaturation. *Advan. Protein Chem. 23:* 121.

Tristram, G. R., and R. H. Smith. 1963. The amino acid composition of some purified proteins. *Advan. Protein Chem. 18:* 227.

Von Hippel, P. H., and Kwok-Ying Wong. 1964. Neutral salts: the generality of their effects on the stability of macromolecular conformations. *Science 145:* 577.

ENZYMES

Acker, L. 1962. Enzymic reactions in foods of low moisture content. *Advan. Food Res. 11:* 263.

Bradley, D. F. 1966. Relation between structure and activity of biopolymers. *Trans. N.Y. Acad. Sci.,* Ser. II *28:* 788.

Brock, T. D. 1967. Life at high temperatures. *Science 158:* 1012.

Dixon, M. 1961. General introduction. In *Production and Application of Enzyme Preparations in Food Manufacture.* S.C.I. Monograph No. 11, p. 3, Soc. Chem. Ind., London.

Florkin, M., and E. H. Stotz, eds. 1964. *Comprehensive Biochemistry,* Vol. 13. Elsevier Publ. Co., New York.

Hammes, G. G. 1968. Relaxation spectrometry of enzymatic reactions. *Accounts Chem. Res. 1:* 321.

Lund, D. B., O. Fennema, and W. D. Powrie. 1969. Enzymic and acid hydrolysis of sucrose as influenced by freezing. *J. Food Sci. 34:* 378.

McLaren, A. D. 1957. Concerning the pH dependence of enzyme reactions on cells, particulates and in solution. *Science 125:* 697.

Neurath, H., K. A. Walsh, and W. P. Winter. 1967. Evolution of structure and function of proteases. *Science 158:* 1638.

Reed, G. 1966. *Enzymes in Food Processing.* Academic Press, New York.

Schultz, H. W., ed. 1960. *Food Enzymes.* Avi Publ. Co., Westport, Conn.

Schwimmer, S. 1962. Theory of double pH optima of enzymes. *J. Theor. Biol.* 3: 102.

S.C.I. Monograph No. 11. 1961. *Production and Application of Enzyme Preparations in Food Manufacture.* Soc. Chem. Ind., London.

Tappel, A. L., D. S. Miyada, C. Sterling, and V. P. Maier. 1956. Meat tenderization. II. Factors affecting the tenderization of beef by papain. *Food Res. 21*: 375.

Wilder, C. J. 1962. Factors affecting heat inactivation and partial reactivation of peroxidase purified by ion-exchange chromatography. *J. Food Sci. 27*: 567.

COLLAGEN, GELATIN

Anonymous. 1967. Microcrystalline technology used with three more polymers. *Chem. Engr. News,* p. 26, Apr. 24.

Assoc. Official Anal. Chemists. 1965. *Official Methods of Analysis,* 10th ed. Washington, D.C.

Battista, O. A., N. Z. Erdi, C. F. Ferraro, and F. J. Karasinski. 1967. Colloidal macromolecular phenomena. Part II. Novel microcrystals of polymers. *J. Appl. Polymer Sci. 11*: 481.

Bogue, R. H. 1922. *Chemistry and Technology of Gelatin and Glue.* McGraw-Hill Book Co., New York.

Bogue, R. H. 1923. Conditions affecting the hydrolysis of collagen to gelatin. *Ind. Eng. Chem. 15*: 1154.

Bornstein, P. 1968. Collagen: relatively invariant (helical) and variable (non-helical) regions. *Science 161*: 592.

Dahlberg, A. C., D. C. Carpenter, and J. C. Hening. 1928. Grading of commercial gelatin and its use in the manufacture of ice cream, II. *Ind. Eng. Chem. 20*: 516.

Eldridge, J. E., and J. D. Ferry. 1954. Studies of the cross-linking process in gelatin gels. III. Dependence of melting point on concentration and molecular weight. *J. Phys. Chem. 58*: 992.

Ferry, J. D. 1948. Protein gels. *Advan. Protein Chem. 4*: 1.

Friedman, L., and W. N. Shearer. 1939. The effect of non-electrolytes upon the time of setting of gelatin gels, I. *J. Am. Chem. Soc. 61*: 1749.

Gelatin Manufacturers Institute of America, Inc. 1964. *Standard Methods for the Sampling and Testing of Gelatins.* 501 Fifth Ave., Room 1101, New York, N.Y.

Hall, D. A. 1961. *The Chemistry of Connective Tissue.* C. C. Thomas, Springfield, Ill.

Harrington, W. F., and P. H. Von Hippel. 1961. The structure of collagen and gelatin. *Advan. Protein Chem. 16*: 1.

Idson, B., and E. Braswell. 1957. Gelatin. *Advan. Food Res. 7*: 235.

Klein, L., B. D. Garg, and C. J. Nowacek. 1969. Evidence for an isotopic steady state in soluble collagens. *Biochem. Biophys. Res. Comm. 34*: 8.

Lloyd, D. J., J. H. Marriott, and W. B. Pleas. 1933. The swelling of protein fibers, Part I. The swelling of collagen. *Trans. Faraday Soc. 29*: 554.

Marks, E. M., D. Tourtellotte, and A. Andux. 1968. The phenomenon of gelatin insolubility. *Food Technol. 22*: 1433.

McClain, P. E., E. Kuntz, and A. M. Pearson. 1969. Application of stress-strain behavior to thermally contracted collagen from epimysial connective tissues. *J. Agr. Food. Chem. 17*: 629.

Melcher, A. H. 1969. Histologically demonstrable bound lipid apparently associated with relatively stable, mature collagen fibres. *Gerontol. 15*: 217.

Moran, T. 1926. The freezing of gelatin gels. *Proc. Roy. Soc. (London) A112*: 35.

Moran, T. 1932. The hydration or combined water of gelatin. *Proc. Roy. Soc. (London) A135*: 411.

Page, R. C., and E. P. Benditt. 1969. Collagen has a discrete family of reactive hydroxylysyl and lysyl side-chain amino groups. *Science 163*: 578.

Piez, K. A. 1966. Collagen. In *The Physiology and Biochemistry of Muscle as a Food*, E. J. Briskey, R. G. Cassens, and J. C. Trautman, eds., p. 315. U. of Wisc. Press, Madison, Wisc.

Sponsler, O. L., J. D. Bath, and J. W. Ellis. 1940. Water bound to gelatin as shown by molecular structure studies. *J. Phys. Chem. 44*: 996.

Tiemstra, P. J. 1968. Degradation of gelatin. *Food Technol. 22*: 1151.

Veis, A. 1964. *The macromolecular chemistry of gelatin.* Academic Press, New York.

CHAPTER 4

Starch and Other Polysaccharides

ELIZABETH OSMAN

Polysaccharides are found in living organisms, in which they perform a wide variety of functions. Some of these substances, such as starch, pectin, or plant gums, are added to food mixtures, often in more or less purified forms, to bring about desired physical characteristics in the foods, usually through increasing viscosity or forming a gel. Others play important roles in structure of plant and animal tissues and the changes these tissues undergo during cooking. Knowledge of the chemical and physical properties of a number of polysaccharides is therefore important for control of the texture of many food products. Before the individual members of this group of substances are discussed, consideration of some of the general properties of the group as a whole should prove helpful.

CHEMICAL STRUCTURE

Monosaccharide Units

The term *polysaccharide*, meaning "many sugars," comes from the fact that a single molecule of one of these substances will, upon hydrolysis, yield a large number of monosaccharide molecules. If all the resulting molecules are alike, the polysaccharide is known as a homoglycan (glycan being another word for polysaccharide). Some of the most abundant polysaccharides, including starch and cellulose, are of this type. If more than one monosaccharide is produced by hydrolysis, the polysaccharide is classed as a heteroglycan. However, unlike protein molecules, which usually contain as many as 20 kinds of amino acid units, the heteroglycans rarely contain more than 3 or 4 kinds of monosaccharide units, and frequently only 2.

The monosaccharide units are most frequently hexoses, for example,

151

D-glucose (**I**), or pentoses, for example, D-xylose (**II**), but closely related substances such as D-galacturonic acid (**III**), N-acetyl-D-glucosamine

HC=O	HC=O	HC=O	HC=O	HC=O
HCOH	HCOH	HCOH	HCNHCOCH$_3$	HCOH
HOCH	HOCH	HCOH	HOCH	HCOH
HCOH	HCOH	HOCH	HCOH	HOCH
HCOH	CH$_2$OH	HCOH	HCOH	HOCH
CH$_2$OH		COOH	CH$_2$OH	CH$_3$
(I)	(II)	(III)	(IV)	(V)

(**IV**), or L-rhamnose (**V**) are also found. Occasionally sulfate or phosphate groups are attached to one of the monosaccharide groups by an ester linkage. The presence of one of these strongly acidic groups or of the more weakly acidic carboxyl group of a uronic acid exerts an important influence on the physical properties of the polysaccharide.

The monosaccharide units are held together by acetal linkages between the carbonyl (aldehyde or ketone) group of one unit and one of the hydroxyl groups on the adjacent unit. If on each monosaccharide unit only one hydroxyl group, in addition to the carbonyl group, is linked to another monosaccharide unit, the polysaccharide is linear or straight chain. If more than one hydroxyl in some of the monosaccharide units is linked to another unit, branching occurs. The branches may be only single units along an otherwise linear molecule, as shown in Figure 1*a*, or they may give rise to a more treelike structure, such as that of amylopectin (Figure 1*b*), one of the polysaccharides that compose starch, or even a bushy structure, such as that of glycogen (Figure 1*c*).

Molecular Weight

Polysaccharides also differ widely in the size of the molecules and their molecular weight. To understand why quite different values for the molecular weight of a single polysaccharide, such as the amylose fraction of the polysaccharide mixture known as starch, are reported in the literature, it is necessary to consider some of the difficulties involved in its measurement. First, the molecular weight of a particular type of polysaccharide, for example, amylose, differs with its source. Potato amylose, for example, is a much larger molecule than that of corn. Therefore, unless the source, as well as the type, of polysaccharide is the same, differences in molecular weight are to be expected. Second, to isolate a polysaccharide from a natural source and purify it completely, and then to disperse it in the form of single molecules, overcoming the

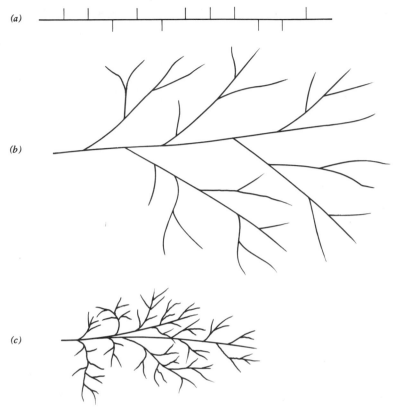

FIGURE 1. Schematic drawings of typical branched polysaccharides. (*a*) Guaran; (*b*) amylopectin; (*c*) glycogen.

strong tendency of the hydroxyl groups of different molecules to associate through hydrogen bonding, and, at the same time, to avoid any degradation of the molecules, presents a tremendous problem. Many of the values, especially in the older literature, were obtained on materials that had undergone considerable degradation. Others may have been derived from systems in which the material was not completely free from intermolecular association. Finally, a single sample of a polysaccharide often contains molecules of widely different molecular weights. In methods for determining molecular weight that depend on an actual count of the number of molecules in a given weight of the sample, such as end-group determinations or measurements of osmotic pressure, the smallest molecules affect the results as much as the largest. The values are known as *number-average molecular weights*. In methods that employ such physical measurements as viscosity measurements, light scattering, or certain types of sedimentation, the larger molecules are of much greater importance. Each molecule affects the resultant value in proportion to its molecular weight, leading to a figure known as the *weight-average molecular weight*. In general, the values obtained by one of these latter methods are much more nearly related to the properties and potential uses of the materials than are number-average molecular weights. If all the polymer molecules in a sample were of the same length, the number-average and weight-average values would be the same, but actually such a situation does not exist. Therefore, although it is important to recognize that the molecular weight of a polysaccharide has a very considerable effect on its physical properties, it is also important to use caution in comparing reported molecular weights and to take into consideration how the measurements were made and what the experimenters actually determined.

EFFECT OF STRUCTURE ON PHYSICAL PROPERTIES

All polysaccharides, regardless of the monosaccharide units from which they are built, have large numbers of hydroxyl groups that attract water, that is, are hydrophilic. The molecules of water that are in direct contact with the hydroxyls along the polysaccharide chains may be partially immobilized through hydrogen bonding. Other molecules of water not in actual contact with the polysaccharide may be held somewhat immobilized by secondary forces. These water molecules cause the polysaccharide to remain in a more or less extended form with little or no tendency to form a tight coil or ball.

When the hydrated polysaccharide moves about in solution, bombarded by molecules of the solute, it effectively sweeps through a large, roughly spherical volume (Figure 2). As a result, the extended, hydrated molecules, even when present in very low concentration, will come into contact with one another and give the solution a viscosity decidedly greater than that of the solvent. As the concentration of polysaccharide is increased, the viscosity increases rapidly.

Branched polysaccharides also become hydrated, but the sphere of solvent that moves with the dissolved polymer is much smaller than for a linear polymer of the same molecular weight (Figure 2). It therefore has a smaller effect on viscosity. Examination of Figure 1 will make clear why this effect differs with the degree of branching. When the branches consist of single monosaccharide units only, the effect of these stubby branches in lessening the coiling of the molecule may balance the result of the somewhat shorter actual length of the chain.

When linear polysaccharide molecules twist and turn in solution,

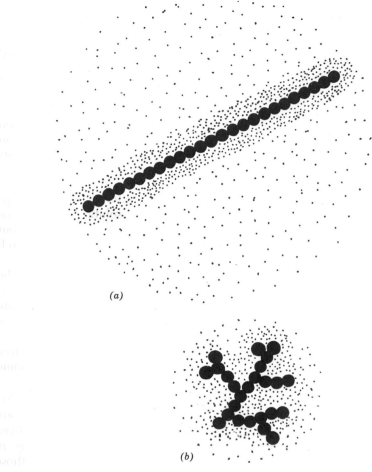

FIGURE 2. Schematic drawing showing volumes swept by gyrating polysaccharides of the same molecular weight. (*a*) a linear polysaccharide; (*b*) a highly branched polysaccharide.

they frequently collide with such force that the enveloping atmosphere of water is sheared from large sections of their length. These bare sections of the polysaccharide molecules may then adhere to one another rather than to new molecules of water. Further movement along the two chainlike molecules may bring larger sections together, and a single polysaccharide molecule may thus form bonds with others of its kind at several points along the chain. If this effect occurs in polysaccharide dispersions of the concentration found in most food systems, the result is an interwoven meshwork that holds the water both through attraction of those hydroxyls not involved in the intermolecular bonding of the polysaccharide molecules and also by means of the porous structure of the three-dimensional meshwork. The structure will be recognized as that of a gel, which is an important structure affecting the texture of foods.

Some movement of the portions of the polysaccharide chains between points of attachment continues after a gel has formed and results in a growth of the areas of attachment as more of the monosaccharide units along the chains become oriented in a crystal pattern. This growth is comparable to the growth of crystals in a sugar solution after nuclei form. As these areas of attachment grow, fewer of the hydroxyl groups in the polysaccharide chains are available for hydration, and the regions between the chains grow smaller. The gel shrinks and squeezes out some of the water, a process known as syneresis. This process in starch is known as *retrogradation*.

If the polysaccharide solution or dispersion is very dilute, so that the individual molecules do not become entangled to form a gel, the same general process results in the formation of a precipitate. Such dilute solutions of polysaccharides are seldom encountered in foods, but a precipitate formed in this way is frequently found in bottles of starch indicator solutions used in the chemical laboratory as a test for free iodine by formation of the characteristic blue color of the starch-iodine complex.

Branching of polysaccharide molecules is very effective in preventing gel formation. Even very short, stubby branches (see Figure 1a) are sufficient to fend off colliding molecules and prevent the chains from becoming oriented so they can associate and produce a gel. Only in extremely concentrated dispersions, far more concentrated than those that are commonly found in foods, are the molecules of a branched polysaccharide packed sufficiently tightly to produce a gel.

Acid groups distributed along a polysaccharide chain have a pronounced effect on its behavior, which may vary with conditions, depending on whether these groups are weakly or strongly acidic. If the groups are weakly acidic carboxyl groups such as are found in pectins and in some of the vegetable gums and seaweed polysaccharides, which will be discussed later, the properties of the solution are strongly affected by pH. In neutral solutions these carboxyl groups exist as salts. If the cations are monovalent, such as sodium, the salt is largely ionized, so that negative charges are distributed along the polysaccharide chain (see Figure 3a). These charges repel one another and keep the molecules in an extended form. In addition, the carboxylate ions tend to cause

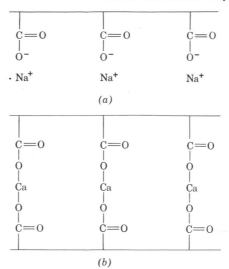

FIGURE 3. Salts of acid polysaccharides. (a) Sodium salt, (b) calcium salt.

increased hydration. As a result, the solution is highly viscous. At the same time, the charges keep the chains from associating to form a gel or a precipitate. If, however, the cations are polyvalent, such as calcium, they tend to form insoluble salts by forming bridges between adjacent chains (see Figure 3b), giving rise to gels or precipitates.

When the pH of the solution of such a polysaccharide containing weakly acidic groups is lowered to about 3 or less, the carboxyl groups exist in their acid form, and are only very slightly ionized. It then behaves as an uncharged linear polysaccharide. The molecules tend to associate readily to produce gels or precipitates. Probably the most familiar example of this effect of pH is the formation of fruit jelly, which will be discussed later.

Those polysaccharides, such as some of the gums and seaweed polysaccharides used in foods, which have strongly acidic groups along the polysaccharide chain, are much less influenced by pH than those with weakly acidic groups. The reason is that the ionization of the strongly acidic groups is not greatly depressed even at very low pH values. In other words, these groups carry a negative charge at any pH.

The effects of structure on the behavior of polysaccharides are summarized in the following statements:

1. At the same concentrations, solutions of linear polysaccharides

have higher viscosities than solutions of branched polysaccharides of the same molecular weight.

2. Molecules of linear polysaccharides may associate through intermolecular bonding to form precipitates in very dilute solutions or gels in more concentrated solutions; branches or side chains on the molecules inhibit this association.

3. Like ionic charges distributed along the polysaccharide molecules repel one another and keep the chains extended. This extension of the chains, coupled with the increased hydration about the charged groups, causes increased viscosity. The charged groups also repel those of other like molecules, inhibiting intermolecular association which would result in gel formation and possibly ultimate syneresis or retrogradation. Strongly acidic groups, such as sulfate or phosphate, are ionized even in the acid form, and therefore show these characteristics even at low pH values.

4. Carboxyl groups, being only weakly acidic, are only slightly ionized in acidic solutions and are therefore able to form gels at low pH values.

The whole subject of the influence of structure on the properties of polysaccharides has been discussed in greater detail by Whistler (1959).

STARCH

Starch is quantitatively the major constituent of cereals, which form the greater part of the food of a large portion of the world's people. Of the cereals, wheat, rice, and corn (maize) are used in the greatest quantities. Other staple foods such as potatoes, taro root, and legumes, including a wide variety of beans and peas, are also rich in starch. Whether these products are used in their native form or ground into flour, or whether their starch is isolated in a more or less pure form and added to other foodstuffs, an understanding of the properties of starch is of great importance in obtaining the desired texture in the many foods in which it is present.

Nutritionally, starch furnishes only energy to the body rather than material for tissue replacement. However, its presence in sufficient quantity in the diet conserves the much less prevalent, more expensive proteins for tissue building, diminishing their utilization as a source of needed energy. While the effectiveness of carbohydrates in preventing ketosis in a situation in which the body metabolism involves protein and fatty acids almost exclusively, as in starvation, has long been recognized, the only effect that needs to be considered in the ordinary diet of a normal person is the regulation of calories.

Molecular Structure

The term starch is applied to not one, but two, polysaccharides that occur in nature in tiny granules. Both molecular species may be found intimately associated in a single granule. Both, upon complete hydrolysis, yield only D-glucose. One, however, is a linear polymer, *amylose,* and the other a branched polymer (see Figure 1*b*), *amylopectin.* A third closely related substance, *glycogen,* with a still more highly branched structure (see Figure 1*c*), is the form in which carbohydrate storage occurs in the animal body.

Amylose

In amylose, the D-glucose units, occurring as 6-membered (pyranose) rings formed through reaction of the aldehyde group with the hydroxyl on carbon 5 of the same unit, are bound together through an acetal linkage between the aldehyde group of one monosaccharide unit and the hydroxyl on carbon 4 of another. The stereoconfiguration on carbon 1 is of the alpha form, and the result is known as an alpha-glycosidic linkage (a linkage to the carbonyl group of a sugar in the alpha-configuration). As a result, the disaccharide repeating unit in starch is the maltose unit (Figure 4).

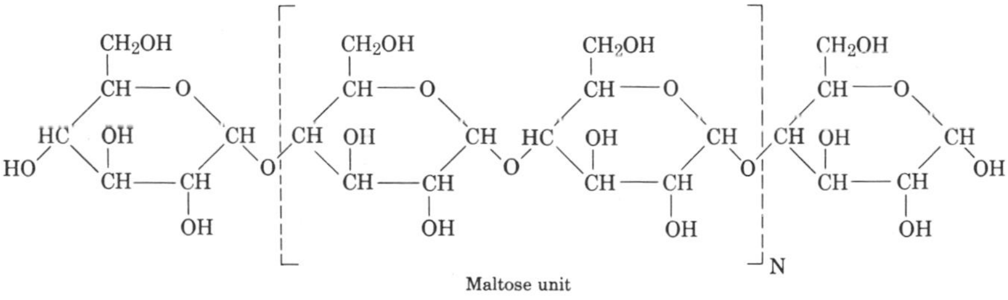

FIGURE 4. Structure of amylose.

Some of the difficulties in measuring the molecular weights of polysaccharides in general have already been discussed. Usually the amyloses from roots and tubers have been found to have higher molecular weights than those from cereals. Use of improved techniques for isolating amylose from a single plant source, for example, the potato, has led in recent years to the recognition that these molecules are much larger than was previously believed. Number-average molecular weights obtained by osmotic pressure measurements have increased from about 250,000 to 1.1 million (Greenwood, 1956) and a weight-average molecular weight of 1.9 million, obtained by measurement of light scattering, has been reported (Killion and Foster, 1960).

Foster (1965) has discussed the considerable evidence that indicates that amylose in solution assumes the form of a long flexible coiled spring, a loose helix that can be bent into wormlike configurations. When the molecule complexes with a material such as iodine or one of the emulsifiers that forms a core within the helix (to be discussed later), the helix becomes more rigid and rodlike. In addition to the many physical measurements that indicate such a configuration, observation of a three-dimensional molecular model of amylose shows that it falls naturally into a helical form.

Amylopectin

The chemical structure of amylopectin is basically the same as that of amylose except that the aldehyde groups of some of the D-glucose units are bonded to hydroxyls of other units at carbon 6, in addition to those bonded at carbon 4 (see Figure 5), giving rise to a branched structure (see Figure 1b).

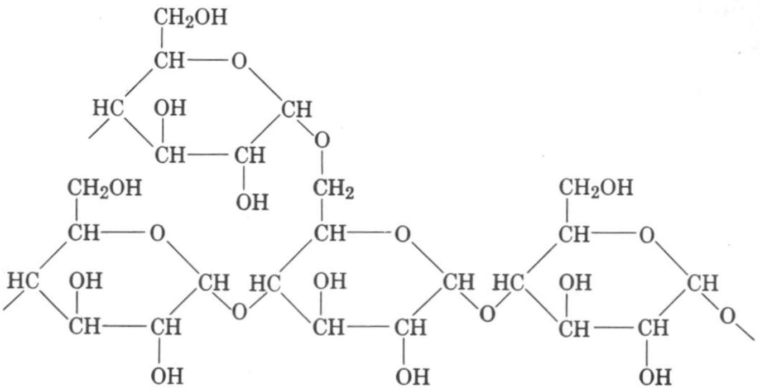

FIGURE 5. Point of branching in amylopectin molecule.

Present knowledge of the fine points of the structure of amylopectin is much less advanced than that of amylose, partially because its great size and branched structure make it more difficult to purify and study. Foster (1965) pointed out that amylopectin isolated by the techniques presently available is extremely heterogeneous insofar as molecular weight and probably degree of branching are concerned. Certainly differences in the properties of starch pastes and white sauces prepared from purified amylopectins from different plant sources (Osman and

Cummisford, 1959) indicate that botanical species has as much or more influence on the properties of amylopectin as of amylose.

Chemical determinations for nonreducing end groups (that is, those D-glucose units that are bound to others through only their aldehyde, but not their hydroxyl, groups) show such an end group for every 20 to 25 D-glucose units for practically all the amylopectins that have been examined by this method. These figures have frequently been interpreted as indicating a branch length of 20 to 25 units, without recognizing that an undetermined number of these units occur in inner rather than outer branches and that they are averages, giving no indication of the homogeneity of the branch lengths. More complete information about the branching of amylopectin from different varieties of starches present in foods might be very valuable in explaining the differences known to exist between starches.

Amylopectin has long been thought to be a much larger molecule than amylose, but number-average molecular weights obtained by osmotic pressure or reducing end-group measurements varying from about 50,000 to one million have not borne out this assumption. Foster (1965) has discussed the difficulties in applying these techniques to amylopectin and has concluded that they do not give valid results.

Weight-average molecular weights for amylopectin obtained by the light-scattering method, reported by a number of investigators, have also been discussed by Foster (1965). He points out that the sensitivity of this method increases, if anything, with increasing molecular weight, rather than decreasing, as the osmotic pressure method does. Values obtained by this method for different amylopectins have ranged from about 10 million to 100 million. Foster also reported sedimentation studies (using ultracentrifugation) that imply an extremely broad distribution of molecular weights within a single sample of amylopectin.

A comparison of values reported for the intrinsic viscosities of amylose and amylopectin form an excellent example of the effect of branching in polysaccharides on hydration and the resulting viscosities of their solutions. In spite of its greater size, the viscosities reported for amylopectin are actually lower than those reported for amylose, indicating the more compact structure of the molecules in solution (Foster, 1965).

Structure of the Starch Granule

A unique feature of starch that is of the utmost importance in determining its action in food products is its almost universal occurrence in nature in the form of discrete bundles or granules. In higher plants starch formation occurs inside the plastids, characteristic organelles of the plant cells. In some plants, only one granule is produced within a single plastid, in others, several. In the granule, the starch forms an insoluble source of energy that can be made available gradually to the plant through the action of enzymes. Because of the importance of starch to the living plant, botanists have been attempting for many years to untangle the complex sequence of events that result in its formation. Much has been learned, but much remains a mystery. Badenhuizen (1965) and Akazawa (1965) have reviewed the present status of the problem.

Although the granules swell to varying degrees when heat is applied in the presence of water, as in the cooking of food systems, only conditions far more severe than those normally encountered in food processing will completely eliminate all traces of granular structure, and the swollen granules can be observed by microscopic examination of the products. This swelling, or gelatinization, of the granule will be discussed later, but first a closer look at the unswollen granules is necessary.

Most starches contain both amylose and amylopectin within the granule. Usually the amylose represents between 20 and 30 percent of the total starch. Although in starches from different botanical sources these two types of molecules differ somewhat in molecular weight and probably, at least in the case of amylopectin, in some of the fine points of structure, they are sufficiently alike to have many properties in common. It is therefore remarkable that each plant species has it own specific type of starch granule almost as characteristic as a fingerprint (Table 1). In fact, the plant source of a sample of starch can frequently be identified with a high degree of certainty merely by examination under the microscope. However, there are some, such as corn and grain sorghum starches of both the ordinary and waxy varieties, that cannot be distinguished by appearance alone. Staining the sample with a very dilute iodine solution makes it possible to differentiate between the ordinary and waxy varieties; the amylose content of the ordinary varieties causes them to be stained blue by iodine, whereas the waxy varieties, which are composed entirely of amylopectin, are stained red. Gelatinization temperatures, to be discussed later, must usually be determined to distinguish between corn and grain sorghum starches.

Photographs of some of the most common varieties of starch found in foods (Figure 6) illustrate some of these differences in appearance. That all granules in a given starch sample are not exactly alike is readily apparent. Instead they differ, like individual members of a family. But the family resemblance is strong, and the sample can usually be readily distinguished from that of starch from a different species of plant.

TABLE 1. Characteristics of Starch Granules[a]

Source	Range of Sizes (in Microns)	Average Size (in Microns)	Appearance
Corn	4–26	15	Polygonal; almost continuous distribution of sizes.
Waxy corn	5–25	15	Polygonal; almost continuous distribution of sizes.
Grain sorghum	6–30	15	Polygonal; almost continuous distribution of sizes.
Barley	2–35		Mixture of large and small granules, round or elliptical.
Rice	3–9	5	Small, polygonal.
Wheat	2–38	20–22	Mixture of small round and large lenticular granules.
Potato	15–100	30	Large, with heavy striations about eccentric hilum, resembling oyster shells.
Sweet potato	15–55	25–50	Polygonal; small granules predominate, some large.
Tapioca (cassava)	5–36	20	Round or oval, frequently truncated on one side.

[a] Data from Whistler and Smart (1953) and Kerr (1950).

In most granules a single spot or the intersection of two lines or creases may be seen. This point is known as the hilum. More often than not it occupies an eccentric rather than a central location. Many starches, including potato starch, show a series of striations about the hilum that are characteristic and aid in the identification of the particular starch. The possible cause of the development of these striations during the development of the granule in the plant has been discussed in some detail by Badenhuizen (1965).

The exact arrangement of the amylose and amylopectin molecules within the granule is not completely understood, but the schematic presentation made by Meyer and Bernfeld in 1940 (Figure 7) seems to be as consistent with the behavior of the granule as any other which has been proposed. Here the two types of molecules, amylose and amylopectin, are intermingled, with crystalline regions holding them together in a sort of accordion arrangement that may be stretched tangentially as water penetrates the granule, causing it to swell. A singe large molecule of either type may pass through more than one of these crystalline

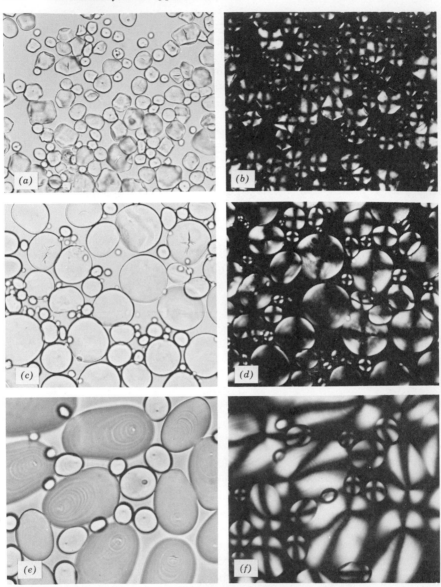

FIGURE 6. Photomicrographs of common starches, showing same fields under normal and polarized light all at same magnification. (*a*) Corn starch, (*b*) corn starch (polarized light), (*c*) wheat starch, (*d*) wheat starch (polarized light), (*e*) potato starch, and (*f*) potato starch (polarized light). (From Wivinis and Maywald, 1967.)

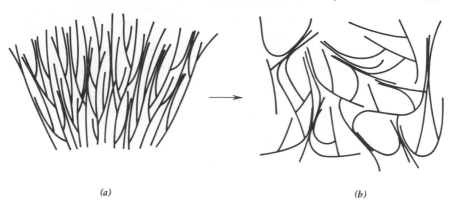

(a)   *(b)*

FIGURE 7. Segment of starch granule before and after swelling. (*a*) Unswollen segment; (*b*) swollen segment. (After Meyer and Bernfeld, 1940.)

regions as well as through several intervening amorphous regions. Such a structure is in accord with observations that only part of the starch in the granule is crystallized. Sterling (1960), on the basis of X-ray diffraction studies, reported the crystallinity of air-dried potato starch as 21 percent; Rundle et al. (1944) had earlier estimated that the crystalline portion of most ordinary native starches comprised 50–60 percent of the total starch. This degree of molecular orientation, or crystallization, is sufficient to cause the granule to be birefringent so that it can be observed under plane polarized light between the prisms of a polarizing microscope. Modern investigations indicate that the structure of alternating crystalline and amorphous regions is relatively uniform throughout the granule, and that older theories of alternate layers of amylose and amylopectin, a concentration of amylopectin in the outer part of the granule or a membrane, probably of cellulose, around the granule are untenable.

Swelling of the Starch Granule

Gelatinization Range

In water at temperatures below 60° C (the exact temperature depending on the variety of starch), no obvious change occurs in native starch granules. Small amounts of water may enter the amorphous regions of the granule, but the strong intermolecular bonds in the crystalline areas remain intact and prevent any noticeable swelling of the granule. Destruction of these intermolecular bonds by mechanical or chemical treatment permits swelling of the granules, or of fragments of the granule remaining after the treatment, in cold water. In pregelatinized starches, used in such products as instant puddings and pie fillings, the granular structure has been almost completely eliminated. The intermolecular bonds have been disrupted by cooking of the starch and the swollen granules have been broken up during subsequent drying under conditions that involve mechanical shearing action, usually roll-drying. Parts of the resulting particles are readily hydrated to give an effect analogous to granular swelling, but, because the fragments are so much smaller than the whole granules, and because in some regions retrogradation (an irreversible crystallization to be discussed later) has occurred, the effect of the hydration on viscosity is greatly reduced.

When aqueous suspensions of starch granules that have not been subjected to any of the treatments mentioned are heated, no apparent change occurs until the water reaches a temperature, usually between 60 and 70° C, that is dependent on the particular starch being examined. At this temperature a few of the granules, usually the largest ones, swell very rapidly, and examination under polarized light shows that they have simultaneously lost their birefringence. As the temperature continues to rise, other granules in the sample undergo the same rapid swelling until, within a temperature range of 10 to 15° C, all have swollen. These changes can be observed under a microscope equipped with a hot stage (a small electric hot plate with a tiny hole in the center to allow the passage of light, and equipped with a built-in thermometer). Polarizing prisms in the microscope are needed for observation of the loss of birefringence. The temperature range over which the swelling of all the granules in the microscope field occurs is known as the gelatinization range. It is characteristic of the particular variety of starch being examined and serves as a means of identification (see Table 2).

Certain other changes occur simultaneously, or nearly so, with the initial swelling of the starch granules. One of these is an increase in the clarity of the starch suspension, which may be measured quantitatively by a sudden change in light transmission. Another change at the gelatinization temperature that can be observed only in a very concentrated suspension is an increase in viscosity. Unless the granules are packed together very tightly, no increase in viscosity is noticed until a considerably higher temperature has brought about much greater swelling, because the viscosity increase is caused by the swollen granules being sufficiently close together to have their movement inhibited.

Finally, a change that has been little used as a measure of gelatinization temperature, but that is of great significance in the baking of yeast breads, is the increased susceptibility of the starch to enzyme attack.

TABLE 2. Gelatinization Ranges of Various Food Starches[a]

Source	Temperature at Loss of Birefringence (°C)		
	Initiation	Midpoint	Termination
Corn	62	66	70
Waxy corn	63	68	72
High-amylose corn (55 percent amylose)	67	80	—[b]
Grain sorghum	68	73.5	78
Waxy sorghum	67.5	70.5	74
Barley	51.5	57	59.5
Rice	68	74.5	78
Rye	57	61	70
Wheat	59.5	62.5	64
Pea (green garden peas of normal amylose content)	57	65	70
Potato	58	62	66
Potato (heat-moisture treated)	65	71	77
Tapioca	52	59	64

[a] From Osman (1967).
[b] Some granules still birefringent at 100° C.

Although amylases can attack raw starch to a limited extent, dependent on both the type of starch and the source of the enzyme (Gates and Sandstedt, 1953), the greater accessibility of the starch to the enzyme following gelatinization makes the action much more rapid. The extent of the action of the hydrolyzing enzymes, the amylases, during baking depends on the rate at which the temperature in the bread is rising and on the source of the particular amylases present, for the activities of amylases from different sources differ, as do the temperatures at which they are destroyed. In general, amylase activity in bread can be described as increasing very rapidly with the gelatinization of the starch and continuing to increase for a short time with rising temperature until the rate of destruction of the enzyme through heat denaturation overtakes the increase in activity brought about by the temperature increase.

The gelatinization of starch granules may be strongly affected by the presence of some substances in the water surrounding them. Care must therefore be taken in using data for gelatinization of starch in pure water in interpreting results observed in food systems. Small amounts of noncarbohydrate materials, for example, lipids, proteins, and the like,

are closely associated with starch in the plant cell, in some cases probably occluded in the starch granule, and are not entirely eliminated
during commercial refining procedures (see Gracza, 1965), or even
during most laboratory purification. Several studies on starch from which
the lipids have been almost completely eliminated by special extraction
techniques show that these materials, for example, exert an effect on
the swelling of the starch granules and on the properties of the resulting
pastes. Other minor constituents undoubtedly have effects, also. However, unless otherwise indicated, most studies on granular starch have
been carried out without removal of these contaminants. The results
are probably more comparable to those in food systems than if all such
materials were removed, since these natural contaminants are in no
way objectionable in food and therefore no attempt is made to remove
them from food grade starches. But recognition of the presence of these
minor constituents is sometimes helpful in interpreting data.

Continued Swelling and Viscosity Increase

The first rapid swelling, or gelatinization, of the starch granule is
followed by continued swelling as the temperature of the starch suspension continues to rise, provided that additional water is available to
enter the granule. In some food systems, particularly in bread, the extent
of swelling of the granules beyond the initial gelatinization is greatly
limited by the amount of water present.

As the granule swells, it becomes increasingly fragile. If agitation is
kept to a minimum and the suspension is sufficiently dilute so that the
swollen granules can move freely, most natural starches can be heated
to 100° C with little rupture. As the temperature rises still higher, they
may be observed to implode, that is, they collapse or cave in, rather
than exploding. The implosion is followed by a gradual breakdown into
fragments. Long before rupture of the granules occurs, a progressive
leaching out of soluble starch, chiefly the shorter chains of amylose,
begins. The granules may be regarded as bags of soluble starch solution
surrounded by more soluble starch solution. The preferential separation
of amylose into the surrounding water served as the basis of most of the
early methods for fractionating starch, but the dissolved material was
not entirely pure amylose, and the undissolved material was quite
impure amylopectin.

In more concentrated suspensions of starch, such as those usually
found in food systems, any very strong agitation causes the fragile,
swollen granules to be pulled past one another with sufficient force to
cause their rupture. The extent to which such breakdown of the granules
is brought about in food preparation varies widely, not only because of

the differences in the starches used and their concentrations, but also because of the wide differences in the temperatures to which they are heated and the agitation they receive. The temperature in the top of a double boiler rarely rises much above 95° C. This temperature is sufficiently below that reached when a starch-containing mixture in a saucepan is boiled over direct heat to cause the granules to be appreciably less swollen and fragile. Final temperatures far below 95° C have frequently been reported for products cooked in steam-jacketed kettles of the type frequently used in institutions, and one can only assume that the swelling of the starch must be greatly reduced. On the other hand, some processing in commercial plants, particularly in the canning industry, involves autoclaving at temperatures considerably above 100° C. Add to these differences in temperature the differences in agitation that are used, all the way from infrequent stirring of a product in a double boiler to fairly vigorous mechanical agitation in large cookers, and the differences that have been observed by different investigators using different conditions are readily understandable.

The most noticeable change that occurs in the characteristics of starch-containing food products such as gravies or cornstarch puddings when they are heated is the increase in viscosity. This change is primarily caused by the swelling granules and the difficulty they encounter in moving past one another. The soluble starch that is leached out of the swollen granules into the unabsorbed water between them undoubtedly has some effect, but a minor one. Of greater importance is the extent to which the swollen granules have been ruptured by the shearing action of the agitation, since fragments of granules have far less effect on viscosity than do the intact swollen granules.

Because such a suspension of swollen starch granules, fragments of granules, and dissolved starch molecules does not show the properties of true Newtonian viscosity described in Chapter 2, the terms "apparent viscosity" and "consistency" have sometimes been used. More often, however, the term viscosity is used without further definition, on the assumption that those studying such a system are aware that it cannot be expected to show Newtonian behavior.

For accurate comparisons of the viscosity changes in different starches, or in the same starch under different conditions, during heating in an aqueous system, identical conditions of heating and agitation must be used. Several instruments that provide such conditions, together with a device for measuring and continuously recording the viscosity changes, have been devised. Those most commonly used are the Brabender amylograph and the Corn Industries Viscometer. Although the stirring, sensing, and recording mechanisms of the two instruments are quite different (see Smith, 1965), probably the most important difference is that in the rate of heating and the final temperature reached.

In the Brabender amylograph a thermoregulator controls the increase in temperature in the cooking vessel, allowing it to rise at a constant rate of 1.5° C per minute. The maximum temperature to which the instrument is designed to take the mixture is 95° C, a temperature quite comparable to that reached in a double boiler or, in most cases, in a steam-jacketed kettle. But it is lower than that usually attained over direct heat or during autoclaving. The sample can be maintained at 95° C for as long as desired, or cooled at a controlled rate of 1.5° C per minute.

In the Corn Industries Viscometer, the sample mixture is heated in a stainless-steel beaker surrounded by a water bath maintained at a constant temperature. Although a few studies have been made in which the temperature of the water bath has been held at 100° C, allowing the temperature in the sample mixture to reach 95–98° C, most studies with this instrument which have been reported have used a bath temperature of 92° C. The final temperature within the sample has then been about 90° C, appreciably lower than that usually attained in food systems.

In most starch mixtures, the granules are swelling rapidly and are very fragile in the range of 90–100° C. The record of the viscosity changes in the system has been interpreted (Katz, 1938) as representing the combination of two changes in the starch granules that are occurring at the same time in this temperature range, a progressive swelling of some and a breakdown of others. The curve continues to rise until the collapse and fragmentation of granules becomes the dominant effect. The shape of the curve, the final viscosity, and any measurements, such as gel strength, that may be made on the cooked sample will usually be greatly influenced by the final temperature of the mixture and how long it is maintained. They may also be affected by the length of time involved in reaching that temperature and by differences in agitation. Although much information of great value in the study of food systems has been obtained with these and similar instruments, recognition of the effects of these factors is essential in comparing reported studies and in applying them to interpretation of changes occurring in actual food processing.

Concentration is another factor that greatly influences the viscosity changes during heating, often termed *hot-paste viscosity*. Sufficient viscosity develops to register on the instrument only when the granules have swollen enough to hinder the movement of one another. Obviously, less swelling of the individual granules is needed to bring about such hindrance to movement when more granules are present. As a result,

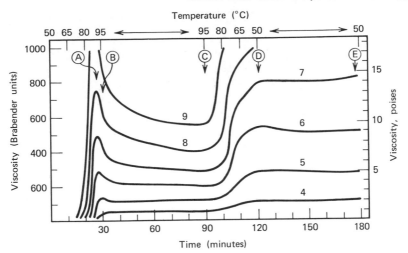

FIGURE 8. Effect of concentration on amylograph curves of cornstarch. Numerals indicate concentration in g per 100 ml. (From Smith, 1967.)

the higher the concentration, the lower is the temperature at which an increase in viscosity is recorded (see Figure 8) until, in suspensions in which the granules are tightly packed, the increase in viscosity occurs simultaneously with the initial swelling of the granules at the gelatinization temperature. Concentration also affects the shearing effect the moving granules exert on one another and thus the rapidity with which they are broken down, and consequently the rate of decrease of the viscosity (see Figure 8). The need for taking concentration into account in comparing hot-paste viscosity curves is thus illustrated.

Calculation of the concentration of starch in any system must be done on the basis of dry substance because starch in contact with air absorbs a quantity of water that is in proportion to the relative humidity of the air. For most starches at normal relative humidities, this water amounts to about 10 to 14 percent of the weight of the starch. In some uses of starch, advantage is taken of this ability of starch to absorb moisture. For example, specially dried starches are added to powdered sugar and to baking powder to take up moisture from the air in contact with these substances, thereby preventing caking of the finely pulverized sugar and, in the case of baking powder, reaction of the acid ingredient with the bicarbonate.

Prevention of Lumps in Starch-Thickened Products. For each granule in a starch paste or a starch-thickened food product to swell freely and not adhere to others around it, water must completely surround it when the swelling begins. If, instead, clumps of starch granules are present, the granules on the surface of the clump will take up water and gelatinize first, forming an almost impervious layer about the dry granules on the inside. A somewhat similar effect occurs if the partially swollen granules are allowed to clump together, as on the sides or bottom of a cooking vessel in the absence of any scraping action during cooking. These effects apply not only to refined starches, but also to cereal flours, which are chiefly starch.

Separation of starch granules in food preparation is almost always accomplished by one of the following three methods:

1. Separation of the granules by water, or other aqueous liquid such as milk or fruit juice, at a temperature below the gelatinization temperature of the starch. Usually the liquid used is cold, but it may be lukewarm or slightly warmer without causing difficulty in most systems. In any case, the mixture must be stirred to keep the starch suspended until the granules have swollen enough so that they will not settle.

2. Separation with sugar. If the volume of sugar used far surpasses that of the starch, as in puddings and pie fillings, thorough mixture of the starch and sugar will cause the water to completely surround the granules when it dissolves the sugar.

3. Separation with fat. Although fat is effective in keeping the starch granules from clumping together, two precautions should be taken. If the fat has water with it, as frequently occurs in meat drippings used for making gravy, it must be cooled enough so that the starch will not start to gelatinize before the granules are separated. If hot fat alone is used, the mixture should not be held at the elevated temperature before addition of water if maximum thickening by the starch is desired. High temperatures cause dextrinization of the starch, a thermal degradation that causes some of the starch molecules to be severed, allowing the granules to fragment instead of swelling freely. If browned flour is desired in order to lend color to a gravy, the need for limiting the extent of the browning and for using more flour must be recognized.

Gel Formation

If a starch-thickened mixture is stirred during cooling, forces of attraction between the starch molecules cause it to become more viscous (see Figure 8). If it is allowed to stand without stirring, there is a tendency for intermolecular bonds to form (Figure 9). If the starch is of the waxy variety, containing only branched amylopectin molecules, the intermolecular association is too slight to be of any permanence unless the paste is very concentrated, containing 30 percent or more of

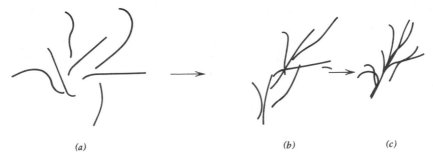

(a)   (b)   (c)

FIGURE 9. Gel formation and retrogradation. (a) Solution; (b) gel; (c) retrograded.

the starch, causing the ends of the branched molecules to be packed tightly together. But with ordinary, amylose-containing starches, such intermolecular bonding occurs readily and produces a three-dimensional meshwork or gel even at relatively low concentration. K. H. Meyer (1942 and 1950) has described the bonding of a starch gel as involving the formation of small crystalline regions from portions of both amylose and amylopectin molecules, both within the swollen granules and, of greater importance, in the aqueous solution between the granules. This involvement of molecules or parts of molecules in the space between the granules explains why the formation and characteristics of the gel are affected by such conditions as time and temperature of cooking (Woodruff et al., 1931 and 1933) and agitation, which influence the leaching of starch molecules from the swollen granules. Sterling (1956) has pointed out that the ability of a gel to withstand a certain amount of deformation before it breaks can be attributed to the amorphous regions between the crystalline bonding areas. The portions of the starch molecules in these regions can be stretched or compressed to a limited degree.

The gel formation becomes progressively stronger during the first few hours after it is prepared, but after about 16 hours little further change occurs (Kesler and Bechtel, 1954; Teegarden, 1961). Stronger gels are formed at lower temperatures, but Teegarden showed that when the temperature of a cornstarch gel that had been stored at 5° C was raised to 25° C, the gel strength was approximately the same as that of a gel that had been held only at the higher temperature.

A wide variety of instruments have been used for testing starch gels. Some of these have been discussed by Kesler and Bechtel (1954) and by Teegarden (1961). They have measured many different properties of the gels, including their deformation under a load, their ability to retain the shape of the vessel in which they were formed, their ability to resist cutting action, and their resistance to breaking under stress. Measurement of any one of these properties gives only a partial picture of the characteristics of the gel. All the methods that have been used leave much to be desired.

The method that has been most widely used by the starch industry is measurement of the force required to remove an embedded disk from the gel. Although the method is crude, the results obtained with it give information that has proved valuable in predicting the behavior of starches in many practical applications. The center of a disk of standard size, about that of a penny, is attached to the end of a rod and suspended in the hot paste at a standard depth. After the gel has formed and been allowed to stand for a standard length of time, the force required to remove the disk is measured. To prevent a tough skin from forming on the top of the gel, thereby impeding removal of the disk, a thin layer of mineral oil is placed on top of the hot paste immediately after the disk is inserted. The method has been described by Kerr (1950).

With starch-water pastes, aging of the gel before testing is usually carried out at room temperature. Because of the perishability of food systems, refrigeration is desirable, preferably in a constant temperature bath. However, because the gel cannot be refrigerated while the test is being made and because the strength of the gel is greatly affected by temperature, as has been mentioned, great care must be taken to have the gels at exactly the same temperature when the tests are being made.

Retrogradation

The formation of intermolecular association of starch molecules to form a gel may be considered as the formation of crystal nuclei on which additional segments of starch molecules may be deposited slowly to form crystalline regions of increasing size. As increasingly long portions of the molecules are pulled together by this association, the water-filled regions between them become smaller. The gel shrinks and water is forced out, just as water is forced from a sponge when it is squeezed. The forcing out of the liquid is an example of syneresis (see Chapter 2), and the increased association of the starch, with the accompanying changes in its properties, is termed *retrogradation*. When applied to starch, the term does not imply a backward movement of the starch molecules to their original position within the starch granule. This would be impossible because of the enormous disruption of the original orientation of the molecules during the swelling process. Instead, it means a return to a more orderly, partially crystalline state, but one quite different from the original.

Two of the most important factors that influence the rate of retrogradation are temperature and the size and shape of the starch molecules. Although many factors, especially other ingredients present, probably influence somewhat the temperature at which retrogradation occurs most rapidly in a particular system, the consensus is that it is close to 0° C. Many systems that show little tendency to retrograde at room temperature or under refrigerated storage have been found to be unstable, that is, to retrograde, when frozen and thawed. Apparently the change occurs most rapidly as the temperature changes during the freezing and thawing action, and a common practice for examining systems for freeze-thaw stability is measurement under standard conditions of the number of cycles of freezing and thawing the sample will withstand before syneresis is observed.

In food systems, retrogradation of starch almost always results in deterioration of quality. Many of the early studies of retrogradation followed the recognition that it constitutes what is undoubtedly the most important change that occurs during the staling of bread. In recent years, with the development of the frozen-food industry and of home freezing of foods, many studies have been related to problems with frozen starch-thickened foods such as gravies, sauces, and puddings involving syneresis and development of a curdled appearance.

One interesting development of these studies has been the accumulation of considerable evidence that, although amylopectin will not form a gel except at very high concentrations in which the linear ends of the branches are in close contact, it is involved in staling (Schoch and French, 1947) and in the syneresis of frozen products (Hanson et al., 1951 and 1953; Osman and Cummisford, 1959). Heating of bread that has staled under conditions that have not allowed an appreciable amount of water to be lost through evaporation renews its fresh texture. Although complete reversal of the curdling of sauces thickened with amylopectin was not observed by Osman and Cummisford, it was greatly reduced. They added support to the theory that long end-branches are probably involved in retrogradation during freezing and thawing by finding that aqueous pastes and white sauces thickened with the more highly branched polysaccharide, glycogen, with its shorter end-branches, were stable to this treatment.

The use of surface-active agents such as monoglycerides to reduce loss of compressibility in bread during aging, and of various modifications of starch to increase freeze-thaw stability, will be discussed later.

Characteristics of Some Food Starches

Differences in the size, shape, and gelatinization temperatures of starches from different botanical sources have already been discussed. In the study of their use in foods, the differences in the viscosity and gel strength they produce is of even greater importance. The data recorded in Table 3, in which concentrations of starch that produced nearly the same maximum viscosity in the Corn Industries Viscometer were used, illustrate some of the differences in these properties. More than three times as much wheat starch as potato starch was needed to produce the same maximum viscosity. The concentration of tapioca and waxy sorghum starches used were nearly the same, but tapioca reached its maximum viscosity at a temperature 20° lower than waxy sorghum. Wide variations in the extent of viscosity decrease during a 20-minute cooking period beyond maximum viscosity was observed for the unmodified starches, and even more for the modified starches and the flours studied. In most cases the increased fragmentation of the granules and leaching of soluble starch from the swollen granules during the 20-minute cooking period past maximum viscosity resulted in gels of greater strength. The waxy starches, as noted earlier, failed to produce gels. Potato and tapioca starches likewise failed to yield gels under the conditions used in this study, but other investigators have reported gel formation by these starches. Although the presence of amylases in flours may affect the behavior of the starch, the rapid heating in the Corn Industries Viscometer to temperatures above those at which cereal amylases are destroyed minimized their effects, and the differences between the flours and their refined starches must be attributed largely to the other constituents of the flours.

Unmodified Starches

Wheat Starch. In the United States and the other wheat-growing areas of the world, the source of the greatest amount of starch in the diet is wheat because of the use of wheat flour in bread and, to a lesser extent, other baked products such as cakes, cookies, and crackers. The role of starch in the staling of baked products by means of retrogradation has already been discussed. Much less attention has been paid to its importance in producing the characteristics of the freshly baked products. In general the proteins of the flour have been considered the important factor in these foods. But a gradually increasing number of investigations are recognizing that starch is of much greater importance than formerly thought.

Rotsch (1953) made bread of good grain, texture, and volume from wheat, corn, or potato starch in combination with certain polysaccharide adhesives, including gelatinized potato starch. Jongh (1961) used a small amount of glyceryl monostearate instead of a polysaccharide adhesive to give the dough plastic properties and a structure to retain the gas evolved. More recently Howard and co-workers (1968) have substi-

TABLE 3. Properties of Starch-Water Pastes Having Nearly the Same Maximum Viscosity in Corn Industries Viscometer[a,b]

Starch or Flour	Concentration (Percent Dry Substance)	At Maximum Viscosity			Cooked 20 Minutes Beyond Maximum Viscosity		
		Temperature (°C)	Viscosity (g-cm)	Gel Strength (g-cm)	Temperature (°C)	Viscosity (g-cm)	Gel Strength (g-cm)
Unmodified Starches							
Potato	1.96	90	105	0	95	49	0
Waxy corn	2.98	89	105	0	95	65	0
Waxy rice	3.13	87	110	0	96	106	0
Waxy sorghum	3.42	91	108	0	96	65	0
Tapioca	3.54	71	108	0	94	59	0
Arrowroot	4.37	80	103	87	96	85	115
Sorghum	4.66	94	110	76	97	73	136
Corn	4.90	91	113	52	95	77	142
Rice	5.49	94	101	31	97	54	30
Wheat	6.44	92	105	345	94	62	440
Modified starches							
Cross-linked waxy corn[c]	4.15	93	103[d]	0	96	115	0
Thin-boiling corn (60-fluidity)	8.26	85	111	115	94	0	210
Thin-boiling wheat (59-fluidity)	10.50	82	111	434	94	3	1440
Flours							
Waxy rice	5.48	70	97	0	92	25	0
Rice	5.57	93	100	11	97	77	15
Wheat	9.27	83	108	26	95	5	88

[a] Taken from Osman and Mootse (1958).
[b] Water bath around cooking vessel maintained at 100° C.
[c] Stabilizer W-13, manufactured by American Maize-Products Co.
[d] Viscosity at which change from rapid to slow increase occurred.

177

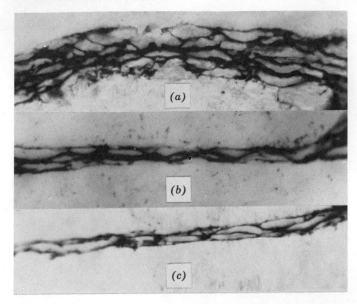

FIGURE 10. Orientation and elongation of starch granules in cross-sections of three bread films. (From Sandstedt, 1961.)

tuted granular starch entirely for cake flour in a layer-cake formulation. They reported that inclusion of polyvalent cations, soluble proteins, and surface-active lipids was needed to give the necessary stability to the batter emulsion during the early stages of baking.

A more detailed description of the changes that starch undergoes has been presented elsewhere (Osman, 1967). However, mention of a photomicrographic study by Sandstedt (1961) is of special interest. He showed that in the unbaked dough, the lenticular starch granules are oriented parallel to the surface of the gluten film surrounding the gas cells. He pointed out that adhesion of the protein to the granule surface must be strong to prevent leakage of gas from the cells and to prevent the granules from being forced out of the film by the increasing pressure of the gas. When the granules are gelatinized during baking, they undergo only limited swelling because of the small amount of water present. However, they become softer and more flexible, and, with the expansion of the gas cells, they are greatly stretched and are even more completely oriented with the surface of the gluten film (see Figure 10). Substitution of starches other than wheat gave products that were inferior to that with wheat starch. Substitution of glass beads of a size comparable to that of starch granules allowed fair retention of gas, resulting in a loaf of only moderately reduced size, but the collapsed cells in the interior suggested that the needed rigidity of the cell walls failed to develop, possibly because water was not removed from the gluten as it was by gelatinizing starch granules.

Although the proteins in wheat flour are of unquestionable importance, these studies indicate that other film-forming substances can be used to replace them in baked products with considerable success, but nothing has yet been found to replace the starch. Of practical importance is the possibility of more satisfactory baked products for those individuals who cannot tolerate wheat gluten in their diets.

Use of cake flour, with its lower protein content, instead of all-purpose flour has long been known to yield more tender baked products. Further reduction of the protein content by substitution of refined wheat starch for part of the cake flour in a number of baked products has been reported to produce improvement. As an example, Dubois (1959) reported that use of wheat starch as a replacement of 30 per cent of the cake flour in an angel food or other foam-type cake gave significant improvement in volume, grain, texture, and eating properties, as well as in freshness retention.

Corn and Grain Sorghum Starches. Because of their abundance and low cost, corn and grain sorghum starches are the most widely used refined starches in this country. Sorghum starch has a somewhat higher gelatinization temperature than corn starch (see Table 2) but, except for cases in which this is an important factor, their properties are so nearly the same that they can be used almost interchangeably (see Table 3). They give opaque pastes of higher viscosity than wheat starch at the same concentration. The pastes have the short (nonmucilaginous) character typical of nonwaxy cereal starches, and they yield stiff gels. Unless they have received special treatment, they have a characteristic cereal flavor. They undergo extensive retrogradation, especially when frozen and thawed. However, in those food products in which greater clarity, freeze-thaw stability, or resistance to gel formation are not factors, they are usually the starches used. In addition to their use for thickening and gel formation, they find such miscellaneous uses as serving as the mold in which gumdrops are formed and for "dusting" in baking operations.

Waxy Corn and Waxy Sorghum Starches. Like ordinary corn and sorghum starches, waxy corn and waxy sorghum starches are very much alike (see Table 3) except for the slightly higher gelatinization temperature of the latter (see Table 2). Although their greater paste clarity, high water-binding capacity, and resistance to gel formation and retrogradation suggest their use in food products, the stringy, mucilaginous character of their pastes makes use of the unmodified starches in foods unsatisfactory except in a very few products in which they are used in conjunction with other starches. Elimination of this undesirable property by cross-linking will be discussed later.

Rice Starch. Rice is the main food of more than half the world's population. Approximately 90 percent of the total dry substance of rice is starch. The attempts of a number of investigators to correlate the characteristics of the starch in different varieties of rice with the quality of the cooked rice have been discussed elsewhere (Osman, 1967). In brief, a number of properties such as amylose content and gelatinization temperature of the starch show correlation with the cooking quality of most varieties, but there are numerous exceptions. These have led some investigators to suggest that a number of factors are involved. Webb and coworkers (1963), for example, found that certain characteristics of amylograph curves, particularly the transition temperature (temperature of initial increase in viscosity), peak viscosity, and resistance to decrease in viscosity during a 10-minute holding period at 95° C, were useful in evaluating rice, but were of even greater value when considered together with the amylose content and the gelatinization temperature. Dawson and her co-workers (1960) suggested that fats, proteins, minerals, and cell-wall carbohydrates may influence cooking quality.

The tender, opaque gels formed from rice starch appear to offer no particular advantage in food products, so little refined rice starch is consumed in food in the United States. In the study of foods, the starch is chiefly of interest in relation to its effect on the cooking of the whole rice kernel.

Waxy Rice Starch and Waxy Rice Flour. Waxy rice flour holds a unique place among natural starches and flours because of the much greater freeze-thaw stability of the white sauces and puddings in which it is the thickening agent. This stability has frequently been attributed to the starch component of the flour, but data on sauces prepared with purified waxy rice starch have shown them to be considerably less stable than those prepared with the flour (Hanson et al., 1951; Osman and Cummisford, 1959), although more so than those prepared with other starches used in the studies. It seems clear that other ingredients in the flour, in addition to the starch, contribute to the freeze-thaw stability. Introduction of modified and derivatized starches specially designed for use in frozen foods have lessened the importance of this unique flour.

Potato Starch. The high viscosity produced by potato starch has already been mentioned, as well as its low tendency to form gels. A theory that has been proposed to explain the latter characteristic is that its unusually long amylose molecules tend to coil back on themselves instead of intermeshing with others to produce a gel. Another unusual feature of potato starch is its high phosphorus content. Unlike the phosphorus of cereal starches, which has been found to exist largely in phospholipids associated with the granule but not chemically bound to the starch molecules, the phosphorus in potato starch is present as dihydrogen orthophosphate groups esterified to the amylopectin fraction. These negatively charged groups attached to the starch molecules make potato starch more affected by cations than are other starches. It gives pastes of longer (stringier) body and greater clarity than those of cereal starches.

Potato starch is used much more in certain potato-growing areas of Europe than it is in the United States, so it is not surprising that it contributes some of the characteristics of native foods of these areas. It is used in a type of pudding known as Danish dessert, in some Swedish and German style breads, and in matzoh (unleavened bread eaten at Passover). It is also used in a number of other foods, but most of that manufactured in the United States is used outside the food industry.

What causes some potatoes to be "mealy" and others "waxy" is not yet entirely clear, but the concentration of starch in the cells seems to be a major, although not the only, factor. It appears that when the starch content of the cells is high, its gelatinization causes the cells to swell and become more nearly spherical. Contact between adjacent cells in this form is greatly reduced and they can easily be pulled apart. Sterling and Bettelheim (1955) suggested that, although the starch content is the chief cause of cell separation, it is counteracted to some degree by the calcium content and the molecular size of the pectic substances in the middle lamella and the cell wall. They thus accounted, at least in part, for the lack of complete correlation between starch content and mealiness.

Tapioca Starch. Tapioca starch that has not been either chemically modified or formed into partially gelatinized "pearls," or small pellets, is unsuitable for most food uses because of its stringy, cohesive quality. However, in the modified or pelleted form it retains the high degree of paste clarity and the bland flavor that are typical of root starches. The chemically modified starch is used in a variety of commercially prepared foods such as pie fillings and baby foods, as well as in starch blends used in salad dressings.

Pearl tapioca has long been used as a thickener for cream-type and fruit puddings. It is prepared by spreading the damp starch on iron plates, where it is heated, with constant stirring, to partially gelatinize the granules and agglomerate them into irregular pellets. On cooling, these become hard and translucent.

Separation of the pellets of tapioca, to prevent their clumping, can be accomplished by any of the techniques used with granular starch or flour. However, since it is usually used in puddings and pie fillings, the separation is usually brought about by thorough mixing with sugar and liquid. Stirring after the starch begins to gelatinize should be kept at a minimum to prevent development of a stringy texture through disintegration of the pearls. Penetration of water into the pellets is so slow that overnight soaking in water, prior to mixing with the other pudding ingredients, and long cooking are necessary. A form of much smaller particle size allows elimination of the soaking period and much more rapid cooking, while also reducing the stringy character found in the untreated starch.

Modified and Derivatized Starches

Chemically modified or derivatized starches are not sold as such on the retail market because they are designed for specialized purposes rather than the general use that the homemaker requires of starch. However, they are present in many of the commercially prepared foods and food mixes available to the homemaker, and are also used in institutional food preparation. Modification of starch by mild degradation has long been practiced. This treatment with an acid or an oxidizing agent cleaves the molecules sufficiently to cause the granules to fragment and produce much reduced viscosity during cooking. Cross-linked, phosphate-derivatized, and pregelatinized starches are among the somewhat later developments in food starches. As more is learned about the chemical and physical properties of starch and their relation to its behavior in various uses, new modifications are being developed to meet special requirements.

Acid-Modified Starches. A suspension of ordinary granular starch is heated below its gelatinization temperature in very dilute acid to produce "thin-boiling" starches. The term is derived from the fact that this treatment hydrolyzes enough molecules in the granules to cause them to fragment when they are heated in water, thus preventing the great increase in viscosity that results when unmodified granules are heated. However, the strength of the gel that forms is, if anything, improved and its clarity increased. The starch is thus well suited for one of its major uses, the production of gumdrops and similar confections. It forms a very fluid hot mixture that is easily poured into molds, and then sets to a relatively rigid gel. The molds are prepared by impressing the desired shapes in a layer of redried unmodified cornstarch with which a small amount of edible oil has been thoroughly blended to help the starch retain the shape of the impressions. This dried starch absorbs some moisture from the starch jelly as it sets. It can be redried and used again.

Oxidized Starches. Manufacture of oxidized starches is very similar to that of acid-modified starches except that alkaline hypochlorite is used instead of acid, resulting in cleavage of the molecules by oxidation rather than by hydrolysis. The products of the two processes are much alike, except that the oxidized starches usually give more tender gels.

Cross-Linked Starches. The stringy, mucilaginous character of products thickened with waxy varieties of starches and, to a lesser degree, with root starches, has been mentioned. This is brought about by the high water-binding capacity of these starches, resulting in rapid swelling and breakdown of the granules. Control of the swelling can be brought about to any extent desired by introduction of intermolecular bonds, which effectively tie the granule together. In this way, the undesirable stringy character of the starch paste can be eliminated without interfering with its desirable clarity and resistance to retrogradation. Like the unmodified waxy starches, however, those that have been cross-linked are not stable to freeze-thaw treatment unless they have received additional treatment to cover up some of the hydroxyl groups. If large numbers of free hydroxyl groups are available to form intermolecular hydrogen bonds, the starch retrogrades under the conditions of freezing and thawing, but some waxy starches that have received additional treatment such as acetylation or propionylation in addition to the cross-linking have given good performance in frozen foods.

The cross-linkages most often used in food starches are either of the phosphate ester type, formed by reaction of the starch with phosphorus oxychloride or water-soluble metaphosphates, or of the ether type, formed by reaction with epichlorohydrin. Both types depend on the reaction of hydroxyl groups on two different starch molecules with the same molecule of reagent.

The clarity of paste of the cross-linked waxy starches is a particular asset when they are used to thicken foods such as fruit pie fillings in which the sight of individual food particles adds to the attractiveness of the product, and the lack of gel formation is valued in such canned foods as prepared fruit pie fillings. Increased resistance of cross-linked starches to breakdown in acid media makes them useful in the production of commercially prepared salad dressings.

Starch Phosphates. Reduction of the intermolecular association of starch molecules, which causes retrogradation, through esterification of the hydroxyl groups has been mentioned in connection with improving the freeze-thaw stability of cross-linked starches. Introduction of ionic groups carrying the same charge and thus repelling one another is perhaps even more effective in this respect. Monoesterified phosphates have been used for this purpose in food starches. In one method (Neukom, 1958 and 1959), monoesterified groups are introduced under conditions that cause some degradation of the starch and yield a cold-water dispersible product. This derivatized starch has been reported to have excellent freeze-thaw stability both in a starch-water paste (Albrecht et al., 1960a) and in a white sauce formula (Albrecht et al., 1960b). In another method (Kerr and Cleveland, 1959), both monoesterified phosphate and cross-bonding diesterified phosphate can be formed simultaneously or in sequence in almost any ratio desired. When both types of esterification are introduced into waxy starches, all the advantages previously mentioned for cross-linked waxy starches plus greatly enhanced freeze-thaw stability result.

Pregelatinized Starches. The trend toward quickly prepared convenience foods has led to the wide use of pregelatinized starches. These starches, which have been precooked and dried, usually on hot rolls, have the common property of being cold-water dispersible. A wide variety of natural, modified, and derivatized starches have been subjected to this treatment; the products form dispersions that reflect the characteristics of the raw starch but are not entirely like the freshly cooked pastes. The drying process is usually accompanied by considerable breakdown of the swollen granules as well as some retrogradation. As a result, production of a given viscosity requires a considerably greater weight of pregelatinized than of raw starch of the same kind, and a somewhat different texture is produced.

Packaged "instant" pudding and cream pie filling mixes probably form the largest food uses of pregelatinized starch. These are mixtures of the starch with sugar and flavoring, together with salts that produce enough viscosity in the milk to which the mixture is added to hold the starch particles in suspension until they are hydrated.

A number of advantages from use of particular pregelatinized starches in other foods have been described. One of interest is retention of fresh fruit flavor in fruit pie through elimination of cooking by thickening the juice with pregelatinized cross-bonded waxy cereal starch.

Effects of Other Ingredients on Starch

Most foods are complex mixtures of ingredients. Determination of what the ingredients are and how each changes when heated alone or in water forms only the first step toward understanding the entire system. A second step that must precede any detailed comprehension of the interaction of all the ingredients in a system is the investigation of how a single ingredient is affected by another. Without such a step-by-step approach, erroneous conclusions can easily be drawn. Starch is one food constituent that is greatly influenced by many other ingredients, and these influences are important to the study of starch-containing foods.

Sugars

Many sweet puddings, sauces, and pie fillings are thickened with starch in the form of either an isolated starch or flour. That sugar not only provides the desired sweetness, but also affects the rate of thickening of the product during cooking and its final consistency, has long been recognized. The earliest studies were concerned with sucrose, but some later studies have included other sugars. They have shown that all the sugars commonly present in foods impede swelling of the starch granule, apparently by competing with the starch for the water present. The extent of the effect of different sugars, however, varies greatly, especially at high concentrations. Microscopic studies have shown that the various sugars, in addition to retarding the swelling of the granules, greatly extend the gelatinization range. Cornstarch granules in water alone lose their birefringence below 70° C (see Table 2), but in 50 percent sugar solution, a considerable number of birefringent granules were present at 85° C, more in solutions of disaccharides than in those of monosaccharides (Savage, 1968). In solutions of disaccharides, a few birefringent granules were present at 95° C. This difference in the effects of mono- and disaccharides was also observed in the effects of sucrose, lactose, D-galactose, D-glucose, and D-fructose on the swelling power of starch, in which the starch was allowed to swell to the maximum extent in the sugar solution at 75, 85, and 95° C, then centrifuged, and the volume of the swollen granules measured. However, maltose, for some unknown reason, allowed as much swelling at the higher temperatures as the monosaccharides.

This difference in the effects of 50 percent solutions of mono- and disaccharides on cornstarch had previously been reported by Bean and Osman (1958) in a study of hot-paste viscosity (Figure 11). The anomalous effect of maltose was also observed in this study. Lower concentrations of sugar had much less effect (Figure 12). For all sugars, concentrations above about 10 percent reduced the strength of the gels formed by the pastes on cooling. With 50 percent concentrations of disaccharides, no gel structure could be observed, and with the monosaccharides, only very weak gels were formed.

These studies indicate that direct substitution of one sugar for another on an equal weight basis cannot be made without affecting the physical properties of a starch-thickened product. Miller and Trimbo (1965) have also shown that substitution of D-glucose or invert sugar for sucrose in a white layer cake formula prevented the defect known as "dipping," that is, a concave surface, as did other treatments that caused the starch to gelatinize and increase the viscosity of the batter at a lower tempera-

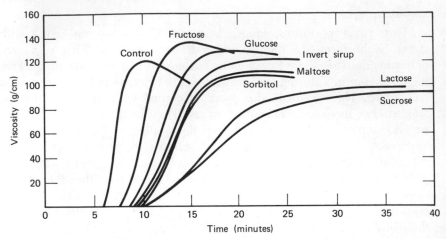

FIGURE 11. Effect of different sugars on gelatinization of five percent cornstarch in a Corn Industries Viscometer with water bath at 100° C. (From Bean and Osman, 1959.)

ture. Unfortunately, the monosaccharides also caused browning of both crust and crumb to an extent considered excessive for a white cake.

Increasing amounts of added sucrose were shown by Hester, Briant, and Personius (1956) to raise the temperature at which aqueous suspen-

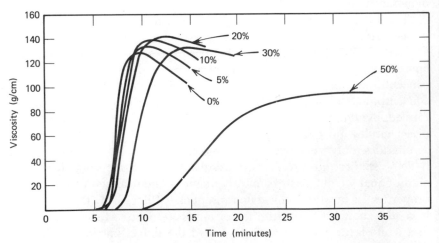

FIGURE 12. Effect of different concentrations of sucrose on gelatinization of five percent cornstarch in a Corn Industries Viscometer with water bath at 100° C. (From Bean and Osman, 1959.)

sions of soft and hard wheat flours, as well as isolated wheat starch, caused an increase in apparent viscosity to be recorded by the amylograph. The marked differences between the shapes of the viscosity curves obtained with the flours and the starch undoubtedly reflect the interaction of the starch with the numerous other constituents of the flours, such as proteins, together with the effect of the sugar on the changes occurring in some of these other ingredients, as well as starch, during heating.

Acids and Alkalies

In most foods, the pH value lies between 4 and 7. Variations within this range produce only minor effects on the swelling and breakdown of starch granules and the resultant viscosity of the mixture (see Figure 13). Because foods are almost never very alkaline, the effect of alkalies

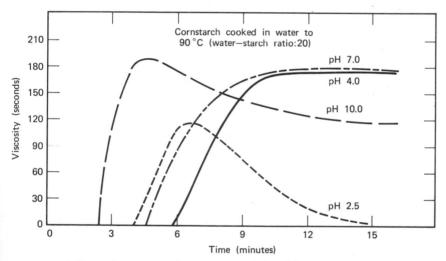

FIGURE 13. Effect of pH on gelatinization and breakdown of cornstarch. (From Corn Industries Research Foundation, 1964.)

in increasing starch gelatinization is of only theoretical interest in the study of foods. Foods that are acid because of the presence of fruit juices, vinegar, or other acid ingredients are, however, common, and the effects of lower pH values on starch are important.

Breakdown of the starch granules because of some hydrolytic cleavage of the starch molecules usually results in a lower maximum viscosity during cooking, followed by a rapid thinning. This effect has presented a great problem in the commercial production of salad dressing. Although granules of some varieties of natural starch are somewhat more resistant to breakdown in acid media than others, the most effective means of combating this problem is by the use of the more acid-resistant cross-linked starches, as has already been mentioned.

In sweetened products such as fruit pie fillings, the effect of the acid is reduced to a considerable degree by the high sugar concentration. Campbell and Briant (1957) showed that increasing concentrations of citric acid from 0.05 to 0.20 N caused the maximum viscosity of a wheat starch paste to be greater and to occur at a lower temperature, but also to break down more rapidly. Addition of high concentrations of sugar, by reducing the swelling of the granules (and thereby access of the acid solution to much of the starch), retarded the hydrolysis. As a result of the slower hydrolysis, the maximum viscosity was higher than without the sugar present, and, with all but the highest level of acid used, the thinning of the paste was somewhat slower. Results with the highest concentration of citric acid (Figure 14) show the delayed swelling caused by the high concentration of sugar, even with a relatively high concentration of acid. One practical conclusion that can be drawn from this study is that in preparing a lemon pie filling, the effect of the high sugar concentration in retarding the swelling of the starch may cause

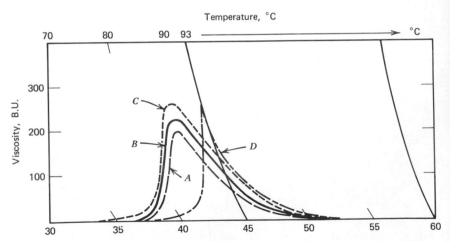

FIGURE 14. Effect of citric acid and sucrose on gelatinization of starch from un-bleached soft wheat flour heated in an amylograph to 93° C. A, 0.200 N citric acid solution; B, 10 g sucrose/100 ml 0.200 N citric acid solution; C, 20 g sucrose/100 ml 0.200 N citric acid solution; D, 40 g sucrose/100 ml 0.200 N citric acid solution. (From Campbell and Briant, 1957.)

insufficient cooking to be a more frequent cause of a too thin filling than overcooking with resulting hydrolysis.

In commercial and institutional preparation of fruit pie fillings, cross-linked waxy starches are frequently used because of their resistance to hydrolysis, as well as the greater clarity of their pastes and the elimination of gel formation. Their resistance to hydrolysis is especially important in canned pie fillings because of the high temperatures required in processing.

Although reaction between unswollen starch granules and the acid in prepared mixes such as that for lemon pie filling is slow, it is sufficient to present a shelf-life problem unless the acid is segregated from the starch during storage by coating the acid with an inert material or adding it in tablet form.

Salts

In general, starches are much less sensitive to the presence of ions than are proteins. This is because most starches do not have charged groups built into the molecular structure. An exception, which has been mentioned previously, is potato starch, in which some of the hydroxyl groups of the amylopectin fraction are esterified with orthophosphate groups. The negative charge carried by these groups makes potato starch much more affected by the presence of cations than are other starches, which have no such ionizing groups. For example, 0.00001 N sodium chloride has been reported to reduce the development of viscosity of potato starch during heating, although 0.1 N sodium chloride had little effect on cornstarch.

Although the concentration of salts in some common food ingredients such as milk is high enough so that they undoubtedly affect the behavior of starch, these systems are little understood at the present time. In milk and in many other food systems, the effects of the salts on the proteins present are so much greater than on the starch that the effects on the latter are difficult to distinguish.

Many reports of the effects of salts on starch may be found in the literature, but they often appear to contradict one another. This is because most of the studies were made before the advent of modern instruments for controlling the heating and stirring of the mixture while changes in viscosity are automatically recorded. The effects of sodium sulfate are greater and more complex than those of many salts but indicate why different cooking conditions may produce very different effects. Examination of Figure 15 shows that at 90° C the viscosities of the samples containing either 0.5 N or 1.0 N sodium sulfate are very much lower than the control sample of starch in distilled water. On the

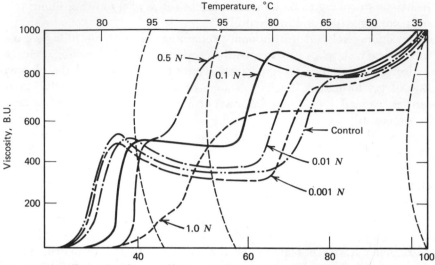

FIGURE 15. Effect of sodium sulfate on gelatinization of seven percent cornstarch heated in the amylograph to 95° C. (From Osman, 1967.)

other hand, these same concentrations of sodium sulfate produce higher viscosities than the control in mixtures held at 95° C for 15 minutes, with the viscosity of the 0.5 N solution being much greater than that of the 1.0 N solution. After only five minutes at 95° C, the viscosity of the sample containing 0.5 N sodium sulfate is appreciably higher than that of the control, whereas that containing 1.0 N sodium sulfate is very much lower. It is a small wonder that the data reported by different investigators who made measurements on viscosity or on the volumes of the swollen granules after cooking procedures that varied from one laboratory to another are not in agreement. When the variety of starch used has not been specified and one does not know whether it is potato or cereal starch, the results can be even more confusing.

At the present time about all that can be said concerning the effects of salts on starch in food systems is that in most cases the concentration of salts is low enough so that they are probably not as great as those caused by other substances present. On the other hand, the effects are not so small that they should be completely ignored. A somewhat more detailed discussion of the matter has been published elsewhere (Osman, 1967).

Fats and Surface-Active Agents

In a discussion of the effects of fats on the swelling of starch granules and the resulting viscosity changes, a distinction must be made between the fats that contain emulsifying agents (as most modern shortenings do) and those that do not.

The effects of 11 natural and hydrogenated fats and oils on a 6 percent cornstarch paste were studied by Osman and Dix (1960). These fats included soybean oil and five hydrogenated soybean oils, corn oil and two hydrogenated corn oils, cottonseed oil, and prime steam lard. The iodine numbers, indicating the degree of unsaturation of these fats and oils, varied from 38 to 132, and their physical appearance at room temperature ranged from oils to a very hard, brittle fat. However, the effects of all were the same. None either increased or decreased the maximum viscosity that was obtained when the mixtures were heated in the Brabender amylograph, but all had the same effect in lowering the temperature at which the maximum viscosity was reached. The temperature at maximum viscosity (92° C for the control sample) became progressively lower as more fat was added until it reached 82° C when the weight of the fat equaled 9 to 12 percent that of the starch-water mixture. Larger amounts of fat had little additional effect, probably because no more could be well dispersed in the mixture. The strength of gels prepared from the samples that had been held 15 minutes at 95° C did not appear to differ substantially from control samples, although the results obtained were somewhat erratic, probably because separated fat or oil prevented formation of a homogeneous gel structure. It should be noted that in these fats, as in most fats commonly used in food, the carbon chains of the fatty acid groups consisted almost entirely of 16 to 18 carbon atoms. It is possible that triglycerides with shorter fatty acid groups might differ in their effect.

Monoglycerides, which are constituents of most shortening, are usually discussed in terms of their emulsifying properties, which improve the dispersion of fat in an aqueous medium. But they have other effects on starch-containing foods, which have led to their use in a variety of commercially prepared products. Several of these have been discussed by Brokaw (1962). Addition of monoglycerides prevents gel formation in a variety of canned sauces, gravies, and soups. Dehydrated potatoes, either granules or flakes, to which monoglycerides have been added have better texture after reconstitution. Spaghetti and rice are reported to be less sticky when monoglycerides have been added. A variety of surface-active agents, including monoglycerides and polyoxyethylene monostearates, retard the firming of bread and other baked products on standing.

The mechanism by which these effects are produced is not clear, although many studies have been made of the effects of surface-active agents on granular starch, on amylose and amylopectin, and on starch-containing foods.

A wide variety of nonionic surface-active agents of the general type used in foods have been shown to form complexes with amylose (Osman, Leith, and Fleš, 1961). These complexes have the same general structure as the amylose-iodine complex responsible for the characteristic blue color produced when iodine is added to starch, but the complexes of surface-active agents are colorless. The amylose molecules, ordinarily present in solution as long, flexible, loose coils, assume the more rigid, more tightly coiled form of helices having cores of the surface-active agents (Figure 16). When the amylose molecules are tied up in this

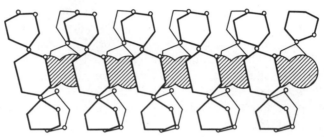

FIGURE 16. Model of an iodine-filled amylose helix. (Rundle, Foster, and Baldwin, 1944.)

way, they cannot form the intermolecular bonding necessary for gel formation and retrogradation. Such complexing of the amylose therefore appears to be at least partially responsible for the effectiveness of monoglycerides in preventing gel formation in starchy foods.

Considerable evidence has been accumulated to show that the effect of surface-active agents in reducing the firming of bread on standing cannot be explained by complexing of the amylose. Schoch and French (1947) showed that most of the amylose in bread becomes insoluble during baking and is therefore not available to take part in the subsequent staling reaction. Their investigation led them to conclude that the firming is caused by an association of the amylopectin molecules. Because this can presumably occur only between the ends of the branches, fewer bonds can be formed between adjacent molecules. With fewer bonds involved, the association cannot be as stable as between linear amylose molecules, and can therefore be broken more easily. These conclusions agree with the well-known fact that bread that has become firm but not dry can be made softer by heating, since the energy provided by the heat is enough to break the bonds between amylopectin molecules, but would not reverse the retrogradation of amylose. Involvement of amylopectin rather than amylose in staling was also shown by a study by Noznick, Merritt, and Geddes (1946) in which they prepared bread from flour in which the wheat starch was replaced by waxy maize starch (entirely amylopectin). This elimination of amylose did not prevent staling. On the other hand, bread prepared from flour in which part of the starch had been replaced by cross-linked starch had increased firmness (Prentice, Cuendet, and Geddes, 1954; Bechtel, 1959) and increased crystallinity (Zobel and Senti, 1959), and was judged by organoleptic tests to have the characteristics normally associated with staling (Bechtel, 1959), thus supporting the hypothesis that bread staling does involve intermolecular association of the amylopectin. Just how surface-active agents inhibit this association is still a matter of conjecture.

The presence of certain surface-active agents causes a marked increase in the temperature at which the viscosity increases in a mixture of starch and water, as well as the temperature at which appreciable swelling of the granules occurs (Gray and Schoch, 1962; Thompson, 1968). It also markedly decreases the strength of gels formed from the resulting pastes on standing. Osman and Dix (1960) had found the same effects in mixtures that contained soybean oil in addition to the starch, water, and surface-active agent (Table 4). However, two compounds, methyl alpha-D-glucoside 6-laurate and lecithin, used in the latter mixture, had the opposite effect, although they were later shown (Osman, Leith and Fleš, 1961) to be capable of forming complexes with amylose. No explanation that has yet been proposed appears adequate to explain all the observed effects.

Proteins

Starch and protein are frequently both present in the same food. In some cases, such as legumes and wheat flour, the combination is produced in the growing plant from which it is obtained. In others, such as cornstarch pudding, the protein has been added in the form of such ingredients as milk or eggs. Most discussions of the changes that occur during food preparation treat the two substances separately, as though each is completely independent of the other. But some data have been reported that suggest that the presence of protein and its condition affect the characteristics normally associated with changes in the starch.

When a series of starch-water pastes and white sauces was prepared with the same samples of various starches, the white sauces were, in general, more stable to freezing and thawing than the corresponding pastes, indicating some effect from the milk solids (Osman and Cummisford, 1959). Although white sauces prepared with waxy rice starch

TABLE 4.   Effect of Surface-Active Agents on Starch Pastes Containing Fat[a,b]

Ester	Temperature at Maximum Viscosity (°C)	Gel Strength (g-cm)
Glyceryl monopalmitate	94	186
Glyceryl monostearate	96	150
Methyl alpha-D-glucoside-6-laurate	75	105
Methyl alpha-D-glucoside-6-palmitate	88	78
Methyl alpha-D-glucoside-6-stearate	92	73
3-Palmitoyl-D-glucose	92	
3-Stearoyl-D-glucose	½ minute at 96	62
Ascorbyl palmitate	96	123
Sorbitan monostearate	94	132
Sucrose monostearate	2 minutes at 96	91
Polyoxyethylene monostearate (MYRJ 45)	1 minute at 96	43
Polyoxyethylene monostearate (MYRJ 52)	no maximum	18
Sucrose dipalmitate	84	59
Sucrose distearate	90	58
Sucrose ester (Seqol 260)	87	84
Polyoxyethylene sorbitan monooleate	91	130
Polyoxyethylene sorbitan monostearate	92	118
Methyl glucoside distearate	89	85
Methyl glucoside tallow emulsifier No. 2210	90	105
Methyl glucoside tallow emulsifier No. 2275	90	107
Lecithin	77	443
Sorbitan tetrastearate	84	379
None (6.5 percent starch paste with 6 percent soybean oil)	81	608

[a] From Osman and Dix (1960).

[b] Surfactant substituted for 6 percent of the soybean oil of the basic mixture (that is, its weight was 0.36 percent that of the starch-water mixture).

were considerably more stable to this treatment than those prepared from other natural and many modified starches, they were less stable than those prepared from waxy rice flour. The same differences between the starch and flour of waxy rice had been reported in the data of Hanson, Campbell, and Lineweaver (1951). These studies indicated that other components of the flour and those of milk exerted an influence on the starch.

A comparison by Hwang (1960) of the amylograph viscosity curves produced by cornstarch in water, in five percent lactose solution, and in a natural protein-free milk system (Figure 17) with viscosity curves

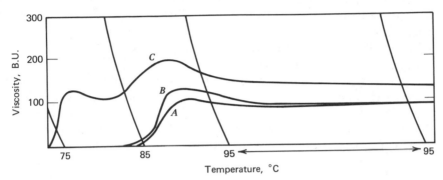

FIGURE 17. Gelatinization of five percent cornstarch in (A) water, (B) five percent lactose solution, and (C) a natural protein-free milk system. (From Hwang, 1960.)

from cornstarch in samples of skim milk (Figure 18), indicated the importance of the effect of milk proteins on viscosity, although they also showed that other constituents of the milk could affect the starch. Stalder (1961) obtained data that indicated that the two types of curves shown in Figure 18, produced by pasteurized skim milk from different sources, were probably the result of different temperatures used in pasteurization. When the temperature of pasteurization is raised appreciably above 161° F (71.7° C), the temperature required for high-temperature-short-

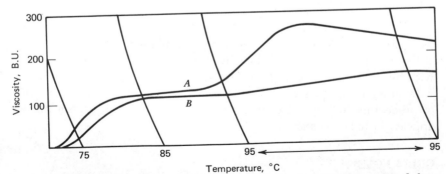

FIGURE 18. Gelatinization of five percent cornstarch in two samples of pasteurized skim milk. (From Hwang, 1960).

time pasteurization, appreciable denaturation of the whey proteins may occur. The samples of milk that gave Curve A could be altered to give Curve B by heating them (prior to mixing with the starch) to 176° F (80° C). Temperatures approaching this figure are not uncommon in commercial pasteurization. It is thus obvious that, in addition to the natural variation in milk constituents discussed in Chapter 10, one must consider possible differences in heat treatment as factors contributing to differences in the properties of products containing milk, at least when starch is also present.

Grant (1968) found that the effect of preheating milk on the viscosity of a starch-milk system remained substantially unchanged when sugar was added to produce a cornstarch pudding of the blanc mange type, that is, without egg. She found that preheating the milk for 30 minutes at 113° F (45° C) or 149° F (65° C) had no effect, but that 171° F (77° C) had almost as great an effect as 203° F (95° C). Results in Table 5 for some representative puddings cooked in an amylograph,

TABLE 5.   Effect on Cornstarch Puddings of Preheated Skim Milk

Milk Sample	Treatment	Maximum Viscosity (B.U.)	Final Viscosity[a] (B.U.)	Gel Strength[b] (g)
A	Raw	550	410	244
	Preheated	330	330	147
B	Raw	470	380	186
	Preheated	310	310	131
C	Raw	440	370	176
	Preheated	295	295	121

[a] After 15-minute holding at 95° C.
[b] By imbedded-disk method.

using a 15-minute holding period after the temperature reached 95° C, show the effect of the 95° C heat treatment of the milk prior to mixing with the starch and sugar. They also show the variation that is obtained with different samples of milk. Grant also demonstrated that the effect of preheating milk is not confined to systems containing starch but also appears in baked custards.

CELLULOSE

Not only is cellulose the most abundant of all natural organic substances, but it is also constantly being produced by the growth of vegetable matter. In the form of partially crystalline microfibrils, it forms the basic structural material of the cell walls of vegetable tissues. The cellulose microfibrils are embedded in an amorphous gel composed largely of noncellulosic polysaccharides, together with a small amount of protein. Changes in the properties of these cell-wall constituents and of the intercellular substances are largely responsible for changes in the texture of fruits and vegetables during maturation, storage, and cooking.

Molecular Structure

Cellulose, like amylose, is a linear polymer of D-glucopyranose units with 1,4-linkages; that is, it is held together by glycoside bonds between the carbonyl group of one unit and the hydroxyl group on carbon 4 of the adjacent unit. However, the steric configuration of the linkage on carbon 1 is beta in cellulose rather than alpha, as it is in amylose. The disaccharide repeating unit in cellulose is therefore cellobiose (see Figure 19a). The configuration of the glycosidic linkage should not be confused with the term "alpha cellulose," used to designate high-quality cellulose, insoluble in 17.5 per cent sodium hydroxide at 20° C, and used in research work.

As with other polysaccharides, determination of the average molecular

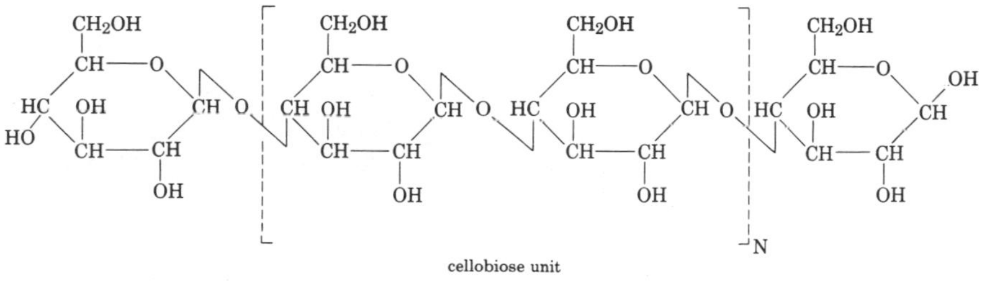

cellobiose unit

FIGURE 19a.   Structure of cellulose.

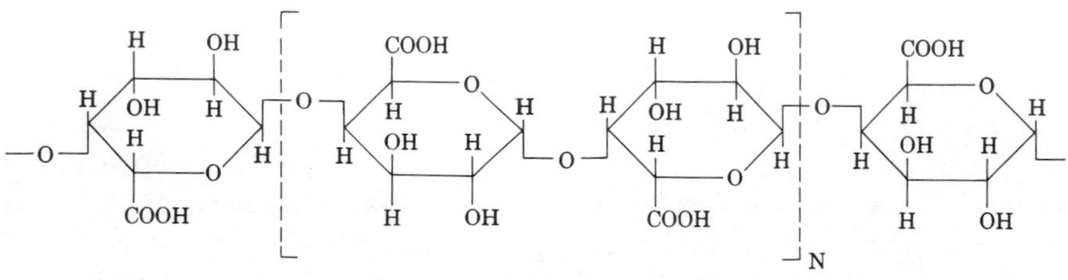

FIGURE 19b.   Chain of anhydrogalacturonic acid units in pectic acid.

weight of cellulose is difficult and depends on the technique used as well as the source and previous treatment of the sample. Many values have been reported, all of them very large. In its native state, cellulose exists in fibrils in which the major portion of it is in a crystalline arrangement. The crystalline areas, sometimes referred to as crystallites or micelles, include portions of many individual cellulose molecules. Between the crystalline areas are regions in which the molecules exist in a disordered, amorphous arrangement. A single molecule may pass through several regions of complete order (crystalline) and complete disorder (amorphous).

Cellulose, like other polysaccharides, has a strong affinity for water. Samples exposed to normal atmospheric conditions, although appearing to be dry, ordinarily contain about 8–9 percent water. However, solution, which involves disruption of the crystalline regions, occurs only in liquids that are able to break the powerful forces between the cellulose molecules in these regions. Such disruption of the crystalline regions does not occur under the conditions that prevail in food preparation, and the softening of the cell walls of vegetable materials must be attributed to solution of the supporting substances present.

Cellulose Ethers

Ethers of cellulose are prepared by first causing the cellulose to swell in strong alkali and then adding an alkyl halide or sulfate. Although each D-glucose unit in the cellulose molecule has three hydroxyl groups, most of the cellulose ethers used in foods are substituted on less than two thirds of the hydroxyls present. The solubility of the product is influenced by several factors, including its molecular weight, its degree of substitution, and the uniformity of the substitution.

Cellulose ethers used in foods are water soluble and have many of the properties of natural vegetable gums. They are used largely for their hygroscopic and thickening properties. Use in foods of methylcellulose and of hydroxypropylmethylcellulose (in which part of the hydroxyl groups are substituted by methyl groups and part by hydroxypropyl groups) have been discussed by Greminger and Savage (1959) and Glicksman (1963). Aqueous solutions of the common grades of methylcellulose differ from those of most polysaccharides and their derivatives by forming gels when they are heated.

Sodium carboxymethylcellulose (commonly referred to as CMC) is prepared by treating cellulose with sodium hydroxide and then reacting it with sodium monochloroacetate. It is probably the most widely used synthetic gum in the food industry and has found a broad range of applications. Its solutions, like those of most gums, become less viscous at high temperatures, but regain their viscosity on cooling. The solutions become less stable at pH values below 5. Addition of calcium ions to the solution produces a haze, and ferric or aluminum ions produce a gel or precipitate.

One of the largest food uses of CMC is as a stabilizer in the manufacture of ice cream, in which it is frequently used in combination with carrageenan, a gum derived from seaweed that is discussed later in this chapter. It helps to retard the growth of ice crystals and to make the melted product more viscous. Its use in this and other food products has been reviewed by Glicksman (1963).

Microcrystalline Cellulose

An interesting product that has become available for use in foods within the last decade is microcrystalline cellulose. The amorphous regions between the crystalline areas in cellulose fibers are more easily hydrolyzed than the crystalline areas, in which the cellulose molecules are tightly packed. Partial hydrolysis of the cellulose leaves the crystalline areas intact in the form of tiny rodlike microcrystals. This product is dried to yield a white, crystalline powder. It is used in this form in pharmaceutical tableting, and can also be used as a carrier to aid in uniform dispersion of spices, essential oils, and color in foods. However, most of that used in foods contains 8–12 percent sodium carboxymethylcellulose to aid in dispersion in aqueous systems and to serve as a protective colloid. It has been recommended as a bodying agent and a retardant of crystal growth in frozen desserts. In emulsions, the solid particles coat the droplets and also thicken the aqueous phase. Another use is as a foam stabilizer in aerosol products.

HEMICELLULOSES

The cell walls of plants contain a number of polysaccharide materials other than cellulose. Pectic substances, which will be discussed later, form one group of these materials. Another that must be recognized is the group known as the hemicelluloses. The term is a somewhat unfortunate one because structurally these materials bear little relation to cellulose, but it does indicate their close association with cellulose in plant materials. The primary definition for this group of substances rests more on solubility than on chemical structure. The term is generally used to designate "water-insoluble cell wall polysaccharides of land plants except cellulose and pectin" (Whistler and Smart, 1953). Although insoluble in water at neutral pH, they are soluble in aqueous alkali. They may be divided according to chemical structure into two groups, (1) those composed of only unmodified pentose and hexose units and (2) those that contain some uronic acid units, together with unmodified pentose and/or hexose units.

Probably the most common member of this group of substances is xylan, a polymer composed almost, if not entirely, of xylose units. Another common hemicellulose is composed largely of xylose units, together with a small amount of D-glucuronic acid. However, other types may be found with other unmodified monosaccharide and uronic acid units.

The presence of these substances in the cell walls helps to explain the considerable effects of the pH of cooking water on the softening of vegetables, especially the mushy texture that appears so rapidly in the presence of alkali.

PECTIC SUBSTANCES

The heterogeneous nature of the pectic substances and the difficulties encountered in isolating them in pure condition has led to much confusion and apparent contradiction in discussions of them. A significant contribution toward clarifying the situation was the work of the nomenclature committee of the Division of Agricultural and Food Chemistry of the American Chemical Society (1944), which resulted in the following widely used definitions.

1. *Pectic substances.* These are complex colloidal carbohydrate derivatives that occur in or are prepared from plants and contain a large proportion of anhydrogalacturonic acid units that are thought to exist in a chainlike combination. The carboxyl groups of polygalacturonic acids may be partly esterified by methyl groups and partly or completely neutralized by one or more bases.

2. *Protopectin.* This is the water-insoluble parent pectic substance that occurs in plants and that upon restricted hydrolysis yields pectin or pectinic acids.

3. *Pectinic acids.* These are colloidal polygalacturonic acids containing more than a negligible proportion of methyl ester groups. Pectinic acids, under suitable conditions, are capable of forming gels with sugar and acid or, if suitably low in methoxyl content, with certain metallic ions. The salts of pectinic acids are either normal or acid pectinates.

4. *Pectin.* These are water-soluble pectinic acids of varying methyl ester content and degree of neutralization that are capable of forming gels with sugar and acid under suitable conditions.

5. *Pectic acids.* These are pectic substances mostly composed of

colloidal polygalacturonic acids and essentially free from methyl ester groups. The salts of pectic acids are either normal or acid pectates.

These definitions, drawn largely from studies on citrus products, appear to describe the structures of the major portions of the various pectic substances and to explain their properties (see Figure 19b). However, the difficulty of removing all traces of neutral (nonacidic) sugar units from purified pectin preparations has long led chemists to question whether covalent linkages binding these groups to the anhydrogalacturonic acid chains in nature were hydrolyzed during purification procedures. Recent evidence indicates that they are, that a variety of neutral sugar groups are actually present in covalent linkage in purified pectic acid (see Abersheim, 1965). Moreover, the association between the pectic substances and the hemicelluloses in cell walls is such that some investigators believe it likely that in the plant the two are bonded together to form a continuum of polysaccharides and that the various substances that have been isolated are the result of breaking covalent bonds during extraction from the plant source (Albersheim, 1965). This noncellulosic material forms the matrix in which the cellulose fibrils are embedded and to which they may even be bonded. The picture is far from clear, but represents one of the fascinating frontiers of plant study. Pectic substances are also present in the intercellular layer in the form of salts, largely of calcium.

The studies on fruits and vegetables that have been reported deal with these noncellulosic materials in terms of the substances that are obtained by various methods of extraction, that is, the hemicelluloses and, especially, the various pectic substances, because at present, techniques are not available to demonstrate the actual situation within the plant itself. Staining techniques used in microscopic examination are helpful in showing the location of pectic substances within the plant, but are not able to resolve such questions as how they are associated with other materials.

Changes in the pectic substances occur during the ripening of fruits. Studies on apples and pears have shown that the amount of protopectin decreases more or less rapidly after the fruit is picked, as it becomes softer; an increase in the soluble pectin occurs simultaneously, indicating the conversion of protopectin to pectin (Spencer, 1965). This change is followed by a period during which the amounts of both pectic substances remain constant, before a final decrease in pectin as the fruit becomes mealy. Similar changes have been observed in other fruits and vegetables, although the development of lignin, an insoluble noncarbohydrate cementing substance, in many vegetables causes them to become less tender as they mature and to acquire a woody texture. A loss of methyl ester groups from the pectin also occurs in some cases. Addition of a calcium salt such as calcium chloride causes the formation of insoluble salts of pectic substances and is used to add firmness to some canned or frozen fruits and vegetables, especially canned tomatoes.

Although some fruit juices contain enough pectin for gel formation in the presence of adequate acid and sugar, most jellies and jams prepared commercially or in the home employ purified pectin isolated from the peel of citrus fruits or the pomace of apples. The pulp of sugar beets is considered a possible future source of this material. Acid is used commercially to extract the pectin. The product is undoubtedly somewhat degraded from the form in which it occurs in the plant tissue, but it has the gel-forming properties needed for jelly and jam making. The finished product is available in the form of a solution or as a powder. The powder is mixed with dextrose (D-glucose) hydrate to standardize its gel-forming properties, since each batch produced has its individual strength. Dextrose also aids its dispersion in water without lump formation.

Pectins for High-Sugar Jellies and Jams

Grading of pectin does not refer to color or purity, but rather to the ability of the pectin to form a gel. The grade is the ratio by weight of the sugar to pectin which will yield a high-sugar gel of standard strength provided that the jelly-making process, composition, and pH are as defined (Bender, 1959). This measurement depends not only on the particular method of measuring the gel strength, such as removal of an embedded disk, breakthrough with a plunger, or sag of the unmolded jelly, but also on such factors as completeness of dispersion of the pectin, solids content, amount and kind of acid and salts present, whether the acid is added before or after cooking, and the temperature of storage after setting. Although not completely defined, these conditions are relatively standard among pectin manufacturers. One pound of a 100-grade pectin will form a standard gel with a mixture containing 100 pounds of sugar. Present commercial grades for liquid pectin are about 5.0 or 5.5 and for powdered pectin, about 150 or 200.

In a neutral or only slightly acid dispersion of pectin molecules, most of the unesterified carboxyl groups are present as partially ionized salts. Those that are ionized produce a negative charge on the molecule which, together with the hydroxyl groups, causes it to attract layers of water. Addition of acid converts the carboxyl ions to mostly unionized carboxylic acid groups, with much less attraction for water. Added sugar, by attracting water to itself, further lessens the hydration of pectin molecules.

Thus an unstable dispersion is formed that, on cooling, forms a gel, a continuous meshwork of pectin holding the aqueous solution. The pectin molecules are partially associated with one another and partially hydrated. The gel is reversible and liquifies when it is heated. ·

The degree of methylation, that is, the percentage of galacturonic acid groups that are present in the form of their methyl esters, affects the rate at which gel formation takes place; a higher degree of methylation causes slower setting. Possibly other factors, such as the length of the molecules, may also exert an effect. A slow-set type is generally preferred for commercial jelly making because it allows enough acid to be used for satisfactory tartness without causing the jelly to set before it can be filled into the containers. It also allows any air bubbles to rise, thus improving clarity. A more rapidly setting type is preferred for jams, preserves, and marmalades because it quickly produces enough thickening to hold fruit and pulp particles uniformly distributed throughout the mixture instead of floating to the top. A slow-set pectin is used for making confectioner's jelly—clear, varicolored gumdrops, which are essentially jelly of high solids concentration.

Pectin for Low-Sugar or Sugar-Free Gels

In solutions of pectinic or pectic acids in which the degree of methylation is about 30 or below, gel formation can be brought about by the addition of calcium or other divalent cations without the addition of sugar. The presence of some sugar is said to increase firmness and to decrease syneresis, but it is not essential and, if used at all, can be used in very limited quantity. Gel formation depends on the formation of calcium salts involving carboxyl groups on different pectinic or pectic acid molecules, thus bringing about an intermolecular bonding and meshwork without the aid of sugar. When some sugar is present, the amount of calcium required to form a firm gel is reduced. These gels, like high-sugar jellies, are reversible and melt when heated (Bender, 1959).

Low-methoxyl pectins can be used when it is desirable to limit the amount of sugar in a gel to give the desired flavor or for dietary reasons. They also have uses in food such as the preservation of shape and reduction of drainage in frozen strawberries.

VEGETABLE GUMS

In its broad sense, the term gum is applied to a wide variety of materials with "gummy" characteristics. These include such hydrophobic substances as rubber, chicle for chewing gum, and rosin, as well as a large group of hydrophilic substances that are plant polysaccharides or their derivatives. It is this latter group that constitutes the vegetable gums widely used in the food industry today. The term has come to apply to all polysaccharides or their derivatives that can be dispersed in water and swell to produce gels or very viscous solutions or dispersions. Under this definition, these dispersions need not necessarily be gummy or tacky; those that are slimy or mucilaginous are also included. The important characteristics are their hydrophilic nature and ability to form dispersions of high viscosity even at low concentrations.

Certain derivatives of cellulose and starch can be classified as gums under this definition, as can pectin. In addition, a wide variety of polysaccharides of this type are obtained as plant exudates or as extracts from seaweeds or seeds. More recently, some polysaccharides prepared by the action of microorganisms have entered the picture. It is beyond the scope of this chapter to discuss this broad field of substances in any detail. Rather, an attempt will be made to point out their wide variety in chemical structure and physical characteristics, opening the way for the reader who is interested to pursue the subject further. There are many references available, including those by Whistler and Smart (1953), Whistler and BeMiller (1959) and Glicksman (1969).

Gum Arabic

Gum arabic is an exudate of several species of acacia trees in Asia and Africa, especially in the Sudan, and has been used for various purposes for at least 4000 years. It is obtained by cutting off limbs or making incisions in old, diseased, or injured trees. Healthy trees with plenty of water produce little gum. Chemically, it is a highly branched polysaccharide containing units of L-arabinose, L-rhamnose, D-galactose, and D-glucuronic acid in a structure so complex that it is not yet fully known. In fact, the suggestion has been made that it is actually not one substance but a mixture. Its ability to give solutions of high viscosity and its inability to crystallize, together with the fact that it is nontoxic, odorless, colorless, and tasteless, have led to a variety of uses in the food industry, especially in confectionery. Gum drops were originally produced from gum arabic, but are now made from thin-boiling starches or pectins. But gum arabic still finds numerous uses because of its ability to retard or prevent crystallization of sugar and to serve as an emulsifier.

Gum Tragacanth

Gum tragacanth is another exudate gum that has been used since ancient times. It is obtained from small, thorny shrubs in semidesert areas of the Near East. It, too, has a highly complex structure that has so far defied all attempts at complete analysis. It has a water-soluble fraction that has been named tragacanthin and a larger fraction, called bassorin, that remains as a swollen gel or gellike dispersion. It is used for its thickening power and its stabilizing action on suspended matter. It stabilizes emulsions over wide ranges of pH and temperature.

Gum Karaya

Gum karaya, the exudate of a tree of India, was originally introduced as an inexpensive substitute for gum tragacanth, but has found additional uses because of its own unique properties. Like the other exudate gums mentioned, it has a complex chemical structure composed of many different varieties of monosaccharide units. Although the gum can be dissolved if it is autoclaved, at normal temperatures it does not dissolve but absorbs water to swell to many times its original size. Coarse granulation produces a discontinuous, grainy dispersion, but a finely powdered gum, in spite of the individual particle swelling, yields an apparently homogeneous dispersion. It is this latter form that is used in French dressings, sherbets, cheese spreads, ground meat preparations, and as a meringue stabilizer.

Locust-Bean Gum

Locust-bean gum is the material of the white, semitransparent endosperm of the seed of the carob, a tree of the Mediterranean area. It is composed largely of a type of polysaccharide known as a galactomannan, which consists of a straight chain of D-mannose units to which single units of D-galactose are attached on approximately every fourth or fifth mannose unit. It dissolves in either hot or cold water to form a very viscous, mucilaginous solution that does not gel. It is recommended for use in the manufacture of ice cream, certain cheese products, and sausages. It also is said to have a beneficial effect on certain baked products, especially bread made from flour deficient in gluten.

Guar Gum

A recent addition to the list of gums available for food uses is guar gum, or guaran. It is a galactomannan, like locust bean gum, from which it appears to differ only in the number of galactose units attached to the chain of mannose units. In guaran, galactose units appear to be attached to about half the mannose units, possibly on alternate mannose units in the chain. It is obtained from the guar plant, which has been grown in India and Pakistan for centuries, and was introduced into the United States early in this century; but its potential as a source of a valuable gum was not recognized until the late 1940's. Its properties and usefulness in food products closely resemble those of the more expensive locust bean gum.

Agar

Agar is best known by college students because of its use in the microbiology laboratory. However, it has many other uses, including that in foods. It is extracted from seaweeds, certain red algae. Most agar originally came from Japan, where it was discovered, but some is now manufactured in other countries, including the United States. Determination of its structure has been complicated by the fact that more than one type of polysaccharide is present, but it now appears that the major constituent, called "agarose," is composed of alternating units of D-galactose and 3,6-anhydro-L-galactose (L-galactose units in which the hydroxyl groups on carbons 3 and 6 within the same unit have reacted to form an ether linkage), with sulfate groups on about every tenth D-galactose unit. Calcium and magnesium ions are associated with native agar, but can be replaced by other ions. Dry agar of high purity is practically insoluble in water at room temperature, but is slowly dissolved in boiling water. The resulting solutions gel at temperatures relatively far below those at which the gels melt. Uses in foods are related to its emulsifying, stabilizing, and gelling properties, and to the heat-resistance of its gels.

Carrageenan

A somewhat related seaweed polysaccharide is extracted from another red alga known as Irish moss, which is widely distributed along ocean shores in many parts of the world. The gum from Irish moss, carrageenan, can be separated into two parts called kappa- and lambda-carrageenans. The former can be precipitated from a dilute solution of the gum by the addition of potassium salts; the lambda-carrageenan remaining in solution is thought to be a mixture of polysaccharides. Apparently both fractions contain D-galactose units; in the kappa fraction, there are also units of 3,6-anhydro-D-galactose. In both fractions sulfate groups are attached to many of the monosaccharide units and can react with cations. It is these sulfate groups that cause its properties to be affected by cations present in a mixture and to affect, in turn, any other components, such as casein, whose properties are also related to the ionic environment. Advantage is taken of both its viscosity and its gel-forming properties in its various food applications. It is used in many dairy products, especially chocolate milk, in which it is very effective in keeping the cocoa particles in suspension. It has also found many other applications in foods.

Algin

Algin is the broad name given to various derivatives of alginic acid, the most common of which is its sodium salt. It is found in brown algae, of which one species, *Macrocystis pyrifera* or giant kelp, found in the temperate zones of the Pacific Ocean, is the principal commercial source. For many years it was thought that the repeating unit in alginic acid was entirely D-mannuronic acid, but more recently it has been found that part of the units (the percentage varying with the species of brown algae) are L-guluronic acid. Algin is soluble in either hot or cold water. The carboxyl groups of the uronic acid units cause it to be affected by the type of cations present. This effect of ions is reduced or eliminated by esterifying all or part of the carboxyl groups with propylene glycol. Thus a wide range of properties is possible. Algin has many food uses, especially in dairy products.

ANIMAL POLYSACCHARIDES

Polysaccharides occur in animal tissues in far smaller amounts than in plants. Glycogen, which has already been discussed because of its structural relation to starch, has long been recognized as the form in which the animal body stores glucose for release in response to energy demands. But only in relatively recent years has the importance of other polysaccharides in body functions been recognized. Nearly all the research on these other polysaccharides has been directed at their role in the living body rather than at their possible effects on the properties of flesh used as food. Mention of those occurring in muscle tissue is made here chiefly as a reminder that they are present and may be found, at some future time, to be of greater importance than is now recognized.

Giffee (1960) has described the ground substance in which the connective tissue proteins are imbedded as a mixture of soluble proteins and a variety of complex polysaccharides, including chondroitin sulfates and hyaluronic acid. In the formation of new fibrous tissue, deposition of chondroitin sulfate is followed by the appearance of reticulin fibers, which gradually thicken as the tissue matures. As the fibers grow, the proportion of polysaccharide decreases.

At least three chondroitin sulfates, designated A, B, and C, have been recognized. They all contain units of N-acetyl-D-galactosamine and a uronic acid; sulfate ester groups are also present. The uronic acid groups in chondroitin sulfates A and C are D-glucuronic acid; that in chondroitin sulfate B is L-iduronic acid. The arrangement of these groups in the molecule has led to many conflicting proposals, but it now appears

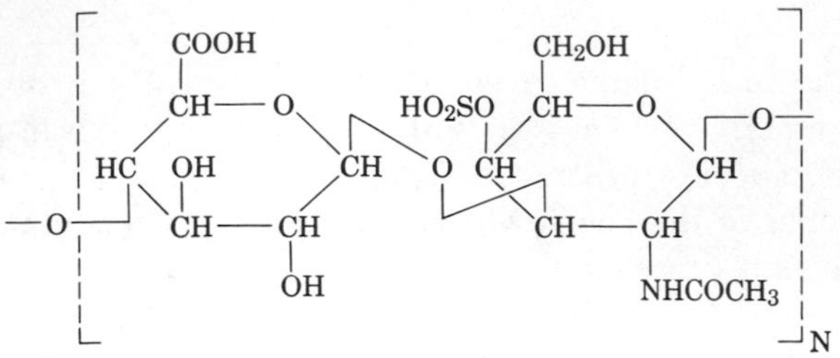

FIGURE 20.   Repeating unit of chondroitin sulfate A.

that the repeating unit in chondroitin sulfate A is as shown in Figure 20, and that for chondroitin sulfate C is the same except that the sulfate ester group occurs on carbon 6 rather than carbon 4 (White, Handler, and Smith, 1968).

Hyaluronic acid is closely related to chondroitin sulfate, being composed of equal parts of N-acetyl-D-glucosamine and D-glucuronic acid. Its structure is shown in Figure 21.

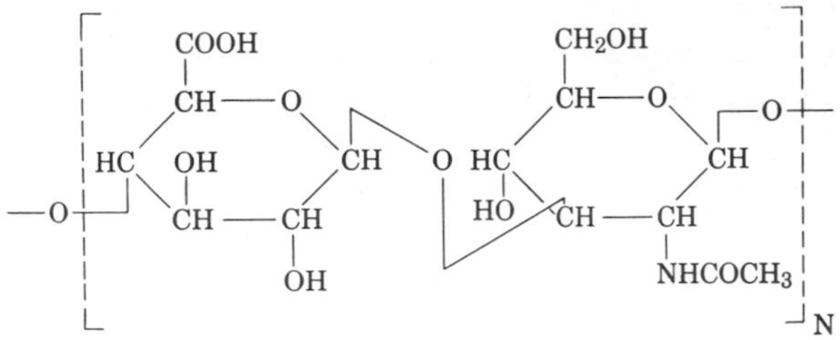

FIGURE 21.   Repeating unit of hyaluronic acid.

Many other polysaccharides have been isolated from the animal body, but none of them appear to occur in the parts of the animal used as food.

References

Akazawa, T. 1965. Starch, inulin, and other reserve polysaccharides. In *Plant Biochemistry*. J. Bonner and J. E. Varner, eds., p. 258. Academic Press, New York.

Albersheim, P. 1965. Biogenesis of the cell wall. In *Plant Biochemistry*. J. Bonner and J. E. Varner, eds., p. 298. Academic Press, New York.

Albrecht, J. J., A. I. Nelson, and M. P. Steinberg. 1960a. Characteristics of corn starch and starch derivatives as affected by freezing, thawing and storage. I. Simple systems. Food Technol. *14*: 57.

Albrecht, J. J., A. I. Nelson, and M. P. Steinberg. 1960b. Characteristics of corn starch and starch derivatives as affected by freezing, thawing and storage. II. White sauces. Food Technol. *14*: 64.

Badenhuizen, N. P. 1965. Occurrence and development of starch in plants. In *Starch: Chemistry and Technology,* Vol. I. R. L. Whistler and E. F. Paschall, eds. p. 65. Academic Press, New York.

Bean, M. L., and E. M. Osman. 1959. Behavior of starch during food preparation. II. Effects of different sugars on the viscosity and gel strength of starch pastes. Food Research *24*: 665.

Bechtel, W. G. 1959. Staling studies on bread made with flour fractions. V. Effect of a heat-stable amylase and cross-linked starch. Cereal Chem. *36*: 368.

Bender, W. A. 1959. Pectin. In *Industrial Gums.* R. L. Whistler and J. N. BeMiller, eds., p. 377. Academic Press, New York.

Brokaw, G. Y. 1962. Distilled monoglycerides for food foaming and for starch complexing. Can. Food Ind. *33*, No. 4: 36.

Campbell, A. M., and A. M. Briant. 1957. Wheat starch pastes and gels containing citric acid and sucrose. Food Research *22*: 358.

Corn Starch. 1964. Corn Industries Research Foundation, Washington, D.C.

Dawson, E. H., O. M. Batcher, and R. R. Little. 1960. Cooking quality of rice. Rice J. *65*, No. 5: 16.

Dubois, D. K. 1959. Wheat starch: a key to better cakes. Baker's Digest *33*, No. 6: 38.

Foster, J. F. 1965. Physical properties of amylose and amylopectin in solution. In *Starch: Chemistry and Technology,* Vol. I. R. L. Whistler and E. F. Paschall, eds., p. 349. Academic Press, New York.

Gates, R. L., and R. M. Sandstedt. 1953. A method of determining enzymatic digestion of raw starch. Cereal Chem. *30*: 413.

Giffee, J. W. 1960. Chemistry of animal tissues: Carbohydrates. In *The Science of Meat and Meat Products.* American Meat Institute, p. 137. W. H. Freeman and Co., San Francisco and London.

Glicksman, M. 1963. Utilization of synthetic gums in the food industry. Adv. Food Research *12*: 283.

Glicksman, M. 1969. Gum Technology in the Food Industry. Academic Press, New York.

Gracza, R. 1965. Minor constituents of starch. In *Starch: Chemistry and Technology,* Vol. I. R. L. Whistler and E. F. Paschall, eds., p. 105. Academic Press, New York.

Grant, V. M. 1968. The effects of heat treatment of milk on selected food systems. Unpublished M. S. thesis, University of Iowa.

Gray, V. M., and T. J. Schoch. 1962. Effects of surfactants and fatty adjuncts on the swelling and solubilization of granular starches. Staerke *14*: 239.

Greenwood, C. T. 1956. Aspects of the physical chemistry of starch. Adv. Carbohydrate Chem. *11*: 335.

Greminger, G. K., Jr., and A. B. Savage. 1959. Methylcellulose and its derivatives. In *Industrial Gums*. R. L. Whistler and J. N. BeMiller, eds., p. 565. Academic Press, New York.

Hanson, H. L., A. Campbell, and H. Lineweaver. 1951. Preparation of stable frozen sauces and gravies. Food Technol. 5: 432.

Hanson, H. L., K. D. Nishita, and H. Lineweaver. 1953. Preparation of stable frozen puddings. Food Technol. 7: 462.

Hester, E. E., A. M. Briant, and C. J. Personius. 1956. The effect of sucrose on the properties of some starches and flours. *Cereal Chem. 33*: 91.

Howard, N. B., D. H. Hughes, and R. G. K. Strobel. 1968. Function of the starch granule in the formation of layer cake structure. Cereal Chem. *45*: 329.

Hwang, Q.-S. 1960. A comparison of some characteristics of milk samples with their action on starch-milk pastes. Unpublished M. S. thesis, University of Illinois.

Jongh, G. 1961. The formation of dough and bread structure. I. The ability of starch to form structure, and the improving effect of glyceryl monostearate. Cereal Chem. *38*: 140.

Katz, J. R. 1938. Viscosity of starch pastes—the changes therein due to continued heating and stirring, and their relation to the sizing of cotton yarns. Textile Research 9: 69.

Kerr, R. W. 1950. *Chemistry and Industry of Starch*. Academic Press, New York.

Kerr, R. W., and F. C. Cleveland, Jr. 1959. Orthophosphate esters of starch. U.S. Patent 2,884,413; Chem. Abstr. *53*: 16569 (1959).

Kertesz, Z. I., G. L. Baker, G. H. Joseph, H. H. Mottern, and A. G. Olsen. 1944. Report of the Committee for the Revision of the Nomenclature of Pectic Substances. Chem. Eng. News *22*: 105.

Kesler, C. C., and W. G. Bechtel. 1954. Physical methods of characterizing starch. In *Starch and Its Derivatives*, 3rd ed. J. A. Radley, ed. p. 402. John Wiley & Sons, New York.

Killion, P. J., and J. F. Foster. 1960. Isolation of high molecular weight amylose by dimethylsulfoxide dispersion. J. Polymer Sci. *46*: 65.

Meyer, K. H. 1942. Recent developments in starch chemistry. In *Advances in Colloid Science*, Vol. I. E. O. Kraemer, ed., p. 143. Interscience Publishers, Inc., New York.

Meyer, K. H. 1950. *Natural and Synthetic High Polymers*, 2nd ed., p. 477. Interscience Publishers, Inc., New York.

Meyer, K. H., and P. Bernfeld. 1940. Recherches sur l'amidon. VII. Sur la structure fine du grain d'amidon et sur les phénomènes du gonflement. Helv. Chim. Acta *23*: 890.

Miller, B. S., and H. B. Trimbo. 1965. Gelatinization of starch and white layer cake quality. Food Technol. *19*: 640.

Neukom, H. 1958. Pudding mix. U.S. Patent 2,865,762; Chem. Abstr. *53*: 5538 (1959).

Neukom, H. 1959. Phosphate-modified starches. U.S. Patent 2,884,412; Chem. Abstr. *53*: 15612 (1959).

Noznick, P. P., P. P. Merritt and W. F. Geddes. 1946. Staling studies on breads containing waxy maize starch. Cereal Chem. *23*: 297.

Osman, E. M. 1967. Starch in the food industry. In *Starch: Chemistry and Technology*, Vol. II. R. L. Whistler and E. F. Paschall, eds., p. 163. Academic Press, New York.

Osman, E. M., and P. D. Cummisford. 1959. Some factors affecting the stability of frozen white sauces. Food Research *24*: 595.

Osman, E. M., and M. R. Dix. 1960. Effects of fats and nonionic surface-active agents on starch pastes. Cereal Chem. *37*: 464.

Osman, E. M., S. J. Leith, and M. Fleš. 1961. Complexes of amylose with surfactants. Cereal Chem. *38*: 449.

Osman, E. M., and G. Mootse. 1958. Behavior of starch during food preparation. I. Some properties of starch-water systems. Food Research *23*: 554.

Prentice, N., L. S. Cuendet and W. F. Geddes. 1954. Studies on bread staling. V. Effect of flour fractions and various starches on the firming of bread crumb. Cereal Chem. *31*: 188.

Rotsch, A. 1953. Uber die Bedeutung der Stärke für die Krumenbildung. Brot Gebaeck 7: 121.

Rundle, R. E., L. Daasch, and D. French. 1944. The structure of the "B" modification of starch from film and fiber diffraction diagrams. J. Amer. Chem. Soc. *66*: 130.

Rundle, R. E., J. F. Foster, and R. R. Baldwin. 1944. On the nature of the starch-iodine complex. J. Amer. Chem. Soc. *66*: 2116.

Sandstedt, R. M. 1961. The function of starch in the baking of bread. Baker's Digest *35*, No. 3: 36.

Savage, H. L. H. 1968. Effects of certain sugars and sugar alcohols on the swelling of corn starch granules. Unpublished M. S. thesis, University of Iowa.

Schoch, T. J., and D. French. 1947. Studies on bread staling. I. The role of starch. Cereal Chem. *24*: 231.

Smith, R. J. 1967. Characterization and analysis of starches. In *Starch: Chemistry and Technology*, Vol. II. R. L. Whistler and E. F. Paschall, eds., p. 569. Academic Press, New York.

Spencer, M. 1965. Fruit ripening. In *Plant Biochemistry*. J. Bonner and J. E. Varner, eds., p. 793. Academic Press, New York.

Stalder, M. J. 1961. The amylograph viscosity of starch-milk pastes: effects of source and preheating of milk. Unpublished M. S. thesis, University of Illinois.

Sterling, C. 1956. Strain retardation in starch jelly candies. Food Research *21*: 491.

Sterling, C. 1960. Crystallinity of potato starch. Staerke *12*: 182.

Sterling, C., and F. A. Bettelheim. 1955. Factors associated with potato texture. III. Physical attributes and general conclusions. Food Research *20*: 130.

Teegarden, S. M. 1961. The effects of storage time and temperature on the gel strength of cornstarch pastes. Unpublished M. S. thesis, University of Illinois, Urbana, Illinois.

Thompson, C. M. 1968. Physical properties of cornstarch paste as affected by degree of saturation of added monoglyceride. Unpublished M. S. thesis, University of Iowa.

Webb, B. D., H. M. Beachell, and J. V. Halick. 1963. Use of the amylograph test in evaluating breeding selections and new varieties of rice for specific uses. Abstr. Amer. Assoc. Cereal Chem., 48th Ann. Meeting, Minneapolis.

Whistler, R. L. 1959. Factors influencing gum costs and applications. In *Industrial Gums*, R. L. Whistler and J. N. BcMiller, eds., p. 1. Academic Press, New York.

Whistler, R. L., and J. N. BeMiller, eds. 1959. *Industrial Gums*. Academic Press, New York.

Whistler, R. L., and C. L. Smart. 1953. *Polysaccharide Chemistry*. Academic Press, New York.

White, A., P. Handler and E. Smith. 1968. *Principles of Biochemistry*. McGraw-Hill Book Co., New York.

Wivinis, G. P., and E. C. Maywald. 1967. Photographs of starches. In *Starch: Chemistry and Technology*, Vol. II. R. L. Whistler and E. F. Paschall, eds., p. 649. Academic Press, New York.

Woodruff, S., and L. Nicoli. 1931. Starch gels. Cereal Chem. *8*: 243.

Woodruff, S., and L. R. Webber. 1933. A photomicrographic study of gelatinized wheat starch. J. Agr. Research *46*: 1099.

Zobel, H. F., and F. R. Senti. 1959. The bread staling problem. X-ray diffraction studies on breads containing a cross-linked starch and a heat-stable amylase. Cereal Chem. *36*: 441.

CHAPTER 5

Fats as Cooking Media, Shortening Agents, and Components of Pastry

MARION BENNION

The principal uses of fats in food preparation are (a) to give textural qualities, including body and smooth mouth-feel, and to give flavor in the addition of fats to vegetables, as spreads on bread, and as components of mayonnaise and salad dressings; (b) to act as a medium for transferring heat in cooking foods by frying; (c) for shortening or tenderizing and/or leavening in muffins, cakes, pastries, and other baked products; and (d) as one phase of emulsions in such products as mayonnaise, gravies, and some sauces. For the first use, flavor may be a very important deciding factor in choice, along with cost. Examples are butter or bacon fat for vegetables in preference to salad oil or hydrogenated fat. For frying and shortening, the chemical and physical characteristics of the fat are important.

CLASSIFICATION OF LIPIDS

Lipids are a group of organic substances covering a wide variety of compounds that are commonly associated together on the basis of insolubility in water and solubility in fat solvents such as ether and chloroform. Lipids include liquid and solid fats, waxes, sterols, and related compounds. A generally accepted classification of lipids (Harper, 1967) is presented in Table 1. Triglycerides are quantitatively the most important constituents of natural fats.

213

TABLE 1. Classification of Lipids (Proposed by Bloor)

A. Simple lipids	Esters of fatty acids and an alcohol.
1. Fats or triglycerides	Esters of fatty acids with glycerol.
2. Waxes	Esters of fatty acids with alcohols other than glycerol.
B. Compound lipids	Esters of fatty acids and alcohols containing additional groups.
1. Phospholipids	Combination of fatty acids, glycerol, phosphoric acid, nitrogen base, and other substances. Includes lecithins, cephalins, and sphingomyelins.
2. Cerebrosides or glycolipids	Compounds of fatty acids, carbohydrate, and nitrogen base but no phosphorus.
3. Other compound lipids	Aminolipids, sulfolipids, lipoproteins, and the like.
C. Derived lipids	Products of hydrolysis of simple or compound lipids. Includes fatty acids, glycerol, and sterols.

Glycerides

Monoglycerides containing long-chain fatty acids are surface-active substances, having both polar (water-soluble) and nonpolar (fat-soluble) groups, and are important in the food industry as emulsifiers. Diglycerides are less polar and exhibit properties more like those of triglycerides.

In a simple triglyceride the three fatty acids combined in the glyceride are the same; in a mixed triglyceride more than one kind of fatty acid residue is present. Although the simple triglycerides, such as tristearin, are theoretically possible, they are not often found in appreciable amounts in natural fats. The two terminally linked fatty acids are known as α- and the center one as β-. If the two α-acids are the same the molecule is symmetrical; if different it is unsymmetrical.

Many combinations of fatty acids are possible in a triglyceride. If only four different fatty acids are present in a fat, 40 chemically distinct triglycerides are possible. Natural fats with only four fatty acids are rare. Vander Wal (1960) points out that butter has at least 28 different fatty acids, theoretically capable (with random distribution) of existing in nearly 15,000 distinct triglycerides. Usually, however, distribution of fatty acids in natural fats is not completely random. Blank and Privett (1964) found some 35 triglyceride types, of which there could be many members, in milk fat. The fatty acids appeared to be nonrandomly distributed.

The arrangement of the fatty acids on the glycerol molecule affects the performance of fats in food preparation by creating differences in crystal formation as well as melting point. The distribution of fatty acids in natural triglycerides varies widely but appears to be highly organized in most fats and oils. The effects that may be produced by differences in distribution may be illustrated by comparing cocoa butter and mutton tallow (Devine and Williams, 1961). The fatty acid composition is similar in these two fats, but the cocoa butter is hard and brittle with a relatively low and sharp melting point (30–34° C), whereas mutton tallow is plastic and greasy and melts over a wide range with a higher final melting point (45–50° C). These differences may be attributed to the fact that most of the glycerides of cocoa butter contain a molecule each of palmitic, oleic, and stearic acids with oleic acid in the β-position. In tallow the fatty acid distribution is more random and a greater variety of glycerides occurs. Changes evidently occur in cocoa butter during processing. By use of thin-layer chromatography of cocoa bean and cocoa butter lipids, Levanon et al. (1967) reported that fermentation of cocoa beans did not influence lipid content, but additional lipid fractions appeared during industrial preparation of cocoa butter.

The fatty acid composition of animal body fats is influenced to some degree by feed as well as by species of animal (Hawthorn and Leitch, 1962). Change in body fat with dietary fat is more pronounced in non-ruminant animals. Peanuts or soybeans fed to hogs produce soft fat. The iodine value of lard from lots of hogs on control and various soybean and soybean product diets varied from 63.6 to 83.4 (Lowe et al., 1938). Not only is the lard from pigs fed certain feeds soft, but the fat of the meat and bacon is also soft and oily. Chung and Lin (1965) fed peanut or hydrogenated coconut oil to pigs. They found that with the higher linoleate diet (peanut oil), more linoleic acid was deposited in all body parts, but only small proportions of lauric and myristic acids were present in body tissues even though large amounts were consumed in hydrogenated coconut oil. The dietary fatty acid changes were reflected to the greatest extent in the vital organ tissues, next in the depot fats, and least in the muscles. Lard made from outer back fat is softer, that is, has fewer saturated fatty acids and more unsaturated ones, than lard made from leaf or perinephric fat (that around the kidney). Also, outer back fat is softer than inner back fat (Hilditch and Williams, 1964).

Hilditch and Williams (1964) report comparatively slight effects on the fatty acid composition of milk fats from cows fed various fatty oils. Milk fats of cows fed high linoleate diets showed little increase in this fatty acid. Dietary triglycerides undergo a number of changes in the rumen of cows before absorption. Parry et al. (1964) fed cows 15 percent safflower oil and produced a large increase in total unsaturation of the milk fat, but most of this was due to an increase in oleic acid. Large decreases in milk production resulted with safflower oil in the diet. It does not appear to be practical to increase the proportion of polyunsaturated fatty acids in milk fat by changing the diet of the cow.

In early studies Cruikshank (1934) found that the extent of unsaturation of the fat of chicken was influenced readily by the fat in the feed. The unsaturated dietary fat also had a marked effect on increasing the unsaturation of the lipids in eggs from these hens. Later studies by several workers (Feigenbaum and Fisher, 1959; Fisher and Leveille, 1957; and Wheeler et al., 1959) have demonstrated an increase in linoleic acid content of egg lipids with the feeding of unsaturated oils. However, Brown and Page (1965) reported that eggs with increased amounts of polyunsaturated fatty acids had no advantage over ordinary eggs in a diet designed to reduce serum cholesterol levels in humans.

The pure triglycerides, except those containing shorter chain acids than caprylic, are devoid of odor and taste. Deodorization during processing of crude fats and oils removes the relatively volatile compounds chiefly responsible for undesirable odors and flavors.

Fatty Acids

In nature a very wide range of fatty acids may be incorporated into triglyceride molecules. Some fatty acids that occur naturally in only small quantities may be produced in larger amounts during processing procedures such as hydrogenation of liquid fats. Examples would include production of fatty acids in which the usual *cis* configuration around a double bond has been changed to *trans* and production of "isoacids" by the shifting of a double bond from its original to another position (Jones et al., 1965). Hilditch and Williams (1964) point out that oleic acid is the most widespread of all natural fatty acids, occurring at levels greater than 30 percent in many fats and being found in all natural fats thus far studied (1964). With the exception of isovaleric acid (found in fats of the dolphin and porpoise) and sterculic and malvalic acids (found in a few seed fats), all fatty acids present in natural fats in more than trace amounts contain even numbers and unbranched chains of carbon atoms. Traces of some odd-numbered and branched-chain acids have been found in animal fats (Hilditch and Williams, 1964).

Hilditch and Williams (1964) list more than 50 "chief acids found, as major and minor components, in natural fats" and adds that the list is not complete. A major component acid is defined as one composing from about 10 percent upwards of the total fatty acids combined in a fat. Some fatty acids are found only in traces; some are found in very large quantity in only one source. Many natural fats contain 5, 6, or 7 acids in major and minor proportions; milk fat and fish oils may contain 12 to 15 such fatty acids. Additional acids are present in trace amounts. Some fatty acids, such as lauric (forming a large proportion of the fat of the laurel kernel) and myristic (sometimes forming as high as 75 percent of the Myristicacea, nutmeg family), have been given popular names that designate their source as a major component. When one saturated acid is present in fairly large amounts, subsidiary portions of the saturated acids next higher and lower in the homologous series are often observed also (Hilditch and Williams, 1964).

Saturated Acids

Saturated fatty acids have the general formula $C_nH_{2n}O_2$ or $C_nH_{2n+1}COOH$. Some of the more important saturated fatty acids are listed in Table 2. Butyric, caproic, caprylic, and capric are found in milk fat (Hilditch and Williams, 1964). Lauric and myristic acids are major constituents of coconut and palm kernel oils (Devine and Williams, 1961). Of the saturated acids, Hilditch and Williams (1964) state that palmitic is undoubtedly the characteristic member of the group. It may constitute 15–50 percent of the total fatty acids of many fats and is completely absent from few, if any, of the natural fats. Stearic acid is abundant in ox and sheep depot fats. Arachidic, behenic, and lignoceric acids are found in small amounts in Leguminosae seed fats.

Unsaturated Acids

The general formula $C_nH_{2n-1}COOH$ describes the monoethenoid acids, of which oleic is representative. Palmitoleic acid is another member of this group. The diethenoid acid, linoleic ($C_nH_{2n-3}COOH$), is nearly as widespread as oleic but occurs in smaller quantity in many fats. Cottonseed, corn, soybean, and safflower oils are common exceptions to this, however, with the linoleic acid content being considerably higher than oleic (Iverson, 1965). Linolenic acid, with the general formula $C_nH_{2n-5}COOH$, is the most usual form of triethenoid C_{18} acid found in seed fats (Hilditch and Williams). It makes up 50 percent of the total fatty acids of linseed oil. Several unsaturated fatty acids are listed in Table 2.

PHYSICAL AND CHEMICAL PROPERTIES

Solubility

Fats are insoluble in water and only slightly soluble in lower alcohols. They are readily soluble in ether, chloroform, benzene, and carbon tetrachloride. Solvent extraction, utilizing the solubility of fats in certain

TABLE 2. Common Fatty Acids

Common Name	Systematic Name	Structural Formula
	Saturated Acids	
Butyric	n-Butanoic	$CH_3(CH_2)_2COOH$
Isovaleric	3-Methyl-n-Butanoic	$(CH_3)_2CH\ CH_2COOH$
Caproic	n-Hexanoic	$CH_3(CH_2)_4COOH$
Caprylic	n-Octanoic	$CH_3(CH_2)_6COOH$
Capric	n-Decanoic	$CH_3(CH_2)_8COOH$
Lauric	n-Dodecanoic	$CH_3(CH_2)_{10}COOH$
Myristic	n-Tetradecanoic	$CH_3(CH_2)_{12}COOH$
Palmitic	n-Hexadecanoic	$CH_3(CH_2)_{14}COOH$
Stearic	n-Octadecanoic	$CH_3(CH_2)_{16}COOH$
Arachidic	n-Eicosanoic	$CH_3(CH_2)_{18}COOH$
Behenic	n-Docosanoic	$CH_3(CH_2)_{20}COOH$
Lignoceric	n-Tetracosanoic	$CH_3(CH_2)_{22}COOH$
	Unsaturated Acids	
Palmitoleic	Hexadec-9-enoic	$CH_3(CH_2)_5CH:CH(CH_2)_7COOH$
Oleic	Octadec-9-enoic	$CH_3(CH_2)_7CH:CH(CH_2)_7COOH$
Linoleic	Octadeca-9,12-dienoic	$CH_3(CH_2)_4CH:CH\ CH_2CH:CH(CH_2)_7COOH$
Linolenic	Octadeca-9,12,15-trienoic	$CH_3CH_2CH:CHCH_2CH:CHCH_2CH:CH(CH_2)_7COOH$
Arachidonic	Eicosa-5,8,11,14-tetraenoic	$CH_3(CH_2)_4CH:CHCH_2CH:CHCH_2CH:CHCH_2CH:CH(CH_2)_3COOH$

solvents, has found increasing application in their commercial production (Kirschenbauer, 1960). The insolubility of fats in water is the basis for the ability of liquid fats to form emulsions with water. Fats and oils have a greasy feel and produce characteristic transparent spots on paper.

Specific Gravity

The specific gravity of fats varies with molecular weight and degree of unsaturation. All the naturally occurring fats have a specific gravity of less than 1.0. The average specific gravity of some edible fats at $25°/25°$ C is tabulated (Mehlenbacher, 1960) below.

Fat	Specific Gravity
Corn oil	0.915–0.920
Cottonseed oil	0.916–0.918
Peanut oil	0.910–0.915
Lard	0.908–0.913
Beef tallow	0.903–0.907

Melting and Solidification Points

Since food fats do not consist of single constituents but are complex mixtures of different triglycerides, they do not have sharp melting points, but melt gradually over a temperature range. Also, the solidifying point of a fat is lower than the melting point, the difference in the two often being great. A sample of butter melted at $34.5°$ C but congealed at $22.7°$ C. This difference corresponds to the period of gradual softening occurring during the phase transition from a solid fat to a liquid oil (Mehlenbacher, 1960). When melted fats are added to a batter or other product, they do not solidify as rapidly as they would if the melting and solidification points were the same.

The melting point of a triglyceride is influenced by the kinds of fatty acid radicals in the molecule, particularly with respect to the degree of unsaturation and the length of the carbon chain of the fatty acid. Fats containing more unsaturated-component fatty acids, such as corn oil, tend to have lower melting points; those with more short-chain saturated acids, such as coconut oil, usually have intermediate melting points; and those with more long-chain saturated fatty acids, such as mutton tallow, usually have higher melting points. The chief distinction between fats and oils, as these terms are commonly used, is that at ordinary temperatures, $18–24°$ C, the fats are solid and the oils are liquid.

Hydrogenation

Hydrogenation is the process by which hydrogen, in the presence of a suitable catalyst such as finely divided nickel, is added to unsaturated carbon bonds of fats. This processing may be used to achieve a variety of results, depending on the conditions of operation used (Hoerr, 1967). The melting point of the fat is raised by hydrogenation. New fatty acid components, not in the original mixture, may be produced. Transisomerization at some of the double bonds produces higher melting compounds. For example, the elaidic acid isomer may be produced from oleic acid. Also, depending on operating conditions, some migration of double bonds occurs, producing a greater diversity of molecular types. This may influence the crystal formation and plasticity in addition to the hardening effect of a lower iodine value.

The hydrogenated vegetable oil shortenings commonly used throughout the United States are not completely hydrogenated. A completely hydrogenated fat is very hard and brittle, like china. Regular hydrogenated shortenings may contain 22–50 percent saturated, 45–75 percent monounsaturated, and 6–15 percent polyunsaturated (two or more double bonds) fatty acids. "Special" shortenings, having the appearance of regular hydrogenated shortenings, may contain 22–48 percent polyunsaturated, with 20–33 percent saturated and 27–55 percent monounsaturated fatty acids (Special Shortenings, 1964).

Crystal Formation and Polymorphism

There is a relationship between chemical composition and physical structure and between physical structure and performance of fats in food preparation. Hoerr (1967) suggests that as we learn more about these relationships we will be able more effectively to produce fats with special properties tailored for specific uses in food preparation. Fats can solidify in more than one crystal form; they are polymorphic. Each crystal form has its own melting point, crystal structure, and solubility (American Meat Institute, 1960). At least three crystal forms seem to exist in most triglycerides. The form with the highest melting point is usually designated as β, that of the lowest melting point as α, and that in between as β′. The numbers I, II, III, and so on are also used to designate the various forms. Through the use of X-ray diffraction, Wille and Lutton (1966) identified six polymorphic forms of cocoa butter, with two of these being fleeting and not readily characterized. They point out that the normal state of cocoa butter in chocolate is apparently V, a β-phase. When chocolate is stored at temperatures of 70–80° F, bloom (a white or gray overall appearance) often develops. Samples with bloom were state VI, whereas bright samples were V. The authors emphasize, however, that it is not known at present whether the change from V to VI is the cause of bloom or just coincidental. Normal procedure in handling chocolate involves tempering or holding the melted chocolate product at a high enough temperature (about 90 ° F) to destroy all low-melting polymorphs, coating centers with the chocolate, and then chilling rapidly to solidify the coating. A relatively stable crystal form is produced by this procedure.

If triglyceride molecules are all very much alike, they can pack themselves closely in a crystal lattice and may easily change from lower-melting to higher-melting polymorphic forms. A mixture of many different triglyceride molecules cannot pack together as closely, and transformation to higher-melting forms is impeded. Ordinary lard contains a limited number of different triglycerides and has three or four different crystal states. It forms relatively large, high-melting crystals that may be used to good advantage in flaky pastry but that do not cream well. A shortening with small, lower-melting crystals, due to a greater variety of triglycerides in the mixture, may be more desirable for a shortened cake (Hoerr, 1967). Fats that are cooled relatively rapidly, with agitation, tend to form smaller crystals and give a smooth appearance, whereas larger crystals are formed with slow cooling at higher temperatures.

Rearranged or catalytically interesterified lard is prepared by redistributing the fatty acid radicals among the triglyceride molecules in a more random fashion. The crystals in this lard are smaller and have creaming properties comparable to good-quality hydrogenated shortening. Interesterification may be carried out at a lower temperature and directed toward the production of more trisaturated glycerides, since some will crystallize out at lower temperatures, thus changing the equilibrium of the reaction mixture and causing even more trisaturated molecules to be formed and crystallize. According to Braun (1960), this process results in a better plastic range because of lesser amounts of disaturated monounsaturated glycerides. Interesterification has also been used on mixtures of nonhydrogenated vegetable oils with small amounts of highly hydrogenated fats. This gives firmness to the blend and yet preserves linoleic acid content. As a result of experiments with rats, Alfin-Slater et al. (1966) concluded that these interesterified fats are at least equal nutritionally to other similar edible fats of equivalent essential fatty acid content.

Iodine Value

The iodine value or number is the number of grams of iodine absorbed by 100 grams of fat or other substance. The iodine, or other halogen, is added to the unsaturated bonds. Jamieson (1943) states that the iodine number of a fat may indicate the class to which it belongs. The nondrying oils have iodine values below 100; they include avocado, almond, cocoa butter, castor, olive, palm, coconut, and peanut. The semidrying oils have iodine values between 100 and 130; they include corn, cottonseed, sesame, wheat, oat, rice, rye, and many others. The drying oils, which include linseed and soybean, have iodine values above 130. Butterfat has an iodine value of 30–40, lard of 63–69, and vegetable-fat shortenings of 70–81 (Technical Committee, 1959). Solid "special" shortenings, containing larger amounts of polyunsaturated fatty acids, may have iodine values of 85–115 (Special Shortenings, 1964).

Refractive Index

The refractive index is the degree of deflection caused in a ray of light in passing from one transparent medium to another. The refractive index of fats is related to molecular structure and unsaturation. However, for the same type of oil, variations due to unsaturation are greater than variations from all other causes (Mehlenbacher, 1960). Since the determination can be made easily and rapidly, the refractive index is a convenient means of determining the extent of hydrogenation of fats during the hydrogenation process.

Acidity

Uncombined or free fatty acids may occur in fats. Triglycerides may be hydrolyzed by lipase or free fatty acids may be produced during the heating of fats in such processes as frying. The amount of free fatty acid may be expressed as a percentage (calculated as oleic) or as an acid value. The acid value is defined as the number of milligrams of KOH required to neutralize the free fatty acids in one gram of fat.

Smoking Temperature

When fats are heated to high temperatures, some decomposition occurs and eventually a point is reached at which visible fumes are given off. This is the smoke point. It is defined as the lowest temperature at which the volatile gaseous products of decomposition are being evolved at sufficient rate to be visible (Mehlenbacher, 1960). Definite conditions of sample size, surface area, degree of illumination, rate of heating, and the like are specified in the official procedure of the American Oil Chemists' Society for determination of smoke point. Fats vary in the temperature at which smoking begins. Those that smoke at low temperatures are not pleasant to use for frying because of the odor and irritating effect of the fumes. The decomposition products may also give an unpleasant flavor to the food. Hence it is preferable to use fats with relatively high smoking temperatures for frying.

One of the changes occurring when fats are heated at high temperatures is a hydrolysis of some triglyceride molecules to produce free fatty acids and glycerol. The glycerol may then be decomposed, losing two molecules of water and forming acrolein. Acrolein, which is volatile at these high temperatures, is an aldehyde that has a sharp odor and is irritating to mucous membranes of the nose and throat and to the eyes.

Smoking temperatures and free fatty acid percentages of several fats are presented in Table 3. In an early study, Blunt and Feeney (1915)

TABLE 3.   Smoking Temperatures and Percent Free Fatty Acids of Some Edible Fats (Bennion and Hanning, 1956)

Kind of Fat	Smoke Point (° C)	Free Fatty Acid, as Oleic (Percent)
Steam rendered lard	189	0.33
Continuous process lard	215	0.11
Cottonseed oil	229	0.11
Peanut oil	230	0.12
Combination shortening I[a]	191	0.13
Combination shortening II[a]	177	0.03

[a] Contained rearranged lard plus vegetable fats and mono- and diglycerides.

pointed out an inverse relationship between free fatty acid content and smoke point, lower smoke points being associated with higher acidity. Others (Lantz and Carlin, 1938; Lowe et al., 1940; and Morgan, 1942) have reported similar relationships, although smoke points are influenced by additional factors as well. These include the presence of mono- and diglycerides and of small particles such as flour, which decrease smoke points. When fats are heated in containers so shaped to produce a comparatively large surface area, the smoke points will also be lowered.

RANCIDITY

The term rancidity is often used in a general sense to designate the development of any disagreeable odor and flavor in fats and oils or fatty phases of foods. The term may be applied differently in the fat and dairy industries to refer to spoilage or deterioration brought about in a particular manner. Here, "rancidity" includes off-flavors and odors in fats produced through specified chemical reactions such as oxidation and hydrolysis.

Rancidity is detected organoleptically as readily as by chemical and physical tests, for no tests have been devised that are sensitive enough to follow the development of rancidity in its very early stages. All standards used for the detection of rancidity are ultimately related to smell and taste. Hence scientific investigation of rancidity meets many problems.

Prevention of rancidity is an important consideration in the processing, preparation, and storage of many foods. Any product that contains fat, even in small amounts, may be susceptible to spoilage of this type. Foods that may be particularly involved include crackers, cookies, breakfast cereals, confectionery products, butter, cheese, whole dried milk and eggs, solid and liquid fats, salad dressings, nuts, potato chips, meats— especially when cured—fish, frozen prepared products, dried vegetables, and even some frozen vegetables. Although the fat content of most vegetables is very low, it may be a source of off-flavors in dried and frozen forms.

Lea (1939) has listed four types of rancidity in fats as changes caused by (a) absorption of odors, (b) action of microorganisms, (c) action of enzymes, and (d) atmospheric oxidation. The first three are designated as the lesser causes of rancidity. Lipids of milk may undergo deterioration by development of (a) rancidity caused by hydrolysis of triglycerides with lipases and (b) oxidized flavor from autoxidation (Webb and Johnson, 1965). Autoxidation of milk lipids is much like that of lipids in other food products but may be complicated by the complex composition of dairy products as well as processing and manufacturing procedures.

Oxidative types of rancidity seem to create the most problems in the deterioration of lipid materials in food products. These types have been grouped by Lundberg (1962) as (a) common oxidative rancidity, typically occurring in fats used as shortening; (b) flavor reversion, resulting from combination with less oxygen than in common oxidative rancidity; (c) enzymatic oxidations, such as by action of lipoxidase; and (d) oxidized flavors in milk and milk products, which process appears to be different enough to warrant separate categorization.

Hydrolytic Rancidity

Lipases may attack fats directly, producing free fatty acids and glycerol. The flavors developed by lipase action depend on the composition of the fat. Hydrolytic rancidity is particularly important in butter and products containing milk fat because hydrolysis releases short-chain fatty acids such as butyric, caproic, and capric, resulting in particularly disagreeable flavors and odors. The short-chain fatty acids are volatile at room temperature. Some of these acids may be detectable by smell and taste even when present in very small amounts. Although hydrolysis may produce long-chain free fatty acids, these do not usually contribute substantially to off-flavors unless oxidation also occurs. Free fatty acids may act as a type of catalyst for oxidative changes. Since lipase is destroyed by heat, hydrolytic rancidity is most commonly encountered in products that are not heated in processing to a temperature high enough to destroy the enzyme.

Soapy Flavors

Soaps and glycerol are formed when fat is saponified. Usually this occurs at high temperatures. For example, baking powder biscuits containing an excessive amount of soda may have a soapy flavor. However, over a long period of time, as in the storage of dry flour mixes, some fats will react with $NaHCO_3$ to form soaps at low temperatures. A soapy flavor in some foods of high fat content may be attributed to the formation of ammonium soaps, the NH_3 for the reaction being derived from protein in the product.

Oxidative Rancidity

Autoxidation or the development of oxidative rancidity in fats involves the spontaneous taking up of oxygen by unsaturated fatty acid components. The rate at which oxidation occurs varies with the fat and the conditions of storage. In most countries oxidative rancidity is considered undesirable from an esthetic point of view, but this preference is probably a cultivated one. In some parts of the world where refrigeration is still uncommon, a product may be considered suspect if it does not have a rancid flavor. A second reason why oxidative rancidity may be undesirable concerns possible harmful effects of eating oxidized fats. Very highly oxidized products have produced some toxic effects in animals, but more research is needed to clearly assess the nutritional effects of mildly oxidized fats. Oxidized fats cause some destruction of certain fat-soluble vitamins and carotene and possibly other nutrients in the diet (Lundberg, 1962). The average American diet probably does not contain sufficient rancid fat to seriously interfere with availability of vitamins, however.

Mechanism of Autoxidation

The autoxidation of food fats is autocatalytic; the reactions proceed at an accelerating rate as oxidation progresses. The period of time before the uptake of oxygen becomes appreciable and before off-odors become detectable is known as the induction period. During this period oxidation evidently takes place very slowly and products of oxidation accumulate gradually to the point where they can be organoleptically detected. Once the induction period is over, oxidation occurs with increasing rapidity. The length of the induction period varies for different fats and oils and for different samples of the same fat. It is probably related to most of the factors that influence the rate of the reaction, in general. The end of the induction period is not sharply defined for all fats.

Various mechanisms have been proposed over the years for the addition of oxygen to fats in the primary reaction of oxidative rancidity. The hydroperoxide hypothesis of autoxidation is the most favored mode of oxidation at the present time. Purified hydroperoxides from autoxidized fats have been isolated. These do not have unpleasant odors and flavors. A large number of secondary reactions also occur in the oxidative deterioration of lipids. The rancid flavors and odors evidently come from the many substances produced at this stage. Much more research is needed to clarify these secondary reactions.

A free-radical chain mechanism has been proposed for hydroperoxide formation (Schultz, 1962). It involves an initiation reaction to produce free radicals, and propagation reactions. If the reaction is to be terminated stable, nonradical products must be formed.

Initiation:

$$\text{RH (organic substance)} \xrightarrow{\text{activation}} \text{R} \cdot \text{ (free radical)} + \text{(H)}$$

Propagation:

$$\text{R} \cdot + \text{O}_2 \longrightarrow \text{RO}_2 \cdot$$
$$\text{RO}_2 \cdot + \text{RH} \longrightarrow \text{R} \cdot + \text{ROOH}$$

Termination:

$$\text{RO}_2 \cdot + \text{X (free radical or}$$
$$\text{free radical inhibitor)} \longrightarrow \text{inactive end products or}$$

In monounsaturated fatty acids the reaction is initiated by the removal of a hydrogen atom from the carbon atom adjacent to a double-bonded carbon. Oxygen is added to the resulting free radical. This in turn may react with another unsaturated fatty acid to form a hydroperoxide and propagate the chain reaction.

$$-\text{CH}_2-\text{CH}=\text{CH}- \xrightarrow{-\text{H}} -\text{CH} \cdot -\text{CH}=\text{CH}- \xrightarrow{+\text{O}_2} -\text{CH(OO}\cdot)-\text{CH}=\text{CH}-$$

$$\xrightarrow{+(-\text{CH}_2-\text{CH}=\text{CH}-)} -\text{CH(OOH)}-\text{CH}=\text{CH}- \quad + \quad -\text{CH}\cdot-\text{CH}=\text{CH}-$$

The rate of oxidation of nonconjugated polyunsaturated fatty acid components is much higher than that of monoethenoic systems because of the activation of a methylene group by two adjacent double bonds (Lundberg, 1962). After the abstraction of a hydrogen atom from the carbon between the double-bonded carbons of linoleic acid, resonance may cause the double bonds to shift, creating three possible free radicals to which oxygen may be added to form hydroperoxides.

(a)   —CH=CH—CH· —CH=CH—

(b)   —CH=CH—CH=CH—CH·—

(c)   —CH·—CH=CH—CH=CH—

The mechanism of the initiation reaction in lipid oxidation is not well understood. Hydroperoxide decomposition, and presence of other pro-oxidants, as heavy metals, have been thought to have an influence. Privett and Blank (1962) suggest that the autoxidation of polyunsaturated lipids is initiated by a discrete reaction occurring prior to the formation of stable hydroperoxides. This reaction did not necessarily involve metals and it was not inhibited by α-tocopherol.

Secondary reaction products in oxidizing fats include many carbonyl compounds, acids, and other substances evidently formed through decomposition and further oxidation of the hydroperoxides (Lundberg, 1962). Many of these products are of low molecular weight and appear to contribute to the off-flavors and odors. Classes of monocarbonyls that included alkanals, alk-2-enals, and alk-2,4-dienals were found by Gaddis et al. (1966) in autoxidized lard.

Tests for Stability

The most important cause of spoilage of food fats involves the development of oxidative rancidity. It has been customary to refer to the first products formed in this decomposition as peroxides, but this term may include any primary decomposition products. Mehlenbacher (1960) cites two criteria necessary in the overall evaluation of the stability of a fat: (a) a test to indicate the condition of the fat at the time of examination and (b) a test to indicate the length of time that the fat may be expected to resist oxidation. Tests to evaluate the present condition of a fat involve the quantitative measurement of one or more of the products of oxidation such as peroxides, aldehydes, or ketones. One such test determines the peroxide value expressed as milliequivalents of reactive oxygen per 1000 grams of fat or as millimoles of peroxide per kilogram of fat (1 millimole = 2 milliequivalents). The Kreis test was used in commercial practice for some time. It evidently measures certain aldehydes. The thiobarbituric acid (TBA) test involves measurement of the red color produced by the reaction of 2-thiobarbituric acid with malonaldehyde in the oxidizing fat (Yu and Sinnhuber, 1964). Pohle et al. (1964) studied the relationship of peroxide value and TBA value to the development of undesirable flavor in fats. Their data indicated that the flavor score cannot be estimated for any given fat from either the peroxide value or the TBA value. Either test could be used to follow the development of off-flavors in any one product, but the values may be different from one product to another.

Methods to indicate the length of time the fat may be expected to remain stable are based on accelerating oxidation usually with the use of heat, with or without the presence of excess air or oxygen. Some measure of degree of oxidation, such as peroxide value, may be made at intervals, or organoleptic evaluation of the odor may indicate the endpoint. Tests of this type include the active oxygen method (heating with aerating), the Schaal or oven test method (holding at 70° C), and oxygen absorption methods using an ASTM oxygen bomb (absorption of oxygen by sample in the bomb) (Mehlenbacher, 1960). Pohle et al. (1964) compared the results of various stability tests with data from a storage test at 85° F evaluated organoleptically at intervals for development of rancidity. Since the various fats studied behaved differently, they concluded that the laboratory tests could not be used as an index of shelf stability except for a given type of fat for which the relationship between the laboratory test and shelf stability was already known. Laboratory tests would need to be used carefully in quality-control programs.

Factors Affecting Lipid Oxidation

Autoxidation may be easily influenced by several different factors. The structure of the fatty acids in a glyceride affects the rate of oxidation, fats containing more polyunsaturated fatty aeids being more susceptible. Raghuveer and Hammond (1967) reported a decrease in the rate of autoxidation of mixtures of triunsaturated glycerides and tridecanoin by interesterification which gave a more random distribution of fatty acids. They theorized that the concentration of the unsaturated fatty acids on the 2-position of glycerol stabilized a fat toward autoxidation. However, the work of Zalewski and Gaddis (1967) showed that transesterification of lard did not affect its resistance to oxidation. They suggested that decreases in stability were due to decomposition of tocopherol in air, and small increases were probably due to formation of reducing substances.

Traces of heavy metals, such as Cu, Fe, and Co, may be active as prooxidants, reducing the length of the induction period. The metal catalysts seem to increase the rate of formation of free radicals (Schultz, 1962). Food lipids usually contain trace amounts of metals, and it may be very difficult to remove them completely. Some fats contain an aqueous phase with nonfatty materials. Lea (1939) found that metallic salts dissolved in this aqueous phase affected the rate of oxidation. Copper was 20 times more active than iron.

Hematin compounds are powerful catalysts affecting oxidation. Hematin-catalyzed oxidative rancidity is important in the deterioration of cooked meats (Younathan and Watts, 1959), where it seems to be confined to muscle lipids.

Light accelerates the development of rancidity in fats. Ultraviolet and short-wave visible light (blues) are the most harmful in accelerating rancidity. They probably function mainly by photolysis of peroxides to free radicals (Schultz, 1962). Ionizing radiations are also potent accelerators of fat oxidation.

Moisture content may influence the oxidative susceptibility differently in various foods. The low moisture content of cereals (Elder, 1941) to keep them crisp seems to favor rancidity development. On the other hand, dried whole egg, egg yolk, and milk keep better with a low moisture content, two percent or less.

Common salt shows an oxidation accelerating effect in some foods, evidently depending on the free moisture in the system (Schultz, 1962). In cured salted meats the catalysis may be substantial. Apparently the effect is due to an activating influence on prooxidants already present rather than a direct effect (Mabrouk and Dugan, 1960).

Flavor Reversion

The term flavor reversion apparently originated from observations of processed marine oils developing or "reverting" to a fishlike flavor during subsequent storage (Daubert and O'Connell, 1953). The term is a misnomer when applied to other oils, such as refined soybean, since these develop off-flavors different from those in the original crude oil. In other words, they do not "revert." The name, however, has been rather firmly established in use. Flavor reversion in edible fats may be defined as flavor deterioration occurring with less oxidation than is required to produce oxidative rancidity or as spontaneous change characterized by the appearance in the refined product of an objectionable flavor prior to the onset of typical rancidity. Fats containing fatty acids with three or more double bonds, such as soybean and linseed oils and various fish oils, are particularly susceptible. Buttery, beany, grassy, painty, and fishy are terms used to describe flavors of reverted soybean oil. Soybean oil is used in large quantities in the United States as refined oil and in the manufacture of margarines and shortenings. Soybean oil shortenings are also susceptible to reversion. Daubert and O'Connell (1953) report that if the proportion of soybean oil in shortenings and margarines is below 25–35 percent, detectable reversion ordinarily does not occur. The initial quality of the soybean oil has an important effect on its stability when made into shortening. There is less reversion with some than with other oils. Linolenic acid and its derivatives are generally recognized as the most important precursors of reversion flavors (Lundberg, 1962).

Methods developed for reducing the flavor reversion of soybean oil include (a) separating into high-iodine number and low-iodine number fractions; (b) inactivation of metallic impurities; (c) selective hydrogenation; and (d) controlled deodorization procedures (Lundberg, 1962). Reduced contact with air and light in processing, and storage in dark bottles, also have a protective effect.

Enzymatic Oxidations

Lipoxidase activity is the most extensively studied enzymatic oxidation. This enzyme catalyzes the peroxidation of unsaturated fatty acids with the *cis-cis* 1,4-pentadiene system, such as linoleic, linolenic, and arachidonic acids. The hydroperoxides formed in this reaction show optical activity, indicating that the enzyme participates in the formation of each hydroperoxide. It does not appear to be a chain reaction in the same sense as autoxidation. The enzyme responsible for the deterioration of frozen peas during storage of the unblanched product appears to be lipoxidase (Lundberg, 1961).

Antioxidants

An inhibitor of autoxidation of a fat is known as an antioxidant, and an accelerator as a prooxidant. Fats always contain at least traces of various substances, some of which may act as antioxidants. Antioxidants present in small quantities are able to prevent or greatly retard the oxidation of fats by inhibiting the chain reaction of autoxidation. Antioxidants may be divided broadly into two groups—primary antioxidants and synergists. The primary antioxidants operate directly to inhibit autoxidation, possibly by donating a hydrogen to the oxidizing fatty acid free radical, thus breaking the chain reaction. Most of the primary antioxidants commonly used in foods are *ortho* and *para* di- and polyphenolic compounds (Lundberg, 1962). They are effective at extremely low levels. At high levels they may accelerate oxidation. For this reason Chipault (Lundberg, 1962) suggests that they are most effective in animal fats containing little natural stabilizer and less effective in vegetable oils that may already contain optimum amounts of naturally occurring antioxidants, such as tocopherols. Most primary antioxidants are inactivated during the baking or frying of foods. The addition of branched groups, as tertiary butyl radicals, in positions next to hydroxyl groups retards destruction by high temperatures and improves "carry-through" antioxidant properties in cooked foods. Butylated hydroxyanisole has been found to have some carry-through effect in fried foods (Kraybill et al., 1949).

Phenolic antioxidants used in foods include the following:

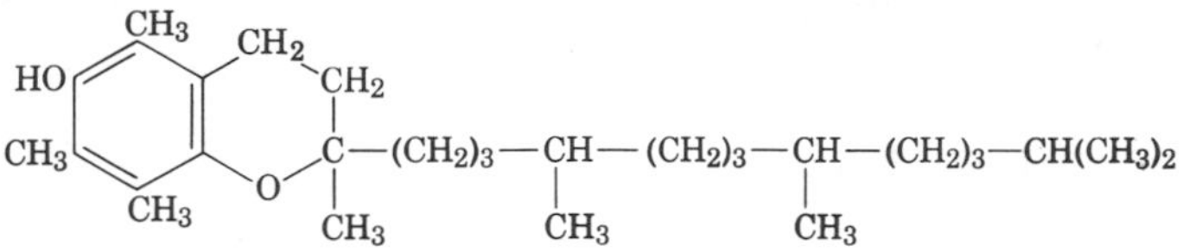

α-tocopherol

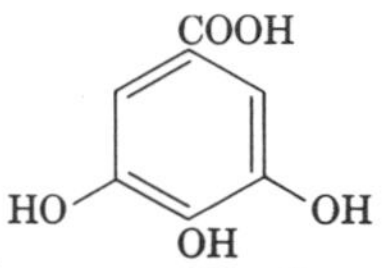

gallic acid

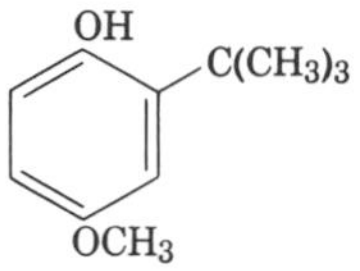

3-butylated hydroxyanisole (BHA)

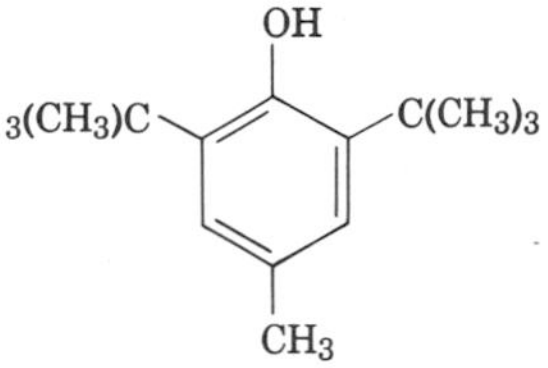

butylated hydroxytoluene (BHT)

Synergists are compounds that by themselves have little effect on the oxidation of fat but that enhance or prolong the antioxidant action of primary antioxidants. They may be organic or inorganic compounds and usually are acidic in character. Synergists include phosphoric, citric, and sulfuric acids, ascorbic acid, lecithin, and some amino acids. They may act by regenerating primary antioxidants, by binding prooxidant metallic ions, or by inhibiting decomposition of hydroperoxides (Lundberg, 1962).

The ingredients combined with fat in baked goods and other products may have anti- or prooxidative action. The protective or adverse action may vary under different conditions. Spices (Chipault et al., 1952) exhibit antioxidant properties, those of rosemary and sage being pronounced. Lecithin and flours such as soy, oat, corn, and unbleached wheat flour possess some antioxidant properties, but they are far from ideal antioxidants. Desirable qualities of food antioxidants include (a) effectiveness in low concentrations; (b) easy incorporation; (c) non-toxicity; (d) contribution of no objectionable flavor, odor, or color; (e) carry-through properties; (f) ready availability; and (g) reasonable cost.

A mixture of antioxidants and synergists is usually used in food products. The mixture gives greater potency with smaller total quantity of antioxidant. Better antioxidant systems are still needed. Thompson and Sherwin (1966) investigated the activity of several antioxidants, both approved and at present unapproved for food use, in stabilizing unsaturated vegetable oils. They found several experimental stabilizers with high-potency antioxidant activity for which further evaluation appeared to be desirable.

CHANGES IN FATS DURING HEATING

Most fats appear to withstand normal cooking conditions and temperatures without major objectionable changes. If fats are abused in use under conditions of continued high temperatures, there may be undesirable changes in flavor, odor, and nutritional value, however.

Changes During Cooking

Several studies have indicated that changes occurring in fats during ordinary baking of various flour mixtures are negligible. In an early study Masters and Smith (1914) reported that the changes occurring in the fat of cooked pastry were slight, unless the pastry was very thin or overcooked. Chang et al. (1952) used lard, the least stable of the plastic fats, in biscuits, pastry, and gingersnaps. The fatty acid content of these baked products did not differ significantly from that of the fat in the dough. A number of commercial mixes for baked products were analyzed for their fat content and their fatty acid composition by Ostwald (1963). A few representative cake mixes were baked and the finished cakes also analyzed. Baking did not appreciably affect the fatty acid composition.

Phillips and Vail (1967) were interested in the effect of baking on the fatty acid composition of products containing corn oil or a corn oil margarine, as well as products containing hydrogenated vegetable shortening. They investigated the effect of oven heat on the fatty acid composition of pastry wafers, biscuits, sugar cookies, plain cake, and chocolate cake when the three different shortenings were used. They reported no important changes in degree of unsaturation during baking. The ratio of linoleic acid to all other fatty acids showed a very small decrease in pastry and biscuits made with corn oil.

Warner et al. (1962) studied the nutritional value of fats in well-done cuts of meat. They reported that cooking did not alter the biologic value of the fats as measured by rat-feeding studies.

Changes During Frying

Fats that have been heated to very high temperatures for long periods of time may undergo chemical and physical changes that influence their performance as frying fats as well as their nutritional quality. Some of the changes that may occur are (a) an increase in free fatty acids, (b) a decrease in iodine number, (c) an increase in refractive index, (d) a decrease in smoke point, (e) an increase in peroxide value, (f) an increase in carbonyl value, (g) a decrease in melting point, (h) a darkening of color, (i) an increase in viscosity, (j) an increase in foaming, and (k) polymerization of the fat. (Bennion and Hanning, 1956b; Goodman and Block, 1952; Krishnamurthy et al., 1965; Perkins and van Akkeren, 1965; Rock and Roth, 1966; Rust and Harrison, 1960; Sahasrabudhe and Bhalerao, 1963; and Wishner and Keeney, 1965.)

Many studies of heated fats have been done with what are called "laboratory-heated fats." The fats have been heated in the laboratory, with or without air or oxygen, at high temperatures of 200–300° C for several days in most cases (Crampton et al., 1956; Firestone et al., 1961; Perkins, 1960; Schultz, 1962). These fats have not had food fried in them; they have been heated alone. Growth depression and toxic effects have been reported when these fats or certain fractions of them were fed to experimental animals. Larger molecules produced by polymerization of the fat at these high temperatures do not appear to be absorbed from the digestive tract, while absorbable nonlinear monomers produced by the heating evidently cause toxic effects in rats (Friedman et al., 1961).

Other studies have concentrated on changes in fats actually used for frying. Poling et al. (1960) and Rice et al. (1960) found that commercially used frying fats fed to rats at 20 percent levels did not produce adverse biological symptoms. They emphasize the differences between laboratory-heated fats and frying fats and the importance of studying fats under regular conditions of use whenever possible. Thompson et al. (1967) conducted a limited survey of fats commercially used for deep-fat frying. Their results suggested, by differences in the degree of increase in viscosity, color, free fatty acid, peroxide value, and non-urea-adduct-forming esters and the degree of decrease in iodine value and content of unsaturated fatty acids, that some food processors maintain their frying fats in good condition, while others abuse and damage theirs.

A few studies have compared changes in the fat absorbed by the food with changes in the fat in which the food was fried. There are many differences between modern food fats and those used in some of the studies done 30 to 50 years ago, and this should be kept in mind in interpreting the results of early studies. Woodruff and Blunt (1919) found a greater decrease in iodine values and a greater increase in free fatty acids and reducing substances in absorbed fat than in the fat in which the foods were fried. King et al. (1936) also reported that the percentage of free fatty acid in fat extracted from potato chips was greater than in the frying fat. Kilgore and Luker (1964) reported a lower linoleic acid content of fat extracted from potatoes than of fat used to fry them at the end of a 10-hour frying period. Since the apparent composition of absorbed fat may be changed by dilution with fatty materials present in the food product being fried, real changes in absorbed fat are difficult to measure.

Potato chips contain more water than do doughnuts or fritter-type batters. As the product is being cooked, part of the moisture lost from the food bubbles through the fat in the form of steam. Porter et al. (1932) emphasize that with more water in the fat, the formation of free fatty acids is increased. Goodman and Block (1952) reported that in commercial frying of doughnuts, the free fatty acid content of the frying fat reached 0.74 percent through normal continuous frying with fresh fat added at regular intervals. Lowe et al. (1940) compared changes after cooking doughnuts or potato chips in different samples of the same fat. After frying potato chips, the iodine number was lower, the free fatty acids (with one exception) were higher, and the smoke point was higher than after frying doughnuts. The fats discolored to a greater extent after frying doughnuts than after frying potato chips. Bennion and Hanning (1956a) found some similar changes in comparing the frying of potatoes and a fritter-type batter. However, the batter caused a more pronounced increase in free fatty acid as well as a decrease in smoke point. The color of the fat darkened markedly with batter frying, whereas little change in color was noted when potatoes were fried for a similar period of time. Later studies (Bennion and Park, 1968) showed that the presence of egg yolk in the batter was responsible for the pronounced darkening of the frying fat as well as the larger increase in free fatty acid. Phospholipids from the egg yolk probably diffuse into the frying fat. Their decomposition at the high frying temperatures may help to explain the darkening with the frying of doughnuts and batters.

During frying at high temperatures, some polymerization of the fat molecules may occur. An estimate of the degree of polymerization is sometimes made by measuring the percent non-urea-adduct-forming fatty acids (NUAF). Urea will form a complex or will adduct with normal straight chain fatty acids but will not form a complex with fatty acids that have been changed by branching, cyclizing, or polymerizing. These would be non-urea-adduct-formers. Rock and Roth (1966) found a direct relationship between the amount of non-urea-adduct-formers and the increase in viscosity of fats used for frying. NUAF compounds have been suggested as a cause of loss of nutritional value in heated fats (Firestone et al., 1961; Friedman et al., 1961). Values from 0.50 to 5.36 percent have been reported in commercial samples of used frying oils (Sahasrabudhe and Bhalerao, 1963; Thompson et al., 1967). Values up to 3.1

percent have been reported in small scale frying (Bennion and Park, 1968). The significance of these values in human nutrition has not been determined.

Changes in fatty acid composition of fats used for frying have been studied. Rather large decreases in polyenoic fatty acids of fats used for commercial frying were reported by Fleischman et al. (1963) in comparing fatty acid composition of the used fats with analysis of the same brand of fat before use. However, no significant change in fatty acid composition was found by Wishner and Keeney (1965) after frying 3400 grams of potatoes (100 minutes frying time). Bennion (1967) found a small (1–2 percent) decrease in linoleate as a percent of the total measured fatty acid esters after frying a fritter-type batter in both corn oil and hydrogenated vegetable shortening for $8\frac{1}{2}$ hours. Thompson et al. (1967), however, emphasize that calculating the fatty acids of frying fats as a percent of the total fatty acids determined by gas chromatography may not be reliable because hydroxy, keto, dibasic, and polymeric acids that may be produced during deep fat frying cannot be eluted under the normal conditions of chromatography and would not be measured. If frying fats are not abused in use, the change in fatty acid composition would appear to be small.

Fat Absorption by Fried Foods

The chief factors governing the amount of fat that will be absorbed by a food during frying are (a) the time and temperature of cooking, (b) the total surface area of the food, (c) the composition and nature of the food, and (d) variation in smoking temperature of the fat used.

In general, the longer a food is cooked, the greater the fat absorption. There will be some exceptions to this. For instance, with some foods cooked at high temperatures, coagulated material or a hardened crust may prevent greater fat absorption with longer cooking. Other foods may lose fat during cooking. Examples might be breaded pork chops and fat chicken. Temperature of the cooking fat affects fat absorption indirectly. At low temperatures the tendency is to cook food longer to obtain the desired browning of the food. Fat absorption is, therefore, increased. Cooking doughnuts for three minutes at 170°, 185°, and 200° C gave no significant differences in fat absorption (Lowe et al., 1940). The color of the doughnuts was quite different, however.

In the frying of doughnuts, with other things being equal, the greater the surface area, the greater the fat absorption. The total surface area of doughnuts may be increased by stretching the dough in handling and by cracks on the surface of the dough. The thicker the doughnut is rolled, the smaller is the total surface area in proportion to the weight of the doughnut. In the frying of a fritter-type batter, the absorption of fat was greatly decreased by leaving the baking powder out of the batter (Bennion and Park, 1968). The surface area of the fritters was much less without baking powder.

Different types and proportions of ingredients in a product may influence the amount of fat absorbed in frying. Increasing the fat and/or sugar in doughnuts resulted in greater fat absorption. Increasing the egg gave a softer dough that tended to absorb more fat. On the other hand, coagulation of the increased egg protein tended to decrease fat absorption. The final result was the sum of these two antagonistic effects and the effect of other factors (Lowe et al., 1940). The addition of egg to a fritter-type batter containing no added shortening caused significantly greater fat absorption by the batter (Bennion and Park, 1968). Fat absorption of doughnuts was found to be less if the dough temperature were near 26° C and greater if it were near 24° C. Increased handling and rerolling of the dough decreased fat absorption (Lowe et al., 1940).

Lowe et al. (1940) reported a significant negative correlation between fat absorption and the smoking point of the fat. Greater absorption occurred in doughnuts cooked in fats with lower smoking points.

THE SHORTENING POWER OF FATS

Fats may be added to doughs and batters for the purpose of producing a finished product that is tender and breaks apart easily. The strands or masses of gluten in the product are "shortened" or retarded in their development by the fat, which is insoluble in water. Fats may be quite differently dispersed in various baked products. In shortened cakes they are often quite finely dispersed; in pastry and biscuits they may be dispersed in relatively large particles. Various fats may differ markedly in their shortening abilities. Attempts have been made to explain these differences. One theory suggests that the fat covering the largest surface area has the greatest shortening power. Several factors affect the surface area covered by a fat. Among these are (a) the nature of the fat, (b) its concentration, (c) the temperature, and (d) the manipulation and extent of mixing.

The Nature of the Fat

The theory of shortening relating to the surface area covered by fats has been developed from the work of Langmuir, Harkins, and their co-workers (Harkins and Cheng, 1921; Harkins et al., 1920; and Langmuir, 1917) on cohesion, adhesion, interfacial tension, and molecular attraction between water and organic liquids. Polar groups or polar molecules are strongly attracted to each other. Water is polar. Molecules like fats, proteins, and starch contain some polar groups (the groups containing oxygen, double bonds, nitrogen, sulfur, phosphorus, and the like). Fats also contain nonpolar groups (the hydrocarbon chains). Langmuir (1917) found that when a small quantity of liquid fat was placed on a large, clean surface of water, it spread rapidly until a definite area was covered, then showed little tendency to spread further. The cause of the spreading appeared to be the attraction of the polar groups of the fat for water. If the whole molecule were attracted by water, the fat would be soluble in water.

Langmuir (1917) measured the length of the fatty acids and the fat molecule, and the area of the water covered by them. The thickness of the fatty acid and triglyceride films was related to the chain length of the fatty acid residues. The area covered by the saturated acids, palmitic, stearic, and creotic, was practically the same, yet the number of carbon atoms in the chain of each is 16, 18, and 26, respectively. The carboxyl group was apparently attracted to the water and the hydrocarbon chains extended into the air above the water surface. A fat molecule containing three saturated fatty acids covered the same water surface as the three fatty acids. The glycerol portion of the triglyceride molecule was evidently held against the water surface with the hydrocarbon chains of the acids in the air. The unsaturated acids covered much greater areas per molecule than the saturated ones. Apparently some of the double bonds were attracted to and held to the surface of the water. However, linoleic acid, with two double bonds, covered approximately the same area as oleic (one double bond), but linolenic, with three double bonds, covered more surface than either oleic or linoleic. It has been suggested that the greater tenderizing power of unsaturated liquid fats in such products as pastry may be due to a greater spreading of the liquid fat over the flour surface because of the attraction of the double bonds. It has been difficult, however, to closely correlate fat constants, such as iodine value, and tenderness of pastries (Hornstein et al., 1943).

It has been suggested that the plasticity of a fat is related to its shortening power (Hornstein et al., 1943). In a plastic or moldable fat, such as lard and hydrogenated vegetable shortenings, both solid and liquid phases are present. Depending on the fatty acid composition and distribution, as much as 70–85 percent of the glycerides may be liquid and only about 15–30 percent crystallized in solid form at ordinary temperatures. Both chemical composition and physical structure affect the liquid/solid ratio and thus the plasticity of a fat. The size of the crystals in the solid phase, which for a given fat will be affected by the conditions of crystallization, also affects plasticity. More plastic fats will presumably spread more easily and cover greater flour surface, thus effecting more shortening. Plasticity is also significant in the capacity of a fat to incorporate air during creaming or mixing.

Concentration

If other factors are equal, the shortening power is increased as the concentration of the fat is increased. When the concentration of fat is relatively large in a baked product, tenderizing differences between various fats will probably be little noticed. Their smaller differences are obscured at high fat concentrations.

Temperature

At higher temperatures the plasticity of fats is increased and they become softer. They spread more readily and the area of flour and other ingredients covered is larger with the same amount of mixing than at lower temperatures where the fat is less plastic. This change in plasticity is related to the effect of increasing temperatures on the liquid/solid ratio of the fat. The plasticity of some fats is much more sensitive to temperature change than other fats. For example, butter, natural lards, and certain commercial shortenings each present different patterns of change in plasticity with increasing temperatures. The melting points of the constituent triglycerides influence these patterns. Fats of high liquid-fat content and low high-melting-point solids content probably vary little in plasticity over ordinary temperature ranges.

At higher temperatures gluten absorbs water and develops more readily. This greater development of gluten might offset the tenderizing effect of the more mobile plastic fat covering a greater surface area of the flour.

Manipulation

Creaming, cutting, or stirring plastic fats softens them. They may then spread more easily, as indicated above. The thoroughness with which fat is mixed with flour, the amount of stirring after liquid is added, and the manner of rolling and handling dough may also influence the spreading and the shortening power of a fat. Increased mixing or handling after the addition of liquid may increase gluten development and counteract the increased shortening resulting from greater dispersion of fat.

The creaming of plastic fats, whereby air is incorporated, has special significance when these fats are used as shortening agents in cakes. Air cells formed in the fat during mixing are expanded during baking by carbon dioxide and steam. When the fat is more finely dispersed in the cake batter by an emulsifier such as monoglycerides, the air cells formed in the fat are smaller and more numerous, resulting in increased cake volume (Carlin, 1944).

PASTRY

The Bailey shortometer is an instrument designed to measure the force required to break (breaking strength) small wafers of plain pastry, crackers, or cookies (Bailey, 1934). It has been widely used in studying factors affecting tenderness of pastry. Flakiness, as well as tenderness, is a characteristic generally considered desirable in pastry. The two properties are influenced somewhat differently by ingredients and methods of manipulation.

Tenderness of Pastry

Many of the studies of tenderness in pastry have been concerned with a comparison of the shortening power of various fats. Fisher (1933) found lard to have the greatest shortening power of the plastic fats tested in pastry. Using 41 and 44 percent fat (based on weight of flour), she found that the shortening value of 5 lards, 2 hydrogenated cottonseed oils, 1 hydrogenated lard, an animal stearin, and 1 all-vegetable oil compound as determined by breaking strength with the Bailey shortometer approximately paralleled their congealing points, those fats with the lowest congealing points having the greatest shortening power. In a comparison of the shortening power of several fats, Hornstein et al. (1943) reported that a hydrogenated vegetable oil gave the most tender pastry, with refined steam-rendered lard, butter oil, and a butter sample producing similar results in second place. In third place were another hydrogenated vegetable oil, a hydrogenated lard, and another butter. Oleomargarine from vegetable fat was in last place. Butter and margarine were corrected for moisture content when compared with the other fats. Denton and Lowe (1924) found that in general the fats having the highest percentage of unsaturated glycerides gave the shortest pastries. Breaking and crushing strengths of pastries for a variety of fats tested are reported in Table 4. From the data it can be seen that the order for different fats varies in some cases according to whether the crushing or the breaking average is taken.

Advances in food technology are apparent in the types of shortenings available today. Hydrogenation, addition of emulsifiers, and plasticizing techniques are used in the preparation of many fats. These changes in modern fats should be kept in mind when interpreting results of earlier studies. Matthews and Dawson (1963) reported on the performance

TABLE 4.   Breaking and Crushing Strength of Different Pastries Made under Standardized Conditions (Denton and Lowe, 1924)[a,b]

Kind of Fat[c]	Melting Point (° C)	Grams to Break	Grams to Crush
Puff pastry shortening	61.0	612	1380
Nutmargarine	28.4	644	1096
Puff pastry shortening (moisture-free)		592	1000
Butter, sample I	34.7	530	902
Butter, sample II		525	802
Mineral oil, purified		418	635
Nutmargarine (moisture-free)		340	554
Coconut oil		333	588
Commercial coconut fat	19.5	334	537
Lard, all leaf, sample II[d]	44.6	350	532
Lard, all leaf, sample I		344	477
Lard, largely leaf, sample I	40.6	327	487
Lard, largely leaf, sample III		276	527
Hydrogenated cottonseed oil		317	506
Lard, bulk	45.4	316	466
Cottonseed oil, emulsion made of oil and water		266	528
Lard, second grade	41.4	261	398
Butter, moisture-free, curd removed		268	387
Cottonseed oil		249	399
Corn oil		240	399
Chicken oil or fat		233	375

[a] Each figure represents an average of 48 tests. The temperature of the ingredients when mixed was 80° F.

[b] Experimental work on pastry done at the Bureau of Home Economics, Washington, D.C.

[c] Modern food fats may differ markedly from fats used in this early study.

[d] Average of 96 tests.

in pastry and baking powder biscuits of several fats produced for the retail market. Pastries made with liquid fats were nearest their optimum scores for tenderness at 45 percent levels of fat (based on weight of flour), while solid fats were best at 51 percent levels. Lard produced a more tender pastry than the two samples of hydrogenated shortening tested, but the hydrogenated fats were better shortening agents in biscuits than was lard. Good-quality products could be made with either solid or liquid fats when the appropriate amount of fat and mixing technique were used.

In general, the breaking strength of pastry was found by Lowe et al. (1938) to be related to the iodine value of the fat from which it was made, the fats with higher iodine values, hence the most unsaturation, producing the most tender pastries. However, most of the fats tested in this study were lards. Other factors also affect the breaking strength. It is difficult to directly relate the shortening power of fats to their chemical and physical constants when a wide variety of fats is compared.

Increasing the amount of fat results in a more tender pastry. Many of the research studies on pastry tenderness have used a relatively "lean" mixture in order to more easily detect differences in tenderness resulting from various treatments. Matthews and Dawson (1963) suggested that a level of 41 percent fat was best for studying performance in pastry.

The texture of lards (Lowe et al., 1938), whether smooth or grainy, if from the same source, produced no significant differences in breaking strength. Pastries (Bernds, 1937) made from lard at room temperature (24–26° C, average dough temperature 27.4° C) had the lowest breaking strength, 9.25 ounces; those from fat at refrigerator temperature (5° C, dough temperature 25° C) were intermediate, with a breaking strength of 10.17 ounces; and those made with melted fat (60° C, dough temperature 30.5° C) had the highest breaking strength, 11.42 ounces. The fat at the lowest temperature would be the least thoroughly mixed with the flour, whereas the warmest fat elevated the temperature of the flour and dough so that hydration of the flour probably occurred more rapidly.

In studying the effect of different flours on pastry tenderness, Davis (1921) found that soft winter wheat (protein content from six percent or less to approximately nine percent) produced pastry with the lowest shortometer values. Denton et al. (1933) also showed that the breaking strength of pastry increased with increased protein content of flour. Pastry flour is made from soft wheat flours of low protein content. The gluten of pastry flour is less viscoelastic than that of harder wheat flours; thus pastry flour gives a more tender pastry than all-purpose or bread flours if the conditions under which the pastries are made are standardized.

Increasing the water in a given recipe decreases the tenderness of pastry (Swartz, 1943). If both fat and water are increased, the result depends on the proportion of each used, but unless the increase in fat is very small, the resulting pastry is more tender, the fat having a greater effect than the water.

Hirahara and Simpson (1961) reported a relationship between breaking strength of pastries and the microscopic appearance of gluten in the raw doughs. In a standard dough, the gluten was described as having "delicate strands with cloudy edges and finger-like structures attached to them." In doughs where gluten was formed in definite strands or "clumps" or where more gluten was present than in the standard dough, the breaking strength of the pastry wafers was higher. Doughs with excess manipulation, those with excess water, and those freezer-stored for 90 days while wrapped in aluminum foil gave baked wafers with significantly higher breaking strength values than those from the standard dough.

Shortometer Measurement of Tenderness

In a study on frozen pastry, Briant and Snow (1957) reported that shortometer values indicated small differences not detected by a taste panel when measurements were made on two-inch wafers. These differences, however, were not considered of practical importance. Rose et al. (1952) stated that two members of a panel judging pastry could only detect variances of three to four ounces or more breaking strength. However, Matthews and Dawson (1963) reported a highly significant negative correlation between tenderness scores judged by panel members and breaking-strength values of pastry. Measurements with the shortometer are somewhat variable. In order to compensate for this, a large number of samples should be measured for each pastry variation.

Flakiness

Flakiness depends on the flour being in layers, with fat in varying concentrations in these layers. Water presumably is imbibed more readily by the portion of the flour not coated so thoroughly with the fat. The absorption of water by the flour allows some gluten to be formed. The layers of dough are separated by the production of steam and probably to a lesser extent by the expansion of air in baking. The proportion of fat as well as its consistency affects the flakiness. Enough fat should be available to coat the flour to some extent for tenderizing and also to form small lumps less completely dispersed. In a plastic fat with both liquid and solid phases, the liquid portion possibly coats the flour during the mixing process and some of the solid portion forms discrete particles with flour adhering to them, which are flattened in rolling and melt into the layers of dough on baking. Since water forms the steam, its proportion in relation to the amount of flour and fat is important in the production of flakiness, as well as in the development of gluten. An indication of comparative flakiness may be gained by measuring the height of a stack of pastry wafers where the unbaked doughs were rolled to the same thickness.

Matthews and Dawson (1963) found a significant correlation between flakiness and tenderness in pastry. Pastries that scored high in flakiness also scored high in tenderness. These relationships were evident in both judging-panel scores and breaking-strength values. The use of oils or melted fats that may be more completely dispersed in the dough is usually expected to give a less flaky (more mealy) and more tender pastry. However, very flaky as well as very tender pastry is usually obtained with liquid fats by students in our laboratory classes. Flaky pastry from liquid fat requires more force for breaking than does the mealy type made with liquid fat.

Hard-wheat all-purpose flour tends to give a flaky pastry and soft-wheat flours a more mealy pastry. Folding and rerolling pastry increases flakiness, although it decreases tenderness and may cause the flakes of dough to be closer together or more compact. Sometimes small pieces of fat are rolled between layers of dough to help prevent increased toughness. Attenuation of gluten to a slight extent may aid in holding steam, thus forcing the layers of dough apart.

Mixing and Manipulation

Certain techniques in preparation may affect the breaking strength of pastries and would need to be carefully controlled in conducting experiments to determine the comparative shortening power of different fats. Thorough mixing of fat and flour up to an optimum amount increased tenderness (Bernds, 1937), as indicated in Table 5. The optimum time of mixing was obtained in a shorter time with the softer lard than with the harder hydrogenated lard. Increased mixing time after adding the water produced greater breaking-strength values (Table 5). Swartz (1943) reported that the breaking strength of pastry was increased with increased mixing time after adding water when the fat and water were cold, but there was little effect under the conditions of this study when all ingredients were at room temperature. Increased manipulation should bring a greater opportunity for hydration and development of gluten. With fat at room temperature, the increased plasticity may produce more complete covering of the flour so that gluten hydration is less complete.

Table 5 shows that pastry rolled immediately had the least breaking strength. The dough felt soft and tender and was rather easily broken. As the dough stood for varying lengths of time up to two hours, it became more firm and elastic, and pastry baked from it showed increased

TABLE 5.   Practices Found to Affect Breaking Strength of Pastry (Bernds, 1937)

	Breaking Strength of Pastries Made With:	
	Prime Steam-Rendered Lard (Ounces)	Hydrogenated Lard (Ounces)
Time of mixing fat and flour (minutes)		
2.5	8.44	11.15
3.0	7.88	11.01
3.5	7.93	10.04
Time of mixing water with fat-flour (seconds)		
15	7.34	9.01
30	8.68	10.77
45	9.10	12.21
Time after mixing before rolled		
Immediately	8.10	
30 minutes	9.77	
2 hours	11.12	
24 hours	10.54	
Age of pastry before testing (hours)		
$\frac{1}{2}$	8.34	10.32
1	8.38	11.79
2	8.60	11.92
4	8.56	12.60
24	8.26	11.34

breaking strength. The "aging" of baked pastry before testing up to two or three hours also increased the breaking strength. Probably because of staling, standing overnight resulted in decreased breaking strength and loss of crispness.

Baking temperatures at 15° intervals from 185° to 245° C gave no significant differences in breaking strengths, but the pastries baked at the highest temperatures were judged more palatable (Bernds, 1937).

Many different methods of mixing have been suggested for making pastry and satisfactory products may be produced by most of them.

References

CLASSIFICATION AND STRUCTURE

Blank, M. L., and O. S. Privett. 1964. Structure of milk fat triglycerides. *J. Dairy Sci. 47*: 481.

Brown, H. B., and I. H. Page. 1965. Effect of polyunsaturated eggs on serum cholesterol. *J. Am. Dietet. Assoc. 46*: 189.

Chung, R. A., and C. C. Lin. 1965. Fatty acid content of pork cuts and variety meats as affected by different dietary lipids. *J. Food Sci. 30*: 860.

Cruikshank, E. M. 1934. Studies in fat metabolism of the fowl. *Biochem. J. 28*: 965.

Devine, J., and P. N. Williams, eds. 1961. *The Chemistry and Technology of Edible Oils and Fats.* Pergamon Press, New York.

Feigenbaum, A. S., and H. Fisher. 1959. The influence of dietary fat on the incorporation of fatty acids into the body and egg fat of the hen. *Arch. Biochem. Biophys. 79*: 302.

Fisher, H., and G. A. Leveille. 1957. Observations on cholesterol, linoleic, and linolenic acid content of eggs as influenced by dietary fats. *J. Nutr. 63*: 119.

Harper, H. A. 1967. *Review of Physiological Chemistry*, 11th ed. Lange Medical Publications, Los Altos, California.

Hawthorn, J., and J. M. Leitch, eds. 1962. *Recent Advances in Food Science*, Vol. I. Butterworth's, London.

Hilditch, T. P., and P. N. Williams. 1964. *The Chemical Constitution of Natural Fats*, 4th ed. John Wiley and Sons, Inc., New York.

Iverson, J. L. 1965. Fatty acid content of vegetable oils, unusual oils, marine oils, and margarines. *J. Assoc. Offic. Agri. Chemists 48*: 902.

Jones, E. P., C. R. Scholfield, V. L. Davison, and H. J. Dutton. 1965. Analysis of fatty acid isomers in two commercially hydrogenated soybean oils. *J. Am. Oil Chemists' Soc. 42*: 727.

Levanon, Y., S. M. O. Rossetini, M. Raskin, and M. T. P. Mesquita. 1967. Thin-layer chromatographic study on the lipid components of cocoa beans and cocoa butter. *J. Food Sci. 32*: 609.

Lowe, B., P. M. Nelson, and J. H. Buchanan. 1938. The physical and chemical characteristics of lards and other fats in relation to their culinary value: I. Shortening value in pastry and cookies. *Iowa Agri. Expt. Sta. Res. Bulletin 242.*

Parry, R. M., Jr., J. Sampugna, and R. G. Jensen. 1964. Effect of feeding safflower oil on the fatty acid composition of milk. *J. Dairy Sci. 47*: 37.

Vander Wal, R. J. 1960. The glyceride structure of fats and oils. *J. Am. Oil Chemists' Soc. 37*: 595.

Wheeler, P., D. W. Peterson, and G. P. Michaels. 1959. Fatty acid distribution in egg yolk as influenced by type and level of dietary fat. *J. Nutr. 69*: 253.

PHYSICAL AND CHEMICAL PROPERTIES

Alfin-Slater, R. B., L. Aftergood, H. Hansen, R. S. Morris, D. Melnick, and C. M. Gooding. 1966. Nutritional evaluation of inter-esterified fats. *J. Am. Oil Chemists' Soc. 43*: 110.

American Meat Institute. 1960. *The Science of Meat and Meat Products.* W. H. Freeman and Co., San Francisco.

Bennion, M., and F. Hanning. 1956b. Effect of different fats and oils and their modification on changes during frying. *Food Technol. 10*: 229.

Blunt, K., and C. M. Feeney. 1915. The smoking temperature of edible fats. *J. Home Econ. 7*: 535.

Braun, W. Q. 1960. Inter-esterification of edible fats. *J. Am. Oil Chemists' Soc. 37*: 598.

Hoerr, C. W. 1967. Changing the physical properties of fats and oils for specific uses. *Baker's Dig. 41*: 42 (Dec.).

Jamieson, G. S. 1943. Vegetable fats and oils. *Am. Chem. Soc. Monograph Series,* No. 58, 2nd ed. Chemical Catalog Co. (Reinhold Pub. Corp.)

Kirschenbauer, H. G. 1960. *Fats and Oils,* 2nd ed. Reinhold Pub. Corp., New York.

Lantz, C. W., and G. T. Carlin. 1938. Stability of fats used for deep fat frying. *Oil and Soap 15*: 38.

Lowe, B., P. M. Nelson, and J. H. Buchanan. 1940. The physical and chemical characteristics of lards and other fats in relation to their culinary value. III. For frying purposes. *Iowa Agri. Expt. Sta. Res. Bulletin* 279.

Mehlenbacher, V. C. 1960. *The Analysis of Fats and Oils.* The Garrard Press, Champaign, Illinois.

Morgan, D. A. 1942. Smoke, fire, and flash points of cottonseed, peanut, and other vegetable oils. *Oil and Soap 19*: 193.

Official and Tentative Methods of Analysis, 3rd ed., including additions and revisions. American Oil Chemists' Society, Chicago.

Special shortenings. 1964. *J. Am. Med. Assoc. 187*: 766.

Technical Committee, Institute of Shortening and Edible Oils Inc. 1959. Composition of food fats and oils. *J. Am. Oil Chemists' Soc. 36*: 181.

Wille, R. L., and E. S. Lutton. 1966. Polymorphism of cocoa butter. *J. Am. Oil Chemists' Soc. 43*: 491.

RANCIDITY

Chipault, J. R., G. R. Mizuno, J. M. Hawkins, and W. O. Lundberg. 1952. The antioxidant properties of natural spices. *Food Res. 17*: 46.

Daubert, B. F., and P. W. O'Connell. 1953. Reversion problems in edible fats. *Advan. Food Res. 4*: 185.

Elder, L. W., Jr. 1941. Rancidity in flaked breakfast cereals. *Oil and Soap 18*: 38.

Gaddis, A. M., R. Ellis, and G. T. Currie. 1966. Carbonyls in oxidizing fat. VIII. Effect of the Pool and Klose method on monocarbonyl precursors in autoxidized lard. *J. Am. Oil Chemists' Soc. 43*: 147.

Kraybill, H. R., L. R. Dugan, Jr., B. W. Beedle, F. C. Vibrans, V. Swartz, and H. Rezabek. 1949. Butylated hydroxyanisole as an antioxidant for animal fats. *J. Am. Oil Chemists' Soc. 26*: 449.

Lea, C. H. 1939. Rancidity in edible fats. *Dept. Sci. Ind. Res. (Brit.) Food Investigation, Special Report* 46. Chemical Pub. Co., New York.

Lundberg, W. O., ed. 1961. *Autoxidation and Antioxidants*, Vol. I. Interscience Publishers, New York.

Lundberg, W. O., ed. 1962. *Autoxidation and Antioxidants*, Vol. II. Interscience Publishers, New York.

Mabrouk, A. F., and L. R. Dugan. 1960. A kinetic study of the autoxidation of methyl linoleate and linoleic acid emulsions in the presence of sodium chloride. *J. Am. Oil Chemists' Soc. 37*: 486.

Mehlenbacher, V. C. 1960. *The Analysis of Fats and Oils*. The Garrard Press, Champaign, Illinois.

Pohle, W. D., R. L. Gregory, and B. van Giessen. 1964a. Relationship of peroxide value and thiobarbituric acid value to development of undesirable flavor characteristics in fats. *J. Am. Oil Chemists' Soc. 41*: 649.

Pohle, W. D., R. L. Gregory, T. J. Weiss, B. van Giessen, J. R. Taylor, and J. J. Ahern. 1964b. A study of methods for evaluation of the stability of fats and shortenings. *J. Am. Oil Chemists' Soc. 41*: 795.

Privett, O. S., and M. L. Blank. 1962. The initial stages of autoxidation. *J. Am. Oil Chemists' Soc. 39*: 465.

Raghuveer, K. G., and E. G. Hammond. 1967. The influence of glyceride structure on the rate of autoxidation. *J. Am. Oil Chemists' Soc. 44*: 239.

Schultz, H. W., ed. 1962. *Lipids and Their Oxidation*. Avi Publishing Co., Westport, Connecticut.

Thompson, J. W., and E. R. Sherwin. 1966. Investigation of antioxidants for polyunsaturated edible oils. *J. Am. Oil Chemists' Soc. 43*: 683.

Webb, B. H., and A. H. Johnson. 1965. *Fundamentals of Dairy Chemistry*. Avi Publishing Co., Westport, Connecticut.

Younathan, M. T., and B. M. Watts. 1959. Relationship of meat pigments to lipid oxidation. *Food Res. 24*: 728.

Yu, T. C., and R. O. Sinnhuber. 1964. Further observations on the 2-thiobarbituric acid method for the measurement of oxidative rancidity. *J. Am. Oil Chemists' Soc. 41*: 540.

Zalewski, S., and A. M. Gaddis. 1967. Effect of transesterification of lard on stability, antioxidant-synergist efficiency, and rancidity development. *J. Am. Oil Chemists' Soc. 44*: 576.

CHANGES IN FATS DURING HEATING

Bennion, M., and F. Hanning. 1956a. Decomposition of lard in the frying of French-fried potatoes and of fritter-type batters. *J. Home Econ. 48*: 184.

Bennion, M., and F. Hanning. 1956b. Effect of different fats and oils and their modification on changes during frying. *Food Technol. 10*: 229.

Bennion, M. 1967. Effect of batter ingredients on changes in fatty acid composition of fats used for frying. *Food Technol. 21*: 1638.

Bennion, M., and R. L. Park. 1968. Changes in frying fats with different foods. *J. Am. Dietet. Assoc. 52*: 308.

Chang, I. C. L., L. Y. Tchen, and B. M. Watts. 1952. The fatty acid content of selected foods before and after cooking. *J. Am. Oil Chemists' Soc. 29*: 378.

Crampton, E. W., R. H. Common, E. T. Pritchard, and F. A. Farmer. 1956. Studies to determine the nature of the damage to the nutritive value of some vegetable oils from heat treatment. IV. Ethyl esters of heat-polymerized linseed, soybean and sunflower seed oils. *J. Nutr. 60*: 13.

Firestone, D., W. Horvitz, L. Friedman, and G. M. Shue. 1961. Heated fats. I. Studies of the effects of heating on the chemical nature of cottonseed oil. *J. Am. Oil Chemists' Soc. 38*: 253.

Fleischman, A. I., A. Florin, J. Fitzgerald, A. B. Caldwell, and G. Eastwood. 1963. Studies on cooking fats and oils. *J. Am. Dietet. Assoc. 42*: 394.

Friedman, L., W. Horvitz, G. M. Shue, and D. Firestone. 1961. Heated fats. II. The nutritive properties of heated cottonseed oil and of heated cottonseed oil fractions. *J. Nutr. 73*: 85.

Goodman, A. H., and Z. Block. 1952. Problems encountered in the commercial utilization of frying fats. *J. Am. Oil Chemists' Soc. 29*: 616.

Kilgore, L. T., and W. D. Luker. 1964. Fatty acid components of fried foods and fats used for frying. *J. Am. Oil Chemists' Soc. 41*: 496.

King, F. B., R. Loughlin, R. W. Riemenschneider, and N. R. Ellis. 1936. The relative value of various lards and other fats for the deep fat frying of potato chips. *J. Agri. Res. 53*: 369.

Krishnamurthy, R. G., T. Kawada, and S. S. Chang. 1965. Chemical reactions involved in the deep fat frying of foods. 1. A laboratory apparatus for frying under simulated restaurant conditions. *J. Am. Oil Chemists' Soc. 42*: 878.

Lowe, B., P. M. Nelson, and J. H. Buchanan. 1940. The physical and chemical characteristics of lards and other fats in relation to their culinary value. III. For frying purposes. *Iowa Agri. Expt. Sta. Res. Bulletin 279*.

Masters, H., and H. L. Smith. 1914. The changes in the character of fats during the process of cooking. *Analyst 39*: 347.

Ostwald, R. 1963. Fat content and fatty acids in some commercial mixes for baked products. *J. Am. Dietet. Assoc. 42*: 32.

Perkins, E. G. 1960. Nutritional and chemical changes occurring in heated fats: A review. *Food Technol. 14*: 508.

Perkins, E. G., and L. A. van Akkeren. 1965. Heated fats. 4. Chemical changes in fats subjected to deep fat frying processes: Cottonseed oil. *J. Am. Oil Chemists' Soc. 42*: 782.

Phillips, J. A., and G. E. Vail. 1967. Effect of heat on fatty acids. *J. Am. Dietet. Assoc. 50*: 116.

Poling, C. E., W. D. Warner, P. E. Mone, and E. E. Rice. 1960. The nutritional value of fats after use in commercial deep-fat frying. *J. Nutr. 72*: 109.

Porter, F. R., H. Michaels, and F. G. Shay. 1932. Changes in fats during frying. *Ind. Eng. Chem. 24*: 811.

Rice, E. E., C. E. Poling, P. E. Mone, and W. D. Warner. 1960. A nutritive evaluation of over-heated fats. *J. Am. Oil Chemists' Soc. 37*: 607.

Rock, S. P., and H. Roth. 1966. Properties of frying fat. 1. The relationship of viscosity to the concentration of non-urea adducting fatty acids. *J. Am. Oil Chemists' Soc. 43*: 116.

Rust, M. E., and D. L. Harrison. 1960. The effect of method of care on the frying life of fat. *Food Technol. 14*: 605.

Sahasrabudhe, M. R., and V. R. Bhalerao. 1963. A method for the determination of the extent of polymerization in frying fats and in fats extracted from fried foods. *J. Am. Oil Chemists' Soc. 40*: 711.

Schultz, H. W., ed. 1962. *Lipids and their Oxidation*. Avi Publishing Co., Westport, Connecticut.

Thompson, J. A., M. M. Paulose, B. R. Reddy, R. G. Krishnamurthy, and S. S. Chang. 1967. A limited survey of fats and oils commercially used for deep fat frying. *Food Technol. 21*: 405.

Warner, W. D., P. N. Abell, P. E. Mone, C. E. Poling, and E. E. Rice. 1962. Nutritional value of fats in cooked meats. *J. Am. Dietet. Assoc. 40*: 422.

Wishner, L. A., and M. Keeney. 1965. Comparative study of monocarbonyl compounds formed during deep frying in different fats. *J. Am. Oil Chemists' Soc. 42*: 776.

Woodruff, S., and K. Blunt. 1919. Changes in fats absorbed by fried foods. *J. Home Econ. 11*: 440.

SHORTENING POWER OF FATS

Carlin, G. T. 1944. A microscopic study of the behavior of fats in cake batters. *Cereal Chem. 21*: 189.

Harkins, W. D., and G. C. Cheng. 1921. The orientation of molecules in surfaces: VI. Cohesion, adhesion, tensile strength, tensile energy, negative energy, interfacial tension and molecular attraction. *J. Am. Chemists' Soc. 43*: 35.

Harkins, W. D., G. L. Clark, and L. E. Roberts. 1920. The orientation of molecules in surfaces, surface energy, absorption, and surface catalysis: V. The adhesion work between organic liquids and water. *J. Am. Chemists' Soc.* 42: 700.

Hornstein, L. R., F. B. King, and F. Benedict. 1943. Comparative shortening value of some commercial fats. *Food Res.* 8: 1.

Langmuir, I. 1917. The constitution and fundamental properties of solids and liquids: II. Liquids. *J. Am. Chemists' Soc.* 39: 1848.

PASTRY

Bailey, C. H. 1934. An automatic shortometer. *Cereal Chem.* 11: 160.

Bernds, M. W. 1937. Factors affecting the shortening power of fat in pastry. M. S. Thesis, Iowa State College Library.

Briant, A. M., and P. R. Snow. 1957. Freezer storage of pie shells. *J. Am. Dietet. Assoc.* 33: 796.

Davis, C. E. 1921. Shortening, its definition and measurement. *Ind. Eng. Chem.* 13: 797.

Denton, M. C., B. Gordon, and B. Sperry. 1933. Study of the tenderness in pastries made with flours of varying strengths. *Cereal Chem.* 10: 156.

Denton, M. C., and B. Lowe. 1924. The shortening power of fats. Unpublished paper. Bureau of Home Economics.

Fisher, J. D. 1933. Shortening value of plastic fats. *Ind. Eng. Chem.* 25: 1171.

Hirahara, S., and J. I. Simpson. 1961. Microscopic appearance of gluten in pastry dough and its relation to the tenderness of baked pastry. *J. Home Econ.* 53: 681.

Hornstein, L. R., F. B. King, and F. Benedict. 1943. Comparative shortening value of some commercial fats. *Food Res.* 8: 1.

Lowe, B., P. M. Nelson, and J. H. Buchanan. 1938. The physical and chemical characteristics of lards and other fats in relation to their culinary value: I. Shortening value in pastry and cookies. *Iowa Agri. Expt. Sta. Res. Bulletin* 242.

Matthews, R. H., and E. H. Dawson. 1963. Performance of fats and oils in pastry and biscuits. *Cereal Chem.* 40: 291.

Rose, I., M. E. Dressler, and K. A. Johnston. 1952. The effect of the method of fat and water incorporation on the average shortness and uniformity of tenderness of pastry. *J. Home Econ.* 44: 707.

Swartz, V. 1943. Effect of certain variables in technique on the breaking strength of lard pastry wafers. *Cereal Chem.* 20: 121.

CHAPTER 6

Fruits and Vegetables

HELEN CHARLEY

Fruits and vegetables are the edible parts of plants. Frequently only one part of an individual plant is used for food, but there are fruits and vegetables representing every part of a plant. The chemical composition and structural makeup of the edible part of a plant affect its textural quality as a food.

STRUCTURAL COMPONENTS OF FRUITS AND VEGETABLES

Gross Anatomy

A plant consists of root and stem. In those plants that yield fruits and vegetables, roots are underground and stems usually aerial. Appendages that develop from stems of plants include leaves, flowers, and the fruits that develop from flowers. An enlarged underground stem, such as in the white potato, is called a tuber.

Plant Tissues

The cell is the basic structural unit of plants. Each part of a plant—root, leaf, and fruit—is an assemblage of masses of cells of different types and arrangements. One small section of a plant may be of tissue of a single type, the cells of which are alike, but most tissue is morphologically complex.

Three types of tissue systems are commonly distinguished in plants—dermal, vascular, and ground or fundamental (Esau, 1965). A continuous layer of epidermal cells forms a protective surface on stem, leaf, and fruit. The presence of cutin, a highly hydrophobic fatty acid polymer, on the surface of epidermal cells restricts water loss from fruits and vegetables. The cutin and associated waxes are responsible for the "bloom" on freshly harvested fruits and vegetables. As a vegetable like the potato matures, the epidermis is replaced by corklike periderm, which serves the same purpose. Two main types of vascular tissue systems are present throughout the plant, the xylem and the phloem. Both are concerned with conduction, the vessels and the tracheids of the xylem with water and the cells of the phloem with food. Parenchyma cells are the main type found in the edible parts of plants, although specialized collenchyma cells that provide support for the plant and sclerenchyma cells that give mechanical strength to plant tissue may be present also (Esau, 1965). Parenchyma cells are in the main polyhedral in shape. They tend to be isodiametric, although they may be much elongated as are those found in pears around the gritty deposits of sclerenchyma cells known as sclereids. Parenchyma cells make up the photosynthetic tissue in the mesophyll of green leaves and the edible portion of the potato, and they predominate in the flesh of fruits such as the apple, peach, and pear.

Plant Cell Structure

Cell Wall

The cell wall is an elastic support and a confining structure for the contents of the cell. Cellulose comprises the skeletal framework for this wall. This polysaccharide is a polymer of β-D glucose residues with a glycosidic linkage between carbon atoms 1 and 4 as in cellobiose (see p. 197 in Chapter 4).

Fragment of a cellulose molecule: a cellobiose residue

Molecules of cellulose with an estimated chain length of a few thousand glucose residues (Mühlethaler, 1961) are long enough to be seen with the light microscope, but their narrow width makes them amicroscopic (Frey-Wyssling and Mühlethaler, 1965). Cellulose molecules in parallel arrangement form bundles called microfibrils that have been demonstrated by the electron microscope. Evidence of three-dimensional, orderly, close-packing of cellulose molecules, typical of crystallinity, has been shown at intervals along the microfibril by means of X-ray diffraction. Lateral association of cellulose molecules in the micelles, as the crystalline regions are called, is attributed to hydrogen bonding. Micellar areas in the microfibrils alternate with amorphous areas. Aggregates of microfibrils give rise to macrofibrils that are visible in the light microscope (Mühlethaler, 1961).

Interstices in the matrix of cellulose in the cell wall contain material that is amorphous in character. The cell wall has been compared to steel-reinforced concrete, the cellulose fibrils like steel rods giving tensile strength and the amorphous material like concrete resisting compression (Sterling, 1963). Materials of an amorphous nature in cell walls include pectic substances and hemicelluloses. The latter are a heterogeneous group of polysaccharides in which pentose sugars and uronic acids predominate.

Elasticity of the walls of parenchyma cells of the potato tuber has been demonstrated (Falk et al., 1958). Parenchyma cells usually have thin primary walls. A small amount of hydroxyproline-rich protein has been reported in the primary cell wall (Lamport, 1965). The primary walls are characterized chiefly by appreciable quantities of pectic substances. Pectic substances are polymers of α D-galacturonic acid united by a 1,4-glycosidic linkage as shown.

Polygalacturonic acid fragment (R = H or CH₃)

The extent to which molecules of pectic substances are polymerized varies. In addition, the carboxyl groups of the uronic acid residues may be free or esterified. Pectic molecules from some sources may contain minor amounts of such neutral monomers as arabinose, galactose, rhamnose, and xylose, according to McCready and Gee (1960) and Barrett and Northcote (1965). In addition, pectic substances from some sources may contain acetyl radicals esterified with secondary alcohol groups.

Polymers of galacturonic acid of colloidal dimensions in which the carboxyl groups are essentially unesterified are called pectic acids; those in which some methoxyl groups are present are called pectinic acids. Pectins are those pectinic acids with a high proportion of methyl ester groups. The greater the methyl ester content, the more readily does the molecule disperse in water. Both pectic acids and low-ester pectinic acids react with divalent ions to form insoluble pectates and pectinates, respectively. In addition, insoluble forms of pectic substances designated protopectin predominate in immature fruits. The nature of protepectin and the reason for its insolubility remain to be clarified. The status of our knowledge of protopectin is found in a review by Joslyn (1962). See Chapter 4, p. 200 for further discussion of pectic substances.

Collenchyma cells have heavily thickened walls inside the primary walls that are especially reinforced at the corners with layers of cellulose alternating with layers of pectic substances (Mühlethaler, 1961). Strands of such cells are found as support in stems and along the midribs and veins of leaves. The presence of cells of this type gives a fibrous character to plant tissue, as does the presence of elongated sclerenchyma fibers, cell walls of which are often lignified (Esau, 1965). Lignin consists of polymers of aromatic nuclei. Other amorphous material that may be deposited along with lignin and may contribute to the toughness of the cell wall are proanthocyanins (leucoanthocyanins). The presence of these phenolic compounds in an insoluble form has been demonstrated in the skin coat of a broad bean (Bate-Smith, 1958). Like pectic substances, these incrusting substances are amorphous. Unlike them, they are unaltered by cooking.

Intercellular Spaces

As a rule, cells do not fit together perfectly where three or more adjoining ones meet. This discontinuity of the middle lamella gives rise to intercellular spaces that permeate plant tissue and provide access for the cells to the external environment. Exchange of gases between the cell and the environment takes place by way of these intercellular spaces. Dimensions of intercellular spaces in plant tissue vary; in apples they may exceed the dimensions of the parenchyma cells, while in peaches they are relatively small. Reeve (1953) reported that 20 to 25 percent of the volume of an apple is intercellular space, compared to 15 percent for fresh peaches (Weier and Stocking, 1949) and approximately 1 percent in potato tubers (Burton and Sprague, 1950). The great number of large, gas-filled intercellular spaces accounts for the opaqueness of raw apple tissue in contrast to the translucency of plum tissue, for example. The opaqueness of raw potato is due to refraction of light by starch grains (Crafts, 1944) rather than to gas-filled intercellular spaces.

Cytoplasm

Immature plant cells and mature parenchyma and collenchyma cells contain a transparent jellylike colloidal sol of living matter called cytoplasm. Dissolved in the watery medium of this cytoplasm are substances in true solution and others, like protein, that are colloidally dispersed. In the cytoplasm, in addition to the nucleus, are inclusions called plastids and smaller ones called mitochondria.

Plastids are of three types, classed according to color. Chloroplasts are found in parenchyma cells of the green parts of plants, especially in the mesophyll of the leaf where photosynthesis takes place. These saucer- or disk-shaped bodies with diameters of 4 to 10 microns and thicknesses of 1 to 2 microns (Park, 1965) have a granular appearance when viewed under the light microscope due to stacks of disklike lamellae called grana. Chlorophyll is located in the grana. Chlorophyll-free plastids that contain yellow or orange pigments are called chromoplasts. Leucoplasts are colorless plastids, some of which, as in the potato, the cotyledon of legumes and the endosperm of cereals, are specialized for storing starch. These are given the name of amyloplasts. Mitochondria, present in the cytoplasm, contain oxidative enzymes essential for respiratory activities in the cell (Esau, 1965).

Vacuole

Immature cells are filled with cytoplasm, but as parenchyma cells mature, one or more vacuoles develop. These spaces are filled with a fluid called cell sap. Dissolved in the aqueous medium are salts, sugars, organic acids, soluble pigments, and in the cells of certain plants, phenolic compounds commonly referred to as tannins. When more than one vacuole is present, wispy strands of cytoplasm traverse the cell-sap area. In mature parenchyma cells, the vacuolar space occupies most of the cell, the cytoplasm being confined to a narrow layer around the periphery.

Cell Membranes

Separating the cell wall from the cytoplasm within the cell is a thin membrane called the plasmalemma. A second membrane that delimits the cytoplasm from the cell sap is the vacuolar membrane or tonoplast. Both membranes are differentially permeable and help to regulate the water content of the cell.

TEXTURE OF FRUITS AND VEGETABLES

Turgor and Texture

The moisture content of plant tissue makes an important contribution to the complex of characteristics in fruits and vegetables referred to as texture (Sterling, 1963). Water, the chief constituent in living tissue, is adsorbed by the macromolecules in the cell wall and in the cytoplasm and its inclusions (Stocking, 1956). Water is found also in high proportions in the vacuole. Here the cell sap with its soluble constituents is surrounded by a thin layer of protoplasm that is confined between the protoplasmic and the vacuolar membranes. This living material acts as a selectively permeable layer to regulate the water content of the cell. The amount of water in the vacuole fluctuates markedly, depending on the access of the plant tissue to moisture in its environment.

The presence of highly hydrophilic macromolecules in the cell and especially of solutes in the cell sap reduces the activity of water molecules (A_w), their free energy, to a level below that of pure water. When fruit or vegetable tissue is placed in water, water molecules move across the selectively permeable membranes. These molecules move from an area of higher free energy to one of lower free energy. Osmotic pressure is the hydrostatic pressure that would be necessary to make the chemical potential of water within the vacuole equal to that of pure water, that is, to prevent the movement of water due to osmosis (Bennet-Clark, 1959).

When a cell has imbibed water due to osmosis, the inflated vacuole presses the cytoplasm against the cell wall. The aqueous contents distend the cell, which is confined by the elastic wall. The inwardly directed pressure of the stretched wall is equal to and opposite the outwardly directed hydrostatic pressure within the cell. This latter is called turgor pressure (Bennett-Clark, 1959). The pressure that turgid cells exert on one another gives erectness to growing plants and crispness to harvested fruits and vegetables. Turgor makes a more important contribution to the texture of some foods such as lettuce and watermelon than it does to others like apple and carrot, in which the structural elements of the cell wall make a more important contribution.

Cells become turgid when plant tissue has access to water either through the roots of growing plants or when harvested fruits and vegetables are in contact with water. Turgor (and crispness) may be maintained by storing fruits and vegetables in an atmosphere saturated with water vapor. When the relative humidity of the air is low and the vapor pressure of the water within the cells exceeds that in the surroundings, moisture will be lost from the cells. As a result, the tissues become limp and flaccid. When the actual turgor pressure is less than the potential turgor pressure, that is, the osmotic pressure, a diffusion pressure deficit results within the cells. This means that water will be drawn into the cells of such wilted tissue if they have access to it. The more concentrated the solutes in the cell sap, the greater the osmotic pressure, and the lower the turgor pressure, the greater the diffusion pressure deficit.

When plant tissue is placed in contact with water in which the free energy has been reduced by high concentrations of salt or of sugar, liquid is drawn from the cells by osmosis. Such is the origin of the syrup that accumulates around slices of frozen peaches or strawberries packed in sugar, of the beads of liquid that appear on the surface of salted, sliced cucumbers, or of the liquid around shredded cabbage that has been salted in preparation for making kraut. Water relationships in living cells, either in the growing plant or in harvested fruits and vegetables, are complex. A thermodynamic treatment of the subject is given by Dainty (1963).

Structure and Texture

Components that make up cell walls and their structural orientation contribute to the uniqueness of the texture of fruits and vegetables (Sterling, 1963). Both cell walls and intercellular bonding material responsible for cell adhesion give mechanical strength to plant tissues and influence their resistance to chopping, grinding, and chewing. While fruits and vegetables are similar in both composition and structure, they do differ in respect to the physiological state at which they are considered optimum for eating. Fruits are consumed mainly when they are mature and approaching senescence, while most vegetables are at their peak when harvested in an immature state (Reeve and Brown, 1966). Cells of young, rapidly growing tissues of vegetables and the soft flesh of fruits show little secondary wall thickening. Most vegetables, as they mature, become less succulent, less tender, and more fibrous. Cell walls thicken and lignin accumulates, especially in vascular tissue. Lignified cells in vegetables that are near maturity give a woodiness to the tissues that is unpalatable if not inedible. The stringiness of the core of parsnips and carrots, of beet root, and of the leaves of spinach is due to the presence of appreciable quantities of lignin. Lignified tissue resists cooking. Lignin is usually absent from the edible parts of fruits. The sclereids of pears are an exception. These sclereids, once parenchyma cells, are almost completely filled with lignin and cellulose (Sterling, 1954). Textural changes occur in fruits as they mature, just as they do in vegetables, except that as fruits ripen they become less firm, softer and juicier.

Textural Changes in Ripening Fruits

The theory that the softening of fruits as they ripen is associated with changes in the pectic substances is widely accepted. According to the theory, change in the texture of fruits from the firmness of the green to the softness of the ripe condition is the result of conversion of insoluble pectic substances (protopectin) to water-dispersible (usually referred to as soluble) forms through the action of pectin-degrading enzymes. Demethylation of the polymers by pectin methylesterase followed by hydrolysis of glycosidic linkages by polygalacturonase could account for diminished cell adhesion as fruits ripen. Apples were among the first fruits to be studied from the standpoint of textural changes associated with ripening.

Apples

Pectinesterase appears to be widely distributed in plant tissue, but Griffin and Kertesz (1946) could find no evidence of polygalacturonase in apples. Instead, they proposed that the increase in soluble pectin and the decrease in tensile strength as apples ripened could be effected by ascorbic acid or by hydrogen peroxide derived from the oxidative breakdown of ascorbic acid. Later, Doesburg (1957) reported that the methyl ester content of the pectin changed only slightly and the total pectin and the chain length not at all as apples (two varieties) ripened. The percent of soluble pectin did increase, however. He proposed that a lowering of the pH of the cell wall by an exchange of ions (hydrogen or potassium) from the cell with the calcium bound by the pectic substances might result in the increase in soluble pectin and in softening of the fruit as it ripens. Gee et al. (1959), on the basis of a histochemical study, reported an increase in methyl ester content in both apples (Golden Delicious and Gravenstein) and in pears (Bartlett) as the fruit went from green-immature, through green-mature and to the hard ripe stage, and then a decrease as the fruit passed to the firm ripe and to the soft ripe stages. Woodmansee et al. (1959) reported that as apples (Red Delicious and Stayman) progressed from full size but unripe to senescent and soft, the apparent equivalent weight of the pectic substances and the degree of esterification decreased and the ratio of soluble to total pectin increased. Kertesz et al. (1959) reported that a higher cellulose content distinguished firmer apples from softer ones, but that the softening that accompanied ripening could not be accounted for on the basis of changes in the cellulose of the fruit. Wiley and Stembridge (1961) presented evidence that a decrease in starch was associated with softening of apples as they ripened.

Pears

Pears, another pome fruit, have had their share of investigation of textural changes associated with ripening. Most of the work has been done on the Bartlett variety. Commercially, pears are harvested when full size but firm and held in cold storage near 31° C before they are ripened. If they are held in cold storage much beyond the optimum of 30 to 40 days before they are removed to ripen at 65 to 70° F, certain changes in texture associated with normal ripening do not take place (Hartman et al., 1929).

McCready and McComb (1954) reported that the intrinsic viscosity of the pectin in Bartlett pears dropped from 6.0 in the green to 1.5 in ripe fruit, an indication of a reduction in the length of the pectin polymer on ripening. The percent of carboxyl groups that were esterified dropped from 89 to 43. The percent of pectic substances unextractable by 0.5 percent Versene (a substance that is used to sequester divalent ions) was 63 in unripe and 40 in ripe pears, the same values as reported for avocados, which were analyzed in the same study. Esterification of the carboxyl groups was 100 percent in unripe and 32 percent in ripe avocados. Polygalacturonase activity, undetected in unripe fruit, was high in both ripe pears and ripe avocados. The intrinsic viscosity of pectins from the ripe fruit was approximately one fourth that of the pectins from the corresponding green fruit. The results in this study suggest that depolymerization of pectic substances accompanies ripening. Thinning and collapse of parenchyma cells of pears on ripening has been reported by Sterling (1954). Esau et al. (1962) studied the changes in the pectic constituents in Bartlett pears as they ripened both on and off the tree. In both cases they found that total pectin decreased as the fruit ripened. The water-soluble fraction increased in fruits ripened off the tree but decreased in those left on the tree. The fraction not extractable by water, which they termed protopectin, increased in those ripened on the tree and decreased in those detached. The degree of esterification decreased as fruits ripened either on or off the tree.

Peaches

A number of studies have been concerned with textural changes in the ripening peach, no doubt in part because of the marked difference between clings and freestones. Addoms et al. (1930) reported that ripe cling peaches contained twice as much insoluble protopectin as did ripe freestones. Nightingale et al. (1930) reported a decrease in protopectin, without a corresponding increase in soluble pectin, as freestone peaches matured to the soft ripe stage. McCready and McComb (1954), who analyzed Elberta peaches in addition to the pears and avocados referred to above, found that the intrinsic viscosity of pectin from ripe peaches was less than half that from the green ones, which indicated a decrease in polymerization of the pectin molecules. However, they were unable to demonstrate polygalacturonase activity in the ripe fruit. Postlmayr et al. (1956) compared clings at four stages of maturity and freestones at three. In clings, the fraction unextractable with water was approximately two thirds of the total pectic substances, and this fraction changed little as the fruit matured from the firm ripe to the ripe stage and the pressure dropped from 10.4 to 5.14 pounds. Approximately half of the water-insoluble pectic material in clings was soluble in 0.5 percent Versene, suggesting that divalent ions were involved in its insolubility in water. In freestones, the proportion of pectic substances extractable by cold water increased as the fruit ripened and the pressure dropped from 11.92 to 0.85 pounds.

Reeve (1959) studied histologically the pectins in the ripening peach. Approximately 75 to 80 percent of the carboxyl groups were esterified up to the time the fruit attained mature size but was still green. Then esterification increased until it was near 100 percent at the hard ripe stage. Upon further ripening and softening, the percent of esterified groups decreased. Thickness of the cell wall was associated with the degree of esterification of the pectin, which was greatest at the hard ripe stage, after which the walls became thinner. No difference was observed histologically between clings and freestones, and the author suggested that constituents in the cell wall other than pectic substances might account for the difference in texture. Sterling and Kalb (1959) analyzed freestone peaches (Elbertas) at five stages of ripeness from full-sized, light-green and hard to yellow and very soft. They found that the total pectic substances decreased as the fruit ripened. The proportion of acid-soluble pectic substances decreased, that of the water-soluble fraction increased, and the methoxyl content of both fractions decreased as the fruit ripened. They proposed that solubilization of pectic substances as fruits ripen could be due either to depolymerization of the galacturonic acid polymer or to the decrease in free acid that occurs as many fruits mature. They theorized that a decrease in the acidity would favor dissociation of unesterified carboxyl groups in pectic substances and consequently their dispersibility in water. Shewfelt (1965) studied one variety of cling and five varieties of freestone peaches at four stages of postharvest ripeness. In the cling peach, the Versene-insoluble fraction accounted for the highest proportion of total pectic substances and the water-soluble portion the least. In freestones, the water-soluble fraction increased rapidly with ripening, while in clings this fraction changed little.

The change in texture as a fruit ripens is obviously a complex phenomenon. Most of the papers cited above point to an increase in the proportion of water-dispersible pectic substances as fruits ripen and the tissues soften. Pinpointing the cause or causes of this increase must await additional work.

Effects of Cooking on Texture of Fruits and Vegetables

Effects on Turgor

When fruits and vegetables are cooked, heat denatures the proteins of the cytoplasm and of the cell membranes, which lose their selective permeability. Once the cell is killed, water passes out of and into the cell by diffusion rather than by osmosis. The vacuoles lose water and the cooked tissue loses its turgor and becomes limp and flabby. Tissue frequently weighs less when cooked than it did in the raw state even though it was completely covered with water during cooking.

In addition to its effect on turgor, cooking also causes the expansion of intercellular gases, which escape and are replaced by steam. When this steam condenses, liquid is drawn into the intercellular spaces (Crafts,

1944). This accounts for the translucency of cooked plant tissue in contrast to the opaqueness of the raw.

Effects on Cell Adhesion

An early attempt to account for the tenderizing of plant tissue by cooking was that of Simpson and Halliday (1941). Two vegetables, carrots and parsnips, were steamed for periods of 20 and 45 minutes. These authors reported that cooked vegetable tissue yielded less protopectin and more pectin than the raw and that microscopic sections of cooked tissue stained with ruthenium red to show pectic substances appeared less dense than the raw. Sterling (1955) prepared photomicrographs of apple, carrot, and potato tissue that had been steamed for 20, 40, and 60 minutes. Separation of some of the cells in the cooked tissue was observed, attributed to solubilizing of pectic substances in the middle lamella, but there was no evidence of fracture of the cell wall as suggested by Simpson and Halliday.

The effect of the acidity of the cooking medium on the texture of cooked plant tissue was investigated by Doesburg (1961). Apple, beet, cauliflower, potato, and turnip tissues were boiled in citrate buffer adjusted to different pH values. Cooked tissue was firmest when the pH of the cooking medium was 4.0 to 4.5. As the pH decreased from 4.0 to 3.0, softness of the cooked tissue increased, as did the percentage of pectic substances in soluble form. Because the molecular weights of the pectic substances remained high, the author suggested that possibly hydrolysis of other cell-wall constituents in the more acid medium had freed the pectic substances. As the pH of the cooking medium increased above 4.5, the cooked tissue again was increasingly softer and the proportion of water-soluble pectin greater. In this case, the author theorized that the increased solubility of pectic substances at the higher pH values might be due either to depolymerization of the pectin molecules or to binding of calcium ions by the citrate buffer. In an early study on the culinary quality of apples, Pfund (1939) found that of the varieties that she studied, the apples that were highest in pH (3.7 or above) usually remained whole during baking, while the lower the pH of the apple, the more likely it was to crack and lose its shape. Sterling (1968) cooked xylem tissue from carrots in water at pH values from 3 to 8 and reported that separation and collapse of cells increased as the pH increased. Firmness of tissue decreased as the pH increased, although there was a plateau between pH 4 and 6. Monovalent cations in the cooking water facilitated softening of the tissues, presumably because of greater dispersion of polysaccharides in the cell wall, while divalent ions firmed it.

Regardless of how cooking tenderizes plant tissue, the cooking temperature has a marked effect on the time required to weaken the intercellular material and decrease cell adhesion. Diced carrots that required 19 minutes to reach the just-done stage when boiled in a saucepan needed only 50 seconds in a pressure saucepan at 15 pounds of steam pressure to make the carrots equally tender (Borchgrevink and Charley, 1966).

Texture of Cooked Apples

Certain varieties of apples tend to retain their shape when cooked, while others slough or disintegrate into a sauce. Reeve and Leinbach (1953) attempted to relate the composition of eight varieties of apples to the texture of the cooked fruit. They noted that as apples cook, intercellular gases expand, and the bubbles escaping from the tissue cause frothing. In spite of the internal pressure developed during cooking, some varieties (Winesap and Newton Pippen) remained firm and intact and the cells did not separate readily, while at the other extreme a variety like Gravenstein cooked to a sauce in a short time. Neither the ratio of soluble to insoluble pectic substances nor the acidity of the apple could account for the differences in cooking quality. Apples that sauced readily also sloughed when raw slices were vacuum-infiltrated with cold water. The authors suggested that during cooking the expanding and escaping gases mechanically aided the separation of cells in the varieties in which the middle lamella was weak. Reeve (1953) investigated the size of the cells, the amount of intercellular spaces, and the cell-wall surface of apples of five of the varieties studied above. While the Gravenstein variety had larger cells, more intercellular space, and more cell-wall surface than did Winesap or Newtown Pippen, Rome Beauty (which resembled the last two varieties structurally) cooked to a sauce almost as readily as did the Gravenstein. Because of the inconsistent relationship between structural features and cooked texture, the author suggested that the strength of the intercellular material was a major factor determining the texture of the cooked apple. Kirkpatrick et al. (1959) examined fixed, stained sections of cooked apple tissue and reported structural changes in the cell walls which they characterized as "flaky breakdown." This was observed in Rome Beauty, Golden Delicious, and Stayman more often than in Jonathan and Red Delicious varieties. "Flakes" were more pronounced in the hypodermal cells of the skin than in the interior of the apple. The "flakes" appeared to contain cellulose, and the authors suggested that cooking might have altered the cellulose of the cell wall.

Sugar in Cooked Fruit

The firming of fruit tissue cooked in heavy syrup is well established (Sterling, 1968). When raw fruit first comes in contact with syrup, water is withdrawn from cells by osmosis until heat destroys the selective permeability of the cytoplasmic membranes. Thereafter, translocation of soluble solids and of liquid takes place by diffusion. Sterling and Chichester (1960) studied the disposition of sugar in cooked fruit tissue. They showed by means of C^{14}-labeled glucose that sugar from the syrup around cooked fruit is found in higher concentration in the cell walls than in the fluid within the cells. This is true in parenchyma cells, but especially in the thickened walls of vascular elements. They suggested that sugar hydrogen-bonds to pectic substances, cellulose, and hemicelluloses in the cell wall. They postulate that the concentration of sugar attained in the cell wall is influenced by the number of hydrogen bonding sites, and that sugar is adsorbed by the cell against a concentration gradient until an equilibrium is reached between the tendency of the sugar molecules to join and to leave the hydrogen-bonding sites on the cell wall. The high concentration of sugar adsorbed by cell wall constituents lowers the activity of water in the cell. This leads to reentry of water from the syrup into the cell and to some extent compensates for water withdrawn originally from the live cells by osmosis when they came in contact with the syrup. A similar uptake of sugars by cell walls of canned fruit followed by uptake of water from the syrup presumably accounts for the increase in drained weight of canned fruit that begins within a few days after processing (Sterling, 1959).

Textural Quality of Cooked Potatoes

The culinary quality of potatoes, and in particular the texture of the cooked product, has been the subject of numerous studies. The literature is voluminous and the issue is far from settled. The texture of cooked potatoes may vary from one extreme described as waxy, pasty, sticky, or soggy to another, variously characterized as mealy, granular, floury, or dry. Some mealy potatoes also slough badly. Separation of starch-filled cells, individually or in clusters, characterizes mealy potatoes, in contrast to waxy potatoes, in which the cells adhere. Because cell separation is believed to be due to failure of intercellular material of the middle lamella, a number of studies have attempted to relate the pectic content of potatoes to texture in the cooked product. Early work pursuing this line was reviewed by Weier and Stocking (1949). Using newer methods for pectin analysis, Bettelheim and Sterling (1955b) found no clear-cut, direct relationship between various pectic constituents of the nine varieties of potatoes they analyzed and the cooked texture.

Starch accounts for the major solids in the potato, and this component has been studied extensively in relation to cooked quality. It has been known for some time that the specific gravity of the potatoes and the dry matter, which is mainly starch, are related. Bettelheim and Sterling (1955a) confirmed the results of earlier work that high specific gravity and high starch content of the tubers tend to be associated with mealiness in the cooked product. However, these authors found that differences in the starch content alone could not account for differences in texture of the cooked potatoes. They concluded that their data did show that the starch content and the calcium content of the tuber and the intrinsic viscosity of the pectic fraction that was soluble in a calcium-sequestering agent (Calgon) could account for more than 90 percent of the differences in texture observed in the potatoes they analyzed. They theorized that swelling of starch grains with the resultant rounding of potato cells that favors cell separation is opposed by the calcium content of the tuber and the size of the pectic polymers available to contribute to cell adhesion (Sterling and Bettelheim, 1955). The interrelation of these three factors determines whether the potato cells separate or adhere upon cooking.

The relation of the size of the starch grains to the mealiness of the tuber has been investigated. Briant et al. (1945) reported that the higher the percentage of small starch grains, the less mealy the tuber. A high correlation between high specific gravity of potato tubers and percentage of large starch grains and between low specific gravity and percentage of small starch grains was found by Sharma and Thompson (1956). Unrau and Nylund (1957a) found no association between the size of the starch grains and the mealiness of potato. These same authors (1957b) found that a high amylose content of the starch and mealiness were positively correlated. A high correlation between starch content and cell size and between mealiness and cell size was reported by Barrios et al. (1963). Russet Burbank, a variety that tends to be mealy, had the largest cells, the highest percentage of total starch, and the highest percentage of large starch grains of the four varieties they studied. Geddes et al. (1965) examined maturing potato tubers and found that, as the tubers matured, the average size of the starch grains increased, as did the percentage of amylose. Larger starch grains gelatinized at a lower temperature. They concluded that "fundamental properties of a sample of potato starch are determined essentially by the size of the granules." Earlier, Briant et al. (1945) had reported that starch from mealy tubers gelatinized at a somewhat lower temperature than did that from soggy tubers.

Starch grains differ in size from one part of the tuber to another, according to Reeve (1967). Starch grains in the storage parenchyma cells inside the vascular ring are the largest. Those in the central pith or water core are somewhat smaller, and those in the storage parenchyma outside the vascular ring are the smallest. The smaller number of starch grains in the water core accounts for its translucency. According to this author, both the cells and the starch grains of the Russet Burbank are larger than those of the White Rose, a variety that tends to be waxy.

Wager (1963) has suggested that phytic acid (phytin) may be involved in the change in texture when potatoes are cooked. He suggests that in mature tubers phytic acid binds calcium ions and so renders pectic substances in the middle lamella soluble. He found more phytin in the bud end than in the stem end of the potato. Lancaster and Sweetman (1932) had reported that the bud end cooked sooner than the stem end.

Textural Defects in Heated Snap Beans

Two textural defects have been observed in green beans that were heat processed in cans. In one, sloughing—breakdown in the layer of parenchyma cells of the pod just underneath the skin—causes the pod to separate into layers and gives it an undesirable texture. The other defect, "squeaky beans," refers to the sound made when the teeth penetrate the too firm flesh of the pod. Both defects are believed to be related to the blanching treatment given the beans prior to packing for heat processing (Van Buren et al., 1960; Sistrunk and Cain, 1960). Blanching is believed to influence the proportion of water-soluble to water-insoluble pectic substances (pectates and pectinates) through its action on the pectin methylesterase in the beans. If beans are either unblanched or overblanched, they are likely to slough; if underblanched, they are likely to be squeaky. It appears that the pectin methylesterase in the beans, which catalyzes the deesterification of the pectic substances, requires some heat for activation (Van Buren et al., 1962). If allowed to act too long, however, excessive demethylation of pectic substances takes place, and an excess of insoluble pectates and pectinates that forms as a result makes the bean pods too firm. Unblanched beans and those blanched at a temperature high enough to inactivate the enzyme are likely to slough because of the high proportion of high-methoxyl, water-soluble pectin.

Texture of Cooked Dried Peas and Beans

Under some circumstances dried beans and peas are difficult to tenderize by cooking. Storage temperature appears to be a factor influencing cookability. Dried beans that had been stored for one year at 75° F had tougher skins and firmer cotyledons when cooked than did those stored at 40° F (Dawson et al., 1952). Moisture content of the stored beans affects cookability. A high moisture level (above 13 percent) in beans stored 6 months or longer at 77° F had a deleterious effect on both flavor and texture, according to Morris and Wood (1956). Dried beans were not difficult to cook when stored for 2 years at a moisture content below 10 percent. Burr et al. (1968) found that the moisture content and the storage temperature were interrelated. Moisture content made less difference in the cookability of dried beans when the storage temperature was low (40° F), and storage temperature was less critical when the moisture content of the beans was low.

Hard- and soft-cooking dried peas differ in that the latter contain more phytic acid (inositol hexaphosphate), according to Mattson et al. (1950). Phytic acid is present in uncooked peas as a water-soluble salt, probably potassium phytate (Crean and Haisman, 1963). As peas cook, the phytate complexes with calcium and magnesium ions that would otherwise form insoluble salts with pectic substances in the cell wall and the middle lamella. The insoluble calcium magnesium phytate (phytin) apparently does not contribute to cell adhesion. Crean and Haisman found that calcium ions in the cooking water reduced the amount of phytate available to bind divalent ions in the peas. Because phytate ions bound less than half of the divalent cations in peas, these authors concluded that a high level of phytate would not necessarily make dried peas cookable, although a low level would make them hard to cook in the presence of small amounts of divalent ions. Rosenbaum (1966) proposed that cookability of peas depended on the ratio of phytic acid to calcium.

PLANT ACIDS

The cell sap of most plant tissue is slightly acidic due to the presence of acids or acid salts, of which there are a number. Malic and citric are the main aliphatic acids in most plants. Other acids, also intermediates in the TCA (Krebs) cycle, include aconitic, *iso*citric, fumaric, *a*-ketoglutaric, oxalacetic, and succinic (Ranson, 1965). Oxalic and tartaric are two other aliphatic acids, not a part of the TCA cycle, that are found in certain plants. Aromatic acids that occur in plants include benzoic, quinic, shikimic, and chlorogenic. Formulas for the acids named above are given.

Monocarboxylic Acids

Formic	$HCOOH$
Acetic	CH_3COOH
Propionic	CH_3CH_2COOH
Butyric	$CH_3CH_2CH_2COOH$
Valeric	$CH_3CH_2CH_2CH_2COOH$
Caproic	$CH_3CH_2CH_2CH_2CH_2COOH$

Dicarboxylic Acids

Oxalic

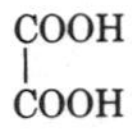

$$\begin{array}{c} COOH \\ | \\ COOH \end{array}$$

Succinic

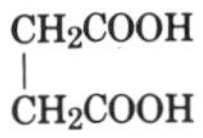

$$\begin{array}{c} CH_2COOH \\ | \\ CH_2COOH \end{array}$$

Fumaric

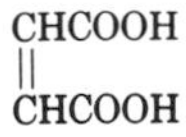

$$\begin{array}{c} CHCOOH \\ \| \\ CHCOOH \end{array}$$

Oxalacetic

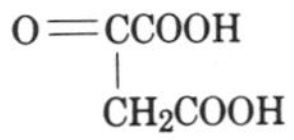

$$\begin{array}{c} O{=}CCOOH \\ | \\ CH_2COOH \end{array}$$

α-ketoglutaric

$$\begin{array}{c} CH_2COOH \\ | \\ CH_2 \\ | \\ O{=}CCOOH \end{array}$$

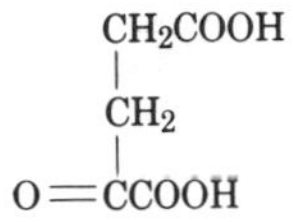

Hydroxycarboxylic Acids

Malic

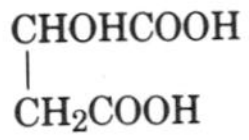

$$\begin{array}{c} CHOHCOOH \\ | \\ CH_2COOH \end{array}$$

Tartaric

$$\begin{array}{c} CHOHCOOH \\ | \\ CHOHCOOH \end{array}$$

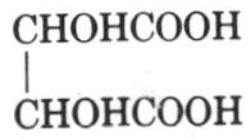

Tricarboxylic Acids

Citric

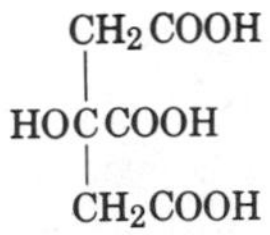

$$\begin{array}{c} CH_2\,COOH \\ | \\ HOC\,COOH \\ | \\ CH_2COOH \end{array}$$

Isocitric

$$\begin{array}{c} HO\,CCOOH \\ | \\ CHCOOH \\ | \\ CH_2COOH \end{array}$$

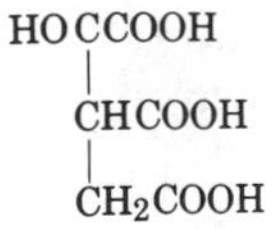

Aconitic

$$\begin{array}{c} COOH \\ | \\ C{=}CHCOOH \\ | \\ CH_2COOH \end{array}$$

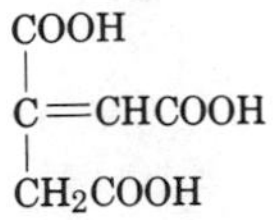

Aromatic Acids

Benzoic

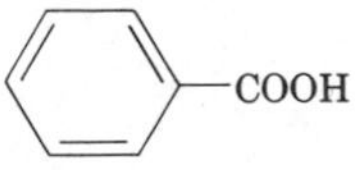

Shikimic

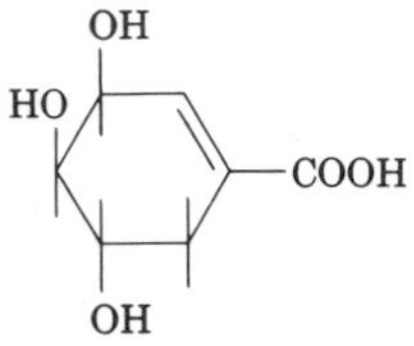

Quinic

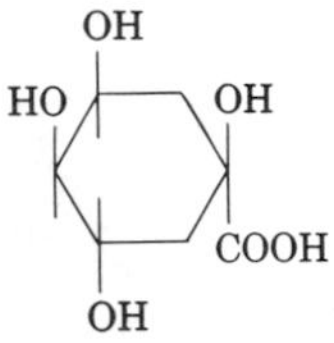

Chlorogenic

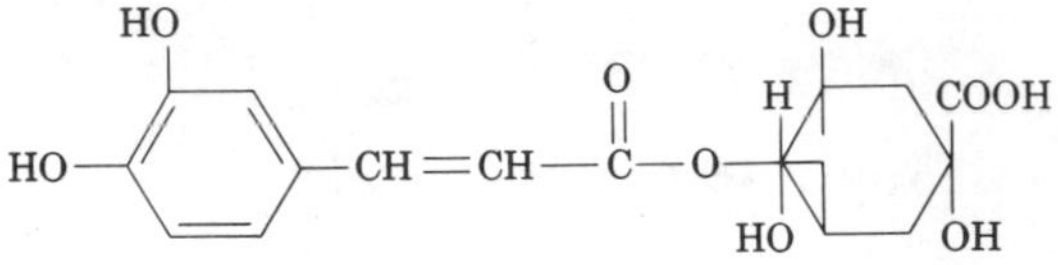

Volatile Acids

In cooking, the organic acids in plants may be divided into two classes, volatile and nonvolatile. Volatile acids escape from the liquid as vapor during cooking. The odor of acetic acid when vinegar is heated is well known. Masters and Garbutt (1920) first suggested that volatile acids were liberated when vegetables were cooked. The monocarboxylic acids listed on p. 268 are volatile. Amounts of each of the first four acids on the list that appeared in various fractions of distillates obtained from approximately 40 ml 0.1 N acid diluted to 110 ml are given in Table 1 (Gillespie and Walters, 1917). The amount of volatile acids found in different plants varies; it varies in different parts of the same plant also. Asparagus, cabbage, cauliflower, and peas were used to determine the comparative quantity of volatile acids evolved during three five-minute periods. The amount was always greatest during the first five minutes of cooking.

Nonvolatile Acids

The nonvolatile acids escape into the cooking water. This can be demonstrated readily for fruits by tasting the water in which they are cooked or for vegetables by determining the pH of the cooking water before and

TABLE 1. Percentage of Original Acid in Various Fractions of Distillate
(110 ml of Dilute Solutions Distilled)

Volume of Distillate (ml)	Formic	Acetic	Propionic	Butyric
10	4.2	6.4	11.2	16.4
20	8.5	13.0	22.2	31.2
30	13.2	19.7	32.7	44.8
40	18.2	26.7	42.9	56.6
50	23.4	34.1	52.7	67.3
60	29.3	41.6	62.0	76.2
70	36.0	49.9	70.9	84.0
80	43.6	58.7	79.1	90.1
90	53.0	68.5	86.7	94.8
100	65.3	79.9	93.6	97.8

after the vegetable is cooked. The major portion of the acids liberated
from fruits and vegetables during cooking does not volatilize. Vegetables
vary in the extent to which they alter the pH of the cooking water because of differences in acidity of the raw vegetable. Acidity or alkalinity
of the cooking water will influence the final pH, too. See the discussion
of purity of water in Chapter 1.

Occurrence

While a number of organic acids may appear in any one fruit or vegetable, one acid usually predominates. Why one acid predominates in a
particular plant tissue and why certain acids accumulate in such high
concentrations (from a biological standpoint) are unanswered questions.
MacLennan et al. (1963) used 1-C^{14} acetate to label the carboxyl carbons
of intermediates in the TCA cycle. They concluded that individual acids
in many instances were located far from the turnover pool of intermediates involved in respiration. These authors suggested that the major
portion of an acid found in high concentration in a plant cell was not a
part of the turnover pool but instead was found in the vacuoles that
served as "sinks" for the acid.

Early work on the acid content of fruits and vegetables was done by
Hartmann and Hillig (1934). They reported the citric and malic acid
contents of 29 fruits and 29 vegetables. The pH of 27 fruits was reported
by Goldmann (1949), and the occurrence of the main organic acids in
plants was summarized by Thimann and Bonner (1950). Literature on
the occurrence of some 75 organic acids in higher plants was tabulated
by Buch (1960). Malic and citric acids predominate in most fruits and
vegetables.

Fruits

Apples

Hulme (1958) listed 13 different acids that had been reported in apples up to the date of his review. The list included quinic acid, identified in apples by this author (1951). Kenworthy and Harris (1960) analyzed three varieties of apples from Michigan (McIntosh, Red Delicious, and Golden Delicious) and Golden Delicious from Washington. They found that the variety and the growing area made a difference in both the kind and the amount of organic acids present. While malic was the main acid in McIntosh and in Golden Delicious apples from Michigan, it was not found in Red Delicious, in which *m*-tartaric acid was the main one. In the Golden Delicious apples from Washington, malic acid was supplanted by indole-3-acetic acid as the main one.

Bananas

Steward et al. (1960) reported that in Gros Michel bananas, malic and citric were the chief acids, with some succinic. Keto acids identified included pyruvic, oxalacetic, and α-ketoglutaric. Miller and Ross (1963) reported that malic and citric acids were the main ones in Dwarf Cavendish bananas, too, and that these two accounted for as much as 80 percent of the total acids. In 1964, Wyman and Palmer found that malic accounted for approximately 65 percent of the total; citric (plus phosphoric) for approximately 20 percent; and oxalic for about 10 percent of the acids in Gros Michel bananas. Traces of other acids were present.

Berries

Citric was identified as the main acid in strawberries and in red and black raspberries (Nelson, 1925). The first two contained small amounts of malic acid also. Whiting (1958) determined the nonvolatile organic acids in a number of berries. Gooseberries contained approximately the same amounts of citric and malic acids. Citric acid was the dominant one in red and black currants, loganberries, raspberries, strawberries, and elderberries, although some malic acid was present in these berries too. Blackberries, both wild and tame, contained malic acid but no citric. Instead, these two berries contained *iso*citric acid and its lactone, these last two accounting for almost half of the total acid present. Gooseberries, blackberries, and elderberries contained small amounts of shikimic and quinic acids.

Markakis et al. (1963) tentatively identified 16 organic acids in blueberries. The main ones were citric, chlorogenic, malic, quinic, and phosphoric. In boysenberries the main acid was citric, but some malic and a small amount of *iso*citric were present, too, according to Rohrer and Luh

(1959). Concentrations of the various acids found in cranberries included approximately 1 percent citric, 0.5 percent to 0.9 percent quinic, approximately 0.26 percent malic, and 0.065 percent benzoic (Fellers and Esselen, 1955).

Citrus Fruits

The main acid in lemons is citric (45 to 65 mg/ml), but some malic acid is present (1.5 to 4.3 mg/ml), according to Sinclair and Eny (1945). These authors found that the concentration of free acid increased and the pH decreased as the fruit matured. In Valencia oranges the citric acid content increased during early development, but the concentration of this acid decreased as the fruit matured. The concentration of malic acid changed little, thus indicating continued production of this acid as the fruit increased in size. Sinclair et al. (1945) reported that the concentration of malic acid per milliliter of orange juice (with one exception) varied little (1.40 to 1.77 mg/ml), but that citric acid varied widely (8.38 to 25.39 mg/ml). Ting and Deszyck (1959) reported the presence of l-quinic acid in orange, grapefruit, tangerine, lemon, and lime. Clements (1964) reported the citric and malic acid contents of a variety of citrus fruits. Three lots of navel oranges varied in citric acid content from 0.56 to 0.93 gm/100 ml of juice. The higher value was near the 0.98 gm/100 ml for the Valencia orange juice analyzed, near the 0.86 gm/100 ml and 1.22 gm/100 ml for the two lots of tangerine juice, and near the 1.19 gm/100 ml for Texas pink grapefruit juice. Two other varieties of grapefruit had citric acid contents near 2 gm/100 ml of juice, while the two lots of lemons analyzed were near 4 gm/100 ml. The concentration of malic acid was low in all these fruits. Only in limes (Palestine sweet) did malic acid concentration exceed that of citric acid (0.20 gm/100 ml versus 0.08 gm/100 ml). Ting and Vines (1966) determined the acids in Hamlin oranges and in Marsh grapefruit. They reported the presence of eight acids, the main ones being citric, malic, and quinic. Quinic acid content decreased as the fruit matured. The concentration of citric acid in the oranges dropped after a high in the summer, while in the grapefruit this acid showed no seasonal trend, although it did increase on a per-fruit basis. Although the concentration of malic acid decreased in both fruits after a high in May, it increased on a per-fruit basis as the fruit developed, in the orange particularly. The citric/malic acid ratio decreased as the fruit ripened.

Grapes

Malic is the predominant acid in grapes (Concord and wine types), which contain high proportions of tartaric acid also (Nelson, 1925; Peynaud and Maurie, 1953).

Peaches

David et al. (1956) reported that malic, citric, and quinic were the main acids in cling (Halford and Peak) peaches and in freestones (Faye Elbertas). Acids increased as the fruit developed and then decreased as it ripened, citric more so than malic in clings. Ripe clings had a higher ratio of malic to citric acid than did freestones. Li and Woodroof (1968) reported that citric acid accounted for 58 to 71 percent of the total acid in shipping-ripe peaches (three varieties), malic acid 29 to 44 percent, and succinic 0.6 to 0.9 percent. Quinic acid was not determined. At the soft ripe stage the proportion of malic acid, which varied from 53 to 75 percent, exceeded that of citric acid.

Pears

Nine organic acids had been reported in pears up to the time of Hulme's review (1958). Dame et al. (1956) reported that citric and malic were the main acids in Bartlett pears. Both decreased as the pears ripened, malic more than citric.

Pineapple

Gortner (1963) found that the citric acid in pineapple increased as the fruit ripened. Malic acid content fluctuated according to the weather. This author suggested that malic acid was metabolized following periods of sunshine and accumulated during cloudy weather. Singleton and Gortner (1965) reported that malic acid exceeded citric in immature fruit but that citric rose steadily, and during the last month the citric acid content of the fruit was three times that of the malic acid content.

Rhubarb

Pucher et al. (1937) found that *l*-malic was the main acid in rhubarb, followed by oxalic and a small amount of citric. Andrews and Viser (1951) reported that rhubarb (fresh-weight basis) contained 0.275 percent oxalic acid.

Vegetables

Asparagus

Citric was the main acid found in asparagus, followed by malic (Dame et al., 1959). The taller the spears above the ground, the higher the citric/malic acid ratio. Minor acids identified included fumaric, succinic, α-ketoglutaric, and glycolic.

Broccoli

The acids reported in broccoli were *l*-malic, citric, and small amounts of oxalic and succinic (Nelson and Mattern, 1931).

Carrots

Malic was reported to be the main acid in carrots by MacLennan et al. (1963).

Potato

Schwart et al. (1962) identified the following acids in potato: aspartic, chlorogenic, citric, glutamic, malic, oxalic, and phosphoric.

Squash

Lewis and Elbert (1964) identified citric and malic as the main acids in winter squash (three varieties). The trace of fumaric identified at harvest disappeared on short storage.

Spinach

Nelson and Mottern (1931) reported that the main acid in spinach was oxalic (0.31 percent of the fresh weight), but that small amounts of *l*-malic and citric acid were present. Pierce and Appleman (1943) reported the following concentrations of acids in spinach leaves: 362 to 380 meq of total acid per 100 grams of dried leaf, 280 to 309 meq of oxalic acid, 7 to 9 meq of malic acid, and 4 to 11 meq of citric acid. Andrews and Viser (1951) reported an oxalic acid content of spinach of 1.057 percent. New Zealand spinach and beet greens also contain high concentrations of oxalic acid (Ryder, 1930).

Tomatoes

Rice and Peterson (1954) found that citric was the main acid in tomato juice (9 lots analyzed). This acid accounted for approximately 65 percent of the total, malic acid about 5 percent, and pyrrolidone carboxylic approximately 30 percent. Villarreal et al. (1960) reported that citric acid made up 73 to 80 percent of the total acid in canned Pearson tomato juice. Some malic was present, and pyrrolidone carboxylic acid made up 15 to 20 percent of the total. The authors suggested that the last was formed when the juice was processed. Citric acid content of the juice decreased from 0.346 percent for firm ripe tomatoes to 0.254 percent for soft ripe ones. The pH of the tomatoes increased from 4.35 for firm ripe ones to 4.60 for soft ripe ones. A range in pH from 4.30 to 4.50 and in citric acid content from 0.35 to 0.46 percent was reported for eight varieties of tomatoes by Hamdy and Gould (1962).

PLANT PIGMENTS

Fruits and vegetables have special appeal in part because of the bright, attractive colors of the pigments that they contain. The main classes of plant pigments are the carotenoids, the chlorophylls, and the flavonoids. The last is a diverse group that includes the anthocyanins, flavones, flavonols, flavanols, leucoanthocyanins, and related phenolic compounds. The carotenoids and the chlorophylls are fat soluble and are found in the plastids. The water-soluble flavonoids are dissolved in the cell sap.

If fruits and vegetables are improperly handled, these pigments may undergo changes that result in either a less colorful or an unattractive product. For an understanding of the nature of the changes that affect the color of the pigments and how these changes are brought about, knowledge of their structure is essential.

Carotenoids

Structure and Color

Carotenoids are yellow, orange, or red pigments so named because the first member of the group to be isolated was from carrots. One subgroup of the carotenoids, the carotenes, are hydrocarbons and the other, the xanthophylls, are oxygen derivatives of the carotenes. The commonly occurring carotenoids are composed of eight isoprene residues (Goodwin, 1955). They have a skeleton of 40 carbon atoms that includes an 18-carbon central portion with 4 methyl groups attached as side chains. Two end groups, either ring structure or open chain, attached to this central portion serve as distinguishing features for individual carotenoids. The carotenoids are polyunsaturated compounds, a number of them with 11 conjugated double bonds as shown for lycopene and beta-carotene. Lycopene is an open-chain carotenoid, while beta-carotene, the most commonly occurring isomer of the carotenes, has ring closure at either end of the molecule.

Color in these pigments is due to the oscillation of electrons the length of the unsaturated chain (Zechmeister, 1960). Carotenoids absorb light in the colored region of the spectrum, and each molecule has a characteristic absorption curve determined by its chemical makeup. The number of double bonds influences the color (Karrer and Jucker, 1950). Lycopene with the same number of conjugated double bonds as beta-carotene but with two additional double bonds in the molecule has a deeper color than does beta-carotene. These additional double bonds make the difference between the orange color of carrots, in which beta-carotene predominates, and the red of tomatoes, in which lycopene is the main carotenoid. Gamma-carotene, in which one end of the molecule is closed in a ring like beta-carotene and the other end open like lycopene, is intermediate in color between the two. Shifting one double bond out of conjugation (from between carbons 5' and 6' to between carbons 4' and 5') shifts the hue of the pigment toward yellow. Thus, alpha-carotene with

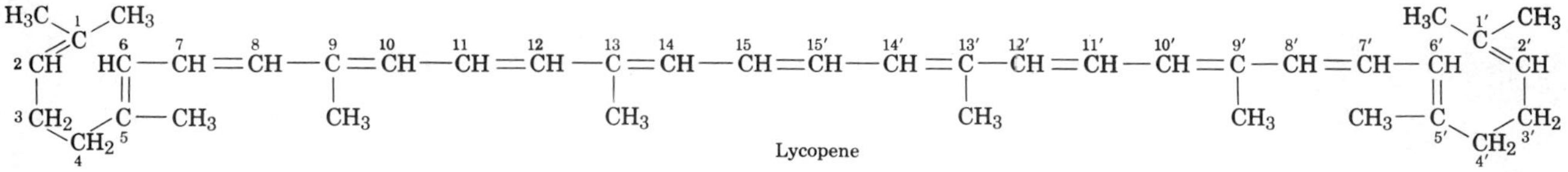

Lycopene

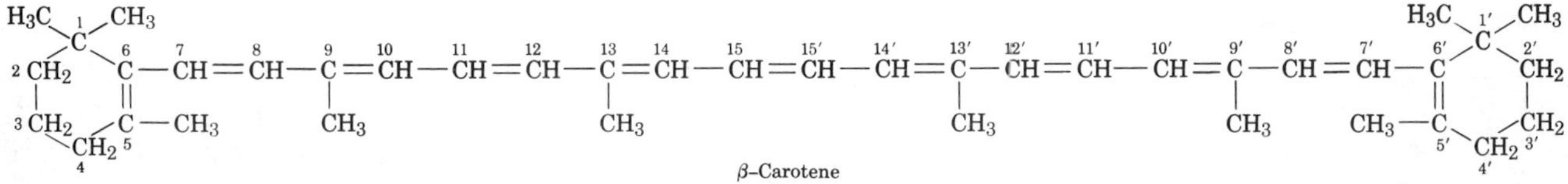

β-Carotene

(Zechmeister, 1962.)

11 double bonds but only 10 in conjugation has a more yellow and less orange hue than beta-carotene (Zechmeister, 1960). Zeta-carotene, which is 7, 8, 7′, 8′-tetrahydrolycopene and thus has fewer double bonds than lycopene and only 7 in conjugation, is a pale yellow in contrast to the deep red of lycopene. Phytofluene (hexahydrolycopene) with only 5 conjugated double bonds and phytoene (octahydrolycopene) with 3 conjugated double bonds are colorless polyenes. Observed under ultraviolet light, these carotenoids fluoresce blue.

The shape of the carbon chain, which influences the length of the molecule and the distance the electrons oscillate, affects the color of the pigment. Most carotenoids are synthesized in the more stable *trans* configuration. Where steric hindrance does not preclude it, energy in the form of heat or light may cause the extended and rod-shaped *trans* form of the molecule to assume one or more bent, *cis* configurations. Two isomeric *cis* forms of beta-carotene are neo-beta-carotene U and neo-beta-carotene B. The former is 9 mono*cis* and the latter is 9, 13′ di*cis,* according to Zechmeister (1962). The all-*trans* form is a vivid orange, the mono*cis* is shifted towards the yellow, and the di*cis* is even paler.

Xanthophylls include lutein (3, 3′-dihydroxy-alpha-carotene), zeaxanthin (3,3′-dihydroxy-beta-carotene), cryptoxanthin (3′-hydroxy-beta-carotene), and violaxanthin (3,3′-dihydroxy-5,6,5′,6′-diepoxy-beta-carotene). Individual carotenoids and their stereoisomers may be separated chromatographically by suitable combinations of adsorbents and developing reagents. The concentration of the eluted pigments may be measured spectrophotometrically.

Beta-carotene can give rise to two molecules of vitamin A, the split in the molecule occurring between carbons 15 and 15′. Alpha-carotene, gamma-carotene, and cryptoxanthin yield one molecule of vitamin A each. Neo-beta-carotene B has approximately half the vitamin A value of the all-*trans* form (Kemmerer and Fraps, 1943).

Distribution

Most vegetables and fruits contain a complex mixture of carotenoids. Carotenoids are found in yellow fruits and vegetables and in the grana of the chloroplasts of green leafy tissue, where they are masked by the chlorophyll until the tissue becomes senescent. The carotenoid content of fruits increases during ripening, although part of the intensification of color is due to loss of chlorophyll.

Freestone (Elberta) and cling (Halford) peaches have a similar carotenoid content, qualitatively, according to Curl (1959). In clings, three xanthophylls, violaxanthin, cryptoxanthin, and one first identified in peaches and called persicaxanthin, account for approximately half of the total carotenoids. Beta-carotene and lycopene account for approximately 10 percent each. Twenty-one carotenoids were identified in fresh pineapple, with violaxanthin contributing 50 percent of the total and beta-carotene 9 percent (Morgan, 1966).

Violaxanthin makes up approximately half the total carotenoids in navel oranges and beta-carotene less than one percent (Curl and Bailey, 1961). Qualitatively the carotenoids in valencia oranges are similar to those in navel oranges. Major carotenoids reported for Italian prunes are violaxanthin (35 percent), beta-carotene (19 percent), lutein (16 percent), and cryptoxanthin (7 percent), together with 20 minor ones (Curl, 1963). Beta-carotene is the chief carotenoid pigment in muskmelons with an orange flesh, accounting for approximately 85 percent of the total (Curl, 1966).

Lycopene contributes to the color of pink grapefruit and is the major carotenoid in Ruby Red grapefruit, making up 40 percent of the total carotenoids, with beta-carotene accounting for 27 percent (Curl and Bailey, 1957). Lycopene is the predominant pigment in watermelon (Zechmeister and Polgár, 1941), rose hips, and most tomatoes. Three genes are involved in determining the color of tomatoes, which may be yellow or orange (tangerine) as well as red. In yellow tomatoes, where beta-carotene synthesis predominates, the gene for lycopene formation is recessive, r, while in orange and red fruits this gene is dominant, R (Porter and Lincoln, 1950). Synthesis of lycopene in the all-*trans* form and the formation of a red tomato is controlled by a dominant gene, T, while the recessive form, t, permits the synthesis of prolycopene, a poly-*cis* form, and the formation of an orange tomato (Zechmeister and Went, 1948). Synthesis of lycopene may be suppressed in the red genotype, if mature but green-colored fruit is exposed to temperatures above 30° C. A temperature of 19° C is optimum for lycopene formation and normal reddening (Went et al., 1942).

The main pigment in red bell peppers is capsanthin (35 percent), a 6-keto carotenoid with one ring a cyclopentane. This is the predominant pigment in paprika also. Capsorubin, a 6,6'-diketo carotenoid with both rings as cyclopentanes, is present but in smaller concentration (6.4 percent), as are beta-carotene (11.6 percent), violaxanthin (9.9 percent) and cryptoxanthin (6.7 percent) (Curl, 1962). Keto carotenoids are absent from green bell peppers, in which the major carotenoid pigments are lutein (40.8 percent), beta-carotene (13.4 percent), violaxanthin (13.8 percent), and neoxanthin (15.1 percent) (Curl, 1964).

Carotenoids are found in high concentration in many varieties of carrots and are more abundant in the phloem than in the central core. The major carotenoids are beta-carotene and alpha-carotene. Gamma-carotene, zeta-carotene, phytoene, phytofluene, and lycopene are present in some varieties. A wide range in crude carotene content of 7 to 12 micrograms per gram for light-colored carrots to 100 to 170 micrograms per gram for those highly pigmented has been reported (Smith and Otis, 1941). Fourteen garden varieties of carrots averaged 54 micrograms per gram, somewhat over half of which was beta-carotene, according to Harper and Zscheile (1945). One variety contained 108 micrograms per gram. Crude carotene content of carrots analyzed by Kemmerer et al. (1945) averaged 96 micrograms per gram, 62 percent of which was beta-carotene and 29 percent alpha-carotene. The carotenes of carrots are found diffused throughout the cytoplasm, in association with starch grains, and as "carotene bodies" that assume a variety of shapes including flakes, needles, spirals, and ribbons (Weier, 1942). These can be observed under the microscope in free-hand sections. Part of the carotene is believed to be associated with protein.

In green leaves, xanthophylls are more abundant than are the carotenes. Lutein is the predominant xanthophyll in green, leafy tissue. The main carotene is beta-carotene, which makes up approximately three fourths of the total carotenes in leafy vegetables (Kemmerer et al., 1945).

Stability of Carotenoids

Carotenoid pigments are susceptible to oxidation. Dehydrated plant tissue such as carrots, when exposed to air, loses color due to oxidation of the highly unsaturated molecules. This fading occurs in both freeze-dried and heat-dried carrots, but fading can be decreased if the vegetable is blanched prior to drying (Reeve, 1943). Thus, unblanched dehydrated carrots stored for 6 months contained 9 mg of carotene per 100 grams dry weight, and blanched samples averaged 54 mg per 100 grams. This protective effect of blanching is attributed to the disruption of the lipoprotein complex in the cells and the dissolving of carotene in the freed fat, which collects in globules.

The carotenoids in fruits and vegetables have been considered stable to ordinary cooking procedures. Martin et al. (1960) reported nearly 100 percent retention of carotene when fresh or frozen broccoli was cooked. Cooking methods that were compared included a pressure saucepan, a large amount of boiling water, a small amount of water, both cold start and boiling, and microwave. Complete retention of the carotene in frozen peas, whether cooked by microwave or by conventional heating, was reported by Eheart and Gott (1964).

Carotenoid pigments are known to be susceptible to *trans-cis* isomerization when exposed to either heat or light, especially in the presence of acid (Karrer and Jucker, 1950). Thus, boiling carrots for 30 minutes resulted in an increase in *cis* isomers of beta-carotene in the cooked product. Neo-beta-carotene U increased from one percent in the raw carrots to two percent in the cooked ones, and neo-beta-carotene B increased from three percent in the raw carrots to 11 percent in the cooked ones (Kemmerer et al., 1945). Color and carotene content of carrots cooked in a saucepan (19 minutes) and in a pressure saucepan (50 seconds), both to the just-tender stage, and those overcooked in a pressure saucepan (2 minutes) were compared (Borchgrevink and Charley, 1966). Those cooked in a saucepan had the highest concentration of all-*trans* beta-carotene, and those overcooked in the pressure saucepan had the lowest. Neo-beta-carotene B content was highest in those overcooked in the pressure saucepan and lowest in those cooked in a saucepan. Those cooked in the pressure saucepan for 50 seconds were intermediate. These differences were reflected in the color of the cooked carrots, those from the saucepan having a red-orange hue, while the hue of those overcooked in the pressure saucepan was shifted toward the yellow.

The change in color of pineapple from the orange-yellow of the raw to the lemon-yellow of the canned is attributed to the shift of the predominant 5,6 epoxy-carotenoids to 5,8 epoxides. The isomerization is catalyzed by acid, and heat favors the shift (Singleton et al., 1961).

Rutabagas are one vegetable in which the color is intensified by cooking. The raw vegetable contains poly-*cis* lycopene, part of which is shifted to the all-*trans* form by cooking (Hanson, 1954).

Chlorophylls

Structure

A molecule of chlorophyll consists of four 5-membered pyrrole groups arranged to form a porphyrin ring as shown (Bogorad, 1965). An atom of

Chlorophyll *a*,
Chlorophyll *b*, — CHO at carbon marked *

magnesium in the center of the molecule is chelated by the four nitrogens of the pyrrole groups. The numbering system used to designate the carbon atoms in this part of the molecule, sometimes referred to as the porphyrin head, is given. The color of the unsaturated chlorophyll is dependent on the resonance of the conjugated double bonds, of which there are 10. Because of the ring structure, these double bonds also migrate around the ring (Wald, 1959).

In addition to the porphyrin head, a feature that the pigments myoglobin and chlorophyll have in common, chlorophyll is a methyl, phytyl ester. The methyl group is attached to the carboxyl adjacent carbon 10 and the phytyl group to the propionic acid residue of which carbon 7 is a part. The phytyl group, which is twice as long as the dimensions of the porphyrin ring (ca-20 Å versus 10 Å, Frey-Wyssling and Mühlethaler, 1965), is visualized as being positioned at an angle to the plane of the porphyrin ring. This phytyl portion of the molecule is responsible for the solubility of chlorophyll in fat and in such fat solvents as acetone, benzene, and alcohol.

Two forms of chlorophyll are found in vegetables and fruits. Chlorophyll *a* has a methyl group attached at carbon 3, while in chlorophyll *b* an aldehyde group (—CHO) replaces this methyl group. The two forms of the pigment differ in hue, chlorophyll *a* being bright blue-green and chlorophyll *b* yellow-green. Chlorophyll *a* exceeds chlorophyll *b* in most fresh plant tissue.

Location

Chlorophylls are found in high concentration in the chloroplasts of the mesophyll cells of the leaf. These green photosynthetic pigments, together with the carotenoids, are found in the grana of the chloroplasts (Park, 1965). These structures act as photoreceptors to trap light energy and convert it to chemical energy. Chlorophylls and carotenoids constitute five to six percent of the chloroplasts, and the two chlorophylls are present in a ratio of three parts chlorophyll *a* to one part chlorophyll *b* (Wolken, 1959). Chloroplasts are approximately half protein and one third fat (Frey-Wyssling and Mühlethaler, 1965). The three components, protein, fat, and pigments, are laid down in the grana in layers called lamella. Current theories of the submicroscopic structure of the chloroplasts have been reviewed by Frey-Wyssling and Mühlethaler (1965).

Stability

Changes in the chlorophyll molecule that may affect the color include loss of magnesium, removal of phytyl and methyl ester groups, and oxidation of the ring. Chlorophylls are sensitive to degradation by acid (Joslyn and Mackinney, 1938), particularly carboxylic acids such as are present in fruits and vegetables (Aronoff, 1953). In fresh, raw tissue, acids and pigments are in separate compartments within the cell, but treatment such as cooking that alters the permeability of cell membranes permits contact of acid and pigment. Magnesium in the chlorophyll molecule is displaced and is replaced by two hydrogen atoms. Magnesium-free molecules are referred to as pheophytins; those from chlorophyll a are pheophytin a and those from chlorophyll b are pheophytin b. Pheophytin a is a grayish green and pheophytin b a dull yellowish green. Loss of magnesium from the molecule, especially from chlorophyll a, leads to marked alteration in the color of chlorophyll-rich foods. While neither is recommended in foods, copper or zinc ions can replace the displaced magnesium and restore the green color of chlorophyll.

When green vegetables are put into boiling water, the immediate effect is an intensification of the color. Expulsion of gas from intercellular spaces, which in the raw vegetable refract light and dull the color, is one factor. Change in the condition or distribution of the constituents in the grana has been suggested as another factor (Mackinney and Weast, 1940). The bright green of the undercooked tissue may in the cooked vegetable become a dull olive green. The speed and extent of change in color is influenced by several factors.

The length of the heating period influences the alteration of the pigment. Sweeney and Martin (1958) measured loss of chlorophylls a and b when broccoli was cooked for periods of 5, 10, 15, and 20 minutes. Chlorophyll a was degraded more rapidly than chlorophyll b, to the greater detriment of the color. At the end of 5 minutes of cooking, retention of chlorophyll a was approximately 80 percent and of chlorophyll b 90 percent. At the end of 10 minutes, retentions were 45 percent and 87 percent, respectively. At the end of 20 minutes less than one third of the chlorophyll remained, and, what was even worse from the standpoint of color, the ratio of chlorophyll a to chlorophyll b had dropped from 1.77 in broccoli cooked for 5 minutes to 0.65 in that cooked for 20 minutes. Mackinney and Joslyn (1940) had reported earlier that chlorophyll a was converted to pheophytin 7 to 9 times faster than was chlorophyll b.

The hydrogen ion concentration of the vegetable influences the speed and extent of conversion of chlorophylls to pheophytins. Sweeney and Martin (1961) reported a high retention of chlorophyll in cooked frozen spinach of 72.2 percent and in cooked frozen peas of 67.6 percent, both vegetables having high pH values of 6.8 and 7.0, respectively. Retention in cooked green beans was 26.7 percent and in Brussels sprouts 20.7 percent, these vegetables having lower pH values of 6.2 and 6.3, respectively. Furthermore, when green beans were cooked in water buffered to elevate the pH, the higher the pH, the better the retention of chlorophyll, up to pH 7. The higher the pH, the faster the vegetable was tenderized, also. Cooking green vegetables in a large amount of boiling water to dilute the acid and with the pan uncovered, especially during the first few minutes, to eliminate volatile acids, are two practical techniques for minimizing the effects of acid on the color of cooked green vegetables.

The temperature used to blanch green vegetables may affect the conversion of chlorophyll to pheophytin. In one study (Van Buren et al., 1964), in which green beans were held subsequent to blanching, conversion of chlorophyll to pheophytin was greater in those blanched for 2 minutes at 70° C than in either those unblanched or those blanched at 100° C. The greater conversion of chlorophyll to pheophytin accompanied a decrease in the pH of the beans and a decrease in the water-dispersible pectin. These observations led the authors to suggest that activation of the pectin methylesterase at 70° C and the resulting demethylation of the pectic substances was responsible for the decrease in pH and the greater conversion of chlorophyll to pheophytin.

The effect of blanching on the retention of chlorophyll in green beans during subsequent frozen storage was reported by Walker (1964). Beans were blanched in boiling water for periods of 20, 30, 45, and 60 seconds and for 2, 3, 5, and 10 minutes. Conversion of chlorophylls to pheophytins increased linearly up to 3 minutes' blanching time, after which the conversion leveled off. Blanched beans were held in frozen storage at −10° C for 20 days. Loss of chlorophyll varied with the blanching treatment. Blanching times of 45 seconds and 1 minute gave best retention of chlorophylls. Loss of chlorophylls in unblanched and in underblanched green beans was attributed in part to conversion of chlorophylls to pheophytins but chiefly to oxidation of chlorophylls as a result of peroxidation of lipids in the beans. The two blanching times that gave the best retentions of chlorophylls were sufficient to completely inactivate both catalase and peroxidase in the green beans. Loss of chlorophylls in overblanched beans was attributed to "heat initiation of other systems," which resulted in oxidation of the chlorophylls.

Chapman et al. (1960) compared fresh and frozen broccoli cooked by both microwave and by boiling in a small amount of water. Cooking times for 1 pound of fresh broccoli to achieve optimum tenderness in the stems was 6 minutes by microwave and 13 minutes by boiling. Comparable cooking times for 20 ounces of frozen broccoli were 13 minutes by microwave and 11 minutes by boiling. The color of fresh broccoli cooked electronically was judged slightly better than that cooked by boiling, but the panel ranked frozen broccoli cooked by boiling above that cooked electronically. Gordon and Noble (1959) had reported better retention of the color of cabbage and broccoli cooked by boiling (in a large amount of water) than by microwave. The color of vegetables cooked by microwave was similar to that of vegetables cooked in a pressure saucepan.

An esterase enzyme, chlorophyllase, which is specific for catalyzing the hydrolysis of the phytyl ester linkage of chlorophyll has been identified in spinach (Weast and Mackinney, 1940), but is reported to be absent from beans and peas (Mackinney and Weast, 1940). The optimum temperature for the activity of this enzyme is 75° C (Weast and Mackinney, 1940). The chlorophyllides (phytyl-free chlorophylls) that result resemble their parent chlorophylls in color, but they have become soluble in water. It is believed that the amount and activity of the enzyme varies as the plant matures.

Chlorophyllase is active during the fermentation of cucumber pickle stock. The dull olive-green color of the cured pickle stock is the result of the conversion of chlorophylls to chlorophyllides that subsequently lose their magnesium to form pheophorbides due to the acids (lactic mainly) formed during fermentation. Pheophorbides predominate over pheophytins in cured pickle stock. The greatest degradation of chlorophyll occurs during the first week of the curing process (Jones et al., 1962).

Alkaline cooking water will saponify both the phytyl and the methyl ester groups of chlorophyll (Willstätter and Stoll, 1928). The salt of the free carboxylic acid that results, called chlorophyllin, is soluble in water and is a brilliant green color. Vegetables cooked in alkaline water may have a mushy texture because of the breakdown of hemicelluloses.

Flavonoid Pigments

Flavonoid pigments and related compounds are widely distributed in plant tissue. They are found in the vacuole of the cell dissolved in the cell sap. Flavonoids have a basic $C_6C_3C_6$ skeleton and consist of two benzene rings and a three-carbon chain that, together with oxygen, form a part of the central ring.

$C_6 C_3 C_6$ skeleton of flavonoid compounds

The ring on the left is designated the A ring and that on the right the B ring. The numbering system is included; carbons in the B ring are given prime numbers. The classes of flavonoid pigments include the flavones for which the entire group is named, the flavonols (flavones with a hydroxyl group substituting in the 3 position), the flavanols, the flavanones, the anthocyanins, and the proanthocyanins (leucoanthocyanins). Differences in the state of oxidation of the central ring differentiate the different classes of flavonoids as shown (Bate-Smith, 1950).

Flavone	Flavonol	Flavanone	Flavanols	Anthocyanidin
			Catechins Proanthocyanidins	

Substitutions in both the A and in the B ring differentiate the individual pigments within each subgroup of flavonoids. In the majority of flavonoids, the A ring has the hydroxyl substitution pattern of phloroglucinol and the B ring that of catechol, but other substitution patterns are found also.

Anthocyanins

Anthocyanins are red, purple, or blue pigments found in the cell sap of a number of fruits and in a few vegetables. Anthocyanins are responsible for the bright red skins of radishes, the red skins of potatoes, and the dark purple skin of eggplant. The color of red cabbage is due to the presence of an anthocyanin that is confined to layers of cells on the surface of the leaf. Fruits that contain anthocyanin pigments include blackberries, red and black raspberries, blueberries, cherries, currants, Concord and other red grapes, pomegranate, ripe gooseberries, and the red skin of apples.

Structure and Color

Anthocyanins are 2-phenyl benzopyrylium compounds. The anthocyanins are glycosides, and the sugar-free pigments, the aglycones, are designated anthocyanidins. The three commonest anthocyanidins are pelargonidin, cyanidin, and delphinidin. All three pigments have hydroxyl groups at carbon 3 and at carbons 5 and 7 in the A ring. They differ in the substitution in the B ring. Pelargonidin has one hydroxyl group at carbon 4'; cyanidin has one hydroxyl group at 4' and a second one at carbon 3'; and delphinidin has hydroxyl groups at carbons 3', 4', and 5'. Cyanidin is the most widely occurring aglycone, and it tends to occur

Pelargonidin

Cyanidin

Delphinidin

in plants that are woody rather than herbaceous. The color of the pigment shifts from the red of pelargonidin to the blue of delphinidin because of additional hydroxyl groups. Methoxyl groups replace hydroxyl groups in some anthocyanidins, and this shifts the hue towards the red. Methoxyl-3'-cyanidin (peonidin) is not as blue as cyanidin, and methoxyl-3'-delphinidin and methoxyl-3', 5' delphinidin (malvidin) are not as blue as delphinidin. The presence of a sugar residue attached by glycosidic linkage to one or more of the hydroxyl groups shifts the hue towards the red, too, but a bioside is bluer than a monoside. Most of the pigments in this group appear naturally as glycosides; pelargonidin-3-glucoside is pelargonin, cyanidin 3-glucoside is chrysanthemin, and cyanidin 3,5-glucoside is cyanin. The glycosides are more stable than the aglycones. The sugar moiety may be either a monoside or a bioside. Glucose is the sugar most often present; less frequently it is galactose and rhamnose. The common position of attachment is at carbon 3 and often at carbon 5, also. Acylated anthocyanins have a cinnamic acid esterified with a hydroxyl group either of the aglycone or of the sugar moiety. Such is the pigment of red cabbage, rubrobrassicin, which is cyanidin 5-glucoside, 3-sophoroside (a diglucoside) acylated with ferulic acid (Harborne, 1964). Each modification of the aglycone affects not only the color but also its stability and its ability to react to various treatments.

Reactions

Anthocyanins and anthocyanidins are amphoteric substances. Many of them undergo such dramatic changes in color with change in hydrogen ion concentration that an early worker, Tswett, characterized them as vegetable chameleons (Blank, 1947). When these pigments are dissolved in dilute acid, the oxygen of the ring carries a positive charge and the structure is called an oxonium or more recently a flavylium ion. Anthocyanins are present in plant tissue in this form because of the acidic cell sap. In acid media (pH 3.0 or less) where the pigment exists as the flavylium ion, the hue is shifted toward the red. As the acidity is decreased, the pigment shifts to the quinone form and becomes the violet color base in weakly acidic or weakly basic media. Near neutral, the violet color base is in equilibrium with the colorless pseudobase forms. The pigment is more stable as a flavylium ion than as a pseudobase form, which is unstable and susceptible to oxidative degradation. In a definitely alkaline medium, the blue salt of the color base forms (Blank, 1958). The effects on the molecule of differences in hydrogen ion concentration are illustrated with cyanidin, the most commonly occurring anthocyanidin (Robinson, 1942; Blank, 1958).

The pigment from red cabbage gives a wider range in colors than most, as it changes from red in acid media to green in alkaline media (Wolf, 1956). All anthocyanin pigments do not change so dramatically in color with change in pH. A minimum of four hydroxyl groups in the molecule and an unsubstituted hydroxyl group at the 4′-position favor the shift in color due to change in pH. Thus the pigment in cultivated strawberries, which is mainly pelargonidin 3-monoglucoside (Sondheimer and Karash, 1956) and so has only three free hydroxyl groups, shifts less in hue with a change in pH than does blackberry juice, in which the chief anthocyanin pigment is cyanidin-3-monoglucoside (Karrer and Pieper, 1930) or in Concord grape juice, in which the main pigments are delphinidin-3-monoglucoside and cyanidin-3-monoglucoside and their acylated (*p*-coumaric acid) derivatives (Ingalesbe et al., 1963).

Anthocyanins that have two or more adjacent, unsubstituted hydroxyl groups react with iron, aluminum, or tin to form greenish, blue, or slate-colored complexes. These metal chelates, the color of which depends on the metal involved and the chelation sites on the pigment, make the food unattractive. The effect of iron on the color of anthocyanin pigment can be demonstrated readily by shredding red cabbage with a nonstainless blade. Iron from the blade reacts with the pigment in the cabbage to form a dark blue complex. Acid will dissociate the iron-pigment chelate, as can be demonstrated by applying lemon juice to the discolored cabbage. The acid shifts the pigment to the red flavylium ion.

Because they react with metals, foods that contain anthocyanins are processed in enameled-lined tinned cans instead of in plain tin ones. Anthocyanin-containing foods may cause pitting and perforation of the can, however. Small exposed areas of the two metals, such as at the seams or in imperfections in the enameled lining, together with the acidic fruit juice form an electrolytic cell that permits localized corrosion of the can. Anthocyanins contribute to the corrosion either by binding metal ions as they are dissolved by the acid or by removing hydrogen and so acting as a depolarizer (Cruess, 1958).

While alteration in pH may bring about reversible changes in the color of anthocyanin pigments, profound and irreversible changes which result in deterioration of color may occur in the anthocyanin pigments in thermally processed fruit products. The pigment in strawberry preserves is markedly labile, a factor that limits the shelf life of the product or may make it unsalable. Factors involved in the destruction of pigment in strawberry preserves have been the subject of numerous studies. Loss of the bright red color of the freshly made product is due not only to a decrease in the pelargonidin-3-monoglucoside but to development of a brownish degradation product as well (Meschter, 1953). A number of factors influence the rate at which the pigment decomposes and the color deteriorates. A high storage temperature, a high pH, oxygen in the head space, the presence of sugars, and the presence of ascorbic acid in the preserves all favor the destruction of anthocyanin pigment. Storage of the preserves at refrigerator temperature (4° C) increases the shelf life sixfold over storage at room temperature and sixtyfold over storage in a warm place (38° C). Aerobic oxidation of ascorbic acid in the preserves induces oxidation of the anthocyanin, leading to an undesirable brown color (Sondheimer and Kertesz, 1953). These authors suggested that H_2O_2 arising from the oxidation of ascorbic acid to dehydroascorbic acid might be responsible for the oxidation of the pigment. A low pH favors retention of color (Meschter, 1953; Lukton et al., 1956), presumably by keeping the pigment shifted from the unstable pseudobase to the more stable flavylium form (Sondheimer, 1953). A low pH is particularly advantageous when oxygen is present in the headspace (Lukton et al., 1956). Sugars, especially fructose, accelerate the destruction of the pigment. Degradation products of sugar are thought to be responsible, and both furfural and hydroxyfurfural have been shown to promote degradation (Meschter, 1953; Tinsley and Bockian, 1960). Anthocyanins in heat-processed black raspberries are subject to degradation, too, and appear to be influenced by the same factors as the anthocyanin in strawberries (Daravingas and Cain, 1968).

Enzyme-Catalyzed Degradation

The existence of an anthocyanase-decolorizing enzyme was first reported by Huang (1955). Crude enzyme preparations from strains of *Aspergillus* effected varying degrees of decolorization of the anthocyanin pigments from a number of berries. Pigment from blackberries was especially labile. The enzyme was inactivated by heating at 80° C for 15 minutes. Decolorizing of the pigment was pH dependent, although the enzyme was active over the pH range for most fruits. Oxygen was not involved in the decolorization, but susceptibility of the decolorized form of the pigment to oxidation was not ruled out. Huang suggested that decolorization involved both hydrolysis of the glycoside and subsequent shift of the flavylium ion of the aglycone into a colorless pseudobase form (2-carbinol) or its ketone tautomer, as shown:

Flavylium ion   2–Carbinol base   Ketone

All pseudobases are susceptible to oxidation, and at a given pH the shift from pseudobase back to flavylium ion occurs less readily with an aglycone than with a glycoside. Huang suggests that anthocyanase might be used to eliminate excess pigment that might otherwise precipitate in bottled juices from highly pigmented fruits or to eliminate pigment completely and thus make white wine from blue or red grapes.

Van Buren et al. (1960) reported the presence of an anthocyanin-degrading enzyme in sour cherries. When this fruit is bruised, the bruised spots "scald," that is, the skin loses color, the flesh underneath becomes pale pink, and the bruised spots eventually turn brown. The authors suggested that anthocyanase comes in contact with the pigment in the bruised tissue and causes the decolorization but not the subsequent browning. They reported that cherry anthocyanase required oxygen for its action, and that it was activated by the presence of catechol. Dekazos (1966) reported that bruised spots on cherries stored in an atmosphere of oxygen turned brown, but the skin did not lose color. On the other hand, bruised cherries stored in an atmosphere of nitrogen did not brown, but the skin over the bruised area was decolorized. In the latter case migration of the pigment from the skin was attributed to permeability of the cytoplasmic membranes in the bruised areas induced by anaerobic respiration. Sakamura et al. (1965) reported that the anthocyanase enzyme in eggplant that decolorized eggplant anthocyanin (delphinidin-3-*p*-coumarylrutinoside-5-glucoside) was a polyphenolase (see page 296) and that the pigment was oxidized by the polyphenolase from mushrooms and potatoes as well. The authocyanase did not split off the sugar moiety as did the fungal anthocyanase studied by Huang. Ascorbic acid depressed the decolorization brought about by eggplant anthocyanase (see page 302).

Flavones and Flavonols

Structure

Flavones and flavonols are 2-phenylbenzopyrone compounds with a double bond between carbons 2 and 3 and one linking the oxygen to the carbon at position 4. Flavonols are flavones with a hydroxyl group substituted at the 3-position. Glycosides of flavones and flavonols, chiefly with glucose and rhamnose, are widely distributed in plants. Flavones (and flavanones) tend to occur in herbaceous plants, while flavonols are more likely to be found in woody ones (Bate-Smith, 1954). Many anthocyanin-containing plants contain appreciable quantities of flavones or flavonols, and these may act as copigments to modify the color of the anthocyanins.

Three flavonol aglycones are kaempferol, quercetin, and myricetin, with hydroxylation patterns analogous to pelargonidin, cyanidin, and

Kaempferol   Quercetin

Myricetin

delphinidin, respectively. All three flavonols contribute to the color of green tea brew (Roberts et al., 1956). Quercetin and its derivatives are the most widely distributed of the flavonols.

Color

These yellow or ivory pigments are basic, and they react with acid to form salts. Gripenberg (1962) suggests for the structure of such a salt of a flavone the resonance hybrid, as shown:

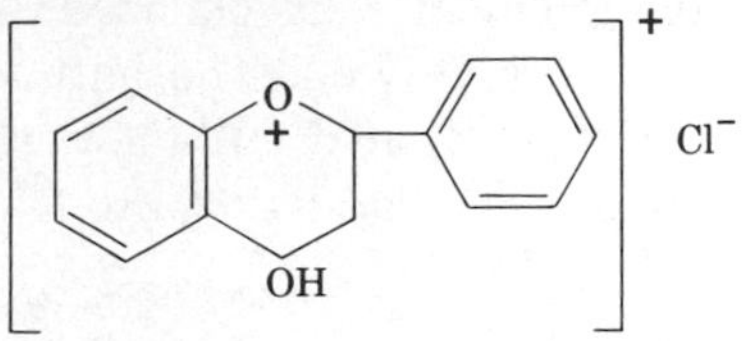

In intact fruit and in acidic cell sap these pigments are stable. Alkali intensifies the color of these pigments. The cooking water from vegetables, even white ones like cauliflower and onions, may have a yellow color if the water is alkaline.

Reactions

Flavones and flavonols that have *ortho*-dihydroxy groups are able to chelate metals, as are anthocyanins. Dark-colored complexes form with iron. Aluminum chelates are bright yellow or brown (Bate-Smith, 1954; Swain, 1962). The yellow tint of the water from green leafy vegetables or onions with yellow skins that have been cooked in an aluminum pan is due to a flavone-aluminum chelate. Ferric complexes are greenish, bluish, reddish, or brownish, depending on the number and position of the hydroxyl groups on the molecule (Bate-Smith, 1954). Proposed chelation sites for quercetin are as follows (Bate-Smith, 1954):

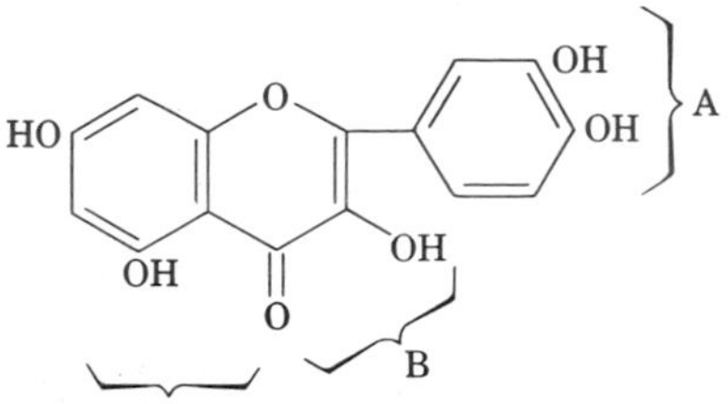

Bright-yellow crystals occasionally observed in canned asparagus are deposits of a flavonol, rutin, which is a 3-rhamnoglucoside of quercetin (Dame et al., 1959). Rutin has limited solubility in water at room temperature. At the elevated temperature used for processing and particularly if the concentration of rutin in the raw asparagus is high, sufficient rutin will dissolve so that the packing liquid is supersaturated at room temperature. Rutin then precipitates. Deposits of rutin have been observed when asparagus is processed in glass containers. If the vegetable is processed in tinned containers, enough of the metal dissolves so that a stannous-rutin complex forms that is more soluble than the rutin. This complex gives the liquid around the asparagus a bright yellow color, but no precipitate forms.

Far more objectional than the yellow precipitate of rutin in canned asparagus is the darkening (blackening) of some lots on exposure to air (Davis et al., 1961). Discoloration is believed to be due to oxidation of a ferrous- to a ferric-rutin complex. Asparagus that discolored was higher in pH, higher in iron, and lower in tin than that which did not discolor. Use of a 0.1 percent citric acid solution as a packing medium prevented discoloration either by lowering the pH or by sequestering iron.

Antioxidant Properties

The ability of these pigments to chelate metals suggested that they might be effective as antioxidants, a role that has been demonstrated for some, including quercetin. Crawford et al. (1961) modified the quercetin molecule by selective alkylation and demonstrated the importance of free *ortho*-hydroxyl groups at positions 3′ and 4′ and also the importance of the hydroxyl group at the 7 position, both points substantiated by Pratt and Watts (1964). Both groups of workers concluded that the effectiveness of such flavonoids as antioxidants resided chiefly in their ability to act as free radical acceptors and so break the chain reaction in autooxidation. (See page 230.)

Flavanones

This group of flavonoids differs from flavones and flavonols in that the double bond existing between carbons 2 and 3 of the first two is missing in the flavanones. While a variety of flavonoids occur in citrus fruits, these fruits are unique for their high concentration of flavanones, which are present as glycosides. Flavanones occur most abundantly in the peel and in the white albedo, but they are present in the edible part of the fruit also. Flavanone pigments are colorless in the acidic fruit. Their contribution to the taste of citrus fruit is discussed in the section on flavor.

Flavanols

The flavanols have a central pyran ring and are hydroxy-flavans. Two subgroups of the flavanols are the catechins and the proanthocyanins (leucoanthocyanins).

Catechins

The catechins are flavan-3-ols, of which catechin is the simplest member. Catechin ($3',4',5,7$-tetrahydroxy flavanol) has a hydroxyl substitution pattern analogous to the anthocyanin aglycone, cyanidin, and the flavonol aglycone, quercetin. Catechin has two asymmetric carbon atoms, C_2 and C_3, so both ($+$)-catechin and ($-$)-catechin are known as well as their epimers, ($-$)-*epi*catechin and ($+$)-*epi*catechin. Only ($+$)-catechin and ($-$)-*epi*catechin appear naturally (Swain, 1965).

Catechin, 2, 3–*trans*
epicatechin, 2, 3–*cis*

Gallocatechin, 2, 3–*trans*
epigallocatechin, 2, 3–*cis*

Gallocatechins have hydroxylation patterns in the B ring analogous to delphinidin. Both catechins and gallocatechins may be esterified with gallic acid to yield catechin gallate and gallocatechin gallate (Swain, 1965).

Gallic acid

Catechin gallate, R=H
Gallocatechin gallate, R=OH

Proanthocyanidins

The second subgroup of flavanols are the flavan-3,4-diols. The commonest C_{15} flavan-3,4-diol is leucocyanidin, which has a hydroxylation pattern in both the A and the B rings analogous to cyanidin and catechin.

Leucocyanidin (a proanthocyanidin)

Other leucocanthcyanins have the hydroxylation pattern of delphinidin, and still others have a hydroxylation pattern unlike any of the common anthocyanidins. When such flavan-3,4-diols are heated in an acid medium, they are converted, by a process that involves dehydration and oxidation, to the corresponding anthocyanidins. The term "leucoanthocyanin" has been used to denote such colorless precursors (Bate-Smith and Swain, 1953), but currently the term "proanthocyanidin" is favored (Freundenberg and Weinges, 1962).

Both flavan-3-ols and flavan-3,4-diols can condense with themselves or with each other to form dimers, oligomers, or polymers. The tentative structure for a proanthocyanidin that is a dimer of leucocyanidin and catechin is proposed by Geissman and Dittmar (1965).

A dimeric proanthocyanidin

Bate-Smith (1954) suggested that proanthocyanidins might be the source of the pinkish color sometimes observed in overcooked stewed pears. Joslyn and Peterson (1956) demonstrated the presence in Bartlett pears of proanthocyanidin that yielded cyanidin, and Luh et al. (1960) reported that a pinkish coloration was more often observed in canned pears that had a higher "tannin" content and in those with a lower pH. Both factors would favor the conversion of the leucocyanidin to cyanidin, as would overprocessing or failure to cool cans promptly.

Both flavan-3-ols and flavan-3,4-diols are most likely to occur in plants that are woody rather than herbaceous (Bate-Smith, 1954). Among the plants used for food, tea contains flavanols in the highest concentration. Phenolic compounds account for 30 percent of the weight of the dried green leaf (Roberts, 1958), and flavanols account for two thirds of this. The main flavanol in tea is gallocatechin gallate. Many fruits contain flavanols, too. These compounds are of interest because of their contribution to the aspect of food quality known as astringency, to be discussed in the section on flavor of fruits and vegetables.

Although the flavanols are colorless compounds, under certain circumstances they may be the source of discoloration in fruits and vegetables. Like other *ortho*-dihydroxy and vicinal trihydroxy compounds, the flavanols react with metal ions to form dark-colored complexes. Furthermore, they are of concern because of their participation in enzymatic browning.

The term "tannin" is often loosely applied to the phenolic compounds that contribute both to astringency and to enzymatic browning.

Phenolic Compounds and Enzymatic Discoloration of Fruits and Vegetables

Rapid browning or, on occasion, blackening of fresh fruit and vegetable tissue when cellular organization is disrupted by cutting, bruising, or other injury is due to the action of a copper-containing enzyme or enzyme complex on phenolic substances in the tissue (Joslyn and Ponting, 1951). The enzyme, officially ortho-diphenol: oxygen oxidoreductase, is also known by a variety of trivial names. These include cresolase, tyrosinase, catecholase, phenolase, polyphenolase, and polyphenoloxidase.

Polyphenoloxidase(s)

Polyphenoloxidase(s), or multiple forms of the same enzyme, catalyze(s) the oxidation of certain polyphenolic compounds prior to their participation in the formation of brown or dark gray polymers. Jolley and Mason (1965) demonstrated that the enzyme from mushrooms exists in five different forms. These authors suggest that multiple forms of the enzyme may be due to configurational changes in the protein molecule, to different degrees of polymerization of identical subunits, or to various combinations of different subunits. The latter might account for the fact that the enzyme from certain sources such as potatoes and mushrooms (Palmer, 1963) can catalyze the oxidation of both monohydroxyphenols and dihydroxyphenols, while that from others such as bananas (Palmer, 1963) and pears (Tate et al., 1964) acts only on dihydroxyphenols. Even greater heterogeneity was reported for mushroom phenolase and for that from potatoes by Constantinides and Bedford (1967), and these workers reported three forms of the polyphenolase enzyme in apples (Golden Delicious). Most polyphenoloxidase enzymes can catalyze the oxidation of a number of substrates but still be most active for a specific polyphenolic compound—for example, banana polyphenoloxidase for 3,4-dihydroxyphenylethylamine (Palmer, 1963).

Polyphenoloxidase enzymes of a number of fruits and vegetables have been studied. The enzyme from potatoes was the first to be isolated, but mushrooms are a more concentrated source. Polyphenoloxidases are present in apples, apricots, cherries, peaches, and pears (Joslyn and Ponting, 1951), bananas (Palmer, 1963), dates (Maier and Metzler, 1965), avocado and eggplant (Knapp, 1965), and sweet potatoes (Scott and Katlan, 1957), but are absent from citrus fruit, melon, and tomatoes (Joslyn and Ponting, 1951; Ponting, 1960).

In intact fruits and vegetables, enzyme and substrate are separated, and only in post-mortem cells in the presence of oxygen do enzyme and substrate come into contact. Harel et al. (1964) reported that apple polyphenoloxidase was either in or on the surface of both chloroplasts and mitochondria, although Walker and Hulme (1966) suggested that association of polyphenoloxidase enzyme with particulate fractions of the cell could be an artifact of the extraction procedure. Joslyn and Goldstein (1964) reported that polyphenoloxidase enzyme was found in the tannin cells of persimmons.

Substrates for Polyphenoloxidase

Baruah and Swain (1959) tested a number of phenolic compounds as possible substrates for potato polyphenoloxidase. This enzyme catalyzed the oxidation of two monohydric phenols, *para*cresol and tyrosine, both with *para*-substituted —CH_2 groups, as well as a number of *ortho*-dihydroxyphenols. Among the latter were caffeic acid, catechol, chlorogenic acid, dihydroxyphenylalanine, pyrogallol, quercetin, and myricetin. Flavonol glycosides were not substrates for this enzyme, possibly because the sugar moiety interfered with the orientation of the molecule on the surface of the enzyme.

A number of workers have attempted to identify the specific substrate(s) in individual fruits and vegetables. Thus, Weurman and Swain (1953) identified chlorogenic acid as the substrate for the polyphenoloxidase in apples (Bramley's seedling) and pears (Conference), and Siegelman (1955) identified (—)-*epi*catechin as the main substrate in the skin of apples (Grimes Golden and Delicious) and in pears (Bartlett). Skins of pears contained (+)-catechin, too. Williams (1955) identified chlorogenic acid, *epi*catechin, and proanthocyanidins in a "high tannin" cider apple. Both (+)-catechin and (—)-*epi*catechin were identified in Bartlett pears by Nortje (1966). El-Sayed and Luh (1965) found chlorogenic acid in apricots, together with a derivative of coumaric acid and lesser amounts of quercetin, catechin, and *epi*catechin. The substrate in bananas, found in especially high concentration in the peel, is 3,4-dihydroxyphenylethylamine, abbreviated dopamine (Palmer, 1963). Chlorogenic acid and (+)-catechin are found in both freestone and in cling peaches, in addition to proanthocyanidins that are the predominant phenolic constituents (Johnson et al., 1951; Craft, 1961; and Luh et al., 1967). In ripening dates, dactylifric acid (3-*o*-caffeoylshikimic acid) and its isomers are the main substrates for the polyphenoloxidases present (Maier and Metzler, 1965). Chlorogenic acid is present in sweet potatoes (Uritani and Miyano, 1955) and both chlorogenic acid and tyrosine in white potatoes (Swain et al., 1966). Thus chlorogenic acid is a prominent *ortho*-dihydroxy compound widely distributed in fruits and vegetables.

It no doubt serves as a substrate of polyphenoloxidase in fruits and vegetables that turn brown when injured, although Siegelman (1955) found that the oxidative products from catechins acted on by apple polyphenoloxidase contributed more to browning than did those from chlorogenic acid. Chlorogenic acid when hydrolyzed yields caffeic and quinic acids.

Chlorogenic acid (caffeoylquinic acid)

Possible contributions of the oxidation products of proanthocyanidins to enzymatic browning should be considered, according to Swain (1962). Craft (1961) reported that the leucoanthocyanin from peach, as well as chlorogenic acid and catechin, was browned by peach polyphenol-oxidase. However, Griffiths (1959) found that the polyphenoloxidase from banana did not brown the proanthocyanidin from this fruit, and Maier and Metzler (1965) reported that the proanthocyanidin in dates was not a substrate for the polyphenoloxidase present in the fruit.

Action of Polyphenoloxidase Enzyme

Conversion of colorless polyphenolic substrates in fruits and vegetables into dark-colored products involves a number of changes in the molecule including enzymatic oxidation, rearrangement, nonenzymatic oxidation, and finally polymerization. The proposed changes are illustrated with one substrate, 3,4-dihydroxyphenylethylamine (dopamine) in banana (Palmer, 1963).

Only the first step involves the enzyme polyphenoloxidase. The substrate in bananas is analogous to 3,4-dihydroxyphenylalanine (dopa), an intermediate in the enzymatic conversion of tyrosine to melanin (Raper, 1928; Lerner, 1953).

Tyrosine
(Colorless)

3, 4-Dihydroxyphenylalanine
(Dopa)
(Colorless)

Enzymes from some plant tissue such as potatoes are able to effect the conversion of such monohydroxyphenols as tyrosine to dihydroxyphenols. The dopa formed enzymatically from tyrosine found in potatoes undergoes changes similar to those for dopamine in bananas. The cut surface of bananas or uncooked potatoes soon after exposure to air takes on a pinkish color, due to accumulation of reddish dihydroindole-quinone (dopachrome). Rearrangement of this substance to dihydroxyindole takes place less rapidly, and this is followed by oxidation to purplish indole-5,6-quinone, which polymerizes to brown and finally to gray-black melanin (Palmer, 1963; Swain et al., 1966). Dark spots sometimes observed in raw potatoes are believed to be due to the formation of melanin as a result of bruises that permit enzyme, tyrosine and oxygen to come into contact.

Discoloration similar to that which occurs on the surface of raw potatoes is observed sometimes in beets that have been blanched to facilitate peeling and then sliced and held prior to canning. Darkening does not occur in slices of raw beet nor in those adequately blanched. In an attempt to pinpoint the source of the trouble, Clark and Moyer (1955) demonstrated that as heating times in boiling water for sliced beets increased by 10- or 20-second intervals, blackening increased up to a point and then diminished with additional heating. Presumably some heating was required to disrupt the cellular organization to bring substrate, enzyme, and oxygen together. Boscan et al. (1962) isolated polyphenoloxidase from beets and reported that the enzyme brought about rapid oxidation of tyrosine and dihydroxyphenylalanine, both of which were isolated from beets along with two unidentified polyphenolic compounds. Darkening has also been reported in the cambial layer of sweet potatoes exposed to the air after lye peeling (Scott and Katlan, 1957). Darkening occurred when the tissue was heated to temperatures between 60 and 90° C. Presumably this is hot enough to kill the cells and inactivate respiratory enzymes but leave the polyphenoloxidase still active. These authors reported that sweet potatoes high in carotenoids were less susceptible to this type of discoloration.

While the prevention of enzymatic discoloration is of primary concern in most plant foods, there is one instance in which oxidation of polyphenolic compounds is deliberately promoted. This is in the production of black tea from green leaves. The leaves are said to be fermented, but actually oxidation takes place after the green leaves are wilted and then bruised by rolling. A polyphenoloxidase in the tea leaf catalyzes the oxidation of two of the flavanols present, (−)-*epi*-gallocatechin gallate and (−)-*epi*gallocatechin, to form orange-yellow theaflavin gallate and theaflavin. On further oxidation, these compounds give rise to rusty brown thearubigens, which may account for 10 percent of the weight of dried black tea and which contribute most to the color (Roberts, 1958).

Darkening of Cooked Potato

Enzymatic discoloration of the exposed surface of raw potatoes should not be confused with after-cooking discoloration of potatoes, sometimes referred to as stem-end blackening. Identifying the nature and causes of this defect engaged the attention of a number of workers over several years (Nutting and Pfund, 1942; Wager, 1955; Bate-Smith et al., 1958; and Hughes and Swain, 1962). This defect is a dark gray coloration that appears more often at the stem than at the bud end of the potato and only after the potato is cooked. Polyphenoloxidase is not involved in this type of discoloration. Evidence indicates that the discoloration is due to a colorless ferrous-chlorogenic acid chelate that, once reducing conditions in the tuber are eliminated by cooking and the tuber is exposed to air, is converted to the black ferric-chlorogenic acid complex responsible for the discoloration (Swain et al., 1966). Heisler et al. (1963) reported a highly significant correlation between the discoloration of tubers and the iron content, and especially the protein-bound iron, which was higher in the stem end than in the bud end of the potatoes. The concentration of chlorogenic acid varies the length of the tuber, as does the concentration of citric acid, a substance that also is able to chelate iron (Hughes and Swain, 1962). While localized high concentrations of chlorogenic acid predisposed the tubers to blackening, this effect was modified by an accompanying high concentration of citric acid, which tended to be higher at the bud end of the potato (Hughes and Swain, 1962). These authors concluded that the chlorogenic acid/citric acid ratio was the best index to the susceptibility of the tuber to stem-end blackening. Some varieties are more susceptible than others to such blackening, and these tend to be higher in chlorogenic acid (Hughes and Mapson, 1966). A cool, wet growing season favors the accumulation of chlorogenic acid in the tuber. Soil is a factor, too. One that favors the uptake of potassium and consequently an increase in citric acid in the tuber reduces the tendency toward after-cooking discoloration. A practical way recommended to prevent after-cooking darkening of susceptible potatoes is to add cream of tartar to the cooking water ($\frac{1}{4}$ teaspoon per pint) or to the potatoes ($\frac{1}{4}$ teaspoon per pound) if they are mashed (Bowman and Hanning, 1949).

Inherent Differences in Enzymatic Discoloration of Fruits and Vegetables

The color of fruits and other vegetables that have undergone enzymatic oxidation may be either brown or gray-black depending on the substrate. Dihydroxyphenols (other than tyrosine, dihydroxyphenylalanine, and dihydroxyphenylethylamine) such as are found in most fruits and vegetables are oxidized by polyphenoloxidase, but they form brown polymers rather than gray-black melanin. Such foods as apples, apricots, cherries, peaches, and pears turn brown, but never black, as a result of enzyme action. While both bananas and potatoes first turn pink and then brown, they darken eventually. Cut surfaces of avocados and eggplant discolor rapidly (Makower and Schwimmer, 1957).

In most fruits and vegetables enzyme-catalyzed browning is not uniform throughout but tends to be localized near vascular tissue. More rapid and intense discoloration in these areas has been reported for avocados and eggplant (Makower and Schwimmer, 1957), for sweet potatoes (Scott and Katlan, 1957) and for beets (Boscan et al., 1962). In addition, the speed and degree of enzyme-catalyzed discoloration is influenced by variety and by differences in the individual fruit or vegetable.

Guadagni et al. (1949) analyzed more than 50 varieties of peaches and concluded that enzyme activity was more important in determining initial browning (first 15 minutes), while total browning depended on the amount of oxidizable tannins. Weurman and Swain (1955) measured total phenols, enzyme activity, and the extent of browning in apples picked at six stages from one month after petal drop to maturity. Total phenols increased 40 percent per apple, but browning decreased 75 percent between first and last picking. The authors concluded that the intensity of browning depended more on enzyme activity than on the concentration of the substrate. Walker (1962) studied 12 varieties of apples, including Gravenstein, Delicious, Golden Delicious, Jonathan, and Granny Smith, and reported wide differences in browning capacity among the varieties, with small differences among apples of a single variety depending on age of the fruit. While the fruit differed in phenolic content, the author reported that extent of browning and phenolic content were not correlated.

Harel et al. (1966) analyzed apples, from fruit set to maturity, for *o*-dihydroxyphenols, for polyphenoloxidase activity, and for browning. Activity of polyphenoloxidase increased for the first 70 days and reached a peak approximately one month after the peak in concentration of phenolic compounds, after which it declined. These authors reported that the extent of browning, which diminished as the fruit matured, correlated better with the concentration of substrate than with the amount of enzyme. Joslyn and Goldstein (1964) reported that in astringent persimmons oxidative browning did not occur in unripe fruit, took place rapidly as the fruit ripened, reaching a maximum as the fruit began to lose its astringency, and then decreased to a low level in the soft ripe fruit. Maier and Metzler (1965) presented evidence that the extent of enzymatic browning in dates was limited by the amount of substrate present, as cut tissue continued to brown upon the addition of catechol. The tyrosine content of potatoes was reported by Mapson et al. (1963) to influence the rate of browning of potatoes more than did the activity of the enzyme. Tyrosine content varied with the variety, but a more important factor was the amount of rainfall. High moisture in the soil favored the accumulation of tyrosine in the tuber (Hughes and Mapson, 1966).

Inhibitors of Polyphenolase Activity

Methods for controlling enzymatic discoloration of fruits and vegetables have been summarized by Ponting (1960). Chilling a food below the optimum for the enzyme ($40°$ C $\pm$ $10°$ C) will retard enzymatic browning. Heat may be used to inactivate the enzyme, but this has the disadvantage of altering the fresh fruit flavor as well as the texture. Enzyme activity is pH dependent. Lowering the pH will retard browning, and below pH 2.5 to 2.7 the enzyme is inhibited (Ponting, 1960). Malic acid is more effective than citric, although adding lemon juice is a convenient way to lower the pH of fruit. Ascorbic acid is often added to fruits to retard enzymatic browning. Its effectiveness depends on its ability to act as an antioxidant. Quinones formed by the enzyme are reduced to the dihydroxyl state by the ascorbic acid, and the latter is concurrently oxidized to dehydroascorbic acid (Bate-Smith, 1954; Tate et al., 1964). The

Ascorbic acid   Dehydroascorbic acid

activity of the enzyme gradually decreases, and if enough ascorbic acid is present the enzyme will be inactivated (Ponting, 1960). Sulfur dioxide has been used for many years to inhibit oxidative browning due to enzyme activity. Dried fruit is often sulfured prior to drying to maintain a bright color. The fruit may be exposed to sulfur dioxide gas, dipped in a solution of sulfur dioxide (sulfurous acid), or dipped in a solution of sulfite, bisulfite, or metabisulfite.[1] A modification of the bisulfite dip to prevent browning of apple slices has been developed. Sliced apples are dipped briefly (45 seconds) in a dilute solution (0.25 percent) of sodium sulfite followed by a 5-minute dip in dipotassium phosphate (K_2HPO_4) (Bolin et al., 1964). Protection against browning afforded by the K_2HPO_4 solution is attributed to the high pH (8) (Nelson and Finkle, 1964). This modification was reported to be superior to dipping sliced apples in a 1 percent solution of sodium bisulfite. Slices stayed white, and, in addition, they were free from SO_2 and did not lose crispness as they did when treated with a 1 percent solution of sodium bisulfite alone.

The chloride ion is known to inhibit the activity of polyphenoloxidase (Samisch, 1935), and a solution of sodium chloride may be used to retard enzymatic browning. Täufel and Voigt (1964) reported that a 0.2 percent sodium chloride solution retarded oxidative browning of apple slices. According to Ponting (1960), sodium chloride may be relied on for temporary inhibition only, as the amount needed to prevent browning permanently would make food unpalatable. Protecting food from oxygen as by vacuum packing will prevent browning. The use of sugar or syrup delays browning, because it retards the diffusion of oxygen to the fruit.

Betacyanins and Betaxanthins

Beet roots contain two groups of water-soluble, vacuolar pigments. One group, the betacyanins, are violet-red pigments that are the main coloring matter in beets. They were so named because the color of beets was for many years attributed to anthocyanins, but supposedly unique ones because they were known to contain nitrogen. A second group of pigments, closely related chemically to the betacyanins although yellow in color, are the betaxanthins. Again they were named for their supposed relationship to the yellow flavonoid pigments in plants. Betacyanins and betaxanthins often occur in the same plant but only in those that belong to the order Centrospermae and never in plants that synthesize anthocyanins. Other flavonoids may occur with betacyanins and betaxanthins in the same plant, however (Mabry, 1966).

[1] Embs and Markakis (1965) presented evidence that sulfite inhibits browning by complexing with quinones formed, thus blocking their subsequent polymerization and formation of brown-colored polymers.

The main violet-red pigment, betanin, is a glycoside from which the aglycone betanidin is obtained by hydrolysis. The structure for beta-

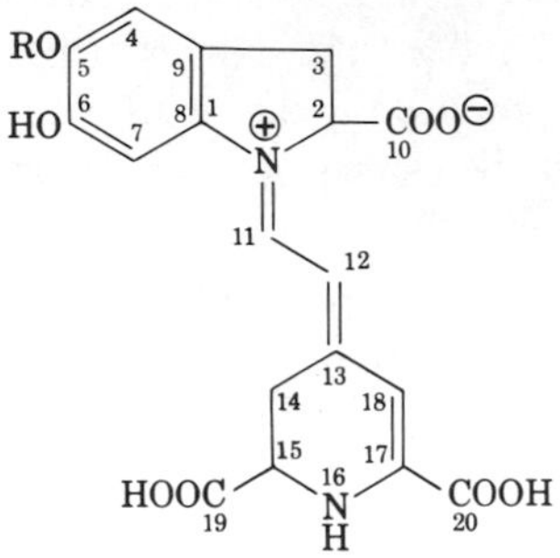

Betanidin, R=H
Betanin, R=glucose

nidin was established by Wyler et al. (1963). Betanidin or isobetanidin, which differs from betanidin only in the configuration at C_{15}, has been identified as the aglycone in most of the betacyanins presently known (Mabry, 1966).

The yellow betaxanthins have not been so extensively studied as the violet-red betacyanins. Piatelli et al. (1965) proposed the following tentative structure for two of the betaxanthins that they isolated from one variety of beet.

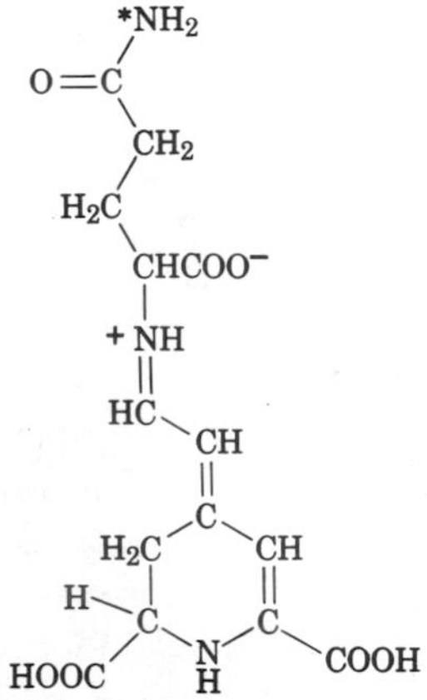

Vulgaxanthin I
Vulgaxanthin II,
* = OH

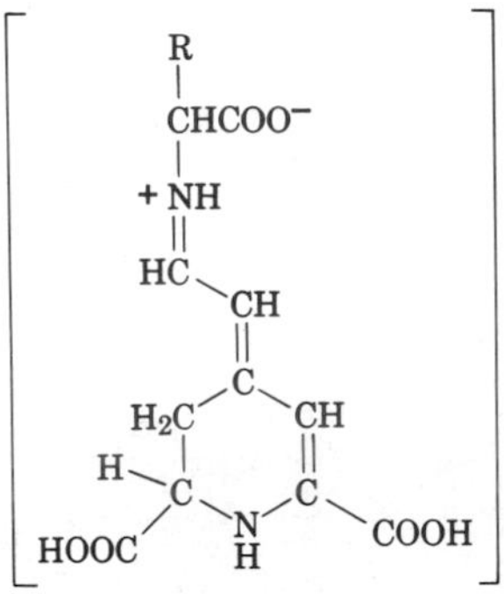

Type formula for
betacyanins and
betaxanthins

These authors suggest that both betacyanins and betaxanthins can be represented as shown above and to the right.

Although the betacyanins in beets are water-soluble, they do not leach from intact, raw beet cells. However, heating denatures cell membranes, and the pigment molecules then diffuse into the cooking water. Betacyanins are sensitive to changes in pH. Peterson and Joslyn (1960) reported that an acid causes a slight shift in the hue of betanidin towards the blue, while a strong base changes the violet-red pigment to yellow.

FLAVOR OF FRUITS AND VEGETABLES

Flavor in fruits and vegetables is a composite of taste, aroma, and mouth feel. Taste contributes more to the overall sensation of flavor in fruits than it does in most vegetables because of the higher concentrations of sugars and of acids in the former. For a discussion of the sweetness of sugars see p. 42, and of pH and titratable acidity, pp. 20–21.

Flavanones and the Taste of Citrus Fruits

One group of flavanoid pigments, the flavanones, are of particular interest because of their contribution to the taste of citrus fruits and because of the relation between chemical structure and taste sensation of certain of these pigments, recently reviewed by Horowitz (1964); Horowitz and Gentili (1969).

One flavanone, hesperidin, is found in high concentration in sweet and bitter oranges, in lemons, and in citrons. The aglycone for hesperidin is hesperetin (3′,5,7-trihydroxy-4′-methoxyflavanone) (Horowitz, 1964). The sugar moiety is rutinose, a disaccharide of L-rhamnose and D-glucose, the same sugar as found in the flavonol, rutin.

Hesperetin (3′ 5, 7 trihydroxy-4′–methoxyflavanone)

The aglycone has the 2S-configuration, so hesperidin is 7-β-rutinoside of 2S-hesperetin. An isomer of hesperidin, neohesperidin, is found in unripe oranges of some varieties. It, too, is a 7-rhamnosylglucoside of hesperetin. Naringin, a third flavanone and the main one in grapefruit, is present also in some varieties of bitter oranges. The aglycone is naringenin (4′,5, 7-trihydroxyflavanone) (Horowitz, 1964). Naringin, like the first two flavanones, is a 7-rhamnosylglucoside.

Naringenin (4', 5, 7–trihydroxyflavanone)

Poncirin, a fourth flavanone and in grapefruit, is a 7-rhamnosylglucoside of isosakuranetin (5,7-dihydroxy-4'-methoxyflavanone) (Horowitz, 1964).

Isosakuranetin (5, 7-dihydroxy-4'–methoxyflavanone)

The three aglycones, hesperetin, naringenin, and isosakuranetin, are tasteless, as is hesperedin. The two glycosides, naringin and poncirin, are very bitter, one fifth as bitter as quinine hydrochloride. The other glycoside, neohesperidin, is approximately one tenth as bitter as naringin. One difference between the three bitter glycosides and the one tasteless one is the type of linkage between the rhamnose and the glucose in the sugar residue. In rutinose, found in hesperidin, carbon 2 of rhamnose is linked to carbon 6 of glucose. In the three bitter flavanone glycosides, carbon 2 of rhamnose is linked with carbon 2 of glucose, leaving free the primary alcohol group on the glucose residue. The disaccharide so formed is called neohesperidose. Naringenin-7-β-rutinoside found in the peel of navel and Valencia oranges has no taste, and another flavanone, the 7-β-rutinoside of eriodictoyl (3',4',5,7-tetrahydroxyflavanone) is not bitter. The presence of neohesperidose in the molecule appears to contribute bitterness. However, the nature of the aglycone also controls the taste. Rhoifolin, a flavonol with a substitution pattern identical with narginin, is not bitter. Horowitz (1964) suggests that only nonplanar aglycones can form glycosides that are bitter. Of interest is the fact that when the central ring of either naringin or hesperidin is opened, the resulting dihydrochalcones are as intensely sweet as the flavanone glycosides are bitter.

Flavanols and Astringency

Astringency is one of a number of tactile sensations (mouth feel) that contribute to the flavor of a food. It is variously characterized as a constricting, shrinking, tightening, "puckery" sensation in the mouth. A food that is excessively astringent is unpalatable, but a limited amount of astringency is desirable in certain foods to keep them from being bland and insipid. The appeal of cider, wine, chocolate, tea, and of many fruits is due in part to an agreeable level of astringency (Bate-Smith, 1954). The sensation of astringency is attributed to the ability of tanninlike substances to react with the proteins in the lining of the mouth and also with the mucoproteins in the saliva, thereby eliminating its lubricating effect (Joslyn and Goldstein, 1964a). Such substances once were thought to be polymers of catechins, but now the majority are considered to be polymers of flavan-3-ol and flavan-3,4-diols (Bate-Smith and Swain, 1953). Cross-linking of the proteins in the mouth by such phenolic compounds is believed to be effected by hydrogen bonds between the hydrogen of the phenolic hydroxyl groups and the oxygen of the keto-imide

$$\text{group} \quad -\!\!\overset{\displaystyle O}{\overset{\displaystyle \|}{C}}\!\!-\!\!\underset{\displaystyle H}{\overset{\displaystyle |}{N}}\!\!- \quad \text{(Gustavson, 1954). The ability of such phenolic sub-}$$

stances to effectively cross-link proteins depends on their size. Small molecules are ineffective, as are large polymers, with astringency being attributed to intermediate-sized oligomers (Swain, 1965), although Geissman and Dittmar (1965) reported that a dimer isolated from avocado seed was astringent.

Most fruits lose astringency on ripening. Two in which this decrease is pronounced are bananas and persimmons. Astringent substances are concentrated in special cells in the persimmons (Joslyn and Goldstein, 1964b) and in latex vessels in the banana (Barnell and Barnell, 1945). When the green fruit is cut, astringent material is found in the liquid that exudes from the cut cells (Barnell and Barnell, 1945). These authors reported that the "active tannin" content of bananas, that is, that capable of precipitating the enzyme diastase, decreased as the fruit ripened and became less astringent. If bananas were chilled, the cells became more permeable and the tannins diffused. Chilled fruit did not lose its astringency.

Since this study of Barnell and Barnell was reported, a number of workers have attempted to account for the change in astringency as fruit ripens. Williams (1955) analyzed a "high tannin" cider apple and found that one third, of the phenolic substances were leucoanthocyanins. Guadagni and Nimmo (1953) analyzed peaches (Elbertas) from three orchards within a 100-mile radius and reported that those grown in the area that was warm and clear had the lowest concentration of total phenolic compounds and were least astringent, while those grown where it was cool and cloudy had the highest total phenolics and were the most astringent. Craft (1961) measured both the extractable proanthocyanidin and that remaining in the pulp of Elberta peaches and reported that both decreased as the fruit ripened from hard-mature to tree ripe, but that the ratio of the two forms was approximately the same at the two stages of maturity.

Nakayama and Chichester (1963) reported a rapid drop in methanol-soluble delphinidin-forming proanthocyanidin as persimmons ripened and lost astringency. Because much proanthocyanidin remained in the extracted pulp even of nonastringent persimmons, these authors concluded that solubility of the proanthocyanidin was the factor that influenced the degree of astringency. An increase in polymerization of phenolic compounds as fruit ripens was reported for bananas by Goldstein and Swain (1963) and for astringent persimmons by Joslyn and Goldstein (1964b). Ito and Joslyn (1965) reported that the proanthocyanidin in the flesh of Gravenstein apples was less highly polymerized and more astringent than that in the peel. Josyln and Goldstein (1964a) suggested that more astringent fruit like bananas and persimmons were those that contained proanthocyanidins that on heating in acid yielded delphinidin.

Aroma

Aroma is a distinguishing aspect of flavor in fruits and in certain vegetables. Constituents that contribute to the aroma may be present in the raw tissue (especially true of fruits), or they may be produced from odorless precursors as the result of either enzyme activity or of heating.

Early work on the chemistry of fruit and vegetable flavors was summarized by Kirchner (1949). More recent work on fruit flavors was reviewed by Teranishi (1966) and on vegetable flavors by Bernhard (1966). Study of the constituents responsible for the aroma of fruits and vegetables has been difficult because of the small quantities involved and because of their instability. Development of the technique of gas chromatography has provided a powerful tool for the separation of volatile constituents in fruits and vegetables. By this means, minute quantities of constituents may be fractionated on capillary columns, and sophisticated sensing devices make possible their identification. Progress relating the significance of compounds so isolated and identified to the characteristic bouquet of a fruit or vegetable as assessed subjectively has lagged, however. What constituents are essential for the characteristic aroma and at what concentration are questions as yet unanswered for most fruits and vegetables.

Fruits

Volatile constituents in fruits that constitute the odorous components include esters, alcohols, acids, aldehydes, and ketones. Volatiles from a single fruit frequently contain a wide assortment of the constituents listed above.

Apples

Thirty components, including 11 esters, 11 alcohols, 5 aldehydes, 1 ketone, and 4 acids, were isolated from the volatiles of McIntosh apples (MacGregor et al., 1964). An essence of Golden Delicious apples yielded an oil with a strong apple aroma in which 56 compounds were identified (Flath et al., 1967). The main components with a characteristic apple odor were ethyl 2-methyl butyrate, hexanal, and 2-hexenal.

Apricots

Tang and Jennings (1967) identified a number of components in the volatiles from apricots (Blenheim) and reported that individually none had the odor of apricots. They suggested that the aroma of apricots was due to an "integrated response" to a number of the components.

Bananas

Issenberg and Wicks (1963) identified a number of alcohols and esters in the volatiles from ripe Gros Michel bananas. McCarthy et al. (1963) attempted to relate the constituents identified in the volatiles from two varieties of banana (Gros Michel and Valery) with the aroma as assessed subjectively. In the early stages of ripening both the gas chromatograms and the flavor profiles were simple. Green and woody or musty elements, which included methyl acetate, pentanone, butyl alcohol, amyl alcohol, and hexyl alcohol, were dominant in immature fruit. As the fruit ripened and the flavor developed, these constituents decreased and the chromatogram became more complex. Aromas from both varieties of fruit were bananalike, that from Valery more so than that from Gros Michel. Compounds present in the chromatogram that contributed to bananalike aroma included amyl acetate, iso-amyl acetate, amyl propionate, and amyl butyrate. Valery had more than did Gros Michel of the fruity components that included butyl acetate, butyl butyrate, hexyl acetate, and amyl butyrate.

Cranberries

The volatiles from cranberries were analyzed by Croteau and Fagerson (1968). These authors reported that benzylaldehyde, benzyl and benzoate esters, and terpenes were the main contributors to cranberry aroma.

Oranges

Acetaldehyde and ethanol were the main water-soluble, volatile constituents reported in Valencia orange juice by Kirchner and Miller (1957). Oil-soluble constituents included the hydrocarbons, limonene and myrcene, in addition to esters, carbonyls, and alcohols. Linalool and *a*-terpineol were the two alcohols present in largest amounts. Teranishi et al. (1963b) reported that the major hydrocarbon found in the low-boiling fraction of orange oil was limonene, while four sesquiterpenes, characterized as mild and delicate, were found in the high-boiling fraction of orange oil. Ethyl 3-hydroxyhexanoate and ethyl acetate were the major esters found by Schultz et al. (1964) in a Valencia orange juice that was low in peel oil. The aroma given off by Hamlin oranges consisted mainly of ethyl esters, chiefly ethyl butyrate, while sesquiterpenes (the chief one valencene) were the main constituents in the aroma from the cuticle (Attaway and Oberbacher, 1968).

Peaches

Jennings and Sevenants (1964a) analyzed the volatiles from peaches and reported the presence of benzaldehyde, benzyl alcohol, γ-caprolactone, γ-octalactone, γ-decalactone, and δ-decalactone. No component isolated from the peaches duplicated peach aroma, although one, γ-decalactone, was reminiscent of peach jam. These authors concluded that peaches lacked "character impact compounds" and that the distinctive aroma of peaches was due to what they characterized as an "integrated response."

Pears

The aroma of Bartlett pears has been analyzed by a number of workers. Hydrolytic products of the esters of pear volatiles consisted of a number of alcohols and acids, with an unsaturated C-10 acid, 2,4-decadienoic acid, the main one (Jennings and Creveling, 1963). Jennings and Sevenants (1964b) had advanced the concept that components in a fruit aroma fell into two classes. Those that serve to differentiate the aroma of one fruit from that of another they designated "character impact compounds," and those that suggest fruitiness but no specific fruit they termed "contributing flavor compounds." They suggested that such compounds as acetaldehyde and hexyl acetate, identified in pear aroma, are in the latter category. Esters of *trans*:2-*cis*:4-decadienoic acid with a sweet, "pear-like" odor they considered "character impact compounds." In view of the fact that a low temperature favors the production in plants of a high proportion of more unsaturated fatty acids (Hilditch, 1951) and because of the demonstrated benefit of holding pears near $-1°$ C for a few weeks between harvest and ripening, Jennings and Sevenants (1964b) suggested that the superior flavor of pears stored at a low temperature might be due to higher concentrations of esters of 2,4-decadienoic acid. Jennings et al. (1964) prepared esters of this C-10 unsaturated acid with alcohols previously identified in hydrolysates of pear esters and reported that ethyl, n-propyl, and n-butyl esters were "very pear-like" but that the n-amyl or n-hexyl esters were not. Heinz et al. (1965) found that the methyl and ethyl esters of trans:2-cis:4-decadienoic acid increased rapidly when fruit attained climacteric peak, reaching a peak one to two days after the peak in production of CO_2 and at the point when pears were of optimum eating quality.

Pineapple

Rodin et al. (1965) isolated from pineapple 2,5-dimethyl-4-hydroxy-3-(2H)-furanone. While this compound was a major component (4 ppm) of the volatiles, when it was added to pineapple juice that had been stripped of odor, it did not enhance the aroma. Other constituents identified in the aroma of pineapple include p-allyl phenol (chavicol), γ-caprolactone (Silverstein et al., 1965), three lactones (γ-butyrolactone, γ-octalactone, and δ-octalactone), acetoxyacetone, a furfuryl alcohol, and a number of esters including methyl esters of β-hydroxybutyric, β-hydroxyhexanoic, and β-acetohexanoic acids and ethyl esters of the last two (Creveling et al., 1968).

Strawberries

Dimick and Makower (1956) analyzed the distillate from Marshall strawberries and reported that about two thirds of the oily fraction or approximately 7 percent of the total essence contained all of the characteristic strawberry aroma and that it could be identified as strawberry at a concentration of 0.1 ppm. Later Teranishi et al. (1963a) reported more than 150 constituents among the more stable volatile components of strawberries. Prominent components include methyl and ethyl acetates, propionates and butyrates, and the acetal, 1,1-dioxyethane.

Vegetables

Each vegetable has a characteristic odor, and most are mild. Those that become strong flavored do so only after the raw tissue is damaged or the vegetable is overcooked. Two groups of vegetables in particular have the potential for becoming strong flavored, those from plants belonging to the genus *Allium* and those of the Cruciferae family, especially those that belong to the genus *Brassica*. Sulfur compounds make an important contribution to the aroma of vegetables of both of these groups.

Sulfur Compounds of Vegetables of the Genus Allium

Vegetables that belong to the genus *Allium* include chives, garlic, leeks, and onions. Of this group of vegetables, the aroma of garlic was the first to be studied. This pungent aroma is derived from an odorless compound in the intact clove that when first studied was given the trivial name of alliin. This odor precursor, a derivative of the amino acid cysteine, was isolated from garlic and identified as (+)-S-allyl-L-cysteine sulfoxide (Stoll and Seebeck, 1950, 1951). In the intact clove this compound is stable, but slicing or crushing brings this substrate into contact with an enzyme alliinase also present in garlic. Alliinase catalyzes the conversion of (+)-S-allyl-L-cysteine sulfoxide to diallyl thiosulfinate, ammonia, and pyruvic acid as shown (Stoll and Seebeck, 1949; Virtanen, 1965).

$$2 \ CH_2{=}CH{-}CH_2{-}\overset{\overset{O}{\uparrow}}{S}{-}CH_2{-}\underset{\underset{NH_2}{|}}{CH}{-}COOH \xrightarrow[\text{Alliinase}]{H_2O}$$

(+)-S-allyl-*L*-cysteine sulfoxide
(Alliin)

$$CH_2{=}CH{-}CH_2{-}\overset{\overset{O}{\uparrow}}{\underset{\underset{CH_2{=}CH{-}CH_2{-}S}{|}}{S}}$$

Diallyl thiosulfinate
(Allicin)

$$+ \ 2 \ CH_3{-}\overset{\overset{O}{/\!/}}{C}{-}COOH \ + \ 2 \ NH_3$$

Pyruvic acid   Ammonia

Diallyl thiosulfinate (2-propenyl-2-propenethiosulfinate) had been isolated earlier from oil of garlic by Cavallito et al. (1944) and given the trivial name allicin. Diallyl thiosulfinate is volatile and is described as garliclike but not unpleasant. Such thiosulfinates are unstable, however, and by disproportionation give rise to a thiosulfonate and a disulfide (Barnard, 1957). The diallyl disulfide from diallyl thiosulfinate is responsible for the characteristic odor of garlic.

$$2 \ \overset{\overset{O}{\uparrow}}{\underset{\underset{CH_2{=}CH{-}CH_2{-}S}{|}}{\underset{CH_2{=}CH{-}CH_2{-}S}{}}} \longrightarrow \underset{\underset{CH_2{=}CH{-}CH_2{-}S}{|}}{\underset{CH_2{=}CH{-}CH_2{-}S}{}} + \underset{\underset{CH_2{=}CH{-}CH_2{-}S}{|}}{\underset{CH_2{=}CH{-}CH_2{-}SO_2}{}}$$

Diallyl thiosulfinate   Diallyl disulfide   Allyl thiosulfonate

Other members of the genus *Allium* (chives, leeks, and onions) contain cysteine sulfoxides, too, but unlike garlic they contain relatively little of the allyl derivatives. Methyl and propyl analogs of the alliin in garlic were identified in onions by Virtenan and Matikkala (1959). Carson and Wong (1961a) established their configuration as (+)-S-methyl-L-cysteine sulfoxide and (+)-S-propyl-L-cysteine sulfoxide.

An enzyme has been isolated from onions that is capable of catalyzing the breakdown of these alkyl cysteine sulfoxides (Schwimmer et al., 1960). This enzyme is unstable in acidic media and has maximum activity in phosphate buffer between pH 8.5 to 8.8, in contrast to the alliinase from garlic, which was active at pH 7.0 (Mazelis, 1963). Chewing or other maceration of onion tissue results in the conversion of cysteine sulfoxides to sulfinates that in turn decompose to yield disulfides.

Carson and Wong (1961b) isolated and identified a number of compounds from macerated raw onions, including alcohols, aldehydes, and ketones, in addition to sulfur compounds that were predominant. These last include propanethiol, hydrogen sulfide, and propyl and methyl derivatives of disulfides and trisulfides. Saghir et al. (1964) analyzed the volatiles from a number of *Alliums*. These authors reported the following percentages of the three sulfide radicals (methyl, propyl, and allyl) in the vapor from raw *Alliums*: 80 to 87 percent allyl, 12 to 19 percent methyl, and 1 percent propyl in garlic; 1 percent allyl, 96 percent propyl, and 3 percent methyl in one variety of onion; 4 percent allyl, 75 percent propyl, and 21 percent methyl in chives; and 5 percent allyl, 67 percent propyl, and 28 percent methyl in leeks. The aroma from garlic was characterized by its high proportion of diallyl disulfide (61 to 74 percent), while chives, leeks, and onions had less than 1 percent; a high proportion of dipropyl disulfide characterized the aroma from onions and to a lesser extent that of chives. Chives contained more of the methyl propyl disulfide than did onions. In the even milder leeks, methyl propyl disulfide accounted for more than half of the sulfides present. The presence of more than one type of alkyl cysteine sulfoxides in these vegetables gives rise to mixed thiosulfinates which accounts for the presence of mixed disulfides.

Yamanishi and Orioka (1955) studied the effects of boiling on the flavor of onions. They reported an increase in n-propanethiol which they suggested derived from n-propyl allyl disulfide. They found n-propane-thiol 50 to 70 times as sweet as sucrose and suggested that this compound contributed to the increased sweetness of onions on cooking.

The lachrymatory substance in onions is derived from another cysteine sulfoxide derivative. This tear-eliciting precursor has been identified as (+)-S-(prop-l-enyl)-L-cysteine sulfoxide (Spåre and Virtanen, 1963).

$$CH_3 - CH = CH - \overset{\overset{O}{\uparrow}}{S} - CH_2 - \underset{\underset{NH_2}{|}}{CH} - COOH$$

(+)-S-(prop-l-enyl)-L-cysteine sulfoxide

An enzyme present in onion (Virtanen, 1965) is capable of cleaving the (+)-S-(prop-l-enyl)-L-cysteine sulfoxide. The products formed are pyruvic acid, ammonia, and, instead of the thiosulfinate obtained from other alkyl cysteine sulfoxides, propenylsulphenic acid, which is the lachrymatory constituent (Spåre and Virtanen, 1963).

$$CH_3-CH=CH-\overset{O}{\overset{\uparrow}{S}}-CH_2-\underset{\underset{NH_2}{|}}{CH}-COOH \xrightarrow[\text{enzyme}]{H_2O} CH_3-CH=CH-\overset{O}{\overset{\uparrow}{S}}-H +$$

(+)-*S*-(prop-1-enyl)-L-cysteine sulfoxide   Propenylsulphenic acid

$$CH_3-\overset{O}{\overset{/\!\!/}{C}}-COOH \quad + \quad NH_3$$

Pyruvic acid   Ammonia

This volatile, irritating compound is unstable, fortunately, and rapidly decomposes to give, first, propenyl alcohol, which is converted to propionaldehyde, some of which condenses to form 2-methyl-2-pentenal, according to Spåre and Virtanen (1963). In addition to decomposition by enzyme, this sulfoxide may cyclize to cycloalliin, a compound identified in the volatiles of onions but one that makes no contribution to odor (Virtanen and Matikkala, 1959b).

$$\underset{\text{Cycloalliin}}{\overset{\overset{\displaystyle O}{\overset{\uparrow}{S}}}{\underset{CH_3HC\diagdown \underset{N}{\underset{H}{\ }}\diagup C}{H_2C\diagup \ \diagdown CH_2}}-COOH}$$

Cycloalliin

According to Schwimmer (1968), the (+)-S-(prop-1-enyl)-L-cysteine sulfoxide is not only the precursor of the lachrymatory factor in minced raw onions, but it is also the precursor of the bitter tasting substance in comminuted tissue of onions and together with the propyl cysteine sulfoxide acts as a precursor for the substances responsible for the biting, burning sensation on the tongue. In fact, this author suggests that most of the odor of raw onions comes from the propenyl precursor.

Sulfur Compounds in Vegetables of the Cruciferae

Most of the vegetables of this family belong to the genus *Brassica*. Included are Brussels sprouts, cabbage, cauliflower, kale, mustard, rutabagas, and turnips. Synge and Wood (1956) reported the presence of (+)-S-methyl-L-cysteine sulfoxide in cabbage, cauliflower, and kale but

$$CH_3-\overset{O}{\overset{\uparrow}{S}}-CH_2-\underset{\underset{NH_2}{|}}{CH}-COOH$$

(+)-*S*-methyl-*L*-cysteine sulfoxide

not in radish (*Raphnus sativa*) nor in cress (*Nasturtium officinale*), two other Cruciferae. Morris and Thompson (1956) analyzed a number of plants for (+)-S-methyl-L-cysteine sulfoxide. They reported values as follows (fresh-weight basis): 117 µg/g in radish, 202 µg/g in young and 43 µg/g in old turnips, 297 µg/g in mustard leaves, 304 µg/g in cabbage, 396 µg/g in Chinese cabbage, and 2380 µg/g in cauliflower. Leaves of kohlrabi contained 558 µg/g and stems 1069 µg/g. In broccoli the (+)-S-methyl-L-cysteine sulfoxide content varied from 851 µg/g in the stem, to 1770 µg/g in leaves, and up to 2406 µg/g in the buds.

Although Cruciferae appeared to lack an enzyme capable of acting on the (+)-S-methyl-L-cysteine sulfoxide, Mazelis (1963) reported the presence of such an enzyme in *Brassica*, for which he proposed the name cysteine sulfoxide lyase. The presence of a lyase in these plants had been overlooked, no doubt, because it is inactive in acidic cell sap, although it is active in alkaline media and remains so up to pH 10.

A second group of sulfur-containing compounds in vegetables of the Cruciferae family are the glucosides of the isothiocyanates (mustard oils). The structure of these compounds was established by Ettlinger and Lundeen (1956) as

$$R-C \overset{\displaystyle S-C_6H_{11}O_5}{\underset{\displaystyle N-O-SO_3X}{}}$$

Type formula for isothiocyanate glucosides

More than 30 mustard oils are known. The embryos of the seeds of Cruciferae are especially rich sources (Kjaer, 1960). These compounds differ from each other depending on the makeup of the R group and on the base attached to the sulfate ion. The best-known isothiocyanate glucoside is sinigrin (potassium myronate). This compound is found in horseradish (Stahmann et al., 1943) as well as in black mustard seed and in cabbage (Kjaer, 1960). In sinigrin the R represents the allyl radical and the X represents potassium, so the formula for sinigrin is

$$CH_2=CH-CH_2-C \overset{\displaystyle S-C_6H_{11}O_5}{\underset{\displaystyle N-O-SO_3K}{}}$$

Sinigrin (potassium myronate)

Present also in tissues of the isothiocyanate-yielding plants is the enzyme myrosinase found in special cells called iodoblasts, in contrast to the isothiocyanate glycoside substrates, which are distributed throughout parenchyma cells (Kjaer, 1960). Cutting or maceration of the tissues is essential to bring enzyme and substrate into contact. Myrosinase, a thioglycosidase, catalyzes the hydrolysis of glucose from the isothiocyanate glycosides (Nagashima and Uchiyama, 1959), after which the remainder of the molecule undergoes electronic rearrangement and the sulfate ion is lost (Ettlinger and Lundeen, 1956; Nagashima and Uchiyama, 1959). The overall reaction in the decomposition of sinigrin is shown (Ettlinger and Lundeen, 1957).

$$CH_2=CH-CH_2-C\underset{N-OSO_3K}{\overset{S-C_6H_{11}O_5}{}} \quad + \quad H_2O \longrightarrow CH_2=CH-CH_2 \quad N=C=S$$

Sinigrin

Myrosinase A

Allyi isothiocyanate
(A mustard oil)

$KHSO_4 \quad + \quad C_6H_{11}O_6$
Potassium   Glucose
acid sulfate

The optimum pH for the action of myrosinase is near neutral (pH 6.5 to 7.5) and the optimum temperature 30 to 40° C (Kjaer, 1960).

White mustard seed contain sinalbin instead of sinigrin found in black mustard seed. In sinalbin the allyl radical of sinigrin is replaced by the *para*-hydroxybenzyl radical (p-$HOC_6H_4CH_2$) (Ettlinger and Lundeen, 1956) and the base sinapine, a choline ester of 3,5-dimethoxy-4-hydroxy cinnamic acid, replaces the potassium of sinigrin (Kjaer, 1960).

$$CH_3O, HO, CH_3O - CH=CH-C\overset{O}{\overset{\parallel}{}}-O-CH_2-CH_2-\overset{+}{N}(CH_3)_3$$

Sinapine

The mustard oil formed from the enzymatic hydrolysis of sinalbin is the isothiocyanate p-$HOC_6H_4CH_2N$ C S. Phenylethyl isothiocyanate was reported in the root of turnip and horseradish (Stahmann et al., 1943), and Challenger (1953) found this mustard oil in garden nasturtium. The main mustard oil from raw cabbage is allyl isothiocyanate, although Bailey et al. (1961) identified four additional isothiocyanates in the aroma of minced raw cabbage. In addition, these workers reported the presence of five sulfides, nine disulfides, and one trisulfide. Isothiocyanates produce a sharp, burning sensation of the tongue. Some isothiocyanates have lachrymatory properties.

Aroma of Cooked Brassica Vegetables

The assertive odor of vegetables of the genus *Brassica* no doubt accounts for the fact that cabbage and cauliflower were the first vegetables to be analyzed as they cooked. Simpson and Halliday (1928) reported that hydrogen sulfide accounted for one fourth of the total volatile sulfur compounds emanating from cooked cabbage. The evolution of hydrogen sulfide during the first seven minutes of cooking was double that evolved during the first five minutes. The yield of hydrogen sulfide from cooked cauliflower was twice that from cooked cabbage. The authors suggested that hydrogen sulfide came from the isothiocyanate present. Dateo et al. (1957) reported that two constituents, dimethyl disulfide and hydrogen sulfide, accounted for the volatile sulfur compounds in the aroma of cooked cabbage. These authors presented evidence that (+)-S-methyl-L-cysteine sulfoxide was the source of the dimethyl disulfide. Under the same conditions of cooking (exhaustively), both cauliflower and broccoli gave off three times as much dimethyl disulfide as did cabbage. Oster-mayer and Tarbell (1960) boiled (+)-S-methyl-L-cysteine sulfoxide with 1 N HCL and proposed the following to account for the reaction products that they obtained:

$$
4\ CH_3-\overset{O}{\overset{\uparrow}{S}}-CH_2-CH-COOH\ +\ 2\ H_2O\ \xrightarrow{\Delta}\ CH_3-\overset{O}{\underset{O}{\overset{\uparrow}{\underset{\downarrow}{S}}}}-S-CH_3
$$

(+)-S-methyl-L-cysteine sulfoxide   Dimethylthio-sulfonate

$$
+\ CH_3-S-S-CH_3\ +\ 4\ CH_3-\overset{O}{\overset{//}{C}}-COOH\ +\ 4\ NH_3
$$

Dimethyl disulfide   Pyruvic acid   Ammonia

These authors reported that the same products were obtained when the hydrolysis was carried out in basic or in neutral medium. In no case did they obtain hydrogen sulfide when (+)-S-methyl-L-cysteine sulfoxide was hydrolyzed. Self et al. (1963) reported large amounts of hydrogen sulfide, methanethiol (methyl mercaptans), and dimethyl sulfide in the aroma of cooked cauliflower and rutabagas. In addition, these workers found large amounts of hydrogen sulfide, dimethyl sulfide, and methane-, ethane-, and n-propanethiol in the vapor from cooked onions and leeks. According to MacLeod and MacLeod (1970), dimethyl sulfide is the primary constituent in the volatiles from cooked cabbage.

Hing and Weckel (1964) identified in the volatiles from cooked ruta-bagas three sulfides—hydrogen sulfide, methyl disulfide, and dimethyl sulfide—in addition to acetaldehyde and ammonia. Isothiocyanates were detected in the uncooked rutabagas.

Asparagus

The sulfur compound in asparagus that gives rise to the methanethiol that appears in the urine soon after the vegetable is eaten has not been determined (Challenger, 1959). A methyl-sulfonium derivative of methionine (Challenger and Hayward, 1954) has been identified in the vegetable.

Celery

Of the 38 constituents identified in the volatiles of celery, 6 appear to make important contributions to the aroma (Gold and Wilson, 1963). These include 4 phthalides (3-isobutylidene-3a,4-dihydrophthalide, 3-isovalidene-3a,4-dihydrophthalide, 3-isobutylidene phthalide, and 3-isovalidene phthalide), *cis*-3-hexen-1-yl pyruvate, and diacetyl. The phthalides produce a burning sensation in the mouth and are slightly bitter.

Cucumbers

Forss et al. (1962) reported that 6 aldehydes (nona-2,6-dienal, non-2-enal, hex-2-enal, hexanal, propanal, and ethanal) were the main components responsible for the odor of cucumbers.

Volatiles from Other Cooked Vegetables

Self et al. (1963) analyzed the low boiling volatiles produced when such mild-flavored vegetables as beans, carrots, celery, corn, parsnips, peas, and potatoes were cooked, as well as the more highly flavored Brussels sprouts, cauliflower, leeks, onions, and rutabagas. All the vegetables yielded a similar array of volatile constituents, qualitatively. In addition to methanol and acetone, these authors reported the presence of hydrogen sulfide in the aroma of cooked beans, corn, parsnips, peas, and potatoes and dimethyl sulfide in the aroma of cooked beans, carrots, celery, corn, parsnips, peas, and potatoes. Small amounts of methanethiol were reported in the aroma of beans, carrots, corn, peas, parsnips, and potatoes. Casey et al. (1962) presented evidence that a number of volatile constituents identified in the aroma of cooked vegetables could arise from the degradation of amino acids by constituents, especially sugars, present in the vegetables. Casey et al. (1963) demonstrated that methanol could arise from the decomposition of pectin and that pectin could act as a methyl donor for the production of dimethyl sulfide.

References

STRUCTURAL COMPONENTS AND TEXTURE

Addoms, R. M., G. T. Nightingale, and M. A. Blake. 1930. *Development and Ripening of Peaches as Correlated with Physical Characteristics, Chemical Composition, and Histological Structure of the Fruit Flesh. II. Histology and Microchemistry.* New Jersey Agr. Exp. Sta. Bull. No. 507. p. 1.

Barrett, A. J., and D. H. Northcote. 1965. Apple fruit pectic substances. *Biochem. J. 94:* 617.

Barrios, E. P., D. W. Newsom, and J. C. Miller. 1963. Some factors influencing culinary quality in Irish potatoes. II. Physical characteristics. *Amer. Potato J.* 40: 200.

Bate-Smith, E. C. 1958. The contribution of phenolic substances to quality in plant products. V. Tannins et anthocyanes. *Qualitas Plantarum et Materiae Vegetabiles.* III/IV: 440.

Bennet-Clark, T. A. 1959. Water relations of cells. In *Plant Physiology* II: 105. F. C. Steward, ed.

Bettelheim, F. A. and C. Sterling. 1955a. Factors associated with potato texture. I. Specific gravity and starch content. *Food Research* 20: 71.

Bettelheim, F. A., and C. Sterling. 1955b. Factors associated with potato texture. II. Pectic substances. *Food Research* 20: 118.

Borchgrevink, N. C., and H. Charley. 1966. Color of cooked carrots related to carotene content. Determinations by chromatographic and spectrophotometric analyses. *J. Am. Dietet. Assoc.* 49: 116.

Briant, A. M., C. J. Personius, and E. G. Cassel. 1945. Physical properties of starch from potatoes of different culinary quality. *Food Research* 10: 437.

Burr, H. K., S. Kon, and H. J. Morris. 1968. Cooking rates of dry beans as influenced by moisture content and temperature and time of storage. *Food Technol.* 22: 336.

Burton, W. G., and W. T. Spragg. 1950. A note on the intercellular space of the potato tuber. *New Phytologist* 49: 8.

Crafts, A. S. 1944. Cellular changes in certain fruits and vegetables during blanching and dehydration. *Food Research* 9: 442.

Crean, D. E. C., and D. R. Haisman. 1963. The interaction between phytic acid and divalent cations during the cooking of dried peas. *J. Sci. Food Agr.* 14: 824.

Dainty, J. 1963. Water relations in plant cells. *Advances in Bot. Res.* 1: 279.

Dawson, E. H., J. C. Lamb, E. W. Toepfer, and H. W. Warren. 1952. *Development of Rapid Methods of Soaking and Cooking Dry Beans.* U.S. Dept. Agr. Bull. No. 1051.

Doesburg, J. J. 1957. Relation between the solubilization of pectin and the fate of organic acids during maturation of apples. *J. Sci. Food Agr.* 8: 206.

Doesburg, J. J. 1961. Relation between the behavior of pectic substances and changes in firmness of horticultural products during heating. *Qualitas Plantarum et Materiae Vegetabiles.* 8 (2): 115.

Esau, K. 1963. Ultrastructure of differentiated cells in higher plants. *Amer. J. Bot.* 50: 495.

Esau, K. 1965. *Plant Anatomy,* 2nd ed. John Wiley and Sons, New York.

Esau, P., M. A. Joslyn, and L. L. Claypool. 1962. Changes in water-soluble calcium and magnesium content of pear fruit tissue during maturation and ripening in relation to changes in pectic substances. *J. Food Sci.* 27: 509.

Falk, S., C. H. Hertz, and H. I. Virgin. 1958. On the relation between turgor pressure and tissue rigidity. I. Experiments on resonance frequency and tissue rigidity. *Physiol. Plant. 11*: 802.

Frey-Wyssling, A., and K. Mühlethaler. 1965. *Ultrastructural Plant Cytology,* p. 36. Elsevier Publishing Company, Amsterdam.

Geddes, R., C. T. Greenwood, and S. Mackenzie. 1965. Studies on the biosynthesis of starch granules. III. The properties of the component starches from the growing potato tuber. *Carbohydrate Research 1*: 71.

Gee, M., R. M. Reeve, and R. M. McCready. 1959. Measurement of plant pectic substances, reaction of hydroxyl amine with pectinic acids. Chemical studies and histochemical estimation of the degree of esterification of pectic substances in fruits. *J. Agr. Food Chem. 7*: 34.

Griffin, J., and Z. I. Kertesz. 1946. Changes which occur in apple tissue upon treatment with various agents and their relation to the natural mechanism of softening during maturation. *Bot. Gaz. 108*: 279.

Hartman, H., F. C. Reimer, and R. K. Norris. 1929. *Further Investigations on the Harvesting, Storing, and Ripening of Pears from Rogue River Valley.* Ore. Agr. Exp. Sta. Bull. 254.

Joslyn, M. A. 1962. The chemistry of protopectin: A critical review of historical data and recent developments. *Advances in Food Research 11*: 1.

Kertesz, Z. I., M. Eucare, and G. Fox. 1959. A study of apple cellulose. *Food Research 24*: 14.

Kirkpatrick, M. E., A. O. Mackey, R. R. Little, R. H. Matthews, and C. E. Falatko. 1959. *Quality of Apples for Household Use. Histological, Chemical, and Palatability Studies.* Home Economics Res. Rept. No. 8. Agr. Res. Service, U.S. Dept. Agr.

Lamport, D. T. A. 1965. The protein component of primary cell walls. *Advances in Botanical Research 2*: 151.

Lancaster, M. C., and M. D. Sweetman. 1932. The relation of maturity, size, period in storage, and variety to the speed and evenness of cooking potatoes. *J. Home Econ. 24*: 262.

Mattson, S., E. Åkerberg, E. Eriksson, E. Koulter-Andersson, and K. Vahtros. 1950. Factors determining the composition and cookability of peas. *Acta Agr. Scand. 1*: 40.

McCready, R. M., and M. Gee. 1960. Determination of pectic substances by paper chromatography. *J. Agr. Food Chem. 8*: 510.

McCready, R. M., and E. A. McComb. 1954. Pectic constituents in ripe and unripe fruit. *Food Research 19*: 530.

Morris, H. J., and E. R. Wood. 1956. Influence of moisture content on keeping quality of dry beans. *Food Technol. 10*: 225.

Mühlethaler, K. 1961. Plant cell walls. In *The Cell.* II: 85. J. Brachet and A. E. Mirsky, eds.

Nightingale, G. T., R. M. Addoms, and M. A. Blake. 1930. *Development and*

Ripening of Peaches as Correlated with Physical Characteristics, Chemical Composition and Histological Structure of the Fruit Flesh. III. Macrochemistry. New Jersey Agr. Exp. Sta. Bull. No. 494.

Park, R. B. 1965. The chloroplast. p. 124. In *Plant Biochemistry,* J. Bonner and J. E. Varner, eds.

Pfund, M. 1939. *The Culinary Quality of Apples as Determined by the Use of New York State Varieties.* Cornell Univ. Agr. Exp. Sta. Memoir 225.

Postlmayr, H. L., B. S. Luh, and S. J. Leonard. 1956. Characterization of pectin changes in freestone and clingstone peaches during ripening and processing. *Food Technol. 10*: 618.

Reeve, R. M. 1953. Histological investigations of texture in apples. II. Structure and intercellular spaces. *Food Research 18*: 604.

Reeve, R. M. 1959. Histological and histochemical changes in developing and ripening peaches. II. The cell wall and pectins. *Am. J. Bot. 46*: 241.

Reeve, R. M. 1967. Suggested improvements for microscopic measurement of cells and starch granules in fresh potatoes. *American Potato J. 44*: 41.

Reeve, R. M., and M. S. Brown. 1966. Some structural and histochemical changes related to frozen fruits and vegetables. *Cryobiology 3*: 214.

Reeve, R. M., and L. R. Leinbach. 1953. Histological investigations of texture in apples. I. Composition and influence of heat on structure. *Food Research 18*: 592.

Rosenbaum, T. M., G. O. Henneberry, and G. E. Baker. 1966. Constitution of leguminous seeds. VI. The cookability of field peas (*Pisum sativum* L). *J. Sci. Food Agr. 17*: 237.

Sharma, K. N., and N. R. Thompson. 1956. Relationship of starch grain size to specific gravity of potato tubers. Mich. Exp. Sta. Quarterly Bull. *38*: 559.

Shewfelt, A. L. 1965. Changes and variations in the pectic constitution of ripening peaches as related to product firmness. *J. Food. Sci. 30*: 573.

Simpson, J. I., and E. G. Halliday. 1941. Chemical and histological studies of the disintegration of cell-membrane materials in vegetables during cooking. *Food Research 6*: 189.

Sistrunk, W. A., and R. F. Cain. 1960. Chemical and physical changes in green beans during preparation and processing. *Food Technol. 14*: 357.

Sterling, C. 1954. Sclereid development and the texture of Bartlett pears. *Food Research 19*: 433.

Sterling, C. 1955. Effect of moisture and high temperature on cell walls in plant tissue. *Food Research 20*: 474.

Sterling, C. 1959. Drained weight behavior in canned fruit: An interpretation of the role of the cell wall. *Food Technol. 13*: 629.

Sterling, C. 1963. Texture and cell-wall polysaccharides in foods, p. 259. In *Recent Advances in Food Science*-3. *Biochemistry and Biophysics in Food Research,* J. M. Leitch and D. N. Rhodes, eds. London: Butterworths.

Sterling, C. 1968. Effect of solutes and pH on the structure and firmness of cooked carrots. *J. Food Technol. 3:* 367.

Sterling, C., and F. A. Bettelheim. 1955. Factors associated with potato texture. III. Physical attributes and general conclusions. *Food Research 20:* 130.

Sterling, C., and C. O. Chichester. 1960. Sugar distribution in plant tissues cooked in syrup. *J. Food Sci. 25:* 157.

Sterling, C. and A. J. Kalb. 1959. Pectic changes in peach during ripening. *Bot. Gaz. 121:* 111.

Stocking, R. 1956. The state of water in cells and tissues. *Handbuch der Pflanzenphysiologie* III: 15.

Unrau, A. M., and R. E. Nylund. 1957a. The relation of physical properties and chemical composition to mealiness in the potato. I. Physical properties. *American Potato J. 34:* 245.

Unrau, A. M., and R. E. Nylund. 1957b. The relation of physical properties and chemical composition to mealiness in the potato. II. Chemical composition. *American Potato J. 34:* 303.

Van Buren, J. P., J. C. Moyer, and W. B. Robinson. 1962. Pectin methylesterase in snap beans. *J. Food Sci. 27:* 291.

Van Buren, J. P., J. C. Moyer, D. E. Wilson, W. B. Robinson, and D. B. Hand. 1960. Influence of blanching conditions on sloughing, splitting, and firmness of canned snap beans. *Food Technol. 14:* 233.

Wager, H. C. 1963. The role of phytin in the texture of cooked potatoes. *J. Sci. Food Agr. 14:* 583.

Wardrop, A. B. 1954. The mechanism of surface growth involved in the differentiation of fibers and tracheids. *Australian J. Bot. 2* (2): 165.

Weier, T. E., and C. R. Stocking. 1949. Histological changes induced in fruits and vegetables by processing. *Advances in Food Research 2:* 297.

Wiley, R. C., and G. E. Stembridge. 1961. Factors influencing apple texture. *Proc. Amer. Soc. Hort. Research 77:* 60.

Woodmansee, C. W., J. H. McClendon, and G. F. Somers. 1959. Chemical changes associated with the ripening of apples and tomatoes. *Food Research 24:* 503.

PLANT ACIDS

Andrews, J. C., and E. T. Viser. 1951. The oxalic acid content of some common foods. *Food Research 16:* 306.

Buch, M. L. 1960. *A Bibliography of Organic Acids in Higher Plants.* U.S. Dept. Agr. Handbook No. 164. 100 pp.

Clements, R. L. 1964. Organic acids in citrus fruits. I. Varietal differences. *J. Food Sci. 29:* 276.

Dame, C., C. O. Chichester, and G. L. Marsh. 1959. Studies of processed all-green asparagus. III. Qualitative and quantitative studies of non-volatile organic acids by chromatographic techniques. *Food Research 24:* 20.

Dame, C., S. J. Leonard, B. S. Luh, and G. L. Marsh. 1956. The influence of ripeness on the organic acids, sugars and pectin of canned Bartlett pears. *Food Technol. 10*: 28.

David, J. J., B. S. Luh, and G. L. Marsh. 1956. Organic acids in peaches. *Food Research 21*: 184.

Fellers, C. R., and W. B. Esselen. 1955. *Cranberries and Cranberry Products*. Mass. Agr. Expt. Sta. Bull. *481*: 13.

Gillespie, L. J. and E. H. Walters. 1917. The possibilities and limitations of the Duclaux method for the estimation of volatile acids. *Am. Chem. Soc. J. 39*: 2027.

Goldmann, M. E. 1949. The pH of fruit juices. *Food Research 14*: 275.

Gortner, W. A. 1963. A short-term effect of weather on malic acid in pineapple fruit. *J. Food Sci. 28*: 191.

Hamdy, M. M., and W. A. Gould. 1962. Varietal differences in tomatoes: A study of a-ketoacids, a-amino compounds and citric acid in eight tomato varieties before and after processing. *J. Agr. Food Chem. 10*: 499.

Hartmann, B. G., and F. Hillig. 1934. Acid constituents of food products. *J. Assoc. Offic. Agr. Chemists 17*: 522.

Hulme, A. C. 1958. Some aspects of the biochemistry of apple and pear fruits. *Advances in Food Research 8*: 297.

Kenworthy, A. L., and N. Harris. 1960. Organic acids in the apple as related to variety and source. *Food Technol. 14*: 372.

Lewis, E. P., and E. M. Elbert. 1964. Organic acids in winter squashes. *J. Food Sci. 29*: 715.

Li, K. C., and J. G. Woodroof. 1968. Gas chromatographic resolution of non-volatile organic acids in peaches. *J. Agr. Food Chem. 16*: 534.

MacLennan, D. H., H. Beevers, and J. L. Harley. 1963. Compartmentation of acid in plant tissues. *Biochem. J. 89*: 316.

Markakis, P., A. Jarczyk, and S. P. Krishna. 1963. Nonvolatile acids in blueberries. *J. Agr. Food Chem. 11*: 8.

Masters, H., and P. Garbutt. 1920. IX. An investigation of the methods employed for cooking green vegetables, with special reference to the losses incurred. Part II. Green vegetables. *Biochem. J. 14*: 75.

Miller, C. L., and E. Ross. 1963. Non-volatile organic acids of the Dwarf Cavendish (Chinese) variety of banana. *J. Food Sci. 28*: 193.

Nelson, E. K. 1925. The non-volatile acids of the strawberry, the pineapple, the raspberry, and the Concord grape. *Am. Chem. Soc. J. 47*: 1177.

Nelson, E. K., and H. H. Mottern. 1931. Organic acids of spinach, broccoli, and lettuce. *Am. Chem. Soc. J. 53*: 1909.

Peynaud, E., and A. Maurie. 1953. Évolution des acides organique dans le grain de raisin au cours de la maturation en 1951. *Ann. Technol. Agr. 2*: 83.

Pierce, E. C., and C. O. Appleman. 1943. Role of ether-soluble organic acids in the cation-anion balance in plants. *Plant Physiol. 18*: 224.

Pucher, G. W., H. E. Clark, and H. B. Vickery. 1937. The organic acids of rhubarb (*Rheum hybridum*). II. The organic acid composition of the leaves. *J. Biol. Chem. 117*: 605.

Ranson, S. L. 1965. The plant acids. In *Plant Biochemistry*, J. Bonner and J. E. Varner, eds., p. 493. Academic Press, New York.

Rice, A. C., and C. S. Pederson. 1954. Chromatographic analysis of organic acids in canned tomato juice, including the identification of pyrrolidone carboxylic acid. *Food Research 19*: 106.

Rohrer, D. E., and B. S. Luh. 1959. Composition and quality evaluation of boysenberries for frozen pies. *Food Technol. 13*: 645.

Ryder, A. E. 1930. The oxalic acid content of vegetables used as greens. *J. Home Econ. 22*: 309.

Schwartz, J. H., R. B. Greenspun, and W. L. Porter. 1962. Identification and determination of the major acids of the white potato. *J. Agr. Food Chem. 10*: 43.

Sinclair, W. B., E. T. Bartholomew, and R. C. Ramsey. 1945. Analysis of the organic acids of orange juice. *Plant Physiol. 20*: 3.

Sinclair, W. B., and D. M. Eny. 1945. The organic acids of lemon fruits. *Bot. Gaz. 107*: 231.

Singleton, V. L., and W. A. Gortner. 1965. Chemical and physical development of the pineapple fruit. II. Carbohydrate and acid constituents. *J. Food Sci. 30*: 19.

Steward, F. C., A. C. Hulme, S. R. Frieberg, M. P. Hegarty, J. K. Pollard, R. Rabson, and R. A. Barr. 1960. Physiological investigation on the banana plant. I. Biochemical constituents detected in the banana plant. *Ann. of Botany*, N. S. 24, No. 93, p. 83.

Thimann, K. V., and W. D. Bonner, Jr. 1950. Organic acid metabolism. *Annual Review of Plant Physiology 1*: 75.

Ting, S. V., and E. J. Deszyck. 1959. Isolation of L-quinic acid in citrus fruits. *Nature 183*: 1404.

Ting, S. V., and H. M. Vines. 1966. Organic acids in the juice vesicles of Florida "Hamlin" orange and "Marsh" seedless grapefruit. *Proc. Am. Soc. Hort. Sci. 88*: 291.

Vallarreal, F., B. S. Luh, and S. J. Leonard. 1960. Influence of ripeness level on organic acids in canned tomato juice. *Food Technol. 14*: 176.

Whiting, G. C. 1958. The non-volatile organic acids of some berry fruits. *J. Sci. Food Agr. 9*: 244.

Wyman, H., and J. K. Palmer. 1964. Organic acids in the ripening banana fruit. *Plant Physiol. 39*: 630.

CAROTENOIDS

Borchgrevink, N. C., and H. Charley. 1966. Color of cooked carrots related to carotene content. Determinations by chromatographic and spectrophotometric analyses. *J. Am. Dietet. Assoc. 49*: 116.

Curl, A. L. 1959. The carotenoids of cling peaches. *Food Research 24*: 413.

Curl, A. L. 1962. The carotenoids of red bell peppers. *J. Agr. Food Chem. 10*: 504.

Curl, A. L. 1963. The carotenoids of Italian prunes. *J. Food Sci. 28*: 623.

Curl, A. L. 1964. The carotenoids of green bell peppers. *J. Agr. Food Chem. 12*: 522.

Curl, A. L. 1966. The carotenoids of muskmelons. *J. Food Sci. 31*: 759.

Curl, A. L. and G. F. Bailey. 1957. The carotenoids of Ruby Red grapefruit. *Food Research 22*: 63.

Curl, A. L., and G. F. Bailey. 1961. The carotenoids of navel oranges. *J. Food Sci. 26*: 442.

Eheart, M. S., and C. Gott. 1964. Conventional and microwave cooking of vegetables. *J. Am. Dietet. Assoc. 44*: 116.

Goodwin, T. W. 1955. Carotenoids. In *Modern Methods of Plant Analysis.* Vol. III, pp. 272–273. Springer-Verlag, Berlin.

Hanson, S. W. 1954. The effect of heat treatment on some plant carotenoids. In *Color in Foods.* U.S. Quartermaster Food and Container Institute. Surveys Progress Military Subsistence Problems. Series I, No. 5, p. 136.

Harper, R. H., and F. P. Zscheile. 1945. Carotenoid content of carrot varieties and strains. *Food Research 10*: 84.

Karrer, R. H., and E. Jucker. 1950. *Carotenoids.* Trans. and revised by E. A. Braude. Elsevier Pub. Co., New York. 384 pp.

Kemmerer, A. R., and G. S. Fraps. 1943. Constituents of carotene extracts of plants. *Ind. Eng. Chem., Anal. Ed. 15*: 714.

Kemmerer, A. R., G. S. Fraps, and W. W. Meinke. 1945. Constituents of the crude carotene of certain human foods. *Food Research 10*: 66.

Martin, M. E., J. P. Sweeney, G. L. Gilpin, and V. J. Chapman. 1960. Factors affecting the ascorbic acid and carotene content of broccoli. *J. Agr. Food Chem. 8*: 387.

Morgan, R. C. 1966. Chemical studies on concentrated pineapple juice. 1. Carotenoid composition of fresh pineapples. *J. Food Sci. 31*: 213.

Porter, J. W., and R. E. Lincoln. 1950. I. Lycopersicon selections containing a high content of carotenes and colorless polyenes. II. Mechanism of carotene biosynthesis. *Arch. Biochem. 27*: 390.

Reeve, R. M. 1943. Microscopy of the oils and carotene bodies in dehydrated carrots. *Food Research 8*: 137.

Singleton, V. L., W. A. Gortner, and H. Y. Young. 1961. Carotenoid pigments of pineapple fruit. 1. Acid-catalyzed isomerization of the pigments. *J. Food Sci. 26*: 49.

Smith, M. C., and L. Otis. 1941. Observations on carotene analysis of vegetables and fruits as a basis for prediction of their vitamin A value. *Food Research 6*: 143.

Weier, T. E. 1942. A cytological study of the carotene in the root of *Daucus carota* under various experimental treatments. *Am. J. Bot. 29*: 35.

Went, F. W., A. L. Le Rosen, and L. Zechmeister. 1942. Effect of external factors on tomato pigments as studied by chromatographic methods. *Plant Physiol.* 17: 91.

Zechmeister, L. 1960. *Cis-trans* isomeric carotenoid pigments. *Fortschr. Chem. Org. Naturstoffe. 18:* 223.

Zechmeister, L. 1962. *Cis-trans Isomeric Carotenoids, Vitamin A, and Aryl-polyenes.* Springer-verlag, Heidelberg. 251 pp.

Zechmeister, L. and A. Polgár. 1941. The carotenoid and provitamin A content of the watermelon. *J. Biol. Chem. 139:* 193.

Zechmeister, L., and F. W. Went. 1948. Some stereochemical aspects in genetics. *Nature 162:* 847.

CHLOROPHYLLS

Aronoff, S. 1953. The chemistry of chlorophyll. *Advances in Food Research 4:* 133.

Bogorad, L. 1965. Chlorophyll biosynthesis. In *Chemistry and Biochemistry of Plant Pigments,* T. W. Goodwin, ed., p. 36. Academic Press Inc., London.

Chapman, V. J., J. O. Putz, G. L. Gilpin, J. P. Sweeney, and J. N. Eisen. 1960. Electronic cooking of fresh and frozen broccoli. *J. Home Economics 52:* 161.

Frey-Wyssling, A. and K. Mühlethaler. 1965. *Ultrastructural Plant Cytology,* pp. 97, 249. Elsevier Publishing Company, Amsterdam.

Gordon, J., and I. Noble. 1959. Comparison of electronic *vs.* conventional cooking of vegetables. *J. Am. Dietet. Assoc. 35:* 241.

Jones, I. D., R. C. White, and E. Gibbs. 1962. Some pigment changes in cucumbers during brining and brine storage. *Food Technol. 16* (3): 96.

Joslyn, M. A., and G. Mackinney. 1938. The rate of conversion of chlorophyll to pheophytin. *J. Am. Chem. Soc. 60:* 1132.

Mackinney, G., and M. A. Joslyn. 1940. The conversion of chlorophyll to pheophytin. *J. Am. Chem. Soc. 62:* 231.

Mackinney, G., and C. A. Weast. 1940. Color changes in green vegetables. Frozen-pack peas and string beans. *Ind. Eng. Chem. 32:* 392.

Park, R. B. 1965. The chloroplast. p. 124. In *Plant Biochemistry,* James Bonner and J. E. Varner, eds.

Sweeney, J. P., and M. Martin. 1958. Determination of chlorophyll and pheophytin in broccoli heated by various procedures. *Food Research 23:* 635.

Sweeney, J. P., and M. E. Martin. 1961. Stability of chlorophyll in vegetables as affected by pH. *Food Technol. 15:* 263.

Van Buren, J. P., J. C. Moyer, and W. B. Robinson. 1964. Chlorophyll losses in blanched snap beans. *Food Technol. 18:* 1204.

Wald, G. 1959. Life and light. *Sci. American 201* (4): 92.

Walker, G. C. 1964. Color determination in frozen French beans (*Phaseolus vulgaris*). 2. The effect of blanching. *J. Food Sci. 29:* 389.

Weast, C. A., and G. Mackinney. 1940. Chlorophyllase. *J. Biol. Chem. 133*: 551.

Willstätter, R., and A. Stoll. 1928. *Investigations on Chlorophyll.* Translation by F. M. Schertz and A. R. Merz. The Science Press Printing Company, Lancaster, Pennsylvania.

Wolken, J. J. 1959. The chloroplasts and photosynthesis. A structural basis for function. *American Scientist 47*: 202.

FLAVONOID PIGMENTS

Anthocyanins

Bate-Smith, E. C. 1950. *Anthocyanins, Flavones, and Other Phenolic Compounds.* Biochemical Symposium No. 3. Cambridge University Press.

Blank, F. 1947. The anthocyanin pigments of plants. *Bot. Rev. 13*: 241.

Blank, F. 1958. Anthocyanins, flavones, xanthones. *Handbuch der Pflanzenphysiologie. 10*: 300.

Creuss, W. V. 1958. Corrosion and perforation in tin plate. In *Commercial Fruit and Vegetable Products,* p. 305. McGraw-Hill Book Co., Inc., New York.

Daravingas, G., and R. F. Cain. 1968. Thermal degradation of black raspberry anthocyanin pigments in model systems. *J. Food Sci. 33*: 138.

Dekazos, E. D. 1966. Anthocyanin in red tart cherries as related to anaerobiosis and scald. *J. Food. Sci. 31*: 226.

Goldmann, M. E. 1949. The pH of fruit juices. *Food Research 14*: 275.

Harborne, J. B. 1964. Plant polyphenols. XI. The structure of acylated anthocyanins. *Phytochemistry 3*: 151.

Huang, H. T. 1955. Decolorization of anthocyanins by fungal enzymes. *J. Agr. Food Chem. 3*: 141.

Ingalesbe, D. W., A. M. Neubert, and G. H. Carter. 1963. Concord grape pigments. *J. Agr. Food Chem. 11*: 263.

Karrer, P., and B. Pieper. 1930. Pflanzenfarbstoffe. XXIV. Der Farbstoff der Waldbrombeere und Grossfrüchtigen Gartenbrombeere. *Helv. Chim. Acta 13*: 1067.

Lukton, A., C. O. Chichester, and G. Mackinney. 1956. The breakdown of strawberry anthocyanin pigment. *Food Technol. 10*: 427.

Meschter, E. E. 1953. Effect of carbohydrates and other factors on strawberry products. *J. Agr. Food Chem. 1*: 574.

Robinson, R. 1942. The red and blue coloring matter of plants. *Endeavour 1*: 92.

Sakamura, S., S. Watanabe, and Y. Obata. 1965. Anthocyanase and anthocyanin occurring in eggplant (*Solanum melangena* L.) III. Oxidative decolorization of anthocyanin by polyphenoloxidase. *Agr. Biol. Chem. 29*: 181.

Sondheimer, E. 1953. On the relation between spectral changes and pH of the anthocyanin pelargonidin-3-monoglucoside. *J. Am. Chem. Soc. 75*: 1507.

Sondheimer, E., and C. B. Karash. 1956. The major anthocyanin pigments of the wild strawberry (*Fragaria vesca*). *Nature 178*: 648.

Sondheimer, E., and Z. I. Kertesz. 1953. Participation of ascorbic acid in the destruction of anthocyanin in strawberry juice and model systems. *Food Research 18:* 475.

Tinsley, I. J., and A. H. Bockian. 1960. Some effects of sugars on the breakdown of pelargonidin-3-glucoside in model systems at 90° C. *Food Research 25:* 161.

Van Buren, J. P., D. M. Scheiner, and A. C. Wagenknecht. 1960. An anthocyanin-decolorizing system in sour cherries. *Nature 185:* 165.

Wolf, F. T. 1956. Absorption spectra of the anthocyanin pigment of red cabbage: A natural wide range pH indicator. *Physiol. Plant. 9:* 559.

Flavones, Flavonols, and Flavanones

Bate-Smith, E. C. 1954. Flavonoid compounds in foods. *Advances in Food Research 5:* 261.

Crawford, D. L., R. O. Sinnhuber, and H. Aft. 1961. The effect of methylation upon the antioxidant and chelation capacity of quercetin and dihydroquercetin in a lard substrate. *J. Food Sci. 26:* 139.

Dame, C. Jr., C. O. Chichester, and G. L. Marsh. 1959. Studies of processed all-green asparagus. IV. Studies on the influence of tin on the solubility of rutin and on the concentration of rutin present in the brines of asparagus processed in glass and tin containers. *Food Research 24:* 28.

Davis, R. B., R. B. Guyer, J. J. Daly, and H. T. Johnson. 1961. Control of rutin discoloration in canned asparagus. *Food Technol. 15:* 212.

Gripenberg, J. 1962. Flavones. In *The Chemistry of Flavonoid Compounds,* T. A. Geissman, ed. Pergamon Press, Oxford, p. 406.

Pratt, D. E., and B. M. Watts. 1964. The antioxidant activity of vegetable extracts. I. Flavone aglycones. *J. Food Sci. 29:* 27.

Roberts, E. A. H., R. A. Cartwright, and D. J. Wood. 1956. The flavonols of tea. *J. Sci. Food. Agr. 7:* 637.

Swain, T. 1962. Economic importance of flavonoid compounds: Foodstuffs. In *The Chemistry of Flavonoid Compounds,* T. A. Geissman, ed. Pergamon Press, Oxford, p. 513.

Flavanols

Bate-Smith, E. C. 1954. Flavonoid compounds in foods. *Advances in Food Research 5:* 261.

Bate-Smith, E. C., and T. Swain. 1953. Identification of leucoanthocyanins as "tannins" in foods. *Chem. & Ind.* (London), p. 377.

Freundenberg, K., and K. Weinges. 1962. Catechins and flavonoid tannins. In *The Chemistry of Flavonoid Compounds,* T. A. Geissman, ed., p. 197. Pergamon Press, Oxford.

Geissman, T. A., and H. F. K. Dittmar. 1965. A proanthocyanidin from avocado seed. *Phytochemistry 4:* 359. Pergamon Press, Oxford.

Joslyn, M. A., and R. Peterson. 1956. Occurrence of leucoanthocyanin in pears. *Nature 178*: 318.

Luh, B. S., S. J. Leonard, and D. S. Patel. 1960. Pink discoloration in canned Bartlett pears. *Food Technol. 14*: 53.

Roberts, E. A. H. 1958. The chemistry of tea manufacture. *J. Sci. Food Agr.* 9: 381.

Swain, T. 1965. The tannins. In *Plant Biochemistry*, J. Bonner and J. E. Varner, eds., p. 552.

PHENOLIC COMPOUNDS AND ENZYMATIC DISCOLORATION OF FRUITS AND
VEGETABLES

Baruah, P., and T. Swain. 1959. The action of potato phenolase on flavonoid compounds. *J. Sci. Food Agr. 10*: 125.

Bate-Smith, E. C., J. C. Hughes, and T. Swain. 1958. After-cooking discoloration of potatoes. *Chem. & Ind.* (Rev.), p. 627.

Bolin, H. R., F. S. Nury, and B. J. Finkle. 1964. An improved process of preservation of fresh peeled apples. *Baker's Dig. 38* (3): 46.

Boscan, L., W. D. Powrie, and O. Fennema. 1962. Darkening of red beets, *Beta vulgaris. J. Food Sci. 27*: 574.

Bowman, F., and F. Hanning. 1949. Procedures that reduce darkening of cooked potatoes. *J. Agr. Research 78*: 627.

Clark, W. L., and J. C. Moyer. 1955. The surface darkening of sliced beets. *Food Technol. 9*: 308.

Constantinides, S. M., and C. L. Bedford. 1967. Multiple forms of polyphenoloxidase. *J. Food Sci. 32*: 446.

Craft, C. C. 1961. Polyphenolic compounds in Elberta peaches during storage and ripening. *Proc. Amer. Soc. Hort. Sci. 78*: 119.

El-Sayed, A. S., and B. S. Luh. 1965. Phenolic compounds in canned apricots. *J. Food Sci. 30*: 1016.

Embs, R. J., and P. Markakis. 1965. The mechanism of sulfite inhibition of browning caused by polyphenol oxidase. *J. Food Sci. 30*: 753.

Griffiths, L. A. 1959. Detection and identification of the polyphenoloxidase substrate of the banana. *Nature 184*: 58.

Guadagni, D. G., D. G. Sorber, and J. S. Wilbur. 1949. Enzymatic oxidation of phenolic compounds in frozen peaches. *Food Technol. 3*: 359.

Harel, E., A. M. Mayer, and Y. Shain. 1964. Catechol oxidases from apple, their properties, subcellular location and inhibition. *Physiol. Plant. 17*: 921.

Harel, E., A. M. Mayer, and Y. Shain. 1966. Catechol oxidases, endogenous substrates and browning in developing apples. *J. Sci. Food Agr. 17*: 389.

Heisler, E. G., J. Siciliano, R. H. Treadway, and C. F. Woodward. 1963. After-cooking discoloration of potatoes. Iron content in relation to blackening tendency of tissue. *J. Food Sci. 28*: 453.

Hughes, J. C., and L. W. Mapson. 1966. Chemical and enzymatic discoloration in potatoes. *Proc. Second Inter. Congr. Food Sci. Technol.,* Warsaw. D. J. Tilgner and A. Borys, eds., p. 119.

Hughes, J. C., and T. Swain. 1962. After-cooking blackening of potatoes. II. Core experiments. *J. Sci. Food Agr.* 13: 229. III. Examination of the interaction of factors by *in vitro* experiments. *J. Sci. Food Agr. 13:* 358.

Johnson, G., M. M. Mayer, and D. K. Johnson. 1951. Isolation and characterization of peach tannins. *Food Research 16:* 169.

Jolley, R. L., Jr., and H. S. Mason. 1965. The multiple forms of mushroom tyrosinase. *J. Biol. Chem. 240:* 1489.

Joslyn, M. A., and J. L. Goldstein. 1964. Changes in phenolic content in persimmons during ripening and processing. *J. Agr. Food Chem. 12:* 511.

Joslyn, M. A., and J. D. Ponting. 1951. Enzyme-catalyzed oxidative browning of fruit products. *Advances in Food Research 3:* 1.

Knapp, F. W. 1965. Some characteristics of eggplant and avocado polyphenolase. *J. Food Sci. 30:* 930.

Lerner, A. B. 1953. Metabolism of phenylalanine and tyrosine. *Advances in Enzymology 14:* 73.

Luh, B. S., E. T. Hsu, and K. Stachowicz. 1967. Polyphenolic compounds in canned cling peaches. *J. Food Sci. 32:* 251.

Maier, V. P., and D. M. Metzler. 1965. Changes in individual date polyphenols and their relation to browning. *J. Food Sci. 30:* 747.

Makower, R. U., and S. Schwimmer. 1957. Enzymatic browning, reflectance measurements, and effect of adenosine triphosphate on color changes induced in plant slices by polyphenol oxidase. *J. Agr. Food Chem. 5:* 768.

Mapson, L. W., T. Swain, and A. W. Tomalin. 1963. Influence of variety, cultural conditions, and temperature of storage on enzymic browning of potato tubers. *J. Sci. Food Agr. 14:* 673.

Nelson, R. F., and B. J. Finkle. 1964. Enzyme reactions with phenolic compounds: Effects of *o*-methyltransferase and high pH on the polyphenol oxidase substrates in apple. *Phytochemistry 3:* 321.

Nortje, B. K. 1966. Some catechins and proanthocyanidins in the cores of Bartlett pears. *J. Food Sci. 31:* 733.

Nutting, H. W., and M. C. Pfund. 1942. Nature of darkening of cooked potatoes. *Food Research 7:* 48.

Palmer, J. K. 1963. Banana polyphenoloxidase. Preparation and properties. *Plant Physiol. 38:* 508.

Ponting, J. D. 1960. The control of enzymatic browning of foods. In *Food Enzymes,* H. W. Schultz, ed., p. 105. Avi Publishing Co., Westport, Conn.

Raper, H. S. 1928. The aerobic oxidases. *Physiol. Rev. 8:* 245.

Roberts, E. A. H. 1958. The chemistry of tea manufacture. *J. Sci. Food Agr.* 9: 381.

Samisch, R. 1935. The measurement of phenolase activity. *J. Biol. Chem. 110*: 643.

Scott, L. E. and A. A. Katlan. 1957. Varietal differences in the catechol oxidase content of sweet potato root. *Amer. Soc. Hort. Sci. Proc. 69*: 436.

Siegelman, H. W. 1955. Detection and identification of polyphenoloxidase substrates in apple and pear skin. *Arch. Biochem. Biophys. 56*: 97.

Swain, T. 1962. Economic importance of flavonoid compounds: Foodstuffs. In *The Chemistry of Flavonoid Compounds*, T. A. Geissman, ed., p. 513. Pergamon Press, Oxford.

Swain, T., J. C. Hughes, and L. W. Mapson. 1966. Discoloration in potatoes and potato products. *Proceedings of Plant Science Symposium, 1966.* Campbell Institute for Agricultural Research. Camden, New Jersey, p. 63.

Tate, J. N., B. S. Luh, and G. K. York. 1964. Polyphenoloxidase in Bartlett pears. *J. Food Sci. 29*: 829.

Täufel, K., and J. Voigt. 1964. Sodium chloride as an inhibitor of enzymic browning of apples. *Nahrung 8*: 80.

Uritani, E., and M. Miyano. 1955. Derivatives of caffeic acid in sweet potato attacked by black rot. *Nature 175*: 812.

Wager, H. G. 1955. Why cooked potatoes blacken. *Food Mfg. 30*: 499.

Walker, J. R. L. 1962. Studies on the enzymic browning of apple fruit. *New Zealand J. Sci. 5*: 316.

Walker, J. R. L., and A. C. Hulme. 1966. Studies on the enzymic browning of apple. III. Purification of apple phenolase. *Phytochemistry 5*: 259.

Weurman, C., and T. Swain. 1953. Chlorogenic acid and the enzymic browning of apples and pears. *Nature 172*: 678.

Weurman, C., and T. Swain. 1955. Changes in the enzymatic browning of Bramley's seedling apples during their development. *J. Sci. Food Agr. 6*: 186.

Williams, A. H. 1953. The tannin of apple juice and cider. *Chem. & Ind.*, p. 540.

BETACYANINS AND BETAXANTHINS

Mabry, T. J. 1966. The betacyanins and betaxanthins. In *Comparative Phytochemistry:* Proceedings of the Phytochemical Group Symposium, T. Swain, ed., p. 231.

Peterson, R. G., and M. A. Joslyn. 1960. The red pigment of the root of the beet (*Beta vulgaris*) as a pyrrole compound. *Food Research 25*: 429.

Piatelli, M., L. Minale, and G. Prota. 1965. Pigments of the Centrospermae. III. Betaxanthins from *Beta vulgaris* L. *Phytochemistry 4*: 121. Pergamon Press, Oxford.

Wyler, H., T. J. Mabry, and A. S. Dreiding. 1963. 189. Zur Struktur des Betanidins. Über die Konstitution des Randenfarbstoffes Betanin. *Helv. Chim. Acta 46*: 1745.

FLAVOR OF FRUITS AND VEGETABLES

Fruits

Attaway, J. A., and M. F. Oberbacher. 1968. Studies on the aroma of intact Hamlin oranges. *J. Food Sci. 33*: 287.

Barnell, H. R., and E. Barnell. 1945. Studies in tropical fruits. XVI. Distribution of tannins within the banana and changes in their condition and amount during ripening. *Ann. Bot. 9*: 77.

Bate-Smith, E. C. 1954. Astringency in foods. *Food 23*: 124.

Bate-Smith, E. C., and T. Swain. 1953. Identification of leucoanthocyanins as "tannins" in foods. *Chem. and Ind.* (London), p. 377.

Bernhard, R. A. 1966. Separation and characterization of flavor components from vegetables. In *Flavor Chemistry*, R. F. Gould, ed., p. 131. Advances in Chemistry Series No. 56.

Craft, C. C. 1961. Polyphenolic compounds in Elberta peaches during storage and ripening. *Proc. Amer. Soc. Hort. Sci. 78*: 119.

Creveling, R. K., R. M. Silverstein, and W. G. Jennings. 1968. Volatile components of pineapple. *J. Food Sci. 33*: 284.

Croteau, R. J., and I. S. Fagerson. 1968. Major volatile components of the juice of American cranberry. *J. Food Sci. 33*: 386.

Dimick, K. P., and B. Makower. 1956. Volatile flavor of strawberry essence. I. Identification of the carbonyls and certain low boiling substances. *Food Technol. 10*: 73.

Flath, R. A., D. R. Black, D. G. Gaudagni, W. H. McFadden, and T. H. Schultz. 1967. Identification and organoleptic evaluation of compounds in Delicious apple essence. *J. Agr. Food Chem. 15*: 29.

Geissman, T. A., and H. F. K. Dittmar. 1965. A proanthocyanidin from avocado seed. *Phytochemistry 4*: 359. Pergamon Press, Oxford.

Goldstein, J. L., and T. Swain. 1963. Changes in the tannins in ripening fruit. *Phytochemistry 2*: 371.

Guadagni, D. G., and C. C. Nimmo. 1953. Effect of growing area on tannin and its relation to astringency in frozen Elberta peaches. *Food Technol. 7*: 59.

Gustavson, K. H. 1954. Interaction of vegetable tannins with polyamides as proof of the dominant function of the peptide bond of collagen for its binding of tannins. *J. Polymer Sci. 12*: 317.

Heinz, D. E., R. K. Creveling, and W. C. Jennings. 1965. Direct determination of aroma compounds as an index of pear maturity. *J. Food Sci. 30*: 641.

Hilditch, T. P. 1951. Biosynthesis of unsaturated fatty acids in ripening seeds. *Nature 167*: 298.

Horowitz, R. M. 1964. Relation between taste and structure of some phenolic glycosides. In *Biochemistry of Phenolic Compounds*, J. B. Harborne, ed., p. 545. Academic Press, London.

Horowitz, R. M., and B. Gentili. 1969. Glycosidic pigments and their reactions. In *Symposium on Foods: Carbohydrates and Their Roles.* H. W. Schultz, R. F. Cain, and R. W. Wrolstad, eds., p. 253. The Avi Publishing Company, Inc., Westport, Connecticut.

Issenberg, P., and E. L. Wicks. 1963. Volatile components of bananas. *J. Agr. Food Chem. 11:* 2.

Ito, S., and M. A. Joslyn. 1965. Apple leucoanthocyanins. *J. Food Sci. 30:* 44.

Jennings, W. G., and R. K. Creveling. 1963. Volatile esters of Bartlett pear. II. *J. Food Sci. 28:* 91.

Jennings, W. G., R. K. Creveling, and D. E. Heinz. 1964. Volatile esters of Bartlett pear. IV. Esters of *trans*:2-*cis*:4-decadienoic acid. *J. Food Sci. 29:* 730.

Jennings, W. G., and M. R. Sevenants. 1964a. Volatile components of peach. *J. Food Sci. 29:* 796.

Jennings, W. G., and M. R. Sevenants. 1964b. Volatile esters of Bartlett pear. III. *J. Food Sci. 29:* 158.

Joslyn, M. A., and J. L. Goldstein. 1964a. Astringency of fruit and fruit products in relation to phenolic content. *Advances in Food Research 13:* 179.

Joslyn, M. A., and J. L. Goldstein. 1964b. Changes in phenolic content in persimmons during ripening and processing. *J. Agr. Food Chem. 12:* 511.

Kirchner, J. G. 1949. The chemistry of fruit and vegetable flavors. *Advances in Food Research 2:* 259.

Kirchner, J. G., and J. M. Miller. 1957. Volatile water-soluble and oil constituents in Valencia orange juice. *J. Agr. Food Chem. 5:* 283.

McCarthy, A. I., J. K. Palmer, C. P. Shaw, and E. E. Anderson. 1963. Correlation of gas chromatographic data with flavor profiles of fresh banana fruit. *J. Food Sci. 28:* 379.

MacGregor, D. R., H. Sugisawa, and J. S. Matthews. 1964. Apple juice volatiles. *J. Food Sci. 29:* 448.

Nakayama, T. O. M., and C. O. Chichester. 1963. Astringency of persimmons. *Nature 199:* 72.

Rodin, J. O., C. M. Himel, R. M. Silverstein, R. W. Leeper, and W. A. Gortner. 1965. Volatile flavor and aroma components of pineapple. I. Isolation and tentative identification of 2,5-dimethyl-4-hydroxy-3(2H)-furanone. *J. Food Sci. 30:* 280.

Schultz, T. H., R. Teranishi, W. H. McFadden, P. W. Kilpatrick, and J. Corse. 1964. Volatiles from oranges. II. Constituents of the juice identified by mass spectra. *J. Food Sci. 29:* 790.

Silverstein, R. M., J. O. Rodin, C. M. Himel, and R. W. Leeper. 1965. Volatile flavor and aroma components of pineapple. II. Isolation and identification of chavicol and γ-caprolactone. *J. Food Sci. 30:* 668.

332   *Food Theory and Applications*

Swain, T. 1965. The tannins. p. 552. In *Plant Biochemistry*, J. Bonner and J. E. Varner, eds. Academic Press, New York.

Tang, C. S., and W. G. Jennings. 1967. Volatile components of apricot. *J. Agr. Food Chem.* 15: 24.

Teranishi, R. 1966. Advances in fruit flavor chemistry. In *Flavor Chemistry*, R. F. Gould, ed. Advances in Chemistry Series No. 56, p. 121.

Teranishi, R., J. W. Corse, W. H. McFadden, D. R. Black, and A. I. Morgan, Jr. 1963a. Volatiles from strawberries. I. Mass spectral identification of the more volatile components. *J. Food Sci.* 28: 478.

Teranishi, R., T. H. Schultz, W. H. McFadden, R. E. Lundin, and D. R. Black. 1963b. Volatiles from oranges. 1. Hydrocarbons. Identified by infra-red, nuclear magnetic resonance, and mass spectra. *J. Food Sci.* 28: 541.

Williams, A. H. 1953. The tannin of apple juice and cider. *Chem. & Ind.*, p. 540.

Vegetables

Bailey, S. D., M. L. Bazinet, J. L. Driscoll, and A. I. McCarthy. 1961. The volatile sulfur components of cabbage. *J. Food Sci.* 26: 163.

Barnard, D. 1957. The spontaneous decomposition of aryl thiosulfinates. *J. Chem. Soc.*, p. 4675.

Bernhard, R. A. 1968. Comparative distribution of volatile aliphatic disulfides derived from fresh and dehydrated onions. *J. Food Sci.* 33: 298.

Cavallito, C. J., J. S. Buck, and C. M. Suter. 1944. Allicin, the antibacterial principle of *Allium sativum*. II. Determination of the chemical structure. *J. Am. Chem. Soc.* 66: 1952.

Carson, J. F., and F. F. Wong. 1961a. Isolation of (+)-S-methyl-L-cysteine sulfoxide and (+)-S-n-propyl-L-cysteine sulfoxide from onions as their N:2,4-dinitrophenyl derivatives. *J. Org. Chem.* 26: 4997.

Carson, J. F., and F. F. Wong. 1961b. The volatile flavor components of onions. *J. Agr. Food Chem.* 9 (2): 140.

Casey, J. C., R. Self, and T. Swain. 1962. The flavor of cooked potatoes: A study of the low-boiling volatiles. In *First International Congress of Food Science and Technology*. London. Vol. III: 369. J. M. Leitch, ed. Gordon and Breach Science Publishers, New York.

Casey, J. C., R. Self, and T. Swain. 1963. Origin of methanol and dimethyl sulfide from cooked foods. *Nature* 200: 885.

Challenger, F. 1953. The biological importance of organic compounds of sulfur. *Endeavour* 12: 173.

Challenger, F. 1959. *Aspects of the Organic Chemistry of Sulfur*, p. 44. New York, Academic Press, Inc.

Challenger, F., and B. J. Hayward. 1954. The occurrence of a methyl-sulfonium derivative of methionine (α-aminodimethyl-γ-butyrothetin) in asparagus. *Chem. & Ind.*, p. 729.

Dateo, G. P., R. C. Clapp, D. A. M. MacKay, E. J. Hewitt, and T. Hasselstrom. 1957. Identification of the volatile sulfur components of cooked cabbage and the nature of the precursors in the fresh vegetable. *Food Research* 22: 440.

Ettlinger, M. G., and A. J. Lundeen. 1956. The structure of sinigrin and sinalbin: an enzymatic rearrangement. *J. Am. Chem. Soc.* 78: 4172.

Ettlinger, M. G., and A. J. Lundeen. 1957. First synthesis of a mustard oil glucoside; the enzymatic Lossen rearrangement. *J. Am. Chem. Soc.* 79: 1764.

Forss, D. A., E. A. Dunstone, E. H. Ramshaw, and W. Stark. 1962. The flavor of cucumbers. *J. Food Sci.* 27: 90.

Gold, H. J. and C. W. Wilson III. 1963. The volatile flavor substances of celery. *J. Food Sci.* 28: 484.

Hing, F. S., and K. G. Weckel. 1964. Some volatile components of cooked rutabaga. *J. Food Sci.* 29: 149.

Kjaer, A. 1960. Mustard oils and their parent glycosides. *Fortschr. Chem. Org. Naturst.* 18: 122.

MacLeod, A. J., and G. MacLeod. 1970. Effects of variations in cooking methods on the flavor volatiles of cabbage. *J. Food Sci.* 35: 744.

Mazelis, M. 1963. Demonstration and characterization of cysteine sulfoxide lyase in the Cruciferae. *Phytochemistry* 2: 15.

Morris, C. J., and J. F. Thompson. 1956. The identification of (+)-S-methyl-L-cysteine sulfoxide in plants. *J. Am. Chem. Soc.* 78: 1605.

Nagashima, Z., and M. Uchiyama. 1959. Possibility that myrosinase is a single enzyme and mechanism of decomposition of mustard oil glucoside by myrosinase. *Bull. Agric. Chem. Soc.* (Japan) 23: 555.

Ostermayer, F., and D. S. Tarbell. 1960. Products of acidic hydrolysis of S-methyl-L-cysteine sulfoxide; the isolation of methyl methanethiosulfonate and mechanism of the hydrolysis. *J. Am. Chem. Soc.* 82: 3752.

Saghir, A. R., L. K. Mann, R. A. Bernhard, and J. V. Jacobsen. 1964. Determination of aliphatic mono- and disulfides in *Allium* by gas chromatography and their distribution in common food species. *Proc. Am. Soc. Hort. Sci.* 84: 386.

Schwimmer, S. 1968. Enzymatic conversion of *trans*-(+)-S-1-propenyl-L-cysteine S-oxide to the bitter and odor-bearing component of onions. *Phytochemistry* 7: 401.

Schwimmer, S., J. F. Carson, R. U. Makower, M. Mazelis, and F. F. Wong. 1960. Demonstration of alliinase in a protein preparation from onions. *Experientia 16*: 449.

Schwimmer, S., and M. Mazelis. 1963. Characterization of alliinase in *Allium cepa* (onion). *Arch. Biochem. Biophys. 100*: 66.

Self, R., J. C. Casey, and T. Swain. 1963. The low boiling volatiles of cooked foods. *Chem. & Ind.*, p. 863.

Simpson, J., and E. G. Halliday. 1928. The behavior of sulphur compounds in cooking vegetables. *J. Home Econ. 20*: 121.

Spåre, C. G., and A. I. Virtanen. 1963. On the lachrymatory factor in onion (*Allium cepa*) vapors and its precursor. *Acta Chem. Scand. 17*: 641.

Stahman, M. A., K. P. Link, and J. C. Walker. 1943. Mustard oils in Crucifers and their relation to resistance to clubroot. *J. Agr. Research 67*: 49.

Stoll, A., and E. Seebeck. 1949. Enzymatic breakdown of S-allyl-L-cysteine sulfoxide to diallyl isothiocyanate, pyruvic acid and ammonia. *Helv. Chim. Acta 32*: 197.

Stoll, A., and E. Seebeck. 1950. Die synthese des natürlichen Alliins. *Experientia 6*: 330.

Stoll, A., and E. Seebeck. 1951. Chemical investigations on alliin, the specific principle of garlic. *Advances in Enzymology 11*: 377.

Synge, R. L. M., and J. C. Wood. 1956. (+)-S-methyl-L-cysteine S-oxide in cabbage. *Biochem. J. 64*: 252.

Virtanen, A. I. 1965. Studies on organic sulphur compounds and other labile substances in plants. *Phytochemistry 4*: 207.

Virtanen, A. I., and E. J. Matikkala. 1959a. The isolation of S-methylcysteine sulphoxide and S-n-propylcysteine sulphoxide from onion (*Allium cepa*) and the antibiotic activity of the crushed onions. *Acta Chem. Scand. 13*: 1898.

Virtanen, A. I., and E. J. Matikkala. 1959b. The structure and synthesis of cycloalliin isolated from *Allium cepa*. *Acta Chem. Scand. 13*: 623.

Yamanishi, T., and K. Orioka. 1955. Chemical studies on the change in flavor and taste of onions by boiling. *J. Home Econ.* (Japan) 6: 45. Cited in Bernhard, 1968.

CHAPTER 7

Meat

PAULINE C. PAUL

Meat and meat products form an important part of the diet. The consumer values them for their contribution to palatability. They are also important for their nutritional contributions, and for their role in the individual and national economy. The concern in this chapter will be primarily with palatability and the numerous variables that affect it.

Naumann (1965) points out the term "meat quality" has many different meanings, depending on the viewpoint of the user, and that the meaning changes with time, depending on public preferences. One of the major problems in meat studies is the difficulty of separating and controlling the numerous variables that affect palatability results. So different studies have often yielded contradictory results, depending on the particular combination of experimental conditions employed. Usually the experimenter has no real control over many of these. In addition, many of these factors are interrelated, so that the results may vary due to the particular combination of treatments and control factors chosen for a given experiment. Or the data collected may be measurements on secondary associated factors rather than primary causes.

One of the first studies to employ careful control of cooking procedures was that of Sprague and Grindley (1907). They advocated the use of internal temperature for determining the desired endpoint in roasting meat. During the 1920s and 1930s a number of conferences on Cooperative Meat Investigations were held. From these came the publication by the Committee on Preparation Factors (1942), which outlined research methods developed for studying meat cookery problems and summarized the results of the committee members' investigations.

Most of the research relating to palatability has concentrated on the voluntary, striated muscles of animals used as major sources of meat— cattle, swine, and sheep—with less emphasis on rabbit. There have also been many studies on poultry and a lesser number on fish. These latter are summarized in the next chapter.

During the past 20 years there has been a tremendous increase in re search studies in many fields relating to voluntary muscle. Much of this has been stimulated by development of new methods of study and analysis, such as X-ray crystallography, electron microscopy, chromatography, electrophoresis, and spectroscopy. These studies are providing a new basis for understanding the structural organization and biochemistry of muscle. The current need is to utilize this information to achieve a better understanding of the muscle mechanisms and systems, and to improve the design of experiments that will eventually result in the ability to predict, with increased accuracy, conditions and treatments necessary to produce the desired end product.

The factors that are recognized as influencing the eating quality and acceptability of meat include the types and treatment of the live animal, slaughtering and carcass characteristics, the various muscles of the carcass, the composition, structure, and function of the muscles, post-mortem changes, cooking methods, processing treatments designed to influence one or more palatability characteristics, and various methods of preservation of meat. The literature related to these is very large, so discussion will be limited to those most closely related to the final preparation of the product for consumption. However, the influence of all should be considered in designing experimental studies involving the cooking of meat. Much of the following discussion applies, at least in the broad sense, to all types of flesh foods, including poultry and fish, although there are differences in details among the various species.

Current changes in techniques of producing, processing, and marketing meat products suggest that results of much of the early research may have little detailed applicability to present market supplies. But this work does furnish valuable background for a better understanding of the nature of the material being investigated.

LIVE ANIMALS

Many factors associated with the living animal influence the amount and quality of meat. Reviews may be found in Hedrick (1968), Lawrie (1966a,b), Palmer (1963), Byerly (1965), Stringer (1970), and the Proceedings of the Reciprocal Meat Conferences and Meat Industry Research Conferences.

Genetic Influences

Species

The major large animals utilized for food include cattle (bovine), sheep (ovine), and swine (porcine). Rabbit provides a smaller portion of the animal protein. Other mammals provide relatively minor amounts, but may be major sources in the food patterns of some cultures.

The shape of the growth curve is similar in all species, but animals having a large mature size usually require a longer time to reach maturity. So animals of the same age but different species may have very different quality characteristics.

The types of fats and fatty acids deposited in the fat depots, and the location and extent of the fat deposits, vary with species, influencing the firmness of the meat and the resistance of the fat to the development of rancidity. Other species differences include susceptibility to stress, at least as evidenced by meat color changes and flavor and texture of the meat.

Breed

Breed variations within a species have been found to influence such items as yield of cuts, lean-fat ratio, intramuscular fat distribution (marbling), firmness of fat, and color, tenderness, and juiciness of cooked meat. The size and relative importance of these differences vary widely among studies, dependent partially on the particular breeds being investigated.

Sire

Differences are often found due to the particular genetic makeup of individual animals within a given breed. Bryce-Jones et al. (1963) reported differences in tenderness, flavor, juiciness, and iodine number of the fat due to sire, and Paul (1962) listed variations in tenderness and average size of beef muscle fibers among animals of similar heredity and management. Mahon et al. (1956) stated that they found more significant differences among individual pigs within a diet group than between the experimental variables being studied. However, Woodhams et al. (1966) reported no influence of sire on palatability characteristics of lamb.

Animal Influences

Sex

Hedrick et al. (1967) have reviewed the many studies on the influence of the hormones associated with sex on the composition of meat animals. There is considerable current interest in the comparative quality of bulls and steers, due to the emphasis on increasing the lean and decreasing the fat content of the carcass. Bull meat appeared to be as acceptable as steer, although the cuts from steers were usually more tender, and some cases had more flavor and juice, the differences becoming more marked with increasing age of the animals (Bryce-Jones et al., 1964; Bailey et al., 1966; Woodhams and Trower, 1965; and Field et al., 1966). In pork, Martin et al. (1968) found significant differences in tenderness, texture, and flavor, due to sex. Pearson et al. (1969) reviewed the problem of "sex odor" in porcine fat. This aroma is found in about two thirds of all boar carcasses, but is of much lower incidence in barrows, gilts, and sows.

Age

Bovine animals are divided, because of characteristics at different ages, into veal (usually less than 3 months of age), calves (3 to 8 months), and beef. A fourth designation sometimes used is that of baby beef (8 to 12 months). Adult bovines may be subdivided into maturity classes that are given letter designations (A to E).

Ovine animals are divided into lamb (less than 14 months of age), yearling (1 to 2 years), and sheep or mutton (over 2 years). Milk lamb is sometimes used to designate ovines under 3 months of age, or lamb may be classified as A for young and B for mature.

Most porcine animals are raised primarily for meat purposes, and are fed to be marketed at about six to seven months of age. The market classes, therefore, are based on weight and sex rather than age.

As the animal increases in age, the ratio of lean, and of fat, to bone increases, the amount of fat increases, and the amount of total moisture decreases in the soft tissues, although the fat content is influenced by the level of feed. So it should be expected that meat from very young animals would give cooked products differing in flavor, tenderness, juiciness, and yield from meat from mature animals. Hedrick et al. (1967) and Guenther (1967) have summarized studies on the changes in meat animal composition during growth.

A generalization often seen is that meat from older animals is less tender due to increasing amounts of connective tissue. However, analytical studies have shown that the lean tissue of very young animals contains the largest percent of connective tissue of any age group, and that after the animal is mature there is little quantitative change in percent of connective tissue, although Helander (1966) reported a small increase in connective tissue protein during old age.

The possibility of increased cross-linking of collagen with increasing age has been investigated in a number of different species. Partington and Wood (1963) proposed possible structures for such cross links. Heikkinen et al. (1964) suggest that there are cross-links of varying strength. Several papers (for example, Goll, 1962) have suggested that increased cross-linking of the collagenous fibers makes the tissue more resistant to the softening influence of heat. This may be why meat from older animals is often less tender.

A number of studies have shown that with increasing age, meat from bovines tends to be darker and redder in color, lower in pH, and less tender (Walter et al., 1965; Simone et al., 1959; Webb et al., 1967; Tuma et al., 1963; and Henrickson and Moore, 1965). However, other workers have found no clear-cut evidence of a relationship between age and palatability factors (Lowe and Kastelic, 1961; Ritchey and Hostetler, 1964; and Norris et al., 1969), while Ho and Ritchey (1967) reported juiciness and softness differences in cuts cooked to 80° C internal temperature but not in those cooked to 61° C. Guenther (1967), in a review of a number of studies, indicates that the increases or decreases with increasing age are not simple, straight-line events, and that results from different studies are often contradictory.

Lawrie (1961) points out that the fat content of bovine muscle tends to increase with age, but that the rate of increase varies markedly at different ages in different breeds. Henrickson and Moore (1965) found that fat content was relatively unimportant in animals under 20 months of age, but had a significant role in tenderness, juiciness, and flavor of older animals. However, Goll et al. (1965) found no effect of marbling on sensory scores for tenderness, juiciness, or flavor, in bovines ranging from A to E in maturity class.

In ovines, Batcher et al. (1962) reported no influence of age from 4 to 14 months on juiciness or shear force. A difference was found in panel scores for tenderness, but the difference was significant only in the rib-loin cut. Paul et al. (1964a) found that cuts from year-old animals generally had higher palatability scores than those from 5½-month-old animals. Woodhams et al. (1966) reported that rib-loins from 17-week-old lambs were more tender than those from 27-week-old animals.

Weight

Weight differences within a small age range are particularly important for hogs, since they are marketed by weight class. A typical study is that of Usborne et al. (1968), who used slaughter weight groups ranging from 72 to 127 kg. They found that the lighter weight groups had significantly better flavor and juiciness.

Treatment Influences

Feed

Several studies on beef (Jacobson and Fenton, 1956; Meyer et al., 1960; Houston et al., 1962; and Henrickson et al., 1965) suggest that high energy content diets yield meat with increased flavor, tenderness and juiciness, but Paul et al. (1964b) found no such trend in lamb. Garrigus et al. (1969) caution that different dietary regimens may produce widely differing growth rates, so the animals vary in age when they reach slaughter weight, and the treatment differences found may be due to age rather than feed. Yeates (1964) found that starvation reduced the size of muscle fibers, with consequent increase in percent of connective tissue, and tougher meat. Hill (1967), as well as Yeates, found that a period of realimentation after starvation permitted recovery of meat quality.

Heck (1958) obtained cured meat with higher palatability scores by feeding hogs a high-sugar diet 48 hours before slaughter, but Wismer-Pedersen (1959a,b) reported that sugar feeding tended to give paler colored bacon and hams, while Bowers et al. (1968) found that sugar feeding gave pork with a higher reducing sugar content, lowered scores for color and firmness, and increased development of brown color. Shorland et al. (1970) reported that lambs fed on white clover species had stronger flavor of fat and lean and more intense odor than those fed on perennial ryegrass.

Mackintosh et al. (1961) found that stilbestrol increased the connective tissue content of lamb muscle, but did not alter the flavor. Johnston et al. (1965) stated that addition of various levels of dietary coumesterol increased the tenderness and juiciness of ovine meat. Hill (1966) reported that stilbestrol decreased the intramuscular fat in beef with no loss in eating quality, while Bryce-Jones et al. (1964) concluded that the sum of the effects of hexosterol on biochemical and biophysical attributes of muscle might be either favorable or unfavorable to eating quality, depending on the source of the meat and the method of cooking.

Exercise

It is generally held that the more heavily exercised muscles of the animal body tend to be less tender. However, Mitchell and Hamilton (1933) reported that exercise decreased the collagen content of muscle, presumably due to hypertrophy of contractile tissue without corresponding increase in connective tissue. Bull and Rusk (1942) found that exercise did not influence flavor or juiciness, and that heavy exercise increased the tenderness of the meat.

Stress

A number of studies have been made on the effects of various stress conditions on the palatability characteristics of the resulting meat. Reviews are given by Hedrick (1965), Lawrie (1966), and Judge (1969). The basic cause for many of the effects observed appears to be treatment influence on glycogen stores, with consequent alteration in the rate and extent of post-mortem glycolysis and in the ultimate pH attained by the muscle.

Lawrie (1966b) pointed out that exercise immediately ante mortem reduced the glycogen level and influenced post mortem glycolysis. Briskey et al. (1959) showed that severe exercise of hogs immediately ante mortem depleted the muscle glycogen and produced high pH meat dark in color and dry in appearance. Sayre et al. (1963b) found that short-term excitement and exercise of swine immediately prior to slaughter produced rapid post mortem glycolysis and yielded muscle with inferior water binding capacity and low color and texture scores.

Other treatments that deplete the muscle glycogen reserves, alter the ultimate pH of the muscle, and influence water binding, color, and firmness of the resulting meat include electrical stimulation (Lewis et al., 1963), abrupt change to a cold environment (Sayre et al., 1961), or elevated environmental temperature (Sayre et al., 1963b).

Howard and Lawrie (1956b) reported that high ultimate pH in beef produced meat with decreased laboratory drip, dark in color, undesirable in flavor, and firm in texture. Bouton et al. (1957) studied beef carcasses representing a range of ultimate pHs, and found that tenderness appeared to be minimal around pH 5.8. Also, cooking losses appeared to be dependent on pH. Searcy et al. (1969) studied porcine animals treated so as to produce pale-soft-exudative (PSE), normal, or dark-firm-dry (DFD) longissimus dorsi. They found no significant organoleptic preference for any of the three. DFD muscle had the smallest roasting loss, greatest total moisture, highest pH, and lowest Warner-Bratzler shear values.

CARCASS, CUTS, AND MUSCLES

Carcass quality usually refers to composition and conformation. The gross composition of the carcass considers the proportion of muscle, fat, and bone. These are influenced by age, weight, breed, and other similar factors. Conformation refers to the proportionate development of different parts of the carcass and to the ratio of meat to bone.

In the past decade, much interest has developed in the breeding and selection of meat animals for increased lean and decreased fat deposition. Fitzgerald (1968) gives the following data as examples of the old and new directions in breeding.

		Old	New
Beef carcass composition—fat		44 percent	26 percent
	lean	43 percent	60 percent
	bone	13 percent	13 percent
Pork carcass characteristics—backfat thickness		2 in.	0.7 in.
	loin eye area	3 sq in.	5.5 sq in.

Descriptions of Carcasses and Cuts

Pictures and diagrams of typical carcasses, wholesale cuts, and many retail cuts may be found in publications of the U.S. Department of Agriculture, National Live Stock and Meat Board, and in textbooks.

Muscles

For many experimental studies, it is necessary to work with known muscles. A number of publications are available to assist in muscle identification. A useful starting point is an animal anatomy text such as Sisson and Grossman (1953). Publications dealing with one species of animal include Tucker et al. (1952), Briskey et al. (1958), Kauffman et al. (1963), and Craigie (1962). Kauffman et al. (1963) list definitions of anatomical terms, and Briskey et al. (1958) describe the porcine muscles according to origin, insertion, and function. Figure 1 shows the location of commonly studied muscles of the beef carcass, and Figure 2 shows how these muscles appear in retail cuts.

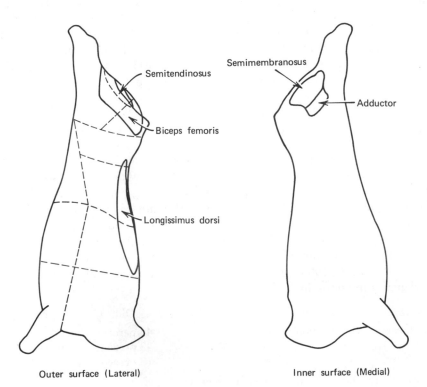

FIGURE 1. Location on beef carcass of muscles most often used in research studies.

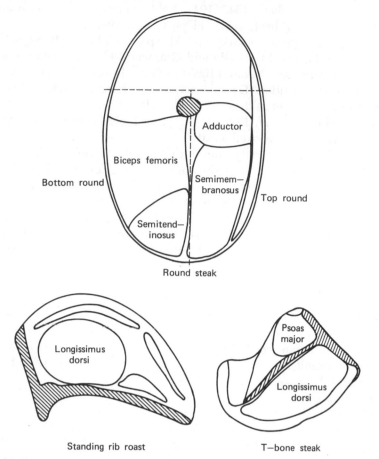

FIGURE 2. Retail beef cuts showing location of muscles most often used in research studies.

Composition and Yields

Composition

Composition of carcass or cuts often refers only to percent fat, lean, and bone, as separated by knife. Callow (1957) points out that this type of composition of the carcass is largely determined by the percent of fatty tissue. More detailed tables are based on chemical analyses for percent ether extract (crude fat), total moisture, crude protein, and in some cases minerals and vitamins. Watt and Merrill (1963) give average values for a wide range of meat items, based on data from many different investigators. Callow (1947, 1948, 1949) summarized data on analyses of mutton, lamb, beef, veal and pigs of varying ages.

For individual species, Clarke and McMeekan (1952), Barnicoat and Shorland (1952), and Marchello and Cramer (1963) list data on analyses of ovine carcasses. Kemp (1965) reviewed New Zealand work on lamb carcass composition. Doty (1962) summarized a number of studies of composition of beef and pork, while Kelly et al. (1968) and Malkus (1965) list data for beef. Pecot et al. (1965) give composition data on beef, from carcass to cooked meat.

Onate and Carlin (1963) found that original backfat thickness of porcine carcasses was a good indicator of cooking losses and yield of fat and lean, but was not related to taste panel scores for flavor, tenderness, and juiciness of rib roasts. Porter et al. (1962) studied beef cuts and found that, within the standard and good grades, carcass weight had a significant effect on yield of cooked meat. They also reported cooked meat yields for a variety of retail cuts, ranging from 79.9 percent for tenderloin steak to 50.3 percent for the third-rib chuck roast.

Methods of Analysis

Measurement of specific gravity is frequently used to estimate fat content of all or parts of the carcass. Garrett and Hinman (1969) obtained correlation coefficients > 0.9 between carcass density and chemical determinations of fat, water, and nitrogen. Powell and Huffman (1968) have reviewed a number of methods of estimating beef carcass composition.

Newer methods being applied to meat samples include spectrophotometric estimation of fat and moisture (Ben-Gera and Norris, 1968) and dye binding for protein content (Moss and Kielsmeyer, 1967). Doty (1962) warns of the "considerable analytical variation in protein analyses" found both between and within laboratories. Kirton et al. (1962), in a study of analysis of lamb carcasses, found that increasing the number of carcasses sampled was more effective in increasing the precision of the data than was increasing the number of samples per carcass.

Inspection and Grading

Inspection

Williams (1968) points out that quality control of meat includes meat hygiene as well as many other factors. He states: "The objective of meat hygiene is to provide wholesome meat and meat products which do not constitute a danger to public health." The federal Meat Inspection Act was passed in 1906. This requires federal supervision of the cleanliness, wholesomeness, and labeling of fresh and processed meat food products for sale in interstate commerce. In 1967, federal legislation was enacted to apply the same inspection standards to meat food products destined for sale within the state where slaughtered. The inspection stamp is placed on each wholesale cut. For example, for the hind quarter of beef, the inspection stamp is placed on the round, rump, short loin, and sirloin. Figure 3 shows the appearance of the inspection stamp.

FIGURE 3. Federal inspection stamp for fresh meat.

Trichinae

Pork may be infected with trichinae, although the actual percentage of animals infected is quite small. Trichinosis is contracted from eating raw, trichinae-infected meat, usually pork.

Ransom and Schwartz (1919) found that live trichinae are quickly destroyed by heating the meat to 55° C. Ransom (1916) found that trichinae are destroyed by freezing, provided that the frozen, infected meat is held at a temperature not higher than −15° C (5° F) for 10 days.

Grading

Federal grading and stamping of meat started in 1927. Periodic changes are made in the names and specifications for the various grades, to reflect changes in production and processing practices, and changing desires of consumers. These changes in the regulations must be kept in mind when comparing recent with older studies based on grade, since the meaning of the grade designations may not be the same. The Livestock Division, Consumer and Marketing Services, U.S.D.A., is responsible for developing and issuing federal grade standards for slaughter animals and carcasses. Official grade standards are published in the Federal Register.

Quality grades for bovine and ovine carcasses are based partly on factors that are considered to indicate the palatability characteristics of the lean. These include color, marbling and firmness of a cut muscle, firmness of fat and lean, color of lean, and amount of fat intermingled with the lean between the ribs (feathering), considered in relation to the apparent maturity of the carcass. The second consideration is the conformation—the relative development of muscular and skeletal systems, influenced to some extent by quantity and distribution of external fat.

Porcine carcasses are graded by the same type of palatability-indicating characteristics, but acceptable belly thickness is used instead of conformation. Carcasses with acceptable-quality lean and acceptable belly thickness are allocated among the four numbered grades, according to the expected yield of the four primal cuts (ham, loin, picnic shoulder, Boston butt) as determined from the average backfat thickness and the length or weight of the carcass.

TABLE 1.   Federal Meat Quality Designations (1969)

Species→	Bovine			Ovine		Porcine
Class→	Steer, heifer, cow	Bull, stag	Veal, calf	Lamb, yearling	Mutton	Barrows, gilts, sows
Grades→	Prime (steer, heifer, only)	Choice	Prime	Prime	Choice	No. 1
	Choice	Good	Choice	Choice	Good	2
	Good	Commercial	Good	Good	Utility	3
	Standard	Utility	Standard	Utility	Cull	4
	Commercial	Cutter	Utility	Cull		Utility
	Utility	Canner	Cull			
	Cutter					
	Canner					

The current grade names are given in Table 1. It will be observed that bovine and ovine species are subdivided into classes based on a combination of age and sex. In both, the older animals are not eligible for the prime grade. Another type of age designation is the maturity class for beef, referred to on p. 341. In addition, beef, lamb and mutton carcasses may be assigned a cutability grade from 1 to 5, depending on the anticipated yield of trimmed retail cuts. The cutability grade is optional. Quality and yield grade stamps are illustrated in Figure 4. An illustrated discussion of current grade and yield standards is given in *Meat Evaluation Handbook* (1969).

(a)   (b)

FIGURE 4. Federal grade stamps for meat. (a) Quality grade; (b) yield grade.

Relation of Grade to Palatability

Williams (1968) concludes that, despite all the research on the subject, there still are not chemical or physical methods, or combinations of methods, by which the palatability of meat can be assessed. Goeser (1961) gave the following summary of tenderness scores for different grades of beef, using a 10 point scale, with 7 rated as the desirable tenderness level.

	Percent Scoring 7 or Above	
Grade	Rib Roasts	Loin Steaks
Choice and good	77	45
Standard	42	25
Commercial	27	5

The Beef Task Force (1968) concluded that visible factors such as finish, conformation, marbling, feathering, and age are relatively easily assessed, but there is great need to identify the hidden factors that affect palatability, and to find methods of measuring them. Perhaps at present the grade designation should be regarded in a statistical sense, with higher grades representing higher probability (but not certainty) that the meat will be more flavorful, tender, and juicy.

Kropf (1968) reviewed a number of studies dealing with the relation of carcass estimates such as maturity, marbling, feathering, percent of fat, and firmness, to flavor, tenderness, and juiciness of lamb, pork, and beef. The results obtained on tenderness and flavor varied widely among studies. However, for marbling score, there did seem to be some indication of relationship to juiciness, at least in pork and beef. Fielder et al. (1963) studied beef cuts fabricated into boned, trimmed units according to tenderness of the muscles. They concluded that prefabrication appeared to minimize grade effects, but agreed with Kropf's suggestion that juiciness appeared to be the palatability factor most affected by grade.

Hoke and Hedrick (1969) reported that in beef of intermediate maturity, meat from choice-grade carcasses was generally more desirable than that from good grade of the same or younger maturity. However, they found that increase in ether-extractable constituents was not consistently associated with greater desirability, so they concluded that this measure of fat content was not suitable for predicting palatability.

Marbling

Marbling consists of the small streaks of fat laid down along the blood vessels within the muscle, and so is a part of the intramuscular lipid. For many years, marbling was believed to be an indicator of desirable eating quality, especially tenderness. However, attempts to relate objective measures such as marbling score or percent ether-extractable material in the muscle tissue to panel scores or shear values have yielded highly variable results, with correlation coefficients ranging from a low of -0.03 to a high of 0.86 **. Investigation of various cross sections within the same muscle has shown considerable variation in extent of marbling within a relatively short distance (Paul, unpublished data). Also, in small, lighter-colored muscles such as those of lamb, it may be difficult to distinguish between marbling and connective tissue unless a fat stain is used. Cover et al. (1956) point out that small fat deposits may be missed in visual assessments, and that ether extraction would include fat deposits along seams of heavy connective tissue, usually not considered to be marbling [compare (b) and (c) of Figure 5]. Most of the percent fat content data is based on ether-extractable material. This includes other lipids beside fat deposits. Also, while the analysis will give the fat content, it does not indicate how the fat is distributed. The action of marbling in influencing tenderness (when it does) may be one of diluting or separating connective tissue fibers and thereby rendering them more susceptible to alteration by heat. And perhaps marbling may only be effective under certain conditions. For example, Bryce-Jones et al. (1963), in a study restricted to sire and environment effects within one breed, found that progeny from two sires had more heavily marbled muscles and more tender meat. Moody (1967) reviews studies on marbling, and gives descriptions of various types of fat cells and methods of measurement.

** highly significant, $p < 0.01$

Slaughter Effects

The techniques used in the conversion from the living animal to the carcass usually include stunning, bleeding, evisceration, cooling and, for beef and lamb, aging for several days. The extent of excitement and nervous stimulation of the animal immediately prior to slaughter can affect the rate of post mortem glycolysis and the ultimate pH attained. The way in which the carcass is hung and the rate of cooling can have an important influence on tenderness. The reasons for these will be discussed in the section on post mortem changes. The discussion here is simply to indicate what some of the results may be.

Slaughter

McLoughlin (1965) and McLoughlin and Davidson (1966) studied the effect of stunning on pH_1 of the longissimus dorsi of pig muscle. pH_1 is the pH measured 30–45 minutes after stunning. Stunning either electrically or with CO_2 increased the tendency for low pH_1 (< 6.0) over that found in those slaughtered without prior stunning. Muscles of $pH_1 < 6.0$ indicate potentially PSE pork.

Cooling

Rate of cooling depends on temperature and rate of air circulation in the chill room, and on the size and composition of the carcass. Gisske (1959) found that flesh thickness in bovines and fat thickness in porcines were the determining factors in rate of cooling. Bowers et al. (1968) compared porcine carcasses chilled at 30° and at 42° F. They reported that muscles chilled at 42° F had lower firmness and color scores than those chilled at 30° F.

Position

The position in which the carcass is suspended during cooling may stretch certain muscles while permitting others to shorten. This affects the degree to which the muscles can contract during development of rigor mortis, the length of sarcomeres, and the tenderness of the meat. Kedlaya et al. (1968) have shown that tension also reduces the linear shrinkage and increases the shrinkage temperature of collagen fibers. Hence different degrees of tension during cooling and "setting" of the carcass may contribute to the variability observed in the extent of softening of collagenous tissues during cooking.

Aging

Beef and lamb are usually held for several days at low temperature, to allow time for the post-rigor softening of the musculature. Larmond et al. (1968) studied the influence of aging time on tenderness of cooked beef. They found that low-finish carcasses held nine days were most tender, and those held two days toughest. At a high finish level, the differences due to aging were not as marked.

Muscles

Differences Between Muscles

There are well-recognized differences among the various muscles of the carcass. Many of these are considered, or known, to influence the palatability characteristics of meat. Ramsbottom et al. (1945) published the first comprehensive survey of tenderness of individual muscles of the beef carcass. By organoleptic rating, they classified longissimus dorsi (LD) as slightly tender, biceps femoris (BF) as medium, semitendinosus (ST) and semimembranosus (SM) as slightly tough, and adductor (Ad) as tough. Hiner and Hankins (1950) classified beef cuts into four tenderness groups: least tender—neck and foreshank; second—round; third—chuck, eighth rib, short loin, and loin end; and most tender—tenderloin. They found little tenderness difference among the SM, ST, and BF of the round.

Muscles vary in their location, size, shape, direction and length of muscle fibers, amount and distribution of connective tissue, and the way in which the muscle fibers are connected through connective tissue in order to fulfill their purpose of supporting and/or moving the animal body. They also vary in average size of individual muscle fibers and muscle fiber bundles. Cassens et al. (1963) reported on the concentration of certain minerals in porcine muscle, and cautioned against using analyses on one muscle to describe the muscle tissue of the entire carcass, since "very large differences may exist in the chemical composition of adjacent muscles." Rogers (1969) has reviewed a number of studies on differences among muscles and within the same muscle, with respect to sampling procedures.

Ritchey and Hostetler (1964) compared properties of cooked LD, BF, SM, and ST muscles of beef. They found that ST was drier and harder than the other two muscles of the round, and when cooked to 80° C, LD muscle fibers adhered more tightly, were more difficult to fragment, and required higher force to shear, than those of the muscles of the round. These findings may be related to differences in connective tissue content and to variations in the microscopic appearance of the muscle fibers after heating (see p. 405). Paul et al. (1970) observed differences in softness and solidity of three muscles in beef rib steaks, and Swift and Berman (1959) noted differences in water retention ability in eight muscles of the bovine carcass.

Briskey et al. (1960) found significant variations in pH, expressible water, glycogen, myoglobin, fat, and total moisture among eight muscles of the porcine carcass, and suggested a moderately strong interrelationship of these factors in regulating the appearance and water-binding properties of pork muscle. Batcher et al. (1962) found the ST usually more tender than the SM in pork.

Red and White Muscles

A range of colors from pale pink to deep red is often observed among different muscles of the same carcass, and in some cases within the same muscle. Muscles are classified as red, white, or intermediate, depending on the proportion of red fibers. Red muscles have more than 40 percent red fibers, have a slower contraction-relaxation cycle, develop higher tension, and exhibit slower post mortem glycolysis. White muscles have less than 30 percent red fibers, high glycolytic activity, less myoglobin, and probably less phospholipid, develop tension more rapidly and attain lower ultimate pH. Beecher et al. (1965) listed serratus ventralis, rectus femoris, interior of BF and ST, and trapezius of the porcine carcass as red muscle, and exterior of BF and ST, LD and gluteus medius as white muscle.

Differences Within a Muscle

Another possible source of variation in meat studies is the differences that may occur between various portions of the same muscle. Beecher et al. (1965) reported that the BF and ST of pork contain different proportions of red and white fibers in the exterior and interior parts. In beef, the posterior portion of the BF contains two parts, one much lighter than the other. Pilkington (1965) studied various parts of the bovine LD, and found that the dorsal segment had larger muscle fibers and smaller muscle bundles, and was more tender than the lateral portion. Harrison et al. (1967) studied anterior, middle, and posterior sections of pork loin, cooked as roasts. They reported differences in size, weight, ratio of bone to muscle, intermuscular fat, cooking time, tenderness, press fluid, and cooking losses. Blumer et al. (1962) and Doty and Pierce (1961) reported marked variation in marbling along the length of beef LD. The latter authors also found differences in amount of fat, autolysis level, and muscle fiber diameter in different portions of the ST. Meyer et al. (1967) reported differences in total moisture and juiciness scores among steaks from three different positions in beef LD. Figure 5 shows differences in shape, size, degree of adhesion among fiber bundles, and amount and distribution of external and internal fat in two cross sections of the same muscle (beef ST).

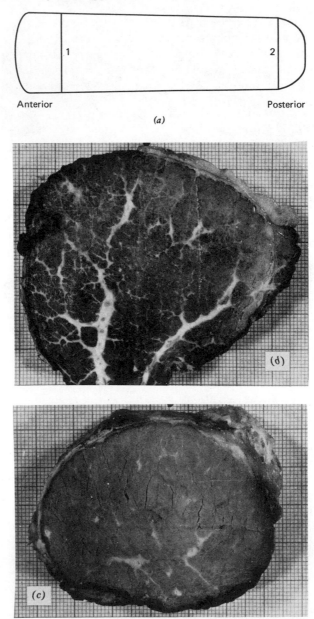

FIGURE 5. Differences in different parts of the same muscle (beef ST). (*a*) Diagram of muscle, to show location of pictures; (*b*) cut surface at position 1; (*c*) cut surface at position 2. Observe differences in shape and size of slice, degree of adhesion between fiber bundles, and amount and distribution of external and internal fat deposits.

MUSCLE COMPOSITION, STRUCTURE, AND WATER BINDING

Composition

The lean portion of muscle is approximately 75 percent water, 18 percent protein, 3 percent fat, 1.6 percent nonprotein nitrogenous compounds, 1.2 percent carbohydrate and its metabolites, 0.7 percent inorganic salts, plus traces of vitamins and other compounds (Lawrie, 1968). Of the 18 percent protein, about 10 percent is made up of the various proteins of the contractile structures, 2 percent is in the connective tissues, and 6 percent is in the sarcoplasm and subcellular organelles. The latter include the soluble proteins of the sarcoplasm (mostly enzymes), myoglobin, and the proteins in such structures as the mitochondria, lysosomes, and sarcoplasmic reticulum. The lipid portion is primarily neutral fat deposits, but also includes small amounts in the muscle cells—lipoprotein, phospholipids, and metabolites. The nonprotein nitrogen includes compounds such as creatine, free amino acids, and nucleotides (ATP, ADP, AMP, and IMP). The carbohydrate-type materials include glycogen, glucose, and various metabolic products from the glycolytic cycle, as well as the mucopolysaccharides of the ground substances.

The composition of any one sample of tissue will vary with such factors as species, breed, age, level of feeding, muscle, and length of time post mortem. For example, Swift and Berman (1959) give the ranges listed in Table 2 for analyses on eight different muscles of five bovine carcasses.

In considering the more detailed information on the components of muscle, the primary emphasis will be on those that have a known or

TABLE 2.   Analyses of Eight Beef Muscles

	Range in Averages
Moisture, percent	70.90–74.75
Fat content, percent	1.85–8.30
Protein ($N \times 6.25$), percent	17.90–22.60
Ca, mg/100 g	3.26–4.40
Mg, mg/100 g	17.09–23.13
Zn, mg/100 g	2.13–7.37
Na, mg/100 g	39.5–64.2
K, mg/100 g	336–436
Fe, mg/100 g	2.16–3.51
P, mg/100 g	154–184
Cl, mg/100 g	40.3–72.9

suspected relationship to palatability and yield of cooked meat. Other compounds are known to be present, but their relationship, if any, to palatability is not clear.

It is difficult to find a consistent classification of the compounds comprising muscle. For example, the sarcoplasmic proteins are those soluble in water or very dilute salt solutions, while the myofibrillar proteins are soluble in more concentrated salt solutions. However, α-actinin, β-actinin, and troponin are all water soluble but occur in the muscle as integral parts of the contractile filaments. The carbohydrate-containing or related substances include such diverse compounds as those of the glycolytic cycle, the ribonucleic acids and ATP, ADP, and AMP, and the acid polysaccharides found in the ground substance. The ether-extractable materials vary from the relatively saturated, neutral triglycerides of the fat depots, through the (often) highly unsaturated, polar lipids of the membranes, to the fat-soluble vitamins and pigments.

Water

Water is the largest single component of muscle by weight. Changes in the amount of water present and the extent to which it is bound by the muscle components is considered to influence the tenderness, texture, and juiciness of meat, as well as the yield of cooked meat. But the relationships between the amount and state of water in meat and the palatability of the product are too complex to be shown by analysis for total moisture content. The properties of water, as discussed in Chapter 1, and the concepts of water binding on colloidal molecules and in gels as given in Chapter 2, should be reviewed. Water binding in muscle will be discussed later in this chapter.

Pigments

The principal red pigments of muscle are myoglobin (Mb) and hemoglobin (Hb). Recent analyses (for example, St-Laurent and Brisson, 1968) have shown that Hb makes up 20 to 30 percent of the total red pigment. The concentration of the red pigments varies with species, breed, feed, anatomical role of the muscle, level of exercise, sex, and age of the animal. Other pigments are present, the most apparent of these being the yellow pigments found in varying quantities in the fat deposits.

Myoglobin is a compact, nearly spherical molecule, with a cleft for the heme prosthetic group. It is recognized that there are several forms of Mb. Quinn et al. (1964) found three and possibly four distinct Mbs, differing in mobility on starch gel, in beef muscle.

The hemes are described by Mahler and Cordes (1966) as "square-planar chelates of Fe, in which the metal can form complexes with two additional ligands." The usual abbreviated notation for the heme group is as follows, with the 4 Ns indicating the pyrrole rings, and the vertical lines the ligand positions 5 and 6.

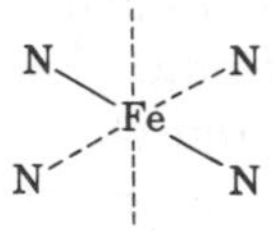

$$
\begin{array}{ccc}
N & \vert & N \\
 & Fe & \\
N & \vert & N
\end{array}
$$

Fe can exist in either the reduced (Fe^{+2}) or oxidized (Fe^{+3}) form. In addition, in normal muscle the reduced form may have either H_2O or O_2 attached in the fifth position. The sixth position is the attachment to globin (G). This gives the three native forms of myoglobin.

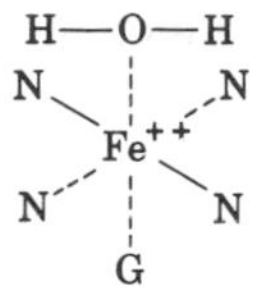

Myoglobin, Mb Bluish–red	Oxymyoglobin, O2Mb Bright red	Metmyoglobin, MMb Brownish red

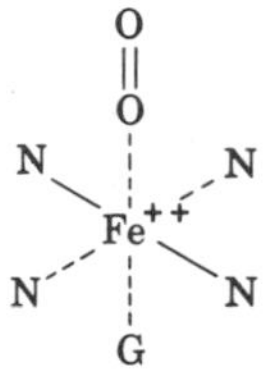

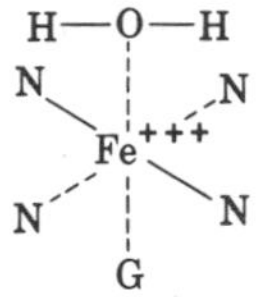

The Fe^{+2} forms are hemochromes, the Fe^{+3} hemichromes. A variety of other forms of these heme pigments may be present in meat, depending on treatments such as curing (nitrosyl-hemochrome, bright pink), heating (denatured globin hemichrome, brown), or breakdown as by bacterial action (degradation products may be yellow, green, or brown). Fox (1966, 1968) has reviewed the chemistry of these pigments from the meat standpoint.

Glycogen, Glucose

The muscles normally contain small amounts of glycogen, glucose, and glucose-6-phosphate, as well as traces of intermediates in the glycolytic cycle. The amounts present will vary with the state of nutrition and activity of the muscle.

Lactic Acid

Lactic acid is the end product of anaerobic oxidation of glucose. On slaughter of the animal, the supply of oxygen to the cells ceases, but the metabolic processes continue. So lactic acid accumulates, and the pH decreases until a point is reached at which the enzymes catalyzing the reactions are inactivated, or the reactants are depleted. The pH of living muscle is considered to be slightly above 7, while the ultimate pH (the lowest pH attained after death) is usually around

5.4–5.5. The post-mortem shift in pH has a marked effect on the water-binding capacity of the meat proteins as well as on the color and flavor of meat.

Dryden et al. (1969) studied broiled beef steaks from triceps brachii, LD,. and SM muscles. They found that lactic acid content averaged around 30 to 35 mg per g of muscle, and was significantly correlated with tenderness, juiciness, shear force, and overall score ($r_{xy} = -0.46^*$, -0.59^{**}, $+0.57^{**}$, and -0.49^*, respectively). They also reported that SM was significantly higher in lactic acid than the other two muscles.

Pentoses

Pentoses are an integral part of essential cellular components such as the ribonucleic acids and ATP and ADP. Degradation of these compounds during cold storage after slaughter may produce small amounts of free ribose.

Mucopolysaccharides

Mucopolysaccharides are very high molecular weight carbohydrates containing uronic acid and acylated hexosamines. These may or may not be sulfated. Fox (1965) states that mucopolysaccharides are probably the most important components of ground substance, the amorphous matrix of connective tissue. They show great variation in type and amount present, depending on the tissue being analyzed and the age of the animal. Lean muscle contains about 2 mg mucopolysaccharide per g of dry, defatted muscle. Most of the mucopolysaccharides occur covalently linked to protein, forming protein polysaccharides. McIntosh (1966) reported chondroitin sulfate as the only mucopolysaccharide in bovine skeletal muscle, but stated that the procedure used appeared not to extract all the protein polysaccharide of the muscle.

The mucopolysaccharides have a large number of negative charges spaced at varying distances along the length of the molecule. Each anionic group has an associated cation—usually Na, K, Ca, or Mg. These give the molecules modified ion exchange properties, so they may function as reservoirs for specific ions or control ion movement across membranes. The mucopolysaccharide molecules also have large water-binding capacity, and marked influence on the viscosity of the systems in which they occur.

Several groups of workers have explored the possibility that the mucoproteins of the ground substance may influence tenderness of meat. It has been suggested that amylases may contribute to tenderizing action

* significant, $p < 0.05$
** highly significant, $p < 0.01$

by attacking the mucopolysaccharides. Thomas (1956) found evidence that some of the hydrolytic action of papain may be on the mucopolysaccharides. Also, ion distribution and water holding capacity are thought to be related to tenderness and juiciness.

Lipids

There are two major types of lipids in muscle, the neutral triglycerides of the fat depots and the polar lipids mainly within the cells. Turkki and Campbell (1967) reported a curvilinear relationship between percent phospholipid in total lipid and percent lipid in muscle, suggesting a minimum concentration of total lipid equivalent to the structural lipids of the cells. In most cases, only three or four fatty acids occur in substantial amounts in the depot fats of the larger meat animals— primarily oleic, palmitic, and stearic. The polar lipids of the cells include phospholipids such as phosphoglycerides, plasmalogens, and sphingomyelin. In addition, glycolipids, cholesterol, and probably other complex lipid molecules are present. The phospholipids of the cells usually make up about 10 to 30 percent of the total lipid of the muscle. Traces of free fatty acids are also present.

A number of studies have reported amounts of lipid and kinds of fatty acids (Duncan and Garton, 1967; Stinson et al., 1967; O'Keefe et al., 1968; Kuchmak and Dugan, 1963; Hornstein et al., 1967; Hubbard and Pocklington, 1968; Terrell et al., 1967; and Lyaskovskaya and Kelmen, 1967). These authors report variations in amount of lipid and in kinds of fatty acids among different species and different animals in a species, and among different depot sites and muscles within a carcass.

The fat depots contain protein as well as lipid, as the fat cells are laid down in a connective tissue framework. Wistreich et al. (1960) present evidence suggesting that most of the adipose tissue proteins of pork are of the collagen type.

Terrell et al. (1967) reported that broiling steaks to 65° C internal temperature decreased the percent of unsaturated esters in subcutaneous fat depots, and (1968) that broiling influenced the fatty acids of the phospholipid portion. They concluded that "alterations in lipids during cooking appear to be, in part, a function of time and temperature."

Hornstein et al. (1961) found that phospholipids of beef and pork develop rancid off-flavors more readily than do the neutral triglyceride fractions on exposure to air. So the phospholipids may have an important influence on stability to oxidative rancidity.

Inorganic Ions

Mitteldorf and Landon (1952) give data on content of 19 mineral elements in 12th-rib samples from each of 7 grades of beef. Berman

(1960) gives a scheme for determining the electrolyte content of beef, and data on 8 elements. Inklaar and Sandifort (1967) give Ca and Mg values for beef, pork and veal, and Lawrie and Pomeroy (1963) list data on Na and K content of pig muscle.

The mineral elements occur either as separate ions, or in a variety of compounds within muscle. In many cases the location is as important as the concentration. Many of the ions influence the water binding and buffering capacity of the tissue. Ca and Mg are essential components of the contraction-relaxation cycle. Fe is a part of the red pigment, and so influences color. Zn is found in some of the enzymes. Berman (1961) reported a highly significant correlation between pH and Zn content of beef, but Cassens et al. (1963) were unable to find any close relation between variation in Zn content and differences in post mortem properties of pork muscle.

Nonprotein Nitrogen

The nonprotein nitrogen-containing compounds make up about one to two percent of muscle substance. These include a group of nucleotides, creatine (C), creatine phosphate (CP), compounds such as carnosine, anserine, and carnitine, and traces of free amino acids. To date, only the nucleotides, C and CP are considered to have significant roles in determining the palatability characteristics of meat.

The nucleotides include the compounds important in the immediate supply of energy for contraction and relaxation, through the high-energy phosphate bonds in adenosine triphosphate (ATP). Adenosine diphosphate (ADP) is also involved in formation of the actin filaments. As the energy cycle runs down post mortem, ATP is split to ADP, then adenosine monophosphate (AMP), inosine monophosphate (IMP), and finally inosine. C and CP are also involved in the energy supply system. The changes in the energy supply cycle post mortem affect the degree of "locking" between myosin and actin filaments and therefore the rigidity of the meat. The nucleotides are also thought to influence the flavor of meat (for example, Dannert, 1966).

Enzyme Systems

Muscle contains a wide variety of enzymes, in keeping with its complex structure and activity. The sarcoplasm is thought to contain over 50 different proteins, mostly enzymes.

Sarcoplasm is recognized as containing a small amount of soluble ATPase. It has been suggested that this ATPase may cause depletion of ATP post mortem, leading to the development of rigor mortis. Nakamura et al. (1969) report the presence of neutral pyrophosphatases (PPase) in the soluble nitrogen fraction of muscle, and suggest that, since pyrophosphates have a marked influence on the water-holding capacity (WHC) of meat, the PPases may affect WHC.

Randall and MacRae (1967) found hydrolytic enzymes in a number of bands on starch-gel electrophoresis of water-soluble proteins of bovine skeletal muscle. They suggested the presence of cathepsins B and C, and leucine aminopeptidase. Cathepsin is the name applied to a group of proteolytic enzymes found in various tissues. Parrish and Bailey (1966) studied the water-extractable cathepsin of muscle. They reported maximum activity at pH 4.0, inactivation by heating to 65° C, and other properties similar to cathepsin D.

It is possible that hydrolytic activity of the enzymes of meat during post-mortem storage may cause, or contribute to, the softening of muscle post-rigor. One difficulty in confirming this is that a small amount of hydrolysis in the right places may produce the softening without producing chemical alterations sufficiently large to be readily detectable by present methods of analysis. Bodwell and Pearson (1964) found no detectable action of bovine muscle cathepsins on myosin, actin, or actomyosin, and suggested that the cathepsins act on the sarcoplasmic proteins. Suzuki and Fujimaki (1968) reported that the catheptic activity extractable from rabbit muscle increased with storage of the muscle. Martins and Whitaker (1968) found no evidence of hydrolysis of rabbit skeletal muscle actomyosin by cathepsin D from chicken leg muscle, but felt that this did not rule out the possible role of cathepsins in post-mortem tenderization, since the softening might be due to other cathepsins or to several acting in combination. Laakkonen et al. (1970) reported finding collagenase activity in raw bovine muscle held for two weeks post mortem.

Myofibrillar Proteins

A summary of information on the myofibrillar proteins is given in Table 3. These data were compiled from several sources (Goll et al., 1969; Briskey, 1967; Donnelly et al., 1966; and Lawrie, 1966).

The myofibrils are made up of 50–55 percent myosin, 20–25 percent actin, 10–15 percent tropomyosin, and 5–10 percent other proteins. The myofibrils are about 1μ in diameter, and there are about 2000 of them in an average fiber of 50μ diameter (Bendall, 1966). They have no outer membrane, but are insoluble at the ionic strength of the sarcoplasm. They may be partly held together by transverse and longitudinal elements of the sarcoplasmic reticulum.

The interaction of myosin and actin to form actomyosin is reversible under appropriate conditions. This is considered the basic reaction of

TABLE 3. Myofibrillar Proteins of Muscle

Protein	Shape	Size	Molecular Weight	Makeup and Role
Myosin	Rod with enlarged "head," 57 percent α-helix	1600 Å long, 30Å diameter	About 500,000	Thick filaments of A band; major role in contraction-relaxation; contains about 7-SH groups per 10^5; made up of subunits, LMM + HMM, ratio 2:1; ATPase
Light meromyosin (LMM)	Rod, 76 percent α-helix, probably 2-stranded coiled-coil	850 Å × 15 Å	About 150,000	Major portion of "tail" of myosin molecule; noncovalently bonded to HMM so that two subunits are easily separated
Heavy meromyosin (HMM)	"Tadpole," 43 percent α-helix		About 200,000	ATPase; "head" and part of "tail" of myosin
HMMS$_1$	Globular, 27 percent α-helix	70 Å long	About 120,000	"Head" of myosin; contains four times as much proline as "tail" portion
HMMS$_2$	Rod, 2-stranded coiled-coil, 73 percent α-helix	450 Å long	About 60,000	"Tail" of HMM
Tropomyosin	Rod, 2-chain coiled-coil, 91 percent α-helix	400 Å × 20 Å	About 70,000	Located in Z line and thin filaments; possibly responsible for structure of Z line; highly charged molecule; resistant to denaturation; may act as core for double helix of F-actin
Actin-G form	Globular, about 30 percent helical	55 Å diameter	50,000–60,000	Aggregates into F-actin of thin filaments
Actin-F form	Double chain of spheres coiled together	Length approximates that of thin filaments	Many millions	Primary structural units of thin filaments; major role in contraction-relaxation; sensitive to Ca++ when complexed with tropomyosin and troponin, so may be trigger mechanism for contraction

TABLE 3. (*Continued*)

Protein	Shape	Size	Molecular Weight	Makeup and Role
Actomyosin (myosin B)				Complex of myosin +1 actin doublet, formed and broken in contraction-relaxation
Troponin A and B				Found in thin filaments; troponin A binds Ca++
α-actinin				Influences cross linking of actin; found in Z line and in thin filaments adjacent to Z line
β-actinin			6500 to 300,000 depending on solvent used	May occur in thin filaments; may act by influencing natural filament length; deterrent to interaction among actin strands, which otherwise tend to form gel
M-protein				Located in middle of H-zone; accelerates lateral aggregation of myosin; holds thick filaments in position in A band

contraction and relaxation. The reaction is influenced by ATP, Mg^{++}, Ca^{++} and temperature. The other proteins—tropomyosin, troponin, α- and β-actinin, and M-protein—appear to function by regulating size and position of the thick and thin filaments and their rates of interaction.

Myosin is easily denatured, and the prevention or control of this denaturation is important in meat quality. F-actin can be depolymerized to the G-form by ATP, ultrasonic treatment, shearing, or freezing. Such depolymerization would disrupt the thin filaments, and probably alter the tenderness and WHC of meat.

Connective Tissue Proteins

Some information on the connective tissue proteins is summarized in Table 4. More extensive discussions may be found in Harding (1965), Piez (1966), Symposium, New York Heart Assoc. (1964), Hall (1961), Goll (1965), and Veis (1965).

Hydroxyproline analyses are widely used to determine connective-tissue content, since collagen and elastin are the only mammalian proteins known to contain this amino acid. Collagen appears to contain 50 to 100 times as much hydroxyproline as does elastin.

Collagen

Collagen is an extremely interesting material, since it not only is considered to play an important role in the tenderness of meat, but also is the source of the gelatin used in many food products. The chemical and physical nature of collagen has already been reviewed in the collagen and gelatin section of Chapter 3.

Elastin

Elastin is a rubberlike protein, usually found in much lower concentration in intramuscular connective tissue than is collagen. It is relatively inert and is not markedly affected by normal food processing and preparation procedures. Winegarden et al. (1952) found that elastin was softened by heating in water, but not to the same extent as collagen.

Elastase is a specific enzyme that degrades elastin. Hall (1962) suggested that enzymic degradation by elastase really involves two enzymes, elastase itself and another that is lipolytic and also releases polysaccharide.

Partridge (1969) summarizes work on the cross-link structures in elastin. Desmocine and isodesmocine are tetra-carboxylic-tetra-amino acids that can form cross-links with up to four peptide chains.

Reticulin

Reticulin is chiefly recognized by its ability to combine with certain histological stains, notably the silver stains. Earlier reports suggested that reticulin was an immature form of collagen. But more recent studies have shown that, although reticulin resembles collagen, it is associated with considerable amounts of lipid-containing myristic acid (Windrum et al., 1955). It is not clear whether this lipid is simply material surrounding the reticulin fibers or is actually part of the molecule. Histological studies suggest that the reticular fibers, and the endoplasmic reticulum in which they are found in muscle, show varying responses to heating, depending on the muscle being studied (Paul, unpublished data).

Ground Substance

Many of the investigations of ground substance have dealt with the polysaccharide portion. However, there is evidence that the polysaccharide and protein moieties are firmly linked (Schubert, 1964; Dorfman, 1964). The protein is not collagen, as it has a very different amino acid makeup, having little glycine and no proline, but a large number of acidic groups (Fitton Jackson, 1964). Ground substance also contains some plasma proteins, and small but significant amounts of glycoprotein.

Muscle Structure

The individual muscle is made up of muscle fibers. The muscle is surrounded by a connective tissue sheath, the epimysium. Within the muscle, the fibers are grouped into bundles or fasciculi. The size of these bundles varies in different muscles and determines to a certain extent the grain or texture of the raw meat. Schmitt and Dumont (1969) present a method for estimating muscle texture according to the size of major subdivisions, the type and number of fiber bundles they include, and the prominence of the perimysium between them.

The connective tissue surrounding the bundles, the perimysium, varies in thickness between and within muscles. The individual muscle fibers within the bundles are also enclosed in a connective tissue framework, the endomysium. Figure 6 shows a cross-section of cooked ovine LD, stretched to show the bundles and perimysium. Figure 7 shows the individual muscle fibers surrounded by the endomysium.

The muscle fibers occupy about three fourths of the volume of the muscle. Fibers increase in size as the animal grows. It is generally agreed that the muscle fibers do not increase in number after the

TABLE 4. Connective Tissue Proteins

Name	Shape	Size	Molecular Weight	Distinctive Composition	Reactions and Role
Collagen	Rod, coiled coil of three helices wound together	Polymer of tropocollagen	Indefinite	Hydroxy groups important in H-bonds, proline rings in shape of molecule. Vertebrate collagen contains about 0.5 percent carbohydrate—at least one galactose residue, often a glucose. Probably cross-linked both intra- and intermolecularly. Degree of cross-linking increases with age.	Shrink temperature, T_s, fiber shrinks to about 1/3 length. T_s usually around 60° C—varies with pH, ions, solvent, rate of heating, stretching force. Major component of tissue supporting contractile fibers and connecting muscles to bones.
Tropo-collagen	Rod, three chains, each left-handed helix, three wound together in right-handed superhelix	2800 Å long, 14 Å diameter	300,000–350,000	About 1/3 glycine, 1/8 proline, and 1/10 hydroxyproline. Small amount hydroxylysine. Configuration of single and triple chains determined by H-bonds and by proline rings.	Building blocks of collagen. Soluble in cold neutral salt solution. Heat to 30° C, triple chain separates into gelatin.

364

TABLE 4. (*Continued*)

Name	Shape	Size	Molecular Weight	Distinctive Composition	Reactions and Role
Elastin	Cross-linked three-dimensional gel		Indefinite	Very low in amino acids with hydrophilic side chains, small amount of hydroxyproline. Cross-linked by desmocine and isodesmocine.	Elastic component of connective tissue, found in small amounts in muscle. Mainly occurs in walls of blood vessels and in elastic ligaments.
Reticulin				Contains lipid, especially myristic acid.	More found in endomysium than in peri- or epimysium.
Ground substance: Protein, polysaccharides, glycoprotein, and the like				Protein bonded to polysaccharide is noncollagenous. Some glycoproteins—may contain glucose, galactose, mannose, hexosamine, fucose, and sialic acid.	Complexed with mucopolysaccharides.

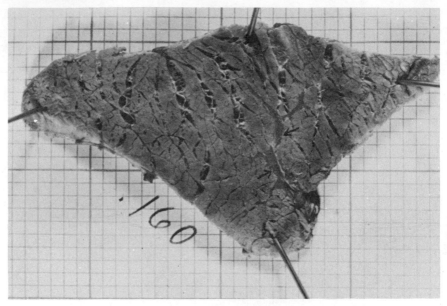

FIGURE 6. Cross-section of lamb LD, at separation between leg and loin. Cooked, stained, and stretched to show muscle bundles, perimysium, and intramuscular fat (arrows). Magnification about 2x.

animal is born, but that the individual fibers grow larger by increase in number of myofibrils (Richter and Kellner, 1963). Joubert (1956) and Hedrick et al. (1967) have reviewed muscle growth in meat animals.

Within and between the muscles fatty deposits occur. The size of the muscle is a function of the size of the muscle fibers and the number and size of fat deposits. These are influenced by species, breed, sex, age, level of nutrition of the animal, and individual animal differences, so considerable variation is possible. Figure 8 shows two rib steaks that represent the extremes in size within a group of eight animals of the same breed, age, sex, and level of feed.

Muscles vary in the direction in which the fibers run, depending on the attachments and the anatomical function. In muscles such as the ST, SM, Ad, psoas and deep pectoral, the fibers run essentially parallel to the long axis of the muscle, from origin to insertion. But in others—for example, LD and BF—the fibers run at an angle, ending on each side of the muscle as a whole, while in the rectus femoris and gastrocnemius, the muscle fibers have their origin on central connective-tissue septa, and angle toward the insertion from both sides. Such muscles must be sampled very carefully for any measurement where fiber orientation is

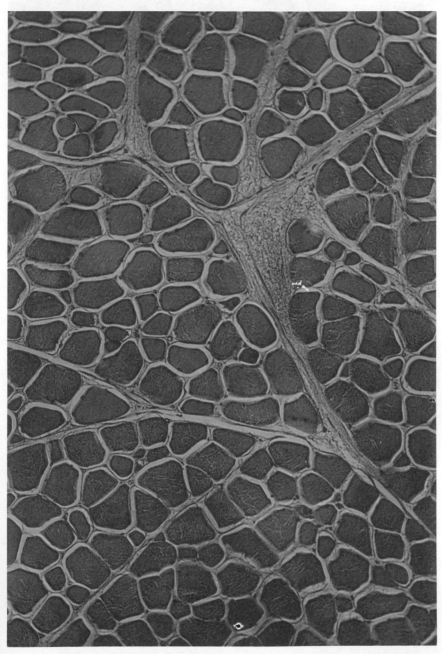

FIGURE 7. Rabbit LD, cooked, showing muscle fibers, endomysium, and perimysium.

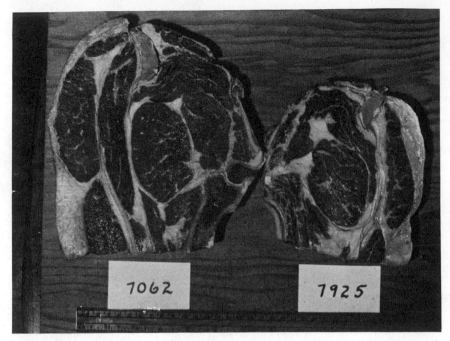

FIGURE 8. Two rib steaks from animals of same breed, age, sex, and management, showing marked differences in size of steaks, intermuscular fat deposits, and muscles.

important. A technique for sampling muscles with slanting fibers is described by Paul (1964).

Muscle Fibers

The description and microscopic appearance of the various structures in the muscle may be found in histology texts such as Bloom and Fawcett (1964). Each muscle fiber is an elongated cylinder with many nuclei. The nuclei are situated peripherally just under the sarcolemma, the sheath enclosing the fiber. Doty and Pierce (1961) have suggested that differences in the sarcolemma may contribute to differences in tenderness of meat. The fibers are usually unbranched. They may run from one end of the muscle to the other, from one end into the interior of the muscle, or entirely within the body of the muscle. So they may be as short as 1 mm, or, in ST of an adult bovine, as long as 25–30 cm. They also vary in diameter, but most appear to fall in the range of 10 to 100μ.

The fibers are made up of myofibrils, which are surrounded by a complex system of tubules and vesicles, the sarcoplasmic reticulum. Voyle and Lawrie (1964) describe the sarcoplasmic reticulum in bovine muscle. The spaces between the fibrils are filled with sarcoplasm, the semifluid material containing many of the enzymes of muscle, as well as other materials such as fat droplets, myoglobin, ATP, and glycogen. Mommaerts (1966) states that the sarcoplasm is not necessarily a solution of uniform concentration, but more probably has some order to the distribution of compounds throughout the muscle fiber. Arnold and Pette (1968) believe that the glycolytic enzymes are not uniformly distributed and probably do not exist in the dissolved state in the muscle.

The fibers also contain several types of granules, such as mitochondria, microsomes, and lysosomes. Each of these structures has some type of membranous bounding surface. Biological membranes are considered to be double-layer structures containing a considerable proportion of lipoprotein. This lipid material is part of the muscle lipid, but very different from that of the neutral fat deposits.

The lysosomes may have considerable importance in determining meat quality, since they contain the major hydrolytic enzymes of the cell—cathepsins, nucleases, and glycosidases. These catalyze hydrolysis of proteins, nucleic acid, and mucopolysaccharides, respectively. These enzymes are generally the type that function best under acid conditions of pH 4.5 to 5.5. The normal post-mortem changes in muscle bring the pH down close to 5.5, a more favorable environment for the hydrolytic activity of these enzymes than that of living muscle. So the lysosomal enzyme systems have a potential role in post-mortem autolysis, tenderization during aging, and production of flavor compounds (Tappel et al., 1965; Tappel, 1966). Changes in enzyme activity can be expected to alter WHC and such palatability characteristics as flavor, tenderness, and juiciness.

Myofibrils

The myofibrils are the cross-striated contractile elements of the muscle, and are made up of sarcomeres. Each sarcomere is bounded by Z lines, and contains one dark band (A), and two half-light bands (I). In the middle of the A band is a lighter area, the H-zone, with a darker line in the center, the M-line. These are illustrated diagrammatically in Figure 9.

The current theory explains the structures in the sarcomere as follows. The light bands contain thin filaments made up mainly of actin, but also of tropomyosin, troponins A and B, and possibly β-actinin. The dark bands contain the thick myosin filaments, the ends of which are thicker than the center, since the myosin molecules are arranged with the heads toward the Z lines. This thinner center produces the lighter H-zone. The dark line in the middle of the H-zone, labeled M-protein, is thought to hold the structures in position so that the I- and A-band filaments

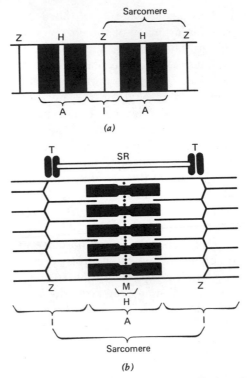

FIGURE 9. Schematic representations of part of a myofibril and of one sarcomere, showing various bands and the structures that are considered to produce the banded (striated) appearance. (*a*) Part of a myofibril; (*b*) one sarcomere, rest length.

interdigitate properly to carry out their function of sliding past one another as the muscle contracts or relaxes. The sarcoplasmic reticulum (SR) and transverse tubules (T) surrounding the fibril are thought to be the pathway by which impulses triggering contraction and relaxation are transmitted to the sarcomeres. This reticular system also contains the structures that release or take up Ca^{++}, an integral part of the contraction-relaxation system.

The sarcomere is usually about 2.5μ long at rest length. It can shorten or elongate considerably during contraction or stretching, as the thin filaments move toward or away from the center of the sarcomere. These changes produce the variations in I-band width observed in muscle fixed at different stages. Much of the current concept of muscle fine structure derives from electron micrographs. Examples of these may be found in such texts as Kurtz (1964) and Freeman and Geer (1964). Stromer and Goll (1967) show the appearance of bovine muscle.

Connective Tissue

Connective tissue is very widely distributed in the animal body. It is considered to have four major parts, the collagenous, elastic, and reticular fibers, and the ground substance. The fibers are often termed "stroma," since they are much less easily dissolved than the other portions of the muscle. In the ensuing discussion, the emphasis is on the fibers and structures that usually represent much larger entities than the molecules discussed in the previous section on composition.

Much of the research on the chemistry, structure, and properties of these has been done with tissues such as tendons, bone, or skin. Detailed investigation of the inter- and intramuscular connective tissues of meat has just begun. While the general pattern is undoubtedly similar, considerable caution should be used in employing results on tendon, for example, to explain changes in the peri- or endomysial connective tissues.

Collagen and elastin contents vary with location and anatomical function of the muscle. Bendall (1967), Vognarová et al. (1968), and Dvořák and Vognarová (1969) give data on collagen and elastin contents of veal, beef and pork. Dvořák and Vognarová (1969) give a range of 0.396 (psoas major) to 3.591 (shank muscles) g hydroxyproline per 16 g nitrogen for beef muscle. Bendall (1967) divides beef muscle into 3 groups according to elastin content—< 0.2 percent, 0.4 to 0.8 percent, and 1–2 percent elastin on a dry, fat-free basis.

Collagen Fibers

These are very widely distributed in muscle, making up a large part of the tendons which connect muscles to bones, the septa between and within the muscles, and the various muscle sheaths. Fine strands of collagen are found even in the endomysium of certain muscles (for example, Paul, 1965) and in the sarcolemma (Kono et al., 1964). Collagen fibers are white and glistening, leading to the designation white fibrous connective tissue.

Collagen fibers appear to be composed of helically entwined filaments that are themselves bundles of large numbers of polypeptide chains. The fibers are wavy, may be branched, and under normal conditions are flexible but inelastic. When heated, the fibers will contract at a specific temperature, T_s, and in many cases will be softened and partially converted to gelatin, becoming soluble in hot water. The fibers also swell and/or dissolve in weak acids and alkalis.

Veis (1961) points out that collagens in different tissues do not have uniform properties, owing to factors ranging from variations in chemical composition to variations in mechanical structural order. Verzár (1963) states that the response of collagen fibers to heat varies with the age of the fiber. Young, newly laid down fibers contract at T_s more rapidly than older ones, but the older ones are stronger and will lift heavier weights. This higher tension of the older fibers is attributed to an increased degree of cross-linking. Piez (1966) suggests that cross-linking may continue with time, to give a continuous three-dimensional structure of great stability. Cross-linking is both intra- and intermolecular.

The order or arrangement of the fibers is a function of the tissue in which they are laid down. In tendon, the fibers run end-to-end, while in mammalian skin the fibers are largely randomly oriented and show no orderly arrangement. Areas can be observed in muscle where one sheet of collagen fibers is superimposed on another with the fibers running at a 90° angle.

Although denatured collagen and gelatin are readily hydrolyzed by many proteolytic enzymes, there are only a few bacterial collagenases that can attack native collagen. Hinrichs and Whitaker (1962) found that ficin, bromelin, papain, and trypsin did not solubilize collagen until after it was denatured by heat, low pH, or high salt concentration. El-Gharbawi and Whitaker (1963) reported that the maximum solubilization of collagen of bovine BF by ficin or bromelain was at pH 7 and 80° C.

Elastin Fibers

These are branching fibers that exhibit rubberlike elasticity. They are normally yellow, hence the common designation of yellow connective tissue. They are found mainly in the walls of blood vessels and in elastic ligaments such as the ligamentum nuchae (neck strap). The amounts found in muscle are usually quite small. Elastin fibers are found mostly between the larger muscle bundles, although in beef ST, they are frequently found throughout much of the perimysium. Hiner et al. (1955) reported that the elastin fibers were smaller in younger animals, and larger and more bunched in muscles that do more work.

The elastin molecules are cross-linked into fibrils and fibers by desmocine and isodesmocine (Partridge, 1966). The formation of desmocine and isodesmocine is a slow process, occurring extracellularly after the peptide chains of elastin are formed. So elastin fibers vary in composition and physical properties with the stage of growth of the animal.

There is disagreement in the literature as to whether elastin tissue is affected by heat up to 100° C. The present consensus seems to be that there are some small effects, but not large enough to have any influence on the tenderness of the tissue. El-Gharbawi and Whitaker (1963) reported that ficin will solubilize elastin even at 20° C.

Reticulin

Much less is known about the reticulin fibers than about collagen and elastin fibers. In muscle they comprise the major portion of the endomysium. They are distinguished from collagen and elastin histologically by different staining properties. They appear to contain about 4 percent bound carbohydrate and 10 percent bound fatty acids, especially myristic acid (Barrens and van Driel, 1962; Sen et al., 1961). Hydrolysis with collagenase appeared to give corresponding peptides from collagen and reticulin, suggesting that the protein part of reticulin may be the same or similar to collagen.

There have been a few studies of the effect of heat on muscle reticulin. Paul (1963), Crow et al. (1967), and Paul et al. (1969) found evidence of partial disintegration of reticulin fibers during cooking of meat. Paul (1963) and Paul et al. (1969) indicate that the extent of change varies among different muscles.

Ground Substance

Ground substance is the collective term for the amorphous material in which the various connective tissue fibers are laid down. It contains considerable mucopolysaccharide combined with protein. The components that have had the most study are hyaluronic acid and the chondroitin sulfates. Hyaluronic acid is believed to be largely responsible for the viscosity of ground substance (Copenhauer and Johnson, 1958). Any alteration in pH or ion concentration that would alter the charge distribution and the shape of the chains would be expected to change the viscosity of the system. This could have marked effects on the integrity of the connective tissues. Banga et al. (1960) treated white connective tissue with an enzyme to remove the protein polysaccharides of the ground substance, and found that the collagen fibers became longitudinally disoriented. And Köhn et al. (1959) stated that, while the carbohydrate-containing components were not necessary for the formation of collagen fibrils, the diameter of the fibrils was influenced by the mucopolysaccharides present.

Fatty Tissue

Sheldon (1969) states that the adipose cell mass is laid down during the early stages of life, and that the number of fat cells does not change, but the size of the cells does. Adipose tissues from different sites in the animal body behave quite differently *in vitro*, so the assumption is that they are different *in vivo*. Fat deposition is influenced by heredity, stage of growth, level of nutrition, exercise, hormones, and sex.

In the development of a fat cell, the cell first shows fine droplets of fat in the cytoplasm. As the droplets grow, they gradually run together into one (or several) large droplet(s) that crowd(s) and flatten(s) the nucleus against one side of the cell.

Fat deposits within the muscle follow the course of the small blood vessels. Hiner et al. (1955) reported that where fatty deposits were found, the collagenous tissue tended to form a fairly loose network between the muscle fibers. With less fat, the collagen fibers were more bunched and solid.

In addition to the fat deposited in adipose cells, muscle fibers are often found to contain, shortly after a meal, very small droplets of fat, apparently coming directly from the blood supply. Other intramuscular lipids are found in the cellular and subcellular membranes, as mentioned previously. Moody and Cassens (1968) point out that the free lipid droplets and membrane lipids may have important effects on postmortem changes, keeping quality, and palatability of muscle.

Water-Binding

The water-binding or water-holding capacity (WHC) of muscle tissue is thought to have considerable influence on the palatability of meat. Raw muscle is approximately 75 percent water, yet none leaks out when a muscle is cut. In fact, the water is difficult to force out even with pressures of 250–500 lbs. per square inch. Many of the techniques used in preparing muscle for consumption as cooked meat cause changes in the ability of the tissue to retain water.

Definitions

The classical meaning of *bound* water or *true bound water* is water that is so tightly held on the molecules that it moves with them in an electric field, and no longer has the characteristic freezing point, vapor pressure, or solvent ability of normal water (see Chapter 2). For example, Riedel (1957) found that not all the water in muscle was frozen at temperatures as low as $-40°$ C. Hamm (1960) estimated that 4–5 percent of the water in muscle is very firmly bound and represents the true water of hydration of the molecules. The remaining water is regarded as free in this context.

More recently, bound and free water and WHC of meat have been studied in two different ways. One type of research has explored the changes in WHC when meat is frozen, cooked, or given other treatments. The changes in WHC are usually measured by pressing a sample of the treated tissue and assessing the amount of fluid forced out by weight change or by spread of fluid on filter paper. Grau and Hamm (1953) proposed this measure; a number of modifications have been used by various investigators since then.

The second area of interest is the ability of muscle to retain added water. These tissues have the capacity, in many cases, to hold water in addition to that present naturally. The tissue is comminuted and mixed with additional water. The mixture may then be treated in various ways, such as adding different amounts and kinds of salts, heating, or chilling. The free water is measured by the amount that drains off, either under normal gravitational force, or with the added force of centrifugation. There are many applicable methods in the literature. As examples, Swift and Berman (1959) give a method using centrifugation, while Jay (1964) used gravitational drainage to measure what he called extract-release volume (ERV).

Mechanism

As in other gels, water is held in muscle tissue by forces such as H-bonds between water and appropriate groups in the molecules, and by capillary attraction in the interstices of the gel structure. Many of the types of molecules found in muscle have a considerable degree of attraction for water. These include the sarcoplasmic, myofibrillar, and connective-tissue proteins, the mucopolysaccharides, the phosphated compounds such as ATP and CP, the carbohydrate materials that supply energy, and the nonprotein nitrogenous compounds.

As has been discussed, muscle is a complex of membranes, fibers, fibrils, and filaments, cross-bonded in a variety of ways. These provide a highly organized structure with spaces where water is immobilized mechanically. Water held in this way is what is termed "bound water" in recent studies of the alterations due to such treatments as heating or freezing. Hoffman (1966) has suggested that intracellular water is in the "ice-like" state. Lockett et al. (1962) described a method for measuring extracellular space, and theorized that, in muscles that have a relatively high proportion of water to protein, the additional water is located in this space.

Altering Water-Binding

There appears to be a continuum from tightly bound to loosely held water. So the amount determined in any given study will vary with the treatments and with the methods of measurement. Riedel (1961) hypothesized that a temperature-dependent equilibrium exists between bound and free water in muscle. This seems to be borne out by studies such as Ritchey and Hostetler (1964) and Ritchey (1965), who noted an increasing shift from bound to free water as the internal temperature of beef LD and BF was increased from refrigerated raw to 80° C. The bound water decreased, while the free water first increased and then decreased as the rate of loss of free water by evaporation exceeded the rate of change from bound to free. Hamm and Iwata (1962) found that 30° C did not influence WHC, but that 50° did and that WHC decreased more rapidly as the temperature was increased to 70 and 90° C. Trumic et al. (1966) stated that increasing temperature decreased WHC even when NaCl and polyphosphates were added.

Both the binding of water onto chemical groups of muscle molecules and the mechanical immobilization of water are altered by a number of factors in addition to heat treatment. The electric field surrounding each molecule is influenced by changes in pH and by changes in kind and/or concentration of ions present. Places where water molecules may be held will be changed by treatments that increase or decrease the amount of cross-bonding between the tissue fibers, or by actual breakage of covalent bonds by proteolysis. Also, any treatment, such as freezing or grinding, that tends to break up the muscle structure will alter the spaces available for immobilizing water. So the degree of water binding will be altered by such treatments as heating, freezing, grinding, degradation of proteins by proteolysis (natural, added, or microbial enzymes) or by heat, addition, subtraction, or translocation of ions such as Na^+, K^+, Ca^{++}, Cl^-, addition of salts such as NaCl, polyphosphates, curing salts, and alteration of pH by adding acids or bases.

Relation to Common Practices

The treatments listed above as influencing WHC frequently occur naturally, or are a part of the preparation of muscle tissue for consumption. The chemical reactions that occur shortly post mortem and during any aging of the meat cause alteration of compounds such as those in the energy-producing cycle; change in pH; and at least small amounts of proteolysis. Sodium chloride, nitrates, nitrites, polyphosphates, and other compounds may be added for curing of pork and beef products, or in preparing sausage mixtures. Grinding is employed for sausage products and for hamburger and ground beef. The softness and wetness of PSE pork is thought to be closely related to loss of WHC paralleling the abnormally rapid rate of pH fall post mortem, and the low ultimate pH usually attained. Freezing, especially at slower rates, decreases WHC and increases thawing drip. And most meat is heated at some step in the total preparation for consumption.

POST-MORTEM CHANGES

The conversion from living muscle to meat involves a series of complex physical and chemical changes that have a profound influence on the quality of the product. In order to understand the current postulates as to these changes, it is necessary to have some comprehension of theories of contraction and relaxation in the living muscle, since many of the same reactions form the basis for post-mortem changes.

Contraction—Relaxation in Living Muscle

The contractile fibers of muscle consist of highly organized filaments composed chiefly of actin and myosin. Earlier theories proposed that muscle fibers shortened or lengthened by changes in the type and degree of folding of these protein chains. Currently, the most widely accepted theory of muscle contraction is based on the interaction of actin and myosin according to the "sliding model" proposed by Hanson and Huxley (1955). Huxley (1969) summarized the recent findings supporting this theory. Several other theories have been reviewed by Slautterback (1966) and by Whitaker (1959).

The change in length of the muscle in contraction or relaxation is thought to be brought about by the interdigitating filaments of actin and myosin sliding past one another, the actin filaments being drawn into the array of myosin filaments as the muscle shortens (contracts), or sliding out as the muscle regains rest length by relaxation. The complex of actin, myosin, tropomyosin, and troponin formed by this junction is actomyosin (also designated myosin B by some authors).

The chemical events that are associated with the formation or dissolution of actomyosin are summarized in a general way as follows. The myosin and actin chains in the resting muscle are kept separate by the plasticizing action of the magnesium complex of adenosine triphosphate (MgATP). Ca^{2+} ions are released from the sarcoplasmic reticulum by nerve impulses to start the contraction cycle. The Ca^{2+} ions release ATP from MgATP, and also stimulate the ATPase activity of HMM. The latter splits ATP to ADP, releasing the energy of the $\sim$P bond and permitting the movement of the actin filaments toward the H zone of the A band. Then the relaxing factor (Marsh, 1952, 1966; Lorand, 1967) promotes the recapture of the Ca^{2+} ions by the sarcoplasmic reticulum, the MgATP complex is re-formed with new ATP, and this in turn breaks up the actomyosin and permits relaxation.

The ATP supply is regenerated by reaction of ADP with creatine

$$CP \quad + \quad ADP \longrightarrow creatine \quad + \quad ATP$$

phosphate (CP). CP is regenerated by means of reactions utilizing energy supplied by the glycolytic cycle. In the anaerobic portion of the glycolytic cycle, energy is released and lactic acid formed from muscle glycogen. Further reactions involving oxygen (aerobic) convert the lactic acid to CO_2 and H_2O.

Development of Rigor

When an animal is killed, many of the physical and chemical reactions of the living cells continue for some time. However, the milieu rapidly becomes anaerobic, as the cessation of blood circulation cuts off the incoming supply of oxygen. In the normal case, this leads to accumulation of lactic acid in the muscle tissue, with a pH shift from around 7.0 to 7.2 to around 5.5. Along with this, the muscles lose their irritability and their soft, pliable nature, and become rigid, stiff, and inflexible. This is termed *rigor mortis*, literally translated "stiffness of death." These changes in pH and in stiffness may follow many patterns, depending on the particular conditions involved, and can have profound effects on the flavor, color, tenderness, and juiciness of the resulting meat.

Chemical Changes

Chemical changes that occur in muscle post mortem have been reviewed by Whitaker (1966), Goll (1968), and Lawrie (1968). The major chemical events include (1) glycolysis, at a rate dependent on factors such as pH, temperature, glycogen supply, and accumulation of end products; (2) decrease in pH with lactic acid formation; (3) decrease in CP concentration to about 30 percent of the initial value as the pH drops to around 6.8; (4) decrease in ATP, as CP supply is depleted; and (5) liberation of NH_3.

Degradation of ATP leads initially to accumulation of ADP, followed by AMP, then IMP, and eventually inosine. When ATP decreases to 50–80 percent of its initial concentration, the muscle loses extensibility and becomes hard.

A number of studies have shown alterations in the muscle proteins as the pH changes and the availability of ions such as Na, K, Mg, and Ca is altered. Scopes and Lawrie (1963) found that some of the sarcoplasmic proteins were denatured within 24 hours after death. These then become susceptible to attack by proteolytic enzymes of the muscle, eventually yielding free amino acids. Lawrie (1968) suggests that these amino acids, along with shifts in Ca^{2+} and K^+ concentrations, increase the WHC of meat. Fujimaki and Deatherage (1964) found that the electrophoretic patterns of sarcoplasmic proteins that remained soluble (undenatured) altered considerably. Whitaker (1966) points out that the pI of several of the myofibrillar proteins is close to 5.4, so the pH shift could induce some denaturation, evidenced by loss of WHC. Also, the formation of actomyosin alters materially the extractability of myofibrillar proteins. Sulzbacher et al. (1960) found that the time of change of extractability varied from one muscle to another, but in general corresponded to the time of onset of stiffening. Disney et al. (1967) noted decreases in protein solubility and in WHC in beef muscles during the first 24 hours post mortem.

The rate and extent of pH change varies with a number of factors. The pH of living muscle is generally regarded as being in the range 7.0 to 7.2. Krzywicki and Ratcliff (1967) introduced the designation pH_1, the muscle pH measured 45 minutes after slaughter, as an approximate index of the rate of post mortem glycolysis in the muscle. The term "ultimate pH" is in general used to designate the lowest pH reached by the muscle post mortem, often around pH 5.5 to 5.8.

Biophysical and Physical Changes

When the animal is slaughtered, the thermodynamic equilibrium of the living muscle is profoundly altered. As the oxygen supply is exhausted, the oxidation-reduction potential drops, and aerobic energy production ceases. These changes are accompanied by loss of ability to maintain (1) body temperature, (2) *in vivo* osmotic equilibrium, (3) membrane permeability and polarization, and (4) normal ion concentrations in various parts of the tissues. The *in vivo* controls on muscle contraction are disrupted by the diminishing supply of ATP, so actin and myosin unite to form actomyosin, the irritability and extensibility of the muscle decrease, and the muscle becomes hard.

Davies (1966) emphasized that there are two aspects to the development of rigor hardness, (1) the shortening or development of tension in a muscle or bundle of muscle fibers, and (2) the loss of extensibility of the fibers. Goll (1968) further subdivides the loss of extensibility into two manifestations, (1) the microscopic, which depends on the ability of the actin and myosin filaments to slide past one another within the sarcomere, and (2) the macroscopic as measured by whether or not the muscle fibers will stretch when a force is applied.

Contraction can cause stiffening of the muscle by shortening if the muscle is free to do so, or by development of isometric tension if the muscles are fixed in length by attachment to the skeleton. Postmortem contraction depends on the muscle being stimulated to contract before the ATP supply is exhausted, since ATP furnishes the immediate energy source to drive the contraction process. If this stimulation occurs while the ATP supply is still plentiful, considerable contraction and/or tension will develop. If the ATP supply is nearly depleted before stimulation, very little shortening or tension development will occur. But any shortening must occur before loss of extensibility is complete, because in the latter case the actin and myosin filaments are no longer able to slide past one another.

Extensibility depends on the presence of MgATP and virtual absence of Ca^{2+}, to permit the actin-myosin bridges to open so the filaments can slide past one another. When the ATP supply is reduced to the point where it can no longer function as a plasticizer, the actin-myosin bridges become fixed, and the muscle can no longer be stretched. This interlocking of the filaments can occur at any degree of overlap, depending on the degree of contraction of the muscle. Huxley (1969) found that the active tension generated by a living muscle decreased to zero when the muscle was stretched enough to eliminate any overlap of actin and myosin filaments. Thus, if the muscle is stretched prerigor until there is little or no overlap of the filaments, very little stiffness of the muscle will be produced by this interlocking. Partmann (1963) reported that when muscle strips were allowed to go into rigor when stretched, they were considerably more tender than strips allowed to age without stretching.

The time course of the loss of extensibility is currently divided into three phases, (1) delay, during which very little change occurs, (2) onset, during which there is a continuous loss of extensibility, and (3) completion, when the muscle becomes virtually inextensible. The length of time for each phase, and for the entire process, varies markedly with factors such as temperature, antemortem stress, and glycogen supply.

Changes in Microscopic Appearance

The changes in the microscopic appearance of bovine muscle fibers after slaughter have been reviewed by Gillis and Henrickson (1967). Paul (1965) reported on changes in rabbit muscle and Cassens et al. (1963b) on those in porcine muscle. The general pattern of changes during the normal development and resolution of rigor is quite similar, although the time intervals vary with species, and marked alterations can be produced by a variety of causes.

Samples taken shortly after death of the animal have poorly differentiated fibers that are straight to slightly wavy (Figure 10). As rigor is initiated, parts of fibers show areas of pronounced contraction, with shortened sarcomeres (Figure 11). As rigor develops, contraction progresses to the formation of rigor nodes. Unstimulated fibers are pulled up in kinks and waves by the shortening of the stimulated fibers (Figure 12). As rigor is resolved, the fibers gradually lose their wavy appearance

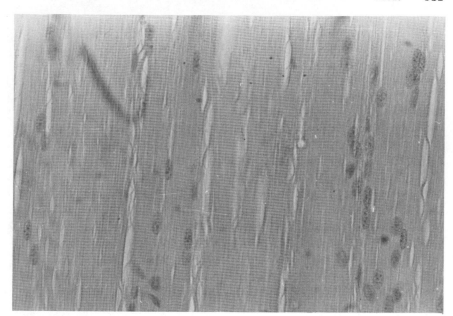

FIGURE 10. Rabbit psoas major, 30 minutes post mortem. Shows poorly differentiated fibers, cross striations in register. Nuclei concentrations indicate edges of individual muscle fibers. Magnification 275x.

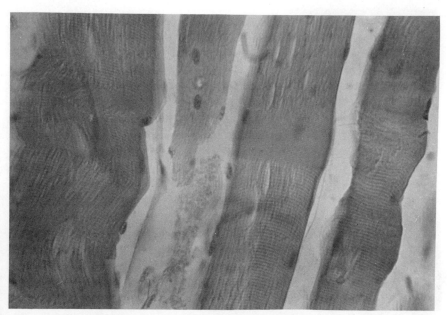

FIGURE 11. Rabbit psoas major, four hours post mortem, showing area of marked contraction (shortened sarcomeres). Magnification 275x.

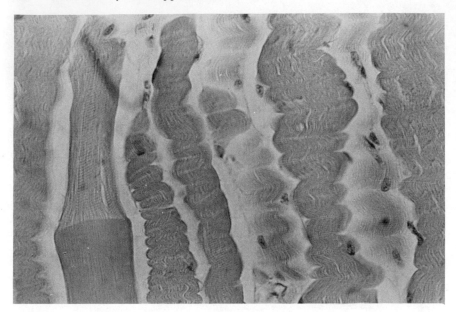

FIGURE 12. Rabbit psoas major, six hours post mortem, showing rigor node, adjacent stretched area in the same fiber, and wavy fibers surrounding contracted one. Magnification 275x.

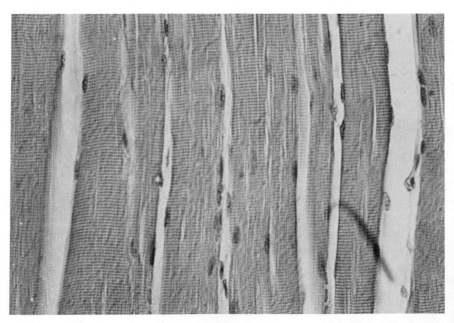

FIGURE 13. Rabbit psoas major, 24 hours post mortem. Fibers almost straight, distinct, and fibrils and cross striations apparent. Magnification 275x.

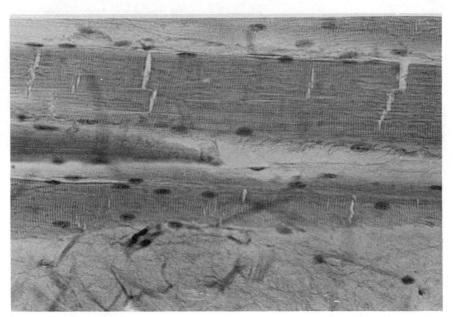

FIGURE 14. Rabbit LD, 48 hours post mortem. Shows breaks at the I band. Magnification 275x.

(Figure 13), the fibers show distinct separations, and the fibrils become more apparent. Rabbit muscles reach this stage within 12 to 24 hours after slaughter, while 4 to 9 days' storage may be needed to produce the same sequence of changes in beef.

With increased storage (aging), breaks and distintegrated areas appear in the fibers (Figure 14). These breaks start in the I band (Figure 14) and are considered to be caused by the disintegration of the Z band and separation of the actin filaments from their connections to the Z structure.

One striking variation in microscopic appearance of rigor is the super-contraction nodes produced by very rapid rigor development (Figure 15). These may be produced by cooking prerigor (Paul et al., 1944, 1952; Ramsbottom and Strandine, 1949; and Weidemann et al., 1967a), thaw rigor or cutting immediately after death (Cassens et al., 1963a), or cold shortening (Weidemann et al., 1967a).

Resolution of Rigor

The traditional method for estimating the development or resolution of rigor is by stiffness or hardness of the muscle, resistance of joints to

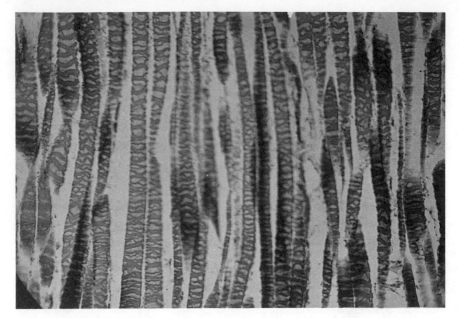

FIGURE 15. Supercontraction nodes in beef psoas, produced by heating muscle prerigor. Magnification 70x.

bending, and similar touch assessments. From this viewpoint, there is a definite change, since the musculature of the carcass does, in most cases, stiffen shortly after death and then eventually soften again.

Because objective methods of measuring the development of rigor have been developed, there has been considerable disagreement as to whether rigor is resolved. It now seems clear that this disagreement stemmed from incomplete understanding of the rigor process. If the development of rigor is defined and measured by disappearance of CP or ATP, or by loss of extensibility, there can be no resolution in these terms, since there is no regeneration of CP or ATP, and the muscle apparently does not regain appreciable extensibility. However, the more recent recognition of the dual nature of the stiffening, as discussed by Goll (1968), demonstrated that the rigidity of the muscle in rigor is due to a combination of contracture or isometric tension, and loss of extensibility. Since the muscle eventually loses its ability to maintain isometric tension and regains at least partial extensibility, it does lose its rigidity, and in this context there is resolution of rigor. Weidemann et al. (1967a) attributed the softening of bovine muscle to ruptured filaments and probable breakage of links between actin and myosin. Goll

(1968) suggested that loss of Z-line structure with rupture of attachments between actin filaments and Z line and weakening of the actin-myosin bridges might be due to limited and very specific proteolysis, possibly catalyzed by proteases released from muscle lysosomes. Goll and Robson (1967) reported that tropomyosin, the most sensitive of the three myofibrillar proteins to attack by proteases, showed no significant proteolysis 312 hours after death of the animal. But Goll (1968) found that short exposure of contracted myofibrils to trypsin in the absence of ATP caused the fibrils to lengthen or relax. Shifts in ion concentration, pH, and temperature to nonphysiological conditions post mortem may also contribute to the resolution of rigor.

Rate and Extent of Post-Mortem Changes

A number of factors can influence the rate and/or extent of the changes that occur in muscle post mortem. These may cause marked alterations in palatability characteristics such as color, tenderness, and juiciness.

Animal and Muscle

Animals of different species appear to go through the development and resolution of rigor at different rates. Herring (1968) states that the onset of rigor mortis in bovine muscle usually occurs within 9 hours, and rigor is completely developed in 12–24 hours post mortem. Rigor in rabbit muscle usually develops within 2 hours and is completely resolved in 12 hours (Paul, 1964). Marsh et al. (1968) give 12 hours as the time required for rigor development in lamb carcasses. Porcine muscle appears to be variable in rigor time, some going into rigor almost immediately after death, others much more slowly. Briskey (1964) gives 4–6 hours as the "normal" time for rigor development in pork.

Part of the variation in the rate of development and resolution of rigor may be temperature variation due to differences in carcass size and in slaughtering procedures. The large bovine carcass cools more slowly than the small rabbit carcass. Porcine carcasses are subjected to heat treatment during slaughtering, to facilitate removal of hair, since the carcass is usually not skinned.

Animals within a species vary in their degree of excitability, and so will respond differently to any ante-mortem stimulation or stress. This influences the rate of glycogen depletion and the degree of contraction of the muscle fibers. For example, Bendall (1966) found that curare injection into pigs immediately ante mortem gave a slow and constant rate of chemical and physical changes post mortem, while a brief electrical stimulation of the excised muscles nearly doubled the rate of change over that of the unstimulated muscles.

The individual muscles within the carcass also vary in rate and extent of post-mortem change, partly dependent on the number of red, white, or intermediate fibers in the muscle, and on factors such as the development of the circulatory system as this influences the oxygen supply to the muscle (Merkel, 1968; Cooper et al., 1969).

Tension on Muscle

Muscles are believed to exert tension during the onset of rigor. Locker (1960a) found that different muscles of the bovine carcass went into rigor at widely differing states of contraction, and concluded that relaxed muscles were more tender than partly contracted ones.

Many muscles of the carcass can shorten during the development of rigor, as they are either attached to connective tissue sheets rather than directly to the skeleton, or are in a slack position due to the way the carcass is suspended. Other muscles may be stretched by the method of hanging. Weidemann et al. (1967b) estimated that the psoas muscle of beef is stretched to approximately 160 percent of its rest length by the usual method of hanging the carcass, and suggested that this contributes materially to the tenderness of this muscle. The degree of contraction, or stretch, as indicated by sarcomere length, is believed to have a major influence on the tenderness of the muscle. Herring (1968) reviewed the relation between degree of muscle contraction and tenderness of meat.

Ramsbottom and Strandine (1949) and Paul and Bratzler (1955) indicated that muscles that were cut or excised before the onset of rigor were tougher than comparable muscles still attached to the skeleton. Eisenhut et al. (1965) studied the effects on sarcomere length of placing the bovine carcass in different positions during post-mortem chilling. They reported that sarcomere lengths of the LD increased with change from vertical suspension, which allowed the LD to contract, to a position involving arching of the spine and stretching of the LD. Herring et al. (1967) investigated the effect of stretch or contraction to produce variations from −48 percent to +48 percent in the length of the sarcomeres of beef ST. They found that post-mortem aging increased the tenderness of all the muscles, but that the contracted muscles did not reach acceptable tenderness levels even after 10 days of aging. Buck et al. (1969) studied the effect of stretching rabbit LD prerigor, and found that the stretched muscles had greater sarcomere lengths and required less force to shear, than those allowed to pass through rigor unrestrained.

Howard and Judge (1968) reported the importance of contracture and sarcomere shortening in bovine muscle as it influences tenderness, but pointed out the possibility of variation in sarcomere length within a muscle and the necessity for sampling several areas. Buck and Black (1968) believe that a contributing factor to the tenderizing effect may be the thinning of connective tissues due to stretching the muscle.

Temperature

The customary procedure is to cool the carcass immediately. The decrease in temperature diminishes chemical reaction rates, influencing the rate of loss of glycogen, CP, and ATP. Large muscle masses cool more slowly than thinner portions of the carcass. Disney et al. (1967) compared ice-cooling and normal air-cooling of beef muscles. Ice-cooling increased the rate of temperature decrease, retarded glycolysis and ATP breakdown, and reduced protein denaturation and loss of WHC.

A number of studies have been made of temperature effects on muscles excised immediately post mortem so that the cooling rates could be controlled. Bate-Smith and Bendall (1949) found that in rabbit muscle, shortening of the muscles increased with increase in the temperature at which rigor developed. Locker and Hagyard (1963) reported a similar finding in beef at temperatures above 17° C, but the shortening effect increased again as the temperature decreased from 17 to 0° C. So the sarcomere shortening influence of temperature on bovine muscle appears to be minimal at about 15–20° C. Busch et al. (1967) suggested that the shortening effect at 37° C might be due to thermal shrinkage of collagen rather than to sliding of the myofilaments of the contractile fibers.

Varying temperature conditions produce different patterns of pH change by altering rate of glycolysis. Cassens and Newbold (1966) found that the decrease in pH and in CP and other acid-labile phosphates in beef muscle was slower at 15° than at 37° C. In a second paper (1967), they reported that at 1° C, an appreciable amount of the ATP still remained in the muscle, and the pH of 6.2 was considerably above the ultimate value of 5.78. Scopes (1960) found that sarcoplasmic proteins are denatured readily below pH 6.0 at 37° C, and that the denaturation of sarcoplasmic protein *in situ* was associated with decreased myofibrillar protein solubility. Sayre and Briskey (1963) reported that sarcoplasmic and myofibrillar protein solubilities decreased with lower pH and high temperature at the onset of rigor, and that the protein solubility was closely related to the juice-retaining properties of muscle.

Cold Shortening

Locker and Hagyard (1963) described the cold-shortening effect that occurs in fresh excised bovine muscle exposed to temperatures between 0 and 8° C. Red muscle appears to be much more susceptible to cold-shortening than white muscle, since only the semitendinosus (the one red muscle) of the rabbit carcass shows this phenomenon. Cassens and Newbold (1967) reported that the delay phase of rigor mortis increased as the temperature decreased from 37 to 15° C but was shorter with lower temperature in the range of 15 to 1° C. Sink et al. (1965) found a high correlation between mean sarcomere length and the duration of the delay phase of rigor in porcine LD. Marsh (1966) suggested that cold shortening may be due to inactivation of the relaxing factor by Ca.

Marsh and Leet (1966) showed that lamb LD is also susceptible to cold shortening. The cold-shortened muscles were less tender than those not cold shortened. However, Parrish et al. (1969b) were unable to demonstrate cold-shortening toughening in bovine LD and SM, and suggested that the thicker fat cover and muscle mass of the bovine carcass may allow internal muscle temperature to remain high enough, even at low ambient temperature, to degrade the energy supplies needed for shortening before the cold-shortening temperature range is reached. Herring et al. (1965) pointed out that three types of shortening could occur in muscle excised prerigor: (1) that associated with excision; (2) that associated with cold shortening; and (3) that associated with the onset of rigor.

Thaw Rigor

Thaw rigor is a condition observed in thawed muscle that was frozen before rigor had developed. If the muscle is frozen before the ATP level has decreased appreciably, and the muscle is then thawed at room temperature, the ATP-ase activity is greatly increased and the muscle contracts vigorously and exudes much fluid (drip). Luyet (1968) observed this thaw-rigor contraction and fluid exudation in single muscle fibers. Bendall (1960) suggested that thaw rigor occurs because of an extensive salt "flux" on thawing, with release of Ca and temporary inactivation of the relaxing factor.

In meat animals, thaw rigor is more apt to occur in species such as lamb and rabbit in which the carcasses are small enough for freezing to occur before rigor is fully developed. Marsh et al. (1968) found that freezing of lamb carcasses very shortly after slaughter caused marked toughening of the meat. This could be eliminated by holding the carcasses for 24 hours at 20° C before freezing, or by storing the frozen cuts for 15 days at a temperature just below the freezing point ($-3°$ C). In the latter case, the glycolytic changes and completion of rigor occurred during the storage at $-3°$. Lawrie (1968) has reviewed thaw rigor and cold shortening in rabbit muscle.

Dark-Cutting Beef

Conditions that result in a very low level of glycogen in the muscles of beef at slaughter will yield meat with a high ultimate pH, since little or no lactic acid will be produced post mortem. The high pH increases the activity of the cytochrome enzymes. Also, the muscle fibers will be tightly packed due to enhanced water binding of the muscle proteins, and so will decrease the ease of diffusion of oxygen. Hence the myoglobin will be principally in the nonoxygenated form, which is dark bluish-red in color. This gives beef a very dark red to almost black color.

PSE Pork

The opposite condition to dark cutting is seen in PSE pork. Such pork is light in color, soft in texture, and wet in appearance. This result also is associated with abnormal rate and extent of pH change post mortem. Briskey (1963, 1964) gives the following patterns of change for porcine muscle:

1. A slow decrease to a high ultimate pH of 6.0 or above yields dark, firm, dry muscle tissue.
2. A gradual decrease in pH to around 5.7, with an ultimate pH of 5.3–5.7 yields normal tissue.
3. A rapid decrease to pH 5.1 to 5.4 in $\frac{1}{2}$ to $1\frac{1}{2}$ hours yields extremely PSE tissue.

In the latter case, pH values below 6.0 may be reached before the temperature of the muscle has fallen below $35°$ C, causing a marked reduction in solubility of the sarcoplasmic and myofibrillar proteins (McLoughlin, 1963; Briskey and Sayre, 1964).

Greaser et al. (1969) showed that the calcium-accumulating ability of the sarcoplasmic reticulum decreased post mortem more rapidly in PSE muscle than in normal muscle, and emphasized the importance of the relaxing factor in determining characteristics of muscle tissue. McClain and Pearson (1969) found that epimysial connective tissue from PSE muscle had lower onset and recovery temperatures for heat shrinkage, had more components melting at low temperatures, and appeared to be less highly cross-linked than epimysial tissue from normal muscles.

Aging

As has been noted, the characteristics of muscle change significantly during the period of development and resolution of rigor. Practical experience over many years has shown that tenderness, juiciness, and flavor of the resulting meat is usually improved by a period of storage or aging, especially in bovine and ovine species. Aging is usually done at 0 to 1.5° C to minimize microbial growth. For beef, the time required for maximum benefit is in the range of 10 to 17 days, for lamb, 3 to 5 days. Various authors have defined the starting time for the aging process differently. Some include all the time postslaughter, others start at the time the carcass reaches cooler temperature, and others at the end of complete rigor development. Davey and Gilbert (1968b) recommend that the aging period be counted from the time the ultimate pH of the musculature is reached.

Palatability Characteristics

Watts (1954) pointed out that the color of meat is principally determined by the amount and state of the pigments, and the transparency of the muscle fibers. The pigment forms shift in accord with the oxidation-reduction conditions within the muscle, and the oxygen supply. Decrease in transparency of the muscle fibers, which is related to loss of water-binding capacity, produces paler-colored meat.

Juiciness of meat is probably dependent on a combination of factors, in which the fat and the water-holding capacity of the muscle proteins play a part. Doty and Pierce (1961), summarizing a number of studies, point out that the fat dispersion during cooking is decreased by aging the raw meat. Hamm (1956) suggested that about $\frac{2}{3}$ of the post-mortem decrease of muscle hydration was due to ATP breakdown, and the remainder to the pH decrease caused by lactic acid production. He also (1959) pointed out the significance of the change in Mg binding in the post-mortem decrease of muscle hydration. Taki (1965) found that the water-holding capacity of bovine LD decreased significantly with storage up to 192 hours post mortem.

Doty and Pierce (1961) state that aging for two weeks improved both the fat and lean flavor of broiled beef rib eye. An additional two-week storage was usually detrimental to flavor. Gunther (1968) noted an increase of low-molecular-weight compounds important in aroma formation, with seven days' post-mortem storage of beef. Lawrie (1968) suggested that the increased amounts of free sugars, amino acids, and hypoxanthine in aged meat might contribute to the altered flavor of the lean. Howard et al. (1960) noted an increase in hypoxanthine level in beef muscle with aging. Enzymic activity and oxidation would be expected to cause changes in the flavor of the fat. Paul et al. (1944) noted rancidity in the fat of beef muscles aged more than nine days.

Tenderness is usually increased by aging. For example, Taki (1965) found that beef LD steaks were more tender at 1 hour than at 24 or 48 hours, but less tender than at 192 hours post mortem, and Doty and Pierce (1961) state that steaks were more tender after 2 weeks' aging. Deatherage and Harsham (1947) showed that tenderness did not increase in a straight-line relation with aging time, the maximum increase in tenderness of beef occurring between the second and seventeenth day, with a slower increase from 17 to 31 days, and little change between 31 and 40 days. They suggested that the different rates might correspond to changes in the contractile fibers and the connective tissue, respectively.

Microscopic Appearance

The decrease in waviness or kinkiness, and the development of broken or granulated muscle fibers, are illustrated in Figures 13 and 14. Disintegration of the fibers would be expected to decrease the resistance of the fibers to shearing. Doty and Pierce (1961) describe an "autolysis rating" based on the frequency and extent of muscle fiber breaks, and state that the autolysis rating increased with aging for all grades and weights of beef carcasses. The increase was greater during the first than during the second two-week aging period. The disintegration of the muscle fibers has been attributed to action of proteolytic enzymes and/or mechanical forces on the fibers stretched by development of rigor nodes or by the tension on the muscle due to position of the carcass. Sharp (1963) suggested that the resistance of the muscle fibers to disintegration after storage at 37° C depended on both the degree of intracellular proteolysis and the denaturation of the proteins. The former tended to weaken the fibers, but the latter appeared to make the fibers stronger.

Szent-Gyorgyi (1952) suggested that the tenderization with aging involved the disintegration of the actin filaments. Paul (1965) observed that the cracks and breaks that developed in the muscle fibers appeared to start in the I band. Weidemann et al. (1967a) concluded that the tendering action was produced by disruption of the actin filaments and probably of the links between the actin and myosin. Davey and Gilbert (1969) noted that aging of fiber pieces caused loss of adhesion between adjacent myofibrils and disruption and frequently disappearance of the Z lines.

Davey et al. (1967) reported that the extent to which beef ages is markedly influenced by the degree of muscle shortening during the onset phases of rigor mortis. In the range of 20 to 40 percent shortening, the extent to which the meat ages decreases with increased shortening, reaching zero at 40 percent shortening.

Storage Temperature

It is customary to age meat carcasses at temperatures just above the freezing point. Whitaker (1959), summarizing a variety of studies, points out that beef is more tender after aging than at 1 to 2 days after slaughter. The time for maximum tenderization varied from 9 to 30 days in different studies (for example, Paul et al., 1944; Rodel et al., 1968; Larmond et al., 1969; and Deatherage and Harsham, 1947).

A variety of techniques have been investigated to permit the use of higher temperatures to increase the speed of aging while minimizing the growth of spoilage organisms. Matz (1962) mentions the use of ultraviolet lamps to reduce the number of microorganisms on the surface of the meat. Wilson et al. (1960a, b) used injection of the antibiotic oxytetracycline, 2 to 3 hours before slaughter, to permit aging of beef at 90, 100, or 110° F. They found tenderness after 24 hours at 110° F nearly comparable to that obtained by aging for 2 weeks at 35° F. Thompson et al. (1968) preceded 30° C storage with 45 minutes in a tunnel dryer at 35° C to dry slightly the outer surface and so retard microbial growth.

Marsh et al. (1968) found that holding lamb carcasses up to 16 hours at 18–24° C before exposure to cold increased the tenderness materially. They suggest that tenderness is more nearly related to presence or absence of sarcomere shortening, rather than to tenderization by aging. Davey et al. (1967) reported that beef sternomandibularis excised within 30 minutes of slaughter achieved maximum aging in $2\frac{1}{2}$ to 3 days at 15° C. They considered aging to start at 24 hours post mortem. They also pointed out that the shortening during the development of rigor mortis determined the extent of tenderization, with muscle allowed to shorten by 40 percent showing no tenderization after 3 days' aging at 15° C.

Parrish et al. (1969b) suggest that the influence of aging time and temperature on tenderness may be related to chronological age, since they found no increase in tenderness of broiled LD or SM steaks due to holding carcasses of 16-month-old bovine animals at 15° C for 48 hours or 21° C for 24 hours plus 5–6 days at 2° C, instead of continuously at 2° C. They also suggest that cooking method may influence the results, since SM roasts did show a tenderness advantage for 24 hours at 15° C for 4 days over continuous 2° C storage.

Changes in Protein Extractability

Alteration in the extractability of the muscle proteins post mortem was noted by Deuticke (1932) and Weber and Meyer (1933). More recently the development of a variety of electrophoretic and chromatographic separation techniques has permitted more detailed studies of these changes. These should assist in the clarification of the nature of these reactions and how they influence palatability characteristics.

The extractability of the myofibrillar proteins has been shown to be least at 24 hours post mortem, then to increase with aging, in both beef and rabbit muscle (Hegarty, 1963; Aberle and Merkel, 1966; Valin, 1968; Davey and Gilbert, 1968a; and Penny, 1968). The presence of actinin and troponin in the extracts from aged muscle is considered to arise from disruption of the Z line and loosening of the attachments of the actin filaments to the Z lines. Penny (1968) found that the changes in the intact muscle differed somewhat from those in isolated myofibrils. Davey and Gilbert (1968a) reported that the extractability varied with pH, so the results from each muscle might differ depending on the ultimate pH attained by that particular sample. Chaudhry et al. (1969) investigated the influence of storage temperatures of 2, 16, 25, and 37° C. They found that solubility increased with aging temperature to 25°, but decreased at 37° C. Paul (1959) found, in beef aged on the carcass at 2° C, that severing the attachments at one end of the muscle so that the muscle was free to contract decreased the extractability of both sarcoplasmic and myofibrillar proteins.

Connective Tissue

Goll (1965) reviewed the studies on changes in connective tissue during post mortem storage. He pointed out that there had been few studies on these, and that the possible role of collagen and elastin in post-mortem tenderization of meat had not been established. Herring et al. (1967a) studied beef muscles from carcasses of differing maturity and reported that neither the amount of collagen present nor its solubility appeared to be significantly affected by aging up to 10 days. McClain et al. (1969), in a study of the extractability of intramuscular connective tissue from bovine and porcine muscles, found that the yield decreased with post-mortem storage up to 3 days. Field et al. (1969) reported that 24 hours' storage reduced the peak melting point and increased the amount melting at lower temperatures in epimysial collagen of porcine muscle.

Possible Bases for Post-Mortem Changes

A number of explanations have been suggested for the post-rigor softening of muscle, but to date the process is not understood. It is possible that a number of factors are involved, including: (1) increased hydration of muscle proteins due to the small increase in pH during aging, the redistribution of ions, and the breakdown of nucleotides; (2) actual, or increased ease of, dissociation of the actomyosin complex; (3) weakening or breaking of the junctions of the thin filaments with the Z line; (4) disintegration of Z lines; (5) weakening or disruption of the sarcoplasmic reticulum within the cell; (6) proteolysis of the muscle proteins; and (7) possible changes in the polysaccharide components. Appreciable connective tissue changes do not appear to occur (Partmann, 1963; Sharp, 1963).

Sharp (1963) and Partmann (1963) report that the pronounced softening of muscle tissue that occurs with long-term storage at 37° C under aseptic conditions is primarily due to proteolysis. However, Partmann points out that under the usual conditions of time and temperature for aging meat, proteolytic changes are small. And Sharp indicates probable differences in autocatalytic activity of muscles due to variations in breed, species, and maturity of the animal.

Studies using temperatures just above freezing and times up to 30 days do show evidence of proteolysis in muscle, with liberation of free amino acids (Scopes and Lawrie, 1963; Davey and Gilbert, 1966; Bowers, 1969; Parrish et al., 1969a; Suzuki et al., 1967; and Locker, 1960b). This proteolysis is considered to occur mainly in the sarcoplasmic proteins, peptides, and other small amino-acid-containing molecules, rather than in the structural proteins. Davey and Gilbert (1966) and Parrish et al. (1969a) reported that this proteolysis showed no relation to tenderness changes. Bowers (1969) suggested that the increase in free amino acids might have a role in the flavor changes that occur during aging. Goll and Robson (1967) reported no significant hydrolysis of tropomyosin, the most susceptible of the three major myofibrillar proteins to proteolytic degradation, even after 13 days' aging.

Davey and Gilbert (1966) state that the hydrolysis that does occur is not due to bacterial action. Cameron and Spector (1961) point out that when cells die they become more acid in reaction and their permeability characteristics are altered. Suzuki and Fujimaki (1968) found that the extractability of the enzymic activity increased during storage of muscle, and considered this change to be due to alterations in the lysosomes. Locker (1960b) states that while there is a considerable quantity of proteolytic enzymes in muscle, the activity is very low as long as the lysosomes are intact, but increases many times when the latter are damaged. Goll (1968) suggests that the softening found in post-mortem muscle may be due to very limited and specific proteolysis of one or more of the myofibrillar proteins, brought about by catheptic enzymes. He cites De Lumen's data showing that there is a large increase in the ATPase activity of myofibrils when they are incubated with lysosomes, and suggests that this may lead to weakening of the actin-myosin interaction, allowing slippage of the myofilaments and loss of ability of the muscle to maintain isometric tension.

Prerigor Processing

A number of recent studies have explored the possibility of fabricating meat cuts before chilling—"hot" processing. Moore et al. (1966) compared roasts from pork loins cut before and after chilling, and found no difference in cooking losses or in shear force. Weiner et al. (1966) studied both fresh pork loins and cured hams. They reported that "hot" cutting produced more tender meat than the conventional process. However, if the loins were cut hot and frozen immediately, they were significantly less tender than the control samples. Mandigo and Henrickson (1966) found that hot-cut hams were more tender, both by panel score and by shear force, than those processed conventionally. Mandigo (1967, 1968) has reviewed the studies on hot processing of pork. The possibility of hot boning of beef is under study at the present time (Davey et al., 1970).

HEATING MEAT

Almost all meat consumed in the United States has been heated, either in processing such as smoking or canning, or in preparation immediately prior to consumption. In many cases meat items are heated more than once. Heat produces marked changes in meat, due to denaturation and coagulation of proteins, melting of fat, alterations in pH and in water-holding capacity, and chemical changes in heat-labile compounds.

A variety of research studies, undertaken for a range of purposes, have included the effects of heating on meat. Because of the large number of variables, such as species, breed, composition and cut of meat, and method and degree of heating, the results do not lend themselves to compact summarization. Rogers (1969) reviewed methods of heating meat, and Paul (1963) summarized the influence of methods of cooking on tenderness.

Heat-Induced Changes in Meat

The type and extent of changes in meat on heating vary with the composition of the meat and with the method and extent of heating.

Matz (1962) pointed out that heat (1) alters the selective permeability of the cell membranes, (2) accelerates the reaction rate of enzymes until the denaturation temperatures of the enzymes are reached, and (3) coagulates the proteins in the temperature range of 57 to 75° C. The range of coagulation temperatures is due to the variety of proteins present, the protective effect of associated colloids and ions, the solubilizing effect of pH away from the IEP, and the dependence of the reaction on time as well as temperature.

General Pattern of Change

Lawrie (1968) states that the most obvious change when meat is heated is the loss of water-holding capacity (WHC), due to denaturation of the sarcoplasmic and myofibrillar proteins. The change is progressive with time and increasing temperature. Hamm (1966), in a review of the influence of heat on muscle protein systems, pointed out that the organization of the proteins into filaments and fibers may cause them to react somewhat differently than they would as purified proteins in solution, due to "the special steric position of each protein, their relatively high concentration in the tissue, and the protective nature of accompanying tissue proteins."

Machlik and Draught (1963) followed the changes in characteristics and in shear force in beef ST muscle. They noted considerable water loss but little change in shear up to 50° C, a marked decrease in shear between 50 and 60° C, especially around 57° C, an increase in shear from 60 to 70° C, and some decrease at about 75° C. They attributed the initial increase in tenderness (decrease in shear force) to collagen shrinkage, the decrease between 60 and 70° C to hardening of the contractile fibers, and the subsequent increase at 75° C to collagen transformation to gelatin. Rogers and Ritchey (1969) noted that rapid changes occur in the internal temperature range of 68 to 77° C when beef steaks are oven cooked. Jones (1968) noted textural changes in beef due to collagen shrinkage between 50 and 60° C, denaturation of myofibrillar proteins between 60 and 80° C, and solubilization of collagen at 100° C. Webb et al. (1961) stated that their data suggest some change in the proteins between 65.6° and 73.9° C, making the meat (pork roasts) less tender. Laakkonen et al. (1970a) believe that the final temperature of the meat is a critical influence on weight loss and tenderness. They state that heating to temperatures lower than the collagen shrink point produces little tendering effect; if the meat is heated to the collagen shrink point, a major increase in tenderness will occur without a large weight loss; if the meat is heated above the collagen shrink temperature, the muscle fibers also will shrink, resulting in higher weight loss and more tightly packed, less tender tissue. These results lend support to the general concept that changes in the myofibrils tend to harden or toughen, while changes in connective tissue tend to soften or tenderize meat.

Changes in Water-Holding Capacity

Many of the studies of heat-induced changes in WHC have utilized some modification of the pressure method developed for raw meat by Grau and Hamm (1953). Others have used the centrifugal method proposed by Wierbicki et al. (1957). Asselbergs and Whitaker (1961) reported that the free moisture of cooked meat decreased with increasing cooking time. Ritchey and Hostetler (1964) investigated the effect of heating to internal temperatures of 61, 68, 74, and 80° C on free and bound water of beef LD and BF steaks. At the lower temperatures, bound water was being freed more rapidly than the free water was being lost, but overall losses of free and bound water were evident at each rise in temperature. The largest percentage of change occurred between 74 and 80° C. The degree of WHC appeared to influence principally juiciness and the softness component of tenderness, since panel scores indicated that the meat was becoming drier and harder with increasing internal temperature. The LD muscle had a higher percentage of free water at 74 and 80° C, suggesting that it was losing water-binding power more rapidly than BF at the higher temperatures. Ritchey (1965) found that, as the internal temperature increased from 68 to 85° C, the rate of loss of free water exceeded the rate of conversion from the bound to the free state, so the loss of total moisture increased. At the same time, the percent of fat in the lean tissue increased. He found no significant correlation between either bound or free water and scores for juiciness or the six components of tenderness, but softness scores were associated with decreased total water and increased fat content.

Hamm (1962) reported that addition of 2 percent NaCl to ground beef muscle increased the initial WHC of the raw meat and retarded the decrease in WHC on heating at 50° C for 60 minutes. Asselbergs and Whitaker (1961) found that the addition of NaCl and sodium polyphosphate ($Na_5P_3O_{10}$) increased the WHC materially, and produced a "rubbery" texture in the cooked meat. Sherman (1961) studied the effect of NaCl, tetrasodiumpyrophosphate, and commercial polyphosphate on the retention of added fluid in ground pork. He reported that up to 2 percent additive, the fluid retention was maximal at 50° C, then decreased continuously as the temperature increased. With 4 percent additive, the temperature at which fluid release commenced varied with the salt used—above 40° C for NaCl, but 65 to 75° C for phosphates, suggesting stronger water binding with phosphates.

Changes in Proteins

Since many different proteins are present, the specific changes and the temperatures at which they occur vary widely. In addition, Cohen (1966) noted that the amount of protein altered at a given temperature varied with the rate at which this temperature was reached, so the extent of change is a function of both time and temperature. In his study, the more rapidly the muscle was heated, the more protein was insolubilized.

Paul et al. (1966) studied the solubility of proteins of rabbit LD after heating at temperatures from 40 to 80° C and times up to 10 hours. They found significant decreases in solubility of sarcoplasmic and myofibrillar proteins after 2 hours at 40° C, after 30 minutes at 45° C, and by the time the tissue had reached 50° C. Beyond these points, solubility of these proteins tended to decrease with either longer time or higher temperature. At the same time, the amount of denatured protein (soluble in 0.1 N NaOH) was increasing. It was also noted that the pH of the meat increased during heating. Bendall (1964) noted that while most sarcoplasmic and myofibrillar proteins were coagulated by the time the temperature reached 62° C, the nature of the coagulum depended on the pH and the ionic strength of the system. Charpentier (1969) found that the denaturation of the sarcoplasmic proteins of pork muscle was greatest at pH 5.5 to 5.8 and temperatures above 40° C.

Laakkonen et al. (1970b), using polyacrylamide gel electrophoresis on water-soluble proteins of beef muscle, found that the slowest-moving anodic proteins changed most rapidly when heated for various times at 37, 45, and 60° C. The myoglobins and myoalbumins were altered significantly only by holding the meat at 60° C. After 6 hours of heating at 60° C, they reported that there were still uncoagulated water soluble proteins (Laakkonen et al., 1970a).

An easily observed change in one segment of the water-soluble proteins is the color change in the red pigments. Machlik (1965) and Draudt (1969) reported a study of the heat denaturation of myoglobin (Mb) and various Mb derivatives in strips of beef ST, in ground beef, and in pure solutions. The maximum precipitation of pigment occurred in the range of 60 to 67° C. Quinn et al. (1964) found that Mb was not noticeably affected by 5 minutes at 55° C. The stability of Mb to temperatures up to 60° C would account for the persistence of the bright pink color in beef cooked to the rare stage, since denaturation destroys the ability of myoglobin to bind oxygen and form red oxymyoglobin. Davies (1962) reported that the denaturation of Mb appeared to occur in two stages at 65° C—a rapid change in the first 15 minutes, followed by slow loss of Mb up to 60 minutes. Machlik (1965) reported that Mb precipitation was greater in intact than in ground muscle, and that purified Mb in solution was more stable to heat (precipitated at a higher temperature) than was the same derivative in ground beef. She found that the state of oxidation of heme Fe, and the ligand associated with the Fe, influenced the thermal stability of purified Mb and of Mb in ground beef, nitric oxide myoglobin being the least stable, carbon monoxide myoglobin and metmyoglobin the most stable. Draught (1969) concludes that the wide differences in the heat precipitation of the various fresh meat pigments indicates that color is likely to be a poor indicator of the actual temperature attained.

Lawrie (1968) states that the susceptibility of the sarcoplasmic enzymes to heat varies. When isolated, hexokinase is inactivated at about 40° C and creatine kinase at about 60° C, while adenylic kinase has been reported as stable to 100° C. El-Badawi et al. (1964) reported that the zinc-containing proteins of beef LD became insoluble at 64° C. It is not known whether the enzyme inactivation temperatures would be the same or different in the intact tissue. Englehardt's (1946) statement that proteins are more resistant to heat in the muscle structure than when isolated is not borne out by Machlik's (1965) and Draudt's (1969) data on myoglobin.

Cohen (1966) states that rabbit myosin denatures in solution at 41–43° C, and actomysin at 45–53° C. Hunt and Matheson (1958) reported that beef muscle fibers retained their contractility after 1 hour at 55° C, but at 70° the contractility was much reduced, and at 100° it was lost completely.

Much of the early work on amount of connective tissue was based on solubility separations. Ritchey and Cover (1962) compared collagen determinations based on solubility of protein (micro kjeldahl) or on hydroxyproline analysis. They concluded that the hydroxyproline method was preferable, especially in cooked meat, since the heat coagulation of muscle proteins could make them less extractable by NaOH, and give too high results in the micro kjeldahl analysis.

It will be recalled that collagen is considered to be denatured at the shrink temperature, T_s, but that higher temperatures are required to break the molecules apart into the soluble gelatin form (see Chapter 3). Lawrie (1968) gives the T_s of collagen in intact meat as 60° C, and that of extracted collagen as 65° C. Bendall (1964) states that the T_s of beef tendon collagen is 64° C. McClain et al. (1969a) reported that the T_s of intramuscular connective tissue from beef LD ranged from 61.4 to 63° C.

McClain et al. (1969b) found that pork and beef epimysial connective tissue lost weight when heated in distilled water, probably due to extraction of water-soluble ground substance and heat-labile collagen. Their data also suggest that cross-links were broken with increasing length of time at 85° C. Goll et al. (1964) noted that the temperature at which collagen changes to gelatin appears to increase with age, since meat from young animals gave more soluble collagen at a lower temperature than did that of older animals.

Ziemba (1961) reported that the resistance of collagen to heat is different in different muscles, being lower in LD than in ST. Ritchey et al. (1963) reported that beef LD contained less collagen than BF, but the rate of conversion of collagen to gelatin appeared to be the same in the two muscles. They found large variations among individual animals in the collagen content and in the percent converted to gelatin during cooking. Ritchey and Hostetler (1965) list the following average values for collagen in beef steaks cooked to various internal temperatures.

Muscle	Collagen N, as g N/100g total N			
	61° C	68° C	74° C	80° C
LD	1.19	0.92	0.76	0.45
BF	2.39	1.88	1.36	0.93

Iyengar et al. (1965) reported greater conversion of collagen to gelatin when cooking in steam under pressure than when cooking in water. The degradation of collagen to gelatin, involving rupture of the cross-links holding the molecules together into fibrils and fibers, would be expected to contribute to softening or tendering of the meat.

Elastin is apparently quite resistant to heat change in the temperatures normally used for cooking meat (Lawrie, 1968). Bendall (1964) points out that elastin polypeptide chains are already randomly oriented and so cannot be heat denatured even at 100° C. Winegarden et al. (1952) found that connective-tissue strips decreased in the force required to shear; in weight; and in length and width, and increased in thickness during heating in water. The changes were greatest in the tissue containing the most collagen, and least in that containing the most elastin, suggesting that the elastin does change, but much less than does the collagen.

Changes in Microscopic Appearance

The changes that occur in microscopic appearance of meat in heating follow a general pattern, but the extent of the changes varies with time, temperature, muscle, and species.

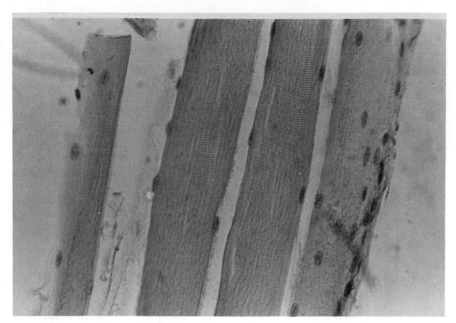

FIGURE 16. Rabbit psoas major muscle, cooked. Note decrease in longitudinal separation of fibrils, in width of fibers, and in length of A and I bands, as compared to Figure 13. Magnification 275x.

As the muscle sample is heated, the contractile fibers shrink in length and in width and the sarcomeres become shorter (Paul, 1963, 1965, unpublished data). An example of this can be seen by comparing Figures 13 and 16. Giles (1968) observed at the electron-microscope level that some of the fine structure of the sarcomere was destroyed at temperatures between 50 and 60° C; at 70° C for 15 minutes, the sarcomeres shrank to 85 percent of their initial length, and had decreased to 60 percent of the original length when the temperature reached 100° C. Hostetler and Landmann (1968) reported that decreases in width of the muscle fibers started soon after heating began, were more rapid at 45° C, and were essentially complete at 62° C. Shrinkage in length began at about 55° C, was marked between 55 and 65° C, and continued slowly as the temperature increased to 80° C. They stated that the width changes appeared to be associated with loss of WHC. The decrease in length, along with the loss of birefringence, which occurred gradually with heating and became complete in the 55–65° C range, seemed to be more closely related to curves of loss of acidic groups on heating given by Hamm and Deatherage (1960). So Hostetler and

FIGURE 17. Rabbit LD, cooked. Shows cracks and breaks in fibers, appearing to occur in the I bands. Magnification 275x.

Landmann theorized that the decrease in width and loss of WHC are related to the early stages of heat denaturation involving unfolding of peptide chains with only small disturbances of the arrangement of the myofilaments, while the decrease in length and loss of birefringence are associated with coagulation and formation of stable cross-links in the myofibrillar and sarcoplasmic proteins. However, they suggest that caution be used in applying these results on free-floating fibers to specific details of heat effects in larger muscle masses.

Another change that can be observed in muscle fibers is the development of cracks and breaks in the fibers, these appearing to occur in the I band, as shown in Figure 17. Giles (1968) noted that on heating beef fillet steak, the myosin filaments of the A band coagulated to a solid mass, while the actin filaments in the I band broke, producing gaps in the sarcomere structure.

In some cases, the fibrils disintegrate, leaving a granular residue within the muscle envelope. This is illustrated in Figure 18. Doty and Pierce (1961) commented on the "erosion" of the muscle fibers of beef

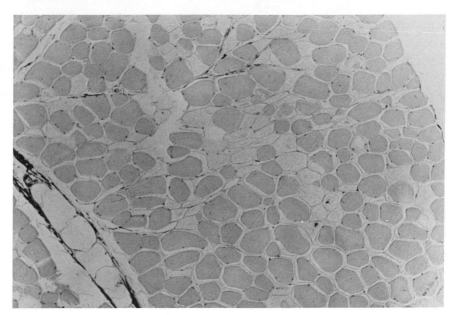

FIGURE 18. Beef BF, heated 45 minutes at 67° C. Note partial to complete granulation of contractile fibers but relative intactness of endomysial reticulum. Magnification 70x.

steaks on heating. Paul (1963, 1965, unpublished data) found that this erosion or granulation appeared much more in beef BF and SM than in beef LD, ST, deep pectoral, or any of the rabbit muscles studied. The tendency of the beef BF muscle to granulate when the LD does not may be related to the general finding of Cover's group that the LD continues to harden as the internal temperature is increased, but the BF becomes more tender and its fibers become mealy and easily fragmented on chewing.

As collagenous tissue is heated, the color taken up from histological stains is altered. Continued heating degrades the collagen from fibrous to granular form (Fig. 19). This has been observed in beef and in rabbit muscle (Paul, 1963, 1965). In the rabbit some of the collagen lost even the granular appearance, becoming an amorphous mass. Giles (1968) noted that some of the beef collagen fibrils were denatured at 70° C, and all were denatured after 100 minutes at 80° C. Buck and Black (1968) found more perimysial connective tissue denaturation in stretched muscle samples than in unstretched controls.

Crow et al. (1967) reported a decrease, due to cooking, in the intactness of the endomysial reticulum in beef LD samples having a low

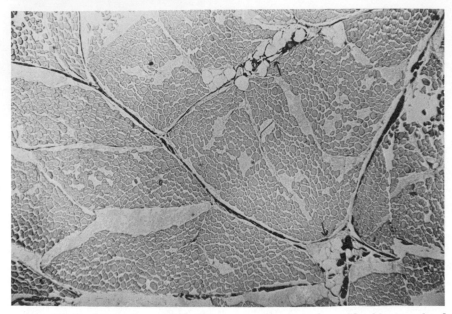

FIGURE 19. Beef trapezius, cooked. Shows some fibrous and considerable granulated perimysial connective tissue, also two areas of empty fat cells (arrows). Magnification 17x.

shear force, but no change in samples having a higher shear. Some evidence of granulation of endomysial tissue was noted in rabbit muscles (Paul, 1965). In beef deep pectoral, the reticulum showed swelling and separation of layers at 75° C (Figure 20) and considerable disintegration after 4 hours at 90° C (Paul, unpublished data). Crow et al. (1967) commented that reticular fibers isolated from liver or spleen could be boiled for one hour without being gelatinized.

When meat is heated, much of the neutral fat is melted out of the fat cells. Wang et al. (1954) noted that the fat from the intramuscular deposits tends to flow in droplets along the path of the heat-degraded collagenous fibers. They stated that the extent of dispersion of fat appeared to be influenced by the amount of fat freed from the fat cells, the muscle being used, the extent of aging of the meat, and probably the time and temperature of cooking. This flow of fat would increase the distribution of fat throughout the lean tissue, and may be one factor contributing to the apparent relation between marbling and juiciness.

Changes in Composition

Since meat cuts change in water and fat content during cooking, it is usually necessary to make fat comparisons on the dry-weight basis

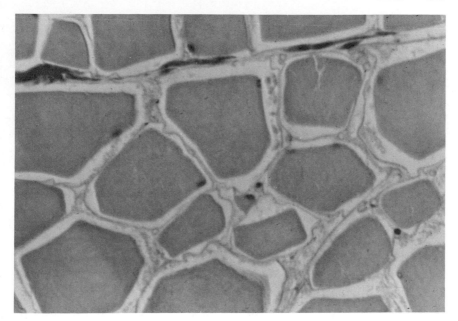

FIGURE 20. Beef deep pectoral, heated to 75° C. Note swelling and separation of endomysial reticulum and some granulation. Magnification 275x.

and nitrogen comparisons on the dry, fat-free basis. Also, in some cooking methods, water and/or fat is added to the meat.

The water content of meat decreases when the meat is cooked. The alteration in the muscle proteins frees water previously immobilized in the protein structures. The amount of this freed water that is lost from the meat depends on the method of cooking, especially on the rate of temperature rise and the internal temperature to which the meat is heated. Some average figures for beef cuts are given in Table 5.

The data in Table 5 also illustrate the fact that cooking often causes an increase in the amount of ether extractable material in the lean portion over that found in raw meat, on the dry basis. This increase in fat in the lean meat has been reported by a number of workers, using a variety of types of meat and methods of cooking. However, Lowe and Kastelic (1961) reported no significant difference between raw and cooked samples, and Bramblett et al. (1959) reported increased fat content in some cooked samples but decreased amounts in others.

Several theories have been advanced to account for this increase in fat in the lean tissue on cooking. It has been suggested that it might be due to infiltration of melted fat from the external fat covering. Weir et al. (1962) reported that removal of the external fat from pork chops

TABLE 5. Average Figures for Percent Moisture and Percent Ether Extract of Raw and Cooked Beef

Cut	Cooking Method	Internal Temperature °C	Percent Moisture		Percent Ether Extract		Source of Data
			Raw	Cooked	Raw	Cooked	
LD	roasted, 149° C oven	70	58.5–69.3	54.4–63.3	8.8–22.2	8.6–19.8	Meyer et al. (1969)
SM	braised	99	72.5–73.9	57.8–58.2	2.0– 2.7	3.4– 4.2	Meyer et al. (1969)
ST	roasted, 149° C oven	60	73.0–74.6	68.2–70.0	7.0–12.7	8.4–14.5	Paul (1962)
ST,		77		63.5–66.6		8.6–14.9	Paul (1962)
lean	roasted, 163° C oven	58	73.9	66.8–67.8	14.5–15.0	19.7–20.1	Woolsey and Paul
only	roasted, 218° C oven	58	73.9	66.1–67.2	13.5–14.7	16.6–18.0	(1969a)

before cooking gave cooked lean with a fat content close to that of the raw. However, Woolsey and Paul (1969a) found that roasted beef ST still showed an increase in fat in the lean in samples where the external fat had been removed before cooking. Another theory is that the heat alteration of the muscle proteins improves the extractability of the fat. But Woolsey and Paul (1969a) reported that use of a polar fat solvent, which would be expected to remove fat from protein complexes in the raw tissue, did not make a significant difference in the amount of fat extracted over that determined by ether extraction.

Campbell and Turkki (1967) reported that the phospholipids were higher in cooked than in raw ground beef or pork. They found no significant changes due to cooking in the fatty acid distribution except that cooking pork increased the linoleate content of the phospholipid fraction. Giam and Dugan (1965) reported essentially no change in fatty acid composition attributable to cooking when beef, pork, and lamb were cooked in boiling water. Chung et al. (1966) reported changes in the fatty acid composition of beefsteaks and pork chops when they were deep-fat fried, the specific changes varying with the fatty acid composition of the frying oil used.

Changes in the nitrogen content of meat during cooking are usually relatively small. Most of the nitrogen that is lost is found in the drippings with dry atmosphere methods, and in the cooking liquid in moist atmosphere methods. Doty and Pierce (1961) reported that 2.0 to 2.5 percent of the total nitrogen was found in the drippings from broiled beefsteaks, mostly in nonprotein nitrogen compounds including some free amino acids. Toepfer et al. (1955) found mostly small amounts of nitrogen in the drippings from a variety of beef cuts.

Methods of Heating

Traditional methods of meat cookery include roasting, broiling (grilling), braising, and stewing. Experimental studies to explore and standardize many details of these methods were summarized by Committee on Preparation Factors (1942). More recently, the availability of new equipment has led to studies utilizing microwave ovens, forced convection ovens, and deep-fat fryers. Also, the need for more exact time and temperature control in detailed studies of chemical and physical changes induced by heat has fostered the development of a variety of techniques for heating small pieces of muscle in thermostatically controlled waterbaths. A number of the techniques that have been employed in heating meat are listed in Table 6.

TABLE 6. Some of the Cuts, Cooking Methods, and Temperatures Used in Meat Research Studies

Source of Heat	Technique	Reference
Conventional oven	1- to 2-pound beef roasts, 300° F oven to 55, 70, 85° C internal	Visser et al. (1960)
	Beef roasts at 125° or 225° C to well done	Cover (1937)
	Beef rib roasts, 300, 350, 400° F oven, 143, 159, 176° F internal	Harries et al. (1963)
	Blade and rump roasts, 225° and 325° F oven to 160° F internal	Nielsen and Hall (1965)
	Beef SM 3 inches thick, 300° F oven, LD 1½ inches thick, 350° F oven, to 176° F internal	Hood et al. (1955)
	Beef ST and BF roasts, 163° C oven to 63° C internal	Paul et al. (1952)
	Beef ST, 163°, 218° C oven, to 58° C internal	Woolsey and Paul (1969a)
	Pork roasts at 325° F to 185 ° F internal	Batcher et al. (1962)
	Pork roasts, 300, 325, 350° F oven, to 120, 125, 130, 135, 140, 145, 150, 160° F internal	Carlin et al. (1969)
	Pork rib and loin roasts, 300, 325, 350, 375° F oven, 170, 185° F internal	Carlin et al. (1965)
	Pork loin roasts, 300, 325, 350, 375, 400° F oven, to 170, 185° F internal	Weir et al. (1963)
	Boned and rolled lamb leg, to about 180° F internal	Headley and Jacobson (1960)
	1-inch steaks from LD, psoas major, quadriceps femoris, at 177° C for varying lengths of time	Lewis et al. (1967)

TABLE 6. (*Continued*)

Source of Heat	Technique	Reference
	"oven broiling"—350° F oven, foil-lined pan, preheated, 1-inch steaks to internal temperature of 142 or 176° F	Cover and Hostetler (1960)
	1-inch beef round steaks at 232° C to 71° C internal; on racks 4 inches above shallow pan	Paul et al. (1956)
	1-inch beef round steaks, 350° F oven for 20, 23, 26, 29 minutes (rare to medium)	Rogers and Ritchey (1969)
	Pork chops, 350° F oven, to 185° F internal	Jacobson et al. (1962)
	Ground beef loaves, 200, 450° F oven	Baity et al. (1969)
	Pork sausage, 400° F oven, 30 minutes	March et al. (1960)
Aluminum foil wrap, conventional oven	Beef roast, foil wrapped, 149° C oven to 77° C internal	Hood (1960)
	1- to 6-pound round roasts, foil wrapped, 30 hours in 63° C oven, 18 hours in 68° C oven	Bramblett et al. (1959)
	Ground beef loaves, loosely or tightly wrapped in foil, 200, 450° F oven	Baity et al. (1969)
	Beef round muscles, foil wrapped, 155, 200° F oven, to 149° F internal	Bramblett and Vail (1964)
Rotary hearth oven	Pork loin roasts, 350° F oven to 167° F internal	Searcy et al. (1969)
Forced convection oven	Ground meat cylinders, at 121° C, with pan of hot water on lower shelf, to 80° C internal temperature	Irmiter et al. (1967)
	Beef sirloin butts, 200, 300° F oven, to 165° F internal	Davenport and Meyer (1970)

TABLE 6. *(Continued)*

Source of Heat	Technique	Reference
Microwave oven	1¼-inch LD and SM steaks to 70° C, with browning unit on for last 3 minutes	Law et al. (1967)
	2-inch pork loin roasts, 3¼ minutes	Moore et al. (1966)
	Top round roasts to 176° F	Marshall (1960)
	Boned and rolled lamb legs, to about 180° F internal	Headley and Jacobson (1960)
	Beef, veal, pork; infra red treatment after microwave cooking, to brown surface	Áldor (1963)
Broiler	Beef at approximately 350° F to 176° F internal	Hood et al. (1955)
	1-inch beef steaks, to 71° C internal	Dryden et al. (1969)
	1¼-inch LD steaks broiled at 149° C to 70° C, turned at 45° C	Law et al. (1967)
	1-inch beef steaks, LD, BF, to 61, 68, 74, 80° C	Ritchey and Hostetler (1965)
	¾-inch beef LD, BF, broiled to well done by color	Cover and Smith (1956)
	½-inch beef rib steaks and pork chops, at 500° F for 5 minutes on each side	Chung et al. (1966)
	½- to 1½-inch thick pork chops, air temperature at upper meat surface, 345° F, to 155, 170, 185° F internal	Goertz et al. (1966)
	Pork chops at 275, 350, 425° F to 185° F internal	Weir et al. (1962)
Combinations	Boneless beef chuck rolls, roast to 43° C internal, refrigerate overnight, slice and broil for serving	Baldwin and Korschgen (1968)
	Round steak, prebrown on surface unit, finish in 500° F oven to 155° F internal	Rodgers et al. (1963)

TABLE 6. *(Continued)*

Source of Heat	Technique	Reference
Pan frying or broiling	Pork slices, 5–7 minutes each side	Penny et al. (1964)
	Pork sausage, pan broil at medium heat 20 minutes	March et al. (1964)
Deep-fat frying	Small cubes of beef, at 121.1° C to 76.7° C internal temperature	Ramsbottom et al. (1945)
	1-inch beef ST and BF slices, at 147° C to 63° C internal	Paul et al. (1952)
	Beef LD strips, at 135° C to 65.5° C internal	Buck and Black (1968)
	1- to 2-pound beef roasts, 100° C fat to 45, 65, 85° C internal	Visser et al. (1960)
	3.2 cm thick LD steaks, 135° C fat to 70° C	Crow et al. (1967)
	$\frac{1}{2}$-inch beef rib steaks and pork chops, 375° F for 10 minutes	Chung et al. (1966)
	Pork chops, 325° F fat to 185° F internal	Jacobson et al. (1962)
Water (liquid or steam)	Blade roasts braised until "fork tender"	Nielsen and Hall (1965)
	1-inch beef LD, BF, braised to 85°, 100° C plus 25 minutes	Cover et al. (1957)
	$\frac{1}{2}$- to $1\frac{1}{2}$-inch thick pork chops, braised in 350, 400° F oven, to 170, 185° F; skillet braised to 155, 170, 185, 185° F plus 15–20 minutes	Goertz et al. (1966)
	Pork slices casseroled (braised) in 185° C oven for $1\frac{1}{2}$ hours	Penny et al. (1964)
	Beef SM, BF steaks, $1\frac{1}{2}$ inches thick, braised to 80° C internal by (a) 10 pounds pressure, (b) 15 pounds pressure, (c) covered pan in 300° F oven; braised to 112.2° C at 15 pounds pressure	Clark et al. (1955)

TABLE 6.   (*Continued*)

Source of Heat	Reference	Technique
	Beef, veal, pork, conventional stewing for 30–60 minutes	Áldor (1963)
Water bath	Samples in plastic bags, evacuated and sealed, heated at 60, 64, 68 or 72° C	Thomas et al. (1966)
	150 g samples in plastic bags at 50, 60, 80° C for 1 hour, 100° C for 1½ hours	Jones (1968)
	2.5 cm slices, 100–130 g, sealed under vacuum in plastic pouches, heated for varying lengths of time at several temperatures	Laakkonen et al. (1970a)
	5.1 cm thick slices beef LD, plastic bags evacuated and sealed, at 60, 64, 68, 72° C, to 1° less than bath temperature plus 12 minutes holding at that temperature	Howard and Judge (1968)
	Pork LD, in steel tubes ⅞ inch internal diameter, 8 inches long, at 140, 150, 160, 180, 190, 200, 210° F, for several hours	Tuomy and Lechnir (1964)
Microscope hot stage	Fibers heated under microscope for observation of changes in length and width	Hostetler and Landmann (1968)

Dry or Moist

Cooking methods for meat are often designated as dry or moist. These terms refer to the atmosphere surrounding the meat, rather than to the meat itself. So the influence is usually on the rate at which heat energy is supplied to the external surface, since water vapor is a more efficient conductor of heat than is dry air. Frying in deep fat is literally a dry-heat method, since the meat is surrounded by liquid fat rather than moisture vapor. But liquid fat is a much better heat conductor than dry air, so again heat energy is supplied more rapidly to the external surface of the meat than in air. The microwave oven is another case of dry heat but very rapid transmission of energy.

Moist and dry methods also differ in the temperature to which the external surface of the meat is exposed. In water vapor, this temperature will not exceed 100° C unless the system is under pressure. With ovens or deep fat, the external surface temperature may be considerably above 100° C. However, again the microwave oven is an exception, since the air in such an oven is not heated. The energy is supplied to the meat as electromagnetic waves, and is converted to heat within the meat itself.

By long custom, dry-heat methods have been recommended for cuts expected to be tender, and moist heat for those expected to be tough. Cuts such as roasts or steaks from the rib, loin, or sirloin; lamb or pork legs; pork, lamb, or veal chops; and ground meat were classed as tender. Other cuts were considered to be less tender because of larger amounts of connective tissue, therefore required long slow cooking in a moist atmosphere to tenderize the meat by degradation of the collagenous tissue. However, changes in the methods of producing meat and in consumer preferences suggest that many of the cuts formerly recommended for moist-heat cooking may be acceptable when cooked by dry heat. Dawson et al. (1959) summarized a number of studies showing such results. Nielsen and Hall (1965) found that beef blade and rump roasts roasted at 225 or 325° F to an internal temperature of 160° F were as tender as, and more juicy than, similar cuts braised until fork-tender.

Cover and co-workers (see for example, Cover and Hostetler, 1960) have shown that the desirability of moist or dry heat varies with the muscle being considered, since beef LD becomes dryer and harder with more extended cooking, while BF becomes increasingly tender.

Roasting

Roasting is a dry-heat method in which the meat is placed on a rack in an uncovered pan and cooked in an oven to the desired stage of doneness. The principal form of energy transmission is by air convection, with minor amounts coming by radiation and by conduction through the metal rack.

A variety of oven temperatures has been used experimentally (see Table 6). The results vary with species, cut, and oven temperature. Temperatures from 300 to 400° F are most frequently recommended for home use. Within this range, Harries et al. (1963) selected 300° F as the preferable temperature for roasting beef ribs for panel evaluation, as the meat was more tender and juicy, although slightly less flavorful, than when roasted at 350 or 400° F. Paul (class data, unpublished) used 400 g of lean ground beef shaped into 3 x 3 x 3-inch cubes as roasts.

Increasing the oven temperature, through the range of 300 to 450° F, decreased the cooking time, increased the cooking losses, and decreased the uniformity of doneness and the amount of the interior remaining pink-colored at the rare stage. Carlin et al. (1965) recommended 325 or 350° F for pork rib or loin roasts, since 300° F required a longer cooking time, and 375° F gave an overcooked appearance to the roasts, with more charring and spattering of fat. All four oven temperatures gave equivalent results for palatability.

Cover (1937) found that beef roasted at 125 or 225° C was more tender at the lower temperature if the roasting time differential was three or more hours, but the longer time increased cooking losses and the meat was dry. Marshall et al. (1960) reported that cooking losses decreased with increasing oven temperature in the range of 200 to 250° F.

Rotary-hearth or forced-convection ovens have been used to increase the temperature uniformity within the oven. Recent studies using these include Searcy et al. (1969) for the rotary hearth oven and Irmiter et al. (1967), Funk et al. (1968), and Davenport and Meyer (1970) for the forced-convection oven. Funk et al. (1966) studied forced-convection roasting of beef loin cuts and found that air circulation shortened the cooking time, increased losses, and decreased flavor and tenderness scores.

Microwave (Electronic) Cooking

Microwave ovens have a dry atmosphere, but the principle of heating is entirely different from that of hot-air ovens. The energy is supplied to the food not as heat, but as high-frequency electromagnetic waves. Materials such as food will absorb this energy. The alternating electric field causes oscillation of the polar molecules of the food, converting the electrical energy into molecular motion and thereby heating the food. These waves can penetrate about two inches, so, if the food mass is not too thick, it will heat relatively uniformly throughout.

Studies on cooking meat in a microwave oven indicate that while the cooking time is much shorter than in a conventional oven, the cooking losses are greater, principally due to greater evaporation losses (Pollak and Foin, 1960; Headley and Jacobson, 1960; and Marshall, 1960) or fat losses (Áldor, 1963). Law et al. (1967) found that cooking losses of beef loin and top-round steaks increased in the following order: conventional roasting < microwave cooking < conventional broiling. Marshall (1960) reported that beef top-round roasts received higher scores for appearance, juiciness, tenderness, and flavor when cooked in a conventional oven than when cooked in an electronic oven. Headley and Jacobson (1960) found that lamb legs did not differ in tenderness, but the meat cooked in the electronic oven appeared more well done and received lower scores for juiciness and flavor. They suggested that the flavor difference might be due to the greater degree of browning in the conventional oven. Áldor (1963) and Law et al. (1967) used infrared irradiation (browning unit) at the end of electronic cooking to increase the surface brownness.

Decareau (1967) pointed out that conventional cooking standards and techniques are not always applicable to microwave cooking. Although the meat heats throughout instead of from the surface inward, a temperature gradient does exist within the piece being cooked, and the thicker the product, the steeper the gradient. So a seven-rib beef roast should be removed from the electronic oven at a center temperature of around 80° F. After the roast is allowed to stand for approximately 45 minutes at room temperature, a temperature in the range of 135 to 145° F will be reached throughout the meat.

Broiling

Broiling involves heating meat primarily by radiant energy from the heat source, with minor amounts from air convection and conduction through the metal rack or other support. This method is usually used with relatively thin cuts of meat, since thick cuts are apt to be overcooked on the surface before the interior reaches the desired stage. This is a rapid method of cooking meat, but the cooking temperature is difficult to control experimentally, since the radiation intensity varies within and among units, and the air temperature of the oven does not reflect the true energy output of the unit. Cover and Hostetler (1960) outline an oven-heating or oven-broiling technique that utilizes roasting of thin cuts in a preheated pan lined with bright aluminum foil. Paul et al. (1956) modified this method to eliminate turning the meat during cooking by using racks with four-inch legs. The latter arrangement is illustrated in Figure 21.

Delayed Cooking Methods

Baldwin and Korschgen (1968) describe the "roasteak" method in which large boneless cuts of beef are roasted at 149° C to an internal temperature of 43° C, chilled overnight, and then sliced and broiled just before serving. Rodgers et al. (1964) compared this method with one that involved prebrowning the meat on a surface unit, then cooking in a 500° F oven (Rodgers et al., 1963), and found that the roasteak samples scored higher for tenderness and general acceptability.

Gaines et al. (1966) reported on delayed-service cookery of top-

FIGURE 21. Use of racks with four-inch legs over shallow, foil-lined pan, for oven broiling of beef steaks. (Univ. of Nebraska photograph)

round beef roasts. All were seared for 1 hour at 425° F, then finished at (a) 300° F, (b) 140° F for 24 hours, or (c) 158° F for 16 hours. The longer cooking periods gave more evaporation, less drip, and less tender meat, but the cuts cooked by the three methods did not reach the same internal temperature [121.6° F for (b), 131° F for (c), and 145.7° F for (a)].

Deep-Fat Frying

Heat transfer is by conduction from the hot fat to the surface of the meat. The rate of heat transfer between fat and meat is much more rapid than the rate of transfer within the meat. So the fat temperature must be adjusted to the thickness of the meat, to avoid formation of a hard crust of overcooked meat at the surface. Paul et al. (1952) used fat at 147° C for beef ST and BF steaks cut 1 inch thick. Visser et al. (1960) used 100° and 110° C for roasts weighing 1 to 2 pounds. Crow et al. (1967) cooked 3.2-cm-thick LD steaks in deep fat at 135° C, and Chung et al. (1966) used 190° C fat for $\frac{1}{2}$-inch-thick beef rib steaks and pork chops.

Braising

For braising, meat cuts are often browned on a surface unit, then covered and cooked at a low temperature until tender. Liquid may or may not be added after browning. The cooking may be completed either on a surface burner or in an oven. Heat transfer is by convection from the moist atmosphere in the pan, and by conduction from the pan surface and/or rack.

This method allows many variations. Paul and Bean (1956) explored a number of these, using 1 inch steaks from beef round muscles. They recommended the following procedure.

1. Brown the steak at 475° F for one minute on each side, using a heavy iron skillet on a thermostatically-controlled surface burner.
2. Place a rack with $\frac{1}{2}$-inch legs under the steak.
3. Add 50 ml water, cover the pan, and place in an oven preheated to 250° F.
4. Cook $\frac{1}{2}$ hour longer than required to bring the internal temperature of the steak to 98° C.

Rogers (1969) recommends omitting the browning step, due to the difficulty of regulating the browning temperature and of browning the meat evenly on all sides.

Bowers and Goertz (1966) explored skillet- and oven-braising of pork chops, using various internal temperatures, and oven temperatures of 350 and 400° F. They found that adding water during skillet-braising had little effect on eating quality, cooking loss or cooking time, but decreased the brownness of the cooked chops.

Because the braising method is primarily one using a water-vapor-saturated atmosphere for cooking the meat, heat is transferred more rapidly to the surface of the meat than in a dry atmosphere. So the meat heats through quite rapidly. The long holding at high temperature degrades the collagenous connective tissue, softening it, and in some muscles also increases the friability of the contractile fibers.

The temperature of the meat does not rise above the boiling point of water unless a closed system under pressure is used. Clark et al. (1955) compared oven and pressure braising and found that $1\frac{1}{2}$-inch beef SM and BF steaks required longer to cook but had similar cooking losses and palatability scores when braised to 80° C in a 300° F oven than when cooked under 10 or 15 pounds of steam pressure. Griswold (1955) concluded that braising in a covered pan in the oven to an internal temperature of 85° C yielded more palatable meat than braising to the same internal temperature under 5, 10, or 15 pounds of pressure.

Stewing

Stewing is usually applied to meat cut into small units. The meat may or may not be prebrowned. It is covered with liquid and cooked slowly for an extended time until tender. It has been suggested that the use of acid liquid such as tomato juice will increase the tenderness of the meat. Subjective and objective tests, however, have indicated that the paired control without acid is usually as tender as the meat to which the acid has been added. In an ordinary cooking period there is not sufficient time for the acid to penetrate into the meat and bring about any appreciable tenderizing effect. Among the factors affecting the time for the penetration of these substances into the meat are (a) the size of the piece of meat, (b) the degree of post-mortem changes in the meat, and (c) the size of the molecule. Griswold (1955) reported that the use of a 1:1 mixture of vinegar and water, with sugar added, as the cooking fluid did not increase the tenderness, and decreased the acceptability of the meat.

Beef broth from a previous cooking as well as 0.2 M or 0.4 M concentrations of combined NaH_2PO_4 and Na_2HPO_4 have been used for cooking beef cubes in several short studies. The tenderizing results depended partly on the size of the beef cubes. There was no difference in tenderness between control and treated samples of large cubes, whereas the treated samples of small cubes were more tender than the controls.

Miller and Harrison (1965) investigated the use of sodium hexametaphosphate as a marinade for LD steaks prior to broiling. They found this treatment of little value in improving the eating quality of the beef.

Foil Wrapping

The use of heavy-duty foil wrap allows the meat to cook in a moist atmosphere. Hood (1960) compared beef roasts cooked in an oven at 149° C to an internal temperature of 77° C, with and without a tight foil wrap. The foil-wrapped roasts had higher cooking losses and were less juicy, less tender, and less satisfactory in flavor.

Higher oven temperatures are often recommended for cooking foil-wrapped meat as compared to comparable unwrapped cuts, since foil is considered to have an insulating effect. Baity et al. (1969) studied the effect of loose and tight wraps on ground beef loaves cooked in ovens at 200° and 450° F. At the low oven temperature, the loose foil wrap had an insulating effect, but tight wrapping did not increase, and in some cases decreased, the cooking time over that for unwrapped loaves. At the high oven temperature, the foil appeared to act as a radiant heat shield and increased the cooking time over that for the unwrapped.

Small Samples

In most methods of meat cookery, different parts of the same cut will experience different degrees of heating. Figure 22 shows time-temperature curves obtained from different positions in a lamb leg

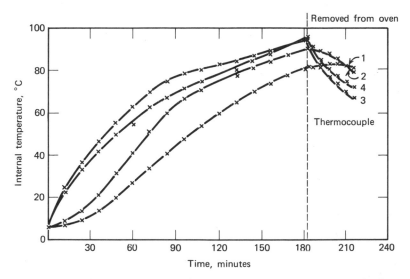

FIGURE 22. Internal temperature, lamb leg, 350° F oven. Thermocouple location: 1 = center of SM, thickest part of leg; 2 = gastrocnemius, thick part of posterior leg; 3 = just under fat cover, anterior portion of leg; and 4 = center of upper leg against bone.

during roasting in a 350° F oven. For more precise measurement of changes due to heating, a number of studies have used small samples. These are usually taken from identified muscles and cut to a specific size with attention to the direction of the muscle fibers. They are placed in glass or metal tubes or in plastic bags, and are heated in a water bath. Changes may be followed during the time required for the temperature of the sample to come up to that of the water bath, or during various periods of holding after the sample attains water-bath temperature, or both.

Hostetler and Landmann (1968) heated isolated muscle fibers on a hot stage under a microscope, so that changes in size and appearance of muscle fibers could be observed. They followed both the changes occurring during heating to 80° C, and during various periods of holding at temperatures ranging from 37 to 77° C.

Heating Endpoint

Following the work of Sprague and Grindley (1907), most studies have utilized temperature at the center of the thickest part of the lean tissue as the endpoint for heating. This may be measured by thermometer or by thermocouple. Even this method does not assure uniform results from one sample to the next. It is frequently difficult to determine the correct location for the thermometer bulb or thermocouple junction so that it will be in the center of the largest lean mass, and not against a fatty deposit or connective tissue. Then, the swelling and contraction of the meat during heating may displace the temperature-sensing element. So it is advisable to check this position during the heating and especially when it appears that the desired endpoint has been reached. Also, when it is desired to investigate the effect of small temperature intervals, the error in the measuring device may be nearly as large as the experimental variable.

Time-Temperature Combination

The stage of doneness at a given internal temperature will vary with the time required to reach that temperature, since one of the major changes in the meat is denaturation of the proteins. Baity et al. (1969), using ground beef loaves, found that a comparable stage of doneness was reached at 164° F internal temperature in a 200° F oven, but at 180° F internal in a 450° F oven, due to the much longer cooking time required at 200° F. Cover and Hostetler (1960) reported that 1-inch steaks were well done at an internal temperature of 176° F when oven-cooked, but at 185° F were medium rare when braised. Paul (class data) compared the muscles of lamb legs when roasted as the intact leg or separated into muscles and the muscles roasted individually. Some typical averages from these experiments are shown in Table 7. Direct comparison could be made between SM muscles cooked in the intact leg or separately, since the endpoint for the whole leg was measured at the center of this muscle. SM from the intact leg was well done, gray-brown throughout, and very tender but somewhat dry. SM cooked separately was medium, still had some pink color in the meat and juice, and was tender and juicy.

TABLE 7.   Average Cooking Time and Losses for Roasting Lamb[a]

Cut	Raw Weight (g)	Cooking Time (Minutes)	Temperature Rise After Cooking (°C)	Cooking Losses (Percent)		
				Total	Drip	Evapo-ration
Intact leg	3515.5	196.5	2.0	29.5	8.3	21.2
Rectus femoris-Vasti	495.0	98.5	1.0	27.3	3.8	23.5
Ad	158.0	45.0	0	23.2	1.1	22.1
Gluteus medius	264.4	35.0	0	17.1	3.2	13.9
BF	427.1	59.0	0.5	28.6	9.1	19.5
SM	346.9	65.0	0	23.2	4.1	19.1
ST	135.1	37.0	0	22.2	8.1	14.1
Castrocnemius	165.0	52.0	0	19.5	3.4	16.1

[a] Intact leg, separate leg muscles; oven temperature 350° F; internal temperature endpoint, 82° C.

Temperature Rise After Cooking

Another source of variation in the use of internal temperature as the cooking endpoint is the increase in temperature that may occur after the meat is removed from the cooking medium. This is most apt to occur with larger pieces of meat that have been cooked by methods that bring the surface of the meat to a considerably higher temperature than that of the interior, so that there is a marked temperature differential between the exterior and the interior. Figure 23 shows the post-heating temperature rise in roasted ground beef loaves. The data in Table 7 shows that the temperature rose in the intact lamb leg and in the two largest individual muscles, but not in the smaller muscles, after removal from the oven. Visser et al. (1960) found it necessary to lower the oil temperature and the endpoint temperatures to obtain the desired stages of doneness in thick pieces of beef cooked in deep fat. Using fat at 100° ± 4° C, they found a temperature rise of about 10° C in meat cooked to 45° C, about 5° C in that cooked to 65° C, and only a negligible rise in meat cooked to 85° C internal temperature.

No definite relation has been established between composition of the meat and the extent of the inner temperature rise after cooking. Composition appears to affect the duration of the temperature rise more

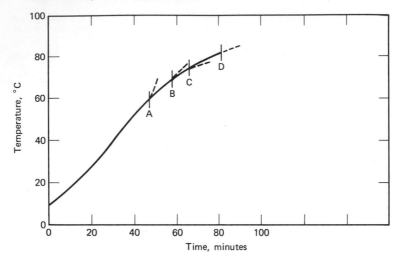

FIGURE 23. 400 g lean ground beef, 3 × 3 × 3 in. cube, roasted at 350° F. A = removed at 60° C internal temperature; B = removed at 68° C; C = removed at 75° C; and D = removed at 82° C. Solid lines = temperature during roasting; dotted lines = temperature rise after removal from oven.

than the extent. Meat containing a great deal of fat, and meat that has a thick layer of fat on the surface, $\frac{3}{4}$–1 inch or more, may take as long as 1 to $1\frac{1}{2}$ hours to reach its maximum inner temperature after the cooking process is stopped, whereas a lean roast of the same shape, and cooked under the same conditions, may take only 12 to 30 minutes.

Time Endpoints

Several studies report cooking small cuts of meat for a constant length of time. Rogers and Ritchey (1969) cooked 1-inch steaks in a 350° F oven for 20, 23, 26, or 29 minutes. They reported the following endpoint temperatures.

Time, Minutes	Average Temperature, °C
20	68.00 ± 4.45
23	73.80 ± 5.40
26	77.05 ± 4.10
29	78.30 ± 4.20

These indicate a range of about 10° C in the endpoint temperature obtained during a specific heating time. Paul et al. (1970) reported a ±10° C range of internal temperatures when 1-inch beef rib steaks were

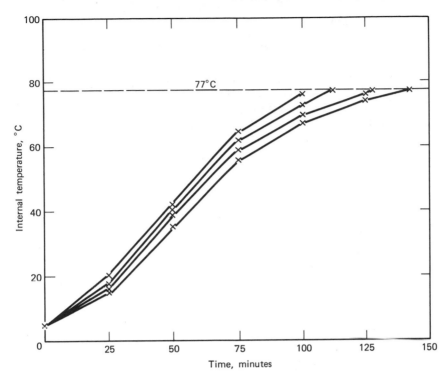

FIGURE 24. Time-temperature curves for internal temperature of small beef ST roasts in a 350° F oven.

cooked in a 400° F oven. Figure 24 shows the time-temperature curves for small roasts cut from a pair of beef ST muscles, roasted at 350° F to 77° C internal temperature. The time required to reach the same internal endpoint varied from 100 to 142.5 minutes. If all four roasts had been removed from the oven when the first one reached 77° C, the internal temperatures of the other three would have been 67, 70, and 73° C.

Directions for cooking often state the time of cooking in terms of minutes per pound. At best this can serve only as a guide, because the following factors affect the time required to cook the meat: (a) the method of cooking; (b) the cooking temperature; (c) the weight, surface area, and shortest distance to the center of the thickest portion of the meat; (d) the stage to which the meat is cooked—rare or well done; (e) the composition of the meat; (f) the degree of post-mortem changes; and (g) the initial temperature of the meat.

Stages of Doneness

The stage of doneness desired and the endpoint selected vary with the type and cut of meat and with the cooking method. In addition, as has been discussed, the degree of doneness at a given heating endpoint may vary with the method of cooking, especially the length of time required and the extent of the interior temperature rise after heating has been terminated.

Beef

Beef may be eaten at any stage from very rare to very well done, depending on the preference of the consumer. The most obvious change is that of internal color, which is dependent on the degree of denaturation and coagulation of the muscle pigments. Very rare beef is a bright red pink, but has lost the translucent appearance of raw meat. Very well done beef is a uniform brownish-gray throughout. Other changes include juiciness, flavor, tenderness, volume, and cooking losses. When rare meat is carved, a considerable quantity of pink juice will flow from the cut surfaces, but no juice flows from very well done meat. Heat-induced changes in flavor precursors are necessary to develop the characteristic meat flavor. The type and extent of these changes vary with the cooking method as well as the stage of doneness.

Rare beef is usually quite tender, unless a cut is used that is high in connective tissue. The muscle fibers usually become more dense and compact with extended cooking, while the heat degradation of collagen increases the tenderness of the connective tissue. In some muscles the muscle fibers tend to disintegrate with extensive cooking (Cover and Hostetler, 1960). Such muscles become very tender on long cooking, but the tenderness is of a different type than in rare beef. The muscle fibers of tender rare beef are soft and juicy, while those of tender very well done beef are dry and crumble into fragments when chewed.

As the meat temperature reaches 63° C, the meat starts to shrink due to coagulation of the proteins and loss of water and fat. Along with this, the cooking losses increase.

Sprague and Grindley (1907) suggested internal temperatures of 55–65° C for rare beef, 65–70° C for medium well done, and 70–80° C for well done. Current practice suggests the use of 58–60° C for rare, 66–68° C for medium rare, 73–75° C for medium, and 80–82° C for well done. Very well done beef is usually produced by braising. In this method the meat temperature frequently reaches 95–100° C, and the meat may be held at that temperature for some time. Harries et al. (1963) selected 160° F (71° C) as the final internal temperature for beef to be tasted cold, since this "gave a product that was sufficiently well cooked to be acceptable to all tasters whilst still retaining sufficient juices to permit good discrimination." Jones et al. (1964) used 165° F for beef scored while still hot, since the meat had a more pronounced red color when hot than when cold. They also reported that steer meat appeared more well done than did bull meat at the same internal temperature.

Other Species

In general, the changes outlined above apply to all meats. Raw veal, pork, and lamb usually are not as intensely colored as raw beef, and so are not as bright a pink at the rare stage, nor as dark a gray when well done.

Older recommendations stated that pork should always be cooked well done (84° C, 185° F). This was to insure destruction of trichina larvae. More recently, this recommendation has been changed to medium (77° C, 170° F). Webb et al. (1961), Weir et al. (1963), Carlin et al. (1965), Pengilly and Harrison (1966), Bowers and Goertz (1966), and Holmes et al. (1966), reported work on palatability of pork roasts and chops cooked to various internal temperatures. All found that as the internal temperature increased, juiciness decreased and cooking losses increased. However, at low internal temperatures the judges found the meat lacking in characteristic pork flavor. There was general agreement that 170° F gave a very acceptable product, with adequate flavor development and good juiciness. In line with the earlier work of Ransom and Schwartz (see p. 347), studies at the Meat Inspection Division, U.S.D.A. (1960) showed that *trichinella spiralis* was completely destroyed at 58.3° C. Carlin et al. (1969) heated pork roasts containing trichina larvae to endpoints of 120, 125, 130, 135, 140, 145, 150, and 160° F. They found viable larvae in all roasts cooked to 130° F or below and in some roasts cooked to 135° F, but no viable larvae in roasts cooked to 140° F or above.

Rate of Heat Penetration

The rate at which the interior of a piece of meat will heat is influenced by a number of factors, including the rate at which energy is supplied, the rate at which it is transmitted to the meat, the shape and size of the sample being heated, its composition, the spatial distribution of areas of lean, fat, connective tissue, and bone, the characteristics of the meat surface, and the changes induced in the meat by heat, including protein denaturation, loss of water, and melting of fat.

Method of Cooking

If the cooking media are the same temperature, the time of cooking depends largely on the rate at which heat is conducted in the particular medium being used. Meat may be cooked in water, steam, air, or fat. The specific heat of water is 1, of steam 0.48, of air 0.24, and of oil 0.41–0.43. Meat reaches a definite interior temperature very much faster in water than in air of the same temperature. See Cover's results, Table 8. Covered containers, in which no water was added initially, form

TABLE 8.   Cooking Time and Losses of Paired Roasts Cooked in Water and in an Oven at the Same Temperature, 90° C[a]

Cut	Interior temperature (°C)	Number of Paired Roasts	Cooking Time		Cooking Losses	
			Oven (Hours)	Water (Hours)	Oven (Percent)	Water (Percent)
Bottom round	80	8	26.4	1.9	41.0	26.1
Top round	80	8	31.8	2.4	42.3	29.9

[a] From B. Lowe, *Experimental Cookery*, 4th ed., 1955. Wiley, New York, p. 238.

steam from fluids escaping from the meat. This steam conducts heat more rapidly than air; hence under otherwise standardized conditions, covered meat heats more rapidly than uncovered meat.

Visser et al. (1960) pointed out that meat heats more rapidly in oil than in air, since heat conductivity of oil is about six times that of air. It should be remembered that heating in a microwave oven is a different situation, since the energy is supplied to the meat in the form of electromagnetic waves rather than directly as heat.

Thermal Conductivity of Meat

A number of studies have been made on rates of heat conduction through the meat itself. Woodams and Nowrey (1968) have reviewed published data on methods of measurement and results obtained for thermal conductivity of a wide variety of food materials. Hill et al. (1967) point out that it is difficult to compare the data obtained by different investigators, since there were differences in the composition of the meat samples used and in the methods of measurement. They concluded that thermal conductivity in meat varies with temperature, moisture content of the meat, and direction of heat flow in relation to the direction of the muscle fibers. In the range of 80 to 150° F, they indicated a degree of uncertainty concerning the composition of the meat, due to weight losses in this temperature zone. Kopelman (1966) also found that thermal conductivity is greater parallel to the fibers than it is perpendicular to them. Morley (1966) lists thermal conductivity values for muscle and fat from $-19°$ to $+37°$ C, and for bone at 0, 19, and 70° C.

Haughey (1968) states: "From an engineering view point, the cooking process is a problem in unsteady state, simultaneous heat and mass transfer." He goes on to point out that cooking time depends on (1) heat transfer to the surface of the meat; (2) internal heat transfer which, by raising the temperature, denatures the proteins and produces the cooked state; and (3) mass transfer resulting from the release of water originally immobilized by the proteins, the diffusion of this water (and possibly also fat) through the meat due to concentration gradients, and the evaporation of water and drip loss from the meat surface.

When meat is roasted in a hot-air oven, the rate of heat penetration usually decreases during a certain range of internal temperatures, then increases again as the upper limit of this range is exceeded. This shows up as a flattening or plateau in the time-temperature curve. The actual range reported by various workers appears to vary with the meat being cooked and the method of cooking. Haughey (1968) reported a marked slowing from 60 to 71° C, with a plateau at about 68° C when roasting beef neck muscle. Irmiter et al. (1967) noted a marked slowing of the rate of heat penetration into ground beef cylinders starting at 55–60° C, with the rate increasing again at 71–74° C. The curve for the lamb leg shown in Figure 22 shows a decreased heating rate from 60 to 82° C. Baity et al. (1969) noted a plateau in the time-temperature curves for beef loaves when roasted in a 200° F oven but not in a 450° F oven. Cover et al. (1957) found that it took longer to oven broil 1-inch LD and BF steaks from 61 to 80° C than from 0 to 61° C. Thus it is obvious that part of the heat energy being supplied to the meat is being utilized for mechanisms other than increasing the temperature. Part of this energy is probably being expended to evaporate the water freed as the proteins denature and coagulate. But Haughey (1968) pointed out that a calculation of the heat balance over the entire roasting period showed that the total heat input was about 25 percent more than could be accounted for by internal temperature rise plus evaporation of water. He suggested that this 25 percent might be energy required to release bound or immobilized water.

Composition of Meat

The results from different studies do not agree as to the effect of the presence or absence of a layer of external fat on the rate of heat penetration. Again, the lack of agreement may be due to the use of different cuts of meat and different heating conditions. Thille et al. (1932) reported that a layer of external fat increased the rate of heating in beef rib roasts cooked in a 225° C oven to an internal temperature of 65° C. Funk et al. (1968) reported that wrapping ground beef cylinders in a layer of fat 0.5 cm thick increased the time necessary to heat the meat to 60° C, but decreased the time required to reach internal temperatures of 70 or 80° C. Woolsey and Paul (1969b) found no significant difference in minutes per pound cooking time for beef ST roasts, depending on whether the external fat cover was left on or removed before roasting. Weir (1960) concluded that external fat cover on pork roasts did not affect rate of internal temperature rise unless the fat cover was very thin. Roasts with 0.1 inch or less of external fat cooked more rapidly than those with a thicker fat layer. Batcher et al. (1962) presented heat penetration curves for pork roasts from carcasses having thick or thin back fat. The curves for the rib roasts showed little difference, but in the picnic shoulder the thick backfat cuts showed appreciably slower rate of heat rise.

The internal composition, especially the amount of fat, also may influence heating rate. Thille et al. (1932) suggested that increasing interior fat may retard heat penetration in beef rib roasts. Weir (1960) found no influence of the amount of marbling on heating rate of pork roasts. Irmiter et al. (1967) and Funk et al. (1968) studied the effect of varying the composition of ground beef cylinders on heating rate. In these the shape and size were constant, and the fat was evenly distributed throughout the meat. Increasing amount of fat decreased the cooking time. Irmiter et al. (1967), from a study of the heating curves, determined that lean meat heated most rapidly in the early part of the cooking (0 to 20 minutes), but that after 25 minutes the rate of temperature rise increased with increasing fat content. Since by this time the internal temperature of the cylinders was above 40° C, this may indicate that solid fat decreases rate of heating, while liquid fat increases it.

Funk et al. (1968) also investigated the influence of bone and of an exterior connective-tissue wrap on heating rates. Bone did not alter the heating rate, except at the next-to-the-lowest fat level in the meat. They regarded the results with the connective-tissue wrap as inconclusive, since heat caused irregular shrinkage of the wrap, which resulted in varying changes in the shape of the cylinders.

Lewis et al. (1967) found that ante-mortem stress increased the rate of heat penetration in 2.5-cm-thick beef steaks. Ante-mortem stress also increased the pH of the steaks and decreased the cooking losses. So they theorized that the increased rate of heating was associated with decreased energy utilization to evaporate the additional water lost from the steaks from unstressed animals.

Skewers

Metal skewers have been suggested as a means of shortening the time for cooking meat. Cover (1941) studied paired round, armbone-chuck, and standing-rib roasts, cooked at an oven temperature of 125° to an interior temperature of 80° C. The use of skewers reduced the cooking time by about 30–45 percent and decreased the weight losses during cooking by about 35 percent. However, the percentage of panel members voting the control as the more tender was 86 percent for rounds, 79 percent for chuck, and 64 percent for rib roasts. Thus greater tenderizing occurred by longer cooking, particularly in the cuts with the higher collagen content. Harries et al. (1963) advised against the use of skewers in experimental studies, since they produce heat-transfer irregularities.

Cooking Losses

Cooking losses are determined by measuring the weight change between raw and cooked meat, and are usually expressed as percent of the raw weight. With some cooking methods, it is possible to separate the total loss into drippings and evaporation. The drippings consist of the material that accumulates in the pan, and the evaporation or volatile losses are calculated from the difference between the total weight change and the weight of the drippings.

As the meat is heated, the denaturation and coagulation of the proteins lessens the water-holding capacity of the tissue. This free water is squeezed out of the tissue as the protein structures shrink. The water carries with it water-soluble materials such as salts, sarcoplasmic proteins, and nonprotein nitrogenous compounds. If the meat is being heated in a dry atmosphere, most or all of the water will be evaporated, forming the major portion of the volatile losses. These losses may also include aromatic compounds and heat-decomposition products of fat and protein. At high cooking temperatures, another source of volatile losses may be fat droplets that are spattered out of the pan onto oven or range surfaces. Drippings, or drip loss, consist primarily of fat that is melted out of the meat by heat. It may also include some water, and the nonvolatile water-soluble materials such as salts and the sarcoplasmic proteins that are heat-coagulated in the pan.

The volume of meat generally decreases on cooking. Bramblett et al. (1959), using beef round muscles, reported that 92 percent of the cuts decreased in length, 83 percent in width, and 69 percent in thickness. Batcher et al. (1962) noted an average decrease of 21 percent in the area of the LD of pork when roasted at 325° F to 185° F internal temperature. Irmiter et al. (1967) found that ground beef cylinders shrank in height and diameter when roasted. Funk et al. (1968) reported that the presence of bone decreased the height skrinkage of the cylinders.

The weight loss during cooking of meat is influenced by a number of factors. These are frequently interdependent, so that the influence of one variable may differ depending on the other conditions chosen. Leverton and Odell (1958) and Toepfer et al. (1955) have published data on cooking losses and compositional changes for a variety of meat cuts and cooking methods.

Internal Temperature

Cooking losses increase as the internal temperature of the meat increases. Cover and Hostetler (1960), Marshall et al. (1960), and Paul (1962) have reported this for different cuts of beef, Webb et al. (1961), Carlin et al. (1965) and Pengilly and Harrison (1966) for pork roasts, and Bowers and Goertz (1966) and Holmes et al. (1966) for pork chops.

Time

Cooking time appears to be one of the critical factors in determining cooking losses. In general, losses increase with longer cooking time for a given cut and cooking method. Paul and Bratzler (1955) obtained this result with beef round steaks fried in deep fat, Paul et al. (1956) and Cover et al. (1957) reported this for braised and for oven-cooked beef steaks from LD and round muscles, and Rogers and Ritchey (1969) for baked beef round steaks.

Oven Temperature

The effect of oven temperature on losses appears to be a complex of time and temperature. At oven temperatures of 200° F or less, the increasing cooking time often increases losses (Marshall et al., 1960; Bramblett and Vail, 1964), although Davenport and Meyer (1970) reported lower losses at 200° F than at 300° F when cooking beef roasts in a forced-convection oven. Above 200° F, the increased rate of evaporation of water and of melting of fat tends to increase losses with increasing external temperature (for example, Woolsey and Paul, 1969b). However, Carlin et al. (1965) reported no significant change of losses when roasting pork at oven temperatures from 300 to 375° F, and Nielsen and Hall (1965) obtained higher losses at 225° F than at 325° F when roasting beef blade cuts. Typical loss data for beef are listed in Table 9.

TABLE 9.   Average Cooking Losses for Beef Roasts

Variables	Total Loss, Percent	Evapo- ration Loss, Percent	Drip Loss, Percent	Source
Stage of doneness				
Beef ST, roasted at				Paul (1962)
300° F to 60° C	13.62	9.82	3.80	
300° F to 77° C	26.76	21.37	5.39	
Beef roasts, 11–12 rib				Lowe (1955)
150° C oven to 55° C	7.7			
150° C oven to 75° C	16.6			
Oven temperature				
Beef ST, roasted to				Woolsey and
58° C, at 163° C	17.6	11.0	6.6	Paul (1969b)
58° C, at 218° C	22.0	14.8	7.2	
Beef roasts, 7–8 rib				Lowe (1955)
at 125° C	9.1			
at 200° C	18.6			

Method of Cooking

The effect of cooking method on losses varies with the cuts and conditions selected. Usually methods that cook the meat in a moist atmosphere increase the losses (Pridgeon, 1954; Paul et al., 1956; and Nielsen and Hall, 1965). However, Weir et al. (1962) reported higher losses for broiled than for braised ½-inch pork chops, and Cover and Smith (1956) higher losses for broiled than braised beef steaks, and higher for roasted than pot-roasted beef roasts. Deep-fat frying (Chung et al., 1966; Pridgeon, 1954; Visser et al., 1960) and pan broiling (March et al., 1961) tend to give higher losses than oven cooking or broiling. Use of a microwave oven usually increases losses over those obtained in conventional roasting, but Law et al. (1967) reported higher losses in broiled LD steaks than in those cooked by microwaves.

Composition of Cut

Orme (1955), Weir (1960), and Batcher et al. (1962) reported that increased external fat increased the drip losses from pork roasts, and Woolsey and Paul (1969b) that the presence of external fat on beef ST roasts increased total and drip losses. Irmiter et al. (1967) and Funk et al. (1968) reported increased drip losses from beef cylinders, and March et al. (1961) noted increased cooking losses in pork sausage as the fat content of the raw meat was increased. However, Irmiter et al.

(1967) noted that the presence of about 30 percent fat appeared to inhibit water loss from ground beef.

Doty and Pierce (1961) reported that a number of factors such as grade and weight of carcass, and rib position from which the steak was cut, influenced drip losses during broiling. They noted that the drip was primarily fat, and concluded that the real determinant of drip loss was the composition of the steak, especially the amount of external and intermuscular fat.

Funk et al. (1968) reported that an external fat wrap decreased the total and volatile losses from ground beef cylinders, but increased the drip. The presence of bone did not influence cooking losses. The addition of a connective-tissue wrap increased drip at lower fat levels (2.4 to 20 percent fat) and decreased evaporation losses at 20 and 30 percent fat levels.

pH

Lewis et al. (1967), using beef steaks, and Meyer et al. (1963) and Searcy et al. (1969), with pork loin roasts, noted that meat of higher pH had lower cooking losses. This is probably a reflection of the fact that increasing pH tends to increase the water-holding capacity of meat. A number of studies (such as Doty and Pierce, 1961) have reported that aging meat decreases the cooking losses. This again may be a pH effect, since the pH of meat usually increases slightly with aging.

PALATABILITY CHARACTERISTICS

The palatability factors usually considered include appearance, color, odor, flavor, juiciness, and tenderness. Appearance and color may be evaluated on either raw or cooked meat. Odor, flavor, juiciness, and tenderness are usually measured on cooked meat. Since the ultimate test of palatability is the human reaction, organoleptic assessment is frequently utilized. In addition, a number of physical and/or chemical measurements may be included. But to date there are no physical or chemical methods that completely measure the eating quality.

The basic principles of panel evaluation and of physical and chemical measurements of eating quality are discussed in Chapters 15 and 16. Harries et al. (1963) outline a procedure for assessing palatability of meat. Beery and Ziegler (1969) describe an apparatus for holding meat samples during broiling and cutting of cooked samples, to obtain uniform pieces for panel evaluation. This appears to be adaptable to a variety of meat cuts and cooking methods.

In scoring meat it is usual to consider first the factors that can be evaluated before eating, so they will be discussed in the order in which a panel member customarily considers them. However, reactions to these factors are usually interrelated, so it is frequently difficult to avoid considerable overlapping.

Appearance

Williams (1968) lists the following as influencing one's reaction to the appearance of raw meat: ratio of lean meat to fat and bone; musculature that is firm, bright in color, free from "drip," and with a minimum of connective tissue; fat that is firm, and uniform in texture and color; and presence of intramuscular fat. The grain of the meat (size of the muscle bundles) and the presence of layers or sheets of connective tissue may also be included in assessment of appearance. Kaess and Weidemann (1967) reported on freezer burn in raw beef, a condition that influences the appearance of meat preserved by freezing.

In cooked meat, appearance may include the presence of juice on the cutting board or plate, the degree of shrinkage, any hardening, drying, or charring of the surface, and the degree of separation of the muscle bundles. This last point may be especially important in meat that is cooked to the very well done stage. Cover and Hostetler (1960) point out that vigorous boiling in such methods as braising or stewing may break the meat into small pieces or strings. This may also occur in certain canned meat items, due to the high temperature treatment required to sterilize the product. Samples for scoring panels are cut so as to present primarily lean or fat tissue, to avoid differences in distribution of lean, fat, connective tissue, and bone.

Color

As indicated earlier, the major pigment of the lean portion is myoglobin (Mb), with a lesser amount of hemoglobin (Hb). The chemical reactions of these pigments are very similar insofar as meat color is concerned, and so will be considered here as Mb only. However, reactions such as autoxidation and denaturation do have different rates for the two pigments, so experimental investigations may need to consider both.

The color of the raw lean may vary from pale pink to dark brownish-red depending on the concentration and chemical state of Mb. The chemistry of the myoglobin pigments has been reviewed by Solberg (1968), Fox (1966), Mackinney and Little (1962), Brown and Tappel (1958), and Schweigert (1956).

The pigments in the fat are principally carotenoids. The color may vary from creamy white to dark yellow, being primarily influenced by the pigment concentration, which is largely controlled by species, breed, and feed.

Raw Meat

Myoglobin (Mb) concentration in muscle tissue is influenced by species, age of animal, and the particular muscle or part of muscle within the carcass. For example, Rickansrud and Henrickson (1967) give the Mb concentration of several beef muscles as follows: BF, 3.64; LD, 3.18; Psoas, 2.40; and ST, 1.99 mg per g of wet tissue.

The influence of pH and of temperature on pork and beef muscle was considered earlier in the discussion of PSE pork and dark-cutting beef. Cook (1968) investigated the color of lamb LD at pHs ranging from 5.2 to 6.8, and temperatures from 0 to 40° C. He reported large variations in muscle color due to the combined effects of pH and temperature.

The chemical state of Mb is usually a function of the extent of oxygenation or oxidation.

$$MbO_2 \rightleftharpoons Mb \rightleftharpoons MMb$$

oxymyoglobin	myoglobin	metmyoglobin
Fe^{++}	Fe^{++}	Fe^{+++}
oxygenated		oxidized
red	purplish red	brown–red

The conversion of red MbO_2 to brown MMb is the major discloration problem of fresh meat. Since the conversion of Mb to MbO_2 is an oxygenation, not an oxidation, the formation of MbO_2 is largely governed by oxygen availability. Respiratory enzymes in the interior of meat consume oxygen. As the oxygen supply is depleted, MbO_2 is converted to Mb. Mb is very labile to oxidation to MMb. Saleh and Watts (1968) found that the autoxidation of Mb to MMb is much more rapid at low oxygen tensions than in air. However, reducing substances (naturally present or added) will continuously regenerate Mb from MMb. So maintenance of the red color of raw meat depends on the supply of O_2 and reducing compounds.

Maintenance of attractive color is one of the major problems in prepackaged meat. Brody (1970) summarized the importance of color in the development of centralized cutting and packaging systems. Packaging materials must permit some passage of O_2, to retain the red MbO_2, but prevent moisture vapor transmission to avoid surface desiccation. Drying of the surface can also cause brown discoloration, due to physical changes that alter the light-reflecting and -absorbing properties of the surface.

Mb can complex with a number of compounds in addition to O_2. The bright red color of carbonmonoxymyoglobin (MbCO) is well known. El-Badawi et al. (1964) found that a mixture of 2 percent CO and 98 percent air was effective in preserving the color of fresh beef for 15 days at 36–38° F. MMb formation at 32° F also is influenced by composition of the atmosphere, being highest at about 1 percent O_2. The shift to MMb is accelerated by surface drying.

Snyder and Ayres (1961), Jay (1966), Naumann (1968), and Zimmerman and Snyder (1969) discuss the role of microbial growth on color of raw meat. Bacterial growth uses up part or all of the O_2 present, lowering the partial pressure of O_2 and favoring the formation of MMb. In addition, bacteria may produce H_2S, which will combine with Mb to form green sulfmyoglobin, or may attack the pigments themselves, degrading the heme structure. Low temperatures to reduce microbial growth also influence the rate of reduction of MMb to Mb, the rate decreasing with decreasing temperature (Hutchins et al., 1967). Meat pigments are very sensitive to discoloration by ozone, so this limits the use of ozone to control microbes (Kaess and Weidemann, 1968).

Studies on the influence of light on the color of meat have given contradictory results. Solberg (1968) has reviewed a number of these papers. Ultraviolet light is generally considered to cause deterioration of fresh meat color. Fluorescent light may or may not cause changes, depending on other conditions.

Cooked Meat

Heating meat denatures the globin portion of the pigment molecule. If O_2 is present, the Fe is oxidized, resulting in a tan-brown hemichrome. If reducing agents are present, the Fe is reduced and a pink hemochrome is produced. Reducing conditions may be produced naturally by release of sulfhydryl groups when the protein is denatured. Bright pink or greenish pigments may be produced if traces of CO or sulfur compounds are present, for example in the gas used as the source of heat. An undesirable red color in cooked meat may also be due to traces of nitrite (Tappel, 1957a). Paul et al. (1964) noted a yellow to green iridescence on the cut surface of cooked lamb.

The reports of Draudt (1969) and Machlik (1966) on the influence of heat on the myoglobin pigments were discussed in the previous section. Bernofsky et al. (1959) found that the major pigment extractable from cooked fresh beef was MbO_2, and that the amount of pigment remaining undenatured depended on the temperature reached by the meat and the length of time it had been held at that temperature. Greene (1969) reported that lipid oxidation in raw meat could result in off-colors in cooked meat.

Brown color in cooked meat may be caused by changes other than those in myoglobin. Pearson et al. (1962, 1966) studied the browning produced by heating fresh pork, and concluded that most of the browning was due to the amino-sugar reaction, but that a small amount appeared to be due to pyrolysis of natural meat sugars.

Nonenzymic browning reactions occur in raw and cooked dehydrated meat. They are more pronounced in heat-dried than in freeze-dried meat, since the latter is not exposed to as high temperatures, and can be dried to a lower moisture level with less damage to rehydration characteristics. However, Gilka (1963) found that most of the browning in stored lyophilized meat was due to reactions between amino acids and sugars, while Goldblith and Tannenbaum (1966) and Zirlin (1968) reported browning due to reactions between proteins and autoxidizing lipids. Bengtsson and Bengtsson (1968) stated that the red color of raw beef could best be preserved in freeze-dried meat by low temperature storage and by avoidance or removal of O_2.

Cured Meat

The characteristic pink color of cured meat is important in such products as ham, bacon, smoked tongue, corned beef, frankfurters and many of the prepared sausage items such as bologna and salami. The bright red pigment, nitric oxide myoglobin (NOMb), is formed by the action of nitrite on myoglobin. In this form it is unstable, but when it is heated the stable denatured nitric oxide myochromogen (DNOMb) is formed (Tappel, 1957b). This occurs when the cured meat is heated to 150° F or higher (Fox, 1966).

A number of factors are important in the production and stability of the desirable cured-meat color. The concentration of nitrite must be sufficient to supply the NO required (Klima and Blanka, 1968). However, excess nitrite promotes the development of green discolorations by degradation of the heme portion of the molecule (Fox and Thompson, 1964). Fox et al. (1967) noted that the temperature of cooking influenced the rate of color formation, the amount of cured meat pigment formed, and its stability during storage. A number of papers have dealt with the influence of various salts, reducing agents, pH, O_2 supply, and curing conditions on the cured-meat color (Walters et al., 1968; Giddey, 1966; Fox and Ackerman, 1968; Fox et al., 1967; and Reith and Szakaly, 1967a).

DNOMb tends to fade when exposed to light and/or air. Draudt and Deatherage (1956), Alm et al. (1961), and Ertle (1969) discuss various phases of this problem and the role of packaging in protecting sliced cured meats. Barton (1967a) states that color fading is due to the conversion of DNOMb to metmyochrome, and that further irreversible oxidation may lead to ruptures of the porphyrin ring, producing grayish-green pigments. Reith and Szakály (1967b) found that breakdown of DNOMb increased with increasing light intensity but was decreased by the use of a CO_2 atmosphere. Cole (1961) suggested that pigment fading in air involved thiol groups and cysteine, while Tarladgis (1962) considered the loss of color to be caused either by lipid oxidation or by light-induced dissociation of the NO from the pigment complex. Shishkina and Moltchanova (1968) found that ultraviolet light accelerated discoloration in cured sausage.

Gardner (1967) attributed discoloration in cooked ham to uneven distribution of curing salts, leading to increased bacterial action. Board and Ihsan-ul-Haque (1965) noted a black discoloration in canned cured meats due to contamination with copper.

Ionizing Radiations

In raw meat, irradiation may produce either intensification of the pink color or development of gray-brown colors, depending on the amount of oxidizing agents present. Irradiation of cooked meat converts the gray-brown pigments to an uncharacteristic red. Tappel (1957c) and Tarladgis and Ehtashan-ud-Din (1965) reported on the identity and nature of the pigments in precooked irradiated meats. Urbain (1969) states that irradiated meats must be protected from oxygen, and that treatment with phosphates such as sodium tripolyphosphate improves color retention. Cured-meat pigment is partially destroyed by irradiation, due to oxidation, but the color may be regenerated if NO is present. To minimize the color changes, O_2-impermeable containers are used, products are held in storage to allow for color regeneration, and extra nitrite is added to cured-meat products.

Methods of Measurement

While Nickerson (1946) is one of the basic references on measurement of food colors, there have been a number of reports on applications specifically to meat. Hegarty (1969) and Hoke and Davis (1970) review conditions for subjective evaluation of color. Quinn et al. (1964), Elliott (1967, 1968), Ockerman and Cahill (1969), Janicki et al. (1967), Dean and Ball (1960), Lane and Bratzler (1962), and Zimmerman and Snyder (1969) illustrate spectrophotometric color analyses on fresh meats, while Barton (1967a,b), Hornsey (1956), and Sidwell et al. (1962) show applications to cured-meat pigments.

Flavor and Aroma

Flavor and aroma are so closely associated that it is difficult to discuss them separately. In fact, flavor is considered to be a complex of taste and aroma, as well as some of the physical sensations produced by food in the mouth.

Flavor and aroma investigations have been concerned principally with cooked meat. However, aroma may be a problem in raw meat if microbiological activity and/or lipid oxidation have produced undesirable odors.

The flavor of cooked meat arises from water- or fat-soluble precursors present in the raw meat. Heating in air promotes reactions among these precursors to produce the flavor and aroma of the cooked meat. Heating in the absence of air produces noncharacteristic aromas. The amine-sugar (Maillard) reaction is considered the major reaction system in meat-flavor production, but may not be the only mechanism by which flavor is developed.

Water extracts of raw meat produce a meaty flavor when heated, but when the intact meat is heated, there is also believed to be some interaction between the water-soluble components and the fibrillar structures. The lipids are thought to contribute certain flavor precursors, and to influence flavor also by modifying taste, mouth feel, and the flavor of other components. They may also act as reservoirs to retain flavor elements that might otherwise be volatilized. Solms (1969) suggests an integrated flavor picture for meat, consisting of amino acids, peptides, and proteins that provide taste and tactile effects; other compounds that act as flavor potentiators or synergists; and the volatile fractions that contribute the odor effects. Lawrie (1966), Tarr (1966), Hornstein (1967), and Broderick (1968) have published general reviews on meat-flavor studies. Cramer (1963) reviewed techniques in meat-flavor research. Kirimura et al. (1969) summarized the contribution of peptides and amino acids, and Forss (1969) the role of lipids.

Separation and Identification of Flavor Compounds

Although it is recognized that a number of factors contribute to the total flavor-aroma sensation, odor is generally regarded as the most important influence. The development of chromatographic techniques for separation and identification of organic compounds has led to a wide interest in the identification of compounds responsible for food flavors. So far, peptides, amino acids, lipids, carbonyl compounds, nucleotides and related compounds, low molecular weight nitrogenous compounds other than amino acids, and the group of carbohydrates and carbohydrate derivatives involved in intermediary metabolism have all been suggested as contributing to the flavor of meats. Hornstein (1967) summarizes chemical research on meat flavor as being concerned with (1) locating sites of flavor production, (2) identifying the precursors, and (3) identifying the flavor compounds produced by heating the precursors.

Hornstein and Crowe (1960, 1961) and Hornstein et al. (1963) studied water- and fat-soluble components of muscle tissue from several species. They suggested that the water-soluble portion gave a meaty flavor common to all species, while the fat portion contained the species-specific flavors. However, later work has suggested that the separations are not so clear-cut. Wasserman (1966) lists a variety of flavor-related chemicals found in meat, and Mills et al. (1969) review the role of Amadori compounds derived from the nonenzymic browning reaction as nonvolatile flavor precursors. Zaika et al. (1968), Zaika (1969), and Mabrouk et al. (1969a) list methods for separation of water-soluble components, Mabrouk et al. (1969b) discuss methods for extracting intramuscular polar lipids, and Issenberg (1969) reviews the use of mass spectrometry, in conjunction with gas chromatography, for identification of volatile components.

Flavor Potentiators

Compounds such as monosodium glutamate and the 5'-nucleotides have been suggested as contributors to meat flavor through potentiating or synergistic action. The 5'-nucleotides such as inosine 5'-monophosphate (IMP) occur naturally in meat, as breakdown products of ATP. However, further breakdown of IMP produces hypoxanthine, which has a bitter flavor.

Kuninaka (1966) summarized recent studies on 5'-nucleotides as flavor enhancers in a variety of foods, and Jones (1969) reviewed their possible roles in meat and fish flavors. There appears to be no strong evidence to date of their contribution to desirable meat flavor. Dannert and Pearson (1967a) analyzed beef, pork, and lamb muscle for IMP. They reported considerable variation in amounts of IMP, depending on the original level in the meat and the length and temperature of storage of the meat. Meyer et al. (1967) found a trend toward increasing flavor desirability with increasing apparent IMP and decreasing hypoxanthine in beef, but the relationships were not outstanding. Dannert and Pearson (1967b) concluded that IMP alone or IMP + GMP (guanosine 5'-monophosphate) caused some improvement in acceptability of frankfurters made from muscle low in IMP, but the influence seemed more closely related to texture than to flavor.

Species-Related Flavors

Hornstein and Crowe (1960, 1963) suggested that the fat accounts for much of the flavor differences among different species of animals. But

Wasserman and Talley (1968) in taste panel tests found that, of beef, pork, and lamb, only lamb fat contained a component that significantly increased identification of lamb flavor. They suggested that texture, color, mouth feel, and other factors might also be involved in the identification of species. Hofstrand and Jacobson (1960) also reported flavor components in the fat of lamb and mutton. Jacobson and Koehler (1963) identified aldehydes, methyl ketones, and possibly 2-methylcyclopentanone in the volatiles collected during roasting of lamb, and stated that all these compounds made important contributions to typical cooked-lamb flavor.

Other Flavor Influences

The amounts of low molecular weight compounds important in flavor development increase during post-mortem aging of beef muscle (Gunther, 1969). Bowers (1969) reported increases in free amino acids during aging of pork, and Golovkin and Vasilyev (1967) studied the changes in volatile aromatic substances in meat during storage. Ingram (1966) reviewed the role of microbial action in the production of desirable meat flavors in aging of fresh meat and in production of certain types of sausage items.

pH is recognized as influencing flavor of meat by its relation to acid or alkaline tastes. In addition, the extent and rate of change of pH post mortem is an indication of the changes in components of intermediary metabolism. Possible relation of these components to meat flavor has already been indicated. Johnson and Vickery (1964) reported that the amount of H_2S released when meat is cooked increases with increasing ultimate pH of the muscle.

Batcher et al. (1969) found flavor differences attributable to age and sex in broth from lamb and yearling-mutton samples, but not in slices of roasted, broiled, or braised meat. Schön and Schön (1966) noted age, degree of fattening, and marbling effects on beef flavor, but Murphy and Carlin (1961) found that pork-chop flavor did not vary with backfat thickness or marbling. Fredholm (1961) pointed out that feeds containing off-flavor fats could cause off flavors in the meat from hogs.

Patterson (1968) identified the major compound responsible for sex odor in pork as 5 α-androst-16-en-3-one. Griffiths and Patterson (1970) investigated olfactory reactions to this compound.

Cooking

The flavor changes that occur on cooking of meat are influenced by the amount and kind of heat applied. In moist heat, exposure to water or steam increases leaching of flavor components from the meat into the broth or drippings. In dry-heat methods, the meat surface is usually exposed to high temperatures. The fluid moving from the interior to the surface of the meat carries soluble components of tissues with it, increasing the concentration of these materials on the surface. Also, fat melts and may cover the surface partially or completely. All these compounds can interact; also, some pyrolysis will occur. The flavor of cooked meat also changes with increasing degree of doneness, finally becoming unpleasant if protein and fat decomposition are carried too far. It has been suggested that the flavor compounds in boiled beef may originate with a small number of compounds by Maillard reactions, and that fat may influence flavor by dissolving and retaining odorous compounds formed during cooking, rather than being a source of flavor compounds itself.

Wasserman (1967) has reviewed the chemistry of cooked-meat flavor, and Landmann and Batzer (1966) the influence of processing procedures. Olson et al. (1959) and Yueh and Strong (1960) reported the formation of H_2S when meat was cooked. Kramlich and Pearson (1960) also noted the presence of sulfur compounds. Hamm and Hofmann (1965) studied the changes in sulfhydryl groups and the effect of heat on the formation of H_2S from beef muscle proteins. Pepper and Pearson (1969) divided beef adipose tissue into water-soluble, salt-soluble and insoluble fractions before heating. Each fraction yielded H_2S on heating, with 71 percent coming from the water-soluble fraction. Tonsbeek et al. (1968, 1969) reported isolation and identification of 4-hydroxy-5-methyl-3(2H)-furanone as a flavor component of beef broth formed during cooking.

March et al. (1961) found that pan-broiled pork sausage received higher flavor scores than that baked in the oven, and suggested that the longer cooking time in the oven might have permitted development of rancidity, or the browned flavor of the surface of the pan-broiled patties might have masked any undesirable flavor. Sanderson et al. (1966) studied the volatile flavor components of roasted and boiled beef. They suggested that the characteristic flavor differences produced by these methods of cooking might be due to differences in amounts of volatile aldehydes and ketones produced. McCrae and Seccombe (1969) reported that roasting lamb legs with or without the fell made no difference in the odor during cooking or in the flavor of the meat.

Development of Off-Flavors

Probably the major cause of off-flavor in cooked meat is the oxidation of lipids. The phospholipids are especially labile to oxidation (Younathan and Watts, 1960), and the heme pigments of cooked meat appear to be active catalysts for this oxidation (Younathan and Watts, 1959). Chang et al. (1961) reported rapid development of oxidative rancidity in beef cooked to 71° C internal temperature and then cooled and sliced. Keskinel et al. (1964) found that cooking permitted the diffusion of O_2 into the deep tissues of meat at the same rate as it did into the surface tissues, making O_2 more available in the interior of cooked than of raw meat. Zipser and Watts (1961) reported that cooking meat to higher temperatures decreased lipid oxidation, probably due to partial pigment destruction and formation of antioxidant substances in the meat.

Greene (1969) noted that lipid oxidation in prepackaged raw beef caused off-odors in the cooked meat. Hornstein et al. (1963) noted rapid development of undesirable aromas in the phospholipid fraction of beef and pork. Dugan (1967) has reviewed the influence of phospholipids on meat characteristics and Pearson (1968) the chemical methods for assessing fat spoilage. Sulzbacher et al. (1968) summarized studies on oxidative rancidity in meat and meat products.

Microbial action can cause flavor and odor changes. Alford et al. (1963) point out that lipases produced by microorganisms can be active catalysts for lipid hydrolysis even at storage temperatures too low for bacterial multiplication. Ertle (1969) reported that any microbiological flavor degradation in the raw stock carried over into such items as bologna and frankfurters.

Shank et al. (1962) noted, in fresh beef rounds, an off-odor associated with an increase in the concentration of short-chain fatty acids, possibly produced by abnormal activity of the tissue enzyme systems. Another source of off-flavors and -odors may be absorption of foreign odors from the storage atmosphere, packaging materials, or other similar sources.

Curing and Smoking

The flavor of cured-meat products varies with the method of curing and the composition of the curing salts. For example, hams may be dry- or wet-cured, or cured by pumping the pickling solution into the meat. These methods vary in the concentration of the curing salts in the final product and in the length of time required for the cure to be effective. In the methods requiring longer curing times, other changes that influence flavor occur. The curing salt mixtures contain sodium chloride and sodium or potassium nitrate. Nitrites may be included and/or may be formed by bacterial action. A variety of other compounds such as sucrose and spices may be added, depending on the type of product being prepared and the individual processor's procedure. Little work has been done to identify the compounds responsible for cured-meat flavor. Cross and Ziegler (1965) and Piotrowski et al. (1970) have reported studies on the volatiles from uncured and cured hams, and Lillard and Ayres (1969) on the volatiles of country-cured hams. McCain et al. (1968) investigated the increase in free amino acids and total ninhydrin-positive materials (NPM) during aging of dry-cured hams. They reported a highly significant correlation between increases in NPM and panel scores for aged flavor, and discussed the relation between the increase in free amino acids and flavor changes.

Smoking also alters the flavor of meat products. Foster and Simpson (1961) reported that the mode of deposition of smoke compounds appeared to be one of absorption of vapors rather than of deposition of particles. Smoking may be done by actual exposure to smoke, or by coating the surface with liquid smoke preparations, or by a combination of the two. Hamid and Saffle (1965), Porter et al. (1965), Wasserman and Fiddler (1969), and Fiddler et al. (1969) have reported studies on the chemical composition of natural or artificial smoke.

Hollenbeck and Marinelli (1963) point out that wood smoke and smoke solutions are highly variable materials. Bratzler et al. (1969) studied the amount of phenol, carbonyl, and acid on smoked bologna, and found that intensity of smoke flavor was most closely related to phenol. Pokorny et al. (1963) reported that the pyrolysis products volatilized below 130° C contained a high percentage of phenolic compounds that had considerable antioxidant activity for meat lipids.

During the smoking process the meat may be heated to different degrees. This also influences flavor and flavor stability. Kemp et al. (1961) studied hams heated from 80 to 140° F during smoking. They found that increasing the internal temperature decreased the development of peroxides and of free fatty acids during subsequent storage.

Freezing and Frozen Storage

Freezing stops bacterial growth, but chemical changes can still proceed slowly. The major effect on flavor is from hydrolysis and from oxidative changes leading to rancidity of the fatty portions. Storage temperature and packaging protection influence the extent of these changes. Mb concentration may influence rate of development of rancidity.

Awad et al. (1968) reported an increase in the percentage of free fatty acids in beef stored at $-4°$ C. They used this high frozen storage temperature to speed up the rate of deterioration. They attributed the increase in free fatty acids to phospholipid hydrolysis. Law et al. (1967) noted an increase in thiobarbituric acid (TBA) number in frozen beef steaks. Tarladgis et al. (1960) and Zipser et al. (1964) have reported significant correlations between TBA numbers and sensory scores for odor. Baldwin and Korschgen (1968) reported that beef roasted to

43° C internal temperature and then frozen, deteriorated slowly in frozen storage, but that dipping slices in antioxidant solution improved the flavor stability.

Salt has a prooxidant effect on meat lipids, so cured meats or fresh meat containing salt has only a short frozen storage life. In pork sausage, Hall et al. (1962) reported that NaCl acted as a prooxidant. Hoynak (1963) stated that the primary site of autoxidation was in the phospholipids and that the heme pigments also accelerate this oxidation. Ellis et al. (1968) found that NaCl, $NaNO_2$, and hematin compounds all acted as prooxidants in frozen pork. Zipser et al. (1964) compared TBA numbers of cured and uncured frozen cooked pork. They reported that the ratio of peroxides to TBA number was 8 to 10 times as high in cured as in uncured pork, and attributed this to the more rapid decomposition of peroxides by the ferric hemes of cooked meat. Sulzbacher and Gaddis (1968) reviewed flavor changes in frozen meat products.

Dehydration and Freeze-Drying

Dehydration of meat at elevated temperatures causes profound changes in all the palatability characteristics, due to extensive changes of proteins and fats and of the muscle structures. The alterations in proteins produce products with only very limited rehydration capacity, so these processes are used only for a few specialty items. Freeze-drying of meat yields products with improved rehydration ability, so there is considerable interest in conditions that produce acceptable eating quality, including flavor.

The major problems in retention of desirable flavor in freeze-dried meat appear to be control of enzyme activity, of oxidation of lipids and possibly proteins, and of nonenzymic browning reactions. Karel (1968) points out that the loss of volatile flavors during the drying operation is much less than expected from a study of volatilization of pure compounds and compounds in model systems. Apparently some mechanism in the food itself decreases the loss of volatile organic materials.

Bird (1965) noted that panel reactions to a number of freeze-dried meat items often included an indication of lack of flavor or of presence of off-flavor. Hirai et al. (1969) compared volatile flavor compounds from fresh and freeze-dried boiled beef. They concluded that deterioration of flavor during freeze-drying and storage was due to changes in amounts of compounds present in the fresh boiled beef, rather than to formation of new compounds.

Enzyme activity has been noted in a number of food materials even when dehydrated to a water content of three percent or lower. Matheson (1962) stated that precooking meat before freeze-drying increased the storage life of meat by inactivating the natural enzyme systems. The precooked products were also less sensitive to changes in moisture content during storage.

Nonenzymic browning can occur at very low water contents. Browning reactions may involve protein and sugar compounds, or protein groups and autoxidizing lipids. Along with the color changes already discussed, marked flavor alterations may occur.

Lipid oxidation is probably the most serious cause of flavor changes in freeze-dried meats. Freeze-dried foods are very susceptible to oxidation, since the porous structure permits easy diffusion of oxygen. Dehydrated foods are also very susceptible to oxidation even at low partial pressures of oxygen, since the oxidation process is accelerated by low water content. It has been suggested that drying meat to <3 percent moisture content can break the monomolecular layer of water associated with the protein molecules (true bound water), and thus alter appreciably the susceptibility to chemical change. Bengtsson and Bengtsson (1968) noted that freeze-dried meat should not be exposed to air before packaging under nitrogen. El-Gharbawi (1965) noted that all his samples, including those stored under N_2, showed oxidative changes. He suggested that these were due to the release of O_2 adsorbed onto the freeze-dried meat. Tappel (1956) suggested that the myoglobin pigment system is involved in oxidative deterioration of freeze-dried beef. Pokorny and Pazlar (1966) concluded that hemoglobin did not have a significant role in catalyzing oxidation in these products.

Irradiation

Irradiation of meat produces off-flavors and odors typical of this method of processing. The extent of the flavor-odor changes depends on the fat content of the meat, the dosage level, the temperature at which the dose was administered, and the time and temperature of storage after irradiation. Some of the volatile materials produced by irradiation appear to be dissipated during storage and/or cooking. Other ways that have been suggested to minimize or obscure off-flavors are addition of NaCl, pepper, sodium ascorbate, or thiamine, or cooking the meat before irradiation.

Different dosage levels may be used to pasteurize the meat surface, extending refrigerated storage life, or to render it sterile. Microorganisms vary in their susceptibility to radiation destruction. As the dosage level is increased, damage to palatability characteristics of the meat also increases. Very high dosage levels are required for inactivation of enzymes. Artar et al. (1961) reported that beef should be heated to internal temperatures of 160–170° F to minimize autolytic changes in proteins, with accompanying changes in flavor and texture during storage. Lea et al. (1960) found that pasteurization doses accelerated lipid oxidation in raw beef. Sterilization doses (Coleby et al., 1961) produced irradiation flavor in raw beef and pork. This changed to stale and bitter flavors during storage. If the meat was irradiated in the frozen state, some protection was afforded. Wick et al. (1961, 1965) have reported isolation and identification studies on the volatile components of irradiated beef, and changes in these during storage. Champagne and Nawar (1969) reported finding the same types of compounds in volatiles from irradiated beef and pork fat.

Merritt et al. (1966), in a review of irradiation damage to lipids, stated that irradiation off-flavors in food fats were different from other off-flavors. Hydrocarbons appear to be the major compounds produced in irradiated meat. While the most obvious source of these is the lipid fraction, some may arise by direct bond cleavage of amino acid moieties of proteins.

Chang et al. (1961) concluded that lipid oxidation products do not contribute significantly to irradiation odor except at high O_2 pressures. Tarladgis (1961) found that lipid oxidation is decreased in irradiated meat because the ferrohemochromogen pigment formed is not an active catalyst for this reaction in the absence of preformed peroxides. Greene and Watts (1966) reported that radiation sterilization partially suppressed lipid oxidation in precooked lean beef. The effect was not as great in pork, possibly due to the greater amount of fat present.

Texture—Tenderness

Szczesniak (1963) defines texture in food as "the broad class of properties related to the structural elements of the food, detectable with the physiological senses." Deatherage (1963) states that "tenderness or toughness of meat is a quality representing the summation of properties of the various protein structures of skeletal muscles." In recent publications, both texture and tenderness are used to refer to the degree of resistance to chewing when meat is eaten. In earlier literature, texture was frequently used to refer to the grain of meat as assessed by visual observation. However, Szczesniak and Torgeson (1965) prefer the use of texture as a more inclusive term than tenderness.

Tenderness (or texture) of meat is a complex sensation. It is determined principally by the mechanical strength of the muscle fibers and connective tissues. However, the sensation of tenderness or toughness may also be influenced by the juiciness of the meat, the water-holding capacity of the proteins, and the amount and distribution of fat (Matz, 1962). So the particular influences that determine tenderness in any given experiment will vary with the meat being tested, the conditions under which the cuts were produced and processed, and the methods used in preparing and testing the samples. A number of reviews on various aspects of meat tenderness have been published by Matz (1962), Harrison et al. (1959), Weir (1960), Hill (1962), and Paul (1965). Both Weir (1960) and Lawrie (1966) indicate that texture-tenderness is probably the most important eating characteristic to the average consumer. Szczesniak and Torgeson (1965), Adam (1964), and Pearson (1968) have reviewed methods of measurement. Bourne (1966) gives a classification of objective methods for measuring texture in a variety of foods.

Methods of Measurement

Cover and co-workers evolved a scoring sheet for panel assessment that includes six elements of tenderness plus juiciness (Cover et al., 1962). They separated the tenderness sensation into the following categories: softness (to tongue and cheek, to tooth pressure); muscle fibers (ease of fragmentation across the grain, mealiness, apparent adhesion between fibers); and connective tissue (amount and softness).

Lowe (1949) proposed chew count as a taste-panel method of assessing tenderness. Panel members are presented with standard-size pieces of meat, and asked to count the number of chews required to reduce the meat to the consistency at which it would normally be swallowed. Harrington and Pearson (1962) pointed out that this method would probably be of value only if the meat being tested contained no tough connective tissue that would be difficult or impossible to chew. They found that some testers were more consistent than others in the use of this method.

The Warner-Bratzler (WB) shear and the Lee-Kramer (LK) shear press are generally used in the United States. These are described in Chapter 16. Other instruments include a portable rotating knife tenderometer (Bjorksten et al., 1967), an adaptation of the WB (Voisey and Hansen, 1967), a slice-tenderness evaluation device (Kulwich et al., 1963), a pressure device (Sperring et al., 1959), a modified pressure device (Alsmeyer et al., 1966), and a modification of the WB machine to give energy measurement at kilowatt-seconds per gram (Áldor, 1965). Bockian et al. (1958), using the grinding technique of Miyada and Tappel (1956), suggested that this method might be improved by the use of a mechanical cubing device for more uniform samples, the use of a recording ammeter for continuous power records, and careful control of the time interval between subjective and objective determinations.

Measurements with these or other physical instruments on raw meat tend to bear little relation to the tenderness of cooked meat as assessed by a taste panel. So the measurements are usually made on cooked meat, and the values obtained frequently correlate well with panel scores. Hinnergardt and Tuomy (1970) have designed a puncture test for raw meat that correlated well with panel assessments on cooked pork LD.

A number of papers give comparisons among these and other instruments, as well as with panel scores. Carpenter et al. (1965) found that the WB shear and the wedge- , denture- , and grinder-tenderometer all showed significant correlations with panel scores for pork. Kropf and Graf (1959) reported significant relationships between WB shear and tenderness scores. Emerson and Palmer (1960) found that WB shear gave a more precise measure of tenderness than did the grinder method. Burrill et al. (1962) and Sharrah et al. (1965a) reported higher correlations for WB shear than for LK shear force with tenderness scores. Sharrah et al. (1965b) noted considerable variability in both instrumental and panel assessment of tenderness. Bratzler and Smith (1963) found little difference between WB shear and the Sperring et al. (1959) press method as predictors of tenderness of cooked beef and lamb.

A number of studies have utilized some modification of the Volodkevitch tenderometer, which measures the force required to force a blunt wedge through a sample of meat (Sale, 1960; Jones, 1968). Marsh et al. (1966), using the instrument designed by Macfarlane and Marer (1966), obtained correlation coefficients ranging from 0.68 to 0.94 between sensory and objective data in a series of studies on lamb. They concluded that the panel values were more nearly linearly related to either the reciprocal or the square root of the shear value than to shear force itself.

Another type of physical measurement is the area occupied by a standard-size sample of meat after being subjected to pressure. Price (1969) measured the spread of a slice of meat under pressure as an estimation of the tenderness. Jedlicka (1966) also used the deformed area of meat under pressure, with a larger area corresponding to greater softness. Paul et al. (1970) used a penetrometer to assess softness as a part of tenderness.

Ma et al. (1961) suggested that tenderness of meat might be assessed by measuring the amount of free leucine and isoleucine in boiling water extracts of muscle. They stated that leucine-isoleucine content increased from less- to more-tender muscles in the beef carcass. However, the psoas major, usually considered the most tender muscle of the carcass, had less leucine-isoleucine than the LD. Hegarty et al. (1968) explored solubility characteristics of the different protein fractions of muscle for relation to tenderness. They found that fibrillar protein solubility was highly correlated with tenderness as measured by shear and by a scoring panel.

Chemical analyses for amount of connective tissue usually have not correlated well with tenderness, since they do not assess the influence of the muscle fibers. Also, most of these have not considered the importance of the degree of cross-linking within the connective tissue in determining the extent to which it will be altered by cooking (Bendall, 1964).

A variety of microscopic methods have been used in attempts to measure tenderness objectively. Measurements on muscle-fiber diameters have usually not included the influence of the amount of stretch to which the muscle was subjected during the development of rigor, so further work is needed to clarify the relationship of fiber diameter to tenderness (Gillis and Henrickson, 1967). Howard and Judge (1968) explored use of sarcomere length as a measure of tenderness, but found that measurement of sarcomere length at one place did not adequately represent the overall contraction state of the muscle.

Hostetler and Cover (1961) studied muscle-fiber extensibility as a means of assessing tenderness. They found high correlations between extensibility and shear force, and extensibility and scores for softness and muscle-fiber characteristics, in LD and BF of beef when cooked to 100° C plus 25 minutes, and in LD but not BF when cooked to 61° C. Extensibility data showed no relation to connective-tissue scores. They pointed out that in a number of cases it was difficult to get usable fibers, especially from the BF muscle.

Sampling

Hostetler and Ritchey (1964) showed that WB shear values were more uniform if the cores were cut parallel to the muscle fibers rather than perpendicular to the cut surface of the steak. Paul and Bratzler (1955) stated that cores $\frac{1}{2}$ inch in diameter gave WB shear values that compared closely with those from the 1-inch cores originally recommended for this instrument. But Dill (1964) found that the use of the smaller cores increased variability of the shear readings. Kastner and Henrickson (1969) reported that cores bored by machine from cooked and chilled muscle were more uniform in diameter than those bored by hand. Davey and Gilbert (1969), using the Macfarlane-Marer tenderometer, recommended that sample size at the shear point be measured carefully and that readings be corrected to a sample cross-section of 1 square cm.

Shear force readings are also influenced by the location at which the core is taken. Rogers (1969) points out the necessity for avoiding obvious connective tissue or fat deposits. A number of studies have shown that force required to shear may vary among different slices of the same muscle and among different locations within a single slice. For example, Carpenter and King (1965) reported shear variations among different cores from the same lamb rib chop, and Alsmeyer et al. (1965) found that cores from the lateral portion were most tender and those from the medial position least tender in pork loin roasts. Smith et al. (1969) also noted the importance of anatomical location in cutting cores from beef rib steaks.

Factors Influencing Tenderness

A number of factors that may influence tenderness have already been discussed in earlier portions of this chapter. The following includes information that bears more specifically on the tenderness of cooked meat.

Field et al. (1969), in a study of bovine epimysial and intramuscular connective tissue, suggested that while hydroxyproline amounts, epimysial thickness, or connective-tissue scores in raw muscle generally did not show significant correlation with shear force on cooked muscle, collagen gelatinization might occur at a faster rate during cooking in LD than in BF as the age of the animal increased. Field et al. (1970) found that heat-labile collagen in both epimysial and intramuscular connective tissue was higher in tender muscles than in tough muscles of cutter- and canner-grade cows. They suggested that tenderness increases with amount of heat-labile collagen in the muscle.

Deatherage (1963) has reviewed the relation of WHC and of shifts in ion binding to tenderness. Webb et al. (1967) reported a significant correlation between WHC values and tenderness scores, and stated that transfer of moisture and mineral ions appeared to be associated with improved tenderization of meat. Deatherage (1963) reported that infusing beef muscle with a solution containing NaCl and $MgCl_2$ increased the tenderness score from 2.0 for the control to 7.5 for the infused sample. Suri (1956) also found that infusion with NaCl solution increased the tenderness of beef and eliminated thawing drip after freezing, suggesting increased WHC of the meat. Rust (1963) reported increased tenderness in beef, and Kamstra and Saffle (1959) increased tenderness in hams after infusion of the raw meat with sodium hexametaphosphate.

It should be recalled that solutions do not penetrate readily into intact muscle tissue. In the studies cited above, the solutions were injected directly into the raw tissue, or perfused throughout the tissue by artery-pumping. Changes in amount and location of ions would be expected to alter the pH and the WHC of the muscle tissue, and could influence tenderness by altering the susceptibility of the protein fibers to heat degradation and/or by influencing the sensation of juiciness through changes in the water-binding capacity of the proteins.

Processing Effects

Freezing and frozen storage may or may not alter tenderness, depending on the type of meat being investigated and the experimental conditions chosen. Sulzbacher and Gaddis (1968) conclude that freezing tends to increase tenderness, provided that the meat is protected from desiccation. Large changes in tenderness during frozen storage usually do not occur, although there is some progressive protein damage. However, Awad et al. (1968), using $-4°$ C as the storage temperature to accelerate deterioration changes, found that freezing and frozen storage caused increase in toughness. McBee (1960) reported that freezing did not increase tenderness of ground beef or steaks, and sometimes decreased it slightly. Smith et al. (1968) reported variable effects of freezing on tenderness of cooked lamb; some cuts requiring less force to shear, others more force. Law et al. (1967) found no change in tenderness of beef steaks with up to nine months' frozen storage. But Smith et al. (1969) suggest that frozen storage, especially for long periods or if the steaks are not protected from desiccation, may cause changes from the unfrozen material. They found no difference in tenderness when steaks were cooked with or without prior thawing. Brown (1962) reported that steaks defrosted at room temperature were less tender than those defrosted in the refrigerator.

Freeze-drying of meat leads to textural changes, the meat often being described as tough, fibrous, stringy, or woody (Bird, 1965; Karel, 1968). Karel (1968) and Bengtsson and Bengtsson (1968b) found that toughness increased with storage at a rate largely determined by the storage temperature and the water content of the meat. The latter authors (1968a) attributed the toughness in freeze-dried raw meat to leakage of fluid onto meat surfaces during drying, forming a gelatinous film that interfered with rehydration. Precooking the meat before freeze-drying decreased development of toughness but did not eliminate it.

Lewis et al. (1963) and Penny et al. (1963, 1964) found that meat of high ultimate pH gave a more tender freeze-dried product, probably due to the increased WHC of the muscle proteins. However, Penny et al. (1964) reported that in some cases freeze-dried pork steaks had a rubbery texture, although they were tender. Strasser (1969) has suggested that changes during storage in the properties of freeze-dried meats could be followed by measurement of the sorption isobar hysteresis, since the sorption isotherms indicate the ability of a dry product to hold water.

Irradiation generally has a tenderizing effect on meat, which may extend to the production of a mushy texture. Braams and Van Herpen (1964) suggest that ionizing radiations may cause covalent-bond rupture so that H-bonds are easily broken when the system is heated. Cooper and Russell (1969) attributed changes in acid-soluble collagen to disruption of the helical structure of the tropocollagen molecule. Pearson et al. (1960a,b) found that irradiation of raw beef allowed protein breakdown due to enzyme activity during storage. Heat inactivation of the enzymes would prevent protein degradation, but not the development of the mushy texture, so the latter did not appear to be due to enzyme-catalyzed proteolysis. Bailey and Rhodes (1964) found a definite tenderizing effect of irradiation on beef and pork, which they considered to be due at least partly to increased solubility of collagen. They stated that doses of < 1 mrad probably would not alter texture appreciably.

Tenderizing Treatments

Treatments that alter the fibrous structure of meat would be expected to increase the tenderness. Mechanical treatments include grinding, chopping, or pounding to break up the muscle fibers and connective tissue. Webb et al. (1962) reported that treatment of beef with sonic vibrations for 10 minutes increased tenderness, especially when used with NaCl brine as a couplant.

Proteolytic enzymes will facilitate rupture of fibers by catalyzing hydrolysis of covalent bonds within and between protein molecules. Bavisotto (1958), Whitaker (1959), and Robinson and Goeser (1962) have reviewed the use of these enzymes for tenderizing meat. The enzyme that has had the widest use is papain. This enzyme has an optimum activation temperature in the range of 60 to 70° C, so most of the proteolytic activity occurs during cooking of the meat. Accordingly, the length of time required to cook and the internal temperature to which the meat is heated will influence the amount of tenderization. Holding cooked meat at warm temperatures may lead to overtenderization and a mushy texture. Another factor in obtaining a desirable degree of tenderization is the uniformity of distribution of the enzyme throughout the meat. As with salt solutions, the enzyme does not penetrate easily into the intact tissue. So a surface application may give only a surface softening. Piercing the meat after surface application to distribute the enzyme into the interior gives some improvement. A commercial process has been developed for injecting the enzyme into the blood-stream of the animal shortly before slaughter, allowing the circulation to distribute the enzyme (Goeser, 1961). Rice (1970) pointed out that with either method, a holding period for the enzyme to become relatively evenly distributed is advisable, even though the enzymes are not active at refrigerator temperatures. Penny (1960) reported that reconstituting freeze-dried beef steaks with dilute enzyme solution gave a very satisfactory tendering action, since the enzyme was easily and evenly absorbed throughout the porous structure of the meat.

Juiciness and Water-Holding Capacity

Juiciness of meat is considered to be related to water-holding capacity (WHC). As assessed by a taste panel, juiciness is largely determined by the amount of water present and by the ease with which it can be expressed from the meat as it is chewed. It also may be influenced by flavor, tenderness, and the amount of fat present. Determinations of total moisture content or cooking losses seldom show any significant relationship to juiciness scores.

Juiciness is usually measured by a taste panel, although in some experiments the amount of fluid expressed under pressure has been found to be significantly correlated with juiciness scores.

Juiciness and WHC are influenced by a variety of factors, such as pH, ion concentrations, quality of the meat, aging of the carcass, any protein denaturation induced by treatments such as heating or dehydrating, or treatments such as grinding or freezing that alter the structure of the tissue. Miller et al. (1968) found that WHC was significantly lower at pH 5.5 than at higher pHs, that WHC varied in prerigor, postrigor, and frozen meat, and that WHC decreased with increasing fat level. Woolsey and Paul (1969) found that removing the external fat from meat before roasting increased the amount of fluid that could be pressed from the cooked meat. Dryden et al. (1969) reported a negative correlation between juiciness scores and lactic acid concentration, suggesting lower WHC at lower pH. Sherman (1961) studied the influence of NaCl, phosphates, and heat in WHC of porcine muscle tissue. He reported that fluid retention in the cold depended on the degree of ion absorption and pH. When the tissue was heated, fluid retention decreased as the temperature increased.

Freezing and thawing of meat usually causes loss of WHC as evidenced by the leakage of fluid from the meat during and after thawing. Several studies (for example, Deatherage and Hamm, 1960 and Brendl and Klein, 1967) have shown that meat frozen very rapidly shows little or no thawing drip. Lawrie (1959) states that very rapid freezing (< 1 hour) will almost eliminate drip. This, however, requires either small pieces of meat or very low freezing temperatures, or both. Loss of fluid is considered to be due to rupture of the muscle structure by the formation of large ice crystals. In general, the slower the freezing rate, the larger the crystals.

Awad et al. (1968) reported that storage of meat at $-4°$ C (just below the freezing point) caused progressive insolubilization of myofibrillar proteins and loss of WHC. When meat was stored at -18 to $-23°$ C, Law et al. (1967) found no significant change in juiciness scores up to six months, but a decline in juiciness between six and nine months.

Coleby et al. (1961) and Urbain (1969) reported that sterilization with ionizing radiation led to loss of fluid in prepackaged raw meat. Coleby et al. (1961) stated that fluid loss was increased by higher storage temperatures. Urbain (1969) recommended treatment of the meat with a phosphate to reduce drip.

Freeze-drying also causes loss of WHC; the meat does not rehydrate completely and is considered dry. Wismer-Pedersen (1965) attributed this to formation of electrostatic and H-bonds between the proteins of the myofibrils, reducing the number of sites for H-bonding of water. The effect appears to be greatest at the IEP of the muscle proteins, so treatments that raise the pH of the meat before freeze-drying result in improved WHC.

Emulsifying Capacity

The WHC and the fat-emulsifying capacity of meat materially influence the palatability characteristics of comminuted items such as wieners, salami, bologna, liver sausage, and other similar products. If the WHC is low, the products will lose moisture and shrink during smoking and/or cooking. If the fat is not properly emulsified, it will separate and form greasy layers or pockets within the product. The same factors that influence WHC in intact meat cuts are important in ground meat products. The emulsion stability depends on the character of the proteins and of the fat. Reviews are given by Saffle (1968, 1969).

The meat proteins that are most important in determining the emulsifying capacity are the salt-soluble myofibrillar proteins. Emulsifying capacity has been found to be influenced by pH, amount and type of inorganic ions present, whether the meat is used pre- or postrigor, freezing of the meat, post-mortem aging, the number of microorganisms present, and extraction time and temperature (Saffle and Galbreath, 1964; Graner et al., 1969; Acton and Saffle, 1969; Borton et al., 1968; Swift and Sulzbacher, 1963; Swift, 1965; and Bard, 1965). Swift (1965) described the apparatus commonly used for evaluating emulsifying capacity, and Rongey (1965) outlined a procedure for evaluating commercially prepared emulsions. Townsend et al. (1968) discussed the use of differential thermal analysis in studying the relation of fat melting to emulsion stability.

References

Aberle, E. D., and R. A. Merkel. 1966. Solubility and electrophoretic behavior of some proteins of post-mortem aged bovine muscle. *J. Food Sci. 31*: 151.

Acton, J. C., and R. L. Saffle. 1969. Preblended and prerigor meat in sausage emulsions. *Food Technol. 23*: 367.

Adams, C. H. 1964. Factors that influence tenderness of beef and the development of suitable methods for appraising tenderness. *Dissertation Abstr. 25*: 2435.

Áldor, T. 1963. Behavior of foods under high-frequency radiation (microwave-length range). I. Losses in weight, moisture, proteins and vitamins A and B during preparation of meat by high-frequency radiation only, or with additional infra-red irradiation, in comparison with conventional preparation. *Z. Lebensmitt. Untersuch. 123*: 189.

Áldor, T. 1965. Investigation of consistency of meat by electrical measurement of energy required for mincing. *Z. Lebensmittelunters. u. Forsch. 128*: 15.

Alford, J. A., D. A. Pierce, and W. L. Sulzbacher. 1963. Microbial lipases and their potential importance to the meat industry. *Proc. 15th Res. Conf.*, p. 11. Circ. No. 74. Am. Meat Inst. Found., Chicago, Ill.

Alm, F., I. Ericksen, and N. Molin. 1961. The effect of vacuum packaging on some sliced processed meat products as judged by organoleptic and bacteriologic analysis. *Food Technol. 15*: 199.

Alsmeyer, R. H., J. W. Thornton, and R. L. Hiner. 1965. Cross-sectional tenderness variations among six locations of pork *longissimus dorsi*. *J. Food Sci. 30*: 181.

Alsmeyer, R. H., J. W. Thornton, R. L. Hiner, and N. C. Pollinger. 1966. Beef and pork tenderness measured by the press, Warner-Bratzler, and STE methods. *Food Technol. 20*: 683.

Arnold, H., and D. Pette. 1968. Binding of glycolytic enzymes to structure proteins of muscle. *European J. Biochem. 6*: 163.

Artar, O. G., J. C. R. Li, and R. F. Cain. 1961. Effect of pre-irradiation heating on the flavor and nitrogenous constituents of beef during storage. *Food Technol. 15*: 488.

Asselbergs, E. A., and J. R. Whitaker. 1961. Determination of water-holding capacity of ground cooked lean meat. *Food Technol. 15*: 392.

Awad, A., W. D. Powrie, and O. Fennema. 1968. Chemical deterioration of frozen bovine muscle at $-4°$ C. *J. Food Sci. 33*: 227.

Bailey, A. J., and D. N. Rhodes. 1964. Treatment of meat with ionising radiations. XI. Changes in the texture of meat. *J. Sci. Food Agr. 15*: 504.

Bailey, C. M., C. L. Probert, P. Richardson, V. R. Bowman, and J. Chancerelle. 1966. Quality factors of the *Longissimum dorsi* of young bulls and steers. *J. Animal Sci. 25*: 504.

Baity, M. R., A. E. Ellington, and M. Woodburn. 1969. Foil wrap in oven cooking. *J. Home Econ. 61*: 174.

Baldwin, R. E., and B. M. Korschgen. 1968. Freezer storage effects on beef prepared by an interrupted cooking procedure. *Food Technol. 22*: 1261.

Banga, I., A. L. Zaides, A. A. Tustanovskii, and G. V. Orlovskaya. 1960. Changes in the submicroscopic structure of collagen after the action of collagen-mucoproteinase. *Gerontol. 4*: 187.

Bard, J. C. 1965. Some factors influencing extractability of salt-soluble proteins. *Proc. Meat Ind. Res. Conf.*, p. 96. Am. Meat Inst. Found., Chicago, Ill.

Barnicoat, C. R., and F. B. Shorland. 1952. New Zealand mutton and lamb. II. Chemical composition of edible tissues. *N.Z. J. Sci. Tech.* No. 1, A, *33* (5): 16.

Barton, P. A. 1967a. Measurement of colour stability of cooked cured meats to light and air. I. Development of methods. *J. Sci. Food Agr. 18*: 298.

Barton, P. A. 1967b. Measurement of colour stability of cooked cured meats to light and air. II. Testing the procedure. *J. Sci. Food Agr. 18*: 305.

Batcher, O. M., A. W. Brant, and M. S. Kunze. 1969. Sensory evaluation of lamb and yearling mutton flavors. *J. Food Sci. 34*: 272.

Batcher, O. M., E. H. Dawson, G. L. Gilpin, and J. N. Eisen. 1962. Quality and physical composition of various cuts of raw and cooked pork. *Food Technol. 16*, No. 4: 104.

Batcher, O. M., E. H. Dawson, M. T. Pointer, and G. L. Gilpin. 1962. Quality of raw and cooked lamb meat as related to fatness and age of animal. *Food Technol. 16*, No. 1: 102.

Bate-Smith, E. C., and J. R. Bendall. 1949. Factors determining the time course of rigor mortis. *J. Physiol. (London) 110*: 47.

Batzer, O. J., A. T. Santoro, and W. A. Landmann. 1962. Identification of some beef flavor precursors. *J. Agr. Food Chem. 10*: 94.

Batzer, O. J., A. T. Santoro, M. C. Tan, W. A. Landmann, and B. S. Schweigert. 1960. Precursors of beef flavor. *J. Agr. Food Chem. 8*: 498.

Bavisotto, V. S. 1958. Meat tenderizing by enzymes. *Proc. 10th Res. Conf.*, p. 67. Circ. No. 45. Am. Meat Inst. Found., Chicago, Ill.

Beecher, G. R., R. G. Cassens, W. G. Hoekstra, and E. J. Briskey. 1965. Red and white fiber content and associated post-mortem properties of seven porcine muscles. *J. Food Sci. 30*: 969.

Beef Task Force. 1968. A national program of research for beef. Mimeo. *Research Program Development and Evaluation*, U.S.D.A., Washington, D.C.

Beery, K. E., and J. H. Ziegler. 1969. A simplified and rapid method to uniformly size rib steak pieces for taste panel evaluation. *J. Food Sci. 34*: 480.

Bendall, J. R. 1960. Post mortem changes in muscle. In *The Structure and Function of Muscle*. G. H. Bourne, ed., vol. 3, p. 227. Academic Press, New York.

Bendall, J. R. 1964. Meat proteins. In *Symposium on Foods: Proteins and Their Reactions*. H. W. Schultz, and A. F. Anglemier, eds. p. 225. Avi Publ. Co., Westport, Conn.

Bendall, J. R. 1966. The effect of pre-treatment of pigs with curare on the post-mortem rate of pH fall and the onset of rigor mortis in the musculature. *J. Sci. Food Agr. 17*: 333.

Bendall, J. R. 1966. Muscle as a contractile machine. In *Physiology and Biochemistry of Muscle as a Food*. E. J. Briskey, R. G. Cassens, and J. C. Trautman, eds., p. 7. U. of Wisc. Press, Madison, Wisc.

Bendall, J. R. 1967. The elastin content of various muscles of beef animals. *J. Sci. Food Agr. 18*: 553.

Ben-Gera, I., and K. H. Norris. 1968. Direct spectrophotometric determination of fat and moisture in meat products. *J. Food Sci. 33*: 64.

Bengtsson, O., and N. E. Bengtsson. 1968a. Freeze-drying of raw beef. II. Influence of some freezing and dehydration variables. *J. Sci. Food Agr. 19*: 481.

Bengtsson, O., and N. E. Bengtsson. 1968b. Freeze-drying of raw beef. III. Influence of some packaging and some storage variables. *J. Sci. Food Agr. 19*: 486.

Berman, M. D. 1960. Determination of the proximate and electrolyte content of beef. *Food Technol. 14*: 429.

Berman, M. D. 1961. Factors affecting the water retention of beef. V. Variation of the zinc-containing enzymes. *J. Food Sci. 26*: 422.

Bernofsky, C., J. B. Fox, Jr., and B. S. Schweigert. 1959. Biochemistry of myoglobin. VII. Effect of cooking on myoglobin in beef muscle. *Food Res. 24*: 339.

Berrens, L., and L. M. J. van Driel. 1962. Vergleichende Untersuchungen über menschliches Kollagen und Retikulin. *Naturwiss. 49*: 608.

Bird, K. 1965. Palatability of freeze-dried meats. *Food Technol. 19*: 737.

Bjorksten, J., P. Anderson, K. A. Bouschart, and J. Kapsalis. 1967. A portable rotating knife tenderometer. *Food Technol. 21*: 84.

Bloom, W., and D. W. Fawcett. 1964. *A Textbook of Histology*. W. B. Saunders Co., Philadelphia, Pa.

Blumer, T. N., H. B. Craig, E. A. Pierce, W. W. G. Smart, Jr., and M. B. Wise. 1962. Nature and variability of marbling deposits in *longissimus dorsi* muscle of beef carcasses. *J. Animal Sci. 21*: 935.

Board, P. W., Ihsan-ul-Haque. 1965. Discoloration of canned cured meats caused by copper. *Food Technol. 19*, No. 11: 117.

Bockian, A. H., A. F. Anglemier, and L. A. Sather. 1958. A comparison of an objective and subjective measurement of beef tenderness. *Food Technol.* *12:* 483.

Bodwell, C. E., and A. M. Pearson. 1964. The activity of partially purified bovine catheptic enzymes on various natural and synthetic substrates. *J. Food Sci. 29:* 602.

Borton, R. J., N. B. Webb, and L. J. Bratzler. 1968. Effect of micro-organisms on emulsifying capacity and extract release volume of fresh porcine tissues. *Food Technol. 22:* 94.

Bourne, M. C. 1966. A classification of objective methods for measuring texture and consistency of foods. *J. Food Sci. 31:* 1011.

Bouton, P. E., A. Howard, and R. A. Lawrie. 1957. Studies on beef quality. VI. Effects on weight losses and eating quality of further preslaughter treatments. C.S.I.R.O., Austr., *Div. Food Pres. and Trans. Tech. paper* No. 6.

Bowers, J. A. 1969. Free amino acids in porcine muscle aged one or eight days. *J. Agr. Food Chem. 17:* 902.

Bowers, J. A., D. L. Harrison, and D. H. Kropf. 1968. Browning and associated properties of porcine muscle. *J. Food Sci. 33:* 147.

Bowers, J. A., and G. E. Goertz. 1966. Effect of internal temperature on eating quality of pork chops. I. Skillet and oven braising. *J. Am. Dietet. Assoc. 48:* 116.

Braams, R., and G. Van Herpen. 1964. The effects of ionizing radiations on some fibrous proteins. In *The Structure and Properties of Biomolecules and Biological Systems.* J. Duchesne, ed. p. 259. Interscience Publ. Co., New York.

Bramblett, V. D., and G. E. Vail. 1964. Further studies on the qualities of beef as affected by cooking at very low temperatures for long periods. *Food Technol. 18,* No. 2: 123.

Bramblett, V. D., R. L. Hostetler, G. E. Vail, and H. N. Draudt. 1959. Qualities of beef as affected by cooking at very low temperatures for long periods of time. *Food Technol. 13:* 707.

Bratzler, L. J., and H. D. Smith. 1963. A comparison of the press method with taste-panel and shear measurements of tenderness in beef and lamb muscles. *J. Food Sci. 28:* 99.

Bratzler, L. J., M. E. Spooner, J. B. Weatherspoon, and J. A. Maxey. 1969. Smoke flavor as related to phenol, carbonyl and acid content of bologna. *J. Food Sci. 34:* 146.

Brendl, J., and S. Klein. 1967. Effect of freezing temperature on the hydration capacity of defrosted meat. *Sb. vys. šk. Chem.-Technol. Praze, Potravin E16:* 39.

Briskey, E. J. 1963. Influence of ante- and post-mortem handling practices on properties of muscle which are related to tenderness. *Proc., Meat Tenderness Symp.,* Campbell Soup Co., Camden, N.J.

Briskey, E. J. 1964. Etiological status and associated studies of pale, soft, exudative porcine musculature. *Advan. Food Res. 13:* 89.

Briskey, E. J. 1967. Myofibrillar proteins of skeletal muscle. *Proc., Meat Ind. Res. Conf.,* p. 1. Am. Meat Ind. Found., Chicago.

Briskey, E. J., R. W. Bray, W. G. Hoekstra, R. H. Grummer, and P. H. Phillips. 1959. The effect of various levels of exercise in altering the chemical and physical characteristics of certain pork ham muscles. *J. Animal Sci. 18:* 153.

Briskey, E. J., W. G. Hoekstra, R. W. Bray, and R. H. Grummer. 1960. A comparison of certain physical and chemical characteristics of eight pork muscles. *J. Animal Sci. 19:* 214.

Briskey, E. J., T. Kowalczyk, W. E. Blackmon, B. B. Breidenstein, R. W. Bray, and R. H. Grummer. 1958. Porcine musculature-topography. *Wisc. Agr. Expt. Sta. Res. Bull.* No. 206.

Briskey, E. J., and R. N. Sayre. 1964. Muscle protein extractability as influenced by conditions of post-mortem glycolysis. *Proc. Soc. Exptl. Biol. Med. 115:* 823.

Broderick, J. J. 1968. Progress in meat flavoring. *Cereal Sci. Today 13:* 290.

Brody, A. L. 1970. Shelf life of fresh meat. *Modern Packaging,* Jan.

Brown, W. A. 1962. Effect of an oil coating on the microflora and palatability of frozen-defrosted meat. *Dissertation Abstr. 22:* 2943.

Brown, W. D., and A. L. Tappel. 1958. Pigment-antioxidant relationships to meat-color stability. *Proc., 10th Res. Conf.,* p. 81. Circ. No. 45, Am. Meat Inst. Found., Chicago, Ill.

Bryce-Jones, K., J. M. Harries, and T. W. Houston. 1964. Studies in beef quality. III. Effects of hexoestrol implantation. *J. Sci. Food Agr. 15:* 62.

Bryce-Jones, K., T. W. Houston, and J. M. Harries. 1963. Studies in beef quality. II. Influence of sire on the quality and composition of beef. *J. Sci. Food Agr. 14:* 637.

Buck, E. M., and D. L. Black. 1968. Microscopic characteristics of cooked muscles subjected to stretch-tension during rigor. *J. Food Sci. 33:* 464.

Buck, E. M., D. W. Stanley, and E. A. Comissiong. 1970. Physical and chemical characteristics of free and stretched rabbit muscle. *J. Food Sci. 35:* 100.

Bull, S., and H. P. Rusk. 1942. Effect of exercise on quality of beef. *Ill. Agr. Expt. Sta. Bull.* No. 488.

Burrill, L. M., D. Deethardt, and R. L. Saffle. 1962. Two mechanical devices compared with taste-panel evaluation for measuring tenderness. *Food Technol. 16,* No. 10: 145.

Busch, W. A., F. C. Parrish, Jr., and D. E. Goll. 1967. Molecular properties of post-mortem muscle. 4. Effect of temperature on adenosine triphosphate degradation, isomeric tension parameters and shear resistance of bovine muscle. *J. Food Sci. 32:* 390.

Byerly, T. C. 1965. Meat quality: Genetic and environmental factors in development and performance. In *Food Quality*, G. W. Irving, Jr., and S. R. Hoover, eds., p. 251. Am. Assoc. Adv. Sci. Publ. No. 77, Washington, D.C.

Callow, E. H. 1947. Comparative studies of meat. I. The chemical composition of fatty and muscular tissue in relation to growth and fattening. *J. Agr. Sci. 37*: 113.

Callow, E. H. 1948. Comparative studies of meat. II. The changes in the carcass during growth and fattening, and their relation to the chemical composition of the fatty and muscular tissues. *J. Agr. Sci. 38*: 174.

Callow, E. H. 1949. Comparative studies of meat. III. Rates of fattening in relation to the percentage of muscular and fatty tissue in a carcass. *J. Agr. Sci. 39*: 347.

Callow, E. H. 1957. Ten years' work on meat at the Low Temperature Research Station, Cambridge. *Food Sci. Abstr. 29*: 101.

Cameron, R., and W. G. Spector. 1961. *The Chemistry of the Injured Cell*, Chap. 9. C. C Thomas, Springfield, Ill.

Campbell, A. M., and P. R. Turkki. 1967. Lipids of raw and cooked ground beef and pork. *J. Food Sci. 32*: 143.

Carlin, A. F., D. M. Bloemer, and D. K. Hotchkiss. 1965. Relation of oven temperature and final internal temperature to quality of pork loin roasts. *J. Home Econ. 57*: 442.

Carlin, A. F., C. Mott, D. Cash, and W. Zimmermann. 1969. Destruction of trichina larvae in cooked pork roasts. *J. Food Sci. 34*: 210.

Carpenter, Z. L., R. G. Kauffman, R. W. Bray, and K. G. Weckel. 1965. Objective and subjective measures of pork quality. *Food Technol. 19*: 1424.

Carpenter, Z. L., and G. T. King. 1965. Tenderness of lamb rib chops. *Food Technol. 19*, No. 11: 102.

Cassens, R. G., E. J. Briskey, and W. G. Hoekstra. 1963a. Similarity in the contracture bands occurring in thaw-rigor and in other violent treatments of muscle. *Biodynamica 9*: 165.

Cassens, R. G., E. J. Briskey, and W. G. Hoekstra. 1963b. Electron microscopy of post-mortem changes in porcine muscle. *J. Food Sci. 28*: 680.

Cassens, R. G., E. J. Briskey, and W. G. Hoekstra. 1963. Variation in zinc content and other properties of various porcine muscles. *J. Sci. Food Agr. 14*: 427.

Cassens, R. G., W. G. Hoekstra, and E. J. Briskey. 1963. Relation of pork muscle quality factors to zinc content and other properties. *Food Technol. 17*: 493.

Cassens, R. G., and R. P. Newbold. 1966. Effects of temperature on post-mortem metabolism in beef muscle. *J. Sci. Food Agr. 17*: 254.

Cassens, R. G., and R. P. Newbold. 1967. Effect of temperature on the time course of rigor mortis in ox muscle. *J. Food Sci. 32*: 269.

Champagne, J. R., and W. W. Nawar. 1969. The volatile components of irradiated beef and pork fats. *J. Food Sci. 34*: 335.

Chang, P.-Y., M. T. Younathan, and B. M. Watts. 1961. Lipid oxidation in precooked beef preserved by refrigeration, freezing, and irradiation. *Food Technol. 15*: 168.

Charpentier, J. 1969. Influence de la température et du pH sur quelques caracteristiques physico-chimiques des protéines sarcoplasmiques du muscle de porc; consequences technologiques. *Ann. Biol. Anim. Bioch. Biophys. 9*: 101.

Chaudhry, H. M., F. C. Parrish, Jr., and D. E. Goll. 1969. Molecular properties of post-mortem muscle. 6. Effect of temperature on protein solubility of rabbit and bovine muscle. *J. Food Sci. 34*: 183.

Chung, R. A., J. A. McKay, and C. L. Ramey. 1966. Fatty acid changes in beef, pork, and fish after deep-fat frying in different oils. *Food Technol. 20*: 691.

Clarke, E. A., and C. P. McMeekan. 1952. New Zealand lamb and mutton. I. Anatomical characteristics of lamb and mutton carcasses. *N.Z. J. Sci. Tech.* No. 1, A, *33* (5): 1.

Clark, H. E., M. C. Wilmeth, D. L. Harrison, and G. E. Vail. 1955. The effect of braising and pressure saucepan cookery on the cooking losses, palatability, and nutritive value of the proteins of round steak. *Food Res. 20*: 35.

Cohen, E. H. 1966. Protein changes related to ham processing temperatures. I. Effect of time-temperature on amount and composition of soluble proteins. *J. Food Sci. 31*: 746.

Cole, M. S. 1961. Relation of thiol-groups to the fading of cured meat. *Dissertation Abstr. 22*: 533.

Coleby, B., M. Ingram, and H. J. Shepherd. 1961. Treatment of meats with ionising radiations. VI. Changes in quality during storage of sterilized raw beef and pork. *J. Sci. Food Agr. 12*: 417.

Committee on Preparation Factors, National Cooperative Meat Investigations. 1942. *Meat and Meat Cookery.* Nat. Live Stock and Meat Bd. Chicago, Ill.

Cook, C. F. 1968. Rigor state, freeze condition, pH and incubation temperature and their influence on color development and extract release volume in ovine muscle homogenates. *J. Food Sci. 33*: 200.

Cooper, C. C., R. G. Cassens, and E. J. Briskey. 1969. Capillary distribution and fiber characteristics in skeletal muscle of stress-susceptible animals. *J. Food Sci. 34*: 299.

Cooper, D. R., and A. E. Russell. 1969. The decomposition of soluble collagen by γ-irradiation. *Biochem. J. 113*: 263.

Copenhauer, W. M., and D. D. Johnson. 1958. *Bailey's Textbook of Histology.* 14th ed. The Williams and Wilkins Co., Baltimore.

Cover, S. 1937. The effect of temperature and time of cooking on tenderness of roasts. *Texas Agr. Exp. Sta. Bull.* 542, College Station, Texas.

Cover, S. 1941. Effect of metal skewers on cooking time and tenderness of beef. *Food Res.* 6: 233.

Cover, S., J. A. Bannister, and E. Kehlenbrink. 1957. Effect of four conditions of cooking on the eating quality of two cuts of beef. *Food Res.* 22: 635.

Cover, S., O. D. Butler, and T. C. Cartwright. 1956. The relationship of fatness in yearling steers to juiciness and tenderness of broiled and braised steaks. *J. Animal Sci.* 15: 464.

Cover, S., and R. L. Hostetler. 1960. An examination of some theories about beef tenderness by using new methods. *Texas Agr. Exp. Sta. Bull.* No. 947.

Cover, S., S. J. Ritchey, and R. L. Hostetler. 1962. Tenderness of beef. I. The connective-tissue component of tenderness. *J. Food Sci.* 27: 469.

Cover, S., W. H. Smith, Jr. 1956. Effect of moist and dry heat cooking methods on vitamin retention in meat from beef animals of different levels of fleshing. *Food Res.* 21: 209.

Craig, H. B., A. M. Pearson, and N. B. Webb. 1962. Fractionation of the component(s) responsible for sex odor/flavor in pork. *J. Food Sci.* 27: 29.

Craigie, E. H. 1966. *A Laboratory Guide to the Anatomy of the Rabbit.* U. of Toronto Press, revised ed.

Cramer, R. A. 1963. Feed and meats terminology: a symposium. V. Techniques used in meat flavor research. *J. Animal Sci.* 22: 555.

Cross, C. K., and P. A. Ziegler. 1965. Comparison of the volatiles from cured and uncured meat. *J. Food Sci.* 30: 610.

Crow, R. E., A. M. Mullins, S. L. Hansard, and R. F. Boulware. 1967. Reticular tissue and mast cells in relation to tenderness. *Proc., 20th Recip. Meat Conf.,* p. 42. Nat. Live Stock Meat Bd., Chicago, Ill.

Dannert, R. D. 1966. The determination of 5'-mononucleotides in meats. *Dissertation Abstr. B27:* 1970.

Dannert, R. D., and A. M. Pearson. 1967a. Concentration of inosine 5'-monophosphate in meat. *J. Food Sci.* 32: 49.

Dannert, R. D., and A. M. Pearson. 1967b. Acceptability of frankfurters containing flavor potentiators. *Food Technol.* 21: 777.

Davenport, M. M., and B. H. Meyer. 1970. Forced convection roasting at 200° and 300° F. *J. Amer. Dietet. Assoc.* 56: 31.

Davey, C. L., and K. V. Gilbert. 1966. Studies in meat tenderness. II. Proteolysis and the aging of beef. *J. Food Sci.* 31: 135.

Davey, C. L., and K. V. Gilbert. 1968a. Studies in meat tenderness. 4. Changes in the extractability of myofibrillar proteins during meat aging. *J. Food Sci.* 33: 2.

Davey, C. L., and K. V. Gilbert. 1968b. Studies in meat tenderness. 6. The nature of myofibrillar proteins extracted from meat during aging. *J. Food Sci.* 33: 343.

Davey, C. L., and K. V. Gilbert. 1969. Studies in meat tenderness. 7. Changes in the fine structure of meat during aging. *J. Food Sci. 34*: 69.

Davey, C. L., and K. V. Gilbert. 1969. The effect of sample dimensions on the cleaving of meat in the objective assessment of tenderness. *J. Food Technol. 4*: 7.

Davey, C. L., K. V. Gilbert, and G. R. Schmidt. 1970. Meat Ind. Res. Inst., New Zealand, personal communication.

Davey, C. L., H. Kuttel, and K. V. Gilbert. 1967. Shortening as a factor in meat aging. *J. Food Technol. 2*: 53.

Davies, C. K., Jr. 1962. Effect of heat on the water-soluble proteins of beef skeletal muscle. *Dissertation Abstr. 23*: 418.

Davies, R. E. 1966. Recent theories on the mechanism of muscle contraction and rigor mortis. *Proc., Meat Ind. Res. Conf.*, p. 39. Am. Meat Inst. Found., Chicago, Ill.

Dawson, E. H., G. S. Linton, A. M. Harkin, and C. Miller. 1959. Factors influencing the palatability, vitamin content, and yield of cooked beef. *Home Econ. Res. Rep. No. 9*, U.S.D.A., Washington, D.C.

Dean, R. W., and C. O. Ball. 1960. Analysis of the myoglobin fractions on the surfaces of beef cuts. *Food Technol. 14*: 271.

Deatherage, F. E. 1963. The effect of water and inorganic salts on tenderness. *Proc. Meat Tenderness Symp.*, p. 45. Campbell Soup Co., Camden, N.J.

Deatherage, F. E., and R. Hamm. 1960. Influence of freezing and thawing on hydration and charges of the muscle proteins. *Food Res. 25*: 623.

Deatherage, F. E., and A. Harsham. 1947. Relation of tenderness of beef to aging time at 33–35° F. *Food Res. 12*: 164.

Decareau, R. V. 1967. Utilization of microwave cookery in meat processing. *Proc., 20th Ann. Recip. Meat Conf.*, p. 216. Nat. Live Stock Meat Bd., Chicago, Ill.

Deuticke, H. J. 1932. Kolloidzustandsanderungen der Muskelproteine bei der Muskeltätigkeit. *Z. Physiol. Chem. 210*: 97.

Dill, B. M. 1964. A study of some secondary factors influencing tenderness on the bovine longissimus dorsi muscle. Thesis, Okla. State Univ., Stillwater.

Disney, J. G., M. J. Follett, and P. W. Ratcliff. 1967. Biochemical changes in beef muscle post mortem and the effect of rapid cooling in ice. *J. Sci. Food Agr. 18*: 314.

Donnelly, T. H., E. H. Rongey, and V. J. Barsuko. 1966. Protein composition and functional properties of meat. *J. Agr. Food Chem. 14*: 196.

Dorfman, A. 1964. Metabolism of acid mucopolysaccharides. In *Connective Tissues: Intercellular Macromolecules*, p. 155. Little, Brown & Co., Boston.

Doty, D. M. 1962. Factors in the control of product composition by chemical analysis. *Proc. 14th Res. Conf.*, Amer. Meat Inst. Found., Circ. No. 70, p. 11.

Doty, D. M., and J. C. Pierce. 1961. Beef muscle characteristics as related to carcass grade, carcass weight, and degree of aging. *Tech. Bull. No. 1231*, Ag. Marketing Serv., USDA, Washington, D.C.

Draudt, H. N. 1969. Effect of heating on the behavior of meat pigments. *Proc. 22nd Recip. Meat Conf.*, p. 180. Nat. Live Stock Meat Bd., Chicago, Ill.

Draudt, H. N., and F. E. Deatherage. 1956. Studies on the chemistry of cured meat pigment fading. *Food Res. 21*: 122.

Dryden, F. D., J. A. Marchello, and D. E. Ray. 1969. Relationship of certain chemical constituents of beef muscle to its eating quality. *J. Food Sci. 34*: 57.

Duncan, W. R. H., and G. A. Garton. 1967. The fatty acid composition and intramolecular structure of triglycerides derived from different sites in the body of the sheep. *J. Sci. Food Agr. 18*: 99.

Dugan, L. R. 1967. Phospholipids in meat—methods of isolation and influence on meat characteristics. *Proc. 20th Recip. Meat Conf.*, p. 98. Nat. Live Stock Meat Bd., Chicago, Ill.

Dvořák, Z., and I. Vognarová. 1969. Nutritive value of the proteins of veal, beef and pork determined on the basis of available essential amino acids or hydroxyproline analysis. *J. Sci. Food Agr. 20*: 146.

Eisenhut, R. C., R. G. Cassens, R. W. Bray, and E. J. Briskey. 1965. Fiber arrangement and micro-structure of bovine longissimus dorsi muscle. *J. Food Sci. 30*: 955.

El-Badawi, A. A., A. F. Anglemier, and R. F. Cain. 1964. Effects of soaking in water, thermal enzyme inactivation, and irradiation on the textural factors of beef. *Food Technol. 18*: 1807.

El-Badawi, A. A., R. F. Cain, C. E. Samuels, and A. F. Anglemier. 1964. Color and pigment stability of packaged refrigerated beef. *Food Technol. 18*, No. 5: 159.

El-Gharbawi, M. I. 1965. Chemical and physico-chemical changes in lipids and other constituents of freeze-dried raw beef during storage under modified atmospheres. *Dissertation Abstr. 25*: 7191.

El-Gharbawi, M., and J. R. Whitaker. 1963. Factors affecting enzymatic solubilization of beef proteins. *J. Food Sci. 28*: 168.

Ellis, R., G. T. Currie, F. E. Thornton, N. C. Bollinger, and A. M. Gaddis. 1968. Carbonyls in oxidizing fat. XI. The effect of the pro-oxidant activity of sodium chloride on pork tissue. *J. Food Sci. 33*: 555.

Elliott, R. J. 1967. Effect of optical systems and sample preparation on the visible reflection spectra of pork muscle. *J. Sci. Food Agr. 18*: 332.

Elliott, R. J. 1968. Calculation and presentation of pork muscle colour from reflectance spectra. *J. Sci. Food Agr. 19*: 685.

Emerson, J. A., and A. Z. Palmer. 1960. Food grinder-recording ammeter method for measuring beef tenderness. *Food Technol. 14*: 214.

Englehardt, V. A. 1946. Adenosinetriphosphatase properties of myosin. *Advan. Enzymol. 6*: 147.

Ertle, N. L. 1969. Sausage shelf-life as affected by packaging. *Proc. Meat Ind. Res. Conf.*, p. 175. Am. Meat Inst. Found., Chicago, Ill.

Fiddler, W., A. E. Wasserman, and R. C. Doerr. 1970. An ether soluble fraction of a liquid smoke preparation. *J. Agr. Food Chem. 18*: 310.

Field, R. A., G. E. Nelms, and C. O. Schoonover. 1966. Effects of age, marbling and sex on palatability of beef. *J. Animal Sci. 25*: 360.

Field, R. A., A. M. Pearson, D. E. Koch, and R. A. Merkel. 1970. Thermal behavior of epimysial and intramuscular collagen from normal and PSE pork as related to post-mortem time. *J. Food Sci. 35*: 113.

Field, R. A., A. M. Pearson, and B. S. Schweigert. 1970. Labile collagen from epimysial and intramuscular connective tissue as related to Warner-Bratzler shear values. *J. Agr. Food Chem. 18*: 280.

Field, R. A., M. L. Riley, and Y-O. Chang. 1969. Epimysial connective tissue scores as related to beef tenderness. *J. Food Sci. 34*: 514.

Fielder, M. M., A. M. Mullins, M. M. Skellenger, R. Whitehead, and D. S. Moschette. 1963. Subjective and objective evaluations of prefabricated cuts of beef. *Food Technol. 17*: 213.

Fitton Jackson, S. 1964. Connective tissue cells. In *The Cell, Biochemistry, Physiology, Morphology*, J. Brachet, and A. E. Mirsky, eds., vol. VI, p. 387. Academic Press, New York.

Fitzgerald, M. 1968. Recent developments in the breeding of livestock and their effects on today's meat. In *Current topics in food and nutrition.* Dept. of Home Econ., U. of Iowa, Iowa City, Iowa. p. 179.

Forss, D. A. 1969. Role of lipids in flavors. *J. Agr. Food Chem. 17*: 681.

Foster, W. W., and T. H. Simpson. 1961. Studies of the smoking process for foods. *J. Sci. Food Agr. 12*: 363.

Fox, J. B., Jr. 1966. The chemistry of meat pigments. *J. Agr. Food Chem. 14*: 207.

Fox, J. B., Jr. 1968. Chemico-physical properties of meat pigments as related to color. *Proc. Meat Ind. Res. Conf.*, p. 12. Am. Meat Inst. Found., Chicago.

Fox, J. B., Jr., and S. A. Ackerman. 1968. Formation of nitric oxide myoglobin: mechanisms of the reaction with various reductants. *J. Food Sci. 33*: 364.

Fox, J. B., Jr., and J. S. Thomson. 1964. The formation of green heme pigments from metmyoglobin and methemoglobin by the action of nitrite. *Biochem. 3*: 1323.

Fox, J. B., W. E. Townsend, S. A. Ackerman, and C. E. Swift. 1967. Cured color development during frankfurter processing. *Food Technol. 21*: 386.

Fox, J. D. 1965. Acid mucopolysaccharides of connective tissue—biology and function. *Proc. Meat Ind. Res. Conf.*, p. 40. Am. Meat Inst. Found., Chicago.

Fredholm, H. 1961. Rancidity of pork. Influence of different feeding and cold storage conditions on development of rancidity in fatty tissue of pork. *Acta Agr. Scand. 11*: 335.

Freeman, J. A., and J. C. Geer. 1964. *Cellular Fine Structure.* McGraw-Hill, New York, N.Y.

Fujimaki, M., and F. E. Deatherage. 1964. Chromatographic fractionation of sarcoplasmic proteins of beef skeletal muscle on ion-exchange cellulose. *J. Food Sci. 29*: 316.

Funk, K., P. J. Aldrich, and T. F. Irmiter. 1966. Forced convection roasting of loin cuts of beef. *J. Am. Dietetic Assoc. 48*: 404.

Funk, K., P. J. Aldrich, and T. F. Irmiter. 1968. Rate of temperature rise, physical and chemical properties of ground beef cylinders fabricated from selected muscles of the round. 2. Effect of bone; 3. Effect of surface fat; 4. Effect of surface connective tissue. *Food Technol. 22*: 1183, 1285, 1589.

Gaines, M. K., A. K. Perry, and F. O. Van Duyne. 1966. Preparing top round beef roasts. *J. Am. Dietetic Assoc. 48*: 204.

Gardner, G. A. 1967. Discoloration in cooked ham. *Process Biochem. 2*, No. 3: 49.

Garrett, W. N., and N. Hinman. 1969. Re-evaluation of the relationship between carcass density and body composition of beef steers. *J. Animal Sci. 28*: 1.

Garrigus, R. R., H. R. Johnson, N. W. Thomas, N. L. Firth, R. B. Harrington, and M. D. Judge. 1969. Dietary effects on beef composition. I. Quantitative and qualitative carcass traits. *J. Agr. Sci.*, Camb. *72*: 289.

Giam, I., and L. R. Dugan. 1965. The fatty acid composition of free and bound lipids in freeze-dried meats. *J. Food Sci. 30*: 262.

Giles, B. G. 1968. Effect of heat on meat structure. *Abstr. 14th European Meat Res. Conf.*, p. 25. Am. Meat Sci. Assoc., Chicago, Ill., mimeo.

Giddey, C. 1966. Change in meat pigments in sausage making processes. *J. Sci. Food Agr. 17*: 14.

Gilka, J. 1963. Causes of brown discoloration of lyophilized meat. *Prům. potravin 14*: 589.

Gillis, W. A., and R. L. Henrickson. 1967. Structural variations of the bovine muscle fiber in relation to tenderness. *Proc. Recip. Meat Conf.*, p. 17. Nat. Live Stock Meat Bd., Chicago, Ill.

Gisske, W. 1959. Temperature penetration of carcasses under normal cooling conditions. *Fleischwirtschaft 11*: 978.

Goeser, P. A. 1961. Tendered meat through antemortem vascular injection of proteolytic enzymes. *Proc. 13th Res. Conf.*, p. 56, Amer. Meat Inst. Found. Circ. No. 64, Chicago, Ill.

Goldblith, S. A., and S. R. Tannenbaum. 1966. The nutritional aspects of the freeze-drying of foods. *Proc. 7th Int. Cong. Nutr.*, Vol. 4, p. 432. Vlg. Fr. Vieweg. & Sohn GmbH., Braunschweig, Germany.

Goll, D. E. 1962. Isolation of connective tissue from bovine *biceps femoris* muscle and changes in its physiochemical properties with chronological age. Ph.D. thesis. University Microfilms, Ann Arbor, Mich.

Goll, D. E. 1965. Post-mortem changes in connective tissue. *Proc. Recip. Meat Conf.*, p. 161. Nat. Live Stock and Meat Bd., Chicago, Ill.

Goll, D. E. 1968. The resolution of rigor mortis. *Proc. Recip. Meat Conf.*, p. 16. Nat. Live Stock and Meat Bd., Chicago, Ill.

Goll, D. E., A. F. Carlin, L. P. Anderson, E. A. Kline, and M. J. Walter. 1965. Effect of marbling and maturity on beef muscle characteristics. II. Physical, chemical and sensory evaluation of steaks. *Food Technol. 19*: 845.

Goll, D. E., W. O. Hoekstra, and R. W. Bray. 1964. Age associated changes in bovine muscle connective tissue. I: Exposure to increasing temperature. *J. Food Sci. 29*: 515.

Goll, D. E., W. F. H. M. Mommaerts, M. K. Reedy, and K. Seraydarian. 1969. Studies on α-actinin-like proteins liberated during trypsin digestion of α-actinin and of myofibrils. *Biochim. Biophys. Acta 175*: 174.

Goll, D. E., and R. M. Robson. 1967. Molecular properties of post-mortem muscle. I. Myofibrillar nucleosidetriphosphatase activity of bovine muscle. *J. Food Sci. 32*: 323.

Golovkin, Vasilyev. 1967. Changes in the aromatic substances of meat during refrigerated storage. *Report, 13th European Meat Res. Conf.*, p. 33. Am. Meat Sci. Assoc., Chicago, Ill., mimeo.

Graner, M., V. R. Cahill, and H. W. Ockerman. 1969. The emulsifying capacity of bovine muscle tissue as related to time post-mortem and microbial contamination. *Food Technol. 23*: 1590.

Grau, R., and R. Hamm. 1953. A simple method for the determination of water binding in muscles. *Naturwiss. 40*: 29.

Greaser, M. L., R. G. Cassens, E. J. Briskey, and W. G. Hoekstra. 1969. Post-mortem changes in subcellular fractions from normal and pale, soft, exudative porcine muscle. I. Calcium accumulation and adenosine triphosphatase activity. *J. Food Sci. 34*: 120.

Greene, B. E. 1969. Lipid oxidation and pigment changes in raw beef. *J. Food Sci. 34*: 110.

Greene, B. E., and B. M. Watts. 1966. Lipid oxidation in irradiated cooked beef. *Food Technol. 20*, No. 8: 111.

Griffiths, N. M., and R. L. S. Patterson. 1970. Human olfactory responses to 5α-androst-16-en-3-one—principal component of boar taint. *J. Sci. Food Agr. 21*: 4.

Griswold, R. M. 1955. The effect of different methods of cooking beef round of commercial and prime grades. I. Palatability and shear values. *Food Res. 20*: 160.

Guenther, J. J. 1967. Qualitative characteristics of the meat animal as influenced by physiological maturity equivalents. *Recip. Meat Conf. Proc. 20*: 88.

Gunther, H. 1968. Changes of some protein fraction in beef muscle post mortem. *14th European Meat Res. Conf.*, p. 14. Am. Meat Science Assoc., Chicago, Ill., mimeo.

Hall, D. A. 1961. *The Chemistry of Connective Tissue.* C. C Thomas, Springfield, Ill.

Hall, D. A. 1962. Elastase: a bifunctional enzyme. *Arch. Biochem. Biophys., Suppl. 1*: 239.

Hall, J. L., D. L. Harrison, and D. L. Mackintosh. 1962. Countereffect of sodium chloride and sage on development of peroxide in frozen stored sausage. *Food Technol. 16*, No. 3: 102.

Hall, J. L., and D. L. Mackintosh. 1964. Chlorophyll catalysis of fat peroxidation. *J. Food Sci. 29*: 420.

Hamid, H. A., and R. L. Saffle. 1965. Isolation and identification of the volatile fatty acids present in hickory wood smoke. *J. Food Sci. 30*: 697.

Hamm, R. 1956. The action of adenosine triphosphoric acid on hydration and rigidity of post-mortem beef muscle. *Biochem. Z. 328*: 309.

Hamm, R. 1959. Mineral substances of mammalian muscle. II. The binding condition of magnesium, calcium, zinc, iron and phosphate in muscle post mortem. *Zeit. Lebensmitt. Untersuch. 110*: 95.

Hamm, R. 1960. Biochemistry of meat hydration. *Advan. Food Res. 10*: 355.

Hamm, R. 1962. Chemical and physical changes on heating meat. I. Action of heat in the presence of sodium chloride on the water-binding capacity and the pH value of beef muscle. *Z. Lebensm.-Untersuch.-Forsch. 117*: 20.

Hamm, R. 1966. Heating of muscle systems. In *The Physiology and Biochemistry of Muscle as a Food,* E. J. Briskey, R. G. Cassens, and J. C. Trautman, eds. p. 363. U. of Wisc. Press, Madison, Wisc.

Hamm, R., and F. E. Deatherage. 1960. Changes in hydration, solubility and charges of muscle protein during heating of meat. *Food Res. 23*: 587.

Hamm, R., and K. Hofmann. 1965. Changes in the sulphydryl and disulphide groups in beef muscle proteins during heating. *Nature (Lond.) 207*: 1269.

Hamm, R., and H. Iwata. 1962. Chemical changes in meat on heating. I. Effect of heating in presence of sodium chloride on water-binding capacity and pH value of beef. *Z. Lebensm. Untersuch. 117*: 20.

Hanson, J., and Huxley, H. E. 1955. The structural basis of contraction in striated muscle. *Symp. Soc. Exp. Biol. 9*: 228.

Harding, J. J. 1965. The unusual links and cross-links of collagen. *Advan. Protein Chem. 20*: 109.

Harries, J. M., K. B. Jones, T. W. Houston, and J. Robertson. 1963. Studies in beef quality. I. Development of a system for assessing palatability. *J. Sci. Food Agr. 14*: 501.

Harrington, G., and A. M. Pearson. 1962. Chew count as a measure of tenderness of pork loins with various degrees of marbling. *J. Food Sci. 27*: 106.

Harrison, D. L., L. L. Anderson, J. Baird, C. Pengilly, R. A. Merkel, D. Kropf, and D. L. Mackintosh. 1967. Variation of selected factors from the anterior to posterior of pork loin. *J. Food Sci. 32*: 336.

Harrison, D. L., R. Visser, and L. Schirmer. 1959. A resume of the literature related to factors affecting the tenderness of certain beef muscles. *Contrib. No. 208*, Dept. of Home Econ. (Foods and Nutrition), Rep. 10, Kansas Agr. Exp. Sta., Manhattan, Kan.

Haughey, D. P. 1968. A physical approach to the cooking of meat. *Proc. 10th Meat Ind. Res. Conf.* Meat Ind. Res. Inst., New Zealand, Hamilton, N.Z. mimeo.

Headley, M. E., and M. Jacobson. 1960. Electronic and conventional cookery of lamb roasts: cooking losses and palatability. *J. Am. Dietet. Assoc. 36*: 337.

Heck, M. C. 1958. Influence of preslaughter feeding and holding on meat quality. *Proc. 10th Res. Conf.*, Am. Meat Inst. Found. Circ. No. 45, p. 41.

Hedrick, H. B. 1965. Influence of ante-mortem stress on meat palatability. *J. Animal Sci. 24*: 255.

Hedrick, H. B. 1968. Bovine growth and composition. *Mo. Agr. Expt. Sta. Res. Bull.* No. 928.

Hedrick, H. B., D. W. Zinn, D. E. Zobriskey, and M. E. Bailey. 1967. Quantitative relationships of meat animal composition during growth and development. *Proc. 20th Recip. Meat Conf.*, p. 55. Nat. Live Stock Meat Bd., Chicago.

Hegarty, G. R. 1963. Solubility and emulsifying characteristics of intracellular beef muscle proteins. *Dissertation Abstr. 24*: 2414.

Hegarty, G. R., L. J. Bratzler, and A. M. Pearson. 1963. Relationship of intracellular protein characteristics to beef muscle tenderness. *J. Food Sci. 28*: 525.

Hegarty, P. V. J. 1969. Subjective evaluation of the colour of pig muscle. I. Accuracy of subjective measurements of colour. *J. Sci. Food Agr. 20*: 685.

Heikkinen, E., L. Mikkonen, and E. Kulonen. 1964. Age factor in the maturation of collagen. Cross-links in heat-denatured collagen in tail tendon and skin of rat. *Exp. Geront. 1*: 31.

Helander, E. 1966. General considerations of muscle development. In *The Physiology and biochemistry of muscle as a food*. E. J. Briskey, R. G. Cassens, and J. C. Trautman, eds., p. 19. Univ. of Wisc. Press, Madison, Wisc.

Henrickson, R. L., and R. E. Moore. 1965. Effects of animal age on the palatability of beef. *Okla. Agr. Expt. Sta. Tech. Bull.* No. T-115.

Henrickson, R. L., L. S. Pope, and R. F. Hendrickson. 1965. Effect of rate of gain of fattening beef calves on carcass composition. *J. Animal Sci. 24*: 507.

Herring, H. K. 1968. Muscle contraction and tenderness. *Proc. 21st Ann. Recip. Meat Conf.*, p. 47. Nat. Live Stock Meat Bd., Chicago, Ill.

Herring, H. K., R. G. Cassens, and E. J. Briskey. 1965. Sarcomere length of free and restrained bovine muscles at low temperature as related to tenderness. *J. Sci. Food Agr. 16:* 379.

Herring, H. K., R. G. Cassens, and E. J. Briskey. 1967a. Factors affecting collagen solubility in bovine muscles. *J. Food Sci. 32:* 534.

Herring, H. K., R. G. Cassens, G. G. Suess, V. H. Brungardt, and E. J. Briskey. 1967b. Tenderness and associated characteristics of stretched and contracted bovine muscle. *J. Food Sci. 32:* 317.

Hill, F. 1962. Toughness in meat. *Inst. of Meat Bull.,* Agr. Inst., Dublin, Ireland.

Hill, F. 1966. Chemical composition of muscles from hexestrol-treated steers. *J. Agr. Food Chem. 14:* 179.

Hill, F. 1967. The chemical composition of muscles from steers which experienced compensatory growth. *J. Sci. Food Agr. 18:* 164.

Hill, J. E., J. D. Leitman, and J. E. Sutherland. 1967. Thermal conductivity of various meats. *Food Technol. 21:* 1143.

Hiner, R. L., E. E. Anderson, and C. R. Fellers. 1955. Amount and character of connective tissue as it relates to tenderness in beef muscle. *Food Technol. 9:* 80.

Hiner, R. L., and O. G. Hankins. 1950. The tenderness of beef in relation to different muscles and age in the animal. *J. Animal Sci. 9:* 347.

Hinnergardt, L.C., and J. M. Tuomy. 1970. A penetrometer test to measure meat tenderness. *J. Food Sci. 35:* 312.

Hinrichs, J. R., and J. R. Whitaker. 1962. Enzymatic degradation of collagen. *J. Food Sci. 27:* 250.

Hirai, C., A. Kato, K. O. Herz, and S. S. Chang. 1969. Chemical changes of volatile flavor compounds during storage of fresh and freeze dried boiled beef. *Abstr. 29th Ann. Meeting, IFT,* p. 96. Inst. Food Technol., Chicago, Ill.

Ho, G. P., and S. J. Ritchey. 1967. Effects of animal age on juiciness and tenderness of beef. *Food Technol. 21:* 1278.

Hoffman, J. G. 1966. Infrared microspectrophotometry of tissue cells. *Proc. 19th Reciprocal Meat Conf.,* p. 23. Nat. Live Stock Meat Bd., Chicago, Ill.

Hofstrand, J., and M. Jacobson. 1960. Role of fat in flavor of lamb and mutton as tested with broths and with depot fats. *Food Res. 25:* 706.

Hoke, K. E., and C. E. Davis. 1970. Lighting conditions for evaluation of beef marbling and color. *Food Technol. 24:* 283.

Hoke, K. E., and H. B. Hedrick. 1969. Maturity and carcass grade effects on palatability of beef. *Food Technol. 23:* 330.

Hollenbeck, C. M., and L. J. Marinelli. 1963. Some chemical constituents of smoke flavoring. *Proc. 15th Res. Conf.*, p. 67. Am. Meat Inst. Found., Chicago, Ill.

Holmes, Z. A., J. R. Bowers, and G. E. Goertz. 1966. Effect of internal temperature on eating quality of pork chops. II. Broiling. *J. Am. Dietet. Assoc.* 48: 121.

Hood, M. P. 1960. Effect of cooking method and grade on beef roasts. *J. Am. Dietet. Assoc. 37:* 363.

Hood, M. P., D. W. Thompson, and L. Mirone. 1955. Effect of cooking methods on low grade beef. *Ga. State Exp. Sta. Bull.* N.S. 4, Univ. of Georgia, Athens.

Hornsey, H. C. 1956. The color of cooked cured pork. I. Estimation of the nitric oxide-heme pigments. *J. Sci. Food Agr. 7:* 534.

Hornstein, I. 1967. Flavor of red meats. In *Symposium on Foods: The Chemistry and Physiology of Flavors.* H. W. Schultz, E. A. Day, and L. M. Libbey, eds., p. 228. Avi. Publ. Co., Westport, Conn.

Hornstein, I., and P. F. Crowe. 1960. Flavor studies on beef and pork. *J. Agr. Food Chem. 8:* 494.

Hornstein, I., and P. F. Crowe. 1961. Meat flavors from fat—not lean. *Agr. Res. 9* No. 7: 14.

Hornstein, I., and P. F. Crowe. 1963. Meat flavor: Lamb. *J. Agr. Food Chem. 11:* 147.

Hornstein, I., P. F. Crowe, and M. J. Heimberg. 1961. Fatty acid composition of meat tissue lipids. *J. Food Sci. 26:* 581.

Hornstein, I., P. F. Crowe, and R. Hiner. 1967. Composition of lipids in some beef muscles. *J. Food Sci. 32:* 650.

Hornstein, I., P. F. Crowe, and W. L. Sulzbacher. 1963. Flavour of beef and whale meat. *Nature (Lond.) 199:* 1252.

Hostetler, R. L., and S. Cover. 1961. Relationship of extensibility of muscle fibers to tenderness of beef. *J. Food Sci. 26:* 535.

Hostetler, R. L., and W. A. Landmann. 1968. Photomicrographic studies of dynamic changes in muscle fiber fragments. 1. Effect of various heat treatments on length, width and birefringence. *J. Food Sci. 33:* 468.

Hostetler, R. L., and S. J. Ritchey. 1964. Effect of coring method on shear values determined by Warner-Bratzler shear. *J. Food Sci. 29:* 681.

Houston, T. W., K. Bryce-Jones, and J. M. Harries. 1962. Effects of nutrition on eating quality characteristics and composition of beef. *Abstr. First Internat. Congress Food Sci. and Technol.*, p. 39.

Howard, A., and R. A. Lawrie. 1956b. Studies on beef quality. III. Influence of various pre-slaughter treatments on weight losses and eating quality of beef carcasses. C.S.I.R.O., Austr., *Div. Food Pres. and Trans. Tech.* paper No. 2, p. 52.

Howard, A., C. A. Lee, and H. L. Webster. 1960. Studies on beef quality. IX. Nucleotide breakdown in beef tissue: the extent of formation of hypoxanthine during storage as an indicator of degree of ripening. *Div. Food Pres. Tech. Paper No. 21*, C.S.I.R.O., Melbourne, Austr.

Howard, R. D., and M. D. Judge. 1968. Comparison of sarcomere length to other predictors of beef tenderness. *J. Food Sci. 33*: 456.

Hoynak, P. X., Jr. 1963. Mechanism of the development of rancidity in frozen fresh pork sausage and practicable methods for its inhibition. *Dissertation Abstr. 23*: 4302.

Hubbard, A. W., and W. D. Pocklington. 1968. Distribution of fatty acids in lipids as an aid to the identification of animal tissues. I. Bovine, porcine, ovine and some avian species. *J. Sci. Food Agr. 19*: 571.

Hunt, S. M. V., and N. A. Matheson. 1958. Adenosine triphosphatase and contraction in dehydrated muscle fibers. *Nature 181*: 472.

Hutchins, B. K., T. H. P. Liu, and B. M. Watts. 1967. Effect of additives and refrigeration on reducing activity, metmyoglobin and malonaldehyde of raw ground beef. *J. Food Sci. 32*: 214.

Huxley, H. E. 1969. The mechanism of muscular contraction. *Science 164*: 1356.

Ingram, M. 1966. Symposium on the microbiology of desirable food flavors. I. Introductory remarks, with special reference to meat. *J. Appl. Bact. 29*: 217.

Ingram, M., and A. G. Kitchell. 1968. Salt as a preservative. *J. Food Technol. 3*: 77.

Inklaar, P., and J. Sandifort. 1967. Determination of calcium and magnesium in meat. *J. Food Sci. 32*: 622.

Irmiter, T. F., P. J. Aldrich, and K. Funk. 1967. Rate of temperature rise, physical and chemical properties of ground beef cylinders fabricated from selected muscles of the round. 1. Effect of fat cover. *Food Technol. 21*: 779.

Issenberg, P. 1969. Identification of volatile food components: Some practical observations on mass spectrometry for flavor research. *Food Technol. 23*: 1435.

Iyengar, J. R., S. Kuppuswamy, and D. S. Bhatia. 1965. Effect of cooking on the composition of mutton. *Food Technol. 19* No. 2: 120.

Jacobson, M., and F. Fenton. 1956. Effects of three levels of nutrition and age of animal on the quality of beef. I: Palatability, cooking data, moisture, fat, and nitrogen. *Food Res. 21*: 415.

Jacobson, M., and H. H. Koehler. 1963. Components of the flavor of lamb. *J. Agr. Food Chem. 11*: 336.

Jacobson, M., M. Weller, M. W. Galgan, and E. H. Rupnow. 1962. Factors in flavor and tenderness of lamb, beef and pork, and techniques of evaluation. *Wash. Agr. Exp. Sta. Tech. Bull.* 40, Pullman, Wash.

Janicki, M. A., J. Kortz, and J. Rozyczka. 1967. Relationship of color with certain chemical and physical properties of porcine muscle. *J. Food Sci. 32*: 375.

Jay, J. M. 1964. Release of aqueous extracts by beef homogenates and factors affecting release volume. *Food Technol. 18*: 1633.

Jay, J. M. 1966. Influence of post mortem conditions on muscle microbiology. In *The Physiology and Biochemistry of Muscle as a Food*, E. J. Briskey, R. G. Cassens, and J. C. Trautman, eds., p. 387. U. of Wisc. Press, Madison, Wisc.

Jedlicka. 1966. A method for objective determination of meat softness. *Report 12th European Meat Res. Conf.* Am. Meat Sci. Assoc., Chicago, Ill.

Johnson, A. R., and J. R. Vickery. 1964. Factors influencing the production of hydrogen sulphide from meat during heating. *J. Sci. Food Agr. 15*: 695.

Johnston, W. K., Jr., A. F. Anglemier, C. W. Fox, J. E. Oldfield, and L. A. Sather. 1965. Effects of coumestrol and diethylstilbestrol on the organoleptic quality of lamb. *J. Animal Sci. 24*: 718.

Jones, K. B. 1968. Instrument measurements of changes in meat brought about by cooking. *Report 14th European Meat Res. Conf.*, p. 7. Am. Meat Sci. Assoc., Chicago, Ill.

Jones, K. B., J. M. Harries, J. Robertson, and J. M. Akers. 1964. Studies on beef quality. IV. A comparison of the eating quality of meat from bulls and steers. *J. Sci. Food Agr. 15*: 790.

Jones, N. R. 1969. Meat and fish flavors: significance of ribomononucleotides and their metabolites. *J. Agr. Food Chem. 17*: 712.

Joubert, D. M. 1956. An analysis of factors influencing post-natal growth and development of the muscle fibre. *J. Agr. Sci. 47*: 59.

Judge, M. D. 1969. Environmental stress and meat quality. *J. Animal Sci. 28*: 755.

Kaess, G., and J. F. Weidemann. 1967. Freezer-burn as a limiting factor in the storage of animal tissue. V. Experiments with beef muscle. *Food Technol. 21*: 461.

Kaess, G., and J. F. Weidemann. 1968. Ozone treatment of chilled beef. I. Effect of low concentrations of ozone on microbial spoilage and surface colour of beef. *J. Food Technol. 3*: 325.

Kamstra, L. D., and R. L. Saffle. 1959. Effects of a pre-rigor infusion of sodium hexametaphosphate on tenderness and certain chemical characteristics of meat. *Food Technol. 31*: 652.

Karel, M. 1968. Unsolved problems in chemical stability of freeze-dried foods. *Proc. Meat Ind. Res. Conf.*, p. 119. Am. Meat Inst. Found., Chicago, Ill.

Kastner, C. L., and R. L. Henrickson. 1969. Providing uniform meat cores for mechanical shear force measurement. *J. Food Sci. 34*: 603.

Kauffman, R. G., L. E. St. Clair, and R. J. Reber. 1963. Ovine myology. *Ill. Agr. Expt. Sta. Bull.* No. 698.

Kedlaya, K. J., N. Ramanathan, and Y. Nayudamma. 1968. Studies on the shrinkage phenomenon: XI. Effect of pretanning treatments on shrinkage properties of collagen fibres. *Leather Science 15*: 40.

Kelly, R. F., J. P. Fontenot, P. P. Graham, W. S. Wilkinson, and C. M. Kincaid.

1968. Estimates of carcass composition of beef cattle fed at different planes of nutrition. *J. Animal Sci. 27*: 620.

Kemp, J. D. 1965. Significant lamb carcass research in New Zealand. *Proc. 18th Reciprocal Meat Conf.*, p. 215. Nat. Live Stock and Meat Bd., Chicago, Ill.

Kemp, J. D., W. G. Moody, and J. L. Goodlett. 1961. Effects of smoking and smoking temperatures on the shrinkage, rancidity development, keeping quality and palatability of dry-cured hams. *Food Technol. 15*: 267.

Keskinel, A., J. C. Ayres, and H. E. Snyder. 1964. Determination of oxidative changes in raw meats by the 2-thiobarbituric acid (TBA) method. *Food Technol. 18* No. 2: 101.

Kirimura, J., A. Shimiza, A. Kimizuka, T. Ninomiya, and N. Katsuya. 1969. The contribution of peptides and amino acids to the taste of foodstuffs. *J. Agr. Food Chem. 17*: 689.

Kirton, A. H., R. A. Barton, and A. L. Rae. 1962. Efficiency of determining the chemical composition of lamb carcasses. *J. Agr. Sci. 58*: 381.

Klima, D., and R. Blanka. 1968. Factors affecting the colour stability of hams. *Abstr. 14th European Meat Res. Conf.*, p. 21. Am. Meat Science Assoc., Chicago, Illinois. mimeo.

Köhn, K., W. Grassmann, and U. Hofmann. 1959. On the formation of collagen fibrils from dissolved collagen and the function of the associated components containing carbohydrates. *Z. Naturforsch. 146*: 436.

Kono, T., F. Kakuma, M. Homma, and S. Fukuda. 1964. The electron-microscopic structure and chemical composition of the isolated sarcolemma of the rat skeletal muscle cell. *Biochim. Biophys. Acta 88*: 155.

Kopelman, I. J. 1966. Transient heat transfer and thermal properties in food systems. *Dissertation Abstr. B27*: 1972.

Kramlich, W. E., and A. M. Pearson. 1960. Separation and identification of cooked beef flavor components. *Food Res. 25*: 712.

Kropf, D. H. 1968. Application of research to meat judging activities—Identification of quality and quantity differences. *Proc. 21st Reciprocal Meat Conf.*, p. 251. Nat. Live Stock and Meat Bd., Chicago, Ill.

Kropf, D. H., and R. L. Graf. 1959. Interrelationships of subjective, chemical, and sensory evaluations of beef quality. *Food Technol. 13*: 492.

Krzywicki, K., and P. W. Ratcliff. 1967. The phospholipids of pork muscle, and their relation to the post-mortem rate of glycolysis. *J. Sci. Food Agr. 18*: 252.

Kuchmak, M., and L. D. Dugan, Jr. 1963. Phospholipids of pork muscle tissues. *J. Amer. Oil Chemists' Soc. 40*: 734.

Kulwich, R., R. W. Decker, and R. H. Alsmeyer. 1963. Use of a slice-tenderness evaluation device with pork. *Food Technol. 17*: 201.

Kuninaka, A. 1966. Recent studies of 5′-nucleotides as new flavor enhancers.

In *Flavor Chemistry,* p. 261. Advan. in Chem. Series No. 56. Am. Chem. Soc., Washington, D.C.

Kurtz, S. M., ed. 1964. *Electron Microscopic Anatomy.* Academic Press, Inc., New York.

Laakkonen, E., G. H. Wellington, and J. W. Sherbon. 1970. Low-temperature, long-time heating of bovine muscle. 1. Changes in tenderness, water-binding capacity, pH, and amount of water-soluble components. 2. Changes in electrophoretic patterns. 3. Collagenolytic activity. *J. Food Sci. 35:* 175, 178, 181.

Landmann, W. A., and O. F. Batzer. 1966. Influence of processing procedures on the chemistry of meat flavors. *J. Agr. Food Chem. 14:* 210.

Lane, J. P., and L. J. Bratzler. 1962. Spectrophotometric estimation of met-myoglobin in frozen meat extracts. *J. Food Sci. 27:* 343.

Larmond, E., A. Petrasovits, P. Tallon, and N. W. Tape. 1968. *Abstr., p. 62. 28th Annual IFT meeting,* Inst. Food Technol., Chicago, Ill.

Larmond, E., A. Petrasovits, and P. Hill. 1969. Application of multiple paired comparisons in studying the effect of aging and finish on beef tenderness. *Canad. J. Animal Sci. 49:* 51.

Law, H. M., S. P. Yang, A. M. Mullins, and M. M. Fielder. 1967. Effect of storage and cooking on qualities of loin and top round steak. *J. Food Sci. 32:* 637.

Lawrie, R. A. 1959. Water-binding capacity and drip formation in meat. *J. Refrig. 2:* 87.

Lawrie, R. A. 1961. Studies on the muscles of meat animals. I. Differences in composition of beef *longissimus dorsi* muscles determined by age and anatomical location. *J. Agr. Sci. 56:* 249.

Lawrie, R. A. 1966a. *Meat Science.* Pergamon Press, Ltd., Oxford, England.

Lawrie, R. A. 1966b. Metabolic stresses which affect muscle. In *The Physiology and Biochemistry of Muscle as a Food,* p. 137, E. J. Briskey, R. G. Cassens, and J. C. Trautman, eds. U. of Wisc. Press, Madison, Wisc.

Lawrie, R. A. 1968. Chemical changes in meat due to processing—a review. *J. Sci. Food Agr. 19:* 233.

Lawrie, R. A., and R. W. Pomeroy. 1963. Sodium and potassium in pig muscle. *J. Agr. Sci. 61:* 409.

Leverton, R. M., and G. V. Odell. 1958. The nutritive value of cooked meat. *Misc. Pub. MP-49.* Okla. Agr. Exp. Sta., Stillwater.

Lewis, P. K., Jr., C. J. Brown, and M. C. Heck. 1963. Effect of pre-slaughter treatments on the chemical composition of various beef tissues. *J. Food Sci. 28:* 669.

Lewis, P. K., Jr., C. J. Brown, and M. C. Heck. 1967. The effect of ante-mortem stress on the internal temperature of beef during heating. *Food Technol. 21:* 393.

Lewis, P. K., Jr., M. C. Heck, and C. J. Brown. 1963. Relationship of chemical and physical measurements to organoleptic properties of pork. *Ark. Agr. Exp. Sta. Bull.* No. 667.

Lillard, D. A., and J. C. Ayres. 1969. Flavor compounds in country cured hams. *Food Technol. 23:* 251.

Locker, R. H. 1960a. Degree of muscular contraction as a factor in tenderness of beef. *Food Res. 25:* 304.

Locker, R. H. 1960b. Proteolysis in the storage of beef. *J. Sci. Food Agr. 11:* 520.

Locker, R. H., and C. J. Hagyard. 1963. A cold shortening effect in beef muscles. *J. Sci. Food Agr. 14:* 787.

Lockett, C., C. E. Swift, and W. L. Sulzbacher. 1962. Some relations between the chemical and physical characteristics of bovine muscles. *J. Food Sci. 27:* 36.

Lorand, L. 1967. Relaxing factors of skeletal muscle. *Proc. Meat Ind. Res. Conf.,* p. 29. Am. Meat Inst. Found., Chicago.

Lowe, B. 1949. Organoleptic tests developed for measuring the palatability of meat. *Proc. Recip. Meat Conf. 2:* 111. Nat. Live Stock Meat Bd., Chicago, Ill.

Lowe, B. 1955. *Experimental Cookery,* 4th ed., pp. 242–243. John Wiley and Sons, Inc., New York.

Lowe, B., and J. Kastelic. 1961. Organoleptic, chemical, physical and microscopic characteristics of muscles in eight beef carcasses differing in age of animal, carcass grade, and extent of cooking. *Ag. and H.Ec. Exp. Sta. Res. Bull.* No. 495. Iowa State University.

Lyaskovskaya, Kelmen. 1967. Characterization of intramuscle lipids of various types of slaughter animals. *13th European Meat Res. Conf.,* p. 32. Am. Meat Science Assoc., mimeo.

Luyet, B. J. 1968. Physical changes in muscle during freezing and thawing. *Proc. Meat Ind. Res. Conf.,* p. 138. Am. Meat Inst. Found., Chicago, Ill.

Ma, R. A., M. B. Matlack, and R. L. Hiner. 1961. A study of the free amino acids in bovine muscle. *J. Food Sci. 26:* 485.

Mabrouk, A. F., J. K. Jarboe, and E. M. O'Connor. 1969a. Water-soluble flavor precursors of beef. Extraction and fractionation. *J. Agr. Food Chem. 17:* 5.

Mabrouk, A. F., E. M. O'Connor, and J. K. Jarboe. 1969b. Nonaqueous beef flavor components. Composition of petroleum ether-extractable intramuscular polar lipids. *J. Agr. Food Chem. 17:* 10.

Macfarlane, P. G., and J. M. Marer. 1966. An apparatus for determining the tenderness of meat. *Food Technol. 20:* 838.

Machlik, S. M. 1965. The effect of heat on bovine myoglobin derivatives in model systems and in beef semitendinosus muscle. Ph.D. thesis, Purdue Univ., Univ. Microfilms, Ann Arbor, Mich. No. 66–5286.

Machlik, S. M., and H. N. Draudt. 1963. The effect of heating time and temperature on the shear of beef semitendinosus muscle. *J. Food Sci. 28:* 711.

Mackinney, G., and A. C. Little. 1962. *Color of Foods*. Avi Publ. Co., Westport, Conn.

Macy, R. L. Jr., H. D. Naumann, and M. E. Bailey. 1964. Water-soluble flavor and odor precursors of meat. I. Qualitative study of certain amino acids, carbohydrates, non-amino acid nitrogenous compounds and phosphoric acid esters of beef, pork and lamb. II. Effects of heating on amino nitrogen constituents and carbohydrates in lyophilized diffusates from aqueous extracts of beef, pork and lamb. *J. Food Sci. 29*: 136, 142.

Mahler, H. R., and E. H. Cordes. 1966. *Biological Chemistry*. Harper and Row, New York.

Mahon, P., D. Hogue, P. Lecking, E. Lim, and F. Fenton. 1956. The quality of smoked ham as affected by adding antibiotic and fat to the diet and phosphate to the cure. I. Cooking losses, palatability, separable fat, and shear values. *Food Technol. 10*: 265.

Malkus, L. A. 1965. Changes in carcass composition from 9 to 18 months in heifers fed a fattening ration. *Dissertation Abstr. 26*: 1585.

Mandigo, R. W. 1967. Hot cutting and processing of pork. *Proc. 20th Ann. Recip. Meat Conf.*, p. 270. Nat. Live Stock Meat Bd., Chicago, Ill.

Mandigo, R. W. 1968. High temperature pork processing: cutting, fabricating, handling and yield. *Proc. Meat Ind. Res. Conf.*, p. 41. Am. Meat Inst. Found., Chicago, Ill.

Mandigo, R. W., and R. L. Henrickson. 1966. Influence of hot-processing pork carcasses on cured ham. *Food Technol. 20*: 186.

March, M. S., E. M. Murphy, J. N. Essen, and E. H. Dawson. 1961. Yield, composition, and palatability of pork sausage varying in fat content. *J. Home Econ. 53*: 687.

Marchello, J. A., and D. A. Cramer. 1963. Variation of ovine fat composition within the carcass. *J. Animal Sci. 22*: 380.

Marsh, B. B. 1952. The effects of adenosine triphosphate on the fibre volume of a muscle homogenate. *Biochim. Biophys. Acta 9*: 247.

Marsh, B. B. 1966. Relaxing factor in muscle. In *Physiology and Biochemistry of Muscle as a Food*, E. J. Briskey, R. G. Cassens, and J. C. Trautman, eds., p. 225. U. of Wisc. Press, Madison, Wisc.

Marsh, B. B., and N. G. Leet. 1966. Studies on meat tenderness. III. The effects of cold shortening on tenderness. *J. Food Sci. 31*: 450.

Marsh, B. B., P. R. Woodhams, and N. G. Leet. 1966. Studies in meat tenderness. I. Sensory and objective assessments of tenderness. *J. Food Sci. 31*: 262.

Marsh, B. B., P. R. Woodhams, and N. G. Leet. 1968. Studies on meat tenderness. 5. The effects on tenderness of carcass cooling and freezing before the completion of rigor mortis. *J. Food Sci. 33*: 12.

Martin, A. H., H. T. Fredeen, and J. G. Stothart. 1968. Taste panel evaluation of sex effects on the quality of cooked pork. *Can. J. Animal Sci. 48*: 171.

Martins, C. B., and J. R. Whitaker. 1968. Catheptic enzymes and meat tenderization. I. Purification of cathepsin D and its action on actomyosin. *J. Food Sci.* 33: 59.

Marshall, N. 1960. Electronic cooking of top round of beef. *J. Home Econ.* 52: 31.

Marshall, N., L. Wood, and M. B. Patton. 1960. Cooking choice grade, top round beef roasts. Effect of internal temperature on yield and cooking time. *J. Am. Dietet. Assoc.* 36: 341.

Matheson, N. A. 1962. Enzymic activity at low moisture levels and its relation to deterioration in freeze-dried foods. *J. Sci. Food Agr.* 13: 248.

Matz, S. A. 1962. *Food Texture.* Avi Publ. Co., Westport, Conn.

McBee, J. L., Jr. 1960. Environmental factors affecting the quality of frozen meat. *Dissertation Abstr.* 20: 3685.

McCain, G. R., T. N. Blumer, H. B. Craig, and R. G. Steel. 1968. Free amino acids in ham muscle during successive aging periods and their relation to flavor. *J. Food Sci.* 33: 142.

McClain, P. E., G. J. Creed, E. R. Wiley, and I. Hornstein. 1970. Effect of post-mortem aging on isolation of intramuscular connective tissue. *J. Food Sci.* 35: 258.

McClain, P. E., E. Kuntz, and A. M. Pearson. 1969b. Application of stress-strain behavior to thermally contracted collagen from epimysial connective tissues. *J. Ag. Food Chem.* 17: 629.

McClain, P. E., and A. M. Pearson. 1969. Connective tissue from normal and pale, soft and exudative (PSE) porcine muscles. 2. Physical characterization. *J. Food Sci.* 34: 306.

McCrae, S. E., and C. G. Seccombe. 1969. Cooking odours in the roasting of lamb cuts. *Ann. Res. Report., 1968–69,* Meat Ind. Res. Inst. of New Zealand, Inc., Hamilton, N.Z.

McIntosh, E. N. 1966. Characterization of mucoprotein in bovine skeletal muscle. *J. Food Sci.* 31: 337.

McIntosh, E. N., D. C. Acker, and E. A. Kline. 1961. Influence of orally administered stilbestrol on connective tissue of skeletal muscle of lambs fed varying levels of protein. *J. Agr. Food Chem.* 9: 418.

McLoughlin, J. V. 1963. Studies on pig muscle. II. The effect of rapid post-mortem pH fall on the extraction of the sarcoplasmic and myofibrillar proteins of post-rigor muscle. *Irish J. Agr. Res.* 2: 115.

McLoughlin, J. V. 1965. Studies on pig muscle. 4. pH values in the *longissimus dorsi* muscle of pigs killed under commercial conditions. *Irish J. Agr. Res.* 4: 151.

McLoughlin, J. V., and V. E. J. Davidson. 1966. Relationship between commercial methods of slaughter and the "pH_1" value of porcine *longissimus dorsi* muscle. *Irish J. Agr. Res.* 5: 55.

Meat Evaluation Handbook. 1969. National Live Stock and Meat Board. Chicago, Ill.

Merkel, R. A. 1968. Implication of the circulatory system in skeletal muscle to meat quality. *Proc. 21st Ann. Recip. Meat Conf.,* p. 204. Nat. Live Stock Meat Bd., Chicago, Ill.

Merritt, C., Jr., P. Angelini, M. L. Bazinet, and D. J. McAdoo. 1966. Irradiation damage in lipids. In *Flavor Chemistry,* p. 225. Advan. in Chem. Series No. 56. Am. Chem. Soc., Washington, D.C.

Meyer, B. H., M. A. Mysinger, and L. A. Wodarski. 1969. Pantothenic acid and vitamin B₆ in beef. *J. Am. Dietet. Assoc. 54:* 122.

Meyer, B., J. Thomas, R. Buckley, and J. W. Cole. 1960. Quality of grain-finished and grass-finished beef as affected by ripening. *Food Technol. 14:* 4.

Meyer, D. D., G. E. Vail, V. D. Bramblett, T. G. Martin, and R. B. Harrington. 1967. Vitamin A supplements and hypoxanthine-uric acid and nucleotide content of selected beef muscles. *J. Food Sci. 32:* 289.

Meyer, J. H., E. J. Briskey, W. G. Hoekstra, and K. G. Weckel. 1963. Niacin, thiamin, and riboflavin in fresh and cooked pale, soft, watery versus dark, firm, dry pork muscle. *Food Technol. 17:* 485.

Meyer, K. 1965. Structure and biology of mucopolysaccharides of connective tissue. *Proc. Meat Ind. Res. Conf.,* p. 24. Am. Meat Inst. Found., Chicago.

Miller, E. M., and D. L. Harrison. 1965. Effect of marination in sodium hexametaphosphate solution on the palatability of loin steaks. *Food Technol. 19:* 94.

Miller, W. O., R. L. Saffle, and S. B. Zirkle. 1968. Factors which influence the water-holding capacity of various types of meat. *Food Technol. 22:* 1139.

Mills, F. D., B. G. Baker, and J. E. Hodge. 1969. Amadori compounds as non-volatile flavor precursors in processed foods. *J. Agr. Food Chem. 17:* 723.

Mitchell, H. H., and T. S. Hamilton. 1933. Effect of long-continued muscular exercise upon the chemical composition of the muscles and other tissues of beef cattle. *J. Agr. Res. 46:* 917.

Mitteldorf, A. J., and D. O. Landon. 1952. Spectrochemical determination of the mineral-element content of beef. *Anal. Chem. 24:* 469.

Miyada, D. S., and A. L. Tappel. Meat tenderization. I. Two mechanical devices for measuring texture. *Food Technol. 10:* 142.

Mommaerts, W. F. H. M. 1966. Molecular alterations in myofibrillar proteins. In *The Physiology and Biochemistry of Muscle as a Food,* E. J. Briskey, R. G. Cassens, and J. C. Trautman, eds., p. 277. U. of Wisc. Press, Madison, Wisc.

Moody, W. G. 1967. Lipid accumulation and method for measuring marbling. *Proc. 20th Reciprocal Meat Conf.,* p. 28. Nat. Live Stock Meat Bd. Chicago, Ill.

Moody, W. G., and R. G. Cassens. 1968. A quantitative and morphological study of bovine longissimus fat cells. *J. Food Sci. 33*: 47.

Moore, R. E., R. W. Mandigo, and R. L. Henrickson. 1966. The effect of cutting, chilling, and cooking method on the quality of pork loin. *Food Technol. 20*: 957.

Moss, V. G., and E. W. Kielsmeier. 1967. A method for rapid determination of protein in meat by dye binding. *Food Technol. 21*: 351.

Murphy, M. O., and A. F. Carlin. 1961. Relation of marbling, cooking yield and eating quality of pork chops to back fat thickness on hog carcasses. *Food Technol. 15*: 57.

Nakamura, S., M. Yamaguchi, J. Morita, and T. Yasui. 1969. Muscle pyrophosphatases. *J. Agr. Food Chem. 17*: 633.

Naumann, H. D. 1965. Evaluation and measurement of meat quality. In *Food Quality*, G. W. Irving, Jr., and S. R. Hoover, eds. Publ. No. 77, p. 239. Amer. Assoc. Advance. Sci., Washington, D.C.

Naumann, H. D. 1968. Cutting and packaging of fresh meat. *Proc. Meat Ind. Res. Conf.*, p. 157. Am. Meat Inst. Found., Chicago, Ill.

Nickerson, D. 1946. Color measurement and its application to the grading of agricultural products. *U.S. Dept. Agr. Misc. Pub.* 580, Washington, D.C.

Nielsen, M. M., and F. T. Hall. 1965. Dry-roasting of less tender beef cuts. *J. Home Econ. 57*: 353.

Norris, H. L., D. L. Harrison, L. L. Anderson, B. von Welck, and H. J. Tuma. 1971. Effects of physiological maturity of beef and marbling of rib steaks on eating quality. *J. Food Sci. 36*: 440.

Ockerman, H. W., and V. R. Cahill. 1969. Reflectance as a measure of pork and beef muscle tissue color. *J. Anim. Sci. 28*: 750.

O'Keefe, P. W., G. H. Wellington, L. R. Mattick, and J. R. Stouffer. 1968. Composition of bovine muscle lipids at various carcass locations. *J. Food Sci. 33*: 188.

Olson, L. E., D. A. Greenwood, H. M. Nielsen, and E. B. Wilcox. 1959. Techniques for evaluating the flavor of processed meat. *Food Res. 24*: 696.

Orme, L. E. 1955. The effects of firmness of fat and degree of finish on the evaluation of pork carcasses. M.S. thesis, U. of Tennessee, Knoxville, Tenn.

Onate, L. U., and A. F. Carlin. 1963. Relation of physical and sensory evaluations of pork loin quality to backfat thickness. *Food Technol. 17*: 1461.

Palmer, A. Z. 1963. Relation of age, breed, sex and feeding practices on beef and pork tenderness. *Proc. Meat Tenderness Symposium*, p. 161. Campbell Soup Co., Camden, N.J.

Parrish, F. C., Jr., and M. E. Bailey. 1966. Physicochemical properties and partial purification of porcine muscle cathepsin. *J. Agr. Food Chem. 14*: 232.

Parrish, F. C., Jr., D. E. Goll, W. J. Newcomb II, B. O. deLumen, H. M. Chaudhry, and E. A. Kline. 1969a. Molecular properties of post-mortem muscle. 7. Changes in nonprotein nitrogen and free amino acids of bovine muscle. *J. Food Sci. 34*: 196.

Parrish, F. C., Jr., R. E. Rust, G. R. Popenhagen, and B. E. Miner. 1969b. Effect of postmortem aging time and temperature on beef muscle attributes. *J. Animal Sci. 29*: 398.

Partington, F. R., and G. C. Wood. 1963. The role of non-collagen components in the mechanical behavior of tendon fibres. *Biochem. Biophys. Acta 69*: 485.

Partmann, W. 1963. Post-mortem changes in chilled and frozen muscle. *J. Food Sci. 28*: 15.

Partridge, S. M. 1966. Elastin. In *The Physiology and Biochemistry of Muscle as a Food*, E. J. Briskey, R. G. Cassens, and J. C. Trautman, eds., p. 327. U. of Wisc. Press, Madison, Wisc.

Partridge, S. M. 1969. Elastin, biosynthesis and structure. *Gerontol. 15*: 85.

Patterson, R. L. S. 1968. 5α-androst-16-ene-3-one: —Compound responsible for taint in boar fat. *J. Sci. Food Agr. 19*: 31.

Paul, P. C. 1959. Unpublished data.

Paul, P. C. 1962. Tenderness and chemical composition of beef. I. Variations among animals treated alike. *Food Technol. 16*, No. 11: 115.

Paul, P. C. 1962. Tenderness and chemical composition of beef. II. Variations due to animal treatment and to extent of heating. *Food Technol. 16*, No. 11: 117.

Paul, P. C. 1963. Influence of methods of cooking on meat tenderness. In *Proc. Meat Tenderness Symp.*, p. 225. Campbell Soup Co., Camden, N.J.

Paul, P. C. 1964. The rabbit as a source of experimental material for meat studies. *J. Food Sci. 29*: 865.

Paul, P. C. 1965. Storage- and heat-induced changes in the microscopic appearance of rabbit muscle. *J. Food Sci. 30*: 960.

Paul, P. C. 1965. Current research on meat. *J. Am. Dietet. Assoc. 46*: 468.

Paul, P. C., and M. Bean. 1956. Method for braising beef round steaks. *Food Res. 21*: 75.

Paul, P. C., and L. J. Bratzler. 1955. Studies on tenderness of beef. II. Varying storage times and conditions. III. Size of shear cores: end to end variation in the semimembranosus and adductor. *Food Res. 20*: 626, 635.

Paul, P. C., M. Bean, and L. J. Bratzler. 1956. Effect of cold storage and method of cooking on commercial grade cow beef. *Mich. Agr. Exp. Sta. Tech. Bull. 256*, East Lansing, Mich.

Paul, P. C., L. J. Bratzler, E. D. Farwell, and K. Knight. 1952. Studies on tenderness of beef. I. Rate of heat penetration. *Food Res. 17*: 504.

Paul, P. C., B. Lowe, and B. R. McClurg. 1944. Changes in histological structure and palatability of beef during storage. *Food Res. 9*: 221.

Paul, P. C., L. Buchter, and A. Wierenga. 1966. Solubility of rabbit muscle proteins after various time-temperature treatments. *J. Ag. Food Chem.* *14*: 490.

Paul, P. C., R. M. Mandigo, and V. R. Arthaud. 1970. Textural and histologic differences among three muscles in the same cut of beef. *J. Food Sci. 35*: 505.

Paul, P. C., J. Torten, and G. M. Spurlock. 1964a. Eating quality of lamb. I. Effect of age. *Food Technol. 18*: 1779.

Paul, P. C., J. Torten, and G. M. Spurlock. 1964b. Eating quality of lamb. II. Effect of preslaughter nutrition. *Food Technol. 18*: 1783.

Paul, P. C., J. Torten, and G. M. Spurlock. 1964. Eating quality of lamb. III. Overall comparisons and interrelationships. *Food Technol. 18*, No. 11: 127.

Pearson, A. M. 1963. Objective and subjective measurements for meat tenderness. *Proc. Meat Tenderness Symp.*, p. 135. Campbell Soup Co., Camden, N.J.

Pearson, A. M., L. J. Bratzler, and R. N. Costilow. 1960a. Effects of pre-irradiation heat inactivation of enzymes on palatability of beef and pork. *Food Res. 25*: 681.

Pearson, A. M., L. J. Bratzler, and G. D. Gernon, Jr. 1960b. Effects of pre- and post-enzyme inactivation storage on irradiated beef and pork roasts. *Food Res. 25*: 687.

Pearson, A. M., G. Harrington, R. G. West, and M. E. Spooner. 1962. The browning produced by heating fresh pork. I. The relation of browning intensity to chemical constituents and pH. *J. Food Sci. 27*: 177.

Pearson, A. M., B. G. Tarladgis, M. E. Spooner, and J. R. Quinn. 1966. The browning produced on heating fresh pork. II. The nature of the reaction. *J. Food Sci. 31*: 184.

Pearson, A. M., R. H. Thompson, and J. F. Price. 1969. Sex odor in pork. *Proc. Meat Ind. Res. Conf.*, p. 145. Am. Meat Inst. Found., Chicago, Ill.

Pearson, D. 1968. Application of chemical methods for the assessment of beef quality. III. Methods related to fat spoilage. *J. Sci. Food Agr. 19*: 553.

Pecot, R. K., C. M. Jaeger, and B. K. Watt. 1965. Proximate composition of beef from carcass to cooked meat: method of derivation and tables of values. *Home Econ. Res. Rep. No. 31*, U.S. Dept. Agri., Washington, D.C.

Pengilly, C. I., and D. L. Harrison. 1966. Effect of heat treatment on the acceptability of pork. *Food Technol. 20*, No. 3: 98.

Penny, I. F. 1960. Upgrading of low-grade meat. *Chem. and Ind.*, p. 288.

Penny, I. F. 1968. Effect of ageing on the properties of myofibrils of rabbit muscle. *J. Sci. Food Agr. 19*: 518.

Penny, I. F., C. A. Voyle, and R. A. Lawrie. 1963. A comparison of freeze-dried beef muscles of high or low ultimate pH. *J. Sci. Food Agr. 14*: 535.

Penny, I. F., C. A. Voyle, and R. A. Lawrie. 1964. Some properties of freeze-dried pork muscles of high or low ultimate pH. *J. Sci. Food Agr. 15*: 559.

Pepper, F. H., and A. M. Pearson. 1969. Changes in hydrogen sulfide and sulfhydryl content of heated beef adipose tissue. *J. Food Sci. 34*: 10.

Piez, K. A. 1966. Collagen. In *Physiology and Biochemistry of Muscle as a Food*, E. J. Briskey, R. G. Cassens, and J. C. Trautman, eds., p. 315. U. of Wisc. Press, Madison, Wisc.

Pilkington, D. H. 1965. The relation of firmness to certain other characteristics of beef muscle: Part I. Variation in the physical structure of the *longissimus dorsi* muscle at the twelfth rib and its relationship to firmness and tenderness. II. Relationship of objectively measured firmness and tenderness to the physical structure of the *longissimus dorsi*. *Dissertation Abstr. 26*: 1586.

Piotrowski, E. G., L. L. Zaika, and A. E. Wasserman. 1970. Studies on aroma of cured ham. *J. Food Sci. 35*: 321.

Pollak, G. A., and C. Foin. 1960. Comparative heating efficiencies of a microwave and a conventional electric oven. *Food Technol. 14*: 454.

Pokorný, J., S. Klein, and M. Blomannová. 1963. Smoke process. II. Antioxidant activity of phenolic substances of smoke condensates. *Sborn. praž. vys. školy chem. technol. potravin Technol.* 7,i,91.

Pokorny, J., and M. Pazlar. 1966. Effect of hemoglobin on the autoxidation of lard in water-free media. *Nahrung 10*: 274.

Porter, R. W., L. J. Bratzler, and W. T. Magee. 1962. Yield of cooked edible meat from various retail beef cuts as influenced by carcass weight and carcass grade. *Food Technol. 16*, No. 4: 86.

Porter, R. W., L. J. Bratzler, and A. M. Pearson. 1965. Fractionation and study of compounds in wood smoke. *J. Food Sci. 30*: 615.

Powell, W. E., and D. L. Huffman. 1968. An evaluation of quantitative estimates of beef carcass composition. *J. Animal Sci. 27*: 1554.

Price, M. 1969. Dept. Livestock Husb., U. New England, Armidale, N.S.W., Austr., personal communication.

Pridgeon, M. L. 1954. A comparison of palatability and cooking changes of beef steaks prepared by four methods. M.S. thesis, Michigan State Univ., East Lansing, Mich.

Proceedings, Meat Industry Research Conference. Am. Meat Sci. Assoc., Am. Meat Inst. Found. (annual), Am. Meat Inst. Found., Chicago, Ill.

Proceedings, Reciprocal Meat Conference. Am. Meat Sci. Assoc. (annual). Nat. Live Stock and Meat Bd., Chicago, Ill.

Quinn, J. R., A. M. Pearson, and J. R. Brunner. 1964. Detection and isolation of multiple myoglobins from beef muscle. *J. Food Sci. 29*: 422.

Ramsbottom, J. M., and E. J. Strandine. 1949. Initial physical and chemical changes in beef as related to tenderness. *J. Animal Sci. 8*: 398.

Ramsbottom, J. M., E. J. Strandine, and C. H. Koonz. 1945. Comparative tenderness of representative beef muscles. *Food Res. 10*: 497.

Randall, C. J., and H. F. MacRae. 1967. Hydrolytic enzymes in bovine skeletal muscle. II. Proteolytic activity of the water-soluble proteins separated by starch gel electrophoresis. *J. Food Sci. 32*: 182.

Ransom, B. H. 1916. The effects of refrigeration upon the larvae of Trichinella spiralis. *J. Agr. Res. 5*: 819.

Ransom, B. H., and B. Schwartz. 1919. Effects of heat on Trichinae. *J. Agr. Res. 17*: 201.

Reith, J. F., and M. Szakály. 1967a. Formation and stability of nitric oxide myoglobin. I. Studies with model systems. *J. Food Sci. 32*: 108.

Reith, J. F., and M. Szakály. 1967b. Formation and stability of nitric oxide myoglobin. II. Studies on meat. *J. Food Sci. 32*: 194.

Rice, E. E. 1970. Reaction of connective tissue to meat tenderizers. *Proc. Current Topics Food Nutr. 1970*, Dept. Home Econ., Univ. Iowa, Iowa City. To be published.

Richter, G. W., and A. Kellner. 1963. Hypertrophy of the human heart at the level of fine structure. An analysis and two postulates. *J. Cell Biol. 18*: 195.

Rickansrud, D. A., and R. L. Henrickson. 1967. Total pigments and myoglobin concentration in four bovine muscles. *J. Food Sci. 32*: 57.

Riedel, L. 1957. Calorimetric studies on the freezing of flesh. *Kältetechnik 9*: 38.

Riedel, L. 1961. Bound water in meat. Calorimetric studies on beef with varied water content at temperatures between $-180°$ and $0°$ C. *Kältetechnik 13*: 122.

Ritchey, S. J. 1965. The relationships of total, bound, and free water and fat content to subjective scores for eating quality in two beef muscles. *J. Food Sci. 30*: 375.

Ritchey, S. J., and S. Cover. 1962. Determination of collagen in raw and cooked beef from two muscles by alkali-insoluble, autoclave-soluble protein and by hydroxyproline content. *J. Ag. Food Chem. 10*: 40.

Ritchey, S. J., and R. L. Hostetler. 1964. Characterization of the eating quality of four beef muscles from animals of different ages by panel scores, shear-force values, extensibility of muscle fibers, and collagen content. *Food Technol. 18*: 1067.

Ritchey, S. J., and R. L. Hostetler. 1964. Relationship of free and bound water to subjective scores for juiciness and softness and to changes in weight and dimensions of steaks from two beef muscles during cooking. *J. Food Sci. 29*: 413.

Ritchey, S. J., and R. L. Hostetler. 1965. The effect of small temperature changes on two beef muscles as determined by panel scores and shear-force values. *Food Technol. 19*: 1275.

Ritchey, S. J., S. Cover, and R. L. Hostetler. 1963. Collagen content and its relation to tenderness of connective tissue in two beef muscles. *Food Technol. 17*, No. 2: 76.

Robinson, H. E., and P. A. Goeser. 1962. Enzymatic tenderization of meat. *J. Home Econ. 54*: 195.

Rodel, W., E. Sandner, and L. Zahn. 1968. Post mortem changes of beef. *14th European Meat Res. Conf.*, p. 23. Am. Meat Sci. Assoc., mimeo.

Rodgers, C., M. Mangel, and R. Baldwin. 1963. Comparison of dry-heat cooking methods for round steak. *Food Technol. 17*, No. 7: 111.

Rodgers, C., M. Mangel, and R. Baldwin. 1964. Further comparisons of dry-heat methods for round steak. *Food Technol. 18*, No. 2: 130.

Rogers, P. J. 1969. Standardization of methods of heating and sampling meat. *Proc. 22nd Ann. Recip. Meat Conf.*, p. 166. Nat. Live Stock Meat Bd., Chicago, Ill.

Rogers, P. J., and S. J. Ritchey. 1969. Sensory differentiation of beef tenderness and juiciness components over short intervals of cooking time. *J. Food Sci. 34*: 434.

Rongey, E. H. 1965. A simple objective test for sausage emulsion quality. *Proc. Meat Ind. Res. Conf.*, p. 99, Am. Meat Inst. Found., Chicago, Ill.

Saffle, R. L. 1965. Some comments on emulsifying properties of muscle proteins. *Proc. Meat Ind. Res. Conf.*, p. 94. Am. Meat Inst. Found., Chicago, Ill.

Saffle, R. L. 1968. Meat emulsions. *Advan. Food Res. 16*: 105.

Saffle, R. L. 1969. Stability of meat emulsions. *Proc. Meat Ind. Res. Conf.*, p. 187. Am. Meat Inst. Found., Chicago, Ill.

Saffle, R. L., and J. W. Galbreath. 1964. Quantitative determination of salt-soluble protein in various types of meat. *Food Technol. 18*: 1943.

Sale, A. J. H. 1960. Measurement of meat tenderness. In *Texture in Foods*. Soc. Chem. Ind. Monograph No. 7, p. 103. Soc. Chem. Ind., London, Engl.

Saleh, B., and B. M. Watts. 1968. Substrates and intermediates in the enzymatic reduction of metmyoglobin in ground beef. *J. Food Sci. 33*: 353.

Sanderson, A., A. M. Pearson, and B. S. Schweigert. 1966. Effect of cooking procedure on flavor components of beef. Carbonyl compounds. *J. Agr. Food Chem. 14*: 245.

Sayre, R. N., E. J. Briskey, W. G. Hoekstra, and R. W. Bray. 1961. Effect of preslaughter change to a cold environment on characteristics of pork muscle. *J. Animal Sci. 20*: 487.

Sayre, R. N., and E. J. Briskey. 1963. Protein solubility as influenced by physiological conditions in the muscle. *J. Food Sci. 28*: 675.

Sayre, R. N., E. J. Briskey, and W. G. Hoekstra. 1963b. Effect of excitement, fasting, and sucrose feeding on porcine muscle phosphorylase and post-mortem glycolysis. *J. Food Sci. 28*: 472.

Sayre, R. N., E. J. Briskey, and W. G. Hoekstra. 1963c. Alteration of post-mortem changes in porcine muscle by preslaughter heat treatment and diet modification. *J. Food Sci. 28*: 292.

Schmitt, O., and B.-L. Dumont. 1969. Méthodes d'analyse de la structure musculaire. *Ann. Biol. animale Biochim. Biophys.* 9: 123.

Schön, Schön. 1966. Factors which influence the flavor of beef. *Report 12th European Meat Res. Conf.*, Am. Meat Sci. Assoc., Chicago, Ill. mimeo.

Schubert, M. 1964. Intercellular macromolecules containing polysaccharides. In *Connective Tissues: Intercellular Macromolecules*, p. 119. Little, Brown & Co., Boston.

Schweigert, B. S. 1956. Chemistry of meat pigments. *Proc. 8th Res. Conf.*, p. 61. Am. Meat Inst. Found., Chicago, Ill.

Scopes, R. K. 1960. Influence of post-mortem conditions on solubilities of muscle proteins. *Biochem. J.* 91: 201.

Scopes, R. K., and R. A. Lawrie. 1963. Post-mortem lability of skeletal muscle proteins. *Nature 197* No. 4873: 1202.

Searcy, D. J., D. L. Harrison, and L. L. Anderson. 1969. Palatability and selected related characteristics of three types of roasted porcine muscle. *J. Food Sci.* 34: 486.

Sen, P. B., M. D. Mukherji, and C. Mookerjea. 1961. Histochemical observations on the nature of reticulin. *Indian J. Med. Res.* 49: 1051.

Shank, J. L., J. H. Silliker, and P. A. Goeser. 1962. Development of non-microbial off-condition in fresh meat. *Appl. Microbiol.* 10: 240.

Sharp, J. G. 1963. Aseptic autolysis in rabbit and bovine muscle during storage at 37° C. *J. Sci. Food Agr.* 14: 468.

Sharrah, N., M. S. Kunze, and R. M. Pangborn. 1965a. Beef tenderness: Sensory and mechanical evaluation of animals of different breeds. *Food Technol.* 19, No. 2: 131.

Sharrah, N., M. S. Kunze, and R. M. Pangborn. 1965b. Beef tenderness: Comparison of sensory methods with the Warner-Bratzler and L.E.E.-Kramer shear presses. *Food Technol.* 19, No. 2: 136.

Sheldon, H. 1969. The morphology and growth of adipose tissue. *Proc. Meat Ind. Res. Conf.*, p. 9. Am. Meat Inst. Found., Chicago.

Sherman, P. 1961. Water binding capacity of fresh pork. I. Influence of sodium chloride, pyrophosphate and polyphosphate on water absorption. II. Influence of phosphates on fat distribution in meat products. III. Influence of cooking temperature on the water binding capacity of lean pork. *Food Technol.* 15: 79, 87, 90.

Shishkina, N., and N. A. Moltchanova. 1968. Colour changes of packed cooked-and-smoked sausage during keeping in refrigerated display-cases with various degrees of illumination. *Abstr. 14th European Meat Res. Conf.* Am. Meat Sci. Assoc., Chicago, Ill. mimeo.

Shorland, F. B., Z. Czochanska, M. Moy, R. A. Barton, and A. L. Rae. 1970. Influence of pasture species on the flavour, odour and keeping quality of lamb and mutton. *J. Sci. Food Agr.* 21: 1.

Sidwell, C. G., H. Salwin, M. Driver, and R. B. Koch. 1962. Spectral examination of cured-meat pigments during frankfurter processing. *J. Food Sci.* 27: 9.

Simone, M., F. Carroll, and C. O. Chichester. 1959. Differences in eating quality factors of beef from 18- and 30-month steers. *Food Technol. 13:* 337.

Sink, J. D., R. G. Cassens, W. G. Hoekstra, and E. J. Briskey. 1965. Rigor mortis pattern of skeletal muscle and sarcomere length of the myofibril. *Biochim. Biophys. Acta 102:* 309.

Sisson, S., and J. D. Grossman. 1953. *The Anatomy of the Domestic Animals.* W. B. Saunders Co., Philadelphia. 4th ed.

Slautterback, D. B. 1966. The ultrastructure of cardiac and skeletal muscle. In *Physiology and Biochemistry of Muscle as a Food,* E. J. Briskey, R. G. Cassens, and J. C. Trautman, eds., p. 39. Univ. of Wisc. Press, Madison, Wisc.

Smith, E. C. B. 1935. *Report of the Food Investigation Board,* p. 17. Dept. Sci. Ind. Res. (Brit.).

Smith, G. C., Z. L. Carpenter, and G. R. King. 1969. Considerations for beef tenderness evaluations. *J. Food Sci. 34:* 612.

Smith, G. C., C. W. Spaeth, Z. L. Carpenter, G. T. King, and K. E. Hoke. 1968. The effects of freezing, frozen storage conditions and degree of doneness on lamb palatability characteristics. *J. Food Sci. 33:* 19.

Snyder, H. E., and J. C. Ayres. 1961. The autoxidation of crystallized beef myoglobin. *J. Food Sci. 26:* 469.

Solberg, M. 1968. Factors affecting fresh meat color. *Proc. Meat Ind. Res. Conf.,* p. 32. Am. Meat Inst. Found., Chicago, Ill.

Solms, J. 1969. The taste of amino acids, peptides, and proteins. *J. Agr. Food Chem. 17:* 686.

Sperring, D. D., W. T. Platt, and R. L. Hiner. 1959. Tenderness of beef muscle as measured by pressure. *Food Technol. 13:* 155.

Sprague, E. C., and H. S. Grindley. 1907. A precise method of roasting beef. *Univ. Illinois, Univ. Studies, vol. II,* No. 4.

Stinson, C. G., J. M. deMan, and J. P. Bowland. 1967. Fatty acid composition and glyceride structure of piglet body fat from different sampling sites. *J. Am. Oil Chemists' Soc. 44:* 253.

St-Laurent, G. J., and G. J. Brisson. 1968. Effect of dietary iron and desferrioxamine on blood hemoglobin and on pigment content and color of muscles in veal calves. *J. Animal Sci. 27:* 1527.

Strasser, J. 1969. Detection of quality changes in freeze-dried beef by measurement of the sorption isobar hysteresis. *J. Food Sci. 34:* 18.

Stringer, W. C. 1970. Pork carcass quality. MP123, Extension Division, U. of Missouri, Columbia, Mo.

Stromer, M. H., and D. E. Goll. 1967. Molecular properties of post-mortem muscle. 3. Electron microscopy of myofibrils. *J. Food Sci. 32:* 386.

Sulzbacher, W. L., and A. M. Gaddis. 1968. Meats: Preservation of quality by freezer storage. In *The Freezing Preservation of Foods,* 4th ed., vol. 2, p. 159. D. K. Tressler, W. B. VanArsdel, and M. J. Copley, eds. Avi Publ. Co., Westport, Conn.

Sulzbacher, W. L., A. M. Gaddis, and R. Ellis. 1963. Oxidative rancidity in meat and meat products. *Proc. 15th Res. Conf.,* p. 111. Circ. No. 74, Am. Meat Inst. Found., Chicago, Ill.

Sulzbacher, W. L., R. J. Gibbs, C. E. Swift, and A. J. Fryar. 1960. Protein investigations at the USDA Beltsville laboratory. *Proc. 12th Research Conf.,* p. 61. Circ. No. 61, Am. Meat Inst. Found., Chicago, Ill.

Suri, B. R. 1956. Chemical and physical changes in isolated beef muscle tenderized by infusion with sodium chloride. Ph.D. thesis, Oregon State Univ., Corvallis, Ore.

Suzuki, A., and M. Fujimaki. 1968. Studies on proteolysis in stored muscle. Part II. Purification and properties of a proteolytic enzyme, cathepsin D, from rabbit muscle. *Agr. Biol. Chem. 32*: 975.

Suzuki, A., M. Nakazato, and M. Fujimaki. 1967. Studies on proteolysis in stored muscle. Part I. Changes in nonprotein nitrogenous compounds of rabbit muscle during storage. *Agr. Biol. Chem. 31*: 953.

Swift, C. E. 1965. The emulsifying properties of meat proteins. *Proc. Meat Ind. Res. Conf.,* p. 78, Am. Meat Inst. Found., Chicago, Ill.

Swift, C. E., and M. D. Berman. 1959. Factors affecting the water retention of beef. I. Variations in composition and properties among eight muscles. *Food Technol. 13*: 365.

Swift, C. E., and W. L. Sulzbacher. 1963. Comminuted meat emulsions: Factors affecting meat proteins as emulsion stabilizers. *Food Technol. 17,* No. 2: 106.

Swift, C. E., W. E. Townsend, and L. P. Witnauer. 1968. Comminuted meat emulsions: Relation of the melting characteristics of fat to emulsion stability. *Food Technol. 22*: 775.

Symposium, New York Heart Assoc. 1964. *Connective Tissue: Intercellular Macromolecules.* Little, Brown and Co., Boston.

Szczesniak, A. S. 1963. Classification of textural characteristics. *J. Food Sci. 28*: 385.

Szczesniak, A. S., and K. W. Torgeson. 1965. Methods of meat texture measurement viewed from the background of factors affecting tenderness. *Advan. Food Res. 14*: 33.

Szent-Gyorgyi, A. 1952. The structure and chemistry of muscle. *Proc. Fourth Res. Conf.,* Am. Meat Inst., Chicago, Ill.

Taki, G. H. 1965. Physical and chemical changes occurring in beef, post-mortem, as related to tenderness and other quality characteristics. *Dissertation Abstr. 26*: 5972.

Tappel, A. L. 1956. Freeze-dried meat. II. The mechanism of oxidative deterioration of freeze-dried beef. *Food Res. 21*: 195.

Tappel, A. L. 1957b. Spectral studies of the pigments of cooked cured meats. *Food Res. 22:* 479.

Tappel, A. L. 1957c. The red pigment of precooked irradiated meat. *Food Res. 22:* 408.

Tappel, A. L. 1966. Lysosomes: Enzymes and catabolic reactions. In *Physiology and Biochemistry of Muscle as a Food,* E. J. Briskey, R. G. Cassens, and J. C. Trautman, eds., p. 237. U. of Wisc. Press, Madison, Wisc.

Tappel, A. L., S. Shibko, M. Stein, and J. P. Susz. 1965. Studies on the composition of lysosomes. *J. Food Sci. 30:* 498.

Tarladgis, B. G. 1961. Heat-induced heme-catalyzed lipid oxidation in animal tissues. *Dissertation Abstr. 21:* 2668.

Tarladgis, B. G. 1962. Interpretation of the spectra of meat pigments. II. Cured meats. The mechanism of colour fading. *J. Sci. Food Agr. 13:* 485.

Tarladgis, B. G., and A. M. F. Ehtashan-ud-Din. 1965. Structure of the pigments of precooked irradiated meats. *Nature* (Lond.) *207:* 489.

Tarladgis, B. G., B. M. Watts, M. T. Younathan, and L. Dugan. 1960. A distillation method for the quantitative determination of malonaldehyde in rancid foods. *J. Am. Oil Chemists' Soc. 37:* 44.

Tarr, H. L. A. 1966. Flavor of flesh foods. In *Flavor Chemistry.* Advan. in Chem. Series No. 56, Am. Chem. Soc., Washington, D.C.

Taylor, A. McM., and C. L. Walters. 1967. Biochemical properties of pork muscle in relation to curing. Part II. *J. Food Sci. 32:* 261.

Terrell, R. N., R. W. Lewis, R. G. Cassens, and R. W. Bray. 1967. Fatty acid compositions of bovine subcutaneous fat depots determined by gas-liquid chromatography. *J. Food Sci. 32:* 516.

Terrell, R. N., G. G. Suess, R. G. Cassens, and R. W. Bray. 1968. Broiling, sex and interrelationships with carcass and growth characteristics and their effect on the neutral and phospholipid fatty acids of the bovine longissimus dorsi. *J. Food Sci. 33:* 562.

Thille, M., L. J. Williamson, and A. F. Morgan. 1932. The effect of fat on shrinkage and speed in the roasting of beef. *J. Home Econ. 24:* 720.

Thomas, L. 1956. Reversible collapse of rabbit ears after intravenous papain and prevention of recovery of cortisone. *J. Exp. Med. 104:* 245.

Thomas, N. W., P. B. Addis, H. R. Johnson, R. D. Howard, and M. D. Judge. 1966. Effect of environmental temperature and humidity during growth on muscle properties of two porcine breeds. *J. Food Sci. 31:* 309.

Thompson, G. B., W. D. Davidson, M. W. Montgomery, and A. F. Anglemier. 1968. Alterations of bovine sarcoplasmic proteins as influenced by high temperature aging. *J. Food Sci. 33:* 68.

Toepfer, E. W., C. S. Pritchett, and E. M. Hewston. 1955. Boneless beef: raw, cooked, and served. Results of analyses for moisture, protein, fat, and ash. *Tech. Bull. No. 1137, U.S.D.A.,* Washington, D.C.

Tonsbeek, C. H. T., E. B. Koenders, A. S. M. van der Zijden, and J. A. Losekoot. 1969. Components contributing to beef flavor. Natural precursors of 4-hydroxy-5-methyl- 3(2H)-furanone in beef broth. *J. Agr. Food Chem.* *17*: 397.

Tonsbeek, C. H. T., A. J. Plancken, and T. v. d. Weerdhof. 1968. Components contributing to beef flavor. Isolation of 4-hydroxy-5-methyl-3(2H)-furanone and its 2, 5-dimethyl homolog from beef broth. *J. Agr. Food Chem.* *16*: 1016.

Townsend, W. E., L. P. Witnauer, J. A. Riloff, and C. E. Swift. 1968. Comminuted meat emulsions: Differential thermal analysis of fat transitions. *Food Technol. 22*: 319.

Trumic, Petrovic, Ristin. 1966. Effect of various temperatures of water and solution of sodium chloride and polyphosphates on hydration of ground beef. *12th European Meat Res. Conf.*, Am. Meat Sci. Assoc., mimeo.

Tucker, H. Q., M. M. Voegeli, G. H. Wellington, and L. J. Bratzler. 1952. *A Cross Sectional Muscle Nomenclature of the Beef Carcass.* Michigan State Univ. Press, East Lansing, Mich.

Tuma, J. H., R. L. Henrickson, G. V. Odell, and D. F. Stephens. 1963. Variation in the physical and chemical characteristics of the *longissimus dorsi* muscle from animals differing in age. *J. Animal Sci. 22*: 354.

Tuomy, J. M., and R. J. Lechnir. 1964. Effect of cooking temperature and time on the tenderness of pork. *Food Technol. 18*, No. 2: 97.

Tuomy, J. M., R. J. Lechnir, and T. Miller. 1963. Effect of cooking temperature and time on the tenderness of beef. *Food Technol. 17*, No. 11: 119.

Turkki, P. R., and A. M. Campbell. 1967. Relation of phospholipids to other tissue components in two beef muscles. *J. Food Sci. 32*: 151.

Urbain, W. M. 1969. Fresh meats. *Proc. Food Ind. Symp.*, p. 79. Food Sci. and Technol. Dept., U. of Nebraska, Lincoln, Nebr.

Usborne, W. R., J. D. Kemp, and W. G. Moody. 1968. Effect of liveweight on quality, proximate composition, certain protein components and free amino acids of porcine muscle. *J. Animal Sci. 27*: 584.

Valin, C. 1968. Post-mortem changes in myofibrillar protein solubility. *J. Food Technol. 3*: 171.

Veis, A. 1961. The structure and properties of collagen. *Proc. 13th Meat Res. Conf.*, p. 95. Am. Meat Inst. Found., Chicago, Ill.

Veis, A. 1965. Chemistry and properties of collagen. *Proc. Meat Ind. Res. Conf.*, p. 1. Am. Meat Inst. Found., Chicago.

Verzár, F. 1963. The aging of collagen. *Sci. Am. 208*, No. 4: 104.

Visser, R. Y., D. L. Harrison, G. E. Goertz, M. Bunyan, M. M. Skelton, and D. L. Mackintosh. 1960. The effect of degree of doneness on the tenderness and juiciness of beef cooked in the oven and in deep fat. *Food Technol. 14*: 193.

Vognarová, I., Z. Dvořák, and R. Böhn. 1968. Collagen and elastin in different cuts of veal and beef. *J. Food Sci. 33*: 339.

Voisey, P. W., and H. Hansen. 1967. A shear apparatus for meat tenderness evaluation. *Food Technol. 21*: 355.

Voyle, C. A., and R. A. Lawrie. 1964. The demonstration of sarcoplasmic reticulum in bovine muscle. *J. Royal Micro. Soc. 82*: 173.

Walter, M. J., D. E. Goll, E. A. Kline, L. P. Anderson, and A. F. Carlin. 1965. Effect of marbling and maturity on beef muscle characteristics. I. Objective measurements of tenderness and chemical properties. *Food Technol. 19*: 841.

Walters, C. L., A. McM. Taylor, R. J. Casselden, and N. Ray. 1968. Investigation of specific reducing systems in relation to meat curing. *Brit. Food Mfg. Ind. Res. Assoc., Res. Rept.* No. 139, Leatherhead, Surrey, England.

Wang, H., E. Rasch, V. Bates, F. J. Beard, J. C. Pierce, and O. G. Hankins. 1954. Histological observations on fat loci and distribution in cooked beef. *Food Res. 19*: 314.

Wasserman, A. E. 1966. The composition of meat flavor. *Nat. Provisioner*, Dec. 3.

Wasserman, A. E. 1967. The chemistry of cooked meat flavor. *Proc. 20th Recip. Meat Conf.*, p. 228. Nat. Live Stock Meat Bd., Chicago, Ill.

Wasserman, A. E., and W. Fiddler. 1969. Natural smoke: Composition and properties. *Proc. Meat Ind. Res. Conf.*, p. 163. Am. Meat Inst. Found., Chicago, Ill.

Wasserman, A. E., and A. M. Spinelli. 1970. Sugar-amino acid interaction in the diffusate of water extract of beef and model systems. *J. Food Sci. 35*: 328.

Wasserman, A. E., and F. Talley. 1968. Organoleptic identification of roasted beef, veal, lamb and pork as affected by fat. *J. Food Sci. 33*: 219.

Watt, B. K., and A. L. Merrill. 1963. Composition of foods. U.S.D.A., *Agr. Handbook No. 8*, revised.

Watts, B. M. 1954. Oxidative rancidity and discoloration of meats. *Advan. Food Res. 5*: 1.

Webb, N. B., L. J. Bratzler, and W. T. Magee. 1962. Effects of sonic vibration on tenderness of beef. *Food Technol. 16*, No. 6: 124.

Webb, N. B., O. J. Kahlenberg, H. D. Naumann, and H. B. Hedrick. 1967. Biochemical factors affecting beef tenderness. *J. Food Sci. 32*: 1.

Webb, N. L., N. B. Webb, D. Cederquist, and L. J. Bratzler. 1961. The effect on internal temperature and time of cooking on the palatability of pork loin roasts. *Food Technol. 15*: 371.

Weber, H. H., and K. Meyer. 1933. Das Kolloidale Verhalten der Muskeleiweisskorper. *Biochem. Z. 266*: 137.

Weidemann, J. F., G. Kaese, and L. D. Carruthers. 1967a. The histology of pre-rigor and post-rigor ox muscle before and after cooking and its relation to tenderness. *J. Food Sci. 32*: 7.

Weidemann, Kaess, and Bain. 1967b. Unpublished data cited in Weidemann,

J. F., G. Kaess, and L. D. Carruthers. 1967. The histology of pre-rigor and post-rigor ox muscle before and after cooking and its relation to tenderness. *J. Food Sci. 32:* 7.

Weiner, P. D., D. H. Kropf, D. L. MacKintosh, and B. A. Koch. 1966. Effect on muscle quality of processing pork carcasses within one hour post-mortem. *Food Technol. 20:* 189.

Weir, C. E. 1960. Palatability characteristics of meat. In *The Science of Meat and Meat Products,* Am. Meat Inst. Found., Chap. 6. W. H. Freeman and Co., San Francisco, Calif.

Weir, C. E. 1960. Factors affecting the quality of cooked pork. *Proc. 12th Res. Conf.,* p. 107. Am. Meat Inst. Found., Circ. No. 61, Chicago, Ill.

Weir, C. E., C. Pohl, E. Auerbach, and G. D. Wilson. 1963. Effect of cooking conditions on yield and palatability of pork loin roasts. *Food Technol. 17,* No. 12: 95.

Weir, C. E., A. Slover, C. Pohl, and G. D. Wilson. 1962. Effect of cooking procedures on the composition and organoleptic properties of pork chops. *Food Technol. 16,* No. 5: 133.

Whitaker, J. R. 1966. Summary and discussion of Part IV. In *Physiology and Biochemistry of Muscle as a Food.* E. J. Briskey, R. G. Cassens, and J. C. Trautman, eds., p. 299. U. of Wisc. Press, Madison, Wisc.

Whitaker, J. R. 1959. Chemical changes associated with aging of meat with emphasis on the proteins. *Advan. Food Res. 9:* 1.

Wick, E. L., M. Koshika, and J. Mizutani. 1965. Effect of storage at ambient temperature on the volatile components of irradiated beef. *J. Food Sci. 30:* 433.

Wick, E. L., T. Yamanishi, L. C. Wertheimer, J. E. Hoff, B. E. Proctor, and S. A. Goldblith. 1961. Volatile components of irradiated beef. *J. Agr. Food Chem. 9:* 289.

Wierbicki, E., L. E. Kunkle, and F. E. Deatherage. 1957. Changes in the water holding capacity and cationic shifts during the heating and freezing and thawing of meat as revealed by a simple centrifugal method for measuring shrinkage. *Food Technol. 11:* 69.

Williams, E. J. 1968. Meat and meat products. In *Quality Control in the Food Industry,* S. M. Herschdoerfer, ed., vol. 2, p. 251. Academic Press, New York.

Wilson, G. D., P. O. Brown, W. R. Chesbro, B. Ginger, and C. E. Weir. 1960a. The use of antibiotics and gamma irradiation in the aging of steaks at higher temperatures. *Food Technol. 14:* 143.

Wilson, G. D., P. D. Brown, C. Pohl, L. E. Weir, and W. R. Chesbro. 1960b. A method for the rapid tenderization of beef carcasses. *Food Technol. 14:* 186.

Windrun, G. M., P. W. Kent, and J. E. Eastoe. 1955. The constitution of human renal reticulin. *Brit. J. Exp. Pathol. 36:* 49.

Winegarden, M. W., B. Lowe, J. Kastelic, E. A. Kline, A. R. Plagge, and P. S. Shearer. 1952. Physical changes of connective tissue of beef during heating. *Food Res. 17*: 172.

Wismer-Pedersen, J. 1965. Effect of EDTA and pH on properties of freeze-dried pork muscle. I. Effect of pH and magnesium and calcium ions on freeze-dried myofibrils. *J. Food Sci. 30*: 85.

Wismer-Pedersen, J. 1959a. Influence of feeding and ante-mortem treatment on the quality of cured bacon. *Fleischwirtschaft 11*: 728, 830.

Wismer-Pedersen, J. 1959b. Some observations on the quality of cured bacon in relation to *ante-mortem* treatment. III. Effects on the color of cured hams. *Acta Agr. Scand. 9*: 102.

Wistreich, H. E., E. Karmas, and J. E. Thompson. 1960. Nitrogen content of pork adipose tissue proteinaceous fraction. *Food Technol. 14*: 412.

Woodams, E. E., and J. E. Nowrey. 1968. Literature values of thermal conductivities of foods. *Food Technol. 22*: 494.

Woodhams, P. R., A. H. Kirton, and K. E. Jury. 1966. Palatability characteristics of cross breds as related to individual Southdown sires, slaughter age and carcass fatness. *N.Z.J. Agr. Res. 9*: 268.

Woodhams, P. R., and S. J. Trower. 1965. Palatability characteristics of rib-steaks from Aberdeen Angus steers and bulls. *N.Z.J. Agr. Res. 8*: 921.

Woolsey, A. P., and P. C. Paul. 1969a. External fat cover influence on raw and cooked beef. 1. Fat and moisture content. *J. Food Sci. 34*: 554.

Woolsey, A. P., and P. C. Paul. 1969b. External fat cover influence on raw and cooked beef. 2. Cooking time, losses, press fluid and shear force values. *J. Food Sci. 34*: 568.

Yeates, N. T. M. 1964. Starvation changes and subsequent recovery of adult beef muscle. *J. Agr. Sci. 62*: 267.

Younathan, M. T., and B. M. Watts. 1959. Relationship of meat pigments to lipid oxidation. *Food Res. 24*: 728.

Younathan, M. T., and B. M. Watts. 1960. Oxidation of tissue lipids in cooked pork. *Food Res. 25*: 538.

Yueh, M. H., and F. M. Strong. 1960. Volatile constituents of cooked beef. *J. Agr. Food Chem. 8*: 491.

Zaika, L. L. 1969. Meat flavor. Method for rapid preparation of the water-soluble low molecular weight fraction of meat tissue extracts. *J. Agr. Food Chem. 17*: 893.

Zaika, L. L., A. E. Wasserman, C. A. Monk, Jr., and J. Salay. 1968. Meat flavor. 2. Procedures for the separation of water-soluble beef aroma precursors. *J. Food Sci. 33*: 53.

Ziemba, Z. 1961. Changes of canned meats by the effect of heat treatment. *Przemysl Spozywczy*, No. 1, p. 2.

Zimmerman, G. L., and H. E. Snyder. 1969. Meat pigment changes in intact beef samples. *J. Food Sci. 34*: 258.

Zipser, M. W., T.-W. Kwon, and B. M. Watts. 1964. Oxidative changes in cured and uncured frozen cooked pork. *J. Agr. Food Chem. 12:* 105.

Zipser, M. W., and B. M. Watts. 1961. Lipid oxidation in heat-sterilized beef. *Food Technol. 15:* 445.

Zirlin, A. D. 1968. Oxidation effects in a freeze-dried gelatin methyl linoleate system. Ph.D. thesis, Mass. Inst. Technol., Cambridge, Mass.

CHAPTER 8

Poultry and Fish[1]

HELEN H. PALMER and JANE BOWERS

POULTRY

Birds classified as poultry include chickens, turkeys, ducks, geese, guineas, and pigeons. Most poultry is marketed in the ready-to-cook form; dressed poultry, with blood and feathers removed but with head, feet, and viscera intact, is of little importance in modern marketing. Most ready-to-cook poultry is distributed in the chilled form, although distribution in frozen form is increasing. Primarily because of the seasonal nature of the demand, more turkeys than chickens are distributed in frozen form. Prepared and precooked frozen poultry products are available in increasing amounts and varieties (see Chapter 13).

Classes and Grades of Poultry

Complete information on definitions of classes of poultry and descriptions of the inspection and grading of poultry are contained in the Federal Register (Anon., 1966) and in pamphlets published by the U.S.D.A. Consumer and Marketing Service. Because of improved production methods, young chickens and young turkeys are now marketed at younger ages than those indicated in the definitions.

Classes of chickens include: *Rock Cornish game hens,* young immature chickens, usually 5 to 7 weeks of age; *broilers* or *fryers,* young, tender-meated chickens of either sex, usually 9 to 12 weeks of age; *roasters,* young tender-meated chickens of either sex, usually 3 to 5 months of age; capons, tender-meated, surgically unsexed male chickens, usually under 8 months of age; *hens, stewing chickens,* or *fowl,* mature

---

[1] Helen H. Palmer wrote the section on poultry and Jane Bowers wrote the one on fish.

female chickens with meat less tender than that of roasters, usually more than 10 months of age; *stags,* tougher male chickens, usually under 10 months of age; and *cocks* or *roosters,* mature male chickens. The maximum weight of a ready-to-cook Rock Cornish game hen is 2 pounds. The other classes no longer have weight specifications, since the rapid rate of growth of young poultry has made weight restrictions misleading. Young birds weighing 3 to 4 pounds, for example, are suitable for either frying or roasting.

Classes of turkeys include *fryer-roasters,* young immature, tender-meated turkeys of either sex, usually under 16 weeks of age; *young hens* and *young toms,* female and male tender-meated turkeys, usually under 15 months of age; and *mature* or *old turkeys,* turkeys of either sex, usually over 15 months of age. The designation of sex within the class name is optional for labeling purposes, and the three classes of young turkeys may be designated simply as "young turkeys." Ready-to-cook turkeys are available in several styles: whole, halved, quartered, and cut up.

Duck classes include *broiler ducklings* or *fryer ducklings,* tender-meated young ducks of either sex, usually under 8 weeks of age; *roaster ducklings,* tender-meated young ducks of either sex, usually under 16 weeks of age; and *mature ducks* or *old ducks,* tougher ducks of either sex, usually over 6 months of age. Goose classes include *young geese,* tender-meated birds of either sex; and *mature* or *old geese,* tougher geese of either sex. Classes of guineas include *young guineas* and *mature* or *old guineas.* Pigeons include *squabs,* young, immature pigeons of either sex; and *pigeons,* mature pigeons of either sex.

Poultry destined for movement in interstate commerce is inspected for wholesomeness. Ready-to-cook poultry may be graded for quality and given an individual U.S. letter grade of A, B, or C. Grading for quality is based on the following factors; conformation, fleshing, fat covering, degree of freedom from pinfeathers and vestigial hair, and degree of freedom from tears and cuts, disjointed and broken bones, discoloration of skin and flesh, blemishes and bruises of skin and flesh, and freezer burn.

Composition of Poultry Meat

Poultry meat is a nutritionally excellent food; the proteins of the meat are similar to those of other livestock (Millares and Fellers, 1948; Scott, 1959). The nutrient composition of the edible portions of raw and roasted turkeys of various types and ages have been determined and compared to that of chicken, duck, beef, lamb, and pork (Scott, 1956, 1958). Raw turkey and chicken meat has a relatively high protein content (20 to 24 percent) and a fat content ranging from 1 to 2 percent in the breast meat to 4 to 5 percent in the leg meat (Watt and Merrill, 1963). The fat contains a high percentage of unsaturated fatty acids and low cholesterol content.

Effects of Production, Processing and Storage on Poultry Meat Quality

The qualities desired in cooked poultry meat are tenderness, juiciness, and typical poultry flavor and the absence of off-flavor, microbiological spoilage, and hazards. With the knowledge available from research on poultry management, processing, and storage, these qualities can be readily attained (Klose, 1959a, b; 1964). Young chickens and turkeys available on the retail market are tender unless they have been improperly processed (scalded at too high a temperature or subjected to too strenuous methods of feather removal) or unless they have been inadequately aged (held above freezing temperature an insufficient time for the passing of rigor mortis). They are juicy unless they have been held under improper frozen storage conditions (inadequate protection from dehydration, too high a storage temperature, or too long a storage time). They have a typical poultry flavor and absence of off-flavor if they have been fed with usual commercial feeds and eviscerated promptly after killing. Processing, refrigeration, and freezing operations can be performed in a manner that will minimize microbiological problems.

The most apparent differences in flavor of poultry are probably due to added seasonings and not to the production or processing, since certain seasonings are characteristically used with certain cooking methods. Genetic and dietary factors are generally without much effect on poultry flavor (de Fremery and Sayre, 1968). Fishy off-flavors can be prevented by careful control of the diet, since it has been shown that fishy off-flavor is generally directly related to the amount of highly unsaturated (three or more double bonds) fatty acids in the carcass fat (Klose et al., 1953).

Of the various carcass components including meat, skin, fat, bone, and blood, the meat (muscle) is the best source of flavor; fat contributes to the aroma (Pippen et al., 1954; Lineweaver, 1961). More intense and more desirable chicken flavor has been associated with a low pH range in the meat (Bouthilet, 1949; Brant and Hanson, 1962; and Pippen et al., 1965). Natural pH differences that normally exist in broth after cooking meat from the usual commercial birds are not great enough to affect flavor (Pippen et al., 1965). However, in a test of the effect of pH on flavor, these authors varied pH by addition of acid or alkali, by epinephrine injection to limit post-mortem lactic acid production or by cooking immediately post mortem before much lactic acid could form. A pH difference during cooking affected chicken broth flavor more than did similar differences achieved after cooking. Many compounds have been separated from cooked-poultry volatiles and identified, but the contribution to cooked-poultry flavor has been established for only a few. Hydrogen sulfide and ammonia are among those shown to be important constituents of chicken aroma; volatile carbonyl compounds have been isolated from cooked chicken, and evidence indicates that they may contribute to chicken flavor (Pippen et al., 1958; Minor et al., 1965; and Klose et al., 1966).

Processing of poultry includes killing, bleeding, feather removal, evisceration, chilling, cutting into parts, packaging, and refrigeration or freezing. These procedures have been described in detail by Klose (1959a, b; 1964). Although methods used in any of these operations can affect the ultimate quality of the poultry, the conditions used for some operations are of critical importance, primarily to tenderness of the meat. Birds are killed by severing the carotid arteries. Inadequate bleeding may cause reddening of the skin. Birds are scalded by immersion in water at a temperature ranging from 128 to 140°F to facilitate feather removal. The time and temperature of scalding must be carefully regulated, since improper conditions affect appearance and keeping quality; too high or too long a heat treatment may have a toughening effect on the meat. Feathers are removed by mechanical feather-picking machines. Excessive beating during feather removal has a toughening effect on the meat. Evisceration of the birds usually takes place immediately after removal of the feathers. Poultry is then rapidly chilled to 35° F in ice slush.

There are two types of toughness encountered in poultry. One is related to the age of the bird; poultry becomes less tender as it matures. The other type, that due to inadequate aging, can occur in young birds. After aging for 24 hours at 40° F, all muscles are adequately tenderized, and some are tenderized much earlier (Klose, 1964). Adequate tenderization coincides with the passing of rigor mortis. Toughness can occur in young birds if they are cooked or frozen without adequate aging or if the muscles are cut before aging is completed.

Poultry is marketed in either a refrigerated or frozen condition. Packing requirements for chilled and for frozen poultry have been reviewed by Stewart (1953). Packing materials must be adequate with regard to moisture and gas permeability and rough handling during marketing. Suitable packaging is essential to assure that chilled and frozen poultry are of excellent quality. Of course, chilled poultry has limited shelf life because of spoilage due to bacterial growth. The quality of poultry held in frozen storage can be adequately protected by packaging in moisture-vapor proof material during storage of approximately a year at −18° C. Less favorable conditions of packaging, temperature, or time may lead to deterioration in quality.

The long time required to thaw frozen turkeys in a refrigerator and the inconvenience of thawing them under running tap water have prompted investigation of alternate approaches. These include roasting in the frozen state, freezing the neck and giblets in packages separate from the body, freezing large birds as halves or parts, and thawing at ambient temperature in a double-walled bag (Klose et al., 1959b; Fulton et al., 1967; and Klose et al., 1968).

A comparison of roasting unstuffed turkeys, weighing 20 to 24 pounds, from the frozen state and after thawing was made by Fulton et al. (1967). The neck and giblets were packaged separately from the rest of the turkey and not used in this study. Thawing in a refrigerator at 3 to 6° C (38–42° F) required approximately 46 hours. Thawing of halves, quarters, and pieces required 19–24 hours. Whole birds roasted at 163° C (325° F) without prior thawing to an endpoint of 85° C (185° F) required $2\frac{1}{4}$ hours longer than was required for thawed birds. Roasting times for frozen parts were only $\frac{1}{2}$ to $\frac{3}{4}$ hour longer than for thawed parts. Dryness is usually a defect in the breast meat of the whole birds cooked without prior thawing because of the longer roasting times required.

Klose et al. (1959c) found that halves of turkey fryers could be fried from the frozen state in about one fifth the time required for roasting. Deep-fat frying produced tougher meat than roasting, however, whether or not the birds were adequately aged.

The long thawing time can be safely reduced for unstuffed turkeys by thawing at ambient temperature if the surface temperature of the birds is kept low by insulating with a double-layer paper bag (Klose et al., 1968). The low surface temperature reduces potential bacterial growth during thawing. Commercial plastic-bagged ready-to-cook turkeys ranging in weight from 4 to 22 pounds were thawed at air temperature of 13, 21, and 29° C (55, 70, and 84° F), until the neck and giblets could be removed from the body cavity. Thawing times ranged from 12 to 16 hours for birds of various sizes at an air temperature of 29° C (84° F). The skin-surface temperature of birds in the bags remained below 13° C (55° F) for several hours after thawing of the birds. The authors recommend that frozen 4- to 6-pound birds enclosed in an overwrap not be thawed in air at 21–29° C (70–84° F) for longer than 15 hours and 12- to 24-pound birds no longer than 20 hours. Birds should be refrigerated if not cooked promptly after thawing.

Effects of Cooking on Poultry Quality

Chickens

Studies of the effect of cooking methods on tenderness, juiciness, and flavor of chickens are limited. Unfortunately, interpretation of these studies is complicated by uncontrolled variables, such as bird variation, cooking to different or unknown stages of doneness, and selection of inappropriate sensory testing methods.

Cooking *time* affects tenderness of older birds (hens and roosters) having relatively large amounts of connective tissue. Older birds require an adequate heat treatment for conversion of collagen to gelatin. Control of cooking time is important in young birds because it affects juiciness. An increase in cooking time increases weight loss, dryness of meat, and separation of meat from bone. Little effect of cooking method on flavor has been found.

Chicken can be successfully cooked at a range of cooking *temperatures* in many types of equipment, as is apparent from the following studies. No differences in shear press values of cooked meat were found when 9- to 10-week-old White Rock broilers were cooked to a minimum internal temperature of 85° C by microwave oven, deep-fat fryer, rotary-reel oven, and combinations of two methods. Weight losses were least for the rotary-reel oven (Mickelberry and Stadelman, 1962). Cooking in a microwave oven produced chicken comparable in quality to that using conventional cooking methods and requires from one tenth to one fourth the time (Phillips et al., 1960).

Broiling of chickens at temperatures ranging from approximately 175 to 230° C to an internal temperature of 95° C resulted in no important differences in shear values or cooking losses (Goertz et al., 1964a). Roasting temperatures of 125 and 175° C caused no palatability differences in chicken, although the time required at the lower temperature was more than twice that at the higher. Chickens roasted in uncovered pans lose more weight and require longer cooking times than those in covered pans (Lowe and Keltner, 1937). No significant flavor difference was found in mature hens cooked by pressure, steam, and simmering methods (Swickard et al., 1954). However, differences in shear force, press fluid, tenderness, and moisture, and lack of correlation between objective and sensory tests in this study, indicate that the cooking times used resulted in different degrees of doneness of the meat cooked by the three methods. No important differences were found in fowl simmered with various salts added to the water (Kahlenberg and Funk, 1961).

Unstuffed Turkeys

Appropriate sizes of unstuffed turkeys may be cooked by many methods over a wide range of temperature. They may be roasted, fried, broiled, cooked in a microwave oven, or simmered. The current recommendations for roasting unstuffed turkeys usually specify placing the bird on a rack in an uncovered pan in an oven set at 149–163° C (300–325° F). The lower oven temperature is recommended for large birds (20 pounds or over), to permit adequate cooking of the interior without undue browning of the skin. Turkeys are roasted to the well-done stage, an internal temperature of 82–85° C (180–185° F) in the thigh at the usual roasting conditions. Higher internal temperatures (190–195° F) increase weight losses and decrease juiciness, particularly in the breast meat. A partial covering of aluminum foil or cheese cloth is often recommended to prevent drying of the skin.

When turkey is cooked to the "well-done" stage, the pink color of the raw bird disappears. Since the pink color is most noticeable in the thigh joints, adequate heating can usually be assured by determining temperature in the thigh area. Because thickness of the breast muscle varies with the size and type of bird, the breast temperature may vary considerably at a given thigh temperature. The pink color in the thigh disappears at about 85° C (185° F) when poultry is roasted at an oven temperature of 149–163° C (300–325° F). A slower cooking rate will cause the color change at a lower internal temperature. Bramblett and Fugate (1967) found that at a thigh temperature of 82° C, breast temperatures of 12–24 pound turkeys roasted at 163° C average 73° C (164° F) but ranged from 63° to 81° C (146 to 178° F). For turkeys with a very thick breast muscle, determining the temperature in the thick portion of the breast may be advisable to assure adequate cooking in that area also (Klose et al., 1955, 1959c, 1961). A thermometer or thermocouple centered in the muscle at the beginning of cooking may move as the meat shrinks during cooking. Therefore, when the desired temperature is reached, the thermometer should again be centered by moving it short distances in several directions. If the temperature registered is not lower at other positions, the thermometer has not moved and the bird is considered done. If it registers a lower temperature after being inserted deeper in the muscle, additional cooking is required until the desired temperature is again reached.

Comparisons have been made of the quality, cooking times, and degree of doneness of turkeys cooked under many conditions. No difference was found in shear values of 18- to 20-pound turkeys related to cooking rate (Goodwin et al., 1962). Cooking rate was varied by using oven temperatures of 121 and 149° C. The experiment was designed so that the final internal breast temperatures ranged from 55 to 94° C for birds roasted at both temperatures. Cooking times ranged from approximately 5 to $10\frac{1}{2}$ hours at 121° C and 3 to 6 hours at 149° C. In another study, only one of five comparisons of roasted turkeys and turkeys cooked by other methods (frying, broiling, microwave oven) showed significant differences in flavor intensity (Brant and Hanson, 1962). However, detection of differences in flavor intensity, even in unseasoned meat, is difficult in the presence of differences in juiciness or tenderness. Turkeys roasted to 85° C in the thigh were usually less juicy than turkeys cooked more rapidly by frying, broiling, or microwave heating. Large birds, requiring a relatively long roasting time, were usually less juicy than small birds requiring less time. When the turkey was covered with aluminum foil during roasting, Hoke et al. (1965) found that the breast meat was less juicy, less tender, and more well done; and the thigh meat was more tender than in turkeys roasted without a covering. No important or consistent quality differences were found in Thompson White turkeys, 24 to 28 weeks of age, roasted to 90° C in the breast versus 95° C in the thigh; in chilled versus frozen defrosted birds; or in birds roasted with the breast up or down in the pan (Goertz et al., 1960b). Similar results were obtained in a later study (Goertz et al., 1964b). Whole turkeys and turkey rolls were compared by Augustine et al. (1962).

Wrapping of large turkeys in aluminum foil has been advocated, since cooking time can be reduced by using a high oven temperature without overbrowning. Unwrapped turkeys roasted at the usual oven temperatures (149–163° C) were compared with turkeys wrapped in aluminum foil, roasted at 149 to 260° C by Lowe et al. (1953). The meat of foil-wrapped birds roasted at 232° C was comparable to that of the unwrapped turkeys. The internal temperature of 22- to 24-pound birds reached 85° C in $3\frac{1}{4}$ to $3\frac{3}{4}$ hours in the covered bird, compared to the $5\frac{1}{2}$ to 6 hours required for the uncovered birds. A disadvantage of the foil-wrapping method was that the meat tended to pull away from the bone. Lack of browning was overcome by opening the foil at the end of the cooking period. Goertz et al. (1960a) found that temperatures of 85, 90, and 95° C in the thigh and 85 and 90° C in the breast did not result in differences in flavor and tenderness of turkey halves wrapped in aluminum foil and roasted at 163° C. Broad Breasted Bronze turkey hens were used. Cooking losses and "doneness" increased directly with internal temperature, and to some extent greater losses were reflected in lower scores for juiciness. "Doneness" was determined from the color of the juice, the flavor of the meat, and other subjective factors evaluated prior to and during carving. Turkeys (stuffed) roasted at 163° C (325° F) in uncovered pans were compared by Bramblett and Fugate (1967) to birds roasted at 93 or 232° C (200 or 450° F) covered with aluminum foil. Those roasted at 93° C had less desirable appearance, fell apart in handling, and were less juicy. Those roasted at 232° C were less evenly cooked, the meat appeared steamed, and some portions fell off the bone while other portions were still pink or bloody.

Stuffed Poultry

The heat treatment during roasting of stuffed poultry should be sufficient to destroy food poisoning organisms in the stuffing, to maintain the palatability and desirable appearance of the bird, and to provide an adequate yield of cooked meat. Roasting conditions must be adequate to prevent the multiplication of *Staphylococcus aureus* and production of the heat-stable enterotoxin and to destroy salmonella organisms that may be present. Research has shown that the time for roasting birds to the well-done stage at an oven temperature of 163° C (325° F) is sufficient to satisfy these requirements for unfrozen or thawed turkeys. Holding birds without carving for approximately 20–30 minutes after they are removed from the oven provides an additional safety factor, since the temperature of the stuffing continues to rise as conduction of the heat from the outer to the inner portion continues.

The destruction of food-poisoning organisms is assured either by attainment of a specified temperature in the stuffing or by maintaining the temperature in the stuffing above a temperature of 60° C (140° F) for an adequate time. A final stuffing temperature of 74° C (165° F) is adequate for birds of less than 12 pounds. A stuffing temperature of 68° C (154° F) is adequate for larger birds because the increase in bird diameter results in a relatively long cook. Adequate roasting is also assured by the equivalent of a center temperature of 71° C (160° F) for 10 minutes or by a temperature of 65.6° C (150° F) for 12 minutes (Webster and Esselen, 1956; Angelotti et al., 1960).

Roasting procedures that destroy food-poisoning organisms have been determined for both frozen and thawed stuffed poultry (Esselen et al., 1956; Hoke et al., 1965; Bramblett and Fugate, 1967; and Woodburn and Ellington, 1967). Types of birds and sizes studied included 6- to 24-pound turkeys, 1- to 2½-pound chickens, and 6-pound ducks roasted at oven temperatures from 93 to 232° C (200 to 450° F), uncovered, covered, and wrapped in aluminum foil. Esselen et al. (1956) studied roasting of frozen and thawed turkeys, chickens, and ducks. Initial temperatures were -21 to $-15°$ C (-5 to $5°$ F) for frozen stuffed birds and -1 to $4°$ C (30 to $40°$ F) for thawed birds. Stuffing comprised about one fourth of the total weight. The roasting time required at $163°$ C ($325°$ F) for good quality was longer than the minimum for safety for all weight classes. The 12- to 15-pound turkeys were cooked to $68°$ C ($155°$ F) in the center of the stuffing, as they were overdone if cooked to $74°$ C ($165°$ F); smaller birds were cooked to $74°$ C. The stuffing of the frozen birds was in the "dangerous incubation zone" of 10 to $49°$ C (50 to $120°$ F) for the same or less time than that of the thawed birds. Relative roasting times for frozen versus thawed birds ($163°$ C oven) of the 15-pound class were 8 to $8\frac{1}{2}$ hours versus $5\frac{1}{4}$ to 6 hours. For the 9-pound class they were $6\frac{1}{4}$ to $6\frac{3}{4}$ hours versus $4\frac{1}{4}$ to 5 hours. A limited number of 12-pound turkeys were roasted uncovered and covered at $121°$ C ($250°$ F) and at $232°$ C, with the cover or foil removed during the final 30 to 45 minutes of cooking. The birds roasted by the uncovered-pan method at $163°$ C, whether they were roasted before or after they were thawed, were of better quality than those roasted at $121°$ or $232°$ C.

Hoke et al. (1965) studied roasting methods for two weights of turkeys, 16 to 24 pounds and 13 to 16 pounds, ready-to-cook weight (without neck and giblets). Stuffed birds were roasted in $163°$ C ovens from temperatures of -1 to $2°$ C (30 to $35°$ F) to $91°$ C ($195°$ F) at a depth of 1 inch in the thick anterior portion of the breast. A partial covering of aluminum foil was placed over the breast and legs of the larger birds to prevent overbrowning. When the breast temperature was $91°$ C, the average thigh temperature was $91°$ C for the larger birds and $84°$ C ($183°$ F) for the smaller birds. The larger birds were roasted to a higher temperature than is required, and the light meat was less juicy than that of the smaller birds. Stuffing temperatures ranged from 74 to $87°$ C (165 to $189°$ F) in the larger birds and from 68 to $88°$ C (154 to $191°$ F) in the smaller birds at the end of roasting. Temperatures of all of the latter group reached $74°$ C 20 minutes after removal from the oven. Thus safe heat treatment was achieved in all cases.

Bramblett and Fugate (1967) roasted 12- to 24-pound stuffed turkeys on racks in flat pans at oven temperatures of 93, 163, and $232°$ C (200, 325, and $450°$ F) to endpoints in the thigh of 73, 82, and $82°$ C (163 and $180°$ F), respectively. Birds in the $93°$ C and $232°$ C ovens were covered with aluminum foil. Birds in open pans in the $163°$ C oven were partially covered with foil over the top of the legs and breast when the thigh temperature reached $66°$ C ($150°$ F). Two stuffing conditions were used: (1) stuffing at $35°$ to $38°$ F was placed in chilled birds that were refrigerated overnight; (2) stuffing at 97° to 100° F was placed in birds just before cooking. Average breast temperatures at the end of roasting were 73, 73, and 67° C in the 93, 163, and 232° C ovens. Corresponding stuffing temperatures were 75, 74, and 71° C (167, 165, and 159° F). After a 20-minute hold, the stuffing temperature for all but three of 144 birds had been above 60° C (140° F) for 85 minutes or longer. Turkeys roasted at 93° C required 3 to 6 times longer to cook than did those roasted at 163 or 232° C. Roasting times required for the stuffed birds at 163° were 4, 5½, and 6½ hours for 12-, 20-, and 24-pound birds. Shorter roasting times would be adequate if bird temperature at the start of roasting were higher than 3° C (38° F). The yield of edible meat differed only slightly (46.8 to 47.9 percent) at the different oven temperatures. The 163° C oven temperature was preferred, since the meat was uniformly cooked and had good appearance, flavor, juiciness, and tenderness.

Woodburn and Ellington (1967) evaluated the microbiological safety of the stuffing of medium-weight turkeys roasted at 93 and 232° C, as in the study of Bramblett and Fugate (1967). The high and the low roasting temperatures were selected for further study because they would present better opportunities for survival of pathogenic organisms than would the usually recommended temperature, 163° C. The danger with the low-temperature oven is the possibility that the stuffing temperature would rise so slowly that it would remain for long periods in the range permitting growth and multiplication of organisms. The danger with the high-temperature oven is the possibility that the meat would be cooked before the stuffing reached a temperature high enough to kill pathogens. The stuffing was inoculated with three strains of *S. aureus*. Some birds were stuffed and refrigerated the day before roasting. The stuffing was at 97 to 100° C when it was placed in the chilled birds. Results showed that this procedure is safe if the turkey is cold and the stuffed bird is immediately refrigerated, since the stuffing cools rapidly enough to prevent increases in bacterial count. The type of stuffing had no measurable effect on the growth of organisms. Medium-weight stuffed turkeys cooked at 93° C were safe on the basis of time-temperature conditions during cooking and absence of viable staphylococci in samples taken one hour after the birds were removed from the oven. However, because of the time in a temperature zone that would permit multiplication of staphylococci, roasting of stuffed turkeys larger than 20 pounds at 93° C is unwise. The stuffing of most birds roasted at 232° C received inadequate heating even after 30 to 60 minutes' holding following removal from the oven. The type of stuffing had no measurable effect on growth of organisms.

Poultry Meat Yields

Poultry meat yields, whether raw or cooked, are affected by so many factors of breeding, production, processing, and cooking that generalizations cannot readily be made. However, a thorough survey of this subject has recently been published (Swanson et al., 1964). Data have been compiled relating to chickens, turkeys, and waterfowl; diet, management, and hormone treatment; and processing methods such as preslaughter handling, killing, bleeding, evisceration, chilling, and cooking. Yields are reported for whole birds, parts, and boneless meat. Of particular value for future studies is a section concerning methodology for reporting of yields.

Typical percentage yields of whole eviscerated poultry (including neck and giblets) based on live weights range as follows:

Chickens	
Broilers, fryers, fowl	70–73 percent
Roasters	72–74 percent
Turkeys	
Fryer-roasters, light breeds	75–79 percent
Heavy hens and toms	78–82 percent
Ducklings (7 to 9 weeks)	70–73 percent
Geese (white Chinese,	
10 to 16 weeks)	72–73 percent

Typical percentage yields of cut-up parts of poultry based on chilled ready-to-cook weights range as follows:

	Chicken Fryers (Percent)	Turkeys, Beltsville and Bronze (Percent)
Breast	22–25	30–33
Legs	14–16	12–14
Thighs	15–16	12–14
Wings	12–14	10–13
Back	14–18	21–23
Neck	5–8	3–4
Giblets	6–8	5–7

Typical percentage yields of cooked poultry based on ready-to-cook weights range as follows:

	Chicken, Halves or Whole (Percent)	Turkey, Halves or Whole (Percent)
Roasted, fried, or broiled		
With bone	72–79	72–79
Edible meat	53	55
Stewed, braised, boiled, or pressure- cooked		
With bone	62–75	69–76
Edible meat	47–51	54–57

Pinkness in Well-Done Poultry

The occasional pinkness that occurs near the surface of well-done poultry is not due to undercooking (Pool, 1956). Rather, it is due to a type of reaction that has been used for many years in developing pink color of cured meat. Hemoglobin in the chicken meat combines with carbon monoxide and nitric oxide to form bright red compounds. Most flames generate small amounts of either or both of these, and the color can also develop in poultry in electric ovens when the heating element operates at a very high temperature. The pink color develops in birds roasted uncovered in contact with the atmosphere in the oven and is in no way deleterious.

Prepared and Precooked Poultry

Chapter 13 includes information about prepared and precooked frozen poultry products such as turkey rolls and roasts, stuffed turkeys, fried chicken, poultry dinners, creamed chicken and turkey, chicken a la king, and precooked duck and goose products.

Poultry Research Methods

For research on poultry cooking methods, uniform raw material, including birds of the same breed, age, and weight, from a flock raised under controlled conditions of feed and management are used. Of equal importance are uniform processing conditions (Lowe, 1948; Klose, 1964). Even when such conditions are observed, unexplained variations in tenderness may occur. Tenderization occurs at different rates, and tenderness differences are most apparent with short aging periods. Because of this variation in tenderness, six to eight birds are needed in poultry research for each imposed variable (Klose et al., 1959c; Pool et al., 1959).

Half birds are usually used to avoid the error introduced by bird variation (Paul et al., 1959). However, the birds must be adequately aged before being halved, because cutting the breast muscle before the passage of rigor mortis may cause the cut half to be tougher than the uncut half (Lowe, 1948; Koonz, et al., 1954; and de Fremery and Pool, 1960).

Sensory Test Methods

The muscles within a single bird differ in composition, appearance, tenderness, and flavor. Therefore, for evaluation of the quality of poultry meat by sensory tests, each judge receives a designated portion of a muscle or muscles. Tenderness and juiciness differences between birds may interfere with evaluation of flavor differences in poultry meat. Therefore, flavor tests are often made on broth instead of on meat (Pippen et al., 1954; Peterson, et al., 1959). Deboned rolls of meat of equal size can be used to eliminate tenderness and juiciness differences that might result from the different cooking times required for birds of different sizes (Hanson et al., 1959). The flavor, tenderness, and juiciness differences in poultry can be evaluated by small laboratory panels, but consumer preference or acceptability can only be adequately evaluated by panels representative of the consumer population (White et al., 1964; Hanson et al., 1965).

Physical Test Methods

Shear resistance determined by the Warner-Bratzler shear apparatus or the Kramer shear press correlates with sensory evaluation of poultry tenderness when birds differ in tenderness due to processing or aging. Studies showing the relation between shear resistance readings from the Warner-Bratzler apparatus and sensory evaluation of tenderness include those of Stewart et al. (1941), Carlin et al. (1949), Koonz et al. (1954), Paul et al. (1959), Klose et al. (1961), and White et al. (1964). Similar comparisons between the Kramer shear press and panel evaluation include those of Shannon et al. (1957), Dodge and Stadelman (1960a), and Hanson et al. (1965). The Warner-Bratzler apparatus has been used without parallel panel evaluations by Pool et al. (1959) and de Fremery and Pool (1960); the Kramer apparatus has been similarly used by Goodwin et al. (1961), Marian and Stadelman (1958), and Dodge and Stadelman (1959, 1960b). Discussions of these and other texture devices have been published (Friedman et al., 1963; Szczesniak, 1963) and are referred to in Chapter 16.

A method of measuring connective-tissue tenacity of poultry meat has been recently devised (Pool, 1967). The method measures the force required to tear the meat apart, independent of the force required to shear across the fibers. This force is inversely related to cooking time and is a measure of the toughness associated with the connective tissue of old fowl. The measurement shows good correspondence with sensory-panel evaluation of cohesiveness of meat.

Histological studies have been extensively used to elucidate tenderness and texture differences in poultry (Hanson et al., 1942; Stewart et al., 1945; and Lowe, 1948). Histological tests showed, for example, the relationship between rigor mortis development, rigor nodes in the muscle, and toughness in chickens; they also showed the breaks within the muscle fiber and granular-type structure associated with the passing of rigor mortis and the development of tenderness (Hanson et al., 1942).

Chemical Test Methods

Biochemical methods are being used to study the influence of postmortem changes on the development of tenderness in poultry meat. Research is designed to determine the chemical basis of changes during which the initially tender poultry meat toughens and then becomes tender in the course of the aging process (de Fremery, 1966). The studies include determination of the metabolic changes that occur during rigor mortis, such as the breakdown of glycogen and adenosine triphosphate and the decrease in pH of the meat. They show the relationship between acceleration of glycolysis and toughness and they also show that in the absence of glycolysis, poultry meat is tender without aging. Thus, the acceleration of glycolysis that occurs during some processing treatments (elevated temperature, freezing and thawing, and cutting the muscles) is related to toughness in fully aged meat (de Fremery, 1960, 1963, 1966).

FISH

The proteins and lipids of fish and the effects of storage on protein denaturation and lipid changes in fish muscle have been studied extensively and are reviewed. However, there is a lack of literature on the relation of those factors to palatability of fish. A few studies on the effects of certain cooking methods on the eating quality of fish have been made, and those are reviewed in the last part of this section on fish.

Fish, like other vertebrates, have three major kinds of muscle—smooth, cardiac, and skeletal. The skeletal muscles make up the bulk of the fish (other than its skeleton) and are arranged segmentally. The muscle segments or myotomes are separated by myocomma (connective tissue). In the embryo, the myotomes of the somites grow ventrally until each meets the one from the opposite side on the mid-ventral line. There is an equal number of myotomes and vertebrae that alternate with each other, each muscle mass spanning half of each of two adjacent vertebra. Fish muscle cells are short and their ends are inserted into layers of connective tissue. In cooked fish this arrangement results in "flakes" where the connective-tissue sheets gelatinize and free the coagulated "flakes" of muscle cells.

The muscle fibers appear microscopically similar in overall structure to the skeletal muscle fibers of higher animals. In studying muscle-cell dimensions of cod, Love (1958a) found that the number of segments was independent of the size of the fish, and that the fiber lengths from one myotome were proportional to the body length of the intact fish. Average fiber widths from different parts of the fillet followed the same pattern as fiber lengths, being largest at about 12 myotomes from the point of severance of the head and decreasing anteriorly and posteriorly.

Gross Composition

The proximate chemical composition of seafood is similar to that of land animals. The principal constituents are moisture, 66–84 percent; protein, 15–24 percent; lipid, 0.1–22 percent; and mineral substances, 0.8–2 percent (Jacquot, 1961). Water content usually is inversely related to lipid content, and together they comprise about 80 percent of the total weight.

The lipid content has been used to classify fish as fat or lean, but a strict distinction between fat and lean fish should not be made because of individual variation and the many factors that affect lipid content. Thurston et al. (1959) analyzed 21 species of freshwater fish for proximate composition, and found wide variation in composition among the different species of fish and among individual fish within a single species. Oil in fillets ranged from 0.7–63.5 percent, moisture from 29.8–84.1 percent, protein from 5.9–22.1 percent, and ash from 0.41–1.48 percent.

Recently, Stansby and Hall (1967) compiled data on the chemical composition of fish commercially important in the United States and categorized fish on the basis of oil and protein content as follows:

1. Low oil (<5 percent)-high protein (15–20 percent)—most common category; for example, cod.
2. Medium oil (5–15 percent)-high protein—second most common category; for example, salmon.
3. High oil (>15 percent)-low protein (<15 percent); for example, trout.
4. Low oil (<5 percent)-very high protein (>20 percent), not a common category, but several species in it are highly important commercially; for example, tuna and halibut.

5. Low oil (<5 percent)-low protein (<15): category for shellfish such as clams and oysters.

Species of fish were grouped into those categories, but may fall into other categories under certain conditions. Factors that may cause variation in composition include feeding, locality, size, age, and the season in which fish is caught.

The difference in composition attributable to seasonal variation may be related to many factors such as stage of sexual development and feeding conditions. Although Jangaard et al. (1967) reported no seasonal variation in the amount of flesh lipids of cod from inshore waters, other authors have noted differences in composition of fish caught in different seasons. Stansby and Lemon (1941) reported that the concentration of oil in mackerel varied as much as elevenfold between fish caught in the spring when the concentration was low and those caught in the summer when the concentration was high. Some seasonal variation in free amino acids in muscle tissue has been found. In May–July, taurine concentration peaked at 350–450 mg/100 g and fell to 100–150 mg/100 g in December–February (Jones, 1954). Seasonal variation in the composition of cod may be linked to the physiological processes taking place in the animal's body during the reproduction activities. During the spawning period, there was a 20 percent decrease in fat and a 5 percent decrease in protein, paralleled by a 10 percent increase in water solubles and a 5 percent increase in moisture in the muscle (Dambergs, 1964).

Differences in composition attributable to sex do not exhibit a constant pattern and may be subject to seasonal variation. Dambergs (1963) detected slight differences in the composition of male and female cod fillets, but measurements of the constituents were made during the "resting" period when differences were at a minimum.

The composition of the flesh tissue varies with the anatomical location. Thurston and Groninger (1959) found that the percentage of oil was generally lower near the tail than near the head. In studying various sections of cod, Dambergs (1963) found that the head end was richest in protein, the midsection contained the most water solubles, and the tail end contained more fat and water than other parts.

Red and White Muscle

Underneath the skin of many fish, particularly in the region of the lateral line, a layer of heavily pigmented, reddish muscle is present. The proportion of the red to white muscle varies considerably from species to species and from section to section in individual fish. Fraser et al. (1961) found that in cod and haddock the dark muscle made up 8 percent of the flesh in the tail section and only 1 percent of the middle section of the fillet. They also found that the dark lateral band of muscle contained 2 percent lipid, compared with 0.7–0.8 percent for the lighter muscle. Dark muscles of halibut had higher lipid content and nonprotein nitrogenous extractives, and lower water and protein than light muscle (Mannan et al., 1961). Dark muscles of cod contained three times as much lipid material as did white muscle, but the composition of the lipid material was similar (Bligh and Scott, 1966).

Red muscle may act as a storehouse for fat, glycogen, and other metabolites. Levels of inorganic and total acid-soluble phosphorus were lower in red than in white muscle of cod, and in exhausted fish, energy reserves were depleted to low levels in white muscle, whereas in red muscle, glycogen levels were maintained (Fraser et al., 1966). Belinski and Jonas (1966) reported greater lecithinase activity in the pigmented lateral muscle of trout than in white muscle. Nucleotide change from inosine monophosphate to hypoxanthine occurred earlier in the red muscle of swordfish than in white muscle (Dyer et al., 1966). In contrast to those reports, Fraser et al. (1968) reported that post-mortem rates of degradation of inosine monophosphate to hypoxanthine were similar in both red and white muscle of mackerel.

It was stated that dark muscle of cod contained two times as much α-tocopherol in proportion to lipid as did white muscle (Ackman and Cormier, 1967), and that it contained more fat and B vitamins (except for niacin) than white muscle (Brackkan, 1956).

Lipids

Fish oils, according to Tsuchiya (1961), consist mostly of triglyceryl esters of fatty acids and minor proportions of free fatty acids, vitamins, coloring matter, hydrocarbons, sterols, and phosphatides. However, Garcia et al. (1956) reported that in cod and haddock muscle the triglyceride fat comprised about 3 percent of the total lipid; choline phosphatides, 35 percent; ethanolamine phosphatides, 7 percent; cholesterol and cholesterol esters, 13 percent; waxes and alcohols, 13 percent; free fatty acids, 6 percent; inositol lipids, 2 percent; and unidentified lipids, 21 percent. It should be noted that the samples contained only about 0.6 percent lipid material.

Besides fatty acids that occur both in vegetable oils and land-animal fats (palmitic, stearic, and oleic acids), fish oils contain saturated and unsaturated fatty acids of the C_{20}, C_{22}, and C_{24} series. The percentage of saturated fatty acids may be from 15–40 percent (Stansby and Hall, 1967; Tsuchiya, 1961). The main saturated fatty acid is palmitic, with small amounts of myristic and stearic. Of the unsaturated fatty acids, oleic is widely distributed in fish oils and several polyenoic acids are present. Highly polyunsaturated fatty acids with four or more double bonds per molecule occur commonly in fish. Ackman and Eaton (1966) studied the fatty acid composition of Atlantic herring oil and found the proportions of the saturated, monounsaturated, and polyunsaturated fatty acids to be 20, 60, and 20 percent, respectively. Hexadecanoic acid averaged about 60 percent of the total saturated fatty acids.

In general, seawater fish oils have a relatively complex composition and contain great proportions of C18, C20, and C22 fatty acids; whereas freshwater fish oil contains smaller amounts of C20 and C22 unsaturated acids than seawater fish oils, but greater amounts of palmitic acid and C18 unsaturated acids. Gruger et al. (1964) reported lower percentages of total polyunsaturated fatty acids that contained 4, 5, and 6 double bonds in freshwater fish (70 percent) than in marine fish (88 percent). The average linoleic acid content for freshwater fish was 4.8 percent and for marine species, 1.5 percent; eicosapentaenoic acid averaged 5.8 percent for freshwater fish and 9.7 percent for marine species. The amount of constituent fatty acids varied widely among species—1.6–8.0 percent myristic, 9.5–33.4 percent palmitic, 2.0–11.2 percent palmitoleic, 5.2–29.1 percent oleic, 0.7–10.5 percent eicosenoic, 5.0–21.5 percent eicosapentaenoic, 0.2–11.6 percent docosenoic, and 5.9–26.2 percent docosahexaenoic acids.

Protein

Fish muscle proteins can be classified according to the extraction with various media. The sarcoplasmic proteins can be extracted with water or a weak salt solution and comprise about 16–22 percent of the total protein (Dyer and Dingle, 1961). This fraction contains enzymes and comes mostly from the sarcoplasm and interstitial fluid.

Another fraction that can be extracted with electrolyte solutions of ionic strengths greater than 0.5 contains the contractile material of the muscle (myofibrillar) and comprises about 75 percent of the total protein (Dyer and Dingle, 1961). Three principal myofibrillar proteins are myosin, actin, and tropomyosin. Myosin, in fish as well as mammals, is the most abundant fraction and makes up about 40 percent of the total protein of cod (Connell, 1962). Most properties (size, shape, and amino acid composition) of cod myosin are similar to rabbit myosin (Connell, 1958 and Connell and Howgate, 1959), but Connell (1954) reported different ultracentrifugal properties for the two myosins. Buttkus (1966) found the sedimentation coefficient of trout myosin to be similar to that of cod and rabbit. The isolated protein had two enzyme activities, adenosine triphosphatase and acetyl cholinesterase. The amino acid composition of myosin from white muscle of trout was similar to that of rabbit and had a molecular weight of 500,027 ± 44 (Buttkus, 1967).

The ratio of myosin to actin has been reported to be about 2–4:1 (Connell and Howgate, 1959). This proportion is similar to that of mammal tissue. The amount of actin in cod muscle was estimated to be about 15–20 percent.

Yields of tropomyosin vary from 1.8–2.6 percent of the total muscle protein (Dyer and Dingle, 1961). Hoogland et al. (1961) reported that the amino acid composition of cod tropomyosin was similar to that of other vertebrates except that aspartic acid values tended to be higher for cod.

The portion of the muscle that remains insoluble after extraction with salt solution, sometimes called stroma, is made up largely of myocommata (connective tissue), vascular tissue, and probably fiber membranes or sarcolemma. Fish collagen contains more hydroxy groups than does bovine collagen (Gustavson, 1955). Eastor (1957) reported that fish collagen was similar to mammalian collagen in distribution of amino acids. However, fish collagen contained less proline and hydroxyproline and more serine and threonine than mammalian collagen.

The quantity of collagen in the muscle varied from about 3 percent in gadoids to about 10 percent in elasmobranchs (Dyer and Dingle, 1961), as compared with 17 percent for mammals. The low amount of connective tissue present in fish muscle probably accounts for the flakiness and tenderness of the muscle.

Post-Mortem Changes

Rigor mortis occurs in fish, as in mammals, after death, but generally has a shorter duration than in mammals. It starts about one to seven hours after death (Amlacher, 1961). Rigor is influenced by environmental factors. Fish stored in ice have a longer duration of rigor than those not iced, and immediate slaughter of fish after capture extends rigor.

Biochemical changes associated with rigor mortis are important factors influencing the quality and characteristics of both fresh and frozen fish. Size and condition of the fish, feed, degree of struggle, holding temperature, physical handling, and time elapsed after death and before freezing affect the post-mortem changes in fish as similar conditions affect post-mortem changes in mammals.

With the onset of rigor, there is a decrease in muscle pH, caused by the appearance of lactic acid. Freshly killed fish may have a slightly alkaline pH, but reach ultimate pH values of 6.2–6.5 (Amlacher, 1961) during rigor. Those pH values are higher than most pH values reported for mammalian tissue.

In a review of post-mortem changes in glycogen, nucleotides, sugar phosphates, and sugar in fish muscle, Tarr (1967) gave two routes for glycogen breakdown, (1) by the Embden-Meyerhof (glycolytic) pathway (the same sequence of enzymes that is operative in mammalian muscle), and (2) by an amylolytic route. Glycogen degradation is, in part, dependent on the degree of activity of the fish during capture. MacLeod and Simpson (1927) reported initial glycogen levels of 0.5 percent or more in "rested" muscle, and decreased amounts of glycogen with the formation of lactate, depending on the degree of struggling during capture. Black et al. (1962) reported muscle glycogen level in "rested" trout muscle to be 0.25–0.12 percent of the wet weight of muscle, and in fish severely exercised for 15 minutes, 0.04 percent. With the depletion of glycogen there was a sudden accumulation of muscle pyruvate and lactate. Lactate levels were low (7–28 mg/100 g) and high-energy phosphate compounds were high in relaxed cod muscle (anesthetized), whereas unexercised fish had higher lactate levels (100 mg/100 g) and lower levels of high-energy phosphate compounds (Fraser et al., 1966).

Trawled cod muscle contained little or no glycogen in contrast to average levels of 200 mg/100 g found in brailed trapped cod (Fraser, 1965). The trawled fish also had a significantly lower average adenine nucleotide content and higher ammonia and lactate levels than did brailed fish.

Chalkiness

A type of musculature similar to PSE (pale, soft, exudative) pork has been observed in fish, halibut in particular (Tomlinson et al., 1965 and 1966). A condition in which the flesh is dull, white, opaque, soft, and flabby is called "chalkiness." The flesh of normal and potential chalky fish were indistinguishable when caught. The change was related to the pH of the muscle, taking place when the pH fell to about 6.0 or lower, and was accompanied by a marked decrease in extractability of both myofibrillar and sarcoplasmic protein. During storage in ice there was an increase in free drip, and water decreased more in chalky than in normal halibut muscle. There was a consistent trend for drip to increase with decreased pH of filleted cod, and with increased feed and water temperature. The pH levels were dependent on season of catch and glycolysis (MacCallum et al., 1967).

Freezing and Storage

Generally, fish gradually deteriorate in quality upon frozen storage. When fish are thawed after frozen storage, a large amount of drip may be formed. Less is formed in fresh fish or in rapidly frozen fish stored for a short period of time. Toughening of the muscle fibers also occurs during freezing. It is thought that during the freezing process, water is frozen out as ice, the moisture that remains associated with the protein micelles becomes more and more concentrated in salts, the amount of moisture is decreased, and dehydration of the protein occurs.

Alteration of fish muscle during frozen storage was studied by estimating the amount of protein dissolved by neutral five percent sodium chloride and the soluble protein-nitrogen in the muscle (Ironside and Love, 1958; Love and Ironside, 1958; and Love, 1958b). Soluble protein declined steadily during the storage of the fish, and it was suggested that the concentrated tissue salts still in liquid solution at the low temperatures brought about the reduced solubility.

Another method for measuring cold-storage changes in muscle was developed by Love and Mackay (1962). Muscles samples were submitted to a homogenization procedure, and then the optical density of the homogenate was measured. The resulting value was related to the proportion of muscle cells destroyed, and so to the extent of protein denaturation. Using this technique, it was found that after being thawed, the muscle cells became more difficult to rupture with a homogenizer as storage time increased.

Both the cell-fragility and the protein-extractability methods were used to assess the changes in muscle protein that occur when cod were kept in ice, and the results of the two methods did not agree (Love et al., 1965). It was concluded that cell fragility changed independently of protein extractability; binding together of myofibrils was the agent causing changes in cell-fragility readings, while binding together of structural protein molecules and perhaps myofilaments was a factor related to changes in protein extractability.

Connell (1966) found that the aldolase activity of cod and haddock flesh was reduced significantly by freezing and thawing, and fell progressively during storage at $-14°$ C. During both rigor mortis and frozen storage at $-14°$ C, much of the aldolase activity became inextractable in water. It was suggested that during rigor mortis, the enzyme, which is normally water-soluble, becomes attached to the fibrillar part of the muscle so that it can no longer be extracted completely in water.

In addition to changes in the protein fraction of fish muscle during freezing and storage, there also are changes in the lipid components. Free fatty acid content increased from 5 to 326 mg/100 g of tissue because of hydrolysis of phosphatidyl ethanolamine and phosphatidyl choline during nine months' storage of cod at $-12°$ C (Bligh and Scott,

1966). After five weeks of storage in ice, 70 percent of the phospholipids in cod were hydrolyzed to free fatty acids. Lecithin and phosphatidyl ethanolamine were hydrolyzed at the same rate (Lovern et al., 1959).

In cod and halibut, there was development of free fatty acids and an increase in peroxide values after nine months of storage (Dyer, 1951). The development of free fatty acids in stored frozen halibut was higher at $+10°$ F than at $-10°$ F (Dyer and Fraser, 1959). When appreciable lipid hydrolysis occurred on storage, usually the actomyosin values and taste-panel scores decreased. Contrary to most studies, no loss in actomyosin extractability or taste-panel acceptability up to $1\frac{1}{2}$ years' storage of cod at $-10°$ F was noted.

Some study of freezing fish pre- and postrigor has been made. Prerigor frozen cod were found to be less denatured (loss of salt-solubility of the protein) than were postrigor ones (Love, 1962). Prerigor frozen cod became less soluble in salt solution than postrigor fish when the muscle was able to contract freely upon thawing or when small pieces were thawed quickly. If fragments were thawed slowly or whole fillets or entire fish were used, the contraction did not take place and the protein was not affected. The salt-solubility of fresh prerigor muscle was always low compared with that of postrigor muscle, and it was found that if prerigor muscle went into rigor as fillets, not as whole fish, the salt solubility remained low. On the basis of appearance, odor, and texture of cod, freezing prerigor fish was preferable to freezing postrigor fish.

Other factors related to the storage of fish have been reported. Muscle from the tail section stored at $0°$ C became rancid faster than did muscle from the head or center section, and rancidity was greater in fish caught in the winter and early spring than in the summer or fall (Castell and MacLean, 1964). Hansen (1964) reported differences in the storage life of male and female trout. Fish of both sex caught in September kept equally well when stored in ice, but in March females could be kept three days longer than males.

Cooking Methods and Palatability

Little work has been reported on the effects of various cooking procedures on the eating quality of fish. Dyer and Fraser (1964) studied three cooking methods using cod fillets. The taste panel could discriminate better between samples frozen under several conditions at three different temperatures when fillets were baked or steamed than when fried. Palatability scores of samples stored at higher temperatures were higher when the fish were fried than when they were baked or steamed. Fillets that had been stored at $-9°$ C were rejected when baked, barely

518   *Food Theory and Applications*

acceptable when steamed, and acceptable when fried. Acceptability and cooking losses were similar for fish cooked at 300 and 500° F, but samples cooked uncovered at 300 and 500° F were rated more attractive and palatable than those cooked covered (Armstrong et al., 1960).

Charley (1952) baked one-inch salmon steaks to internal temperatures of 70, 75, 80, and 85° C. Moistness scores and amount of press fluid decreased and cooking losses increased as the temperature increased. There was no difference in the tenderness of the steaks cooked to the four internal temperatures. Steaks cooked to 80 or 85° C generally received higher palatability scores than did those cooked to the two lower temperatures.

Oven temperatures of 350, 400, 450, and 500° F were used by Charley and Goertz (1958) for baking two-pound salmon steaks. The baking temperature had no effect on the histological appearance of the cooked salmon. A 100° F increase in baking temperature resulted in a significant increase in total cooking losses. Oven temperature had no effect on the amount of press fluid or on palatability ratings of the baked salmon. However, some differences attributed to the anatomical location of the steaks was noted. The cut nearest the head received the highest scores for flakiness and the lowest ones for tenderness, whereas the section from the tail was the least flaky and the most tender. The cut from the third quarter was ranked highest and that from the head end lowest for flavor and overall desirability.

References

POULTRY

Angelotti, R., M. J. Foter, and K. H. Lewis. 1960. Time-temperature effects on Salmonellae and staphylococci in foods: II. Behavior at warm holding temperatures. Thermal-death-time studies. U.S. Dept. Health, Education, and Welfare, Robert A. Taft Sanitary Engineering Center, Cincinnati, Ohio, Tech. Report F60-5: 6.

Anon. Aug. 1, 1966. Regulations governing the grading and inspection of poultry and edible products thereof and United States classes, standards, and grades with respect thereto. Federal Register Title 7, Ch. 1, Subchapter C, Part 70.

Augustine, G. M., A. F. Carlin, and C. G. Marquess. 1962. Quality of whole turkey and turkey rolls. *J. Am. Dietetic Assoc. 41*: 443.

Bouthilet, R. J. 1949. A note on the nature of a flavor constituent from poultry meat. *Food Technol. 3*: 118.

Bramblett, V. D., and K. W. Fugate. 1967. Choice of cooking temperature for stuffed turkeys. I. Palatability factors. *J. Home Econ. 59* (3): 180.

Brant, A. W., and H. L. Hanson. 1962. Age, sex, and genetic effects on poultry flavor. Proc. Twelfth World's Poultry Congress, Sydney, Australia: 409.

Carlin, F., B. Lowe, and G. F. Stewart. 1949. The effects of aging vs. aging, freezing, and thawing on the palatability of eviscerated poultry. *Food Technol.* 3: 156.

de Fremery, D., and M. F. Pool. 1960. Biochemistry of chicken muscles as related to rigor mortis and tenderization. *Food Res.* 25: 73.

de Fremery, D., and M. F. Pool. 1963. The influence of postmortem glycolysis on poultry tenderness. *J. Food Sci.* 28: 173.

de Fremery, D. 1966. Relationship between chemical properties and tenderness of poultry muscle. *J. Agr. Food Chem.* 14: 214.

de Fremery, D., and R. N. Sayre. 1968. Poultry: Characteristics and stability of the frozen products, Chapter 6. In *The Freezing Preservation of Foods*, 4th ed., Vol. 2, D. K. Tressler, W. B. Van Arsdel, and M. J. Copley, eds. Avi Publishing Co., Westport, Conn.

Dodge, J. W., and W. J. Stadelman. 1959. Studies on post-mortem aging of poultry meat and its effect on tenderness of breast muscle. *Food Technol.* 13: 81.

Dodge, J. W., and W. J. Stadelman. 1960a. Studies on tenderness evaluation. *Poultry Sci.* 39: 184.

Dodge, J. W., and W. J. Stadelman. 1960b. Relationships between pH, tenderness and moisture levels during early postmortem aging of turkey meat. *Food Technol.* 14: 43.

Esselen, W. B., A. S. Levine, and M. Brushway. 1956. Adequate roasting procedures for frozen stuffed poultry. *J. Am. Dietetic Assoc.* 32: 1162.

Friedman, H. H., J. E. Whitney, and A. S. Szczesniak. 1963. The texturometer —a new instrument for objective texture measurements. *J. Food Sci.* 28: 390.

Fulton, L. H., G. L. Gilpin, and E. H. Dawson. 1967. Turkeys roasted from frozen and thawed states. *J. Home Econ.* 59: 728.

Goertz, G. E., K. Cooley, M. C. Ferguson, and D. L. Harrison. 1960a. Doneness of frozen, defrosted turkey halves roasted to several end-point temperatures. *Food Technol.* 14: 135.

Goertz, G. E., A. S. Hooper, and D. L. Harrison. 1960b. Comparison of rate of cooking and doneness of fresh-unfrozen and frozen, defrosted turkey hens. *Food Technol.* 14: 458.

Goertz, G. E., D. Meyer, B. Weathers, and A. S. Hooper. 1964a. Comparison of two cooking methods. Effect of cooking temperature on broiler acceptability. *J. Am. Dietetic Assoc.* 45: 526.

Goertz, G. E., and M. A. Watson. 1964b. Palatability and doneness of right and left sides of turkeys roasted to selected end-point temperatures. *Poultry Sci.* 43: 812.

Goodwin, T. L., V. D. Bramblett, G. E. Vail, and W. J. Stadelman. 1962.

Effects of end-point temperature and cooking rate on turkey meat tenderness. *Food Technol. 16:* 101.

Goodwin, T. L., W. C. Mickelberry, and W. J. Stadelman. 1961. The influence of humane slaughter on the tenderness of turkey meat. *Poultry Sci. 40:* 921.

Hanson, H. L., G. F. Stewart, and B. Lowe. 1942. Palatability and histological changes occurring in New York dressed broilers held at 1.7° C. *Food Res. 7:* 148.

Hanson, H. L., A. A. Campbell, A. A. Kraft, G. L. Gilpin, and A. M. Harkin. 1959. The flavor of modern- and old-type chickens. *Poultry Sci. 38:* 1071.

Hanson, H. L., A. A. Klose, S. Smith, and A. A. Campbell. 1965. Evaluation of toughness differences in chickens in terms of consumer reaction. *J. Food Sci. 30:* 898.

Hoke, I. M., G. L. Gilpin, and E. H. Dawson. 1965. Heat penetration, quality, and yield of turkeys roasted to an internal breast temperature of 195° F. *J. Home Econ. 57:* 188.

Kahlenberg, O. J., and E. M. Funk. 1961. The cooking of fowl with various salts for precooked poultry products. *Poultry Sci. 40:* 668.

Klose, A. A., H. L. Hanson, E. P. Mecchi, J. H. Anderson, I. V. Streeter, and H. Lineweaver. 1953. Quality and stability of turkeys as a function of dietary fat. *Poultry Sci. 32:* 82.

Klose, A. A., M. F. Pool, and H. Lineweaver. 1955. Effect of fluctuating temperatures on frozen turkeys. *Food Technol. 9:* 372.

Klose, A. A. 1959a. *Poultry Products. ASRE Air Conditioning-Refrigerating Data Book,* Ch. 2. Am. Soc. of Refrigerating Engineers.

Ibid., 1959b, Ch. 16.

Klose, A. A., M. F. Pool, M. B. Wiele, H. L. Hanson, and H. Lineweaver. 1959c. Poultry tenderness. I. Influence of processing on tenderness of turkeys. *Food Technol. 13:* 20.

Klose, A. A., A. A. Campbell, H. L. Hanson, and H. Lineweaver. 1961. Effect of duration and type of chilling and thawing on tenderness of frozen turkeys. *Poultry Sci. 40:* 683.

Klose, A. A. 1964. Poultry products. ASHRAE *Guide and Data Book,* Ch. 43. Am. Soc. of Heating, Refrigerating, and Air Conditioning Engineers.

Klose, A. A., H. H. Palmer, H. Lineweaver, and A. A. Campbell. 1966. Direct olfactory demonstration of fractions of chicken aroma. *J. Food Sci. 31:* 638.

Klose, A. A., H. Lineweaver, and H. H. Palmer. 1968. Thawing turkeys at ambient air temperatures. *Food Technol. 22:* 1310.

Koonz, C. H., M. I. Darrow, and E. O. Essary. 1954. Factors influencing tenderness of principal muscles composing the poultry carcass. *Food Technol. 8:* 97.

Lineweaver, H. 1961. Chicken flavor. *Flavor Chemistry Symposium,* Proc., Campbell Soup Co., Camden, N.J.: 21.

Lowe, B., and F. Keltner. 1937. Studies in cooking frozen poultry. *U.S. Egg and Poultry Mag. 43:* 296.

Lowe, B. 1948. Factors affecting the palatability of poultry with emphasis on histological postmortem changes. *Advances in Food Research 1:* 203.

Lowe, B., M. Edgar, F. Schoenleber, and J. Young. 1953. Cooking turkey in aluminum foil. *Iowa Farm Sci. J. 8:* 326.

Marion, W. W., and W. J. Stadelman. 1958. Effect of various freezing methods on quality of poultry meat. *Food Technol. 12:* 367.

Mickelberry, W. C., and W. J. Stadelman. 1962. Effect of cooking method on shear-press values and weight changes of frozen chicken meat. *Food Technol. 16 (8):* 94.

Millares, R., and C. R. Fellers. 1948. Amino acid content of chicken. *J. Am. Dietetic Assoc. 24:* 1057.

Minor, L. J., A. M. Pearson, L. E. Dawson, and B. S. Schweigert. 1965. Chicken flavor: The identification of some chemical components and the importance of sulfur compounds in the cooked volatile fraction. *J. Food Sci. 30:* 686.

Palmer, H. H. 1968. Prepared and precooked poultry products, Chapter 7. In *The Freezing Preservation of Foods,* Vol. 4, *Freezing of Precooked Foods,* D. K. Tressler, W. B. Van Arsdel, and M. J. Copley, eds., Avi Publ. Co., Westport, Conn.

Paul, P. C., C. I. Sorenson, and H. Abplanalp. 1959. Variability in tenderness of chicken. *Food Res. 24:* 205.

Peterson, D. W., M. Simone, A. L. Lilyblade, and R. Martin. 1959. Some factors affecting intensity of flavor and toughness of chicken muscle. *Food Technol. 13:* 204.

Phillips, L., Delaney, and M. Mangel. 1960. Electronic cooking of chicken. *J. Am. Dietetic Assoc. 37:* 462.

Pippen, E. L., A. A. Campbell, and I. V. Streeter. 1954. Origin of chicken flavor. *Agric. and Food Chem. 2:* 364.

Pippen, E. L., M. Nonaka, F. T. Jones, and F. Stitt. 1958. Volatile carbonyl compounds of cooked chicken. I. Compounds obtained by air entrainment. *Food Res. 23:* 103.

Pippen, E. L., D. de Fremery, H. Lineweaver, and H. L. Hanson. 1965. Chicken broth flavor and pH. *Poultry Sci. 44:* 816.

Pool, M. F. 1956. Occasional pinkness of well-done roast poultry explained. *Poultry Processing and Marketing 62 (1):* 29.

Pool, M. F., D. de Fremery, A. A. Campbell, and A. A. Klose. 1959. Poultry tenderness, II. Influence of processing on tenderness of chicken. *Food Technol. 13:* 25.

Pool, M. F. 1967. Objective measurement of connective tissue tenacity of poultry meat. *J. Food Sci. 32:* 550.

Scott, M. L. 1956. Composition of turkey meat. *J. Am. Dietetic Assoc. 32:* 941.

Scott, M. L. 1958. Composition of turkey meat. II. Cholesterol content and fatty acid composition. *J. Am. Dietetic Assoc. 34:* 154.

Scott, M. L. 1959. Composition of turkey meat. III. Essential amino acid composition. *J. Am. Dietetic Assoc. 35:* 247.

Shannon, W. G., W. W. Marion, and W. J. Stadelman. 1957. Effect of temperature and time of scalding on the tenderness of breast meat of chicken. *Food Technol. 11:* 284.

Stewart, G. F., B. Lowe, and M. Morr. 1941. Post-mortem changes in New York dressed poultry at 35° F. *U.S. Egg and Poultry Mag. 47:* 542.

Stewart, G. F., H. L. Hanson, B. Lowe, and J. J. Austin. 1945. Effects of aging, freezing rate, and storage period on palatability of broilers. *Food Res. 10:* 16.

Stewart, G. F. 1953, July. Packages are different. *Poultry Processing and Marketing 13.*

Swanson, M. H., C. W. Carlson, and J. L. Fry. 1964. Factors affecting poultry meat yield. Minnesota Agr. Exp. Station Bulletin 476.

Swickard, M. T., A. M. Harkin, and B. J. Paul. 1954. Relationship of cooking methods, grades, and frozen storage to quality of cooked mature Leghorn hens. *U.S.D.A. Tech. Bull.,* No. 1077.

Szczesniak, A. S. 1963. Objective measurement of food texture. *J. Food Sci. 28:* 410.

Watt, B. K., and A. L. Merrill. 1963. Composition of foods. *Agricultural Handbook No. 8.* U.S. Dept. Agriculture, Washington, D.C.

Webster, R. C., and W. B. Esselen. 1956. Thermal resistance of food poisoning organisms in poultry stuffing. *J. Milk and Food Technol. 19:* 209.

White, E. D., H. L. Hanson, A. A. Klose, and H. Lineweaver. 1964. Evaluation of toughness differences in turkeys. *J. Food Sci. 29:* 673.

Woodburn, M. and A. E. Ellington. 1967. Choice of cooking temperature for stuffed turkeys. II. Microbiological safety of stuffing. *J. Home Econ. 59* (3): 186.

FISH

Ackman, R. G., and M. G. Cormier. 1967. α-Tocopherol in some Atlantic fish and shellfish with particular reference to live-holding without food. *J. Fish. Res. Bd. Canada 24:* 357.

Ackman, R. G., and C. A. Eaton. 1966. Some commercial Atlantic herring oils; fatty acid composition. *J. Fish. Res. Bd. Canada 23:* 991.

Amlacher, E. 1961. Rigor mortis in fish. In *Fish as Food.* G. Borgstrom, Ed. Vol. I. Academic Press, New York and London.

Armstrong, I. L., E. W. Park, and B. A. McLaren. 1960. The effect of time and temperature of cooking on the palatability and cooking losses of frozen Atlantic codfish fillets. *J. Fish. Res. Bd. Canada 17*: 1.

Belinski, E., and R. E. E. Jonas. 1966. Lecithinase activity in the muscle of rainbow trout. *J. Fish. Res. Bd. Canada 23*: 207.

Black, E. D., A. R. Connor, K. C. Lam, and W. G. Chiu. 1962. Changes in glycogen, pyruvate, and lactate in rainbow trout (Salmo gairdneri) during and following muscular activity. *J. Fish. Res. Bd. Canada 19*: 409.

Bligh, E. G., and M. A. Scott. 1966. Lipids of cod muscle and the effect of frozen storage. *J. Fish. Res. Bd. Canada 23*: 1025.

Brackkan, O. R. 1956. Function of the red muscle in fish. *Nature 178*: 747.

Buttkus, H. 1966. Preparation and properties of trout myosin. *J. Fish. Res. Bd. Canada 23*: 563.

Buttkus, H. 1967. Amino acid composition of myosin from trout muscle. *J. Fish. Res. Bd. Canada 24*: 1607.

Castell, C. H., and J. MacLean. 1964. Rancidity in lean fish muscle. II. Anatomical and seasonal variations. *J. Fish. Res. Bd. Canada 21*: 1361.

Charley, H. 1952. Effects of internal temperature and of oven temperature on the cooking losses and palatability of baked salmon steaks. *Food Research 17*: 136.

Charley, H., and G. E. Goertz. 1958. The effects of oven temperature on certain characteristics of baked salmon. *Food Research 23*: 17.

Connell, J. J. 1954. Studies on the protein of fish skeletal muscle. 3. Cod myosin and cod actin. *Biochem. J. 58*: 360.

Connell, J. J. 1958. Studies on the protein of fish skeletal muscle. 5. Molecular weight and shape of cod fibrillar proteins. *Biochem. J. 71*: 83.

Connell, J. J. 1962. Changes in amount of myosin extracted from cod flesh during storage at $-14°$. *J. Sci. Food Agric. 13*: 607.

Connell, J. J. 1966. Changes in aldolase activity in cod and haddock during frozen storage. *J. Food Sci. 31*: 313.

Connell, J. J., and Howgate, P. F. 1959. Studies on the protein of skeletal muscle. 6. Amino acid composition of cod fibrillar proteins. *Biochem. J. 71*: 83.

Dambergs, N. D. 1963. Extractives of fish muscle. 3. Amounts, sectional distribution, and variation of fat, water-solubles, protein, and moisture in cod fillets. *J. Fish. Res. Bd. Canada 21*: 703.

Dambergs, N. D. 1964. Extractives of fish muscle. 4. Seasonal variation of fat, water-solubles, protein, and water in cod (Gadus morhua L.) fillets. *J. Fish. Res. Bd. Canada 21*: 703.

Dyer, W. J. 1951. Protein denaturation in frozen and stored fish. *Food Research 16*: 522.

Dyer, W. J., and J. R. Dingle. 1961. Fish proteins with reference to freezing. In *Fish as Food*. G. Borgstrom, Ed. Vol. I. Academic Press, New York and London.

Dyer, W. J., and D. I. Fraser. 1959. Proteins in fish muscle. 13. Lipid hydrolysis. *J. Fish. Res. Bd. Canada 16*: 43.

Dyer, W. J., and D. I. Fraser. 1964. Cooking method and palatability of frozen cod fillets of various qualities. *J. Fish. Res. Bd. Canada 21*: 577.

Dyer, W. J., D. I. Fraser, and D. P. Lohnes. 1966. Nucleotide degradation and quality in ordinary and red muscle of iced and frozen Sword fish (Xiphias gladius). *J. Fish. Res. Bd. Canada 23*: 1821.

Eastor, J. E. 1957. The amino acid composition of fish collagen and gelatin. *Biochem. J. 65*: 363.

Fraser, D. I., W. J. Dyer, H. M. Weinstein, J. R. Dingle, and J. A. Hines. 1966. Glycolytic metabolites and their distribution at death in the white and red muscle of cod following various degrees of antemortem muscular activity. *Can. J. of Biochem. 44*: 1015.

Fraser, D. I., A. Mannan, and W. J. Dyer. 1961. Proximate composition of Canadian Atlantic fish. III. Sectional differences in the flesh of a species of Chrondrostei, one of Chimaerae and of some miscellaneous teleosts. *J. Fish. Res. Bd. Canada 18*: 893.

Fraser, D. I., D. P. Pitts, and W. J. Dyer. 1968. Nucleotide degradation and organoleptic quality in fresh and thawed mackerel muscle held at and above ice temperatures. *J. Fish. Res. Bd. Canada 25*: 239.

Fraser, D. I., H. M. Weinstein, and W. J. Dyer. 1965. Post-mortem glycolytic and associated changes in the muscle of trap and trawl-caught cod. *J. Fish. Res. Bd. Canada 22*: 83.

Garcia, M. D., J. A. Lovern, and J. Olley. 1956. The lipids of fish. 6. The lipids of cod flesh. *Biochem. J. 62*: 99.

Gruger, E. H., R. W. Nelson, and M. E. Stansby. 1964. Fatty acid composition of oils from 21 species of marine fish, freshwater fish and shellfish. *J. Amer. Oil Chem. Soc. 41*: 662.

Gustavson, K. H. 1955. The function of hydroxyproline in collagens. *Nature 175*: 70.

Hansen, P. 1964. Fat oxidation and storage life of iced trout. II. The influence of sex and season. *J. Sci. Food Agric. 15*: 344.

Hoogland, P. L., H. C. Freeman, B. Truscott, and A. E. Waddell. 1961. The amino acid composition of cod tropomyosin. *J. Fish. Res. Bd. Canada 18*: 501.

Ironside, J. I. M., and R. M. Love. 1958. Studies on protein denaturation in frozen fish. I. Biological factors influencing the amounts of soluble and insoluble protein present in the muscle of North Sea Cod. *J. Sci. Food Agric. 9*: 597.

Jangaard, H., H. Brockerholl, R. D. Burgher, and R. J. Hoyle. 1967. Seasonal changes in general conditions and lipid content of cod from inshore waters. *J. Fish. Res. Bd. Canada 24*: 607.

Jacquot, R. 1961. Organic constituents of fish. In *Fish as Food.* G. Borgstrom, Ed. Vol. I. Academic Press, New York and London.

Jones, N. R. 1954. Factors affecting the free amino acid composition of fresh and iced skeletal muscle of North Sea codling (Fadus callarias). *Biochem. J. 58*: xlvii.

Love, R. M. 1958a. Studies on the North Sea cod. I. Muscle cell dimensions. *J. Sci. Food Agric. 9*: 195.

Love, R. M. 1958b. Studies on protein denaturation in frozen fish. III. The mechanism and site of denaturation at low temperatures. *J. Sci. Food Agric. 9*: 609.

Love, R. M. 1962. Protein denaturation in frozen fish. VII. Effect of the onset and resolution of rigor mortis on denaturation. *J. Sci. Food Agric. 13*: 534.

Love, R. M., M. M. Aref, M. K. Elerian, J. I. M. Ironside, E. M. Mackay, and M. G. Valera. 1965. Protein denaturation in frozen fish. X. Changes in cod muscle in the unfrozen state, with some further observations on the principles underlying the cell fragility method. *J. Sci. Food Agric. 16*: 259.

Love, R. M., and J. I. M. Ironside. 1958. Studies on protein denaturation in frozen fish. II. Preliminary freezing experiments. *J. Sci. Food Agric. 9*: 604.

Love, R. M., and E. M. Mackay. 1962. Protein denaturation in frozen fish. V. Development of the cell fragility method for measuring cold-storage changes in the muscle. *J. Sci. Food Agric. 13*: 200.

Lovern, J. A., J. Olley, and H. A. Watson. 1959. Changes in the lipids of cod during storage in ice. *J. Sci. Food Agric. 10*: 327.

MacCallum, W. A., J. I. Jaffray, and D. N. Churchill. 1967. Post-mortem physicochemical changes in unfrozen Newfoundland trap-caught cod. *J. Fish. Res. Bd. Canada 24*: 651.

MacLeod, J. J. R., and W. W. Simpson. 1927. The immediate post-mortem changes in fish muscle. *Contrib. Canadian. Biol. Fisheries 3*: 437.

Mannan, A., D. I. Fraser, and W. J. Dyer. 1961. Proximate composition of Canadian Atlantic fish. I. Variation in composition of different sections of the flesh of Atlantic Halibut (Hippoglossus hippoglossus). *J. Fish. Res. Bd. Canada 18*: 483.

Stansby, M. E., and A. S. Hall. 1967. Chemical composition of commercially important fish of the United States. *Fishery Industrial Res.* Vol. 3. No. 4.

Stansby, M. E., and J. M. Lemon. 1941. Studies on the handling of fresh mackerel (Scomber scombrus). *Research Report 1.* Fish and Wildlife Service.

Tarr, H. L. A. 1966. Post-mortem changes in glycogen, nucleotides, sugar phosphates, and sugars in fish muscle. *J. Food Sci. 31*: 846.

Tomlinson, N., S. E. Geiger, and E. Dollinger. 1965. Chalkiness in halibut in relation to muscle pH and protein denaturation. *J. Fish. Res. Bd. Canada 22*: 653.

Tomlinson, N., S. E. Geiger, and E. Dollinger. 1966. Free drip, flesh pH, and chalkiness in halibut. *J. Fish. Res. Bd. Canada 23*: 673.

Thurston, C. E., M. E. Stansby, N. L. Karrick, D. T. Miyauchi, and W. C. Clegg. 1959. Composition of certain species of fresh-water fish. II. Comparative data for 21 species of lake and river fish. *Food Research 24*: 493.

Thurston, C. E., and H. S. Groninger. 1959. Composition changes in Puget Sound pink salmon during storage in ice and in refrigerated brine. *J. Agric. and Food Chem. 7*: 282.

Tsuchiya, T. 1961. Biochemistry of fish oil. In *Fish as Food*. G. Borgstrom, Ed. Vol. I. Academic Press, New York and London.

CHAPTER 9

Eggs

HELEN H. PALMER

Eggs give the characteristic structure, texture, and appearance to many prepared foods. They form elastic films when beaten, incorporating the air needed for leavening in angel cakes, meringues, and souffles. They coagulate during heating, thickening custards or binding pieces of food together in croquettes. They form the framework of popovers when the egg protein stretches with the expansion of steam and coagulates on heating. Yolks are the emulsifying agents in mayonnaise, salad dressing, and cream puffs. The structure and composition of eggs, their coagulating and foam-forming functions, and the effects of processing and storage on their culinary quality are reviewed in this chapter. Their emulsifying function is reviewed in Chapter 12, and the freezing of egg-containing cooked products in Chapter 13.

THE STRUCTURE OF SHELL EGGS

Eggs consist of approximately 11 percent shell, 58 percent white, and 31 percent yolk. The shell, a porous structure, is primarily calcium carbonate. The thin semipermeable shell membrane has two layers; the air cell at the large end is formed by separation of the two membranes as the contents shrink during cooling. The condition of the shell and the membrane influence moisture and CO_2 loss, breaking strength, and susceptibility to microbial invasion. The egg white is composed of three layers, a thin layer next to the shell, a thicker viscous layer within it, and a thin layer surrounding the yolk. The chalazae are dense cordlike strands of white, mostly mucin, one on each side of the yolk. They anchor the yolk near the center of the egg and allow it to revolve. The yolk is separated from the white by the vitelline membrane.

CONSUMER GRADES AND WEIGHT CLASSES OF SHELL EGGS

Shell eggs are sorted on the basis of quality and weight. Eggs in lots such as dozens or cases may be identified by grades that are intended to indicate quality. The consumer grades for eggs are U.S. Grade AA or Fresh Fancy Quality, U.S. Grade A, and U.S. Grade B. The regulations permit a tolerance of not over 15 percent for eggs below the specified quality at point of origin and not over 20 percent at destination. There is no tolerance for inedible eggs. The weight classes of U.S. consumer grades for shell eggs are jumbo, 30 ounces; extra large, 27 ounces; large, 24 ounces; medium, 21 ounces; small, 18 ounces; and peewee, 15 ounces (U.S. Dept. Agric., 1967).

THE CULINARY QUALITY OF SHELL EGGS

Physical quality of shell eggs from the standpoint of food preparation refers to the properties that produce the desired structure, appearance, and flavor in egg-containing products. Eggs with a firm, thick white that closely surrounds the yolk are more satisfactory for poaching and frying than eggs with thin whites that spread readily when opened. Such eggs of high physical quality also produce thick, stiff custards, and angel, sponge, and layer cakes of good volume (Pyke and Johnson, 1940; 1941; Harns et al., 1953, 1954b; and Jordan et al., 1954). The established standards for judging the interior quality of *intact* eggs are based on four factors that can be evaluated while eggs are twirled ("candled") in front of a light in a darkened room: yolk centering and movement; clarity, firmness, and defects of the white; unbroken shell and its "normality"; and depth and regularity of the air cell. These factors do not necessarily measure nutritional, palatability, or culinary quality of eggs, but they are representative of other factors, impossible to judge in the intact egg, that deteriorate at relatively the same rate (Baker and Forsythe, 1951). Consumers generally recognize the characteristics evaluated in the standards and interpret them as expected (Noles and Roush, 1962). Other methods of judging the quality of intact eggs have been tested but generally were not considered satisfactory. These have included radio-frequency and torsion-pendulum methods. A photoelectric apparatus for detecting green-rot fluorescence is useful only as a supplement to the usual methods, and a spectrophotometric method for detecting blood is useful only in eggs with white shells (Norris and Brant, 1952; Rowan et al., 1958; Mercuri et al., 1957; and Brant et al., 1953).

Physical characteristics can be used to estimate the quality of *opened* eggs. These include albumen height; yolk index, the ratio of the height to the width of the yolk; albumen index, the ratio of albumen height to width; albumen area index, an estimate of the spreading of thick albumen; the percentage of thick and thin white; and the Haugh unit, a number based on the logarithm of albumen height with correction for egg weight (Haugh, 1937). Brant et al. (1951) favored the Haugh unit. Changes in the unit, determined from the height of the thick white and the weight of the egg, are closely associated with changes in appearance of the opened eggs. Candled quality has been shown to correlate with albumen index, yolk index, albumen scores, and pH in stored eggs (Sauter et al., 1953). Combinations of egg white variables and egg weight were suggested by Eisen (1962) for evaluating quality.

Some physical changes begin to take place in the egg as soon as it is laid. The thick white becomes less viscous and jellylike, gradually changing from one that closely surrounds the yolk to a thin, watery white that spreads readily; and the yolk tends to flatten. A number of possible mechanisms for the thinning of egg white during storage have been proposed. These include proteolysis, reduction of S-S bonds, and interaction of mucin and lysozyme. The increase in thinning is correlated with an increase in alkalinity, and alkaline hydrolysis of the disulfide bonds of ovomucin to yield a lower molecular weight protein may be responsible for the thinning (Donovan, 1967). The pH of egg white ranges from approximately 7.6 immediately after eggs are laid to 8.9 to 9.4 after storage. In unprotected eggs the pH changes rapidly during the first few days after lay and then remains relatively constant (Sharp, 1937; Feeney et al., 1951; Meehan et al., 1962). The pH of the yolk is 5.9 to 6.1 in freshly laid eggs and rises to about 6.8 after long storage (Feeney et al., 1951). The rise in pH of the white is due to CO_2 loss. The rate of loss is affected by the storage temperature, time, and partial pressure of CO_2 in the atmosphere and permeability of the shell (Cotterill, 1958).

The water loss from eggs during storage depends on the temperature, air movement, relative humidity of the surrounding atmosphere, and shell treatments that affect permeability. The treatments generally consist of spraying or dipping the eggs in colorless, tasteless mineral oil shortly after they are laid. Weight loss is reduced, the loss of CO_2 is decreased, and low pH and the initial albumen index level are maintained (Sharp, 1937; Grant, 1948; Evans and Carver, 1942; Gibbons, 1950; Korslund et al., 1957; and Goodwin et al., 1962). The treatment has no adverse effect on the performance of the eggs in sponge cakes, plain cakes, custards, and angel cakes (Carlin and Foth, 1952; Sauter et al., 1954b). Angel cakes made from unoiled eggs stored at room temperature or above shrink during the last stages of baking and after removal from the oven (Harns et al., 1953; Meehan et al., 1962). Oiling on the day eggs are laid prevents the decrease in angel cake volume; the benefits are correlated with maintenance of low pH of the white.

Heat treatments designed to retard changes in shell eggs may have detrimental effects on the performance of eggs in foods. Thermostabilization, a method of heating eggs in water or oil at 54 to 60° C, proposed by Funk (1950), increases the candle grade and the viscosity of the white, but is only used in special circumstances, since it increases the difficulty of separating the yolk and the white, decreases egg white yield, and decreases egg white whipping rate, volume of foam, and volume of angel cakes. The performance of thermostabilized eggs in sponge cakes, plain cakes, and custards is unaffected (Goresline et al., 1952; Carlin and Foth, 1952; and Hard et al., 1963). Immersion of shell eggs for two to three seconds in water at 100° C has no effect on egg white whipping and angel cake baking properties (Feeney et al., 1954b).

The season of the year and the age and breed of the birds have been implicated in some small differences in egg quality and performance. Eggs laid in winter retain their physical quality better than those laid in summer (Hunter et al., 1936; Sauter et al., 1954a; and Jones et al., 1961). The performance of the yolk in foaming tests, sponge cakes, and layer cakes does not vary with the age of the birds. However, egg whites from 18–21-month-old layers produced angel cakes of slightly lower volume than those from younger layers, possibly because of the lower solids content of the whites (Kline et al., 1965). Thick white content of eggs can be increased by breeding (Knox and Godfrey, 1940). Feed composition does not affect the albumen index (King et al., 1936a; Jordan et al., 1962).

Flavor differences in eggs are most important in soft-cooked, poached, and scrambled eggs and in custards, since egg flavor is not masked in those foods as it is in more highly seasoned foods (Sauter et al., 1953; Banwart et al., 1957; and Harns et al., 1954a). The breed of the hen and the season of the year have little or no effect on egg flavor (Sauter et al., 1954a; Harns et al., 1954a). Supplements of 10 percent corn oil or beef tallow in the feed of the hen had no important effect on egg flavor, but diets containing fish meal, linseed oil, and cod liver oil cause off-flavors in eggs (Jordan et al., 1960). Eggs stored near odorous substances can absorb odors and exhibit flavor changes. Flavors and/or odors can be absorbed from washing solutions, but the off-flavors decrease after eggs are held in cold storage (Forsythe, 1952). Oil treating and heating do not retard flavor changes of shell eggs during storage even though they do retard physical changes, as noted previously (Banwart et al., 1957).

Shell color is a breed characteristic and is not related to egg quality. Fresh egg white has an opalescent appearance and a greenish cast, attributed to riboflavin; as the pH rises, the white becomes clearer. Yolk color ranges from very pale through deeper yellow to a deep orange. Carotenoid pigments, primarily xanthophyll, are responsible for the yellow color of the yolk. The intensity of pigmentation depends largely on the feed and its pigment content and is influenced only slightly by heredity (Palmer and Kempster, 1919; Peterson et al., 1939; Wilcke, 1938; and Marusich et al., 1960).

The food processing industry prefers yolks of uniform color to insure uniformity of color in foods in which yolks are the coloring agents. Eggs with deeply pigmented yolks are in demand for those foods in which it is illegal to add artificial coloring. The grass eaten by farm flocks formerly provided xanthophylls desired for deep yolk color. The color can be obtained by addition of appropriate carotenoids to the ration; removal of the supplement will again cause production of lighter-colored yolks. Direct addition of carotenoid pigments to egg yolk is advocated because of the extra cost, inefficiency of pigment transfer from feed, instability and variation in pigment content in natural feeds, and biological differences in the hen's ability to deposit pigment (Forsythe, 1963).

An occasional off-color in eggs, salmon- or olive-colored yolks and pink whites, is related to the feed of the birds. Ingestion of derivatives of cottonseed causes egg-color changes and increases permeability of the vitelline membrane and convergence of the pH of the whites and yolks (Heywang et al., 1955; Masson et al., 1957; Shenstone and Vickery, 1959; and Kemmerer et al., 1961, 1962, 1963). Pink white results from diffusion of iron from the yolk to form the iron-conalbumin complex; the salmon-colored yolks results from the pink color combined with the natural yellow of the yolk.

THE COMPOSITION OF EGGS

Egg contents consist of approximately 65 percent white and 35 percent yolk. When eggs are broken under commercial conditions, the liquid yolk contains about 15 percent white. The yield of white under these conditions is 55 to 57 percent; the yolk portion is 43 to 45 percent. The chemical composition of eggs has been reviewed by Parkinson (1966).

Egg White

The egg white consists of about 87.6 percent water, 10.9 percent protein, 1.1 percent carbohydrate, and traces of fat (Watt and Merrill, 1963). Proteins make up 82.8 percent of the 12 percent solids in the egg white; other components include small amounts of sugar and minerals and a trace of fat.

Ovalbumin, which constitutes about 63 percent of the protein of egg white, is a glycoprotein with a molecular weight in the region of 45,000; its isoelectric point is pH 4.6 to 4.8. It has been available in crystalline form for many years. Ovalbumin is denatured when subjected to heat; and by adsorption at surfaces or in films, shaking, or the action of various denaturing agents. Native ovalbumin contains virtually all of the sulphydryl groups in egg white. Denaturation of ovalbumin is necessary, however, to make them all detectable or reactive. Ovalbumin in food preparation serves to provide sufficient heat-denaturable protein to maintain the structure of baked products. A long whipping time is necessary to form a foam from ovalbumin alone. Although angel cake can be made with ovalbumin alone, other egg white proteins are needed to provide the characteristic quality of a cake made from complete white (MacDonnell et al., 1955).

The globulins, about 8 percent of egg white protein, include three components. The isoelectric points of two of these are pH 5.6 and 6.0 and of the other, lysozyme, pH 10.5 to 11.0 (Longworth et al., 1940; Forsythe and Foster, 1950). Lysozyme lyses certain microorganisms, a property that contributes to the resistance that the intact egg shows to bacterial invasion. Its molecular weight is about 17,000. The purified form is relatively stable to most denaturing agents and conditions but is readily inactivated by a variety of other chemical reagents and by copper in a weakly alkaline solution (Alderton et al., 1945, 1946a; Fraenkel-Conrat, 1950; and Feeney et al., 1956). The globulins are important for their foam-forming property and because they coagulate during heating. Removal of globulins from egg white decreases the foaming rate and produces angel cakes of lower volumes. Replacement of the globulins restores cake volume and partially restores the beating rate (MacDonnell et al., 1955). Chicken egg white has three to four times more lysozyme than does duck egg white and almost twice as much as turkey egg white (Smolelis and Hartsell, 1951; MacDonnell et al., 1954). Duck egg whites accordingly have poor whipping properties and produce angel cake of low volume. The addition of lysozyme and other globulins to duck egg white at the level present in chicken egg white enables the duck egg white to make essentially normal cake (MacDonnell et al., 1955).

Ovomucin, a mucoprotein responsible for the jellylike character of egg white, comprises about 2 percent of the egg white protein; there is more mucin in thick than in thin white (McNally, 1933; Hughes and Scott, 1936; and Young, 1937). Its virus antihemagglutinin activity provides biochemical evidence of a relationship between chalazae, yolk membrane, and ovomucin and also indicates comparable amounts of ovomucin in chicken and turkey egg white and lower amounts in duck egg white (Sugihara et al., 1955). Mucin is implicated in the damage that occurs to the foaming properties of egg white as a result of mechanical or shear stress during egg white processing (MacDonnell et al., 1950; Forsythe and Bergquist, 1951). Thus, if egg whites are homogenized, the whip time required to reach a given specific gravity increases with increase in homogenization pressure. Homogenized whites produce cakes of lower volume than do unhomogenized whites. Microscopic examination by Forsythe and Bergquist (1951) showed membranes in thick white but no fibers. They suggested that ovomucin fibers are formed by the curling of the membranes during stirring. Blending produced a rapid decrease in fiber length, followed by a slow drop to a constant length of 200 microns. High-speed centrifugation did not harm egg white unless it was carried out in equipment permitting the action of high shear forces. Then functional performance was reduced as observed in homogenization. Ovomucin stabilizes egg white foams at a short whip time (MacDonnell et al., 1955). Removal of globulins and mucin increased whip time and resulted in angel cakes of low volume. Replacement of the mucin alone decreased the required whip time but had no effect on cake volume; increasing the whip time used for these whites decreased the angel cake volume.

Approximately 12 percent of the protein of egg white is the glycoprotein ovomucoid. It has a molecular weight in the region of 27,000–29,000 and its isoelectric point is pH 3.8–4.5. It has unusual heat stability and can be heated for an hour at 100° C with little viscosity change or denaturation as indicated by protein solubility. Ovomucoid has been identified as the inhibitor in egg white of the proteolytic enzyme, trypsin (Lineweaver and Murray, 1947; Fredericq and Deutsch, 1949a, b; and Fraenkel-Conrat et al., 1949).

Approximately 0.05 percent of egg white protein is avidin, the basic protein that binds biotin and thereby makes it biologically unavailable. Its isoelectric point is pH 10; its molecular weight is in the region of 48,000–66,000. It is insoluble in water but soluble at low salt concentrations. It is fairly stable to pH changes but is inactivated by heat under the usual conditions of egg preparation (Eakin et al., 1941; Gyorgy et al., 1941; Wooley and Longworth, 1942; Green, 1963; and Parkinson, 1966).

Conalbumin comprises about 12 percent of the protein of egg white; its molecular weight is about 80,000. Conalbumin binds iron; one molecule of HCO_3^- or $CO_3^=$ per metal ion is required for formation of the complex (Alderton et al., 1946b; Shade et al., 1949; and Warner and Weber, 1953). Combination of conalbumin with iron inhibits the growth of certain microorganisms that require iron. Below pH 5.8 the complex does not occur; at pH 7.3 the complex is stable at 60° C for an hour but is destroyed at 70° C (Shade and Caroline, 1944). Low concentrations of citrate interfere with the complex above pH 8.0 (Feeney and Nagy, 1952; Warner and Weber, 1953). The iron complex of conalbumin is more resistant to denaturation by heat and to physical and chemical treatments than is the metal-free protein (Azari and Feeney, 1958; 1961), a characteristic used as the basis of an egg white pasteurization method (Cunningham and Lineweaver, 1965). The combination of conalbumin and iron produces a pink color in the white. This color occasionally develops from contact of egg white with iron during processing, but it disappears when the conalbumin is denatured during heating. Conalbumin interacts with lysozyme to form a soluble complex (Ehrenpreis and Warner, 1956).

Egg Yolk

Yolk consists of about 49 percent water, 16 percent protein, 32 percent fat, and traces of carbohydrate. Approximately 30 to 33 percent of the yolk solids are protein, 62 percent are lipids, and 2.9 percent are ash (Everson and Souders, 1957; Watt and Merrill, 1963).

The proteins of yolk are present mainly as lipoproteins, loosely combined with the lipids of the yolk. Two phosphoproteins, vitellin and vitellenin, and the lipids with which they are combined, comprise the lipoproteins. Lipovitellin contains about 22 to 26 percent lipid; lipovitellenin contains about 40 to 50 percent lipid. Lipovitellin comprises 16 to 18 percent of the egg yolk solids; lipovitellenin comprises 12 to 13 percent (Parkinson, 1966). Another phosphoprotein, phosvitin, contains about 10 percent phosphorus and constitutes 5 to 6 percent of the yolk solids (Mecham and Olcott, 1949). Livetins, water-soluble proteins, comprise 4 to 10 percent of the egg yolk solids. A number of enzymes have also been shown to exist in the protein fraction (Lineweaver et al., 1948; Shepard and Hottle, 1949).

Lipids of three general types exist in egg yolks. Triglycerides constitute about 46 percent of the egg yolk solids; phospholipids, 20 percent; and sterols (mainly cholesterol), 3 percent (Brooks and Taylor, 1955; Parkinson, 1966). The two phospholipids present in the largest amount are lecithin (phosphatidylcholine) and cephalin (phosphatidylethanolamine (Martin et al., 1963; Parkinson, 1966). Much of the lipid portion exists in combination with proteins as the lipoproteins, referred to above.

The lipoproteins of yolk are of particular interest in the freezing of eggs because they are probably responsible for the gelation that occurs in yolk and whole egg during frozen storage (Feeney et al., 1954a; Powrie et al., 1963). The lipoproteins containing lecithin (lecithoproteins) contribute to the emulsifying ability of egg yolk that is essential for the production of the characteristic structure of mayonnaise, salad dressings, Hollandaise sauce, cream puffs, and other bakery products (Sell et al., 1935; Schulz and Forsythe, 1967).

COAGULATION AND THE THICKENING FUNCTION OF EGGS

The terms denaturation, coagulation, and gelation are used to describe changes in egg proteins and egg products. Denaturation refers to the loss of specific properties of the native protein; gelation means the formation of a gel structure; coagulation refers to the conversion from a fluid to a solid. In food preparation coagulation is usually caused by heat or mechanical agitation; gelation is usually caused by heat or cold. The time, temperature, and other factors that influence coagulation affect the consistency of cooked eggs and egg-containing foods. Egg white changes from a clear, transparent mass to a white, opaque one during coagulation. The temperature at which this change occurs increases with an increase in the heating rate. At a moderate heating rate the change becomes apparent at about 60° C and the white becomes firmer as the temperature is elevated. Egg yolk usually begins to thicken near 65° C but does not reach a state at which it does not flow until about 70° C.

Dilution of egg proteins elevates their coagulation temperature. Salts such as lactates, chlorides, sulfates, and phosphates aid in producing gelation; they may be added before or after heating. If they are added after heating, curdling may occur during the addition. If egg white is dialyzed so that the salt content is lowered, the albumin does not coagulate on heating (Lepeschkin, 1922). However, if dialyzed egg albumin is heated, coagulation occurs when salts are added. The addition of sugar elevates the temperature of gelation, coagulation, and curdling and retards surface denaturation of egg white. Its effect is proportional to the amount added. The coagulation process is endothermic. During heating of a custard, the temperature may remain stationary or may drop when coagulation occurs. A later rise in temperature indicates approach of the curdling point.

Eggs Cooked in the Shell

The time for cooking eggs in the shell depends on the doneness desired, the initial temperature of water and egg, the quantity of water in relation to size of the egg, and the rate of heating. Uniformly hard-cooked egg requires 25–35 minutes at 85–90° C or at least 12 minutes at 98–100° C.

The peeling difficulty occasionally encountered in hard-cooked eggs is related to the pH of the egg white (Meehan et al., 1961). Sections of cooked white may adhere to the shell unless the pH of the white is 8.9

or higher. Early oiling of the eggs to stabilize internal quality during storage retards pH rise above 8.5 and thus contributes to the difficulty (Hard et al., 1963).

The dark greenish color that forms on the surface of the yolk during the cooking of shell eggs in hot water is due to the formation of ferrous sulfide (Tinkler and Soar, 1920). Egg white contains about 0.03 mg of iron per 100 g, and egg yolk contains 5 to 6 mg per 100 g. Egg white contains approximately 211 mg of sulfur per 100 g; and egg yolk approximately 214 mg per 100 g (Everson and Souders, 1957; Schaible et al., 1944, 1946; and Johnston, 1956). The sulfur of the white is more heat labile than is that of the yolk. Considerable H_2S is evolved during prolonged heating of the white and diffuses to the yolk because of its lower temperature and pressure. Reaction with the iron of the yolk forms FeS. Yolk washed free of white and made alkaline turns green when cooked, indicating that sulfur from the white is not necessary for the reaction (Salwin et al., 1953). The amount of H_2S evolved during the cooking of eggs depends on pH of the egg and the conditions of heating. The sulfur is split off more readily at an alkaline pH. The pH of the yolk, which is acid before cooking, becomes alkaline after cooking. An increase in cooking time and temperature increases the amount of H_2S evolved. Tinkler and Soar showed that formation of FeS takes place very slowly until the yolk reaches 70° C. It is seldom formed in eggs cooked 1 to $1\frac{1}{4}$ hours at 70° C or in eggs cooked 30 to 35 minutes at 85° C. Rapid cooling of eggs after 15 minutes in boiling water prevents most green-color development, but the color develops if the eggs are cooled slowly. Placing the eggs in cold water lowers the pressure at the surface, and the H_2S diffuses to the surface. Immediate cooling of eggs is usually beneficial, but after 30 minutes in boiling water, the green color develops in spite of cooling.

Poached and Fried Eggs

Eggs that do not spread or flatten are desirable for poaching or frying. Since the white and yolk tend to flatten after removal from the shell, the best appearance is obtained if the egg is broken just before cooking. Water near the boiling point when the egg is added insures rapid coagulation of the outer portion of poached eggs; cooking is completed at a lower temperature.

Plain or French Omelets; Scrambled Eggs

The basic ingredients of these products are eggs, milk, and salt. They are mixed only enough to blend. Scrambled eggs are stirred occasionally during preparation to coagulate the mixture in large sections. French omelet is manipulated only enough to assure that no fluid egg remains;

the finished product is a continuous disc, slightly moist on the upper surface.

Scrambled eggs prepared from fresh shell eggs do not develop greenish-black discoloration during holding on a steam table, because the initial pH of 7.3 to 7.5 rises only to 7.5 to 8.3 on cooking (Kline et al., 1953). However, scrambled eggs prepared from dehydrated eggs may develop discoloration under these conditions if the pH is above 8.6. Discoloration is rare below that pH (Kline et al., 1953; Salwin et al., 1953). An iron cooking utensil may also contribute to discoloration.

Custards

The basic ingredients and proportions in soft and baked custards are one cup of milk (244 g), one egg (48 g) and two tablespoons of sugar (25 g). Baked custards, cooked without stirring, are firmer than stirred or soft custards and appear to be gels. Most of the heat-coagulable protein in custards is furnished by the egg; about 0.75 percent of the milk protein is heat coagulable. When substitutions are made on the basis of two yolks or two whites for one whole egg, the egg white custard thickens at a lower temperature and the egg yolk custard thickens at a higher temperature. However, on a weight basis, yolk has more thickening power than white. An increase in the proportion of sugar raises the gelation temperature and decreases stiffness of the custard, and vice versa. Sugar has a protective influence on protein structure and diminishes the rate of heat denaturation.

When heat is applied to the custard mix, the first change probably involves structural changes in the egg protein, followed by association or aggregation to form a gel. The temperature of maximum gelation varies with the proportion of ingredients, the rate of cooking, the quality of the eggs, and the pH of the mixture. Thus, no recommended endpoint temperature can be given. If the temperature is held at the gelation point or carried beyond this point, the custard shows syneresis. Since the gelation reaction is endothermic, the temperature of the thickening custard will remain constant at one point during heating if the rate of heating is relatively slow. If cooking is not stopped until the temperature starts to rise again, rapid cooling is advisable to prevent curdling. The more slowly a custard is cooked, the lower is the temperature at which it reaches serving consistency. A slow rate of cooking is preferred, since thickening is evident for some time before the curdling point is reached. With slow cooking, custard reaches serving consistency at 80 to 84° C. Curdling may occur between 85 and 87° C. With rapid heating, less than three minutes, custard generally curdles at about 89° C. The stiffness of custards has been correlated with the quality (Haugh units) of the eggs.

Pie Fillings

A major problem in preparing custard pie is the soaking of the filling into the crust. Prevention of this defect has not been completely successful; recommendations include an increase in egg content from 1 to 1.5 per cup of milk to lower the coagulation temperature of the mix, and warming the milk before adding it to the mix to shorten the time of cooking.

Fillings of butterscotch, lemon, chocolate, banana, and coconut cream pies thickened with egg yolk and a starchy cereal thickening agent occasionally become thin after standing. In making this type of filling, the scalded milk is usually cooked with the sugar and cornstarch or flour until thick. The hot mixture is added to the beaten yolks. If the temperature of the mixture drops below 80° C during mixing and the mixture is not reheated, the egg yolks will not be adequately coagulated and the filling will become thin. A thin filling may also occur in lemon pie filling if too little starch is used, but this defect is usually evident before the starch mixture is combined with the yolk.

THE FOAM-FORMING FUNCTION OF EGGS

Stable egg foams of optimum volume are essential for production of angel cake, meringues, divinity candy, some souffles and omelets, and sponge cakes. Foams are prepared by whipping, injection of gas, or evolution of a dissolved gas. Part of the egg at the air-egg interface coagulates, giving rigidity to the foam.

Foam stiffness is judged subjectively by appearance, the height of peaks, the extent to which the peak bends when the beater is removed, or the rate of flow when the container is partly inverted. As egg white is whipped, the enclosed air bubbles become smaller, the color changes from a pale greenish yellow (flavin pigment) translucency to an opaque white, and the stiffness and volume increase. The surface appearance changes from moist to dry and dull. Egg yolk and whole egg whip to a less stiff foam than egg white; the yolk in the whole egg produces predominantly yolk-type foam. A skillful operator learns to judge stiffness with surprising proficiency by the appearance of the foam, but for control purposes the extent of whipping of the foam is determined by calculation of specific gravity (weight per unit volume) or specific volume (volume per unit weight). Both are measures of the amount of occluded air in the foam.

Foam stability varies with beating time. With slight beating of egg white, considerable drainage occurs. After longer beating, stability increases and drainage decreases; after still longer beating, drainage increases. These changes are related to the increasing amounts of egg white coagulated at the air-egg interface and to the eventual breaking of egg films with excessive whipping. Optimum whipping time for minimum leakage is usually less than the time for maximum foaming (Bailey, 1935). Foam stability is determined by measuring the drainage from the foam in a given time, or by measuring the volume of foam after drying (Henry and Barbour, 1933; Carney, 1938; Barmore, 1936; Hanning, 1945; and McKellar and Stadelman, 1955). Stability measurements are of limited usefulness, since they cannot be used for prediction of egg white performance.

Conditions of beating influence beating rate. Beating rate is the ratio of specific volume to the beating time; it is expressed as specific volume of foam per second of beating (ml per gm per sec). Egg whites at refrigerator temperature may whip more slowly than at room temperature (Miller and Vail, 1943), but unless the ambient temperature is low, occlusion of air at higher temperatures rapidly raises the foam temperature. Lower surface tension of the egg white at higher temperatures may partly explain the faster whipping.

The type of beater influences the beating rate of egg white foams and their optimum specific volume; the wires and blades of beaters differ considerably. The inability of some beaters to whip thick egg white adequately and a tendency of others to overwhip thin whites may explain differences in foam and angel cake volume reported for thick and thin egg white in early studies (Bailey, 1935). Addition of sugar at an early stage in the beating process decreases the beating rate by decreasing the rate of coagulation at the air-egg interface. Because of the danger of overwhipping egg white on an electrically operated beater at high speed, the steady addition of sugar as soon as beating starts is recommended. For hand-operated beaters, addition of sugar is delayed.

Added Ingredients

Acids or acid salts increase the stability of egg white foams. Cream of tartar, acetic acid, and citric acid produce foams of practically the same stability at pH 8, but at pH 6 the foam containing cream of tartar is most stable and that containing acetic acid is least stable (Barmore, 1934, 1936). Henry and Barbour (1933) reported increased foam volume with an increase in pH in the range of 5.47 to 11.06; pH was varied by the addition of H_2SO_4 or NaOH. Bailey (1935) reported that untreated white produced greater volume at equal time than did white at pH 9.5, 7, 6, or 5 but white at pH 7 or 6 was more stable.

Sugar delays formation of egg white foams by delaying surface coagulation of the egg white and thus making them less susceptible to overbeating. Foams to which sugar is added are smoother and more stable than are foams without sugar (Barmore, 1936; Hanning, 1945).

Salt, 1 gram to 40 grams of egg white, decreased the stability of egg white foams beaten short times, but not of those given longer beating (Hanning, 1945). Sechler et al. (1959) reconstituted egg white solids in distilled water containing 0 to 9 g of salt per two egg whites and found a reduced beating rate with the first increment of salt (0.5 g). Addition of salt increased foam leakage and had no beneficial effect on the ease of reconstituting dried egg white.

Oils and the fat of egg yolk and milk have a detrimental effect on egg white foams. Bailey (1935) found that the foaming power of the white was impaired and leakage increased by less than 0.1 percent added yolk. The effect was greater with added olive oil than with yolk containing the same amount of fat. Refined cottonseed oil (0.01 to 1.0 percent by volume) reduced the volume of egg white foam in proportion to the amount of oil added (Henry and Barbour, 1933). Stability was unaffected by 0.2 percent oil, but a definite breakdown occurred with a 0.5 percent addition. Dizmang and Sunderlin (1933) found milk fat to be detrimental to foam formation. Meehan et al. (1962) showed that, during storage at elevated temperature, yolk or yolk fat did not migrate from the yolk to the white in amounts sufficient to affect the volumes of angel cakes prepared from such eggs.

Angel Cake

The qualities desired in angel cake are good volume, tenderness, fairly even and fine texture or grain, and delicate and pleasing flavor. Optimum volume, tenderness, and texture are affected by the extent of whipping of the whites, the ingredients used, and baking conditions. Because angel cake volume is a sensitive indicator of differences in egg whites, it is widely used as a test of the effects of storage or processing treatments on egg whites.

Angel cake volume depends on whipping the egg white foam to its optimum stage. The optimum foam volume may be less than the maximum to which the foam can be whipped. The enclosed air and the steam produced during baking expand the foam cell walls. Coagulation of the stretched cell walls during baking results in a tender cake of large volume. With insufficient beating, too little air is enclosed in the foam. Expansion of air and steam does not stretch the cell membranes to their full capacity, producing relatively thick cell walls in a tough cake of low volume. An overwhipped foam loses extensibility, cell walls break during baking, and a cake of low volume results.

Although foam and batter specific volume and cake volume usually correlate, whipping to predetermined specific gravity or to a particular foam appearance does not assure optimum cake volume. The beating rate of the meringue (egg white, cream of tartar, and sugar) usually correlates with cake volume (Slosberg et al., 1948). Egg white that foams rapidly produces a cake of high volume, but egg white that beats slowly does not always give a cake of poor volume. Blending egg reduces ovomucin fiber length, increases beating rate, and increases angel cake volume (Forsythe and Bergquist, 1951). A maximum fiber length of not more than 300–400 microns was required for good whipping quality.

To assure that egg white under test conditions is whipped to the optimum stage for maximum cake volume, several cakes are made from whites whipped to different specific volumes by whipping for different lengths of time. The first foam is whipped to the stage judged by the operator to be approximately optimum, and subsequent samples are whipped for longer and shorter periods. Usually the cake volumes of such a series plotted against whipping time will form a curve with a maximum near the center of the time series and smaller volumes for the underwhipped and overwhipped samples (MacDonnell et al., 1955) (Figure 1).

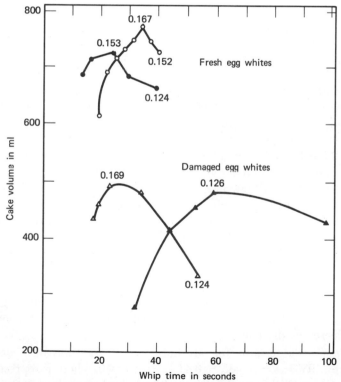

FIGURE 1. Effect of egg white whip time on angel cake volume. Decimal numbers are meringue specific gravities.

In addition to the egg white, the essential ingredients in angel cake are acid (cream of tartar), sugar, and flour. If cream of tartar is omitted, the cake color is yellowish, the texture coarse, the cell walls thick, and the cake tough (Grewe and Child, 1930). Flavone pigments in flour are colorless in acid or neutral media, but yellowish or yellow-green in alkaline media. Tartaric, acetic, and citric acid produce angel cakes of approximately the same texture at pH 8. At pH 6 the acid tartrate produces the least coarse texture in cake, the acetic acid produces a coarse texture, and the citric acid produces an intermediate texture (Barmore, 1936). At a lower pH in the finished cake, the relation of foam stability to texture is even more noticeable. Barmore concluded that there are two functions of acid in angel cake: (1) stabilizing the foam so that the temperature of coagulation is reached before the foam collapses and (2) preventing the extreme shrinkage during the last part of the baking and during the cooling period.

Fine crystalline sugar is used for angel cake because it dissolves rapidly. The optimum amount of sugar depends somewhat on the amount of flour. Flour may vary from 0.2 to 0.4 g per gram of egg white. The smaller amount gives a moist and tender cake; the larger, a drier and less tender one. Excess sugar will prevent coagulation during baking, and the cake will fall. The crust will be sugary, crystalline, and rather dry. From sea level to 1000 feet above sea level the optimum amount of sugar for angel cake is about 1 gram per gram of egg white; this level can be increased to 1.25 grams provided the maximum amount of flour is used. At higher altitudes sugar must be decreased. Part or all of the sugar should be added before any of the flour to improve foam stability.

Cake flour is used in angel cakes as a binder and to provide the starch that gelatinizes in the oven and supplements the egg protein in forming the cake structure. All-purpose flour causes the cakes to shrink excessively and pull away from the sides of the pan during the last of the baking period and during cooling because of the cohesive properties of the gluten. Such cakes are compact and have small volume. Wheat starch has been used recently in place of as much as 30 percent of the flour; such substitution improves cake volume and quality (Dubois, 1959). Flour and starch are folded in at the end of the mixing period. Loss of volume at this stage is related to agitation of the flour-foam system. Increasing the egg or flour in angel cake increases its tensile strength, and increasing the sugar decreases the tensile strength.

An angel cake formula for any habitable altitude has been devised by Barmore (1936): $F - 0.43S - 0.41A - 24.5 = 0$, where F represents flour in grams; S, sugar in grams; and A, altitude in thousands of feet. The cake volume and tenderness increase with altitude. The maximum internal cake temperature decreases with altitude, and the crust color is lighter. No moisture is lost by evaporation by any portion of the cake farther than one cm from the outer edge (Barmore, 1936).

Desirable cakes can be baked at a range of temperatures; the optimum baking time at a given temperature depends on the volume and shape of the pan. At high temperatures the crust sets so rapidly that cake volume is reduced; at low temperatures, the cake structure is unduly long in setting. For a given formula and altitude, the maximum internal temperature is nearly the same regardless of the oven temperature. Continued baking after the maximum temperature is reached increases toughness and dryness of the cake. At a relatively low temperature, baking beyond the optimum time is less serious than at a relatively high temperature.

Meringues and Dessert Souffles

Soft meringues, used as toppings for pies, contain egg white, sugar, an optional acid ingredient, salt, and flavoring. Problems encountered in preparing a desirable meringue topping include leakage, stickiness, beading (drops of liquid on top), and inadequate height. Although the proportion of ingredients, extent of whipping, quality of the egg white, and baking conditions have been implicated in these problems, published research on the subject is limited. Hester and Personius (1949) reported that excessive leakage occurred under conditions producing incomplete coagulation (use of a cold base or a short baking time at a high temperature). Excessive beading occurred under conditions favoring overcoagulation (a hot base and a low-temperature, long-time bake). Levels of 0.8 and 1.6 percent potassium acid tartrate had little effect on leakage, but the higher level increased beading. A wide range of baking temperatures produces satisfactory meringues if baking time is properly adjusted. There is no appreciable expansion of meringues in the oven. Gillis and Fitch (1956) found that the proportion of sugar, the extent of beating of the egg white before the addition of sugar, and the baking conditions affected stability, appearance, and cutting quality of soft meringues. Felt et al. (1956) studied the effect of leakage and slippage of meringue cream pies with variations in formula, preparation methods, fillings, and baking conditions. Most stable meringues were prepared with a hot syrup and vegetable-gum stabilizer, baked at 191° C. Too high a temperature in the meringue produced curdling of the filling.

Sweetened dessert souffles and soft pie meringues lose volume and texture during freezing and frozen storage. Methods of reducing this damage through adjustment of the formulas are described in Chapter 13.

Hard meringues, used as foundations for desserts, contain more sugar than soft meringues (approx. four tablespoons per egg white versus two tablespoons for soft meringues). Sugar is gradually added to the egg white during whipping, and the mixture is beaten to a stiff stage. Because of the high proportion of sugar, underbeating is usually more of a problem than is overbeating. Hard meringues require a long, slow baking, essentially a drying, to develop a crisp, tender texture. They are baked at 100-110° C for one to two hours, depending on their size, and are then dried in the oven for several hours after the heat is turned off. Thoroughly dry meringues retain their crispness during storage in an air-tight container.

Candy

Candies such as nougat and divinity require the foaming and heat-coagulating properties of egg white to produce their typical texture, form, and stability. In candies such as fondant, a small amount of egg white improves stability by preventing sugar-crystal growth during storage. The proportion of egg white and sugar in divinity is important in preventing grainy, crumbly, dry, or powdery textures (Swanson, 1933). The pH of the mixture affects the specific volume of divinity; small amounts of yolk in the egg white have a detrimental effect (Cotterill et al., 1963). (See also Chapter 1.)

Fluffy Omelets and Souffles

The basic ingredients of omelets are eggs, liquid, and salt. The liquids may be water, water with cream of tartar, vinegar or lemon juice, or tomato juice or other vegetable juice. Acid ingredients produce a tender omelet of large volume, but they may also increase whipping time of the white. For fluffy or foamy omelets the beaten yolk is folded into stiffly beaten whites. Insufficient whipping of the whites, insufficient mixing of yolk with white, or delay in cooking causes drainage of liquid from foamy omelets, the formation of a layer on the bottom, and the greenish color of FeS on the underside. Overbeating of white results in loss of extensibility, and volume does not reach its maximum during baking. Rough handling and overmixing of the yolk with the white cause loss of incorporated air.

Souffles consist of beaten yolks blended with a white sauce and beaten whites folded into the mixture. Maximum volume requires whipping the whites to optimum stiffness (stiff but not dry), minimum blending of the whites with the white sauce-yolk mixture, prompt baking after mixing, baking until the center is completely coagulated, and prompt serving after removing the souffle from the oven. The endpoint of baking of souffles is indicated by a temperature rise following a leveling or drop in temperature toward the end of baking. In quantity cookery, the terms souffle and foamy omelet are interchangeable, since the use of a white sauce is specified in both to improve stability (Longree et al., 1962).

Sponge Cake

The qualities desired in sponge cake are good volume, tenderness, texture or grain, and flavor. If the proportion of ingredients is well balanced, the quality of the sponge cake depends chiefly on optimum beating of the egg and sugar. The sugar and whole eggs may be whipped together, or the sugar and yolks may be whipped and the beaten whites folded in after the flour has been added. Excellent sponge cakes may be made from yolks alone if some water is added and the mixture is beaten rapidly with the sugar until it is very light. Probably the most common fault in making sponge cake is insufficient beating of the egg-sugar mixture.

The aeration of egg and sugar is affected by the quality of the egg, the particle size of the sugar, the ratio of egg to sugar, the proportion of sugar in solution at the start of aeration, the size, type, and speed of whip, the ambient, and ingredient temperatures (Farrand, 1957; Pyke, 1941; and Pyke and Johnson, 1940). Farrand (1957) recommends aeration of the mix to a constant overrun (percent increase in volume due to incorporation of air into the mix) rather than for a standard time or to a constant bubble characteristic. He reported that the cake-making properties of an egg cannot be assessed purely by the amount of air that can be incorporated.

The use of cream of tartar to adjust the pH has been recommended, since lemon juice impedes formation of the whole-egg meringue (Pyke and Johnson, 1940). If the lemon flavor is desired, the juice can be added with the flour. Pike and Johnson prepared balanced cake formulas suitable for altitudes from sea level to 12,000 feet. A constant amount of sugar was used to provide satisfactory sweetness; flour and water were increased with increasing altitude.

Methods and apparatus used for measuring quality of sponge and angel cake include seed displacement for determining volume, photography for recording grain, and devices for determining tensile strength, compressibility, and shape (Platt and Kratz, 1933; King et al., 1936b). See also Chapter 16. The use of ungreased and unlined pans reduces errors in volume measurement caused by paper linings that produce concave indentations in the bottom of the cake (King et al., 1936a).

THE EMULSIFYING FUNCTION OF EGGS

The use of egg yolk as an emulsifying agent in mayonnaise, salad dressing, Hollandaise sauce, and cream puffs is discussed in Chapter 2.

THE EFFECTS OF PROCESSING AND STORAGE ON CULINARY QUALITY OF EGG PRODUCTS

Eggs are broken, separated, and processed to increase their usefulness and extend their shelf life. There are standards of identity for egg products such as whole eggs, egg whites, and egg yolks in liquid, frozen, and dried forms. Salted yolks, sugared yolks, and various whole-egg blends are available for special uses. Review articles have been published on various aspects of egg processing and storage (Bergquist, 1964; Conrad et al., 1948; Forsythe, 1953, 1957, 1960, 1963, 1964; and U.S. Dept. Agric., 1969).

PASTEURIZATION

Liquid eggs may become contaminated with pathogenic and spoilage microorganisms that multiply under improper holding conditions and may survive in uncooked foods or in foods given a minimum cooking such as soft scrambled eggs, meringue toppings, and egg drinks (Beloian and Schlosser, 1963). Therefore, egg products are pasteurized under conditions that destroy salmonella organisms in excess of the maximum number expected in these products; the treatment also reduces spoilage organisms (U.S. Dept. Agric., 1969).

Liquid whole eggs have been pasteurized for many years by heating at 60–61° C for $3\frac{1}{2}$ minutes to destroy pathogenic organisms. This treatment has little or no effect on the performance of the eggs in custards, sponge cakes, or mayonnaise (Hanson et al., 1947; Miller and Winter, 1950, 1951), although the combination of pasteurization and freezing may adversely affect foaming power unless the treatment includes homogenization (Sugihara, 1966). Pasteurization has little or no effect on the functional performance of salted or sugared yolks, although higher pasteurization temperatures are required to kill microorganisms in these products than are required for whole eggs (Palmer et al., 1969a, b; U.S. Dept. Agric., 1969).

Liquid whites were not pasteurized until recently at the temperature used for whole eggs because of damage to the egg white proteins by heat treatment. The beating rate of meringue and the volume of angel cake are both impaired by momentary heating to 59° C or by heating to lower temperatures for longer times. There are now five approved processes for pasteurization of liquid egg whites that cause only slight damage to performance of the whites (U.S. Dept. Agric., 1969). One consists of adjustment of the pH of whites to 6.8 to 7.3 and addition of a metal salt so that the whites can withstand the pasteurization conditions used for whole eggs. Two processes involve a combination of peroxide addition and reduced heat treatment to kill the organisms at the normal high pH of egg white. A fourth process involves a combination of heat plus vacuum; the reason for the beneficial effect of the vacuum is not known. A fifth process utilizes the greater killing effect of the high pH of egg white to pasteurize at lower temperatures than are required for whole eggs. Pasteurization causes little or no decrease in volume of angel cakes made from the whites. The beating rate of the whites is decreased, but whipping aids such as triethyl citrate and triacetin can be added to increase whipping rate (Kline et al., 1965).

Dried egg whites can be pasteurized after drying to assure elimination of any recontamination that might occur during packaging of products pasteurized before drying. Dried whites containing not over five percent moisture can be held at 50° C, and whites containing not over three percent moisture can be held at 60–70° C to eliminate large numbers of *Salmonellae* without noticeably impairing functional properties, including angel cake properties (Ayres and Slosberg, 1949; Banwart and Ayres, 1956). Research and experience have shown that a holding period of 7–10 days is adequate for powder containing approximately six percent moisture.

FREEZING

Freezing does not appreciably alter the physical characteristics of uncooked, liquid egg white; after defrosting, the white can be used in the same way as unfrozen white. However, the viscosities of egg yolk and whole eggs increase when they are exposed to temperatures below their freezing point. The viscosity increase (or gelation) is more severe in egg yolks than in whole eggs. The use of frozen plain yolks has been limited in food-manufacturing operations because of the difficulty in blending gelled yolks with other ingredients. Sugar, salt, and other substances have been added to yolks ever since their effectiveness in limiting gelation was reported (Moran, 1925; Thomas and Bailey, 1933). Ten percent by weight of either sugar or salt is the usual amount added commercially. For home freezing, addition and thorough mixing of $\frac{1}{2}$ teaspoon salt or 2 tablespoons sugar per cup of yolk or whole egg adequately limits viscosity increase. The use of these additives restricts the egg products to foods that would normally contain such additives. Even when the additives are used, variable degrees of viscosity increase or gelation occur in comparable lots of egg unless strict control of freezing, storage, and thawing conditions is maintained. The production of eggs of uniform consistency is of particular importance in commercial preparation of foods such as mayonnaise in which the original viscosity of the mix influences the rate at which the emulsion forms and the final stiffness attained.

Gelation of yolk-containing egg products does not occur immediately as the temperature of the product is lowered to the critical range. The freezing point of salted yolks is approximately 1° F. Increases of practical significance in the viscosity of commercially processed salted yolks do not occur until the yolks have been held about 5 days below −10°.F (Palmer et al., 1969a). Viscosity (or gelation) continues to increase during a month of storage below −10° F, but only minor changes take place during further storage. To prevent the major increase in gelation and decrease in their emulsifying property that occurs at −20 or −30° F, commercial salted yolks are usually frozen at −10° F and held at 0° F.

Only a small increase in viscosity occurs in commercially processed sugared yolks held at 0° F. The major viscosity change in sugared yolks occurs below 0° F, at −10 or −20° F (Palmer et al., 1969b). The freezing point of sugared yolks is approximately 25° F.

Although 10 percent by weight of the sugar or salt are added commercially, lesser amounts inhibit viscosity also. Added sugar from 0 to 10 percent has a stepwise effect in limiting viscosity; the more sugar added, the lower the viscosity development. With added salt, however, samples containing 4 percent have a lower viscosity after freezing and thawing than samples containing 10 percent (Figure 2) (Palmer et al.,

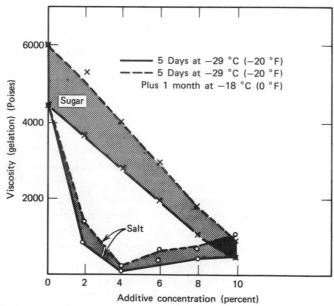

FIGURE 2. Effect of additive concentration on viscosity of thawed egg yolk.

1970). The 10 percent added salt, however, is valuable for its inhibitory effect on the growth of microorganisms.

Although egg yolk gelation has always been considered irreversible, it has recently been shown that the gelation can be partially reversed by heating after thawing (Palmer et al., 1970). Commercially processed egg yolks without added sugar or salt freeze at about 31° F. They gel at temperatures ranging from 10 to − 30° F to such an extent that they will not flow from an inverted container when they are thawed at ambient temperature. The stiffness of the gels, as determined by viscosity measurements, can be reduced more than 50 percent by heating to about 45° C. The heat treatment also improves the beating performance of the thawed yolks. This partial reversal of gelation in egg yolk gels appears to be similar to the "melting" of gelatin gels. Gelatin gels at about 4° C and softens at about 40° C. Egg yolks gel at temperatures below the freezing point, but the yolk proteins coagulate above about 45° C. This coagulation prevents the use of higher temperatures to determine whether the gelation is completely reversible. An increase in holding time at the elevated temperature decreases the gel stiffness slightly, but temperature rather than time is the prime factor in controlling gelation. Gelation of yolks containing sugar or salt is also partially reversed by heat treatment.

DEHYDRATION

Egg powders may be prepared from whole eggs, yolks, or whites. Most commercial powders are spray-dried, although whites are also dried in trays or as a film on a continuous belt. Dehydrated eggs have the advantages over frozen eggs that they can be incorporated in mixes prepared for baked products, that they are convenient, and that they conserve weight and space.

Research in recent years has been designed to overcome the problems of changes in color, flavor, solubility, whipping, and coagulating properties of dried egg products; and their increasing use indicates that the research has been generally successful. Glucose is removed by bacterial or yeast fermentation or enzymatic oxidation before egg white is dried commercially to prevent changes in color, flavor, and performance caused by reaction between glucose and proteins (Stewart and Kline, 1941; Ayres and Stewart, 1947; Mohammed et al., 1949; and Forsythe, 1953). The reaction that occurs between glucose and the protein is called the Maillard or browning reaction. Glucose removal, particularly bacterial desugaring, improves performance of spray-dried whites in angel food cake. Storage of dried whites at 22 and 40° C causes little or no loss in volume of cakes made from fermented whites but 7 to 26 percent loss in those made from unfermented whites (Carlin and Ayres, 1951).

Flavor differences due to the method of glucose removal are unimportant (Carlin and Ayres, 1953; Carlin et al., 1954).

Although natural egg white contains almost no fat, the fat content of commercial whites may be as high as 0.05 percent because of yolk contamination. Drying magnifies the adverse effect of yolk contamination on the foaming properties of egg white (Bergquist, 1964), and whipping aids are used in angel cake mixes in part to counteract the effect of yolk fat. These include anionic surface-active agents such as sodium lauryl sulfate (Mink, 1939) and other additives such as triethyl citrate (Kothe, 1953). Angel cakes prepared from dried whites are improved by modified mixing methods and slight alterations in ingredients. One fourth to one fifth of the sugar is replaced with icing or powdered sugar. Half of the total sugar may be mixed and added with the dried egg white to separate the egg white particles and prevent clumping of the egg particles and incomplete rehydration of the center of the clump. Half of the sugar is added to the flour to facilitate its blending with the other ingredients. The dry-blended egg, sugar, and acid salt are added to the water during low-speed mixing; high-speed mixing is used for foam formation. Approximately a third of the flour is replaced with wheat starch. These modifications improve the volume, texture, and eating quality of the cakes, as is also true for cakes prepared from liquid whites (Pinney, 1960; Miyahara and Bergquist, 1961).

During storage of yolk or whole-egg solids at elevated temperatures, changes in color, flavor, and functional properties may occur. Browning is eliminated by removing the natural glucose before drying, using either yeast fermentation or enzymatic oxidation of glucose to gluconic acid (Kline and Sonoda, 1951; Kline et al., 1951a, b, 1953, 1954). Elimination of glucose also eliminates the off-flavor caused by the reaction of glucose and cephalin of the yolk. Unless oxygen is eliminated, however, an oxidative flavor change occurs during storage. This is reduced, but not eliminated, by removal of glucose. A combination of glucose removal, drying to a low moisture content, and inert-gas packing retards off-flavor development during several months' storage at 37.5° C (Kline et al., 1951b).

Freeze-drying or spray-drying markedly diminishes the foaming power of egg yolk or whole egg at ambient temperature. Joslin and Proctor (1954) showed that the loss of whipping characteristics during drying of dried whole egg occurs in the yolk. Lyophilized yolk whipped with undried white does not foam satisfactorily; lyophilized white whipped with undried yolk foams normally. Microscopic examination of a drying egg film showed breakdown of the fat emulsion and formation of a free surface of oil. The deleterious fraction was removed by treatment of the powder with a fat solvent such as acetone. Solvent-washed powders whipped to voluminous foams characteristic of nondried eggs, indicating that free oil of the dried whole-egg powder is responsible for the anti-foam action. Hawthorne and Bennion (1942) and Bennion et al. (1942) showed that a satisfactory foam could be produced by whipping the reconstituted whole egg at 38–50° C. The addition of carbohydrates such as sucrose to the egg before drying minimizes loss of foaming power and extends shelf life (Brooks and Hawthorne, 1943; Dawson et al., 1945; and Conrad et al., 1948). Approximately 10 percent sucrose (percent of liquid weight) was added, but the additive accelerated off-flavor development. Commercially, corn-syrup solids have been substituted since they produce less off-flavor development at the same concentration. However, recent studies have shown that there is an optimum level for each carbo-hydrate, and flavor stability requires addition of appropriate levels (Kline et al., 1964). Levels above and below optimum increase off flavor. Off-flavor changes are correlated with extractability of the egg lipids.

Whole-egg and yolk solids now available include standard whole-egg or yolk solids, stabilized whole-egg or yolk solids (with glucose removed), fortified whole-egg solids (mixtures of whole egg and yolk in various proportions, commonly 70 percent whole egg and 30 percent yolk), and special blends (Forsythe, 1960). Standard solids are used for layer cakes, doughnuts, sweet doughs, cookies, mayonnaise, and salad dressing. Stabilized solids with glucose removed are used in dried mixes. Fortified whole-egg solids contain slightly less than half egg yolk solids and slightly more than half whole-egg solids. These products are used in the baking industry, and economic considerations influence which type is used. The blends of whole-egg solids include sucrose or some other carbohydrates to improve retention of foaming power. These products dissolve readily and are used in foam-type cakes and cookies.

References

STRUCTURE, COMPOSITION, QUALITY, AND GRADES

Alderton, G., W. H. Ward, and H. L. Fevold. 1945. Isolation of lysozyme from egg white. *J. Biol. Chem.* 157: 43.

Alderton, G., H. L. Fevold, and H. D. Lightbody. 1964a. Some properties of lysozyme. *Fed. Proc. Part II*, 5: 119.

Alderton, G., W. H. Ward, and H. L. Fevold. 1964b. Identification of the bacteria-inhibiting, iron-binding protein of egg white as conalbumin. *Arch. Biochem.* 11: 9.

Azari, P. R., and R. E. Feeney. 1958. Resistance of metal complexes of conalbumin and transferrin to proteolysis and to thermal denaturation. *J. Biol. Chem. 232*: 293.

Azari, P. R., and R. E. Feeney. 1961. The resistances of conalbumin and its iron complex to physical and chemical treatments. *Arch. Biochem. Biophys. 92*: 44.

Baker, R. L., and R. H. Forsythe. 1951. U.S. standards for quality of individual shell eggs and the relationships between candled appearance and more objective quality measures. *Poultry Sci. 30*: 269.

Banwart, S. F., A. F. Carlin, and O. J. Cotterill. 1957. Flavor of untreated, oiled, and thermostabilized shell eggs after storage at 34° F. *Food Technol. 11*: 200.

Brant, A. W., A. W. Otte, and K. H. Norris. 1951. Recommended standards for scoring and measuring opened egg quality. *Food Technol. 5*: 356.

Brant, A. W., K. H. Norris, and G. Chinn. 1953. A spectrophotometric method for detecting blood in white-shell eggs. *Poultry Sci. 23*: 357.

Brooks, J., and D. J. Taylor. 1955. Eggs and Egg Products, Dept. Scientific and Industrial Res., *Food Investigation Special Report No. 60*. Her Majesty's Stationery Office, London.

Carlin, A. F., and J. Foth. 1952. Interior quality and functional properties of oiled and thermostabilized shell eggs before and after commercial storage. *Food Technol. 6*: 443.

Cotterill, O. J., F. A. Gardner, E. M. Funk, and F. E. Cunningham. 1958. Relationship between temperature and carbon dioxide loss from shell eggs. *Poultry Sci. 37*: 479.

Cunningham, F. E., and H. Lineweaver. 1965. Heat stability of egg white and egg white proteins in relation to egg white pasteurization. *Food Technol. 19*: 1442.

Donovan, J. W. 1967. Spectrophotometric observation of the alkaline hydrolysis of protein disulfide bonds. *Biochem. and Biophys. Res. Commun. 29*: 734.

Eakin, R. E., E. E. Snell, and R. J. Williams. 1941. The concentration and assay of avidin, the injury-producing protein in raw egg white. *J. Biol. Chem. 140*: 535.

Ehrenpreis, S., and R. C. Warner. 1956. The interaction of conalbumin and lysozyme. *Arch. Biochem. Biophys. 61*: 38.

Eisen, E. J., B. B. Bohren, and H. E. McKean. 1962. The Haugh unit as a measure of egg albumen quality. *Poultry Sci. 41*: 1461.

Evans, R. J., and J. S. Carver. 1942. Shell treatment of eggs by oiling. I. Effect of time between production and oiling on interior quality of stored eggs. *U.S. Egg and Poultry Mag. 48*: 546.

Everson, G. J., and H. J. Souders. 1957. Composition and nutritive importance of eggs. *J. Am. Dietetic Assoc. 33*: 1244.

Feeney, R. E., R. B. Silva, and L. R. MacDonnell. 1951. Chemistry of shell egg deterioration: The deterioration of separated components. *Poultry Sci. 30*: 645.

Feeney, R. E., and D. A. Nagy. 1952. The antibacterial activity of the egg white protein conalbumin. *J. Bacteriol. 64*: 629.

Feeney, R. E., L. R. MacDonnell, and H. Fraenkel-Conrat. 1954a. Effects of crotoxin (lecithinase A) on egg yolk and yolk constituents. *Arch. Biochem. Biophysics 48*: 130.

Feeney, R. E., L. R. MacDonnell, and F. W. Lorenz. 1954b. High temperature treatment of shell eggs. *Food Technol. 8*: 242.

Feeney, R. E., L. R. MacDonnell, and E. D. Ducay. 1956. Irreversible inactivation of lysozyme by copper. *Arch. Biochem. Biophys. 61*: 72.

Forsythe, R. H., and J. F. Foster. 1950. Egg white proteins: I. Electrophoretic studies on whole white. *J. Biol. Chem. 184*: 377.

Forsythe, R. H., and D. H. Bergquist. 1951. The effect of physical treatments on some properties of egg white. *Poultry Sci. 30*: 302.

Forsythe, R. H. 1952. The effect of cleaning on the flavor and interior quality of shell eggs. *Food Technol. 6*: 55.

Forsythe, R. H. 1963. Chemical and physical properties of eggs and egg products. *Cereal Science Today 8*: 309.

Fraenkel-Conrat, H., R. S. Bean, and H. Lineweaver. 1949. Essential groups for the interaction of ovomucoid (egg white trypsin inhibitor) and trypsin, and for tryptic activity. *J. Biol. Chem. 177*: 385.

Fraenkel-Conrat, H. 1950. The essential groups of lysozyme, with particular reference to its reaction with iodine. *Arch. Biochem. 27*: 109.

Fredericq, E., and H. F. Deutsch. 1949a. Purification and properties of ovomucoid. *Fed. Proc. 8*: 199.

Fredericq, E., and H. F. Deutsch. 1949b. Studies on ovomucoid. *J. Biol. Chem. 181*: 499.

Funk, E. M. 1950. Maintenance of quality in shell egg by thermostabilization. *Missouri Agr. Expt. Sta. Res. Bull. 467*.

Gibbons, N. E. 1950. Preservation of eggs: VII. Effect of age of egg and carbon dioxide content at time of oiling on keeping quality. *Can. J. Research F28*: 118.

Goodwin, T. L., M. L. Wilson, and W. J. Stadelman. 1962. Effects of oiling time, storage position, and storage time on the condition of shell eggs. *Poultry Sci. 41*: 840.

Goresline, H. E., K. M. Hayes, Q. W. Otte. 1952. Thermostabilization of shell eggs: Quality retention in storage. *U.S. Department of Agriculture Circular 898*.

Grant, J. N. Apr., 1948. The secret of oiling eggs successfully. *U.S. Egg and Poultry Mag. 54*: 10.

Green, N. M. 1963. Avidin. 3. The nature of the biotin-binding site. *Biochem. J. 89*: 599.

Gyorgy, P., C. S. Rose, R. E. Eakin, E. E. Snell, and R. J. Williams. 1941. Egg white injury as the result of nonabsorption or inactivation of biotin. *Science 93*: 477.

Hard, M. M., J. V. Spencer, R. S. Locke, and M. H. George. 1963. A comparison of different methods of preserving shell eggs. 2. Effect on functional properties. *Poultry Sci. 42*: 1085.

Harns, J. V., E. A. Sauter, B. A. McLaren, and W. J. Stadelman. 1953. Relationship of egg shell quality and performance of egg white in angel food cakes. *Food Research 18*: 343.

Harns, J. V., E. A. Sauter, B. A. McLaren, W. J. Stadelman. 1954a. Effect of season, age, and storage conditions on the flavor of eggs and products using eggs. *Poultry Sci. 33*: 992.

Harns, V. J., E. A. Sauter, B. A. McLaren, and W. J. Stadelman. 1954b. Comparison of several methods of evaluation of quality in eggs. *Poultry Sci. 33*: 1022.

Haugh, R. R. 1937. The Haugh unit for measuring egg quality. *U.S. Egg Poultry Mag. 43*: 552.

Heywang, B. W., H. R. Bird, and A. M. Altschul. 1955. Relationship between discoloration in eggs and dietary free gossypol supplied by different cottonseed products. *Poultry Sci. 34*: 81.

Hughes, J. S., and H. M. Scott. 1936. The change in concentration of ovoglobulin in egg white during egg formation. *Poultry Sci. 15*: 349.

Hunter, J. A., A. Van Wagenen, and G. O. Hall. 1936. Seasonal changes in interior egg quality of single comb white Leghorn hens. *Poultry Sci. 15*: 115.

Jones, K. B., T. W. Houston, and J. M. Harries. 1961. Studies on egg quality. I. Effects of certain poultry housing systems, age of bird and season. *J. Sci. Food Agr. 12*: 381.

Jordan, R., A. T. Barr, and M. L. Wilson. 1954. Shell eggs: quality and properties as affected by temperature and length of storage. *Purdue Univ. Agr. Exp. Sta. Bull. No. 612*, 59 pp.

Jordan, R., G. E. Vail, J. C. Rogler, and W. J. Stadelman. 1960. Functional properties and flavor of eggs laid by hens on diets containing different fats. *Food Technol. 14*: 418.

Jordan, R., G. E. Vail, J. C. Rogler, and W. J. Stadelman. 1962. Further studies on diets differing in fat content. *Food Technol. 16*: 118.

Kemmerer, A. R., B. W. Heywang, and M. G. Vavich. 1961. Effect of sterculia foetida oil on gossypol discoloration in cold storage eggs and the mechanism of gossypol discoloration. *Poultry Sci. 40*: 1045.

Kemmerer, A. R., B. W. Heywang, H. E. Nordby, and R. A. Phelps. 1962. Effect of cottonseed oil on discoloration of cold storage eggs. *Poultry Sci. 41*: 1101.

Kemmerer, A. R., B. W. Heywang, M. G. Vavich, and R. A. Phelps. 1963. Further studies of the effect of cottonseed oil on discoloration of cold storage eggs. *Poultry Sci. 42*: 893.

King, F. B., E. F. Whiteman, and W. G. Rose. 1936a. Cake making quality of eggs as related to some factors in egg production. *Cereal Chem. 13:* 703.

Kline, L., J. J. Meehan, and T. F. Sugihara. 1965. Relation between layer age and egg-product yields and quality. *Food Technol. 19:* 1296.

Knox, C. W., and A. B. Godfrey. 1940. Five years of breeding for high and low percentages of thick albumen in the eggs of Rhode Island Reds. *Poultry Sci. 19:* 291.

Korslund, J. J., W. W. Marion, and W. J. Stadelman. 1957. Some factors affecting quality loss in shell eggs. *Poultry Sci. 36:* 338.

Lineweaver, H., and C. W. Murray. 1947. Identification of the trypsin inhibitor of egg white with ovomucoid. *J. Biol. Chem. 171:* 565.

Lineweaver, H., H. J. Morris, L. Kline, and R. S. Bean. 1948. Enzymes of fresh hen eggs. *Arch. Biochem. 16:* 443.

Longworth, L. G., R. K. Cannan, and D. A. MacInnes. 1940. An electrophoretic study of the proteins of egg white. *J. Am. Chem. Soc. 62:* 2580.

MacDonnell, L. R., H. L. Hanson, R. B. Silva, H. Lineweaver, and R. E. Feeney. 1950. Shear—not pressure—harms egg white. *Food Inds. 22:* 273.

MacDonnell, L. R., E. D. Ducay, T. F. Sugihara, and R. E. Feeney. 1954. Proteins of chicken, duck, and turkey egg white. *Biochem. Biophys. Acta 13:* 140.

MacDonnell, L. R., R. E. Feeney, H. L. Hanson, A. Campbell, and T. F. Sugihara. 1955. The functional properties of the egg white proteins. *Food Technol. 9:* 49.

Martin, W. G., N. H. Tattrie, and W. H. Cook. 1963. Lipid extraction and distribution studies of egg yolk lipoproteins. *Canad. J. Biochem. Physiol. 41:* 657.

Marusich, W., E. DeRitter, J. C. Bauernfeind. 1960. Evaluation of carotenoid pigments for coloring egg yolks. *Poultry Sci. 39:* 1338.

Masson, J. C., M. G. Vavich, B. W. Heywang, and A. R. Kemmerer. 1957. Pink discoloration in eggs caused by sterculic acid. *Science 126:* 751.

McNally, E. 1933. Relative amount of mucin in thick and in thin egg white. *Prod. Soc. Exptl. Biol. Med. 30:* 1254.

Mecham, D. K., and H. S. Olcott. 1949. Phosvitin, the principal phosphoprotein of egg yolk. *J. Am. Chem. Soc. 71:* 3670.

Meehan, J. J., T. F. Sugihara, and L. Kline. 1962. Relationships between shell egg handling factors and egg product properties. I. Egg white damage at moderate to elevated shell egg holding temperatures. *Poultry Sci. 41:* 892.

Mercuri, A. J., J. E. Thomson, J. D. Rowan, and K. H. Norris. 1957. Use of the automatic green-rot detector to improve the quality of liquid eggs. *Food Technol. 11:* 374.

Noles, R. K., and J. R. Roush. 1962. Consumer egg preferences and their relationship to U.S. standards. *Poultry Sci. 41:* 200.

Norris, K. H., and A. W. Brant. 1952. Radio frequency as a means of grading eggs. *Food Technol.* 6: 204.

Palmer, L. S., and H. L. Kempster. 1919. The influence of specific feeds and certain pigments on the color of the egg yolk and body fat of fowls. *J. Biol. Chem.* 39: 331.

Parkinson, T. L. 1966. The chemical composition of eggs. *J. Sci. Food Agric.* 17: 101.

Peterson, W. J., J. S. Hughes, and L. F. Payne. 1939. The carotenoid pigments. *Kansas Agr. Expt. Sta. Tech. Bull. 46.*

Powrie, W. D., H. Little, and A. Lopez. 1936. Gelation of egg yolk. *J. Food Sci.* 28: 38.

Pyke, W. E., and G. Johnson. 1940. Preparing and baking yellow sponge cake at different altitudes. *Colo. Agr. Expt. Sta. Tech. Bull. 27.*

Pyke, W. E., and G. Johnson. 1941. Relationships between certain physical measurements upon fresh and stored eggs and their behavior in the preparation and baking of cake. *Poultry Sci.* 20: 125.

Rowan, J. D., K. H. Norris, and C. K. Powell. 1958. A method for measuring the rheological properties of eggs. *Food Research* 23: 670.

Sauter, E. A., J. V. Harns, W. J. Stadelman, and B. A. McLaren. 1953. Relationship of candled quality of eggs to other quality measurements. *Poultry Sci.* 32: 850.

Sauter, E. A., J. V. Harns, W. J. Stadelman, and R. McLaren. 1954a. Seasonal variations in quality of eggs as measured by physical and functional properties. *Poultry Sci.* 33: 519.

Sauter, E. A., J. V. Harns, W. J. Stadelman, and B. McLaren. 1954b. Effect of oil treating shell eggs on their functional properties after storage. *Food Technol.* 8: 82.

Schultz, J. R., and R. H. Forsythe. 1967. The influence of egg yolk lipoprotein-carbohydrate interactions on baking performance. *Bakers Digest 41 (2):* 56.

Sell, H. M., A. G. Olsen, and R. E. Kremers. 1935. Lecitho-protein: The emulsifying ingredient in egg yolk. *Ind. Eng. Chem.* 27: 1222.

Shade, A. L., and L. Caroline. 1944. Raw hen egg white and the role of iron in growth inhibition of Shigella dysenteriae, Staphylococcus aureus, Escherichia coli, and Saccharomyces cerevisiae. *Science 100:* 14.

Shade, A. L., R. H. Reinhart, and H. Levy. 1949. Carbon dioxide and oxygen in complex formation with iron and siderophilin, the iron-binding component of human plasma. *Arch. Biochem.* 20: 170.

Sharp, P. F. 1937. Preservation and storage of hens' eggs. *Food Research* 2: 477.

Shenstone, F. S., and J. R. Vickery. 1959. Substances in plants of the order Malvale causing pink whites in stored eggs. *Poultry Sci.* 38: 1055.

Shepard, C. G., and G. A. Hottle. 1949. Studies of the composition of the livetin fraction of the yolk of hens' eggs with the use of electrophoretic analysis. *J. Biol. Chem. 179*: 349.

Smolelis, A. N., and S. E. Hartsell. 1951. Occurrence of lysozyme in bird egg albumins. *Proc. Soc. Exptl. Biol. Med. 76*: 455.

Sugihara, T. F., L. R. MacDonnell, L. R. Knight, and R. E. Feeney. 1955. Virus antihemagglutinin activities of avian egg components. *Biochimica et Biophysica Acta 16*: 404.

U.S. Dept. Agric. 1967. Regulations governing the grading of shell eggs and United States standards, grades, and weight classes for shell eggs, *Federal Register Title 7*, Ch. 1, Subchapter C, Part 56, July 15.

Warner, R. C., and I. Weber. 1953. The metal combining properties of conalbumin. *J. Am. Chem. Soc. 75*: 5094.

Watt, B. K., and A. L. Merrill. 1963. Composition of foods—raw, processed, prepared, *U.S.D.A. Agric. Handbook No. 8*.

Wilcke, H. L. 1938. Recent developments in studies of interior egg quality. *U.S. Egg and Poultry Mag. 44*: 16.

Woolley, D. W., and L. G. Longsworth. 1942. Isolation of an antibiotin factor from egg white. *J. Biol. Chem. 142*: 285.

Young, E. G. 1937. On the separation and characterization of the proteins of egg white. *J. Biol. Chem. 120*: 1.

FUNCTIONAL PERFORMANCE OF EGGS

Bailey, M. I. 1935. Foaming of egg white. *Ind. Eng. Chem. 27*: 973.

Barmore, M. A. 1934. The influence of chemical and physical factors on egg-white foams. *Colo. Agr. Expt. Sta. Tech. Bull. 9*, Fort Collins, Colo.

Barmore, M. A. 1936. The influence of various factors, including altitude, in the production of angel food cake. *Colo. Expt. Sta. Tech. Bull. 15*, Fort Collins, Colo.

Carney, R. I. 1938. Determination of stability of beaten egg albumen. *Food Inds. 10*: 77.

Cotterill, O. J., G. M. Amick, B. A. Kluge, and V. C. Rinard. 1963. Some factors affecting the performance of egg white in divinity candy. *Poultry Sci. 42*: 218.

Dizmang, V. R., and G. Sunderlin. 1933. The effect of milk on the whipping qualities of egg white. *U.S. Egg and Poultry Mag. 39* (11): 18.

Dubois, D. K. 1959. Wheat starch, a key to better cakes. *Bakers' Digest 33* (12): 38.

Everson, G. J., and H. J. Souders. 1957. Composition and nutritive importance of eggs. *J. Am. Dietetic Assoc. 33*: 1244.

Farrand, E. S. 1957. Observations on the aerating properties of egg and the mass production of cakes. *Chem. and Ind. No. 17, April 27*: 500.

Felt, S. A., K. Longree, and A. M. Briant. 1956. Instability of meringued pies. *J. Am. Dietetic Assoc. 32*: 710.

Forsythe, R. H., and D. H. Bergquist. 1951. The effect of physical treatments on some properties of egg white. *Poultry Sci. 30*: 302.

Gillis, J. N., and N. K. Fitch. 1956. Leakage of baked soft-meringue topping. *J. Home Econ. 48*: 703.

Grewe, E., and A. M. Child. 1930. The effect of acid potassium tartrate as an ingredient in angel cake. *Cereal Chem. 7*: 245.

Hanning, F. M. 1945. Effect of sugar or salt upon denaturation produced by beating and upon the ease of formation and the stability of egg white foams. *Iowa State Coll. J. Sci. 20*: 10.

Hard, M. M., J. V. Spencer, R. S. Locke, and M. H. George. 1963. A comparison of different methods of preserving shell eggs. 2. Effect on functional properties. *Poultry Sci. 42*: 1085.

Henry, W. C., and A. D. Barbour. 1933. Beating properties of egg white. *Ind. Eng. Chem. 25*: 1054.

Hester, E. E., and C. J. Personius. 1949. Factors affecting the beading and leakage of soft meringues. *Food Technol. 3*: 236.

Johnston, F. A. 1956. Iron content of eggs. *J. Am. Dietetic Assoc. 32*: 644.

King, F. B., E. F. Whiteman, and W. G. Rose. 1936a. Cake making quality of eggs as related to some factors in egg production. *Cereal Chem. 13*: 803.

King, F. B., H. P. Morris, and E. F. Whiteman. 1936b. Some methods and apparatus used in measuring the quality of egg for cake making. *Cereal Chem. 13*: 37.

Kline, L., T. Sonoda, H. L. Hanson, J. H. Mitchell, Jr., 1953. Relative chemical, functional, and organoleptic stabilities of acidified and glucose-free whole egg powders. *Food Technol. 7*: 456.

Lepeschkin, W. W. 1922. The heat coagulation of proteins. *Biochem. J. 16*: 678.

Longree, K., J. C. White, and B. V. Sison. 1962. Time-temperature relationships of souffles. *J. Am. Dietetic Assoc. 41*: 107.

MacDonnell, L. R., R. E. Feeney, H. L. Hanson, A. Campbell, and T. F. Sugihara. 1955. The functional properties of the egg white proteins. *Food Technol. 9*: 49.

McKellar, D. M. B., and W. J. Stadelman. 1955. A method for measuring volume and drainage of egg white foams. *Poultry Sci. 34*: 455.

Meehan, J. J., T. F. Sugihara, and L. Kline. 1961. Relation between internal egg quality stabilization methods and the peeling difficulty. *Poultry Sci. 40*: 1430.

Meehan, J. J., T. F. Sugihara, and L. Kline. 1962. Relationships between shell egg handling factors and egg product properties. I. Egg white damage at moderate to elevated shell egg holding temperatures. *Poultry Sci. 41*: 892.

Miller, E. L., and G. E. Vail. 1943. Angel food cakes made from fresh and frozen egg whites. *Cereal Chem. 20*: 528.

Platt, W., and P. D. Kratz. 1933. Measuring and recording some characteristics of test sponge cakes. *Cereal Chem. 10*: 73.

Pyke, W. E., and G. Johnson. 1940. Preparing and baking yellow sponge cake at different altitudes. *Colo. Agr. Expt. Sta. Tech. Bull. 27.*

Pyke, W. E. 1941. Factors the baker should consider in preparing the yellow sponge cake. *Cereal Chem. 18:* 92.

Salwin, H., I. Bloch, and J. H. Mitchell, Jr. 1953. Dehydrated stabilized egg. Importance and determination of pH. *Food Technol. 7:* 447.

Schaible, J. J., J. A. Davidson, and S. L. Bandemer. 1944. The iron contents of whites and yolks of eggs from hens fed various iron supplements. *Poultry Sci. 23:* 441.

Schaible, P. J., and S. L. Bandemer. 1946. Composition of fresh and storage eggs from hens fed cottonseed and non-cottonseed rations. III. Iron content. *Poultry Sci. 25:* 451.

Sechler, C., L. O. Maharg, and M. Mangel. 1959. The effect of household table salt on the whipping quality of egg white solids. *Food Research 24:* 198.

Slosberg, H. M., H. L. Hanson, G. F. Stewart, and B. Lowe. 1948. Factors influencing the effects of heat treatment on the leavening power of egg white. *Poultry Sci. 27:* 294.

Swanson, E. L. 1933. Egg whites and sugar crystals, *U.S. Egg and Poultry Mag. 39* (9): 32.

Tinkler, C. K., and M. C. Soar. 1920. The formation of ferrous sulphide in eggs during cooking. *Biochem. J. (London) 14:* 114.

EGG PRODUCTS: PROCESSING AND STORAGE

Ayres, J. C., and G. F. Stewart. 1947. Removal of sugar from raw egg white by yeast before drying. *Food Technol. 1:* 519.

Ayres, J. C., and H. H. Slosberg. 1949. Destruction of Salmonella in egg albumen. *Food Technol. 3:* 180.

Banwart, G. J., and J. C. Ayres. 1956. The effect of high temperature storage on the content of salmonella and on the functional properties of dried egg white. *Food Technol. 10:* 68.

Beloian, A., and G. C. Schlosser. 1963. Adequacy of cook procedures for the destruction of salmonellae. *Am. J. Public Health 53:* 782.

Bennion, E. B., J. R. Hawthorne, and E. C. Bate-Smith. 1942. Beating and baking properties of dried eggs. *J. Soc. Chem. Ind. (London) 61:* 31.

Bergquist, D. H. 1964. Eggs. In *Food Dehydration II. Products and Technology.* W. B. Van Arsdel, and M. J. Copley, eds. Ch. 21, 652–693.

Brooks, J., and J. R. Hawthorne. 1943. Dried eggs: IV, Addition of carbohydrates to egg pulp before drying. *J. Soc. Chem. Ind. (London) 62:* 165.

Carlin, A. F., and J. C. Ayres. 1951. Storage studies on yeast fermented dried egg white. *Food Technol. 5:* 172.

Carlin, A. F., and J. C. Ayres. 1953. Effect of removal of glucose by enzyme treatment on the whipping properties of dried albumen. *Food Technol. 7:* 268.

Carlin, A. F., J. C. Ayres, and P. G. Homeyer. 1954. Consumer evaluation of the flavor of angel cakes prepared from yeast-fermented and enzyme-treated dried albumen. *Food Technol.* 8: 580.

Conrad, R. M., G. E. Vail, A. L. Olsen, G. L. Tinklin, J. W. Greene, and C. Wagoner. 1948. Improved dried whole egg products. *Kansas Agr. Expt. Sta. Tech. Bull. 64.*

Dawson, E. H., D. E. Shank, J. M. Linn, and E. A. Wood. 1945. Effect of storage on flavor and cooking quality of spray-dried eggs. *U.S. Egg and Poultry Mag.* 51: 154.

Forsythe, R. H. 1953. Sugar removal from egg white solids. *Poultry Processing and Marketing, 59 (3)*: 17.

Forsythe, R. H. 1957. Some factors affecting the use of eggs in the food industry. *Cereal Science Today* 2: 211.

Forsythe, R. H. 1960. Eggs. In *Bakery Technology and Engineering*, S. A. Matz, ed. Avi Publ. Corp., Westport, Conn., Ch. 7, 188.

Forsythe, R. H. 1963. Chemical and physical properties of eggs and egg products. *Cereal Science Today* 8: 309.

Forsythe, R. H. 1964. Recent advances in egg processing technology and egg products. *Bakers Digest 38* (5): 54.

Hanson, H. L., B. Lowe, and G. F. Stewart. 1947. Pasteurization of liquid egg products: V. The effect on performance in custards and sponge cakes. *Poultry Sci.* 26: 277.

Hawthorne, J. R., and E. B. Bennion. 1942. Influence of temperature on the beating and baking properties of spray-dried egg. *J. Soc. Chem. Ind. (London) 61*: 151.

Joslin, R. B., and B. E. Proctor. 1954. Some factors affecting the whipping characteristics of dried whole egg powders. *Food Technol.* 8: 150.

Kline, L., and T. T. Sonoda. 1951. Role of glucose in the storage deterioration of whole egg powder. I. Removal of glucose from the whole egg melange by yeast fermentation before drying. *Food Technol.* 5: 90.

Kline, L., J. E. Gegg, and T. T. Sonoda. 1951a. Role of glucose in the storage deterioration of whole egg powder. II. A browning reaction involving glucose and cephalin in dried whole eggs. *Food Technol.* 5: 181.

Kline, L., H. L. Hanson, T. T. Sonoda, J. E. Gegg, R. E. Feeney, and H. Lineweaver. 1951b. Role of glucose in the storage deterioration of whole egg powder. III. Effect of glucose removal before drying on organoleptic, baking, and chemical changes. *Food Technol.* 5: 323.

Kline, L., T. Sonoda, H. L. Hanson, J. H. Mitchell, Jr. 1953. Relative chemical, functional, and organoleptic stabilities of acidified and glucose-free whole egg powders. *Food Technol.* 7: 456.

Kline, L., T. T. Sonoda, and H. L. Hanson. 1954. Comparisons of the quality and stability of whole egg powders desugared by the yeast and enzyme methods. *Food Technol.* 8: 343.

Kline, L., T. F. Sugihara, and J. J. Meehan. 1964. Properties of yolk-containing solids with added carbohydrates. *J. Food Sci. 29*: 693.

Kline, L., T. F. Sugihara, M. L. Bean, and K. Ijichi. 1965. Heat pasteurization of raw liquid egg white. *Food Technol. 19*: 105.

Kothe, H. J. 1953. *Egg white composition.* U.S. Patent No. 2,637,654.

Miller, C., and A. R. Winter. 1950. The functional properties and bacterial content of pasteurized and frozen whole eggs. *Poultry Sci. 29*: 88.

Miller, C., and A. R. Winter. 1951. Pasteurized frozen whole egg and yolk for mayonnaise production. *Food Research 16*: 43.

Mink, L. D. 1939. *Egg material treatment.* U.S. Patent No. 2,183,516.

Miyahara, T., and D. Bergquist. 1961. Modern egg solids for the baker. I. Use of egg white solids. *Bakers Digest 35* (1): 52.

Mohammad, A., H. Fraenkel-Conrat, and H. S. Olcott. 1949. The "browning" reaction of proteins with glucose. *Arch. Biochem. 24*: 157.

Moran, T. 1925. Effect of low temperature on hen eggs. *Proc. Roy. Soc. (London) 98B*: 436.

Palmer, H. H., K. Ijichi, S. L. Cimino, and H. Roff. 1969a. Salted egg yolks. I. Viscosity and performance of pasteurized and frozen samples. *Food Technol. 23*: 1480.

Palmer, H. H., K. Ijichi, H. Roff, and S. Redfern. 1969b. Sugared egg yolks: Effects of pasteurization and freezing on viscosity and performance. *Food Technol. 23*: 1486.

Palmer, H. H., K. Ijichi, and H. Roff. 1970. Partial reversal of gelation in thawed egg yolk products. *Food Technol. 24*: 403.

Pinney, C. F. 1960. Use of dry egg solids in baked foods. *Proc. 36th Annual Meeting,* Am. Soc. Bakery Engineers, 281.

Stewart, G. F., and R. W. Kline. 1941. Dried-egg albumen: I. Solubility and color denaturation. *Proc. Inst. Food Technol.* p. 48.

Sugihara, T. F., K. Ijichi, and L. Kline. 1966. Heat pasteurization of liquid whole egg. *Food Technol. 20*: 1076.

Thomas, A. W., and M. I. Bailey. 1933. Gelation of frozen egg magna. *Ind. Eng. Chem. 25*: 669.

U.S. Dept. Agric. 1969. *Egg Pasteurization Manual,* ARS 74–48.

CHAPTER 10

Milk and Milk Products

MARY PALUMBO

In food preparation, milk is used in many ways and combined with many other foods. Butter and all the different types of cheese are made from it. Meat, vegetables, and cereals may be cooked in it. It is used as a basis for many sauces, which may be combined with eggs, meats, or vegetables. It is used in puddings and in frozen desserts, for soups and for drinks like cocoa and coffee; it is combined with cereals; and it is used in combination with many foods, as in custards, cakes, and bread. One of its important uses is as a food beverage.

Milk from different animals is used for food, but in this country unless the source of the milk is mentioned, it is understood to be cow's milk.

COMPOSITION OF MILK

Numerous studies have been conducted on the composition of milk, as men have attempted to assess its nutritive value, to solve problems in the manufacture of various dairy products, and to understand the role of milk in various prepared food products. A wide array of constituents has been revealed; it is probable that others await discovery. Detailed compilations of the constituents of cow's milk and their concentrations have been made by Jenness and Patton (1959) and McKenzie (1967), but the average gross composition may be summarized as follows: water, 87 percent; fat, 3.9 percent; lactose, 4.9 percent; protein, 3.5 percent; and ash (minerals), 0.7 percent (Watt and Merrill, 1963).

Like many biologically produced foodstuffs, milk varies considerably in composition. These variations are of practical interest, for marketing and manufacturing reasons, as well as of academic interest. The widest variation is in fat content, with protein second. Jenness and Patton (1959) and Corbin and Whittier (1965) have summarized the sources of variations.

(a) Inherited variations. The different breeds of dairy cattle have rather pronounced and characteristic differences in the composition of the milk they produce (Table 1). There are also variations between individual cows within a breed. It appears that the quantity of each constituent (fat, proteins, and lactose) synthesized by the mammary tissue depends to some extent on separately inherited factors.

(b) Nutrition of the cow. The feed of the cow affects the gross composition of milk only slightly, although the concentrations of such minor constituents as vitamin A, carotene, iodine, and some trace metals are decidedly affected.

(c) Seasonal variations and effect of temperature. The fat content of milk shows a pronounced seasonal trend, being higher in winter than in summer. The protein content follows the same trend. Environmental temperatures above 85° F and below 40° F tend to result in increased fat content.

(d) Age of cow. The fat content of milk tends to decline slightly with advancing age.

(e) Stage of lactation. The greatest changes occur at the beginning and end of the period. Colostrum contains more mineral salts, total protein, casein, serum protein, and less lactose, than normal milk.

(f) Disease. Infections of the udder (mastitis) cause a lowering of the concentrations of fat, solids-not-fat, lactose, and casein, and an increasing of serum protein and chloride contents.

(g) Milking procedure. The fat content of milk increases continuously during the milking process.

Different analytical methods frequently influence reported values of gross composition. For example, fat is determined either volumetrically as in the Babcock method or gravimetrically as in the Mojonnier procedure. In the Babcock method, the fat is released from the emulsifying protein by treatment with concentrated sulfuric acid, and the percent fat measured directly in specially calibrated bottles. The Mojonnier procedure involves extraction of the lipid, evaporation of the solvent, and weighing of the residue, all under standardized conditions. There are recognized systematic differences in results obtained by these two methods. Most workers have found that the Babcock fat test is 0.05 to 0.10 percent higher than the Mojonnier result (Jenness and Patton, 1959).

CONSTITUENTS OF MILK

Proteins

Milk contains a number of protein components that differ in composition and properties. The names given to these components have evolved.

TABLE 1.   Composition of Milk of Various Breeds of Dairy Cattle[a]

Breed	Number of Cows	Number of Samples	Average Composition (Percent)				
			Fat	Protein[b]	Lactose[c]	Ash	Total Solids
Holstein	19	268	3.55	3.42	4.86	0.68	12.50
Brown Swiss	17	428	4.01	3.61	5.04	0.73	13.41
Ayrshire	14	208	4.14	3.58	4.69	0.68	13.11
Jersey	15	199	5.18	3.86	4.94	0.70	14.69
Guernsey	16	321	5.19	4.02	4.91	0.74	14.87

[a] Data of Overman et al. (1939).
[b] Total $N \times 6.38$.
[c] Calculated by difference.

gradually as new criteria of purity and methods of separation were applied to the proteins. For an appreciation of the problems of protein nomenclature and the rapid development of our knowledge of the milk proteins, reading of the reports of the Committee on Milk Protein Nomenclature, Classification, and Methodology, of the American Dairy Science Association, is suggested (Jenness et al., 1956; Brunner et al., 1960; Thompson et al., 1965; and Rose et al., 1970).

Milk proteins are generally first subdivided into two groups, the casein fraction, which coagulates in natural souring and with rennet, and the whey or serum protein fraction, which remains after removal of the casein. The casein fraction (referred to as whole casein) is a heterogeneous group of phosphoproteins. It can be subdivided into α-, β-, and γ-caseins, based on electrophoretic mobility under standard conditions. Whole casein contains about 66 percent α-, 29 percent β-, and 5 percent γ-casein (Corbin and Whittier, 1965). α-Casein is itself a complex mixture of proteins with differing functional properties. It includes α_s-caseins, which are coagulated by calcium ion, and ϰ-casein, which is not calcium-sensitive. α_s-Caseins are stabilized in milk by the protective action of ϰ-casein (Waugh and von Hippel, 1956). The whey proteins include β-lactoglobulin, α-lactalbumin, the immune globulins, blood serum albumin, a number of enzymes, proteose-peptones, and some minor proteins of unknown function. Identification and characterization of the milk proteins have been further complicated by the fact, only recently recognized (Aschaffenburg and Drewry, 1957), that several of these proteins exist in more than one genetic variant. That is, two or more forms of the protein exist, differing slightly in amino acid composition, the secretion of which is controlled genetically. A given cow may produce either one or two forms of a particular protein.

Caseins

In order to understand the behavior of the caseins, one must have some knowledge of the characteristics of the component proteins as well as an understanding of the physical-chemical state of these proteins in milk (see Chapter 3). There are, of course, some very large gaps in our information in both these categories, but great strides have been made in recent years.

The largest casein component is α_s-casein, which constitutes 45–55 percent of the skim-milk protein. It has a molecular weight of about 23,000 (Schmidt et al., 1967) and is composed of α_{s_1}-, α_{s_2}- and α_{s_3}-caseins. α_{s_1}-Casein, the principal component, exists in four genetic variants, designated A, B, C, and D (Rose et al., 1970). In solution at about pH 6.5, the α_{s_1}-casein monomer or single unit is roughly spherical in shape (Payens, 1966) and has a random coil configuration (Kresheck, 1965). It tends to associate to form polymers of at least six subunits, probably by hydrophobic bonding (Payens and Schmidt, 1965).

$\varkappa$-Casein, the calcium-insensitive component of α-casein, is a carbohydrate-containing protein with a monomer molecular weight of around 19,000 (Woychik et al., 1966). At neutral pH values, it forms polymers that are insensitive to calcium ion and to changes in temperature (Waugh and von Hippel, 1956). These probably exist as long rods or randomly coiled threads in solution (Payens, 1966). As mentioned previously, $\varkappa$-casein has the ability to stabilize α_s-casein against calcium ion.

β-Casein has a molecular weight of about 25,000 at 4° C, where it exists as a monomer (Payens and van Markwijk, 1963). As the temperature is increased, it polymerizes strongly; at 8.5° C, a polymer consists of about 22 subunits; at 13.5° C, it is much larger. Like $\varkappa$-casein, β-casein polymers exist as extended rods or randomly coiled threads. Kresheck (1965) found no evidence of helical content. β-Casein is precipitated by calcium ion at pH 7 only at temperatures of 37° C or higher. It occurs in a number of genetic variants (Rose et al., 1970).

γ-Casein has the lowest phosphorus content and the highest sulfur content of any of the caseins. Whole γ-casein is composed of pure γ-casein (which occurs in several polymorphs) and three other minor proteins, designated R, S, and TS caseins (Rose et al., 1970).

Casein exists in milk primarily in the form of rather large colloidal particles usually called micelles. These are complexes of protein and salt ions, principally calcium and phosphorus. The size of the casein micelles ranges from about 40 to 300 mμ, although a few larger particles may be found in some milks (Shimmin and Hill, 1964). This corresponds very approximately to particle weights of 1×10^6 to 3×10^9. Together with the fat globules, the micelles give to milk its opalescent or "milky" appearance. The structure of the casein micelles and their interactions with nonmicellar proteins and with milk salts constitute one of the central problems in milk-protein research.

From observations of the shape and association behavior of the caseins in pure solutions and observations of the properties of naturally occurring micelles (Waugh and Noble, 1965), several models of the casein micelle have been proposed. These are reviewed by Rose (1969). These models have in common the essential components α_s-casein, $\varkappa$-casein, and calcium ion, but differ in the nature and extent of β-casein incorporation and in the type of bonding between the casein and calcium phosphate.

The stability of colloidal casein micelles is very important in the manufacture and storage of milk products. To make cheese, it is necessary to destabilize the micelles. Maintenance or recovery of colloid stability is essential for the production and marketing of all beverage milk products.

Whey Proteins

Around 1900, it was discovered that the protein remaining in solution after removal of the casein could be separated into two fractions in half-saturated ammonium sulfate or saturated magnesium sulfate solutions. The fraction insoluble in such solutions was designated "lactoglobulin," and the soluble fraction "lactalbumin." Rowland (1938) observed that if milk is heated, about 80 percent of the whey proteins are changed so that they can be precipitated (along with the casein) by acidification to pH 4.6. He considered that this 80 percent represents "lactoglobulin" and "lactalbumin," and that the remaining 20 percent is a separate protein to which he applied the name "proteose-peptone." The Rowland analytical scheme is still in use, although milk-protein chemists are now discontinuing its terminology. The terms "lactalbumin" and "lactoglobulin" have largely disappeared from the literature as more has been learned about their component proteins. For a description of the composition of these classical fractions, see Jenness et al. (1956). For our purpose, it is sufficient to say that they should not be confused with the "pure" proteins, α-lactalbumin and β-lactoglobulin. The nature of the proteins in the proteose-peptone fraction has not been clearly established.

The largest component of the whey proteins is β-lactoglobulin. Among the milk proteins, β-lactoglobulin has been subjected to the most thorough study, and hence its behavior is best understood. A summary of its chemical and physical properties may be found in McKenzie (1967) and Timasheff (1964). It is very slightly soluble at its isoelectric point (pH 5.3) in the complete absence of salt, but is solubilized by either small concentrations of neutral salt or by changes in pH. Thus, because of the solubilizing effect of milk salts, β-lactoglobulin is not precipitated with casein when acid is added to milk. β-Lactoglobulin contains most of the cysteine, and thus most of the free sulfhydryl (-SH) groups, of milk. The importance of these will be seen when the effects of heat on milk are discussed. This protein exists in three genetic variants—β-lacto-globulins A, B, and C—which differ considerably in properties (Aschaffenburg, 1965). β-Lactoglobulin A has an isoionic point[1] of 5.35; β-lactoglobulin B, 5.45 (Tanford and Nozaki, 1959). A is less soluble than B, and more stable to heat (Bhattacharya et al., 1963; Gough and Jenness, 1962). Both forms have a monomer molecular weight of about 18,000, but their predominant form at moderate concentration near the isoionic point is the dimer, with a molecular weight of 36,000. At pH 4.6 and low temperature, β-lactoglobulin A undergoes octomerization (four dimers associate) to a much greater extent than variants B or C. This property appears to be associated with one extra aspartic acid unit per monomer (Timasheff, 1964).

α-Lactalbumin, the protein of second greatest concentration in whey, shows a more complicated set of molecular habits, reviewed by Timasheff (1964) and McKenzie (1967). It has a molecular weight of 16,200 and an isoelectric point of 5.1. Its tendency to reactions such as ion-binding, association, and polymerization are more marked on the acid side of the isoelectric point than on the alkaline side. Herskovits and Mescanti (1965) have determined the optical rotatory properties of α-lactalbumin. From these data it appears that the native protein has an appreciable content of α-helix. Recently, a biological function of α-lactalbumin has been discovered; it is one of two proteins required for the lactose synthetase enzyme (Ebner and Brodback, 1968).

When skim milk is heated at 95 to 100° C for 30 minutes and then adjusted to pH 4.6 by addition of acid, most of the whey proteins precipitate with the casein, leaving the "proteose-peptone" fraction in solution. Larson and Rolleri (1955) identified by moving boundary electrophoresis three components designated 3, 5, and 8, of increasing mobility, that appeared to be the "proteose-peptones." A number of workers have studied proteins in this group, and their work is reviewed by Groves (1969) and McKenzie (1967). Since components 5 and 8 are

---

[1] The isoionic point is the pH at which the number of acidic groups ionized is equal to the number of basic groups in the cationic form. It is the same as the isoelectric point only if there is no binding of small ions (other than protons).

phosphoglycoproteins found in micellar casein as well as in the serum, Brunner and Thompson (1961) suggested that they should be classified as caseins. At this point, one begins to understand the limitations of such classification systems.

The immunoglobulins, sometimes referred to as euglobulins and pseudoglobulins (differentiation is based on their solubility in water) make up the antibody fraction of milk. They are present in much higher concentrations in colostrum than in normal milk. Some of their chemical and physical properties have been determined by Murthy and Whitney (1958).

The serum albumin of milk is apparently identical to the bovine serum albumin of blood (Polis, Shmukler, and Custer, 1950). Other minor, nonenzymatic proteins of milk include lactollin (Groves, Basch, and Gordon, 1962) and an iron-binding red protein (Gordon, Groves, and Basch, 1962).

A number of enzymes are normal constituents of milk. Although it is sometimes difficult to ascertain which are native constituents of milk and which are of bacterial origin, nineteen types of enzymes have been reported to be found in normal milk (Shahani, 1966). The lipases have been of particular interest to dairy chemists because of the flavors of the fatty acids that they liberate. In milk or butter, these flavors are very undesirable; on the other hand, they may be important in the development of desirable flavors in some cheeses. The number of lipases that occur in milk is not known, but there is accumulating evidence that more than one lipase is present in all raw milk. The principal lipase of milk is a minor protein of the casein complex, found associated with ϰ-casein (Fox, Yaguchi, and Tarassuk, 1967). Lipolysis will be discussed further in connection with milk flavor.

Several types of phosphatases have been reported in milk, but the most thoroughly studied is an alkaline phosphatase that is destroyed by pasteurization treatments. The presence of phosphatase in pasteurized milk therefore indicates either improper pasteurization or postpasteurization contamination with raw milk. Testing milk for phosphatase activity for quality control purposes has been a common practice for 30 years.

Another enzyme that may have particular technical significance is xanthine oxidase. Evidence has been found that it may be involved in the keeping and baking quality of dry milk (Greenbank et al., 1954) and that it can cause a spontaneously oxidized flavor in milk (Aurand and Woods, 1959). However, these relationships are not unquestioned. Hwang, Ramachandran, and Whitney (1967) observed that milk contains both activators and inhibitors of this enzyme.

In addition to lipases, milk also contains amylases and protease.

Shahani (1966) has discussed probable reasons why these and other enzymes of milk do not work spontaneously on their substrates and thus cause rapid deterioration.

Another minor protein fraction of milk is the protein portion of the "membrane" that surrounds the fat globule. This membrane, or interfacial layer, will be discussed further under the subject of the structure of fat globules. The lipid-free protein has been subdivided into two fractions based on solubility in dilute salt solution. The insoluble protein can be solubilized by disulfide-degrading agents (Harwalker and Brunner, 1965). The soluble protein is a mucoprotein, probably heterogeneous, containing higher levels of sialic acid, hexose, and hexosamine than any of the major proteins of milk (Jackson, Coulson, and Clark, 1962).

Lipids

Milk fat is important from several points of view: economics, since it still plays a significant role in determining the price of milk and milk products; nutrition, because it serves as a carrier for the fat-soluble vitamins and contains significant amounts of linoleic and arachidonic acids; and flavor and texture, because these characteristics of milk fat greatly influence consumer acceptance of most dairy products.

Chemical Composition

Milk fat consists chiefly of triglycerides of fatty acids (Table 2). The fatty acid composition of the lipids of cow's milk is shown in Table 3. Variations in this composition may be caused by the same factors that affect general milk composition (see Kurtz, 1965). In general, milk fat is characterized by a relatively high proportion of short-chain fatty acids that are very significant in flavors and off-flavors of milk and milk products. The shortest member, butyric acid, is unique to milk fat. The manner in which the fatty acids are distributed in the triglycerides has not been completely resolved (Kurtz, 1965), but it appears to be of great importance with regard to the physical properties of milk fat. Randomization of the fatty acid distribution consistently results in hardening of the fat (deMan, 1964).

Physical Structure

Most of the fat in milk is in the form of small globules, which average approximately 1 to 5 μ in diameter. These globules are stabilized by a layer or layers of phospholipid and protein that is commonly called the fat-globule membrane. (The use of the word "membrane" to describe this interfacial layer is questioned by some and defended by others, but recent evidence seems to support its use. Since it is generally accepted

TABLE 2. The Lipids of Milk[a]

Class of Lipid	Range of Occurrence (Percent)
Triglycerides	98–99
Diglycerides	0.25–0.48
Monoglycerides	0.016–0.038
Phospholipids	0.2–1.0
Sterols	0.25–0.40
Free fatty acids	0.10–0.44
Cerebrosides	0.013–0.066
Squalene	0.007
Waxes	trace
Fat-soluble vitamins	0.003
Vitamin A	7.0–8.5 µg/g fat
Carotenoids	8.0–10.0 µg/g fat
Vitamin E	2–50 µg/g fat
Vitamin D	trace
Vitamin K	trace

[a] From Jenness and Patton (1959) and Kurtz (1965).

TABLE 3. Fatty Acid Composition of Milk Fat[a,b]

Fatty Acid		
Common Name	Carbon Atoms: Double Bonds	Percent of Total Acids
Butyric	4:0	2.79
Caproic	6:0	2.34
Caprylic	8:0	1.06
Capric	10:0	3.04
Lauric	12:0	2.87
Myristic	14:0	8.94
Pentadecylic	15:0	0.79
Palmitic	16:0	23.8
Margaric	17:0	0.70
Stearic	18:0	13.2
Palmitoleic	16:1	1.79
Oleic	18:1	29.6
Linoleic	18:2	2.11
Linolenic	18:3	0.50
	18:2 c,t conj[c]	0.63

[a] Data from Herb et al. (1962).

[b] Arbitrarily omitted from the table are those acids that constitute less than 0.5 percent of the total fatty acids. Those omitted are odd-numbered acids, branched chain acids, and acids of 20–24 carbon atoms with 0–4 double bonds.

[c] *cis-trans* conjugated.

to mean the materials at the fat/plasma interface, it will be so used here.) Brunner (1965) has discussed the isolation and the chemical and physical characteristics of the fat-globule membrane in detail. The composition of this material has been reasonably well elucidated, although the characterization of the protein fraction is far from complete. However, the organization of these components in the membrane is not completely understood. The types of forces influencing the orientation and interaction of lipids and proteins at this interface are discussed by Gurd (1960) and Brunner (1965). King (1955) has suggested a structure for the fat-globule membrane in which phospholipid molecules are oriented with the hydrocarbon chains extending into the fat phase and the polar groups extending toward the aqueous phase. Adsorbed onto this surface is a layer of protein with most of its polar groups oriented toward the polar phospholipid groups. Another layer of protein might then be adsorbed onto this, with the hydrophobic groups oriented to the hydrophobic (nonpolar) groups of the first layer. The hydrophilic side chains of this second layer of protein would then extend into the aqueous phase. Morton (1954) proposed that the fat-globule surface is covered by an adsorbed layer of cytoplasmic protein, to which is adsorbed a concentrated layer of microsomes (lipoprotein particles). Hood and Patton (1958) obtained electron photomicrographs that they believe support the existence of a lipoprotein subunit structure of the membrane; that is, they visualize distinct lipoprotein entities packed on the surface of the fat globule.

The high-melting triglycerides that King visualized as oriented next to the phospholipid layer are usually referred to as part of the membrane. However, experiments of Vasic and deMan (1966) indicate that this is due to preferential crystallization at the membrane-fat interface at temperatures below the melting point of the fat phase. Since most methods of isolation of membrane material require cooling to permit churning (see the section on churning), these high-melting triglycerides would be crystallized on the internal surface of the membrane.

Lactose

The characteristic carbohydrate of milk is lactose, although trace amounts of glucose, galactose, and other sugars are present. Sources of lactose other than milk are rare, and lactose is present in the milk of nearly all species of mammals (Nickerson, 1965). The structure and some of the properties of lactose have been discussed in Chapter 1.

Because of its relatively low solubility (determined by Whittier, 1944 to be 21.6 g/100 g water at 25° C), the crystallization properties of lactose are of particular importance in the manufacture of several milk products, including ice cream, sweetened condensed milk, and nonfat dry milk. Lactose exists in two isomeric forms, designated α and β (see Chapter 1). At 20° C and rotational equilibrium, a lactose solution is composed of 62 percent β-form and 38 percent α-form. The β-form is much more soluble than the α-form, and therefore at temperatures below 93.5° C, it is the α-form that crystallizes first. As the α-form crystallizes out, β-lactose shifts to the α-form to maintain equilibrium conditions. The α-lactose that crystallizes from aqueous solution is the monohydrate (one molecule of water is associated with each lactose molecule). The crystals are hard and not very soluble, so that when placed in the mouth, they feel gritty. This is the origin of the term "sandy" to describe the defect in texture of ice cream, condensed milk, or processed cheese spread that contains perceptible α-hydrate crystals. Crystals that are 10 μ or smaller are not detected in the mouth. The larger the crystals (above 16 μ), the fewer that can be tolerated without affecting texture (Nickerson, 1965).

When milk is dried rapidly, as in the production of nonfat dry milk, the lactose does not crystallize but exists as lactose glass (amorphous lactose). Lactose glass is very hygroscopic, and absorption of moisture dilutes the glass to the stage where molecular orientation is possible and crystallization occurs. The hard α-hydrate crystals cement the milk particles together, producing the lumpiness and caking of milk powder that has not been protected from moisture.

Lactose is also of interest because of its role in the browning of dairy products. This will be discussed under the effects of heat.

Salts

In the broadest sense, the salts of milk include all constituents except hydrogen and hydroxyl ions that are present as ions or in equilibrium with ions. Thus the term includes the proteins and trace elements of milk. However in the usual usage, the term indicates the major salt constituents that are comprised of the chlorides, phosphates, citrates, sulfates, and bicarbonates of sodium, potassium, calcium, and magnesium. The practical importance of these salts is largely a result of their influence on the condition and stability of the proteins, especially the casein fraction. The trace elements, particularly copper and iron, are important in the development of off-flavors in milk and milk products.

Some of the milk salts are present almost entirely in the dissolved state. Others, especially calcium phosphate, are present in amounts that exceed their solubility in the ionic environment of milk serum. These exist partly in solution and partly in colloidal form. In addition, the milk proteins bind ions, mainly cations. Calcium binding is characteristic of casein, but binding of monovalent ions is not negligible, and some magnesium is bound to casein (Pyne, 1962). Calcium binding by β-lactoglobulin is appreciable (Zittle et al., 1957). Binding of polyvalent anions to proteins is also known to occur (Pyne, 1962).

About 31 percent of the total calcium, 65 percent of the magnesium, 53 percent of the inorganic phosphorus (not including the phosphorus of phosphoproteins and phospholipids), and 94 percent of the citrate are present in the serum of milk. These estimates were obtained by analysis of whey and of sera obtained by centrifugation, ultrafiltration, and dialysis of milk (White and Davies, 1958; Davies and White, 1960). The ionic forms in which the soluble salts of milk exist can be calculated approximately from the composition and the dissociation constants of phosphoric, citric, and carbonic acids, after making allowance for the binding of calcium and magnesium to citrate and phosphate as anionic complexes, and to phosphate as undissociated salts. Jenness and Patton (1959) describe such an approach.

The equilibria among the various forms of salts and ions in milk are affected by changes in temperature, pH, and ionic strength. They are thus partly responsible for changes in the conditions of the milk proteins during heating, souring, or concentrating of milk.

The presence of proteins, phosphate, citrate, and carbon dioxide in milk make it evident that milk has some buffering capacity. Quantitative assignment of buffer capacity of these constituents is rather difficult, however, due to the changes of state that occur when the pH is raised or lowered. As the pH is raised, calcium and magnesium precipitate as colloidal phosphates; when the pH is lowered, the colloidal phosphates are solubilized. Since these changes of state are sluggish, the slope of the titration curves and the position of maximum buffering will depend on the speed of titration (Wiley, 1935).

Vitamins and Other Minor Constituents

All of the recognized vitamins may be found in milk, although some are present only in very small quantities. As one would expect, the fat-soluble vitamins are found in the lipid phase, the water-soluble vitamins in the aqueous phase. The carotene in the fat gives milk a somewhat yellow tinge. Riboflavin imparts a greenish-yellow color to whey. The quantities of most of the fat-soluble vitamins in milk are principally dependent on the amounts of these vitamins in the diet of the cow. The amounts of the water-soluble vitamins and vitamin K, on the other hand, are largely, if not entirely, independent of diet, since these are synthesized by bacteria of the cow's rumen or by her tissues (Hartman and Dryden, 1965).

Other minor constituents of milk are reviewed by Corbin and Whittier (1965) and Jenness and Patton (1959). These include nonprotein nitrogenous substances, various organic acids and esters, sugar phosphates, and dissolved gases.

PHYSICAL PROPERTIES OF MILK

Physically, milk is at once a rather dilute emulsion, colloidal dispersion, and true solution. Its physical properties are essentially those of water, modified somewhat by the concentration and state of dispersion of the solid constituents. In the dairy industry, measurements of the physical properties of milk and dairy products are made to obtain data necessary for design of dairy equipment, to determine the concentration of a constituent or group of constituents, or to assess the extent of chemical or physical changes (Jenness, Shipe, and Whitnah, 1965). However, only a few of the physical properties of milk have a distinct bearing on food preparation; the remainder will be treated very briefly.

pH and Acid-Base Equilibria

The principles of acid-base equilibria are discussed in Chapter 1. The pH of milk commonly falls between 6.5 and 6.7 at 25° C. The temperature of measurement is important, because the pH of milk exhibits a greater dependence on temperature than do such buffers as phosphate or phthalate (Jenness et al., 1965). This phenomenon is probably due to insolubilization of calcium phosphate as the temperature is raised and its solution as the temperature is lowered. As fresh milk stands exposed to the air, the loss of carbon dioxide causes a slight decrease in titratable acidity. The buffer action of milk, which has been mentioned previously, is discussed more fully by Jenness and Patton (1959).

Viscosity

The viscosity of milk and milk products is important primarily from the standpoint of consumer acceptance. In the case of evaporated milk, optimum viscosity lies between the extremes of undesirable gelation and a thinness that permits rising of the fat. In normal fluid milk, the following factors appear to influence viscosity: state and concentration of the protein, state and concentration of the fat, temperature of the milk, and age of the milk (Jenness and Patton, 1959). The most significant contributors to the viscosity of milk are casein and the fat globules. Conditions and treatments that affect the stability of casein are important in the viscosity of milk. Such factors are acidity, salt balance, heat treatment, and the action of various enzymes and bacteria. The effect of milk fat depends on such factors as the amount of fat, the size of the globules, and the extent of clustering of the globules. Whitnah et al. (1956) found that homogenization increases the viscosity of milk. The viscosity of pasteurized milk, both homogenized and unhomogenized, increases with age (Jenness and Patton, 1959).

Surface and Interfacial Tension

The surface tension of milk averages about 50 dynes/cm at 20° C (Jenness and Patton, 1959). This may be compared to water, which has a surface tension of 72.75 dynes/cm at that temperature. The important surface-tension depressants of milk are the proteins and lipids. Jenness (in Jenness and Patton, 1959) found the following surface tensions for a number of fractions from the same lot of milk: rennet whey, 51–52; skim milk, 52–52.5; whole milk, 46–47.5; 25 percent cream, 42–45; and sweet cream buttermilk, 39–40 dynes/cm. Thus, the whey proteins and fat globules were significant in reducing surface tension, as were the fat-globule-membrane materials released during churning into buttermilk. The latter are known to be exceedingly surface-active.

Colligative Properties

The colligative properties of milk, those that depend on the number of solute particles present (see Chapter 1), are remarkably constant. The freezing point of milk is its most useful colligative property and therefore has generated the most interest. It is used to determine whether water has been added to the milk. The average freezing point is about $-0.540°$ C, although milk samples from individual cows might exhibit freezing points between -0.525 and $-0.565°$ C (Jenness and Patton, 1959). A freezing depression of less than $0.5335°$ C (that is, a freezing point higher than $-0.5335°$ C) for a pooled milk sample is taken by the Association of Official Agricultural Chemists to indicate watering. The principal contributor to the freezing-point depression of milk is lactose.

Other Physical Properties

Another physical property that has significant practical aspects is the oxidation-reduction potential of milk. This potential is largely the result of milk's oxygen content, and is lowered by bacteria through use of available oxygen as well as production of reducing substances in the course of their metabolism (Jenness and Patton, 1959). Also important in maintaining the potential is ascorbic acid. Heat treatment of milk also lowers the potential. This appears to be attributable largely to the liberation of sulfhydryl groups on denaturation of β-lactoglobulin (Jenness et al., 1965).

The density, electrical conductivity, thermal conductivity, and heat capacity are of interest primarily to manufacturers and are discussed by Jenness et al. (1965).

FUNCTIONAL PROPERTIES OF MILK

Effects of Heat on Milk

Heat is the most important and universal treatment that milk receives during processing and food preparation. A given quantity of milk may receive two or three or more heat treatments before it is consumed. The most obvious of these is pasteurization. The primary purpose of pasteurization is destruction of all pathogenic bacteria and the bulk of the nonpathogenic organisms. It also inactivates certain enzymes that would otherwise cause development of off-flavors. Unpasteurized homogenized milk quickly becomes rancid due to the increased hydrolytic activity of the lipases.

More severe heat treatment is encountered in the production of evaporated and dried milks. Evaporated milk is forewarmed, concentrated by heating under vacuum, and then heat-sterilized. Forewarming is the process of heating whole milk to temperatures of approximately 88 to 100° C before it is introduced into the vacuum pan for condensing. For reasons that are not well understood, forewarming increases the stability of the concentrated milk to subsequent heating. The purpose of heat sterilization of milk is to destroy all microorganisms and their spores; thus, it is a relatively severe heat treatment, about 116° C for 15 minutes. Such pasteurized or evaporated milk may then be combined with other foods and heated again during food preparation.

The changes that occur in milk during heating are complex and interrelated. Heat treatments that are likely to be used in food preparation may cause denaturation of serum proteins and shifts in the salt system, which in turn affect the casein particles. Combination with other foods may also change the ionic environment of the milk proteins, thus affecting their response to heat treatment. More severe heat treatment, such as that encountered in the production of evaporated milk, may cause degradation of casein and lactose.

Effects on the Salts

Some of the shifts in ionic equilibria that are produced by temperature changes are readily reversible; others are only sluggishly reversible; and still others are not reversible at all. Heat accelerates the loss of carbon dioxide from fresh milk. This loss is considered irreversible, and results in an increase in pH and reduction in titratable acidity. Since calcium phosphate becomes less soluble as the temperature is raised, the equilibrium between colloidal and dissolved calcium phosphate shifts towards the colloidal phase, and the concentration of the ions decreases. This change of state is slowly reversed when the milk is held at low temperatures after heating. Since colloidal calcium phosphate occurs in milk primarily as a part of the casein micelle, it may be presumed that the colloidal calcium phosphate that is formed by heat treatment becomes connected in some way (perhaps adsorbed) to the micelles (Jenness and Patton, 1959).

These heat-induced changes in the milk salts produce slight shifts in the pH of the milk, but in opposing directions. Loss of carbon dioxide causes a decrease in acidity, whereas hydrogen ions are liberated by insolubilization of calcium phosphate. The net effect is usually a slight decrease in pH. At temperatures of $100°$ C and above, lactose and casein degradation result in increased acidity of milk. The higher the temperature of heat treatment, the greater is this effect (Jenness and Patton, 1959).

Effects on the Serum Proteins

Some obvious and practical effects result from heat denaturation of the whey proteins. Heat-induced changes in these proteins are directly or indirectly responsible for development of (1) cooked flavor, (2) increased heat stability (forewarming effect), (3) increased resistance to rennet clotting, and (4) improvement of loaf volume of bread made with milk. The degree of dispersion of the serum proteins is not greatly altered after heat treatment; that is, the denatured protein does not precipitate or form large aggregates, although a portion of it will sediment along with casein in the ultracentrifuge (Sullivan et al., 1957). However, if the charge on the molecules is sufficiently reduced by acidification or by addition of salts, the heated serum proteins will precipitate along with the casein. The rate of denaturation increases with increasing temperature. Figure 1 shows the extent of serum protein denaturation at several temperatures when held for varying lengths of time. Heat treatments required for pasteurization are not sufficient to cause noticeable denaturation of serum proteins.

When milk is heated to approximately $74°$ C, even momentarily, a distinct cooked flavor develops. The intensity of the flavor depends on the temperature and duration of heating. The appearance of cooked flavor closely parallels the increase in reactivity of the sulfhydryl groups of the whey proteins, principally β-lactoglobulin. These groups are apparently occluded or bonded in the native protein so as to be relatively unreactive. When the protein is heated sufficiently, it uncoils or

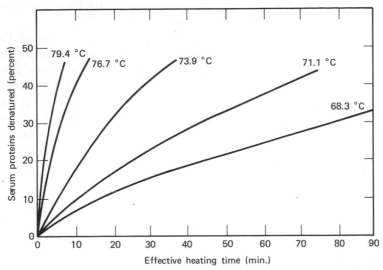

FIGURE 1. Heat denaturation of milk serum proteins in skim milk. (Harland, Coulter, and Jenness, 1952.)

changes in structure so that the sulfhydryl groups are more accessible and more reactive (Jenness and Patton, 1959).

The increase in heat stability of concentrated milk brought about by forewarming is generally thought to be due to denaturation of the serum proteins as well as to favorable changes in the salt system. If the serum proteins are not denatured in the unconcentrated milk, where aggregation is restricted by distance between molecules, their subsequent denaturation during sterilization of the concentrate will result in extensive aggregation (Tumerman and Webb, 1965). In addition, heat denaturation of β-lactoglobulin in the presence of x-casein leads to an association of these two proteins. The occurrence of this complex has been repeatedly demonstrated in pure solutions, but its formation in milk has not been proved at this time (Tessier, Yaguchi, and Rose, 1969). However, β-lactoglobulin does have a distinct effect on the heat stability of the casein micelle at pH 6.5 to 6.9 (Tessier and Rose, 1964).

Heat treatment of milk also affects both its susceptibility to coagulation by rennin and the firmness of the resulting curd. If milk is heated to 65–100° C for 30 minutes, clotting is markedly delayed. Kannan and Jenness (1961) found that this effect is dependent on the presence of β-lactoglobulin. Zittle et al. (1962) demonstrated that the rennin coagulation of x-casein was retarded following heat-induced interaction with β-lactoglobulin. The soft-curd characteristics of heated milk may be due to such a complex, or they may be caused physically by the flocculated serum proteins (Jenness and Patton, 1959).

When incorporated into bread, raw milk slackens the volume of the resulting loaf. This effect can be overcome by heat treatment of the milk. The improvement in baking quality produced by heat treatment has been found to parallel approximately, but not exactly, the denaturation of serum proteins. At least three factors seem to be involved in this phenomenon: (1) a deleterious, unknown protein fraction that follows the immune globulins when serum proteins are fractionated (this fraction is inactivated by heat treatment), (2) a deleterious effect of casein, and (3) a deleterious effect of freshly heated β-lactoglobulin due to the active sulfhydryls that it contains (Jenness and Patton, 1959).

Effects on Casein

Ordinary heating of milk in food preparation does not cause any measurable alteration in the structure of casein itself. In fact, the insolubility of "native" casein at the isoelectric point, its sensitivity to coagulation by electrolytes, and its resistance to conventional denaturing processes, have led a number of investigators to regard casein as an inherently denatured protein (Tumerman and Webb, 1965). This is seen as advantageous to its biological role as a source of nutrition for the young of the species: it is susceptible to fairly rapid proteolytic digestion. However, severe heat treatment will cause destabilization of the caseinate particles; the result is gelation or coagulation to form a three-dimensional network entrapping some of the milk serum.

The only known direct effect of heat on casein is actual decomposition with the release of esterified phosphate and hydrolysis of peptide bonds. While it has not been clearly established that such hydrolytic reactions occur during or are responsible for coagulation, considerable evidence exists supporting a relationship. Several investigators have concluded that there is a complex relationship between coagulation of milk and dephosphorylation of casein (Tumerman and Webb, 1965). When heated together with β-lactoglobulin, ϰ-casein forms a complex that affects the stability of casein micelles. This reaction was discussed in the previous section.

The changes in the salt system of milk during heating have a great effect on the stability of casein. This effect also ensues when other foods are combined with milk, thus changing the salt system. Since casein is stabilized primarily by charge rather than by hydration, it is extremely sensitive to any changes in the ionic environment. The general role of salts in precipitating colloids is discussed in Chapter 2. In view of the complexity of the ionic equilibria and protein interactions in milk, it is not surprising that no relationship has been established between the concentration of individual ions and the stability of the casein micelles in milk.

The pH of the system is perhaps the most important single factor in the stability of casein. At pH 7 or higher, casein is not readily coagulated by heat, due to its negative charge. Below pH 6, it coagulates readily. In between these two values, the complicated relations between hydrogen ions, salts (especially polyvalent ions), β-lactoglobulin, and x-casein determine the stability of casein to heat.

Effects on Lactose

The effects of heat on sugar and sugar-protein solutions are discussed in general in Chapter 1. Lactose participates primarily in Maillard-type browning reactions during heat treatment and storage of milk products, but caramelization of the lactose itself occurs under severe heating such as in sterilization (Nickerson, 1965).

Coagulation

The term coagulation is used here to refer both to the formation of a gel from the colloidal milk sol and to flocculation of the proteins, or curdling (see Chapter 3). Both of these situations result from destabilization of the casein micelles, and the exact result will depend on the extent and conditions of destabilization.

Coagulation by Acid or Salts

Casein in milk represents a largely lyophobic colloid stabilized by its negative charge. Removal of this negative charge obviously destabilizes the micelle. The addition of acid sufficient to lower the pH of milk to 5.2–5.3 will cause coagulation. This drop in pH may be caused bacteriologically, by souring, or chemically, by addition of acids or acidic substances such as lemon or tomato juice. The stabilizing negative charge and slight hydration of the micelle may also be removed by addition of large amounts of salts. For example, casein will precipitate from a saturated solution of sodium chloride. Such high concentrations of sodium chloride or any other salt would not normally be found in food systems. However, the destabilizing effect of salts often works in conjunction with other factors, such as heat, to cause coagulation. Salts may be added to a milk-containing system directly, as with table salt, or indirectly, as with sodium chloride and sodium nitrate in cured meat. The general role of salts in precipitating colloids is discussed in Chapter 2.

Coagulation by Heat

As previously stated, ordinary heating of milk in food preparation does not cause coagulation. However, milk is often heated in the presence of other foods that change the ionic environment of the milk proteins, and coagulation may then occur after a very short period of heating. For example, milk may curdle when certain vegetables are cooked in it. This is probably the result of the acids and salts found in the plant tissues and released into the milk during heating.

Meats and fish may also be cooked in milk. Factors that influence the curdling of such a system are the time and temperature of heating, the salt content of the meat, and the pH of the system. Thus curdling is more likely to occur with cured meat than with fresh meat, and with sour milk (or cream) than with fresh milk. The addition of acid ingredients such as prepared mustard or apples also increases the tendency to curdling. Evaporated milk has less tendency to curdle than does fresh milk, probably because of the previous heating as well as the presence of the stabilizer carrageenan. The curdling can be prevented by the addition of sodium bicarbonate to the milk to increase the pH.

When tomatoes are combined with milk to make cream of tomato soup, coagulation may occur. The manner in which the ingredients are combined, the pH of the tomatoes and the milk, and the time and temperature of heating determine whether curdling occurs.

Coagulation by Rennin

Rennet is a salt extract of the stomach of milk-fed calves that contains the enzyme rennin. The coagulation of milk by rennet is a very old process, but it is not entirely understood. By a mechanism as yet unknown, rennin releases from κ-casein a glycomacropeptide—a large peptide that contains most of the carbohydrate portion of the original molecule. This glycomacropeptide is extremely hydrophilic, which might account for the stabilizing properties of κ-casein and for the loss of micelle stability when it is removed from κ-casein by rennin (Nitschmann et al., 1957). The clotting of milk by rennin is a two-step process: first is the specific action of rennin on casein, and second is the formation of a gel or clot by the modified casein (usually called paracasein) and calcium ions in the milk. These two stages, the enzymatic and the nonenzymatic, may be separated by manipulating the calcium ion concentration. If milk is dialyzed to remove the calcium and then treated with rennin, it will not form a clot. Addition of a calcium salt to this system causes very rapid clotting. A third stage of rennin action, the slow proteolysis of all casein components, was discovered by Alais et al. (1953).

Several factors influence the coagulation of milk by rennin: (a) temperature, (b) hydrogen ion concentration, (c) concentration of casein, calcium ion, and calcium phosphate, (d) previous heat treatment of the milk, and (e) other cations present. The optimum temperature of coagulation is about 40–42° C. At this temperature, coagulation occurs most rapidly and gives the firmest clot. There is no coagulation below 10° C or above 65° C. Berridge (1942) was able to separate the effects of temperature on the two stages of coagulation and show that they are not the same. He found that the enzymatic reaction proceeded at a reduced but reasonable rate at 0° C, but no coagulation occurred below 8° C, regardless of the incubation time. The nonenzymatic stage was shown to have a very high temperature coefficient, with the rate of reaction increasing by a factor of 1.3–1.6 per 1° C. The temperature coefficient of the first stage was of the same order of magnitude as that of most chemical reactions; that is, the reaction rate approximately doubled for an increase in temperature of 10° over the temperature range of 0° to 40° C.

Coagulation proceeds faster and the clot is stronger as the pH is lowered from that of milk to about 5.8 (Ernstrom, 1965). The pH affects the activity of the rennin as well as the stability of the caseinate particles. The concentration of casein influences the strength of the gel, since with more particles a firmer structure may be formed. Fat globules, on the other hand, do not form an integral part of the gel and hence weaken it. As mentioned previously, a minimum concentration of calcium ion is needed before gel formation occurs; a large excess does not make the gel stronger, however. Other cations also affect the rate and extent of coagulation; in general, monovalent ions reduce clotting tendencies, and divalent and trivalent cations hasten coagulation (Ernstrom, 1965). The presence of colloidal calcium phosphate is also important in the formation of a smooth gel.

Previous heat treatment of the milk at temperatures over 65° C reduces the speed of coagulation and the strength of the clot when the milk is treated with rennin. This is an example of hysteresis; not only the temperature at which the milk was heated, but also the length of time between heating and addition of rennet affect the coagulability of the milk. This phenomenon is not entirely understood, but it appears to involve an interaction of β-lactoglobulin with the casein micelle (Kannan and Jenness, 1961; Zittle et al., 1962).

Coagulation by Freezing

Milk can be frozen for limited periods of time (3–4 months) without serious adverse effects. The limitation on storage life is usually the stability of the casein, although there is some flavor change as well. If the milk is concentrated before freezing, the tendency of the casein to flocculate on defrosting is more serious and limits the storage life to a shorter period (6–10 weeks). At first the flocculation is reversible with heat and agitation, but with continued storage it becomes irreversible. An interesting finding concerning casein precipitation in frozen milk is its chronological relationship to the crystallization of lactose. A number of studies have shown that the casein sol retains its normal colloidal dispersion until some of the lactose crystallizes. This relationship is discussed by Doan and Keeney (1965).

Properties of the Fat Globules

Creaming

Milk, after it is drawn from the cow, forms a cream layer upon standing. This is, of course, due to the difference in density between the fat globules and the milk serum. However, if the rate of rise of an average fat globule, 3 to 4 μ in diameter, is calculated according to known physical laws,[2] it is clear that other factors must enter into the phenomenon in order for a cream layer to appear on milk in as little as 30 minutes. The principal factor aiding the creaming process is clustering of individual fat globules. These clusters have a larger effective radius, and therefore rise more rapidly than the same fat globules individually. Sharp and Krukovsky (1939) presented evidence that the clustering of fat globules is due to a substance in milk that they called agglutinin. This substance is absorbed on solid or solidifying fat globules. If milk is separated at low temperature, the agglutinating substance appears largely in the cream; if separation is carried out at 122° F, the skim milk is relatively rich in agglutinin. Dunkley and Sommer (1944) established that the agglutinating substance is a protein that is classified as a euglobulin.

The largest cream layer will be found on milk having a high fat content and relatively large fat globules. Other important factors in creaming are the temperature and agitation history of the milk. The

[2] Stokes' law: $V = \dfrac{2gr^2(d_1 - d_2)}{9\eta}$, where

V = Velocity of rise in cm/sec
r = radius of the sphere in cm
d_1 = density of dispersing medium
d_2 = density of the sphere
g = acceleration due to gravity (981 cm sec^{-2})
η = viscosity of the liquid in poises

agglutinating protein is denatured at temperatures only slightly higher than those used for pasteurization. The effect of agitation depends on its intensity and the temperature at which the milk is agitated (Jenness and Patton, 1959).

Most cream is separated mechanically from the milk by centrifugal force. Although the cream can be separated to contain greater or lesser concentrations of fat, usually the fat globules remaining in the skim milk are 2 μ or less in diameter.

Homogenization

Homogenization has become a standard procedure, the purpose of which is the stabilization of the fat emulsion against gravity separation, or creaming. The process involves forcing milk through small apertures under pressure (about 2000–2500 psi), breaking the fat globules up into smaller ones. This results in an increase in fat globule surface area of four- to sixfold. This increased surface area is one of the basic causes of the altered characteristics of homogenized milk. The newly created fat globules adsorb a mixture of proteins from the plasma phase. Jackson and Brunner (1960) reported the presence of high concentrations of casein and lesser quantities of serum proteins at the fat/plasma interface of homogenized milk. The disintegration of the original fat globules is probably achieved by a combination of several mechanisms. Those proposed are (1) shattering by impact, (2) explosion on release of pressure, (3) shearing between layers of liquid under flow, and (4) cavitation, which is explained as the formation of vapor cavities as the milk leaves the homogenizer valve, followed by collapse of the cavities as the milk passes into a region of higher pressure (Jenness and Patton, 1959). The conditions of homogenization, that is, temperature, pressure, and concentration of fat phase, materially affect the size and dispersion of the ensuing fat globules.

The ramifications of the increased dispersion of the lipid phase and of its resurfaced interfacial boundary are many. Homogenized milk is whiter in appearance, blander in flavor, less susceptible to copper-induced oxidative changes, more sensitive to light-induced deterioration, and possessive of greater foaming capacity and lower curd tension than nonhomogenized milk (Brunner, 1965). Above all, the lipid phase exists as a stabilized emulsoid resisting gravity separation. This effect is not only due to the smaller size of the fat globules, but also to their increased effective density and to the greatly reduced tendency of the fat globules to form clusters that are essential to normal creaming of milk.

Most investigators have observed an increase in the viscosity of milk after homogenization. Whitnah et al. (1956) found that the viscosity increase was greater with increasing pressures of homogenization. The surface tension of milk is also increased by homogenization. The causes of these changes are not known.

Whipping

Like most protein solutions, milk foams because the protein tends to concentrate at the air/water interface. Milk foams are quite unstable. Cream, however, can be whipped under proper conditions to a relatively stable foam. This stability arises from the tendency of the fat globules to clump at the air/liquid interface (Rahn, 1932), giving rigidity to the structure. The protein film (which increases the stability of the whipped cream through its surface denaturation at the air/liquid interface), the fat content, the size of the fat particles, the temperature of whipping, the viscosity of the cream, and the addition of sugar are important factors in the whipping of cream.

For a stable foam there must be sufficient protein to form the stabilizing film around the air bubbles. In homogenized cream so much protein is required at the fat/liquid interface that not enough is left in the plasma to stabilize the air bubbles at the liquid/air interface; hence homogenized cream seldom whips. Other contributing factors are the small size and lack of clumping of the fat globules of homogenized cream.

The fat content of the cream is very important. Cream containing 20 percent fat will whip, but greater volume and stiffness are obtained with increasing fat content up to about 30 percent; above this proportion the whipped cream tends to become buttery and lumpy. In addition, the fat particles must clump, adding stiffness and stability. As the fat particles clump at the liquid/air interface and within the liquid, the increased rigidity that they give the foam permits inclusion of more air bubbles and extension of the films, with the result that the dryness of the foam is increased. This is why cream from milk containing larger fat particles (Jersey and Guernsey breeds) whips somewhat more quickly and to a stiffer foam than cream from other breeds that contains smaller ones.

Low temperatures, 7–8° C (45° F) or lower, favor the whipping of cream (Babcock, 1922), because they (1) induce clumping of the fat particles, (2) keep the fat in the solid state, which gives a firmer structure, and (3) prevent escape of liquid fat onto the air interface where it acts as a foam depressant (see churning theory of King, 1953). Above 10° C (50° F), the decrease in stiffness of whipped cream is in direct ratio to the increase in temperature, so that 30 percent cream will not whip at 22.2° C (72° F).

Dahlberg and Hening (1925) found that increased viscosity increases the whipping properties of cream, but the lowering of the surface tension does not improve the whipping qualities. Aging increases the viscosity of the cream and hence its whipping properties. Pasteurization has a slightly detrimental effect on whipping quality.

Babcock (1922) found that acidity up to 0.3 percent, at which sour taste is evident, had no effect on whipping quality. If acid was added in excess of 0.3 percent, whipping quality decreased, whether added to fresh or aged cream, when the amount added began to curdle the cream. Babcock also observed that the addition of sugar to cream either before or after whipping decreased the stiffness of the cream. Adding the sugar before whipping decreased the volume obtained and increased the whipping time.

Cream of 40–50 percent fat content is sometimes frozen in order to carry excess cream from seasons of surplus to periods of shortage (Doan and Keeney, 1965). Freezing causes a great deal of the fat to separate, which reduces the whipping quality of the cream. The thawed cream is homogenized and mixed with fresh cream for use in ice cream.

Because of its high protein content and viscosity, evaporated milk can be whipped, although the foam obtained is less stable than whipped cream. Lowering the pH to decrease protein solubility improves the stability of whipped evaporated milk.

Churning

Butter may be churned from sweet or sour cream, but in this country commercial butter is made from sweet cream. Churning occurs upon agitation of milk or cream when the fat is partially solid and partially liquid, and thus it is temperature dependent. It is basically a process of phase inversion; cream is an oil-in-water emulsion, whereas butter is primarily of the water-in-oil type. While churning is possible in the absence of air, it is greatly accelerated by air and foaming. The phase inversion is accompanied by release of the protein and phospholipid from the surface of the fat globules into the plasma phase. A theory of the mechanism of churning that accounts for the observed phenomena was proposed by van Dam and Holwerda (1934) and by King (1953), and may be summarized as follows: fat globules concentrate in the air-plasma interface, and a part of the liquid fat immediately spreads out over the interface, cementing the globules into clumps. The liquid fat serves as a foam depressant and, upon repeated formation and destruction of the foam bubbles, butter granules are formed.

Butter

Microscopic studies of butter structure have revealed a continuous phase of liquid-free fat in which there are dispersed fat globules, fat crystals, moisture droplets, and air bubbles (King, 1964). The rheological properties of butter, which are of interest with regard to its spreadability, hardness, and oiling off, depend on the chemical composition of the fat, the physical structure of the butter, and the temperature. More specifically, these properties depend on the ratio of liquid to solid fat, the size and shape of the fat crystals, and the air content of the butter (deMan, 1964). If there is not enough liquid fat to accommodate the globules and crystals and the moisture droplets, the butter will be hard, brittle, and crumbly. An excess of liquid fat is also undesirable, since it causes a soft butter with excessive oiling off (drainage of liquid fat from butter). The ratio of liquid to solid fat is higher when the fat contains more low-molecular-weight and unsaturated fatty acids, and at higher temperatures. The more globular fat in the butter, the less is available to form the continuous phase of liquid-free fat.

To some extent, seasonal variations in chemical composition may be offset by changes in the manufacturing process that impose different physical structures on the finished product. For example, in Denmark, hard winter butter is frequently worked under vacuum, which apparently causes part of the liquid fat to ooze out of the fat globules into the continuous phase (King, 1964). Temperature treatment of the cream may also be manipulated. Different churning processes give butters of different structure and therefore possessing different properties.

The occurrence of polymorphism (see Chapter 5) in milk fat is well established. However, the influence of different polymorphic forms of milk fat on the rheological properties of butter has not been elucidated.

Butter exhibits thixotropic changes on working or stirring (deMan and Wood, 1959). This is due to the breakup of the three-dimensional network of needlelike crystals in the free fat.

FLAVOR

The flavor of fresh milk is very bland and hence difficult to describe. Normal milk is both slightly sweet and slightly salty, due to the presence of lactose and of chloride salts. It is neither sour nor bitter. A faint olfactory component exists, but the compounds responsible for it are not known with certainty. Jenness and Patton (1959) suggested that certain low-molecular-weight compounds present in trace amounts, such as acetone, acetaldehyde, butyric acid, and other free fatty acids, probably contribute to flavor. Milk also contains traces of methyl sulfide, which in low concentrations has a flavor characteristic of fresh milk (Patton, Forss, and Day, 1956). Certain other flavor compounds identified in fresh dairy products may also contribute to the flavor of fresh milk (Parks, 1967).

Among these are (1) diacetyl, an accepted flavor constituent of fresh butter, (2) isovaleraldehyde, observed in fresh cream, (3) 4-cis-heptanal, reported to impart a creamy flavor to fresh butter, and (4) delta-lactones, flavor constituents of butter, shown to occur in pasteurized milk.

Off-Flavors

Undesirable flavors may occur in milk as a result of inhalation or ingestion by the cow of odor substances (barn air, feed, and weeds), microbiological activity, or chemical changes. Volatile flavor substances may be absorbed from the atmosphere during storage.

The contributing role of feeds in abnormal flavors of milk has long been recognized. Odor substances may enter the bloodstream, and hence the udder and the milk, either through the lungs or through the digestive tract of the cow.

Milk is an excellent growth medium for nearly all types of microorganisms, and the chemical changes that they produce cause a wide array of off-flavors. Proper refrigeration and improved sanitation practices have generally extended the keeping quality of fresh milk, and bottled milk is being held longer and longer before use. However, psychrophilic bacteria will sometimes grow in milk at 40 to 45° F sufficiently to affect flavor in four to six days. These bacteria produce bitter, fruity, stale, and putrid types of off-flavors. Sourness and coagulation often do not occur. Psychrophiles are destroyed by pasteurization, but may be reintroduced into the milk on equipment and bottles (Thomas, 1958).

Rancid flavor in milk generally refers to hydrolytic rancidity, which develops as a result of the liberation of fatty acids by milk lipases. Since these enzymes are destroyed by pasteurization, prevention of rancidity is largely a matter of proper handling of raw milk. The lipases of raw milk are inactive at the time the milk is secreted. The inactivity is ascribed (Jenness and Patton, 1959) to the fact that the lipases are present in the aqueous phase and are prevented from contacting the fat by the fat-globule membrane. One of the lipases is irreversibly adsorbed onto the fat-globule membrane when the milk is cooled, whereas another is associated with the casein fraction (Schwartz, 1965). Anything that alters the membrane and permits contact of the lipases with the fat will promote rancidity. Jenness and Patton (1959) list such factors: (1) prolonged and excessive agitation, especially when accompanied by foaming, (2) homogenization, (3) separation (in centrifugal separator), (4) warming cold milk to 80 to 90° F and cooling again to low temperatures, (5) freezing and thawing of milk, (6) secretion of milk during advanced lactation, and (7) addition of small amounts of raw milk to pasteurized, homogenized milk. There are also some milks that develop rancid flavors without any treatment other than cooling of freshly drawn milk. This is termed spontaneous lipolysis, and is discussed by Schwartz (1965). Rancid flavor is most likely to be found in market milk in the late fall and early winter months (Parks, 1967).

Autoxidation of milk lipids results in off-flavors described as cardboard, metallic, oily, and tallowy (Jenness and Patton, 1959). The mechanism of autoxidation is discussed elsewhere in this book. The primary sites of oxidation in fluid milk are the unsaturated fatty acids of the phospholipids. The inhibition of such oxidation by homogenization has been attributed (Parks, 1967) to physical alteration of the fat-globule membrane, of which phospholipids are a major part. Milks vary tremendously in their susceptibility to oxidized flavor. Such factors as trace metals (especially copper), ascorbic acid (at normal concentration of milk), and light tend to accelerate oxidized flavor development. The products of oxidation that result in off-flavors are aldehydes, primarily those 5 to 11 carbon atoms in length (Parks, 1965).

When milk is exposed to light, especially direct sunlight, two distinct off-flavors may develop. One is a typical oxidized flavor (light serves as an energy source to initiate autoxidation) and the other is an activated or sunlight flavor. Sunlight flavor is described as burnt or cabbage, and is known to originate in the proteins of milk. Specifically, the degradation of methionine in the presence of riboflavin is involved. The identity of the compound(s) that are produced and that impart the characteristic flavor has not been clearly demonstrated (Parks, 1967).

The flavor of milk is also affected by heat treatment. Even the relatively mild heating employed for pasteurization causes a slight change in flavor, probably caused by loss of volatile compounds as well as new heat-generated flavor constituents (Parks, 1967). When milk is heated to 74° C or higher, a distinct cooked flavor develops as a result of the sulfhydryl groups activated by denaturation of β-lactoglobulin and proteins of the fat-globule membrane (Hutton and Patton, 1952). The flavor is specifically due to volatile sulfides, and hydrogen sulfide in particular (Jenness and Patton, 1959). Scanlan et al. (1968) investigated the volatile compounds produced by more severe heat treatment. Milk was preheated at 82° C for 30 minutes and then heated to 146° C for four seconds and cooled to 4° C in a tubular heat exchanger. The following compounds were found to be heat-induced: $C_{3,4,5,7,8,9,10,11,13}$ n-methyl ketones, $C_{8,10,12}$ delta-lactones, benzaldehyde, furfural, phenylacetaldehyde, vanillin, oct-1-en-3-ol, n-heptanol, 2-butoxyethanol, maltol, acetophenone, benzonitrile, benzothiazole, and diacetyl. Diacetyl was present in heated milk in amounts exceeding the average flavor threshold. It was also found in much lower concentrations in raw milk. When heat treatment is prolonged or carried out at higher temperatures, heated flavor gives way to caramelized flavor.

Severe heat treatment of milk also produces a tactual flavor defect (Patton and Josephson, 1952). The milk is no longer smooth tasting but imparts a sensation of graininess or chalkiness. This defect is apparently caused by insoluble aggregates of calcium and magnesium with the milk proteins. It is particularly noticeable in dry milk products.

The changes in flavor produced during manufacture of dairy products from milk are many and varied. They may result from heat treatment, addition of flavor compounds (such as salt), or chemical degradation. The flavors of dry whole milk, evaporated milk, and sterile concentrated milk result from heat treatment and chemical changes during storage. Compounds known to contribute to the flavor of these products include ketones, lactones, fatty acids, aldehydes, furfural, and hydroxymethyl-furfural (Parks, 1965).

The flavor of cultured dairy products such as butter, cultured butter-milk, cottage cheese, and sour cream has recently been reviewed by Lindsay (1967). The characteristic culture flavor of these products is primarily dependent on flavor and aroma substances produced by certain lactic-acid-producing bacteria. The most important component of culture flavor is diacetyl, which is produced by bacterial action on the citrate of the milk. Acetic acid, acetaldehyde, methyl ketones, and dimethyl sulfide are also important (Lindsay, 1967). Subthreshold levels of free fatty acids probably contribute to the flavor of sweet cream butter (McDaniel et al., 1969). Butter manufactured from sweet cream does not have a cultured flavor, but distillate of starter flavor may be added during the working process. The characteristic flavor imparted to food when butter is used in cooking and baking is largely due to delta-lactones. These are cyclic compounds formed from 5-hydroxy acids (Day, 1965):

$$
\begin{array}{c}
\text{H}_2 \\
\text{C} \\
\text{H}_2\text{C} \qquad \text{CH}_2 \\
| \qquad\qquad | \\
\text{O}\!=\!\text{C} \quad \text{O} \quad \text{CH} \\
\backslash \\
\text{R}
\end{array}
$$

The flavor of cheese obviously depends on the variety of cheese, but these are too numerous to discuss here. The flavor of Cheddar and blue cheeses will be discussed briefly in a subsequent section.

MILK PRODUCTS

The composition of a large variety of milk products may be found in Bell and Whittier (1965).

Concentrated Milks

The products most commonly seen on the retail market are evaporated milk and sweetened condensed milk. These products are prepared by removal of part of the water from fluid milk; their manufacture is discussed by Hall and Hedrick (1966).

Evaporated Milk

Federal standards of identity require that evaporated milk contain not less than 7.9 percent milk fat and not less than 25.9 percent total milk solids. One pound of evaporated milk is considered equivalent to 2.1 pounds of fluid milk. This product is made by forewarming fluid milk, evaporating under vacuum, homogenizing and filling into cans, and sterilizing at 116° C for 15 minutes. The effect of forewarming was discussed previously. Homogenization is important to obtain a uniform fat emulsion and reduce separation of the fat during storage. The principal defects (Hall and Hedrick, 1966) occurring in evaporated milk are (1) cooked flavor, (2) coagulation, (3) browning or discoloration, (4) gelation or thickening, (5) fat separation, (6) staling, (7) protein settling, (8) mineral-salt separation, and (9) lack of sterility. Browning, gelation, fat separation, and stale flavor are more likely to occur at high storage temperatures. Cooked flavor is caused by the high temperature required for sterilization.

Sweetened Condensed Milk

Sweetened condensed milk is prepared by adding sugar to condensed milk. The sugar is added to preserve the milk without resorting to sterilization. The finished product contains 55.7 percent carbohydrate (11.4 percent lactose and 44.3 percent sucrose) (Watt and Merrill, 1963). One pound of sweetened condensed milk, as made in the United States, is considered equivalent to 2.2 pounds of fluid milk (Bell and Whittier, 1965). Although the product is not sterilized, the milk is preheated before condensing. The purposes (Hall and Hedrick, 1966) of this preheating are (1) to satisfactorily use the evaporator, (2) to destroy pathogenic bacteria and inactivate enzymes (such as lipase), and (3) to provide sufficient viscosity of the product. As the preheated milk is condensed, approximately 18 pounds of sugar are added per 100 pounds of fresh milk. In condensed milk the lactose forms a supersaturated solution. To prevent sandiness in the finished product, it is important that crystallization occur rapidly. Rapid crystallization is usually aided by seeding with very small lactose crystals, pulverized nonfat dry milk, or sweetened condensed milk from a previous batch (Hall and Hedrick, 1966). Agitation, temperature control, and viscosity are also important factors. If the product is cooled too fast, the increase in viscosity may decrease the rate of crystallization.

Dried Milk

A number of milk products may be dried, including whole milk, skim milk, buttermilk, cream, whey, malted milk, and ice-cream mix. Most milk products are dried by roller and spray processes. The drying process employed affects the characteristics of the particles obtained (Hall and Hedrick, 1966). The structural elements in a dried milk particle are: lactose (normally in amorphous form; in certain instantized powders it is partially in a crystalline state), casein micelles and whey protein particles, fat (partly in globules and partly "free"), and air (as spherical cells). The protein, fat, and air are presumably dispersed in a continuous phase of amorphous lactose. However, there are indications of an interconnection between the casein micelles, which thus form a network (King, 1965).

Nearly all nonfat dry milk for home use is instantized (Mori and Hedrick, 1965). The surfaces of milk-powder particles are humidified so that the surface becomes tacky, and then redried. This produces a clustering of the particles in loose, spongy aggregates of low density. The aggregates are free-flowing and readily dispersible in water. Water quickly penetrates the spongy structure of the aggregates, allowing them to sink and disperse, whereas normal milk particles tend to clump and ball up, making lumps difficult to disperse in water (Nickerson, 1965).

Dried whole milk has not been widely used in this country. First, it has been very difficult to disperse even by mechanical means. Second, the flavor of the freshest powder tends to be highly cooked and eggy, with butterscotch or cooked-fat overtones, and finally, deterioration during storage has resulted in flavors characterized as oxidized, tallowy, rancid, stale, burnt-feathery, powdery, fruity, coconut-like, malty, cereal-like and a host of other terms (Mook and Williams, 1966).

Off-flavor development in the fat phase of whole-milk powder has been shown to be due mainly to (1) chemical rearrangement of certain fatty acids to form lactones and methyl ketones and (2) the production of carbonyl compounds as a result of oxidation of other fat components (Mook and Williams, 1966). Special processing techniques can minimize these defects. Another source of off-flavor development is the browning or Maillard reaction between lactose and proteins (see Chapter 1). Control of lactose-protein interaction flavors, generally described as cereal, stale, and the like, is not as simple as the control of fat-off-flavor development. The most important preventives appear to be low moisture, low oxygen, sufficient heat processing for an optimum sulfhydryl group development, and minimal storage times and temperature (Mook and Williams, 1966). Heat treatment of the milk to develop sulfhydryl groups imparts a cooked flavor to the dry milk powder, but results in improved keeping quality because it retards oxidative reactions.

Progress has also been made in improving the dispersibility of whole-milk powder. Rupture of the fat globule membrane during and following processing allows free fat to be absorbed into the powder structure. This migration of the fat results in formation of a water-repellent film in and around the powder particles. Fat migration cannot occur if temperatures are used during drying, handling, and storage of the powder that will maintain the fat as a solid. Migration of fat that is a liquid at the usual temperatures of storage and reconstitution (about 21° C) does not interfere with powder wettability, since the water can penetrate to the soluble powder solids. Thus another means of minimizing this problem is to separate the higher- and the lower-melting portions of the component fat by assigning each to its own powder particles. Other techniques to improve dispersibility are (1) application of surface-active agents to the surface of the powder particles and (2) agglomeration procedures (Mook and Williams, 1966).

Ice Cream

The Federal standard of identity for ice cream states that it must contain at least 10 percent milk fat and 20 percent total milk solids, except where there is a diluting effect of the flavoring material. Not more than 0.5 percent stabilizer and 0.2 percent emulsifier are allowed.

Physically, ice cream is a foam in which the continuous phase is a partially frozen emulsion. The ingredients of ice cream and their functions (Doan and Keeney, 1965) are as follows: (1) *Milk fat,* which imparts a richness or body and helps to insure a smooth-textured ice cream. Low-fat ice cream feels colder in the mouth than does ice cream with more fat. Milk fat also contributes a subtle flavor quality, acts as a carrier for added flavor compounds, and gives desirable tactual qualities. (2) *Milk solids not fat* (MSNF), which contribute flavor, body, and texture. Milk proteins are essential for the formation and maintenance of small, stable air cells. (3) *Sugars,* which contribute sweetness and lower the freezing point so that the ice cream is not frozen solid. Corn sweeteners, which are added along with sucrose, bind water, increase the viscosity of the water phase, and give desirable body. (4) *Stabilizer,* which aids in maintaining a smooth texture by inhibiting large ice-crystal formation between manufacture and consumption. Stabilizers are carbohydrate polymers that bind water, increase the viscosity of the unfrozen portion, and give a heavier body to ice cream. Common stabilizers are carboxymethylcellulose (CMC), locust-bean gum, sodium alginate, propylene glycol alginate, Irish moss or carrageenan, and guar gum. They are usually used in combination because of particular individual properties. (5) *Emulsifiers*, which are monoglycerides or polysorbate esters. These stiffen ice cream by causing agglomeration of fat globules and produce a smoother texture by reducing the size of the ice crystals and air cells.

Manufacture of ice cream involves (1) preparation of the mix, (2) freezing, and (3) hardening. The ingredients are first blended and dispersed to form the mix. The mix is then pasteurized, homogenized, cooled, and pumped into the freezer. In the freezer, it is partially frozen and air is simultaneously whipped into it. The increase in volume due to the incorporation of air is called overrun. The Federal standard of identity requires that ice cream weigh not less than 4.5 pounds/gallon. For a mix that weighs 9.0 pounds/gallon, this means that 100 percent overrun is allowed. Average overrun for packaged ice cream is about 70–80 percent.

The initial freezing point of the mix is -2.8 to $-2.2°$ C. As ice crystals are formed, the freezing point of the remaining solution is lowered because it is becoming more concentrated. The ice cream is discharged from the freezer at -5 to $-6°$ C and filled into containers. Hardening is the final static chilling. It is important that it be done rapidly and without temperature fluctuations so that the ice crystals formed will be small.

The flavor of the finished ice cream is dependent on the flavor of the ingredients. Flavor defects may be due to (1) dairy products of poor quality, (2) excessive or deficient sweetness, (3) excessive, deficient, or atypical flavoring, or (4) displeasing blend. The body and texture are dependent on the freezing process and storage conditions as well as the ingredients. Texture refers to fineness of structure. The size, shape, and number of ice crystals, lactose crystals, and air cells; the quantity of fat; and the agglomeration of the fat globules determine the texture of ice cream. Ice cream having an ideal texture will be very smooth, with the solid particles too small to be detected in the mouth. Temperature fluctuations during storage are most frequently responsible for texture defects. Body implies consistency or firmness, melting resistance, and separation characteristics on melting. The ideal body is that produced by the correct proportion of constituents, proper processing conditions, and proper overrun. The ice cream should melt fairly rapidly at room temperature to a smooth liquid. Body defects are commonly described as crumbly, fluffy, gummy, soggy, and weak, while the common texture defects are coarse, icy, sandy, and buttery. Defects in the flavor, texture, and body of ice cream are discussed in detail by Arbuckle (1966) and Doan and Keeney (1965).

The composition of other types of frozen desserts, such as ice milk, sherbet, and soft-serve ice cream, may be found in Arbuckle (1966). In general, the same principles apply to these products as to ice cream.

Cultured-Milk Products

Cultured-milk products have been known to mankind since antiquity. They are produced by the addition of various bacterial "starter" cultures to milk. These cultures function primarily by carrying out a lactic acid fermentation in the milk. They also produce diacetyl and other compounds that contribute to the flavor of the different cultured products. The lactic acid-forming bacteria include *Lactobacillus acidophilus* and *L. bulgaricus,* and *Streptococcus thermophilus, S. lactis, S. diacetilactis,* and *S. cremoris.* The flavor-producing bacteria include *Leuconostoc citrovorum* and *L. dextranicum,* and *S. diacetilactis.*

Some cultured-milk products are acidophilus milk, Bulgarian buttermilk, yoghurt, cultured buttermilk, sour cream, and sour half-and-half. The basic steps in the manufacture of these different products are the same. The differences in the products arise from differences in the starting milk (high, low, or no butterfat), different bacteria in the starter, and different incubation temperature of the inoculated milk.

Kosikowski (1966) lists the following requirements for producing good cultured-milk products: (1) a source of good-flavored, low-bacteria milk, (2) high heat treatment of the milk, (3) an active, properly functioning, appropriate starter, (4) quick chilling of the cultured product, and (5) high standards of sanitation. The manufacture of cultured buttermilk and yoghurt will be considered to allow illustration of some of the above points.

1.   Cultured buttermilk. Skim or partially skimmed milk is pasteurized at 185° F for 30 minutes and cooled to 72° F. Heat denaturation of the whey proteins by this treatment is desired to increase the viscosity and body of the product. The cooled milk is inoculated with 1.0 percent active lactic starter culture composed of *S. lactis, S. cremoris,* and *L. citrovorum.* The inoculated milk is held at 70–72° F until the titratable acidity is 0.85 percent or higher, or the pH is 4.5 or below (12 to 14 hours). The buttermilk is now cooled to 40° F, rapidly and with minimum agitation, and filled into appropriate containers. The temperature of incubation of the inoculated milk is quite important. The optimum temperature for the growth of flavor-forming bacteria is 68° F, while the optimum temperature for acid-forming bacteria is 86° F. At a temperature below 68° F, insufficient acid is produced and the product is "flat" in flavor. Above 75° F, the acidity becomes excessive and the flavor is "harsh" and "coarse" (Emmons and Tuckey, 1967).

2. Yoghurt. Skimmed, partially skimmed, or whole milk (which may be fortified with 3 percent nonfat dry milk) is heated to 180° F, homogenized, then held at 180–185° F for 30 minutes and cooled to 113° F. This heat treatment of the milk is important, because it controls the extent of whey protein denaturation, which affects the water-binding capacity of the protein and hence the gel structure of the yoghurt. It also stimulates growth of the starter organisms (Emmons and Tuckey, 1967). The cooled milk is inoculated with 2.5 percent of an active culture of *L. bulgaricus* and *S. thermophilus* (or 1.25 percent of each separately). The inoculated mix is filled into individual containers and incubated at 106–108° F for about 3 hours. The yoghurt is then cooled to 45° F. It has an acidity of about 0.9 percent (as lactic acid) and pH of 4.6. Fruit essence may be added at the time of inoculation or solid fruit preserves may be added to the containers before the inoculated milk is filled into them. Yoghurt has an acid flavor and generally a smooth, light custard texture. Yoghurt made with whole milk has a firmer body than that made with skim milk; added nonfat dry milk solids also produce a firmer gel (Emmons and Tuckey, 1967).

Cheese

Like cultured milks, cheeses have been known to mankind since very early times. They represent man's successful attempt to convert a perishable foodstuff, milk, into a much less perishable one, cheese. Cheese production enabled man to preserve the milk from times of high production for times of low production. Cheeses also provide a flavorful addition to the diet. They have been made from the milk of many different mammals, although commonly the milk from the cow, sheep, or goat is used.

Basically cheese is made by forming a curd by the action of rennin or acid on the milk and then ripening the curd by the action of milk and microbial enzymes. This is known as natural cheese. During ripening, all components of the curd, fat, lactose, and protein, are acted on to produce the flavor and texture characteristic of a particular variety of cheese.

The U.S.D.A. has published Federal standards that apply to cheese. Most states follow these regulations, which include minimum curing time (60 days) and temperature (35° F) for ripening cheeses made from unpasteurized milk, varieties that must be made from pasteurized milk, and labeling requirements and composition standards (fat and moisture) for both natural and processed cheeses. These regulations also include a section applicable to imported cheeses.

Cheese may be classified in many different ways. It may be produced from the milk of the cow, sheep, or goat, or even from whey (Gjetost, Mysost). Cheese may be unripened (cream or cottage cheese) or ripened, either by mold (Camembert, Gorganzola, and Blue) or by bacteria (Cheddar and Swiss). One of the most common classifications is on the basis of moisture content, as illustrated in Table 4. Cheese can also be described as natural or processed. Processed cheese is made by blending and heating several lots of natural cheese with a suitable emulsifying agent.

TABLE 4. Classification of Natural Cheese Based on Moisture Content[a]

Consistency	Soft	Semisoft		Hard
Moisture	Very High (80–55 Percent)	High (55–45 Percent)	Medium (45–34 Percent)	Low (34–13 Percent)
Varieties	Cottage Ricotta Impastata Neufchatel Cream	Mozzarella Brie Pizza Blue Camembert	Edam Brick Swiss Cheddar Provolone	Romano Parmesan Dry Ricotta Gjetost Mysost

[a] From Kosikowski, 1966.

The manufacture of natural cheese, regardless of the milk used or the variety desired, involves similar steps. These include:

1. Curd formation. The curd is formed by the addition of rennet extract and suitable starter cultures. Proper temperature is very important during the "setting" period. A lower temperature (21–27° C) of "setting" is used for soft cheeses such as Neufchatel, cream, and cottage cheeses. Cheddar is "set" at 30–31° C and Swiss at 31–34° C. The amount of rennet added and the acidity developed by the starter combined with the "setting" temperature affect the rate of whey expulsion and the rate of formation, the firmness, the elasticity, and other properties of the curd.

2. Curd cutting. This step permits a large proportion of the whey to be expelled. The finer the curd is cut, the greater is the whey expulsion. Swiss cheese curd is cut finer than is curd for Cheddar. Inadequate whey expulsion and drainage results in excess lactose retention and causes excess acidity and defects during ripening. Soon after cutting, a thin continuous film forms that allows for the movement of the whey but retains the fat in the curd.

3. Curd cooking. Heating and agitation hasten the expulsion of the whey from the curd. The curd increases in elasticity, the texture becomes more compact, and the lactic acid bacteria increase in number. Cooking at a high temperature decreases moisture content and causes the cheese to ripen less rapidly. Cheddar curd becomes firmer and more rubbery during cooking (38° C); curds that are heated at higher temperatures, such as those for Parmesan and Swiss cheeses (51–54° C), acquire increased plasticity.

4. Curd drainage. In this step, the curd is permanently separated from the whey.

5. Curd knitting. This is essentially a time step that allows further lactic acid development by the starter and further transforms the curd into the characteristics of the variety being made.

6. Salting the curd. This influences the flavor, moisture, and texture of the variety. It will check lactic acid formation and suppress spoilage organisms. Salting also favors the development of the specific ripening organisms desired.

7. Pressing the curd. Pressing gives the cheese its characteristic shape and compact texture, extrudes free whey, and completes curd knitting.

8. Special steps. Special treatment may be required for a particular variety. These include the addition of special cultures to the milk during cheese manufacture, such as *Propionibacterium shermanii* to Swiss, addition of mold cultures to the mold-ripened Camembert and Roquefort cheeses, and the surface smearing of cultures of *Brevibacterium linens* on surface-ripened varieties such as Brick and Limburger. This also includes holding of ripening Swiss cheese at elevated temperatures to allow eye development (CO_2 formation).

The "green" cheese that is formed by these steps is further changed into the desirable characteristics of the variety by ripening or curing conditions (temperature and relative humidity).

9. Ripening. During the ripening period, the "green" cheese acquires the characteristic flavor and texture of the variety. The components of the "green" cheese, lactose, fat, and protein, are converted into the various compounds of the finished cheese. Lactose is the easiest to consider, in that relatively little is found in newly made cheese, and this is rapidly converted by the microorganisms present into lactic acid. The principal changes involve the fat and protein fractions.

Proteolysis is important to both flavor and texture development during ripening. The proteins of cheese, mostly casein, provide much of the physical structure, body, and texture properties. Protein is degraded to differing extents depending on the variety of cheese and its maturity. In semisoft cheeses a considerable proportion of the casein is converted into soluble forms during curing, and this contributes to softness. Amino acids are liberated from the proteins more rapidly than in hard cheeses, and in most soft varieties, a greater percentage of ammonia is liberated than in hard varieties. The rate and extent of proteolysis increase with increased moisture content. Ripening of Cheddar cheese causes it to lose its tough, rubbery qualities and progress toward a soft and finally almost crumbly texture as proteolysis continues. Proteolysis in ripening cheese can be followed by measuring the amount of water-soluble nitrogen (WSN). In fresh Cheddar cheese, the WSN is about 4 percent of the total nitrogen, while after 4 months' aging the WSN represents 25 percent of the total nitrogen.

The products of proteolysis are associated with the flavor of ripened cheese, but not specifically with the flavor of any particular variety. The polypeptides formed are in themselves bitter in taste and undergo further breakdown to amino acids. These amino acids provide the brothy background flavor of both Cheddar and blue cheese and also are further converted into alcohols, aldehydes, ammonia, amines, sulfur compounds, and others by microbial action.

Hydrolysis and degradation of the lipid components of ripened cheese are important and necessary events of ripening. Milk fat is necessary for flavor development of most cheeses. For example, Cheddar cheese made from skimmed milk lacks Cheddar flavor (Ohren and Tuckey, 1969). Milk fat acts as a solvent for many of the flavor components, can modify the flavor properties of many compounds, and serves as a precursor of a variety of flavor compounds including lactones, methyl ketones, esters, alcohols, and fatty acids. Of the many cheeses, the flavors of blue and Cheddar have been studied most extensively. The work on blue-cheese flavor has progressed to the point where blue-cheese flavor can be formulated and added to products such as salad dressings. Cheddar cheese presents a different story. Although more work has been done on Cheddar-cheese flavor than on blue-cheese flavor, less is known and the flavor cannot be formulated and added to foods.

The flavor of blue cheese (all the mold-ripened cheeses have the same basic pattern) is due to fatty acids (especially C–4 to C–8), methyl ketones (primarily 2-heptanone and 2-nonanone), primary alcohols (principally methanol and ethanol), secondary alcohol analogs of the methyl ketones, esters (especially methyl esters), and a series of miscellaneous compounds. Careful study of the analytical data of blue-cheese flavor compounds has allowed the construction of a synthetic blue-cheese flavor. The amounts of some components have been altered and some have been completely eliminated, but a flavor similar to that of blue cheese has been produced.

According to Kosikowski (1957), "the typical flavor of Cheddar cheese is associated with a pleasant, slightly sweet, aromatic, walnutty sensation without any outstanding single note. In aged cheese, a bitey quality which is neither coarse nor unpleasant gives sharpness to the cheese." Recent work by a group at the National Institute for Research in Dairying in England (McGugan et al., 1968) has shown that the flavor of Cheddar cheese is due to the activity of the starter culture bacteria. They attempted to analyze the neutral volatile compounds responsible for Cheddar flavor and encountered problems typical of those met by other flavor groups. They extracted the neutral volatiles from Cheddar cheese and injected these into a gas-liquid chromatograph. Sensory analysis of the individual compounds as they came off the column showed that none of the individual compounds alone was responsible for Cheddar flavor. Trapping and recombining all the individual compounds as they came off the column failed to give the sensation of Cheddar cheese originally injected. Either some of the specific Cheddar flavor components remained on the column during analysis or passage through the column altered some of them.

Analysis of ripened Cheddar has revealed the presence of numerous flavor compounds not found in unripened cheese. Typical Cheddar flavor is due in part to the free fatty acids and acetate; carbonyls, especially methyl ketones (odd numbered ones from C–3 to C–13); several aldehydes such as methanal, ethanal, propanal, and 3-methyl thiopropanal (methional), which result from transamination and decarboxylation of amino acids by the starter bacteria; methyl mercaptan and dimethyl sulfide (from the breakdown of methional); diacetyl present at less than 1 ppm; alcohols, including ethanol and 2-butanol; and esters, principally the methyl, ethyl, and n-butyl esters of fatty acids.

Processed Cheese

In the manufacture of processed cheese, natural cheeses are heated with an emulsifying agent to yield a product that is more stable microbiologically, that will not undergo further ripening, and that will not separate on further heating. Stability to microbial spoilage is accomplished by the heating step. Some salt can also be added to give a final concentration of 2.5 to 3.5 percent (6 to 7.5 percent salt in the aqueous phase). The heating also stops ripening. The emulsifiers (sodium citrate and disodium hydrogen phosphate) prevent fat separation and retard protein coagulation on further heating.

The manufacture of processed cheese involves heating the natural cheeses to cause an initial separation into fat and serum phases. Then the emulsifiers are added, increasing the dispersion of the protein. This solubilized protein emulsifies the fat to yield a smooth homogeneous mass, which is then poured into molds and allowed to harden. The cheese thus produced will slice better and without crumbling or sticking and will melt more smoothly than natural cheese. However, the heating step drives off flavor volatiles and causes certain chemical changes, so that processed cheese generally has less flavor than natural cheese.

Several of the individual steps in processed-cheese production are quite important. The first is the mixture of natural cheese used. Very young cheese (less than a week old) cannot be stabilized to prevent the loss of fat during the heating step. If too much young cheese is used, the body of the processed cheese will be rubbery and firm, while too much aged cheese yields processed cheese with a weak body and grainy texture. Very young cheese has too small a proportion of water-soluble protein, while aged cheese has an increased proportion of water-soluble protein. Aged cheese also has a stronger and sharper flavor than young cheese. Thus good processed cheese is generally made from a blend of young and aged cheese, giving the desired flavor and texture.

The temperature of heating is also important and affects the firmness of the cheese. Cheese heated to 71° C is firmer than that heated to 65° C. The heating also seems to cause an increase in the proportion of bound water in processed cheese.

The emulsifying salts function to stabilize the product, so that fat does not separate, and to improve the smoothness of body and texture. Citrates and phosphates peptize, or solubilize, the protein, improving its emulsifying ability and the texture of the cheese.

Use of Cheese in Cooked Products

All the factors that affect the plasticity of the cheese when heated for blending, that is, the degree of ripening, the acidity, and the method of manufacture, also affect its blending properties with other ingredients in such dishes as rarebit, cheese souffle, and macaroni and cheese. To these factors may be added the extent of drying, for the cut or grated surface of cheese may dry rather extensively.

Cream cheese, which has a high moisture content, combines readily with sugar, eggs, milk, and sauces for food products. Processed cheese, with its emulsifier and special treatment, also combines readily with sauces for macaroni, potatoes, and souffles. Cheddar cheese may or may not possess excellent cooking qualities. Personius et al. (1944) found that Cheddar cheese of normal fat content shows a progressive improvement in cooking quality over a 12-month period of ripening and a progressive increase in the amount of soluble protein. This improvement is more rapid in a cheese of high moisture content. A cheese of low fat content has conspicuously poor cooking quality. Relatively high temperatures and long periods of heating tend to increase matting, stringing, and toughening of the cheese as well as increasing the separation of the fat.

The blending quality of the cheese appears to be affected by the acidity and hydrogen-ion concentration. Personius et al. (1944) observed a tendency for stringiness between pH 5.0 and 5.6; the cheese separated from the liquid in which it was heated in curdlike particles at pH 4.0 to 5.0; at pH 5.8 to 8.0, the cheese dispersed readily. The authors suggested that removal of the calcium by phosphates in the buffer solution had an effect on the increasing dispersion.

Imitation Dairy Products

Imitation or substitute dairy products are not new, but their use has increased considerably in recent years. In similarity to the dairy product that they replace, these products range from those in which vegetable fat has been substituted for milk fat in a skim-milk base to those that are formulated from entirely nondairy materials. Margarine and vegetable-fat frozen desserts (imitation ice cream) have been in use for the past 25 years, while new products such as vegetable-fat coffee whiteners, whipped toppings, cultured products made in semblance of sour cream, dip bases, milk shakes, and eggnogs have been introduced more recently. The reasons for the use of simulated dairy products are twofold: (1) economics and (2) functional properties. Vegetable-fat products are less expensive and in some cases more functional (Hetrick, 1969). Because of advancements in fat and oil technology, the flavor and stability of fats have been improved. Fats can be tailor-made with respect to physical characteristics such as melting point and favorable solid-fat indices to make the lipid systems more functional for certain specific applications. For example, dried coffee whiteners formulated from nondairy ingredients have considerably longer shelf life than the corresponding dried products made from milk, primarily because of the improved stability of the vegetable fat over milk fat toward oxidation. Likewise, lipid systems in whipped toppings can be formulated to give improved whipping characteristics and stability of whip, and liquid coffee whiteners can be formulated with a freeze-thaw stability that is not attained in the corresponding dairy products. While it might be possible to improve the functionality of the dairy products, present legal restrictions in many cases forbid the addition of necessary materials.

The sale of imitation fluid milk and cream, in liquid, frozen, concentrated, and dried forms, was made illegal in interstate commerce under the Federal Filled Milk Act of 1923. State laws concerning imitation dairy products vary a great deal, with the sale of filled milk being legal in about a dozen states. Imitation fluid milk of the filled variety (in which vegetable fat replaces milk fat in a skim-milk base) would differ from whole milk nutritionally only with regard to fatty acid composition (if vitamins A and D were added). Differences in functional properties have not been studied. Imitation milk of the simulated type (made with vegetable fat, a protein source, a carbohydrate source, an emulsifier, buffer salts, stabilizer, added vitamins, and flavoring) might differ considerably with regard to both nutritional and functional properties. Under present laws, either type of product may be sold under the name "imitation milk" in some states; however, this subject is under discussion at both federal and state levels (see Goddard, 1968).

References

GENERAL

Corbin, E. A., and E. O. Whittier. 1965. The composition of milk, in *Fundamentals of Dairy Chemistry*, B. H. Webb and A. H. Johnson, eds., Avi Publishing Co., Westport, Conn.

Davies, D. T., and J. C. D. White. 1960. The use of ultrafiltration and dialysis in isolating the aqueous phase of milk and in determining the partition of milk constituents between the aqueous and disperse phases. *J. Dairy Res.* 27: 171.

Hartman, A. M., and L. P. Dryden. 1965. The vitamins in milk and milk products, in *Fundamentals of Dairy Chemistry*, B. H. Webb and A. H. Johnson, eds., Avi Publishing Co., Westport, Conn.

Jenness, R., and S. Patton. 1959. *Principles of Dairy Chemistry*. John Wiley and Sons, Inc., New York.

Jenness, R., W. F. Shipe, Jr., and C. H. Whitnah. 1965. Physical properties of milk, in *Fundamentals of Dairy Chemistry*, B. H. Webb and A. H. Johnson, eds., Avi Publishing Co., Westport, Conn.

Nickerson, T. A. 1965. Lactose, in *Fundamentals of Dairy Chemistry*, B. H. Webb and A. H. Johnson, eds., Avi Publishing Co., Westport, Conn.

Overman, O. R., O. F. Garrett, K. E. Wright, and F. P. Sanman. 1939. Composition of milk of Brown Swiss cows. *Ill. Agr. Exp. Sta. Bull. 457.*

Pyne, G. T. 1962. Some aspects of the physical chemistry of the salts of milk. *J. Dairy Res.* 29: 101.

Watt, B. K., and A. L. Merrill. 1963. Composition of foods. U.S. Dept. Agr., *Agriculture Handbook No. 8,* 189.

White, J. C. D., and D. T. Davies. 1958. The relation between the chemical composition of milk and the stability of the caseinate complex. I. General introduction, description of samples, methods and chemical composition of samples. *J. Dairy Res.* 25: 236.

Whitnah, C. H., W. D. Rutz, and H. C. Fryer. 1956. Some physical properties of milk. III. Effects of homogenization pressure on the viscosity of whole milk. *J. Dairy Sci.* 39: 1500.

Whittier, E. O. 1944. Lactose and its utilization: a review. *J. Dairy Sci. 27*: 505.

Wiley, W. J. 1935. A study of the titratable acidity of milk. II. The "buffer curves" of milk. *J. Dairy Res. 6*: 86.

PROTEINS

Alais, C., G. Mocquot, H. Nitschmann, and P. Zahler. 1953. Rennet and its action on the casein of milk. VII. Hydrolysis of non-protein nitrogen and its relation to the primary reaction of rennet-induced curdling of milk. *Helv. Chim. Acta 36*: 1955.

Aschaffenberg, R. 1965. Variants of milk proteins and their pattern of inheritance. *J. Dairy Sci. 48*: 128.

Aschaffenburg, R., and J. Drewry. 1957. Genetics of the β-lactoglobulins of cow's milk. *Nature 180*: 376.

Aurand, A. L., and A. E. Woods. 1959. Role of xanthine oxidase in the development of spontaneously oxidized flavor in milk. *J. Dairy Sci. 42*: 1111.

Berridge, N. J. 1942. Second phase of rennet coagulation. *Nature 149*: 194.

Bhattacharya, S. D., A. K. Roychoudhury, N. K. Sinha, and A. Sen. 1963. Inherited α-lactalbumin and β-lactoglobulin polymorphism in Indian Zebu cattle. Comparison of Zebu and buffalo α-lactalbumin. *Nature 197*: 797.

Brunner, J. R., C. A. Ernstrom, R. A. Hollis, B. L. Larson, R. McL. Whitney, and C. A. Zittle. 1960. Nomenclature of the proteins of bovine milk— First revision. *J. Dairy Sci. 43*: 901.

Brunner, J. R., and M. P. Thompson. 1961. Characteristics of several minor-protein fractions isolated from bovine milk. *J. Dairy Sci. 44*: 1224.

Ebner, K. E., and U. Brodbeck. 1968. Biological role of α-lactalbumin: a review. *J. Dairy Sci. 51*: 317.

Ernstrom, C. A. 1965. Rennin action and cheese chemistry, in *Fundamentals of Dairy Chemistry*, B. H. Webb and A. H. Johnson, eds., Avi Publishing Co., Westport, Conn.

Fox, P. F., M. Yaguchi, and N. P. Tarassuk. 1967. Distribution of lipase in milk proteins. II. Dissociation from ×-casin with dimethylformamide. *J. Dairy Sci. 50*: 307.

Gordon, W. G., M. L. Groves, and J. J. Basch. 1962. Bovine milk "red protein": Amino acid composition and comparison with blood transferrin. *Biochemistry 2*: 817.

Gough, Patricia, and R. Jenness. 1962. Heat denaturation of β-lactoglobulins A and B. *J. Dairy Sci. 45*: 1033.

Greenbank, G. R., L. V. Rogers, C. F. Hufnagel, and M. B. Middleton. 1954. The effect of xanthine oxidase on the properties of dairy products. (A preliminary report.) *J. Dairy Sci. 37*: 644.

Groves, M. L. 1969. Some minor components of casein and other phosphoproteins in milk. A review. *J. Dairy Sci. 52*: 1155.

Groves, M. L., J. J. Basch, and W. G. Gordon. 1962. Isolation, characterization and amino acid composition of a new crystalline protein, lactollin, from milk. *Biochemistry* 2: 814.

Harland, H. A., S. T. Coulter, and R. Jenness. 1952. The effect of various steps in the manufacture on the extent of serum protein denaturation in nonfat dry milk solids. *J. Dairy Sci.* 35: 363.

Herskovits, T. T., and Linda Mescanti. 1965. Conformation of proteins and polypeptides. II. Optical rotatory dispersion and conformation of the milk proteins and other proteins in organic solvents. *J. Biol. Chem. 240:* 639.

Hwang, Quei-Shiow, K. S. Ramachandran, and R. McL. Whitney. 1967. Presence of inhibitors and activators of xanthine oxidase in milk. *J. Dairy Sci.* 50: 1723.

Jenness, R. 1959. Characterization of milk serum protein component 5. *J. Dairy Sci. 42:* 895.

Jenness, R., B. L. Larson, T. L. McMeekin, A. M. Swanson, C. H. Whitnah, and R. McL. Whitney. 1956. Nomenclature of the proteins of bovine milk. *J. Dairy Sci.* 39: 536.

Kannan, A., and R. Jenness. 1961. Relation of milk serum proteins and milk salts to the effects of heat treatment on rennet clotting. *J. Dairy Sci.* 44: 808.

Kresheck, G. C. 1965. The conformation of casein in aqueous solution. *Acta Chem. Scand. 19:* 375.

Larson, B. L., and G. D. Rolleri. 1955. Heat denaturation of the specific serum proteins in milk. *J. Dairy Sci.* 38: 351.

McKenzie, H. A. 1967. Milk proteins. *Adv. Protein Chem. 22:* 55.

Murthy, G. K., and R. McL. Whitney. 1958. A comparison of some of the chemical and physical properties of γ-caseins and immune globulins of milk. *J. Dairy Sci.* 41: 1.

Nitschmann, H., H. Wissman, and R. Henzi. 1957. Über ein Glyko-Makropeptid, ein Spaltprodukt des Caseins, erhalten durch Einwirkung von Lab. *Chimia 11:* 76.

Payens, T. A. J. 1966. Association of caseins and their possible relation to the structure of the casein micelle. *J. Dairy Sci.* 49: 1317.

Payens, T. A. J., and D. G. Schmidt. 1965. The thermodynamic parameters of the association of α_s-casein C. *Biochim. Biophys. Acta 109:* 214.

Payens, T. A. J., and B. W. van Markwijk. 1963. Some features of the associations of β-casein. *Biochim. Biophys. Acta 71:* 517.

Polis, B. D., H. W. Shmukler, and J. H. Custer. 1950. Isolation of a crystalline albumin from milk. *J. Biol. Chem. 187:* 349.

Rose, D. 1965. Protein stability problems. *J. Dairy Sci. 48:* 139.

Rose, D. 1969. A proposed model of micelle structure in bovine milk. *Dairy Sci. Abstr. 31:* 171.

Rose, D., J. R. Brunner, E. B. Kalan, B. L. Larson, P. Melnychyn, H. E. Swaisgood, and D. F. Waugh. 1970. Nomenclature of the proteins of cow's milk. Third revision. *J. Dairy Sci.* 53: 1.

Rowland, S. J. 1938. The determination of the nitrogen distribution in milk. *J. Dairy Res.* 9: 42.

Sawyer, W. H. 1969. Complex between β-lactoglobulin and x-casein. A review. *J. Dairy Sci.* 52: 1347.

Schmidt, D. G., T. A. J. Payens, B. W. van Marwijk, and J. A. Brinkhuis. 1967. On the subunit of α_{s1}-casein. *Biochem. Biophys. Res. Comm.* 27: 448.

Shahani, K. M. 1966. Milk enzymes: Their role and significance. *J. Dairy Sci.* 49: 907.

Shimmin, P. D., and R. D. Hill. 1964. An electron microscope study of the internal structure of casein micelles. *J. Dairy Res.* 31: 121.

Sullivan, R. A., R. A. Hollis, and E. K. Stanton. 1957. Sedimentation of milk proteins from heated milk. *J. Dairy Sci.* 40: 830.

Tanford, C., and Y. Nozaki. 1959. Physico-chemical comparison of β-lactoglobulins A and B. *J. Biol. Chem.* 234: 2874.

Tessier, H., and D. Rose. 1964. Influence of x-casein and β-lactoglobulin on the heat stability of skimmilk. *J. Dairy Sci.* 47: 1047.

Tessier, H., M. Yaguchi, and D. Rose. 1969. Zonal ultracentrifugation of β-lactoglobulin and x-casein complexes induced by heat. *J. Dairy Sci.* 52: 139.

Timasheff, S. N. 1964. The nature of interactions in proteins derived from milk, in *Proteins and Their Reactions*, H. W. Schultz and A. F. Anglemier, eds., Avi Publishing Co., Westport, Conn.

Thompson, M. P., N. P. Tarassuk, R. Jenness, H. A. Lillevik, U. S. Ashworth and D. Rose. 1965. Nomenclature of the proteins of cow's milk—Second revision. *J. Dairy Sci.* 48: 159.

Tumerman, L., and B. H. Webb. 1965. Coagulation of milk and protein denaturation, in *Fundamentals of Dairy Chemistry*, B. H. Webb and A. H. Johnson, eds., Avi Publishing Co., Westport, Conn.

Waugh, D. F., and R. W. Noble. 1965. Casein micelles. Formation and structure. II. *J. Am. Chem. Soc.* 87: 2246.

Waugh, D. F., and P. H. von Hippel. 1956. x-Casein and the stabilization of casein micelles. *J. Am. Chem. Soc.* 78: 4576.

Woychik, J. H., E. B. Kalan, and M. E. Noelken. 1966. Chromatographic isolation and partial characterization of reduced x-casein components. *Biochem.* 5: 2276.

Zittle, C. A., E. S. Dellamonica, R. K. Rudd, and J. H. Custer. 1957. The binding of calcium ions by β-lactoglobulin both before and after aggregation by heating in the presence of calcium ions. *J. Am. Chem. Soc.* 79: 4661.

Zittle, C. A., M. P. Thompson, J. H. Custer, and J. Cerbulis. 1962. ×-Casein— β-lactoglobulin interaction in solution when heated. *J. Dairy Sci. 45*: 807.

FATS

Babcock, C. J. 1922. The whipping quality of cream. *U.S. Dept. Agric. Bull. 1075.*

Brunner, J. R. 1965. Physical equilibria in milk: The lipid phase, in *Fundamentals of Dairy Chemistry*, B. H. Webb and A. H. Johnson, eds., Avi Publishing Co., Westport, Conn.

Dahlberg, A. C., and J. C. Hening. 1925. Viscosity, surface tension, and whipping properties of milk and cream. *New York State Agr. Expt. Sta. Tech. Bull. 113.*

Dam, W. van, and B. J. Holwerda. 1934. Investigations of the churning process. *Verslag. Landb. Onderzoik. 40C*: 175.

Dunkley, W. L., and H. H. Sommer. 1944. The creaming of milk. *Wisc. Agr. Exp. Sta. Res. Bull. 151.*

Gurd, F. R. N. 1960. Association of lipides with proteins, in *Lipide Chemistry*, D. J. Hanahan, ed., John Wiley and Sons, Inc., New York.

Harwalker, V. R., and J. R. Brunner. 1965. Effects of dissociating agents on physical properties of fat globule membrane fractions. *J. Dairy Sci. 48*: 1139.

Herb, S. F., P. Magidman. F. E. Luddy, and R. W. Riemenschneider. 1962. Fatty acids of cow's milk. B. Composition by gas-liquid chromatography aided by other methods of fractionation. *J. Am. Oil Chem. Soc. 39*: 142.

Hood, L. F., and S. Patton. 1968. Electron microscopic observations of the fat globule membrane. *J. Dairy Sci. 51*: 928.

Jackson, R. H., and J. R. Brunner. 1960. Characteristics of protein fractions isolated from the fat/plasma interface of homogenized milk. *J. Dairy Sci. 43*: 912.

Jackson, R. H., E. J. Coulson, and W. R. Clark. 1962. The mucoproteins of the fat/plasma interface of cow's milk. I. Chemical and physical characterization. *Arch. Biochem. Biophys. 97*: 373.

King, N. 1953. The theory of churning. *Dairy Sci. Abstr. 15*: 589.

King, N. 1955. The milk fat globule membrane. Commonwealth Bureau of Dairy Science Tech. Comm. No. 2, Farnham Royal, Bucks, England.

King, N. 1964. The physical structure of butter. *Dairy Sci. Abstr. 26*: 151.

Kurtz, F. E. 1965. Lipids of milk: Composition and properties, in *Fundamentals of Dairy Chemistry*, B. H. Webb and A. H. Johnson, eds. Avi Publishing Co., Westport, Conn.

de Man, J. M. 1964. Physical properties of milk fat. *J. Dairy Sci. 47*: 1194.

de Man, J. M., and F. W. Wood. 1959. Hardness of butter. II. Influence of setting. *J. Dairy Sci. 42*: 56.

Morton, R. K. 1954. The lipoprotein particles in cow's milk. *Biochem. J.* 57: 231.

Rahn, O. 1932. Why cream and egg white whips. *Food Inds.* 4: 300.

Sharp, P. F., and V. N. Krukovsky. 1939. Differences in adsorption of solid and liquid fat globules as influencing the surface tension and creaming of milk. *J. Dairy Sci.* 22: 743.

Vasic, J., and J. M. de Man. 1966. High melting glycerides and the milk fat globule membrane. *Intern. Dairy Congress*, 17th, Munich (Sec. C): 167.

FLAVOR

Aurand, L. W., J. A. Singleton, and G. Matrone. 1964. Sunlight flavor in milk. II. Complex formation between milk proteins and riboflavin. *J. Dairy Sci.* 47: 827.

Day, E. A. 1965. Role of milk lipids in flavors of dairy products, in *Flavor Chemistry*, ACS Symposium, Detroit, April 6–7.

Forss, D. A. 1969. Flavors of dairy products: A review of recent advances. *J. Dairy Sci.* 52: 832.

Hutton, J. F., and S. Patton. 1952. The origin of sulfhydryl groups in milk protein and their contribution to cooked flavor. *J. Dairy Sci.* 35: 699.

Lindsay, R. C. 1967. Cultured dairy products, in *Chemistry and Physiology of Flavors*, H. W. Schultz, E. A. Day, and L. M. Libbey, eds., Avi Publishing Co., Westport, Conn.

McDaniel, M. R., L. A. Sather, and R. C. Lindsay. 1969. Influence of free fatty acids on sweet cream butter flavor. *J. Food Sci.* 34: 251.

Parks, O. W. 1965. Lipids of milk: Deterioration, in *Fundamentals of Dairy Chemistry*, B. H. Webb and A. H. Johnson, eds., Avi Publishing Co., Westport, Conn.

Parks, O. W. 1967. Milk flavor, in *Chemistry and Physiology of Flavors*, H. W. Schultz, E. A. Day, and L. M. Libbey, eds., Avi Publishing Co., Westport, Conn.

Patton, S., D. A. Forss, and E. A. Day. 1956. Methyl sulfide and the flavor of milk. *J. Dairy Sci.* 39: 1469.

Patton, S., and D. V. Josephson. 1952. Observations on the tactual flavor qualities of heated milk. *J. Dairy Sci.* 35: 161.

Patton, S., and D. V. Josephson. 1953. Methionine origin of sunlight flavor in milk. *Science 118*, No. 3060, 211.

Scanlan, R. A., R. C. Lindsay, L. M. Libbey, and E. A. Day. 1968. Heat-induced volatile compounds in milk. *J. Dairy Sci.* 51: 1001.

Schwartz, D. P. 1965. Lipids in milk: Deterioration, in *Fundamentals of Dairy Chemistry*, B. H. Webb and A. H. Johnson, eds., Avi Publishing Co., Westport, Conn.

Thomas, S. B. 1958. Psychrophilic microorganisms in milk and dairy products. *Dairy Sci. Abstr.* 20: 356.

MILK PRODUCTS

Anonymous. 1966. A summary of laws and regulations affecting the cheese industry. *Consumer and Marketing Service*, U.S. Dept. Agric. Handbk. No. 265.

Bell, R. W., and E. O. Whittier. 1965. The composition of milk products, in *Fundamentals of Dairy Chemistry*, B. H. Webb and A. H. Johnson, eds., Avi Publishing Co., Westport, Conn.

Day, E. A. 1967. Cheese flavor, in *The Chemistry and Physiology of Flavors*, H. W. Schultz, E. A. Day and L. M. Libbey, eds., Avi Publishing Co., Westport, Conn.

Doan, F. J., and P. G. Keeney. 1965. Frozen dairy products, in *Fundamentals of Dairy Chemistry*, B. H. Webb and A. H. Johnson, eds., Avi Publishing Co., Westport, Conn.

Emmons, D. B., and S. L. Tuckey. 1967. Cottage cheese and other cultured milk products. *Pfizer Cheese Monographs*, Vol. III. Chas. Pfizer and Co., New York.

Goddard, J. L. Imitation milks and creams. *Federal Register 33 (98):* 7456. May 18, 1968.

Hall, C. W., and T. I. Hedrick. 1966. *Drying Milk and Milk Products.* Avi Publishing Co., Westport, Conn.

Hetrick, J. H. 1969. Imitation dairy products—past, present and future. *J. Am. Oil Chem. Soc. 46:* 58A, 60A, 62A.

King, N. 1965. The physical structure of dried milk. *Dairy Sci. Abstr. 27:* 91.

Kosikowski, F. V. 1957. Cheese flavor, in *Chemistry of Natural Food Flavors: A Symposium.* Quartermaster Research and Engineering Center, Natick, Mass.

Kosikowski, F. V. 1966. *Cheese and Fermented Milk Foods.* Edward Bros., Inc., Ann Arbor, Mich.

Lindsay, R. C. 1967. Cultured dairy products, in *The Chemistry and Physiology of Flavors.* H. W. Schultz, E. A. Day, and L. M. Libbey, eds., Avi Publishing Co., Westport, Conn.

McGugan, W. A., S. G. Howsam, J. A. Elliott, B. Reiter, and M. E. Sharpe. 1968. Neutral volatiles in Cheddar cheese made aseptically with and without starter culture. *J. Dairy Res. 35:* 237.

Mook, D. E., and A. W. Williams. 1966. Recent advances in improving dry whole milk: a review. *J. Dairy Sci. 49:* 768.

Mori, K., and T. I. Hedrick. 1965. Some properties of instantized dry milks. *J. Dairy Sci. 48:* 253.

Ohren, J. A., and S. L. Tuckey. 1969. Relation of flavor development in Cheddar cheese to chemical changes in the fat of the cheese. *J. Dairy Sci. 52:* 598.

Personius, C., E. Boardman, and A. R. Ausherman. 1944. Some factors affecting the behavior of Cheddar cheese in cooking. *Food Res. 9:* 304.

Reiter, B., T. F. Fryer, A. Pickering, H. R. Chapman, R. C. Lawrence, and M. E. Sharpe. 1967. The effect of the microbial flora on the flavour and free fatty acid composition of Cheddar cheese. *J. Dairy Res. 34:* 257.

Tittsler, R. P. 1965. Cheese chemistry, in *Fundamentals of Dairy Chemistry,* B. H. Webb and A. H. Johnson, eds., Avi Publishing Co., Westport, Conn.

CHAPTER 11

Flour

ADA MARIE CAMPBELL

According to the Code of Federal Regulations (FDA, 1968), "flour, white flour, wheat flour, plain flour, is the food prepared by grinding and bolting cleaned wheat, other than durum wheat and red durum wheat." The definition goes on to list permissible chemical additives and specifications regarding granulation and concentrations of moisture and ash. Standards of identity are presented also for enriched, bromated, durum, self-rising, phosphated, instantized, and whole-wheat flours, as well as flour from sources other than wheat. The discussion that follows, except where specified otherwise, deals with white wheat flour.

FLOUR PRODUCTION

Properties of wheat flour vary greatly and are affected primarily by type and variety of wheat, the specific milling operations, and the physical and chemical treatments applied after milling. Agronomists, plant breeders, millers, and cereal chemists have worked together to bring flour science to its present stage. Improvements in quality of wheat, along with developments in the milling and treatment of flour, have made possible the production of flours having specific properties for specific uses.

Wheat

The wheats that are used for flour vary with respect to optimal growing conditions, color of the kernel, and "hardness." Those varieties that may be planted in the fall for maturation the following summer are known as "winter wheats." They require relatively mild winters. Winter wheats may be red or white and soft or hard. In Canada and areas of the northern United States that have severe winters, varieties that can be planted in the spring and will mature quickly for late summer harvesting must be grown. Spring wheats include hard red and hard and soft white varieties, as well as the durums that are used only for semolina products. The terms "hard" and "soft" actually refer to vitreousness of the kernel but often are used to imply protein content, because vitreousness is a function of concentration and nature of protein.

The protein content of wheat is affected by external factors as well as by the inherent differences among wheat varieties. Soil fertility affects the amount of nitrogen available to the plant. Excessive rainfall may decrease the protein content of wheat by leaching nitrogen from the soil. Rainfall and sunshine affect the extent of growth of leaves and stems and thus the proportion of the available nitrogen that is left for the grain. The combined effect of climate and soil fertility on protein concentration is probably greater than the effect of wheat variety.

Principles of Milling

Details of the milling process vary from mill to mill, are subject to change, and are well described elsewhere (Larsen, 1959; Scott, 1966; Shellenberger, 1965; and Wheat Flour Institute, 1965) in terms of general practice. The emphasis herein will be on the principles of milling and on the relationships among kernel structure and composition, present milling practices, and flour properties. Understanding of such relationships should provide a basis for interpretation of future developments.

Cleaning and possibly blending of wheats precede the actual milling process. Cleaning involves several steps, including screening, air aspiration, scouring, and washing. Blending of wheats of different milling characteristics may follow cleaning.

Flour milling involves separation of the endosperm from the other structural parts of the kernel (Figure 1) and subdivision of the endosperm into a fine meal. Separation of the endosperm from the germ and the seed coat is neither a one-step operation nor a completely efficient process. MacMasters (1961) relates kernel structure to the principles of milling. Between the germ and the endosperm is a layer of amorphous "cementing material" contributing to strong adherence of these structural parts. The seed coat is actually not readily removed as an entity but as a part of what commonly is referred to in the milling industry as "bran." Ideally, from the miller's standpoint, the bran includes (1) the pericarp, or fruit coat, which surrounds and adheres strongly to the seed coat; (2) the seed coat; (3) a thin layer of nucellar tissue, which lies just inside the seed coat; and (4) the aleurone, or outer, layer of the endosperm. The aleurone layer adheres more strongly to the nucellar tissue than to the remainder of the endosperm, which is referred to as "starchy endosperm" and is the source of white flour.

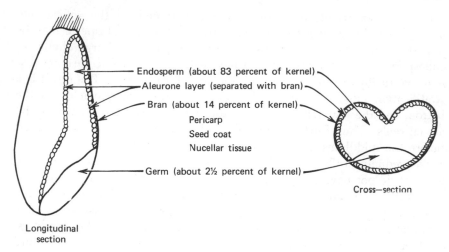

Endosperm (about 83 percent of kernel)
Aleurone layer (separated with bran)
Bran (about 14 percent of kernel)
Pericarp
Seed coat
Nucellar tissue
Germ (about 2½ percent of kernel)

Cross—section

Longitudinal
section

FIGURE 1. Wheat kernel.

Tempering

Tempering of wheat after cleaning expedites separation of the starchy endosperm from the other parts of the kernel. Tempering is the addition of water, usually in steps over a period of 18–72 hours, to a moisture content of 14–19 percent. The treatment causes the brittle, readily pulverized bran to become toughened, probably because of hydration of cellulose and hemicelluloses of the pericarp. At the same time the endosperm becomes more friable. When hydration is accelerated by the application of heat (46–48° C) during the water treatment, the process is referred to as "conditioning" and requires only 8–18 hours. In spite of the beneficial effects of the added moisture, the yield of flour usually represents only about 72 percent of the wheat kernel in the United States, whereas the endosperm constitutes nearly 85 percent of the kernel.

Breaking and Reduction

The tempered or conditioned wheat is subjected to a series of grindings and alternating siftings. Two series of rollers are used: the break rolls and the reduction rolls. The corrugated break rolls exert both shear and pressure forces, producing progressively smaller chunks of germ, bran, endosperm, and bran with adhering endosperm. These fractions are separated from one another by the sifters. Free bran and germ are removed for other uses, primarily as ingredients of animal feeds. Bran is easily removed at this stage because the preliminary tempering causes it to break into rather large, flat particles; germ, because of its high fat content, is not friable or vitreous and is flattened by the rollers into flakes that are readily sifted out. Bran with adhering endosperm may be passed to succeeding break rolls for further separation. Large chunks of endosperm, or "middlings," are purified with the aid of air currents that move vertically through the mass, exerting a lifting effect. The result is a stratification into layers, with the coarsest endosperm particles on the bottom and the low-density bran on top, where it is removed readily by air currents. Thus further removal of the unwanted bran is achieved before the middlings are passed on to reduction rolls.

The reducing rolls to which the chunks of relatively pure endosperm are sent do not have a separating function; they only subdivide further. Thus they exert only a pressure force and are smooth. Their placement becomes progressively closer in order to produce increasingly fine grinding as milling proceeds. Again siftings alternate with the grindings, so that some size classification is achieved. The finest streams are recovered as flour, while the coarser and finer middlings are returned to the coarser and finer reducing rolls respectively.

Selection of Streams

Flour streams may be removed at many points in the milling process, and variations in the combining of streams result in different grades of flour. "Straight flour" is the result of combining all streams, representing in the United States approximately 72 percent of the whole wheat, "Patent" flours result from selection of streams. The lower the proportion selected, the "shorter" is the patent. All-purpose, or family, flour is a rather long patent flour made from either hard or soft wheat. Cake flour is a short patent soft-wheat flour. Combining the streams that are not used for a patent flour produces a "clear" flour; therefore, if a given milling process produces a short patent flour, it also produces a relatively large amount of clear flour (see Figure 2). When 72 percent of the wheat kernel goes into flour, the "extraction rate" is said to be 72 percent. In Europe 80 percent extraction is common. Chemical additives, including enrichment mixtures when used, are added near the end of the line.

Other Physical Treatments

Impact Milling

A development of recent years, impact grinding consists of further reducing particle size of conventionally milled flour by means of special high-speed machinery. Flour is thrown with great force against either pins or baffles and considerable disintegration results. "Pin milling" is a form of impact milling.

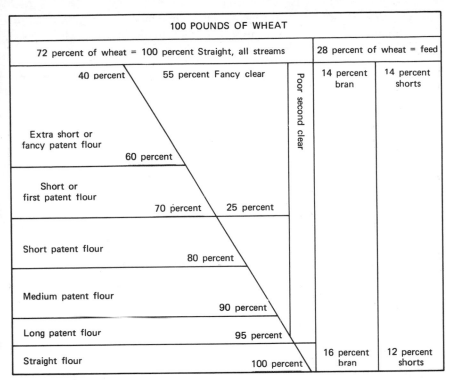

FIGURE 2. Products of wheat milled at 72 percent extraction rate and with different selections of flour streams. (From C. O. Swanson, *Wheat and Flour Quality*. Courtesy of Wheat Flour Institute.)

Air Classification

Another relatively recent development is air classification. Whereas conventional milling involves fractionation of the wheat kernel (that is, separation of the endosperm from the other parts) and subdivision of the endosperm, air classification involves fractionation of the endosperm itself. Conventionally milled flour or flour that has been subjected to impact milling may be classified into fractions that differ as to both particle size and composition. The effectiveness of air classification is due basically to the heterogeneity of the wheat endosperm and the resultant variability in size and composition of particles in conventionally milled flour. The intact endosperm is made up of cells, each containing starch granules embedded in a protein matrix. The cells decrease in size and increase in their content of protein and ash as they radiate outward from the center of the kernel. After milling, some flour particles consist of free starch granules, some of small wedge-shaped pieces of protein matrix, some of intact endosperm cells, and most of aggregates, or chunks of protein matrix with embedded starch (Figure 3). The aggre-

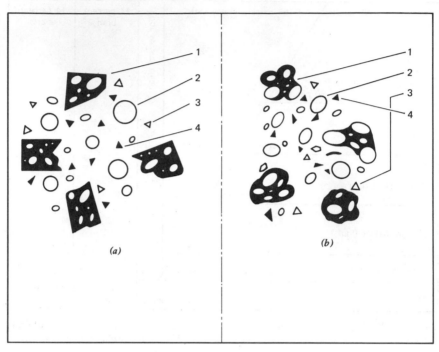

FIGURE 3. Particle types present in soft-wheat and hard-wheat flour. (*a*) Hard-wheat flour, showing, (1) endosperm agglomerates, (2) starch granules, (3) broken starch, and (4) broken protein; (*b*) soft-wheat flour, showing (1) endosperm agglomerates, (2) starch granules, (3) broken starch, and (4) broken protein. (Larsen, 1959.)

gates, of course, vary greatly in size, and the smaller chunks tend to be relatively high in protein. Conventionally milled soft and hard wheat flours differ greatly in their relative proportions of these types of particles; because cells of soft-wheat endosperm are more easily broken than are those of hard wheat, soft-wheat flour normally has a much higher proportion of free starch and protein particles. Particles differ in density as well as size and composition. Air classification involves the application of centrifugal force and the use of air currents in obtaining flours of desired properties from the available material.

As stated by Wichser (1958), "With air classification any flour can be fractionated into its component parts and subsequently reassembled into many totally new flours. . . . From a hard wheat may come a low protein fraction having a baking performance . . . similar to that of an excellent conventionally milled soft wheat cake flour. From a conventionally milled soft wheat flour . . . it is possible to produce a product containing 20–25% protein, . . . as well as one containing less than 3% protein." By means of air classification, the miller thus may tailor-make a flour for any purpose with little dependence on uniformity of the raw material at his disposal. Factors such as soil, climate, and weather, which affect the quality and quantity of wheat protein, have become of decreased importance to the miller who uses air classification.

Agglomeration

Although a patent for an agglomeration process was issued as early as 1915, agglomerated flour was not commercially available until 1963. Several milling companies now have agglomerated family flour on the market. Claus (1964) summarizes the development, underlying principles, and significance of agglomeration. As with air classification, the process is applied following conventional milling. Although the details of the procedure vary, agglomeration essentially involves providing a supply of water in tiny droplets to a mass of moving flour and at the same time providing a means of drying, such as a stream of heated air. In the process flour particles adhere to one another, forming agglomerates that are readily wettable and therefore easily dispersed in water. The agglomerated product, also called "instantized" flour, is free-flowing and dust-free. Agglomerated flours currently on the market need not be sifted, because weight per cup is essentially unaffected by sifting. Products on the market at the time of writing also have higher "cup densities" than most conventional flours, and some recipe adjustment usually is necessary when an instantized flour is used. The future may bring change in that regard because the agglomeration procedure can be altered to produce much variation in the weight of one cup of instantized flour.

Additional Treatments

Chemical

The baking performance of freshly milled flour is not optimal. If the flour is permitted to age over a period of weeks or months, it will improve gradually in baking quality. In the United States chemical treatment is used after milling to accelerate the "maturing" or "improving" process. During natural aging bleaching also occurs, and, as with improving, the effect may be accelerated by the use of chemicals. Most of the chemicals used for bleaching and many of those used for improving are oxidizing agents. Some compounds, notably chlorine dioxide and acetone peroxides, have both a bleaching and an improving effect. Others, for example bromates, iodates, and azodicarbonamide, only improve; still others, such as benzoyl peroxide and nitrogen peroxide, are essentially bleaches.

Pace (1966) summarizes the chemical changes brought about by bleaching and improving agents. The action of bleaches is easily explained because the creamy color of flour is due primarily to the yellow carotenoid pigment xanthophyll and its esters, which are readily oxidized to nearly colorless products. The mechanism by which flour improvement occurs has been more difficult to explain, in spite of the tremendous amount of research that has been carried out. The somewhat simplified explanation that follows seems to represent current consensus based on available evidence, although it undoubtedly is not the whole story. The effect of flour improvers is primarily on flour proteins. The hydrated, cohesive, three-dimensional gluten network in a dough is dependent on cross-linkages in the form of disulfide bonds between protein chains. It seems likely that during dough formation some of these —S—S— bonds are broken by sulfhydryl (—SH) groups, but that new disulfide bonds are formed. (Disulfide-sulfhydryl interchange may occur; for evidence see Kuninori and Sullivan, 1968; Redman and Ewart, 1967; Stewart and Mauritzen, 1966; and Tsen and Bushuk, 1968.) If the net effect is an overly extensive cleavage of disulfide bonds, the resulting dough tends to be sticky, inelastic, and weak. Improvers apparently act by maintaining satisfactory relative proportions of —S—S— and —SH groups, either through oxidation of sulfhydryl groups or through a sulfhydryl-blocking action. Improvers probably differ in their specific reactions. Either an oxidative or a blocking effect would reduce the number of sulfhydryl groups available for disrupting disulfide bonds. The improving action of ascorbic acid, which is a reducing agent, has been a puzzle. According to present theory and recent evidence, this can be explained on the basis of a rapid change of the reduced ascorbic acid to the dehydro form during dough mixing and its acting thereafter as an oxidizing agent.

For a particular flour there is an optimal concentration of improver. Treatment of a flour with the optimal amount of improver results in improved dough-handling properties and increased loaf volume. Overtreatment results in overrigidity of dough structure with a corresponding decrease in loaf volume.

The above discussion of chemical treatment pertains to bread and all-purpose flours. Whereas gaseous chlorine has been replaced by other chemicals for the treatment of bread and all-purpose flours, it has become increasingly important in the treatment of cake flour, particularly if the flour is to be used for high-ratio cakes. For this purpose, sufficient chlorine is used in the bleaching of cake flour to lower the pH of a flour slurry to approximately 4.8. The bleaching effect is only one reason for the treatment. Baking quality is affected greatly by treatment with chlorine; in fact, high-ratio cakes are likely to fall if made with untreated cake flour. Several approaches have been used in the study of the mechanisms involved. Chlorine is known to react with most of the flour components (Whistler and Pyler, 1968) and details of some of the reactions have been established. Much is yet to be learned, however, concerning the reasons for chlorine's beneficial effect on cake flour.

Gamma Irradiation

Relatively low doses of γ-irradiation eliminate insect infestation of wheat and flour; therefore, the use of cobalt-60 for the irradiation of wheat and its products was one of the first food applications of γ-irradiation to be approved by the Food and Drug Administration. An absorbed dose of 20,000–50,000 rad (20–50 krad) was approved in 1963. Later cesium-137 also was approved as a source of γ-irradiation.

Considerable study has been made of the effects of irradiation on the properties of wheat and flour and on organoleptic qualities of flour products. Milner (1957) reported that physical properties of dough, as well as loaf quality, were affected by γ-irradiation of wheat prior to milling. A dosage of 124,000 rep (approximately 114 krad) actually resulted in improved bread quality, whereas treatment at higher levels had deleterious effects. Fifield et al. (1967) reported that γ-irradiation of wheat in doses of 10–175 krad did not affect the milling properties. Biochemical and physical properties were affected little except for decreased sedimentation values with increased radiation dosage. This effect, reflecting a decreased water-imbibing capacity of wheat protein, did not result in changes in physical properties of dough and bread or in organoleptic quality of bread. On the other hand, Miller et al. (1965) reported that cake and bread made from flour irradiated at dosages as low as 20 and 50 krad were less palatable than the controls. Irradiation of the wheat prior to milling gave similar results. Factors such as the type of wheat or flour irradiated and the formula used for the flour product may influence the effect of low-level γ-irradiation and result in contradictory results of studies. With the small irradiation dosages that are feasible, γ-irradiation apparently may, but need not, have serious deleterious effects.

FLOUR COMPONENTS

The average proximate composition of several types of flour is shown in Table 1. The relative protein concentrations are of importance; thus,

TABLE 1.   Average Composition of Wheat Flours[a]

Flour	Percent Water	Percent Protein	Percent Fat	Percent Total Carbo-hydrate	Percent Ash
Whole wheat (from hard wheat)	12	13.3	2.0	71.0	1.7
Straight, hard wheat	12	11.8	1.2	74.5	0.46
Straight, soft wheat	12	9.7	1.0	76.9	0.42
All purpose	12	10.5	1.0	76.1	0.43
Cake	12	7.5	0.8	79.4	0.31

[a] Values from Watt and Merrill (1963).

values are presented on a 12 percent moisture basis for the purpose of comparison. Moisture content actually ranges from 12 to 14 percent and may not exceed 15 percent in the United States. The tendency for fat and ash values to vary directly with the protein concentration is related to the milling process and to the previously mentioned heterogeneity of the wheat kernel. An inverse relationship between protein and carbohydrate concentrations is mathematically inevitable.

Proteins

Wheat proteins have been the subject of much study. Reviews include those of Pence and Nimmo (1964), Pomeranz (1968), Sullivan (1965), and Wall (1967).

The physical properties of wheat endosperm protein are such that wheat flour is particularly well adapted to bread-making. It has long been known that wheat protein is not a chemical entity, but rather that the proteins present in wheat are complex, variable, and diverse. Since Osborne's (1907) early fractionation of wheat-flour proteins into four fractions on the basis of solubility, the more sophisticated methods of electrophoresis, high-speed centrifugation, and column chromatography have been applied to their fractionation. The protein fractions have been subjected to further study, including amino acid analysis, as well as other chemical study. Much remains to be learned concerning the chemical basis for variations in baking quality of flours.

The heterogeneity of the wheat endosperm was mentioned in the section on air classification. Uneven distribution of protein in the endosperm is indicated by analytical values averaging 45 and 11 percent reported by Kent (1966) for a hard-wheat subaleurone and inner endosperm, respectively.

Wheat endosperm proteins may be classed histologically as well as on the basis of solubility and electrophoretic behavior. Related to the endosperm structure, which consists of starch granules embedded in a protein matrix, is Hess's finding (Sullivan, 1965) that the "wedge" protein that fills the interstices between starch granules is different from the "adhering" protein that is bound to the surface of starch granules. Hess found the adhering protein to show no gluten-forming properties. Sullivan (1965) states that both wedge and adhering proteins form gluten and that the gluten properties are affected by the presence of lipid. According to Jones and Dimler (1962), the adhering and wedge proteins have the same components, but the proportions of albumins and globulins are higher in the adhering than in the wedge protein.

The albumins and globulins are referred to as the "soluble proteins." The gliadins and the glutenins, which are more abundant than the soluble proteins, are often referred to as the "gluten proteins" of wheat because of their ability to form gluten, the cohesive, elastic complex that develops when flour is mixed with water.

Albumins

As many as 11 components of this water-soluble fraction of wheat-flour protein have been reported to be detectable by paper electrophoresis. In addition to differing electrophoretically, the members of the group differ in isoelectric point. They are rather similar in molecular size and in amino acid composition. Their tryptophan content is higher than that of other wheat proteins. Although the albumins make up only 6–12 percent of the total flour protein, they apparently contribute to the baking quality of flour. Pence and co-workers (1951) found that when flour was fractionated and then reconstituted with the omission of the water-soluble fraction, baking quality was impaired. Addition of the water-solubles during reconstitution restored the normal baking performance, and most of the effect was traced to the albumin portion of the fraction. The exact mechanism by which the albumins affect a dough still has not been reported and the suggestion has been made recently (AACC, 1970) that the apparent beneficial effect may actually have been attributable to pentosans in the albumin fraction.

Globulins

Representing 5–12 percent of the total flour protein, the globulins of wheat flour are characterized by low tryptophan and high arginine concentrations. They are soluble in dilute salt solutions. At least two, and possibly more, globulins are present. Whether they contribute to the baking quality of flour is a question that has not been definitely answered. Their removal from a flour results in impaired baking performance, but Pence and Nimmo (1964) point out the possibility that the salt solutions used for extracting globulins from flour may affect other flour constituents and thus confound the evidence.

Gluten Proteins

High concentrations of glutamine, asparagine, and proline are characteristic of the major flour proteins, the gliadins and the glutenins. The gliadins, which are prolamines, are soluble in 60–70 percent ethanol; the glutenins are soluble in dilute acids and bases. Components of these fractions have been reported to number anywhere from 4 to more than 20. Huebner and Wall (1966) fractionated wheat gliadin into at least nine components by ion-exchange chromatography. The fractions showed small but significant differences in amino acid composition.

Gliadin and glutenin fractions differ greatly in molecular weight. Gliadins vary within a relatively narrow range, 20,000–50,000, whereas glutenin components have been reported to have molecular weights ranging from 50,000 into the millions. Nielsen and co-workers (1962, 1968) used disulfide cleavage to show that gliadin and glutenin fractions differ in their disulfide linkages. When disulfide bonds of purified gliadin were cleaved by reducing agents, the result was a relatively small decrease in molecular weight. With similar treatment of the glutenin fraction, its average molecular weight was reduced to about 20,000, and heterogeneity of the fraction was greatly reduced. The above findings indicate that disulfide linkages in gliadin are primarily intramolecular and that those in glutenin are intermolecular as well as intramolecular. The large amount of intermolecular bonding to which the glutenin fraction is subject results in macromolecules that do not migrate during electrophoresis. The dependence of molecular weight on the extent of reducing conditions has resulted in confusion as to the number of glutenin components and their properties.

Tracey (1967) points out the lack of information as to the relationship between the low- and the high-molecular-weight gluten proteins in the developing endosperm. It is not known whether maturation involves synthesis of a number of proteins differing in molecular weight and other properties or of relatively few simple proteins that later polymerize. To the extent that polymerization is involved, how much occurs during maturation and how much occurs later when the structure is disturbed is an unanswered question.

Differences in molecular weight, in types of linkages, and in the chains of gliadin and reduced glutenin may be related to their functional behavior in gluten formation. Study of the relationship between wheat protein structure and functional properties has been hampered by problems of separating pure, unmodified fractions. Likewise, study of the possible significance of the relative proportions of gliadins and glutenins has not been fully rewarding because of the great influence of preparation methods on the apparent proportions. Considerable attention has been devoted to the amino acid content of the gluten proteins and to terminal amino acid groups. Again, improved methods of preparation of homogeneous fractions are needed before results can be very meaningful. When such methods are available, the sequence of amino acids in the different polypeptide chains will be an increasingly fruitful area of investigation.

Considerable work in progress at the time of writing is concerned with the extent to which each of the gluten proteins varies among wheat varieties and the actual function of each protein in bread-making. These and other questions perhaps will have been resolved by publication time. The student should refer to the research literature for developments.

Enzymes

Wheat enzymes include amylases, proteinases, lipases, and oxidases. Although poorly characterized thus far, many are in the soluble protein fraction of wheat and thus apparently are albumins or globulins. Enzymes constitute only a small percentage of total flour protein, but they may influence flour properties significantly.

Hydrolysis of starch in wheat is catalyzed primarily by amylases. β-amylase, which is relatively abundant in flour from sound, ungerminated wheat, breaks $\alpha 1,4$ bonds, releasing maltose units beginning at nonreducing ends of chains, and leaving a residue of "limit dextrin" within the branch points of amylopectin molecules. α-amylase also cleaves $\alpha 1,4$ bonds, but in a random fashion, forming dextrins. Raw granular starch is essentially not subject to amylolytic activity, but susceptibility increases during gelatinization. Wheat α-amylase, with a temperature optimum of 60–65° C, is potentially more important in its effect than is β-amylase with its much lower optimum of 48–51° C and early inactivation during gelatinization; however, α-amylase is present only in traces in sound, ungerminated grain. In commercial bread-making, α-amylases of fungal origin often are added for improvement of rheological properties of dough and grain of bread. Fungal α-amylase is inactivated at much lower temperatures than is wheat α-amylase, and thus its concentration can be varied over a wide range without a resulting sticky crumb.

Proteolytic enzymes of at least two types are present in wheat, but their activity is low in flour from North American grain. Limited amounts in added fungal enzyme preparations during commercial bread-making may improve dough-handling properties and result in increased uniformity of browning.

The lipases, which split ester linkages in glycerides, releasing free fatty acids, are most likely to exert an appreciable effect during storage. The resulting hydrolytic rancidity probably is of greater significance in unmilled wheat and in whole-wheat flour than in white flour, because lipase activity is much lower in endosperm than in other tissues of the wheat kernel.

Of the oxidases present in flour, lipoxidase has been studied most. Lipoxidase catalyzes peroxidation of unsaturated fatty acids. The oxidized lipids then react with xanthophyll pigments. Because of the resultant bleaching effect, lipoxidase is sometimes used in the baking industry. Catalase, peroxidase, and ascorbic acid oxidase also are present in wheat, but their activities are low in flour.

Johnson (1965) reviews the use of added enzymes in wheat technology, as well as the activity of enzymes naturally present in flour.

Carbohydrates

Intensive study of wheat carbohydrates has developed more slowly than the study of wheat proteins because carbohydrates were long considered relatively inert components of wheat flour. In recent years, advances in methodology for their study and findings concerning their roles in flour products have been mutually stimulating, and the study of wheat carbohydrates has gained momentum. Recent reviews include those of Kent-Jones and Amos (1967), Medcalf and Gilles (1968), Neukom et al. (1967), Pomeranz (1968), and Shellenberger et al. (1966).

Starch

Starch, by far the major component of flour, represents 75–80 percent of its dry weight. The physical structural unit is the granule, of which there are two general types in wheat: relatively small granules, which tend to be spherical, and larger granules, which are more likely to be lenticular. Stamberg (1939) reported that granules having average diameters of less than 15μ make up nearly 88 percent by number but only 7 percent by weight of a wheat starch; larger granules (mostly 15–35μ) then constitute about 12 percent by number and 93 percent by weight. Distributed throughout the granule are amylose and amylopectin, both polymers of D-glucose. The relative proportions of amylose, the linear polymer with α1,4-linkages, and amylopectin, the branched polymer with α1,4- and some α1,6-linkages, are less variable for wheat starch than for cornstarch. The amylose content averages 25 percent of the starch in wheat, according to Medcalf and Gilles (1968). The chemical and physical properties of starch have been discussed in detail in Chapter 4. The behavior of starch in dough will be discussed later in this chapter.

Cellulose

The strong, woody cellulose that is a major component of wheat bran is essentially removed during milling. The cellulose that is found in the walls of endosperm cells is more likely to appear in flour but is of little consequence because of its low concentration.

Pentosans

Wheat pentosans are polysaccharides with the pentoses arabinose and xylose as major structural components. Crude pentosan preparations from flour contain glycoproteins (Kulp, 1968). Classified as hemicelluloses, the pentosans are found primarily in and just inside the cell walls, and although their concentration is much higher in bran than in endosperm, they may constitute 2–3 percent of white flour. They are of two types, water "soluble" and water insoluble, which apparently differ in branching and in molecular size and shape. About 20–25 percent of wheat flour pentosans are water soluble according to Neukom et al. (1967). Although the water-soluble pentosans may constitute less than one percent of the total weight of flour, they can be important to rheological properties of dough, as will be seen later. The water-insoluble pentosans are less well characterized than the water-soluble ones because of difficulty of isolation and purification in unmodified form.

Dextrins and Sugars

Dextrins, compounds chemically similar to starches but having lower molecular weights, are present naturally in flour in amounts not exceeding 0.2 percent. Sugars are also present in small amounts, normally totalling less than 2 percent. Maltose probably is the most abundant of the sugars naturally present, reaching levels of 0.5–1.0 percent. Small amounts of glucose, fructose, sucrose, and some trioses have been reported, and there is potential for formation of additional amounts of these compounds through enzymatic action when conditions permit.

Lipids

Wheat lipids constitute 1–2 percent of the endosperm. Because of the consequently low concentration in white flour, as well as lack of adequate methods and equipment for study of lipids, the question of their relation to flour quality was neglected for many years. Much work devoted to wheat lipids has been carried out in recent years and has been reviewed by Pomeranz (1967, 1968).

Attempts to relate specific lipids to baking performance of flour have necessitated extensive lipid-fractionation procedures. One method of making a preliminary fractionation of flour lipids involves the use of different solvents for extracting free and bound lipids from flour. Free lipids are readily extracted with petroleum ether, whereas lipids that are bound to starch and protein require a more polar solvent system such as water-saturated butanol or a mixture of chloroform, methanol, and water. Some lipids are so strongly bound to other flour components that their removal in unmodified form is almost impossible. The bound lipids that are extractable by water-saturated butanol are primarily polar lipids, consisting chiefly of phospholipids and the glycolipid digalactosyl glyceride.

Once a preliminary separation of free and bound lipids has been made, the free lipids may be fractionated further by elution from a silicic acid column. Solvents of increasing polarity are passed successively through the column until the highly polar methanol has removed the most polar lipids, the phospholipids and glycolipids. The phospholipids are phosphatidyl choline (lecithin) and the cephalins phosphatidyl serine and phosphatidyl ethanolamine. Although digalactosyl glyceride is present, the chief glycolipid of the free polar lipid fraction is monogalactosyl glyceride. The free polar lipids, particularly the glycolipids, appear to be important to bread-making quality. The less polar compounds of the free lipids are mostly triglycerides, with smaller amounts of mono- and diglycerides, free fatty acids, and nonsaponifiables. The above information concerning lipid fractionation is summarized in Figure 4.

The reason for the particularly strong binding of some flour lipids by other flour components is not known. Some speculation has involved the possibility that the different lipid forms represent some sort of equilibrium during lipid biosynthesis. During maturation of the wheat

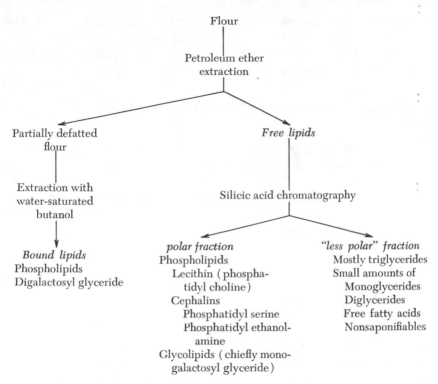

FIGURE 4. Fractionation of wheat-flour lipids.

kernel, the proportion of free polar lipids increases, while free fatty acids and mono- and diglycerides decrease in concentration. Pomeranz (1968) considers it likely that changes in lipids and in proteins occur simultaneously in maturing wheat and that the apparent essentiality of free polar lipids to maximum bread quality may represent an interaction between flour lipids and proteins.

Minerals and Vitamins

The mineral content of the endosperm is only about 0.3 percent, and the concentration of minerals in flour is correspondingly low. The more highly refined the flour, the lower is its ash content. Phosphorus and potassium are the major mineral components of unenriched flour, followed by magnesium and calcium and traces of iron, aluminum, and sulfur. Enriched flour contains iron at a level comparable to that of whole wheat. Calcium is an optional enrichment ingredient.

Although whole wheat contains appreciable quantities of members of the B-vitamin complex, unenriched white flour does not. Enrichment raises the concentrations of thiamin and niacin to levels similar to those in whole wheat and that of riboflavin to a higher level than that in the whole grain.

FUNCTIONS AND BEHAVIOR OF FLOUR COMPONENTS IN DOUGHS

Tremendous scientific resources have been devoted to the study of physical and chemical changes taking place in the wheat proteins during dough mixing, of interactions between wheat proteins and other flour components, and of the relation of these factors to "baking quality" of flour. The complexity of the mechanisms involved has fascinated cereal chemists for a long time.

Proteins

When the gliadin and glutenin proteins are hydrated separately, gliadin is the more extensible and tacky and glutenin the more elastic and tough. Hydrated together, they form a cohesive, elastic three-dimensional gluten network. A bread dough containing optimally developed gluten has truly remarkable properties. Cohesiveness and elasticity are such that bubbles of gas are able to expand without an undue amount of coalescence or of escape to the atmosphere. At the same time, perfect elasticity is undesirable because it would permit a rolled-out dough to draw up into a ball. Optimal gluten development varies with the qualities desired in the final product and represents a rather delicate balance among the many factors that affect dough structure.

If it is remembered that the protein in flour occurs as wedge-shaped pieces of matrix, as the protein portion of intact endosperm cells, and as aggregates of protein and starch granules, it seems obvious that "doughing" must involve, in addition to hydration, some disaggregation and some protein-protein interaction. Gluten proteins take up twice their weight of water during hydration. The disaggregation occurring during the early stages of mixing probably is largely physical, resulting from tearing and shearing forces. With hydration and disaggregation, followed by protein-protein interaction, a continuous gluten matrix forms. The relative insolubility of gluten proteins contributes to their cohering rather than dispersing in spite of their large imbibition capacity.

Figure 5 is a diagrammatic representation of the possible relationship between gliadin and glutenin molecules in gluten. Although surfaces of

Gliadin

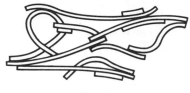

Glutenin

Gluten (gliadin + glutenin)

FIGURE 5. Effect of wheat protein structure on molecular association and properties. (Wall and Beckwith, 1969.)

both gliadin and glutenin molecules have many functional groups and, therefore, the potential for intermolecular association, the compact shape of gliadin molecules limits the possible contact. The "sprawly," elongated structure of glutenin, on the other hand, provides much opportunity for molecular interaction. These differences in molecular interaction are manifest not only in viscosity and other properties of dispersions but also in the properties of films. A film prepared from glutenin is stronger and less subject to elongation than one prepared from gliadin. When gliadin and glutenin are mixed, as in gluten, the desirable intermediate properties result (Wall and Beckwith, 1969).

The molecular structures of gluten proteins permit several types of protein-protein interactions to occur. In Figure 6 the molecular structure is represented with a backbone made of the polypeptide chain, from which extend the side chains characteristic of the different amino acids. The covalent disulfide bonds of cystine can link different polypeptide chains or different portions of single chains; that is, they can provide either inter- or intramolecular linkages. The high concentrations of glutamine and asparagine in gluten proteins contribute to cohesiveness because their free amide groups participate in hydrogen bonding. Dough formation is one of many examples in food science of weak bonds such as hydrogen bonds being so numerous as to have an important total effect. Nonpolar groups such as the side chain of leucine partici-

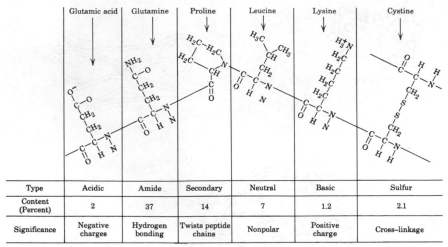

	Glutamic acid	Glutamine	Proline	Leucine	Lysine	Cystine
Type	Acidic	Amide	Secondary	Neutral	Basic	Sulfur
Content (Percent)	2	37	14	7	1.2	2.1
Significance	Negative charges	Hydrogen bonding	Twists peptide chains	Nonpolar	Positive charge	Cross-linkage

FIGURE 6. Representative amino acids in wheat gluten proteins. (Wall and Beckwith, 1969.)

pate with one another in hydrophobic bonding in aqueous media. Salt linkages between charged groups result from the presence of glutamic acid and lysine residues.

Different chemical treatments apparently modify the rheological properties of dough by affecting different types of cohesive bonds. Much of the work on gluten structure has involved disulfide linkages, which are primarily intramolecular in gliadins and both intra- and intermolecular in glutenin components. Some of these disulfide bonds are present before dough mixing is begun; the disulfide content of flour ranges from 7 to 17 μEq/g, as compared with about 1 μEq/g of sulfhydryl (Mecham, 1968). Some disulfide bonds are broken during mixing; some are formed. The relative extents of cleavage and formation of disulfide bonds depend on the presence of reducing and oxidizing agents. Bushuk et al. (1968) state that reducing agents not only decrease the work required for dough formation but also lead to rapid relaxation of the structure; oxidizing agents are important, therefore, for stabilization of the structure. Occluded atmospheric oxygen contributes to oxidation of sulfhydryl groups, apparently through peroxidation of lipids as well as directly, although the role of lipid peroxides as sulfhydryl-oxidizing agents is perhaps relatively minor.

With continued mixing, chemical disaggregation occurs to an extent that varies with the flour and with mixing conditions. The involvement of the various types of protein-protein bonds is of interest to cereal chemists (Tsen, 1967). It has been suggested that differences in doughing properties of flours may be related to the size of protein aggregates present and to susceptibility to disaggregation during mixing.

Mullen and Smith (1968) studied the effect of flour proteins on mixing properties of dough. They used two hard-wheat flours that were similar in protein concentration but different in mixing properties. Their work suggested that changes in solubility, dispersibility, and state of aggregation of protein are important to mixing time. The two flours were inherently different in their level of gliadin, the flour with the lower level showing the longer mixing time and greater stability. The flours differed also in the rate at which protein aggregates apparently were broken down and dispersed, rapid disaggregation favoring short mixing time and thus characterizing "weak" flour.

Lipids

Protein is not the only component of the gluten matrix of a dough. Gluten that has been separated from a dough and then purified and lyophilized contains about eight percent lipid on a dry-matter basis. The much higher concentration of lipid in gluten than in flour is indicative of a high degree of lipid binding by gluten protein during dough formation. Furthermore, the binding is of such a nature as to make the extraction of lipids with organic solvents difficult. The greater the extent of dough development, the greater is the reduction in extractability of lipid. In one of the early studies of lipid binding during dough mixing, Olcott and Mecham (1947) found that excess flour lipids added in amounts up to three times that normally present could be bound during doughing. Phospholipids showed preferential binding, and the glutenin fraction of the gluten was primarily involved.

The nature of the protein-lipid complex has been of interest. Glass (1960) discusses possible types of protein-lipid bonds in a review. Grosskreutz (1961) used electron microscopy and X-ray diffraction to obtain evidence that resulted in a proposed model for gluten structure in dough (Figure 7). According to the proposal, long coiled or folded chains form gluten platelets in which polypeptides have their hydrophilic side chains oriented outward and their hydrophobic groups oriented inward. Interspersed among the protein platelets, according to the theory, are double layers of phospholipid, with each layer attached through saltlike linkages to protein, forming lipoprotein layers. Whereas the dough elasticity is attributable to the coiled and folded protein molecules, slippage is possible because the center of the lipopro-

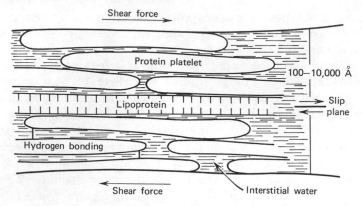

FIGURE 7. Proposed model of gluten sheet structure. (Grosskreutz, 1961.)

tein unit consists of the relatively weak bonds between the phospholipid molecules. If phospholipids are extracted from flour before gluten development, the gluten mass becomes elastic but not plastic.

Binger (1965) reported more recently that the complexes are likely to include metallic ions as well as protein and phospholipid. Binger considers the lipoproteins to exist and function as micelles rather than as sheets. According to Fullington (1969), the metal-containing lipoproteins are formed through chelation of phospholipid and protein on a shared metal ion. Phospholipids have long been recognized as chelating agents. Open coordination positions on lipid-bound metal are available for bonding with other molecules. Proteins of the water extract from flour bind with metal and phospholipid, the extent of binding varying with the protein structure. The specific protein-lipid combinations formed through this type of interaction are not necessarily the same as those resulting in the absence of metal ions.

Considerable recent work has been concerned with the relation of flour lipids to bread quality. Ether extraction of flour has no effect on baking properties when the flour is used in bread containing no shortening. Extraction with water-saturated butanol, however, has a drastic effect on baking quality, resulting in a tight dough that cannot expand properly during fermentation and baking. With restoration of the butanol-extracted lipid to the flour, baking quality is restored. The difference in effect of the two solvents is attributable to the extraction of polar lipids by the highly polar butanol.

When polar lipids are added to flour that has been extracted with water-saturated butanol, the improved baking quality is evidenced by increased loaf volume and improved crumb grain. The total improving effect results from very small additions and within a narrow range, as compared with the effect of added wheat protein, which will increase loaf volume over a wide range of concentration. Pomeranz et al. (1968) interpret these effects to indicate that the inherent bread-making potential of a flour is a function of the gluten protein, whereas lipids fulfill certain functional requirements, and that once those requirements are met, further additions are of no benefit.

Chiu et al. (1968) studied lipid binding in flours that differed inherently in bread-making potential and in flours reconstituted at different protein levels from fractions of a single parent flour, both solvent extracted and unextracted. The bread formula included shortening. Lipid binding during mixing increased with mixing time and with the protein content of the flour, and there was some indication that flour quality as well as quantity influenced the extent of lipid binding in doughs. The reconstituted flours from fractions of unextracted flour showed binding of flour lipids but essentially no binding of shortening lipid during mixing. The reconstituted flours from fractions of extracted flour did show some binding of shortening lipid during mixing, the shortening lipid apparently having substituted for flour lipids that had been removed. With reconstituted flours from both extracted and unextracted flours, binding of shortening occurred during baking, the amount of binding increasing with the protein content. Work underway at present is concerned with the involvement of specific polar and nonpolar lipids in lipid binding, the reasons for differences among the lipids, and the relation of binding of the different lipids to the baking performance of flour.

Carbohydrates

Starch granules become embedded in the gluten matrix during mixing. As gas cells form during fermentation of bread dough, the starch granules become oriented parallel to the gluten films that surround the cells. According to Medcalf (1968), the strong adhesive forces between starch and gluten contribute to continuity of the cell structure. When heat is applied, the gas cells expand and the elastic gluten network stretches accordingly. The starch granules take up water; although the available water is limited and only partial gelatinization occurs, the granules become sufficiently flexible to stretch somewhat along with the gluten. Pyler (1967) describes the behavior of starch in the later stages of heating as consisting of removal of as much water as possible from the gluten, leaving a dehydrated gluten structure that ruptures but is semirigid until coagulated by heat. The starch not only contributes to rigidity through water uptake but also provides the points of weakness at which ruptures in the structure occur. If there were no such ruptures and expanded gases could not escape, negative internal pressures would develop during cooling, resulting in an imploded product! According to Medcalf (1968), starch probably contributes also to increasing stability of the cooling product through association of leached amylose.

Jongh (1961) demonstrated that it is possible to develop an acceptable bread structure in the absence of gluten. Wheat starch and water, in proportions similar to those of a normal bread dough, were mixed with sodium chloride, sucrose, yeast, and various amounts of glyceryl monostearate. The handling and baking procedures were similar to those for ordinary bread. In the absence of glyceryl monostearate the dough could be poured from one container to another. With addition of glyceryl monostearate, the dough became more nearly solid and plastic. Starch bread baked from the dough containing no glyceryl monostearate was sunken in the center and had a coarse, irregular grain; it became hard with cooling. Addition of glyceryl monostearate increased loaf volume and fineness of the grain and decreased rigidity of the crumb; moisture content of the baked bread was increased. Microscopic examination of the crumb revealed that in the absence of glyceryl monostearate, starch granules were elongated in shape and bound to one another on all sides; with addition of glyceryl monostearate, the granules became more nearly normal in shape and points of contact between them decreased in number, resulting in a less compact crumb. Jongh stated that glyceryl monostearate probably was adsorbed on starch granules in the unheated suspension and caused the formation of a continuous flocculum; during heating, the binding between swollen starch granules was probably weakened by the oriented binding of glyceryl monostearate molecules.

Jongh et al. (1968) went on to test the theory that any material causing coherence of ungelatinized starch granules could improve starch breads. Lard, egg albumen, and wheat gluten were shown to have such an effect. The crumb of the baked bread was slightly more elastic when protein was added than when glyceryl monostearate was used.

Pomeranz (1969) still considers gluten essential to bread that is worthy of its name. He recognizes the importance of starch but does not consider it to be *the* flour component essential to bread structure.

Kulp (1968) reviews the properties of wheat endosperm pentosans in relation to their functional behavior. Both the water-soluble and the water-insoluble pentosans are hydrophilic and therefore tend to contribute to dough stiffness by immobilizing free water. Yet the water-soluble pentosans tend to have an improving effect and water-insoluble pentosans an adverse effect on bread quality.

Pentosans interact with protein, probably primarily through hydrogen bonds. Water-soluble and -insoluble pentosans differ as to degree of polymerization and of branching. Kulp postulates that because of these molecular differences, the two pentosan fractions might interact with different proteins: the water-soluble pentosans with proteins that are not essential to dough structure and the water-insoluble fraction with structurally important gluten proteins. Such pentosan-protein interaction would decrease the potential for protein-protein interaction. The adverse effect of the water-insoluble fraction is not necessarily apparent in dough properties but appears during baking when the pentosan-gluten bonds, according to the theory, fail to withstand the stress of dough expansion.

Wheat pentosans affect soft-wheat products also. Gilles (1960) reported that when water-insoluble pentosans were added to a soft-wheat flour of marginal quality, the grain of yellow cake was improved and the volume increased. On the other hand, excessive amounts of either water-soluble or -insoluble pentosans tended to have the undesired effect of reducing the spread of sugar cookies.

The studies cited above are representative of the approaches used to assess the functionality of flour components. Results obtained thus far point up the complexity of protein-lipid interactions. The variability of protein concentration and quality in different flours and the heterogeneity and variability of flour lipids contribute to the complexity. Evidence of protein-carbohydrate interactions further emphasizes the dynamic and variable nature of the forces responsible for dough structure.

TESTS OF FLOUR QUALITY

Understanding of the research literature concerning flour performance requires some background with respect to methods and equipment used in flour studies. The American Association of Cereal Chemists (1962) has adopted official methods for numerous flour and dough tests, as well as baking tests. The development and status of physical dough testing methods and equipment have been reviewed by Brabender (1965) and by Kent-Jones and Amos (1967).

Flour Tests

Routine laboratory analyses on flour include moisture, ash, and nitrogen determinations. These analyses are usually carried out by conventional methods, including AACC 44–15 and 44–40 for moisture, 08–01 for ash, and 46–13 for nitrogen.

Flour color is of special interest in studies of the effects of bleaches.

Methods of evaluation range from visual inspection of wet or dry compressed samples to reflectance measurement in instruments developed particularly for use with flour.

The degree of flour granularity affects other properties of flour, and thus particle size distributions frequently are of interest. Microscopic examination is a somewhat tedious means of obtaining such information. Another procedure sometimes used is sieving through a series of standard-mesh sieves. Most particle-size-distribution data, however, are obtained by sedimentation methods based on the principle that if particles are alike in density, their rate of settling from a suspension varies with their diameters. When the method is applied to flour, the suspension is nonaqueous. Methods differ with respect to the specific suspension medium used, the procedure for assessing rate of sedimentation, and the type of sedimentation (gravitational or centrifugal).

Several flour tests are based on the relation of hydration capacity to quantity and quality of gluten protein. Because hydration capacity varies greatly among different flours and is known to be related to baking performance, attempts have been made, with varying degrees of success, to correlate the results of relatively simple flour tests with the results of baking tests. In a sedimentation test (AACC Method 56–61), a relatively small amount of flour is suspended in a dilute lactic acid-isopropanol solution, and the suspension is allowed to stand in a graduated cylinder. The volume of sediment, read after five minutes, is indicative of hydration capacity. Changes in the viscosity of a flour-water suspension with additions of lactic acid provide another indirect measure of hydration capacity (AACC Method 56–80). A MacMichael viscometer is used. Somewhat more direct and not requiring a viscometer is centrifugation of the acidulated flour suspension and weighing of the solids (Finney and Yamazaki, 1946). The increase in weight, expressed as a percent of the original flour weight, represents the water-retention capacity of the flour.

A lactic acid solution was used in development of the above tests because much of the work has involved hard-wheat flour in relation to performance in bread. Yeast doughs have pHs below 7. Similar tests have been devised especially for soft-wheat flour, which frequently is used in chemically leavened baked products having batter or dough pHs above 7. Dilute sodium bicarbonate solution replaces dilute lactic acid solution and, at least in some instances, gives results that are more predictive of the baking quality of soft-wheat flour than are the tests in acid solution (Finney and Yamazaki, 1953; Yamazaki, 1953).

The amylograph or a similar instrument, the viscograph, is commonly used for heating a flour-water suspension at a uniform rate and recording the change in relative viscosity. The suspension is held in a rotating bowl that has pins rising from the bottom. Suspended into the bowl is the head of the instrument, which contains additional pins to give a stirring effect and also is connected to the recorder. The bowl is rotated at a constant rate, and the suspension exerts an increasing torque on the head as viscosity increases during heating. The increasing torque is recorded on the chart (amylogram or viscogram) as increasing peak height. The changing viscosity is due to gelatinization of starch; because amylolytic action is manifest in decreased viscosity of a starch or flour paste, the instrument is useful in studies concerned with activity of added α-amylase preparations. Further information concerning the amylograph is presented in Chapter 4.

Another physical test for following amylolytic activity is the "falling number test" (AACC Method 56–81), which requires special apparatus obtainable only from a Swedish manufacturer. Falling number is the time in seconds required for the stirrer to fall a given distance through a hot flour paste.

A useful technique for studying the roles of flour components is fractionation of flour, followed by reconstitution. Fractionation is accomplished by different procedures, all involving centrifugation and differing primarily as to whether a dough or a slurry is prepared initially. The products of fractionation are gluten, the water solubles, prime starch, and the "tailings fraction," all in powdered form. The tailings fraction contains the hemicellulosic material, primarily pentosans, as well as damaged and undamaged starch. A goal of all fractionation procedures, of course, is to obtain the fractions with as little modification as possible. Fractionation procedures involving a dough and a slurry respectively are described by Zaehringer et al. (1956) and Sollars (1958). Fractionation of flours that differ greatly in their baking performance has often been followed by extensive chemical and physical testing of the fractions. Reconstitution with systematic omission and substitution of the fractions then provides "flours" from which considerable information may be obtained. In these and other studies of flour, physical tests made on doughs, as well as baking tests, have been of importance.

Dough Tests

The farinograph is a widely used instrument based on the principle that the extent of water absorption by flour during mixing, the consistency of the dough, the time required for the development of maximum dough stiffness, and the resistance of the mixed dough to breakdown all depend on flour "quality." In the farinograph, water is mixed with flour under strict control of the rate of mixing and other conditions. As the mixer shaft rotates, the resistance of the dough to the rotation is transmitted to a recording pen; as the torque increases, the height of the recorder pen increases. The curve may maintain maximum peak height for a time or it may begin to drop immediately, depending on the flour. Typical curves (farinograms) are shown in Figure 8. Farinogram (*a*) is typical of a strong flour and (*b*) of a weaker flour with relatively low tolerance

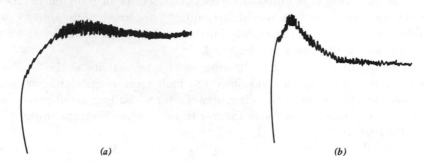

(*a*)   (*b*)

FIGURE 8. Farinograms of (*a*) a strong flour and (*b*) a weak flour.

to continued mixing. Peak height, *a*, in Figure 9 indicates dough consistency; *b* is the time in minutes required for dough development; *c*, the time in minutes that maximum peak height is maintained, is a measure of stability. Dough breakdown may be estimated either as the extent of drop in the curve, *d*, after a given mixing time or as the time required to bring about a specified drop. One of the measurements usually made in using the farinograph is the amount of water taken up by the dough

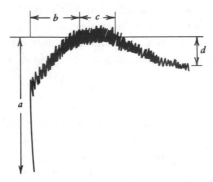

FIGURE 9. Farinogram parameters.

(referred to as "absorption") under otherwise constant conditions of mixing. Because these conditions include dough consistency, that is, a specified peak height, some trial and error is necessary. Occasionally the peak height with water absorption controlled may be of more interest. In either case, dough stability is an important measurement, as is dough breakdown. The time required for dough development may be either controlled, again requiring trial and error, or one of the measurements made.

The mixograph is a recording dough mixer that is somewhat similar to the farinograph. Its graphs (mixograms) provide information similar to that obtained with the farinograph.

The extensigraph measures extensibility of dough and resistance to extension. Extensibility is of special interest in fermented doughs. A condition of the test is that it be made on dough mixed in a farinograph under specified conditions. The mixed dough is shaped into two cylinders and fermented in special holders in the extensigraph. After 45 minutes a dough hook is passed slowly through the center of each dough cylinder while the ends of the dough are held firmly in the instrument. As the dough stretches, a curve such as that in Figure 10 is recorded. Extensi-

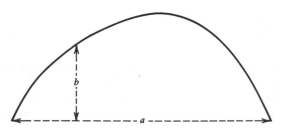

FIGURE 10. Extensigram.

bility of the dough is indicated by the length of the curve in mm, a. The height, b, of the curve 50 mm beyond its origin is a measure of resistance to extension. The "shortness" of the dough relates the two measures: the greater the ratio of b to a, the shorter the dough. The area under the curve indicates the total force exerted on the dough, in general paralleling the "strength" of the flour. The extensigraph is particularly useful in studies of the effect of maturing agents.

Gas production in fermenting doughs has been measured with several instruments, including the fermentograph. This is an ingenious device in which the fermenting dough is contained in a rubber balloon suspended in a constant-temperature water bath and attached to a recording pen.

As carbon dioxide collects in the bag, the increasing buoyancy causes the balloon to rise in the water and the pen to record the rise. The instrument is calibrated so that the resulting graph is a plot of volume of carbon dioxide, in ml, against time.

Baking Tests

Baking performance is recognized as the ultimate criterion of flour quality. Cake flour is evaluated in a cake formula containing no milk and no egg (Kissell, 1959), because such a formula accentuates differences in flour quality. Factors evaluated are optimum liquid level, cake volume, and internal score. Yamazaki (1962) reported that no correlation was found between the above characteristics and flour properties such as ash and protein content, mixogram area, alkaline water retention capacity, pH, and acid viscosity.

For evaluation of straight-grade soft-wheat flour, the cookie-baking test is most satisfactory, cookie spread being the criterion of flour performance. Yamazaki (1953) reported a high negative correlation between cookie diameter and results of the alkaline water retention test. The finding that a relatively early viscosity increase during baking resulted in inferior cookies led to studies of water distribution among dough constituents during the baking process (Yamazaki, 1962). Factors that delay gelatinization of starch were found to favor relatively long maintenance of fluidity and thus increased spread. Application of the cookie-baking test to relatively simple systems showed the mechanism to be complex and to involve an interaction between sugar in the formula and the tailings fraction of the flour. The fact that flours differ in the hydration capacity of their tailings could help explain performance differences in flours that are similar in proximate composition.

Stronger flours are studied in bread formulations. Although water absorption, mixing and fermentation tolerance, and crust and crumb characteristics are of interest, loaf volume provides the most important measure of flour strength. Baking tests have been used for studying the relation of flour strength to wheat variety, to climate and soil, to wheat maturity, to milling and storage practices, and to various physical and chemical treatments.

OTHER FLOURS

Soy Flour

Several types of soy flour, varying chiefly in lipid content, are available. Full-fat and low-fat flours differ in that they contain, respectively, all and part of the fat originally present, or approximately 20 and

7 percent on an 8 percent moisture basis. Defatted soy flour is solvent-extracted to a level of less than 1 percent fat. High-fat flour (12 percent fat on an 8 percent moisture basis) is produced by the addition of oil to defatted soy flour; lecithinated flour results from the addition of lecithin and refined soy oil to defatted soy flour. With the range from less than 1 percent to 20 percent fat, protein concentration ranges from 47 to 37 percent and total carbohydrate from 38 to 30 percent. Ash is much higher in soy flour than in wheat flour, averaging more than 5 percent.

In spite of the much higher concentration of protein in soy flour than in wheat flour, soy flour lacks dough-forming ability. Soy proteins are primarily globulins; soybeans do not contain proteins comparable to wheat gliadin and glutenin. A detailed discussion of the properties of soy proteins is in Wolf's review (1969).

Soy carbohydrate also differs from wheat carbohydrate qualitatively as well as quantitatively. Starch is lacking; the carbohydrates present are fiber, dextrins, pentosans, galactans, sugars, and other oligosaccharides.

The use of soy flour in bread-making has been reviewed by Pomeranz (1966). Particle size, which is variable, is important; coarser flours produce better bread than do the finely powdered flours. Heat treatment of soy flour, which is necessary from a flavor standpoint, has an adverse effect on bread-making potential and the extent of heating must be carefully controlled. Relatively high levels of bromate compensate for the effect of a moderate heat treatment. Soy flour cannot be used as the sole flour in bread. When soy flour is combined with wheat flour in bread-making, the soy flour makes no contribution to the viscoelastic properties of the dough. In addition, water absorption and gas retention are reduced and color and flavor are affected in proportion to the concentration of soy flour.

Rye Flour

Rye flour is graded according to color. As the color varies from light to dark, protein varies from approximately 9 to 16 percent, fat from 1 to 3 percent, total carbohydrate from 78 to 68 percent, and ash from 1 to 2 percent on an 11 percent moisture basis.

Although the proximate composition is rather similar to that of wheat flour and the contents of different types of proteins are not drastically different from those of wheat flour, rye-flour doughs do not behave like wheat-flour doughs. Doughs of rye flour lack a cohesive protein structure, and maturing agents do not have an improving effect. Because of the lack of strength, the doughs have poor gas-retention properties. For the same reason, rye-flour protein cannot be washed out of a dough as can wheat gluten.

The carbohydrate portion of rye flour contains (in addition to starch) fiber, dextrins, sugars, hemicelluloses, and a large quantity of gummy material that apparently consists largely of pentosans. This mucilaginous gum probably is responsible for the stickiness that is characteristic of rye-flour doughs and possibly interferes with development of a cohesive protein structure. "Rye breads" normally contain a rather large proportion of wheat flour because of the above properties of rye flour (Schopmeyer, 1962).

Flours From Other Sources

Flours also may be made from barley, corn, buckwheat, rice, cassava, potatoes, and peanuts. Such flours have relatively limited use in the United States. Some are used in prepared breakfast cereals. Some are minor ingredients in other convenience foods. Most are used to a greater extent in parts of the world where the cultivation of wheat is limited or nonexistent. Kim and deRuiter (1969) developed formulas for breads containing various combinations of flours. Some of the combinations included wheat flour and some did not. Although quality varied tremendously, they considered many of the products to be acceptable.

References

FLOUR PRODUCTION

Claus, W. S. 1964. Flour agglomeration. In *Third National Conference on Wheat Utilization Research*, p. 84. Agricultural Research Service, Washington, D.C.

Fifield, C. C., C. Golumbic, and J. L. Pearson. 1967. Effects of gamma-irradiation on the biochemical storage and breadmaking properties of wheat. *Cereal Sci. Today* 12: 253.

Food and Drug Administration. 1968. Definition and standards for flour. In *Code of Federal Regulations*. Title 21, Part 15.

Kuninori, T., and B. Sullivan. 1968. Disulfide-sulfhydryl interchange studies of wheat flour. II. Reaction of glutathione. *Cereal Chem.* 45: 486.

Larsen, R. A. 1959. Milling. In *The Chemistry and Technology of Cereals as Food and Feed*, S. A. Matz, ed. Chap. 9. The Avi Publishing Co., Westport, Conn.

MacMasters, M. M. 1961. Implications of kernel structure. *Cereal Sci. Today* 6: 144.

Miller, B. S., R. S. Yamahiro, H. B. Trimbo, and K. W. Luke. 1965. Organoleptic quality of cake and bread made from cobalt-60-irradiated flour and flour from irradiated wheat. *Cereal Sci. Today* 10: 80.

Milner, M. 1957. Some effects of gamma irradiation on the biochemical, storage, and breadmaking properties of wheat. *Cereal Sci. Today* 2: 130.

Pace, J. 1966. Chemical changes in flour and dough. Bleachers and improvers. In *The Practice of Flour Milling*, D. Povey, ed. Vol. 2, Chap. 32. The Northern Publishing Co. Ltd., Liverpool, Eng.

Redman, D. G., and J. A. D. Ewart. 1967. Disulphide interchange in dough proteins. *J. Sci. Food Agric. 18*: 15.

Scott, J. H. 1966. The flour milling process (basic). In *The Practice of Flour Milling*, D. Povey, ed. Vol. 1, Chap. 10. The Northern Publishing Co. Ltd., Liverpool, England.

Shellenberger, J. A. 1965. Fifty years of milling advances. *Cereal Sci. Today 10*: 260.

Stewart, P. R., and C. M. Mauritzen. 1966. The incorporation of ^{35}S-cysteine into the proteins of dough by disulphide-sulfhydryl interchange. *Australian J. Biol. Sci. 19*: 1125.

Tsen, C. C., and W. Bushuk. 1968. Reactive and total sulfhydryl and disulfide contents of flours of different mixing properties. *Cereal Chem. 45*: 58.

Wheat Flour Institute. 1965. *From Wheat to Flour*. Wheat Flour Institute, Chicago.

Whistler, R. L., and R. E. Pyler. 1968. Action of chlorine on wheat flour polysaccharides. *Cereal Chem. 45*: 183.

Wichser, F. W. 1958. Air-classified flour fractions. *Cereal Sci. Today 3*: 123.

FLOUR COMPONENTS

AACC. 1970. Composition and functionality in breadmaking. AACC Cereal Seminar, cassette 3, side 1. American Association of Cereal Chemists, St. Paul, Minn.

Huebner, F. R., and J. S. Wall. 1966. Improved chromatographic separation of gliadin proteins on sulfoethyl cellulose. *Cereal Chem. 43*: 325.

Johnson, J. A. 1965. Enzymes in wheat technology in retrospect. *Cereal Sci. Today 10*: 315.

Jones, R. W., and R. J. Dimler. 1962. Electrophoretic composition of glutens from air-classified flours. *Cereal Chem. 39*: 336.

Kent, N. L. 1966. Subaleurone endosperm cells of high protein content. *Cereal Chem. 43*: 585.

Kent-Jones, D. W., and A. J. Amos. 1967. Composition of wheat and products of milling. In *Modern Cereal Chemistry*, p. 1. Food Trade Press Ltd., London.

Kulp, K. 1968. Pentosans of wheat endosperm. *Cereal Sci. Today 13*: 414.

Medcalf, D. G., and K. A. Gilles. 1968. The function of starch in dough. *Cereal Sci. Today 13*: 382.

Neukom, H., T. Geismann, and T. J. Painter. 1967. New aspects of the functions and properties of the soluble wheat-flour pentosans. *Baker's Digest* *41*(5): 52.

Nielsen, H. C., G. E. Babcock, and F. R. Senti. 1962. Molecular weight studies on glutenin before and after disulfide-bond splitting. *Arch. Biochem. Biophys.* *96*: 252.

Nielsen, H. C., A. C. Beckwith, and J. S. Wall. 1968. Effect of disulfide-bond cleavage on wheat gliadin fractions obtained by gel filtration. *Cereal Chem.* *45*: 37.

Osborne, T. B. 1907. *The Proteins of the Wheat Kernel.* Carnegie Institution of Washington, Washington, D.C.

Pence, J. W., A. H. Elder, and D. K. Mecham. 1951. Some effects of soluble flour components on baking behavior. *Cereal Chem.* *28*: 94.

Pence, J. W., and C. C. Nimmo. 1964. New knowledge of wheat proteins. *Baker's Digest 38 (1):* 38.

Pomeranz, Y. 1967. Wheat flour lipids: A minor component of major importance in breadmaking. *Baker's Digest 41 (5):* 48.

Pomeranz, Y. 1968. Relation between chemical composition and bread-making potentialities of wheat flour. In *Advances in Food Research.* Vol. 16, p. 335. Academic Press, New York.

Shellenberger, J. A., M. M. MacMasters, and Y. Pomeranz. 1966. Wheat carbohydrates: Their nature and function in baking. *Baker's Digest 40 (3):* 32.

Stamberg, O. E. 1939. Starch as a factor in dough formation. *Cereal Chem.* *16*: 769.

Sullivan, B. 1965. Wheat protein research. Fifty years of progress. *Cereal Sci. Today 10*: 338.

Tracey, M. V. 1967. Gluten: New light on an old protein. *Cereal Sci. Today 12*: 193.

Wall, J. S. 1967. Origin and behavior of flour proteins. *Baker's Digest 41*(5): 36.

Watt, B. K., and A. L. Merrill. 1963. *Composition of Foods.* Agriculture Handbook No. 8. United States Department of Agriculture, Washington, D.C.

FUNCTIONS AND BEHAVIOR OF FLOUR COMPONENTS IN DOUGHS

Binger, H. P. 1965. Current studies on flour composition and baking quality. *Baker's Digest 39 (6):* 24.

Bushuk, W., C. C. Tsen, and I. Hlynka. 1968. The function of mixing in breadmaking. *Baker's Digest 42 (4):* 36.

Chiu, C., Y. Pomeranz, M. Shogren, and K. F. Finney. 1968. Lipid binding in wheat flours varying in breadmaking potential. *Food Technol.* *22*: 1156.

Fullington, J. G. 1969. Lipid-protein interaction. *Baker's Digest 43 (6):* 34.

Gilles, K. A. 1960. The present status of the role of pentosans in wheat flour quality. *Baker's Digest 34 (5)*: 47.

Glass, R. L. 1960. The role of lipids in baking. *Cereal Sci. Today 5*: 60.

Grosskreutz, J. C. 1961. A lipoprotein model of wheat gluten structure. *Cereal Chem. 38*: 336.

Jongh, G. 1961. The formation of dough and bread structures. I. The ability of starch to form structures, and the improving effect of glyceryl monostearate. *Cereal Chem. 38*: 140.

Jongh, G., T. Slim, and H. Greve. 1968. Bread without gluten. *Baker's Digest 42 (3)*: 24.

Kulp, K. 1968. Pentosans of wheat endosperm. *Cereal Sci. Today 13*: 414.

Mecham, D. K. 1968. Changes in flour protein during dough mixing. *Cereal Sci. Today 13*: 371.

Medcalf, D. G. 1968. Wheat starch properties and their effect on bread baking quality. *Baker's Digest 42 (4)*: 48.

Mullen, J. D., and D. E. Smith. 1968. Protein composition and solubility. *Cereal Sci. Today 13*: 398.

Olcott, H. S., and D. K. Mecham. 1947. Characterization of wheat gluten. I. Protein-lipid complex formation during doughing of flours. Lipoprotein nature of the glutenin fraction. *Cereal Chem. 24*: 407.

Pomeranz, Y. 1969. Bread without bread. *Baker's Digest 43 (1)*: 22.

Pomeranz, Y., M. Shogren, and K. F. Finney. 1968. Functional bread-making properties of wheat flour lipids. 1. Reconstitution studies and properties of defatted flours. *Food Technol. 22*: 324.

Pyler, E. J. 1967. Elements of flour performance. *Baker's Digest 41 (3)*: 55.

Tsen, C. C. 1967. Changes in flour proteins during dough mixing. *Cereal Chem. 44*: 308.

Wall, J. S., and A. C. Beckwith. 1969. Relationship between structure and rheological properties of gluten proteins. *Cereal Sci. Today 14*: 16.

TESTS OF FLOUR QUALITY

American Association of Cereal Chemists. 1962. *Cereal Laboratory Methods.* Seventh Edition. American Association of Cereal Chemists, St. Paul, Minn.

Brabender, C. W. 1965. Physical dough testing: Past, present and future. *Cereal Sci. Today 10*: 291.

Finney, K. F., and W. T. Yamazaki. 1946. Water retention capacity as an index of the loaf volume potentialities and protein quality of hard red winter wheats. *Cereal Chem. 23*: 416.

Finney, K. F., and W. T. Yamazaki. 1953. An alkaline viscosity test for soft wheat flours. *Cereal Chem. 30*: 153.

Kent-Jones, D. W., and A. J. Amos. 1967. Dough testing apparatus. In *Modern Cereal Chemistry*, p. 321. Food Trade Press Ltd., London.

Kissell, L. T. 1959. A lean-formula cake method for varietal evaluation and research. *Cereal Chem. 36*: 168.

Sollars, W. F. 1958. Fractionation and reconstitution procedures for cake flours. *Cereal Chem. 35*: 85.

Yamazaki, W. T. 1953. An alkaline water retention capacity test for the evaluation of cookie baking potentialities of soft winter wheat flours. *Cereal Chem. 30*: 242.

Yamazaki, W. T. 1962. Laboratory testing of flours and cookie quality research. *Cereal Sci. Today 7*: 98.

Zaehringer, M. V., A. M. Briant, and C. J. Personius. 1956. Effects on baking powder biscuits of four flour components used in two proportions. *Cereal Chem. 33*: 170.

OTHER FLOURS

Kim, J. C., and D. deRuiter. 1969. Bakery products with non-wheat flours. *Baker's Digest 43 (3)*: 58.

Pomeranz, Y. 1966. Soy flour in breadmaking. *Baker's Digest 40 (3)*: 44.

Schopmeyer, H. H. 1962. Rye and rye milling. *Cereal Sci. Today 7*: 138.

Wolf, W. J. 1969. Chemical and physical properties of soybean proteins. *Baker's Digest 43 (5)*: 30.

CHAPTER 12

Flour Mixtures

ADA MARIE CAMPBELL

Flour mixtures differ as to consistency; batters have varying degrees of fluidity, and doughs are stiff enough to roll. Largely because of their differences in water:flour ratio, batters and doughs differ as to type of structure. In batter systems, with their relatively high water:flour ratios, water is the continuous phase. The structure of the product depends much less on gluten development than on gelatinization of starch. In bread doughs, with lower water:flour ratios, the gluten matrix is the continuous phase. The matrix consists of the membranes surrounding the gas cells and is continuous because the cells are in contact with one another. Gluten development is extremely important to structure. In doughs of even lower or somewhat higher water:flour ratios than that in bread dough, the importance of the flour protein depends on the other ingredients in the specific mixture. Although the water:flour ratio primarily determines whether gluten or water is the continuous phase, concentrations of other common ingredients of batters and doughs greatly affect the structure of both the unbaked mixtures and the baked products, as will be seen in later portions of this chapter.

Basic proportions, on a volume basis, are shown for several batters and doughs in Table 1. The mixtures are listed in order of increasing proportion of liquid. Although consistency depends to a large extent on relative proportions of flour and water, the position of cake batter in the listing indicates that other factors, such as sugar concentration, affect consistency.

In experimental work, ingredients are weighed. Formulas are usually written on the basis of 100 g of flour; amounts of other ingredients are thus expressed commonly as percent of flour rather than as percent of total formula weight.

Batter and dough products are affected not only by kinds and propor-

TABLE 1. Basic Proportions, on Volume Basis, for Selected Batters and Doughs[a]

	Flour (Cups)	Liquid[b]	Fat (Tablespoons)	Eggs	Sugar	Salt (Teaspoons)	Baking Powder (Teaspoons)
Pastry	1	2 tablespoons	4–5	—	—	$\frac{1}{2}$	—
Shortened cake[c]	1	cups $\frac{1}{4}$–$\frac{1}{2}$	2–4	$\frac{1}{2}$–1	$\frac{1}{2}$–$\frac{3}{4}$ cup	$\frac{1}{8}$–$\frac{1}{4}$	1–2
Yeast bread[d]	1	$\frac{1}{3}$	0–1	—	1 teaspoon–1 tablespoon	$\frac{1}{4}$	—
Biscuits	1	$\frac{1}{8}$–$\frac{1}{2}$	2–4	—	—	$\frac{1}{2}$	$1\frac{1}{4}$–2
Muffins	1	$\frac{1}{2}$	2–3	$\frac{1}{2}$	1–2 tablespoons	$\frac{1}{2}$	$1\frac{1}{4}$–2
Griddle cakes	1	$\frac{3}{4}$–$\frac{7}{8}$	1	$\frac{1}{2}$	0–1 tablespoon	$\frac{1}{2}$	$1\frac{1}{4}$–2
Popovers	1	1	1–2	2–3	—	$\frac{1}{4}$–$\frac{3}{4}$	—

[a] Values from American Home Economics Association Handbook (1971).
[b] Usually milk, except in pastry (water).
[c] Also included: flavoring.
[d] Also included: $\frac{1}{4}$ cake compressed or $\frac{1}{4}$ packet active dry yeast.

tions of ingredients, but also by temperature of ingredients; size and shape of mixing bowl; type of mixing utensil; method of mixing; kind and amount of additional manipulation; size, shape, and material of baking utensil; and temperature and time of baking. The greater the potential effect of these factors on product characteristics, the more critical is adequate control. An example is the effect of the equipment used in mixing and baking on the quality of yeast bread. The amount of manipulation of the dough is relatively large, and manipulation has a tremendous influence on the final product. The counting of mixing strokes, although a beginning, does not constitute adequate control because of the inevitable variability in the strength and effectiveness of strokes. Machine mixing and kneading, with time and speed controlled, are important. The volume, shape, and grain of bread are also affected by such factors as fermentation conditions, oven temperature, and the size and shape of the baking pan, but these conditions are less difficult to control than are hand-manipulative techniques. The worker must be constantly aware of the need for, and problems of, control. A factor that may complicate the interpretation of results, particularly in the absence of adequate control procedures, is the occurrence of many interactions between ingredients and between ingredients and other factors.

YEAST-LEAVENED PRODUCTS

Bread dough was discussed in Chapter 11 in relation to flour performance. Here it will be considered, along with sweet yeast dough, as a mixture of flour and other ingredients.

Ingredients

The essential ingredients of a yeast dough are flour, water, and yeast. Sugar and fat are common additives, and salt is nearly always added. Other ingredients frequently added are milk and, particularly in sweet dough, egg.

Flour

The functions of flour components were discussed in Chapter 11. The elastic, cohesive gluten network that develops when the gliadin and glutenin proteins are hydrated and manipulated is important to the structure of yeast-leavened products. Starch, which becomes embedded in the gluten matrix, provides structural reinforcement. Flour lipids and pentosans, in spite of their low concentrations, also affect the development of dough structure.

Water

In addition to being essential for the hydration of gluten proteins during mixing and for the partial gelatinization of starch during baking, water serves as a solvent for the solutes and a dispersion medium for the yeast. Bakers refer to the added water as "absorption." The greater the content of gluten protein and the "stronger" its quality, the greater is the absorption of a flour. The higher the proportion of water the flour will take, the greater is the storage life of the product (Beaverson, 1966).

Dough properties may be affected by salts in water. Excessively alkaline water can retard the activity of yeast enzymes. Hard waters, containing calcium and magnesium ions, may have a "tightening" effect and soft waters a "loosening" effect on doughs. Whether the effects of the salts are important depends on their concentration in the water and on the strain of *Saccharomyces cerevisiae* used. The nature of the water used in a dough is more likely to be of consequence in commercial bread production than in bread-making in the home. Compensating measures are available to the baker for all of the above types of water content (Maselli, 1960).

Yeast

Yeast of the species *Saccharomyces cerevisiae* is used in the active dry form containing 92 percent solids or in the compressed form containing 30 percent solids. In addition to its usually emphasized function of leavening action, yeast is important to flavor development (Coffman, 1967b; Pence, 1967) and to dough rheology. Cooper and Reed (1968) attribute the rheological effects to a lowering of pH, in part by carbon dioxide, to changes in interfacial tension of dough phases by ethanol, and to dough slackening, possibly through enzymatic reduction of disulfide bonds. Although it once was tempting to attribute the weakening of gluten structure during fermentation to proteolysis, it is known that the yeast-cell enzymes actually do not hydrolyze protein. Pomper's (1969) review includes pertinent references and considerable detail concerning the biochemistry of yeast fermentation.

Yeast fermentation frequently is expressed by the equation $C_6H_{12}O_6 \rightarrow 2CO_2 + 2C_2H_5OH$, which is simply descriptive. Actually carbon dioxide and ethanol are not the only products of alcoholic fermentation, and a series of reactions is involved.

The yeast cell contains many enzymes, and several sugars are available in the dough for carbohydrate metabolism. In addition to the small amounts of free sugars present in the flour, additional maltose becomes available through the action of flour amylases on damaged starch, and sucrose is usually added in small amounts. Among the yeast cell enzymes are maltase and sucrase (invertase), which hydrolyze maltose and sucrose, respectively, to their component monosaccharides. Before the metabolic reactions resulting in carbon dioxide can occur, the sugars must enter the yeast cell. Apparently sugars cross the cell wall primarily through an active transport mechanism. Glucose and fructose enter yeast cells quickly and are metabolized quickly. Yeast invertase acts rapidly, at or just inside the cell wall, and thus sucrose also disappears quickly. In fact, Bohn (1959) reported that 90 percent of the sucrose in a dough was inverted during the first two minutes of mixing. Maltose is utilized more slowly; the rate of transport into the cells and/or availability of the maltose-metabolizing enzymes may be the limiting factor(s). Maltose is fermented more rapidly when it is the only sugar available than when there are hexoses present to be preferentially fermented.

Yeast cells can metabolize either aerobically or anaerobically. The term "zymase," which formerly was applied to "the enzyme" catalyzing fermentation, now is recognized as an inclusive term encompassing all of the metabolic enzymes participating in the various steps and the different pathways of alcoholic fermentation. A dough is likely to have a low level of available oxygen, and the carbon dioxide produced thus results largely from anaerobic metabolism. Products of fermentation are released by the yeast cells to the surrounding medium.

The rate of yeast fermentation increases with temperature up to about 38° C (100° F), the optimal temperature depending on the specific dough system. With an increase in temperature beyond 41° C (106° F), the inactivation rate increases more rapidly than does the reaction rate.

Yeast cells can function over a wide range of external pH. Although anaerobic alcoholic fermentation can occur over the range 2.4–7.4, maximal activity occurs at pH 4.0–6.0, a normal range for yeast doughs. The apparently low dependence of yeast activity on dough pH is explained by the relatively constant pH within the yeast cells themselves (Cooper and Reed, 1968).

The rate of yeast fermentation may be reduced by elevated osmotic pressure. The effect is probably a general interference with metabolism resulting from cell dehydration. Because sugar and salt affect osmotic pressure, the concentrations of yeast, sugar, and salt in a formula need to be considered in relation to each other. For example, a sweet yeast dough needs more yeast and/or less salt than does a dough with a low level of sugar.

Too little yeast results in slow fermentation and a firm crumb. Too much results in a coarse grain and poor flavor.

Sugar

Added sugar, as indicated above, provides substrate for the fermentation reaction but when used in large amounts may actually retard fermentation through its osmotic effect on yeast cells. The retarding effect is a factor to be considered in regard to sweet doughs in which the sugar solution tends to be two to three times as concentrated as that in a bread dough.

By competing with wheat protein for the water present, sugar affects the rate of hydration of gluten proteins. Again this is important only in high-sugar doughs. According to Bohn (1959), the decreased rate of hydration with elevated levels of sugar need not result in decreased extent of hydration if the mixing time is increased to permit maximum dough development.

Inversion of the sucrose that is added to a yeast dough contributes to moisture retention by the baked product because of the extreme hygroscopicity of fructose, and to crust browning because of reactivity of the hexoses in carbonyl-amine browning. Obviously, these effects of inversion depend on the addition of sucrose in amounts in excess of that required for fermentation. Sweet dough products retain moisture longer during storage than does bread because the concentration of residual fructose is higher at a higher level of sucrose. Sweet dough products also may be relatively moist at the end of the baking period because an increased rate of browning lessens the likelihood of overbaking. Volatile flavor components may be better retained for the same reason. The contribution of sugar to sweetness is due to fructose produced through inversion rather than to the sucrose itself (Bohn and Junk, 1960).

Salt

As indicated in the discussion of yeast, sodium chloride provides a means of controlling fermentation, through its osmotic effect on yeast cells. In spite of the low levels of salt used, its total osmotic effect in a bread dough can be as great as that of sucrose because sodium chloride has a much greater effect per unit of weight. An excess may inhibit fermentation unduly. Omission of salt results in extremely rapid fermentation and a product with a "flat" flavor and a harsh crumb. Sodium chloride may affect crumb structure in another way in that it also has a tightening effect on gluten. The mechanism of the effect is not clear.

Shortening

The relation of flour lipids to bread quality was discussed in Chapter 11. The level of added lipid also affects bread characteristics. When Pomeranz et al. (1966) varied the amount of shortening from 0 to 4.5 g per 100 g of flour, loaf volume increased dramatically with additions up to 1.5 g and only slightly thereafter. Improvement in crumb grain accompanied the increase in volume. Fat's lubricating action on the gluten matrix apparently lowers the resistance of the dough to diffusion and expansion of leavening gas, resulting in the increased volume and improved grain. The addition of 3 g of shortening per 100 g of flour resulted in a considerably lower rate of crumb firming during storage than was found with the bread containing no added shortening. According to Beaverson (1966), many bakers consider shortenings of relatively low melting point to favor extended keeping quality.

Other Ingredients

Milk solids contribute to browning of the crust, probably because of the presence of potential reactants for carbonyl-amine browning. The casein fraction increases the moisture-absorbing capacity of the dough and, by thus permitting higher moisture content in the baked bread, reduces the rate of firming during storage (Mykleby, 1960). Eggs, added to sweet doughs, provide color, flavor, and "richness."

Substitution of whole wheat flour or of other flours, such as soy or rye, for a portion of the bread or all-purpose flour in a yeast dough results in decreased volume, inferior grain, and decreased crumb elasticity of the baked bread. The effects increase with level of substitution; usually replacement of more than 40 percent of the flour results in reduction of quality to an unacceptable level.

Commercial breads commonly have dough improvers, yeast foods, and emulsifiers added. Dough improvers are oxidizing agents such as potassium bromate that bakers add instead of, or in addition to, using flour that has been bromated. Yeast foods are salts that may be added to accelerate gas production. "Emulsifiers"—for example, monoglycerides— do not serve the function suggested by the term, according to MacDonald (1968), but rather retard staling. Their action in bread may be related to the observation by Jongh (1961) that monoglyceride added to starch dough appeared to decrease binding between gelatinized starch granules, resulting in a looser crumb. Other theories are mentioned later in the section on bread staling.

Mixing

Straight Dough Process

The yeast, if compressed, is dispersed in water. Until recently, active dry yeast also has had to be hydrated for several minutes in warm (38–46° C, 100–115° F) water. A stable, readily dispersed active dry yeast that can be added with the flour and is not very temperature sensitive is now available. If fresh fluid milk is used, it is scalded in order to denature serum proteins that have a softening effect on gluten. Although the sequence of adding ingredients is not critical, it is convenient to pour the hot milk on fat, sugar, and salt in order to melt the fat, dissolve the sugar and salt, and partially cool the milk. When cooled to approximately 40–45° C (104–113° F), the milk is combined with the yeast if the yeast has been rehydrated. If eggs are used, they usually are added next, and finally the flour is mixed in. The amount should be no more than is needed to give good dough-handling properties. The mixed dough is kneaded until the surface tends to blister. The stronger the flour used, the greater is the amount of kneading that can and should be done.

Sponge Method

Only about half of the flour is added to the yeast and water for the first stage of fermentation. Part of the sugar and/or salt may be added at this stage also. After fermentation of the sponge, the remaining ingredients are added, the dough is mixed and kneaded, and a second fermentation takes place. The sponge method is used more frequently in commercial bread-making than in the home.

Continuous Process

A continuous, automatic dough-making process that was developed for the baking industry is of theoretical interest here. Ingredients are metered into the mixer, from which dough is pumped to the developer for kneading. The developed dough is passed to the divider and extruder and is placed in pans, ready for proofing. The process, omitting the extended fermentation of the dough prior to proofing, is possible for two reasons. (1) One of the ingredients metered into the mixer is a prefermented mixture in the form of either a broth or a liquid sponge. (2) In the developer, which receives the dough as a fluid mass, the mechanical action and the pressure are such that dough structure is developed and carbon dioxide is driven into the gluten matrix, forming the gas-cell nuclei referred to in the following section on fermentation. The net effect is rapid automatic production of a bread having a fine, uniform grain. The fineness of grain is attributed, in addition to the high pressure in the developer, to mixing in a closed system that is also completely filled; thus large air bubbles are not trapped. The air that does enter the mixer, according to deRuiter (1968), is in the form of small bubbles occluded in the flour. Additional gas nuclei are provided by the carbon dioxide in the preferment.

Fermentation

As was discussed in Chapter 11, the mixing of a yeast dough results in a viscoelastic matrix of hydrated protein containing embedded starch granules and trapped gas-cell nuclei. The carbon dioxide formed during fermentation does not produce new gas cells but expands the cells that have been formed during mixing. Diffusion of carbon dioxide into the preformed cells, the gas-cell nuclei, requires a sufficiently high concentration of carbon dioxide to exceed the gas pressure within the bubbles. Optimal rate of fermentation thus is important.

Fermentation to an approximate doubling of volume is best done at a temperature not exceeding 30° C (86° F). Although yeast growth is more rapid at somewhat higher temperatures, so also is that of undesirable microorganisms. During fermentation the dough surface should be protected from drying either by a moist atmosphere or by a thin film of fat. At the end of an adequate fermentation period, a touch with the finger will leave an impression in the dough; dough elasticity causes rapid disappearance of the impression at an earlier stage. The time required for fermentation depends on concentration of yeast, sugar, and salt, and on strength of the gluten structure, in addition to the fermentation temperature. The stronger the gluten structure, the greater is the time required; the weaker the gluten structure, the greater is the possibility of overfermentation and consequent further weakening of the structure.

The fermented dough is "knocked back" or "punched down." The procedure should be more gentle than the terms imply. Its purpose is to force out carbon dioxide, equalize dough temperature, and redistribute the yeast cells and their food supply into a more nearly homogeneous mixture. In addition, this step serves to further subdivide the gas cells and increase the uniformity of their size. This affects the ultimate crumb grain because larger cells expand more readily than smaller ones and variations in size thus become enhanced with loaf expansion (deRuiter, 1968).

After fermentation, the dough is sized, shaped, and placed in pans or on a baking sheet; bakers refer to the sizing step as "scaling" because the individual pieces are usually weighed automatically. The shaping step is also done automatically in commercial bread production. The fermentation that follows is referred to as "proofing." It involves the same reactions as the first fermentation but proceeds more quickly because of the larger supply of yeast cells by this time.

Baking

As indicated in Chapter 11, structural changes occurring during baking of a yeast dough include expansion of gas cells with consequent stretching of the gluten matrix, partial gelatinization of the starch granules embedded in the matrix, removal of water from the gluten by the starch, and coagulation of the gluten. The net effect is a great increase in volume and the development of rigidity. The desired changes are brought about by baking of the proofed loaves or rolls at a relatively high temperature, 204–232° C (400–450° F) for bread and 177–191° C (350–375° F) for rolls of sweet dough. At a low baking temperature the rise in internal temperature is so slow that coagulation of protein and gelatinization of starch are delayed, resulting in impairment of crumb structure. The most obvious effect of an overly high baking temperature is a lessened increase in volume as a result of the rapid crust formation. Reduced thermal conductivity may also be observed along with rapid crust formation when baking temperature is extremely high (Audidier, 1968).

The thermal death point of the yeast cells is about 60° C (140° F) and is reached internally in approximately 25 percent of the total baking time, according to Swortfiguer (1968). Most of the loaf expansion should also take place during this period. The dough rises rapidly in the early stage of baking because of rapid expansion of gases at the high baking temperature. The acceleration of yeast activity prior to inactivation contributes to the supply of carbon dioxide. The rapid rise of the dough is referred to as "oven spring" and is dependent on the elasticity of the gluten structure as well as on the expansion of gases.

In the second stage of baking, which consists of about 50 percent of the baking time, the maximum internal temperature, 98–99° C (209–210° F), is reached, gluten proteins are coagulated, and starch is partially gelatinized. Yasunaga et al. (1968) studied the extent of starch gelatinization during the baking of bread. Their method was indirect, involving measurement of viscosity changes during the heating of bread-crumb slurries. The greater the extent of gelatinization during baking, the less did the viscosity of a crumb slurry increase with heating. They found the extent of gelatinization during baking to increase with the amount of water used and with the internal temperature attained, and to decrease with the addition of glyceryl monostearate to the formula. The extent of gelatinization during baking increased from the loaf center outward because of gradients in the temperature attained.

In the final stage of baking, the internal structure becomes firm. A crust develops through surface drying, and crust browning occurs, primarily as the result of carbonyl-amine reactions. The extent of browning depends on the formula. A formula lacking milk solids and having a low proportion of sugar results in a loaf that browns relatively little. Salem et al. (1967) found different sugar-amino acid combinations to vary greatly in their effect on browning of bread crust.

Evaporation during baking reduces moisture content from about 45 to 35 percent. According to Bushuk (1966), not only does considerable redistribution of water from gluten to starch occur, but a gradient in water content also develops; the center of the loaf is moister than the outer portion at the end of the baking period.

Compounds that are responsible for the characteristic flavor of yeast bread are formed during baking. The activity of yeast and bacteria continues in the early stage of baking. Carbonyl-amine reactions, known to be important to bread flavor, occur in the final stage, as indicated above.

Other Biologically Leavened Doughs

Sourdough Breads

Rye bread is the original example of a sourdough product because rye flour commonly carries the microorganisms that under fermentation conditions convert a sponge of flour, water, and yeast to a "sour mash." The flavor of the mash varies greatly with the environmental conditions and the relative predominance of lactic and acetic acid bacteria; therefore, commercially prepared cultures are used by bakers in the interests of product uniformity.

In a procedure described by Matz (1960), a rye sourdough is prepared from rye flour, water, and a dried culture of acid-forming microorganisms. After an extended period of fermentation (approximately 24 hours), the resulting sourdough is added to a mixture of additional rye flour, white flour, yeast, sugar, shortening, and flavoring adjuncts. Handling thereafter involves procedures typical of conventionally yeast-fermented dough. Rye doughs do not have the mixing tolerance that wheat-flour doughs have, because rye-flour proteins do not form gluten; therefore, the higher the percentage of rye flour used, the more the time and speed of mixing should be reduced.

Pumpernickel is a form of rye sourdough bread made of rye meal, which results from the grinding of the entire berry. No wheat flour is used in its production and it is only slightly leavened. The product, therefore, is dark, compact, and chewy.

It should be noted that in another type of rye bread the true sourdough product is simulated through the addition of organic acids and special flavors to conventionally yeast-fermented dough.

The sourdough French bread that has been produced for more than 100 years in the San Francisco area is particularly interesting. Both leavening and acid development result from use of a natural starter or "mother" sponge. Attempts to duplicate the product elsewhere have not been successful, even with the use of a mother sponge from San Francisco. Kline et al. (1970) and Sugihara et al. (1970) examined commercial sources of natural starter and found the leavening action to be due to a species of yeast that is unusual in its inability to ferment maltose and in its particularly rapid growth at low pH levels. The bacteria responsible for the production of acid were also found to be unusual and have not been identified specifically; their uniqueness lies in part in an absolute requirement for maltose. The art of making sourdough French bread in San Francisco has evolved over a long period of time in bakeries developed specifically for that purpose. Not only are the bread formula and the treatment of the mother sponge unique, but the ovens and the necessary scheduling operations are also entirely different from those in conventional bakeries. Identical bread is not likely to be produced elsewhere unless entirely new bakeries are established; investment in single-purpose bakeries for the production of a bread for which a market develops slowly seems unlikely to be widespread in the immediate future.

Salt-Rising Bread

Salt-rising dough is similar to sourdough in that both yeast and bacterial fermentation occur in its preparation. Apparently the specific microorganisms involved are different from those in sourdough. "Wild yeast" cultures that are able to withstand reconstitution in very hot water are used. The culture used by the baking industry is a dry culture containing both the yeast and the bacteria. In a procedure described by Matz (1960), the total time of fermentation is much shorter than that of sourdough but considerably longer than that of conventional yeast dough. Fermentation temperature is relatively high, ranging from 35 to 46° C (95–115° F), according to Matz.

Bread Flavor

Extensive work on bread flavor has included isolation and identification of compounds in preferments, oven gases, and baked bread. Coffman (1967a) compiled from the literature a list of more than 60 compounds that have been reported to be associated with white-bread flavor; these include acids, alcohols, esters, aldehydes, and ketones. Some are volatile; others are nonvolatile. Research has extended beyond isolation and identification to attempts to assess the relative significance of various compounds with respect to bread flavor and to determine how those that appear most important originate.

The study of factors related to bread flavor is complicated by the subjective nature of bread flavor. In addition, the specific reactions occurring during fermentation vary with fermentation conditions, and the effect of carbonyl-amine browning on flavor depends on the formula, which determines the available reactants. Approaches used in the study of bread flavor and some findings of a variety of investigations have been reviewed by Coffman (1967a,b) and by Pence (1967). In spite of some success in the preparation of natural concentrates having a typical bread aroma, successful synthesis of such concentrates has not been reported at the time of writing. Apparently some of the elusive "minor" components are important qualitatively.

Bread Problems

Faults of Freshly Baked Bread

Martin (1966) lists faults of bread and possible causes, including the following: (1) poor volume, due to insufficient yeast, excessive salt, insufficient water, insufficient fermentation, or an excessively hot oven; (2) excessive volume, due to factors opposite those contributing to poor volume; (3) pale crust, due to overfermentation (that is, too little sugar left for carbonyl-amine reactions) or low oven temperature; (4) dark crust, due to factors opposite those contributing to pale crust; and (5) coarse grain, due to weak flour, overproofing, or low oven temperature.

Bread Staling

The consumer thinks of staling of bread in terms of the sensory qualities that are affected: flavor, aroma, firmness, and opacity of crumb. The cereal chemist thinks of staling in terms of the changes in components that bring about the sensory effects. A rather comprehensive review of the research literature on staling is that of Herz (1965).

Just as the interactions among components contributing to crumb structure in bread are complex, so also are the interactions involved in the process of staling. Criteria used in addition to sensory evaluation in staling studies have included crystallinity, firmness, and crumbliness of crumb, all of which increase during staling, and soluble-starch content and susceptibility to attack by β-amylase, both of which decrease during staling. The complexity of the problem is partially indicated by the fact that, although all of the above changes normally take place during staling, it is possible to manipulate conditions so as to essentially eliminate one of the changes without affecting the others.

According to Jackel (1967), the changes that are referred to as staling of bread begin immediately on removal of bread from the oven. Change in crumb firmness has been a frequently used criterion of staling. Starch retrogradation is known to be involved in the firming of bread crumb. The linear starch molecules that are leached from the granules during the baking process become quite concentrated in the limited amount of water outside the granules. Because the linear molecules do become concentrated in the interstitial spaces and are prone to retrograde, Schoch (1965) believes that amylose retrogradation is essentially complete by the time the bread is cool. He indicates that the loaf is still soft at this point because the granules that are embedded in this gel system are soft. Schoch attributes the subsequent firming largely to a sort of retrogradation of branched molecules within the swollen granules. This retrogradation would involve folding of branches and association between them, resulting in rigid granules. The firming resulting from starch retrogradation is to a large extent reversed by heating. According to Schoch, the amount of heat required, a bread temperature of 50–60° C (122–140° F), is not sufficient to disrupt the hydrogen bonds through which the linear molecules are strongly associated; on the other hand, the energy level is sufficient to reverse the retrogradation of branched molecules, returning the granules to a soft, elastic state and thus restoring softness to the crumb.

Schoch (1965) attributes the crumb-softening effect of monoglycerides to their forming a complex with linear starch molecules within the swollen starch granules; consequently, linear molecules are unable to leave the granules, and less rigidity of crumb structure develops. Other workers favor an effect of monoglycerides and other surfactants on various aspects of moisture transfer at various stages in the life of a loaf of bread (Herz, 1965).

The use of higher moisture levels than are now legal in commercial bread in the United States contributes to a reduced rate of firming. Whatever the level of moisture, the characteristic crumb firming may occur even with no net loss of moisture from the loaf. Transfer of moisture within the crumb and from one part of the loaf to another is associated with staling. Within the crumb, transfer of moisture from starch to gluten occurs during staling; starch decreases in water-holding capacity with aging, while gluten does not (Waldt, 1968).

It can be readily demonstrated that during the staling of bread, water migrates from crumb to crust. The transfer of moisture from crumb to crust results in the crust's becoming soft and leathery while the crumb becomes increasingly firm. This would seem to indicate that the sensory effect as far as the crumb is concerned is essentially a firming resulting from loss of moisture. The situation is not that simple, however. Two loaves of bread, each protected from net loss of moisture, can increase similarly in firmness during storage and yet differ considerably in their ratings of "freshness" after storage. Bechtel et al. (1953) showed this with bread stored in tightly covered cans as intact loaves and with the crust removed. Although the loaves did not differ in firmness after six days of storage, those canned without crusts were given higher ratings for freshness. The migration of water from crumb to crust mentioned above was shown to occur in the intact loaves and did result in firming; however, a comparable degree of firming in the loaves with crust removed was associated with a higher degree of "freshness." This result further pointed up the complexity of the phenomenon of bread staling. The difficulty in consistently correlating a physical test with sensory effects is a problem that remains today in many areas of food research.

Storage temperature affects rate of bread firming. When the temperature of bread is lowered, the rate of firming increases as the freezing point is approached. Pence and Standridge (1955) found that bread stored for one day at 8° C (46° F), a temperature approximating that in many home refrigerators, increased in firmness to about the same extent as bread stored for six days at 30° C (86° F). When the freezing point is actually reached, the rate of firming becomes very low. Obviously, when bread is frozen its temperature should be lowered as rapidly as possible.

Elton (1969) observed a high negative correlation between loaf specific volume (cc/g) and staling rate. This inverse relationship is not yet explained but could be related to the lower concentration (on a volume basis) of crystallizable starch in crumb of higher specific volume. Elton believes that factors that appear to retard staling, for example, increased protein level, actually in many cases act indirectly by increasing specific volume.

Fungal α-amylase was mentioned in Chapter 11 as a possible additive to commercially produced bread. Bacterial α-amylase also may be used and is potentially more effective than fungal α-amylase in retarding the staling of bread. However, bacterial α-amylase is considerably more heat resistant than is the enzyme of fungal origin, and the concentration of bacterial α-amylase in a dough is more critical. If too much is used, a gummy crumb results. The ability of α-amylases to reduce the development of firmness during the storage of bread is an indication that a certain amount of starch breakdown during baking is conducive to enhanced storage life of bread. It has been suggested that a low level of rigidity is maintained by enzymatic attack of links between starch aggregates.

Waldt (1968) reported that the flavor of bacterial α-amylase-treated bread was rated superior to that of untreated bread after four days of storage. Possibly bacterial α-amylase indirectly affects flavor by producing an accumulation of reducing groups and thus decreasing lipid and protein oxidation (Herz, 1965).

Schoch (1965) discusses the phenomenon of loss of natural bread flavor during staling and reversal of the change with reheating of the stored bread. Schoch theorizes that complexing of flavor components with linear starch molecules could occur during staling, resulting in relative imperceptibility of the flavor components. Restoration of flavor with heating would then result from dissociation of the complexes.

Instability of Frozen Dough

Yeast doughs lose gassing power during freezer storage. The effect may be so extreme that the dough fails to rise when thawed. A lesser effect, the necessity of extension of proofing time, may be accompanied by excessive dough weakening during proofing. Kline and Sugihara (1968a, b) reported a study of factors affecting the retention of gassing power during freezer storage of doughs made by the straight-dough and sponge methods. A combination of increased initial level of yeast and reduction of prefreezing fermentation time resulted in considerably increased storage stability of straight doughs. The authors consider the reduced fermentation time, which permits the dough to be frozen before the yeast becomes too vulnerable, to result in a reduction of flavor and other sensory quality characteristics, however.

With the sponge method, freezer storage stability was increased by reduction of sponge fermentation time, chilling of dough during and after mixing, and addition of extra yeast along with the sponge at mixing time. These procedures were more beneficial in combination than singly.

Ring Formation in Frozen Bread

A phenomenon occasionally observed to occur during freezer storage of bread is the development of rather opaque areas a short distance beneath the entire crust surface. In slices of frozen bread the opaque areas are seen as rings that begin $\frac{1}{8}$–$\frac{3}{8}$ inch beneath the surface and extend slowly inward with time. Whereas the slightly enhanced opacity of normal frozen bread is reversed with heating, the greater degree of opacity of the rings that form during storage is not completely reversible. For several years this occurrence was observed and conditions appearing to affect it were noted.

In 1958 Pence et al. reported an extensive study of ring formation in frozen bread. They found rate of freezing and of defrosting to have no effect on the development of rings. Storage temperature had considerable effect; rings appeared in about 2, 4–5, and 11 weeks in loaves stored at -9.5, -12, and $-18°C$, respectively. Omission of shortening or milk solids and addition of emulsifiers had no effect. Addition of gluten and soluble proteins delayed ring formation; addition of starch had an accelerating effect.

Loss of moisture from the loaf was shown not to be a causative factor; with a given bread formula and a given storage temperature, rings developed independently of moisture loss from the loaf. Even with wrapping that completely maintained total moisture content, ring formation occurred. Moisture relationships within the loaf proved interesting. When moisture determinations were made on samples taken from positions *a*, *b*, and *c* (Figure 1), gross redistribution of moisture was not shown to accompany ring formation. However, when the *c* (outer) section was subdivided into sections 1, 2, and 3, it was found that the moisture content of zone 2, the zone most susceptible to ring formation, decreased progressively during storage while that of zone 1 (outermost) increased and that of zone 3 remained unchanged.

The authors concluded that during freezer storage, moisture apparently moves by sublimation and diffusion from the crumb interior to the subcrust region. Microscopic study indicated that the whiteness of the

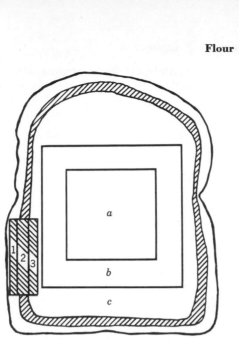

FIGURE 1. Section of bread loaf showing sections sampled for moisture determination. (Pence et al., 1958.)

rings is due to cavities existing in individual starch granules and exerting a light-scattering effect. Pence et al. suggested that the cavities are left in gelatinized granules by sublimation of ice crystals.

Additional information obtained by Pence et al. through various air-drying and lyophilization treatments prior to storage indicated that although the ring area itself is quite low in moisture, ring formation does not occur in very dry areas, explaining the origin somewhat below the crust surface. A white ring beginning considerably below the surface of frozen bread thus may be a criterion of excessive drying out prior to freezing. Rings beginning only a short distance below the surface but continuing inward a considerable distance can be considered indicative of improper freezer storage.

PRODUCTS CONTAINING CHEMICAL LEAVENING AGENTS

Ingredients

Chemical Leavening Agents

Although leavening by yeast involves chemical reactions, the term "chemical leavening agents" is applied to the chemical compounds and mixtures thereof that are added to batters and doughs because of their ability to react chemically, producing leavening gas rapidly. Their reactions are not enzyme-catalyzed; most require heat for maximum gas production. Carbon dioxide is the usual leavening gas and sodium bicarbonate is its usual source.

A source of carbon dioxide other than sodium bicarbonate is ammonium bicarbonate, occasionally used in the baking industry. Ammonium bicarbonate can be decomposed by heat:

$$NH_4HCO_3 \xrightarrow{\text{heat}} NH_3 + CO_2 + H_2O$$

The leavening action is efficient because of the formation of two gases. The unpleasant flavor resulting from a residue of unreacted ammonium bicarbonate and/or nonvolatilized ammonia, however, limits the use of this salt to products that have a large amount of surface area and are baked at high temperatures under well-controlled conditions. Commercially baked cookies represent a successful application.

Sodium bicarbonate can also produce carbon dioxide by decomposition, but the residue has such a disagreeable alkaline off-flavor that in practice sodium bicarbonate is reacted with an acid or an acid salt. The acid reactant releases carbon dioxide from the sodium bicarbonate, with formation of water and a salt of the acid also. The residue depends on the specific acid used and in any case has a more pleasant flavor than that of sodium bicarbonate alone. Although sodium bicarbonate and the acid may be added separately, as in a cake containing sodium bicarbonate and sour milk, more often they are added together as in baking powder. In the interests of stability, baking powders are formulated with acid salts rather than with the acids themselves. Baking powder contains, in addition to sodium bicarbonate and the acid salt, a diluent that is usually finely ground, relatively dry starch. The diluent permits standardization of the baking powder in terms of available carbon dioxide. A baking powder must yield carbon dioxide equal to at least 12 percent of its weight; in most baking powders there is a margin of safety and the actual yield is about 14 percent. The starch also exerts some protective effect against moisture absorption.

The particle size of baking-powder components is of theoretical interest to food-science students. The reactants in a baking powder are likely to react prematurely, with excessive loss of carbon dioxide, if their particles are too small. This is a potential problem in mixes, which may be stored for long periods of time. On the other hand, sodium bicarbonate can cause dark spots on surfaces of baking products because of localized areas of alkalinity. The extent of the effect depends on the opportunity provided for dissolving, which in turn depends on manipulation and on moisture level in the batter or dough, as well as on particle size of the sodium bicarbonate. Moisture level and manipulation tend to be functions of the specific batters and doughs, but the particle size of sodium bicarbonate in baking powder can be varied. A compromise as to particle size usually permits the best combination of protection from both premature reaction and speck formation.

Baking powders are formulated with amounts of sodium bicarbonate and acid such that an excess of neither is left in the product. Extra acid or extra sodium bicarbonate is easily added to the occasional product whose special characteristics are dependent on acidity or alkalinity. Although the theoretical proportions of sodium bicarbonate and a specific acid needed in a baking powder can be calculated on the basis of chemical equivalency if the complete reaction is known, amounts actually needed for neutralization often need to be determined experimentally. In many cases the exact reactions are not known. The actual rate of carbon dioxide release during use is also determined experimentally as a control measure in the production of baking powders.

In the use of a baking powder, a small amount of gas evolution during mixing is desirable for the formation of some gas-cell nuclei. Most of the available carbon dioxide needs to be released during baking before the product becomes firm.

Among the acid reactants used in home-type baking powders are the following salts:

1. Potassium acid tartrate (or potassium bitartrate or "cream of tartar"), $KHC_4H_4O_6$, used in a "tartrate-type" baking powder along with tartaric acid, $H_2C_4H_4O_6$. These are fast-acting acidulants, and a baking powder containing them needs to be used under conditions that minimize the loss of carbon dioxide formed at room temperature. A tartrate baking powder is also relatively expensive. The reactions involved are the following:

$$KHC_4H_4O_6 \ + \ NaHCO_3 \longrightarrow KNaC_4H_4O_6 \ + \ CO_2 \ + \ H_2O$$

Potassium acid   Potassium sodium
tartrate   tartrate (Rochelle salts)

$$H_2C_4H_4O_6 \ + \ 2 \ NaHCO_3 \longrightarrow Na_2C_4H_4O_6 \ + \ 2 \ CO_2 \ + \ 2 \ H_2O$$

Tartaric acid   Sodium tartrate

2. Monocalcium phosphate, $CaH_4(PO_4)_2$, either as the fast-acting monohydrate or in the coated anhydrous form. The coating on the anhydrous form retards action, but some reaction does occur without application of heat. The monohydrate is more likely to be used in "phosphate-type" baking powders and the coated anhydrous form in mixes. Equations cannot be precisely stated because of their variability. For example, the actual reactions probably depend on the relative proportions of monocalcium phosphate and sodium bicarbonate present and are probably affected also by the presence of more than one phosphate (Bennion et al., 1966). What actually happens in baking may be quite different from what happens in a simple mixture of reactants.

3. Sodium aluminum sulfate, $Na_2SO_4 \cdot Al_2(SO_4)_3$, used along with monocalcium phosphate monohydrate in "SAS-phosphate," or "sulfate-phosphate," baking powders. The production of carbon dioxide occurs in at least two steps that are summarized as follows:

$$Na_2SO_4 \cdot Al_2(SO_4)_3 \ + \ 6\,NaHCO_3 \rightarrow 2\,Al(OH)_3 \ + \ 4\,Na_2SO_4 \ + \ 6\,CO_2$$

The reaction occurs only slightly at room temperature but rapidly when heat is applied. Inclusion of monocalcium phosphate monohydrate in the mixture provides for sufficient reaction at room temperature for formation of gas-cell nuclei. SAS-phosphate baking powder is the type most frequently used by homemakers. The different brands on the market differ as to relative amounts of the acidulants.

Other leavening acids are used for special purposes. Sodium acid pyrophosphates, for example, are available in varying degrees of granularity and of temperature dependence; they are used in commercial doughnuts. Pyrophosphates are used also in cake mixes, in combination with monocalcium phosphate. Glucono-delta-lactone is particularly useful in refrigerated and frozen doughs because of its stability (Feldberg, 1959). Glucono-delta-lactone (GDL) is not an acid; it is an inner ester of gluconic acid:

$$
\begin{array}{l}
O{=}C \!\!-\!\!-\!\!-\!\!\rceil \\
\quad | \\
HCOH \quad\;\; | \\
\quad | \\
HOCH \quad O \\
\quad | \\
HCOH \quad\;\; | \\
\quad | \\
HC \!\!-\!\!-\!\!-\!\!\rfloor \\
\quad | \\
CH_2OH
\end{array}
$$

In water, GDL is hydrolyzed slowly to an equilibrium mixture that is 55–60 percent gluconic acid. The rate of hydrolysis increases with temperature, and the extent of hydrolysis becomes complete with neutralization (because removal of reaction products upsets the equilibrium). For these reasons GDL has become a commonly used acidulant, added along with sodium bicarbonate to commercial batters, doughs, and mixes.

In addition to reacting with sodium bicarbonate to produce carbon dioxide gas, leavening acids affect dough and batter rheology, according to Conn (1965); effects on batter viscosity and dough elasticity have been noted. Conn states further that the specific metallic ion provided by the leavening salt can also affect the crumb characteristics, such as resiliency and moistness.

For further detail concerning chemical leavening agents, the reader is referred to the classic writings of Bailey (1940) and Barackman (1931, 1954).

Studies dealing with baking powders in products have included the effects of type and level of baking powder on volume and other characteristics of baked products; relationships between baking powder and such factors as batter or dough stability and batter or dough pH; and interactions between baking powder and other batter and dough ingredients and between baking powder and conditions of mixing and baking. Because of the interactions involved, generalization is difficult. For a given type of baking powder, in a given product, prepared under a given set of conditions (including mixing method, formula, temperature of ingredients, and baking temperature), there is probably an optimal level. Too little can result in low volume and compact crumb; too much can result in increased volume with open, harsh crumb or in a fallen product, depending on the product and extent of the excess. There is a range within which results of variation are not drastic.

Although the different types of baking powder differ in the extent to which they react at room temperature (tartrate, phosphate, and SAS-phosphate in order of decreasing extent), there is little basis for recommending the use of quite different amounts of the different types in a given formula. Substitution of one type for another on an equal-volume basis normally gives satisfactory results. It should be noted, however, that baking powders differ in density. Weights, in grams/teaspoon, for tartrate, phosphate, and SAS-phosphate baking powders are 2.9, 4.1, and 3.2, respectively (AHEA Handbook, 1971).

A word should be said about the use of sour milk or other acidic ingredient as a part of a leavening system. If sour milk is to be substituted in a formula that includes sweet milk and baking powder, two generalizations are useful:

1. One half teaspoon of sodium bicarbonate neutralizes the acid of one cup of sour milk.

2. Sodium bicarbonate, reacting with the lactic acid of sour milk, provides leavening equivalent to that of approximately four times its volume of baking powder.

In a formula calling for $\frac{1}{2}$ cup of milk and $1\frac{1}{2}$ teaspoons of baking powder, substitution of sour milk would require $\frac{1}{4}$ teaspoon of sodium bicarbonate for neutralization. The sour milk plus sodium bicarbonate would provide leavening equivalent to that of one teaspoon of baking powder, leaving $\frac{1}{2}$ teaspoon of baking powder to be added. Even culture buttermilk varies in its degree of acidity, and exercise of some judgment as to the amount of sodium bicarbonate to use is sometimes desirable. Under-neutralization is usually preferable to an excess of sodium bicarbonate. Molasses, another acidic ingredient that might be an ingredient, needs $\frac{1}{2}$–1 teaspoon of sodium bicarbonate/cup for neutralization (AHEA Handbook, 1971).

Batter and dough pH tends to vary somewhat above and below 7.0 for different products. The preceding discussion of substitution implies that the pH of a given batter or dough, as well as total leavening, is important. This is true for several reasons, the most obvious perhaps being flavor. In addition to the flavor effects of the residual salts themselves, some other possible ingredients are affected in flavor by pH. Molasses and chocolate are notable examples. At excessively high levels of alkalinity the typical flavors of molasses and chocolate are lost. Even within a pH range in which all of the products are acceptable, the flavors of gingerbreads and chocolate cakes vary with pH.

Another effect of pH is on color. In light-colored products, the darkness of both crumb and crust increases with pH. Carbonyl-amine browning is accelerated by alkalinity. In products containing molasses and chocolate, pH has an even more dramatic effect on color. Gingerbreads become darker and chocolate cakes redder as pH increases.

Texture is affected by pH, especially in cakes. Relatively high pH may result in crumbly cakes because of the dispersing effect of alkali on gluten. If the excessive alkalinity also represents excessive leavening, grain may be relatively open and irregular.

Flour

As in yeast bread, flour provides structure. The proportion of flour is smaller and the type of flour weaker in most chemically leavened products than in yeast bread, resulting in a softer, crumblier crumb. The crumb also tends to be denser than that of bread because the weaker gluten structure cannot withstand the amount of expansion that occurs in a yeast dough.

Sugar

In high-sugar chemically leavened products—that is, cakes—sugar has a considerable tenderizing effect, apparently exerted during mixing through its competition with gluten for water. In addition, sugar probably contributes to tenderness and elasticity of crumb through its ability to raise the coagulation temperature of protein and the gelatinization temperature of starch. The contribution of sugar to flavor and to moisture retention varies directly with its concentration, which is higher in most chemically leavened products than in bread. When honey is used as part of the sugar, moisture retention is enhanced further because of the hygroscopicity of fructose. Sucrose does not contribute to carbonyl-amine browning of the crust in chemically leavened products because the sucrose is not hydrolyzed as it is in yeast dough.

Shortening

The crumb-tenderizing function of shortening is important in most chemically leavened products. Shortening has the ability to tenderize because it is insoluble in water and it can be spread through a flour mixture, thus interfering with cohesiveness of structure. In batters and some doughs the fat is distributed as globules through the aqueous phase. In biscuits and pastry at least a part of the fat is distributed in pieces that melt during baking and separate layers of other ingredients. In the latter case, a layered crumb results, in addition to the tenderization.

One of the important functions of fat in cake batter is entrapment of air. As will be discussed at greater length in the section on shortened cakes, the air incorporated during mixing has a considerable effect on both the volume and the grain of the baked product.

Softness of crumb increases and rate of crumb firming decreases with increased level of fat. Fat may make a considerable contribution to flavor, for example in products containing butter.

Egg

Egg protein is important to structure in chemically leavened products in which gluten structure is particularly weak. In mixtures such as cakes in which neither the wheat protein nor the egg protein is sufficient to provide the structural strength, the egg may assist the wheat protein in forming cell walls. The lipoproteins of egg yolks are important for their surface-active properties. The effect of egg yolk on flavor and color is obvious. In some products egg contributes to volume and grain through incorporation of air.

Additional Liquid

Although some liquid is provided by egg, additional liquid usually is required to dissolve the sugar and other solutes, hydrate proteins, and partially gelatinize the starch. When milk is used as the liquid, milk solids contribute to carbonyl-amine browning of the crust of baked products. Milk also makes some contribution to flavor.

Shortened Cakes

Cake Formulation

Whereas approximately equal weights of flour and sugar were once common in cakes, formulas with relatively high concentrations of sugar have come to be preferred because of the moist, tender, fine-grained crumb obtained. The term "high ratio" is applied to cake formulas in which the weight of sugar exceeds that of flour. Matz (1960) lists the following rules for formulation of high-ratio cakes:

1. The weight of sugar should be 1.1–1.8 times that of flour.
2. The weight of egg should equal or exceed the weight of shortening.
3. The weight of shortening should fall within the range of 30–70% of the flour weight.
4. The weight of liquid, including water in eggs and milk, should exceed the weight of sugar by 25–35 percent.

With increased sugar concentration, the concentrations of egg and total liquid need to be increased proportionately. As was mentioned previously, sugar competes with gluten for water during mixing and with the starch during baking; egg becomes more important to structure as sugar is increased because of the decreased gluten development. Matz states that rich formulas incorporate air more readily during mixing and thus need less chemical leavening than do formulas that are relatively low in sugar.

(a)   (b)   (c)

FIGURE 2. Vertical cross-sections of cakes made from (a) low-, (b) medium-, and (c) high-sugar formulas. (From Hunter et al., 1950.)

In Figure 2 the effect of sugar level in a plain cake formula is shown in cakes containing hydrogenated shortening and mixed by the conventional method. In raising the level of sugar, Hunter et al. (1950) balanced the formulas by making the appropriate adjustments in other ingredients. All three cakes were acceptable, but it can be seen that they did differ in contour and that grain increased in fineness and uniformity from low- to medium- to high-sugar formulas.

Altitude affects cake formulation. As atmospheric pressure decreases, leavening gases expand more easily. Overexpansion early in the baking period causes rupture of cell walls, coalescence of gas bubbles, and excessive loss of gas. The effect is particularly noticeable with a delicate cake structure, involving at least an irregular grain and possibly a fallen cake. Preventive measures consist of reduction of the amount of leavening agent and strengthening of structure by reduction of sugar or an increase of flour level. An increase in oven temperature favors gas retention. The higher the altitude, the greater are the adjustments needed. The need for adjustment begins at an elevation of about 3000 feet. Recipes for high-altitude cakes have been developed (Dyar and Cassel, 1950).

Some other ingredients that are added to shortened cakes occasionally affect formulation. Yellow cakes that contained 20 g of dried whey per 100 g of flour were softer, moister, and more tender than the controls (deGoumois and Hanning, 1953). The effect of added whey can be sufficient to make reduction of fat content feasible. The addition of whey to a formula necessitates an increase in liquid. An increase in the amount of liquid needed also results from the addition of cocoa or chocolate to a formula.

Methods of Mixing

The conventional, or creaming, method involves creaming the plastic fat alone and then with sugar. Egg is added, followed by alternate additions of portions of the remaining dry ingredients and the milk. Air that is incorporated during the creaming stage forms most of the gas-cell nuclei that determine the ultimate cake structure. A modification of the method involves separate beating of the egg white and its incorporation by folding into the remainder of the mixture.

In the muffin method all of the liquid ingredients, including oil or melted fat, are combined and beaten into the combined dry ingredients. The result is a product with a more breadlike crumb and poorer keeping qualities than cake mixed by other methods. As with the conventional method, a modification involves incorporation of air through the addition of an egg-white meringue as a final step.

The one-bowl method has probably become the most commonly used method. Although there are many modifications, it essentially involves beating all ingredients together until the batter is smooth. One modification is similar except that the liquid is added in two portions rather than all at once. A possible advantage of this modification is improved aeration because of higher initial viscosity. Any version of the one-bowl method lends itself to the use of an electric mixer.

In still another method flour and fat are blended together as the initial step. The sequence of adding other ingredients can vary somewhat, as with the one-bowl method.

Batter Structure

MacDonald (1968) describes the batter of a shortened cake as "an oil-in-water emulsion wherein the continuous phase is an aqueous sugar solution with suspended solids and gases." Whether or not one is willing to consider a dispersion of solid fat in water an emulsion, there is no doubt that fat globules are dispersed throughout an aqueous phase in which some of the other ingredients are in true solution, some in colloidal dispersion, and some in suspension. There is also no doubt that a foam exists in a cake batter. The nature of the foam, however, has been difficult to establish, and evidence has been difficult to interpret. Largely as a result of early microscopic study by Carlin (1944), the foam in a shortened cake batter has been considered for many years to consist of an air-in-fat dispersion. This concept has been difficult to relate to the known importance of the foam structure developed during mixing. It has been recognized that grain of the baked cake is affected by the incorporation and fine dispersal of air during mixing. It has been recognized also that the effect is due to diffusion of leavening gases into the gas-cell nuclei, mostly air cells, during baking, and that batter expansion is thus due to enlargement of existing cells rather than to an increase in the number of cells. In addition, it has been shown that final cake volume is greater when a given amount of incorporated air is finely subdivided than when the same amount of air is distributed as relatively few, large cells. Handleman et al. (1961) explain that if all of the leavening gas that develops during baking diffuses into a small number of cells, a relatively large proportion of those cells will become sufficiently buoyant to rise to the top of the batter and be lost.

The chief difficulty in accepting the preceding ideas and information *in toto* lies in visualizing the diffusion of steam and carbon dioxide through the fat to air cells entrapped in the fat globules. This problem is avoidable if air cells can be considered to be in aqueous dispersion rather than trapped in fat. Relatively new evidence along this line has been provided by Pohl et al. (1968), who freeze-dried cake batter prior to preparation of sections for microscopic study. When they applied the method to the study of cake batters made with many different shortenings, they observed that the air bubbles and fat particles were dispersed separately through the aqueous medium; the air was not trapped in the fat particles (Figure 3). The variance with findings of earlier microscopic studies is probably attributable to immobilization of the batter by freeze-

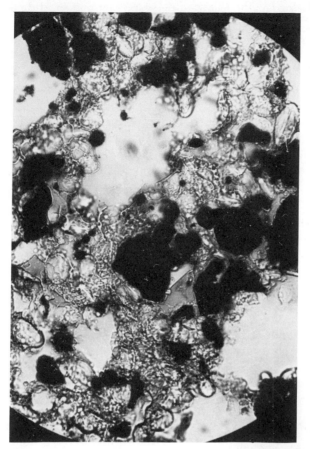

FIGURE 3. Photomicrograph of cake batter. Fat particles (stained black) and air bubbles (clear) are dispersed separately. The starch granules are the discrete bodies seen in the aqueous phase (lacy in appearance). (Pohl et al., 1968.)

drying prior to fixation of fat, infiltration with paraffin, and sectioning. It would seem that sections prepared in this manner should indicate true batter structure more accurately than would those prepared by previous methods in which compression and other distorting forces are inevitable.

This newer concept of the distribution of air in a batter does not minimize the importance of fat and its dispersal. Pohl et al. (1968) postulate that gas pockets form most readily at points of cleavage along fat boundaries. This would explain the increased aeration that may be observed when fat dispersibility is increased, as, for example, with addition of a surfactant to a fat. The kind, amount, and dispersibility of fat also may influence aeration through an effect on batter viscosity. Retention of occluded air is difficult in a batter of very low viscosity; viscosity tends to increase with increased proportion and subdivision of fat.

The source of fat used as shortening probably has less effect on shortening performance than was the case before surfactants came into general use. Monoglycerides, the first surfactants that were added to shortenings to enhance their aeration capacity, are effective in batters mixed by multistage methods. Shortenings containing newer additives such as lactylated monoglycerides are also effective with single-stage mixing. Even liquid shortenings, which alone have antifoaming properties, can become effective aerators with addition of certain surfactants that are "alpha-tending" with respect to crystalline form. Propylene glycol monostearate is an example of such a surfactant. Wootton et al. (1967) suggest that alpha-tending surfactants encapsulate the droplets of dispersed shortening and thus protect the foaming ability of the dispersion. A mixture of stearic acid and propylene glycol monostearate is even more effective in increasing air incorporation by a batter than is propylene glycol monostearate alone.

If the shortening used is not effective in incorporating air, other means must be used. This may involve the incorporation of the egg white as a meringue.

Extent of aeration may be appraised by measurement of density or specific gravity of batter. Density and specific gravity are not identical, but their values and significance are similar. Obviously, batter density and specific gravity decrease as aeration increases. A high negative correlation between batter density and specific volume of cakes was found by Hunter et al. (1950), indicating that aeration can have an important effect on ultimate cake volume. That this relationship might not always hold was apparent in the work of Jooste and Mackey (1952); addition of a surfactant to shortening resulted in increased cake volume but not in decreased specific gravity of the batter. They concluded that the observed volume increase was probably due to greater retention of gas rather than to greater incorporation. As indicated previously, the extent of subdivision of incorporated air, as well as the total air incorporated, can affect the volume of the baked cake. Density and specific-gravity values do not reflect the extent of subdivision of air in the batter.

According to MacDonald (1968), moistness of the baked cake, as well as grain and volume, is probably affected by the foam structure of the batter. The greater the extent of subdivision of air cells, the greater is the surface area on which condensing water vapor can be absorbed.

Dynamics of Baking and Development of Crumb Structure

Howard et al. (1968) state that two stages follow batter aeration in the development of structure in layer cake: (1) thermal stabilization of fluid batter and (2) thermal setting of batter. With the use of a heating stage on a microscope, Carlin (1944) studied the changes that occur during baking of a cake batter. In the early stage of baking, fat melts and some of the air cells coalesce. Ideally, the individual air cells would remain intact, but some coalescence of air cells is inevitable, and this along with batter movement results in some irregularities of texture. The melted fat probably forms films on cell wall surfaces (Jooste and Mackey, 1952). Eventually sufficient coagulation of flour and egg protein occurs to stop batter flow, and finally absorption of water by starch results in the formation of a solid network in which starch granules are embedded in protein.

Trimbo et al. (1966) studied batter flow during baking because of their interest in the surface rings that sometimes form in either ordinary layer cakes or Kissell (1959) formula cakes. The investigation included mix cakes in which the development of rings had been observed only occasionally. Dyed thread and colored batter provided the means of characterizing batter flow. The dyed threads were positioned carefully in the batter and were free to move with the batter during baking. In some tests colored batter was dispensed from a large syringe in horizontal stripes under and over the batter and in vertical stripes up the sides of the pan and at the center. Shifts in position of the colored threads and colored batter during baking provided information regarding batter flow.

Surface rings, when they formed, could be seen near the periphery after about two minutes of baking and moved toward the center. By the end of seven minutes, they had reached their final position. The rings appeared on cakes in which both lateral and vertical batter flow occurred. In mix cakes, most of which did not show ring formation, only vertical expansion occurred. Because most mixes contain gums that increase batter viscosity, Trimbo et al. added gums to nonmix formulas and succeeded in eliminating both lateral flow and ring formation. That viscosity is not the only factor involved, however, was evidenced by high-viscosity pound-cake batter that showed batter flow and by a low-viscosity mix-type batter that showed only vertical expansion.

In layer pans, either round or square, batter flow occurred from the bottom up the sides, across the top, and downward (Figure 4). Trimbo et al. reported that "as baking progressed, the ring and downward movement progressed toward the center of the pan and stopped only when the batter became 'set' in the region outside the ring." Only vertical expansion occurred inside the ring (the "ring" was square in a square pan).

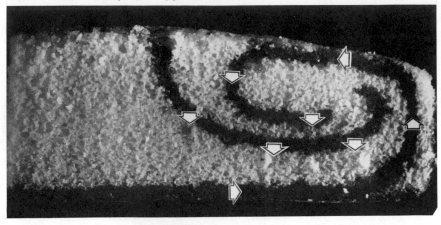

FIGURE 4. Batter flow in white layer cake, as shown in partial cross-section of baked cake. (From Trimbo et al., 1966.)

In a tube pan the flow occurred up the tube and outward across the top, as well as up the outer wall and inward.

The importance of starch gelatinization to cake structure was shown by Miller and Trimbo (1965), who used a commercial white layer cake formula for studying the problem of "dipping," the development of a sunken center during baking. They concluded that prevention of dipping depends basically on adequate gelatinization of starch sufficiently early in the baking process to contribute to high batter viscosity. Particularly in a high-ratio cake, sugar competes with starch for the water, which is relatively limited anyway, and thus gelatinization is retarded. Whether this effect of the relative proportions of sugar and water manifests itself through a dipped cake surface depends on the characteristics of the starch. Miller and Trimbo found that substitution of potato starch, which gelatinizes at a relatively low temperature, for up to 30 percent of the cake flour, resulted in improvement of volume and of other cake qualities. They also showed that starches from various wheat flours differed in their initial gelatinization temperature. With flours having a tendency to produce the dipping effect, an increase in water level and/or reduction of sugar concentration reduced the problem. The effects of varying water above and below the "normal" level and of decreasing sugar below the "normal" level, in the presence of a low level of water, are shown in Figure 5. Both increasing water and decreasing sugar favor gelatinization of starch. Addition of chemicals such as urea and sodium salicylate, which lower the temperature of initial gelatinization of starch, prevented dipping when other factors were critical, but the use of such additives is of theoretical rather than practical significance.

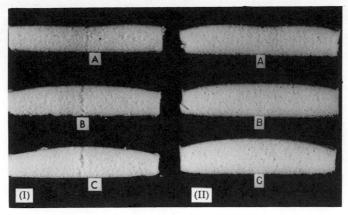

FIGURE 5. Effect of increasing water (from A to C in I) and decreasing sucrose (from A to C in II) on shape of white layer cakes. (From Miller and Trimbo, 1965.)

  I. (sucrose = 140 g/100 g flour)
      (A) 80 percent of "normal" water level
      (B) 100 percent of "normal" water level
      (C) 120 percent of "normal" water level

  II. (water = 80 percent of "normal" level)
      (A) 140 g sucrose/100 g flour
      (B) 130 g sucrose/100 g flour
      (C) 120 g sucrose/100 g flour

The relation of starch to structure in layer cake was also studied by Howard et al. (1968). To formulas containing no flour they added granular starches from several sources. Egg white and/or whole milk provided protein. Starches from different sources varied in performance. The potato starch gelatinized so early that the cake "set" early and had a poor volume. Rice starch, at the other extreme, gelatinized so slowly that most of the starch was only slightly gelatinized at the end of the baking period, and the cake collapsed during cooling. Volume was good with wheat starch, and the best overall results were obtained with mixtures of wheat and rice starches. Substitution of the starches for 100 percent of the flour in this study may account for the less satisfactory performance of potato starch than was reported by Miller and Trimbo (1965). The importance of intact granules was indicated by the poor products obtained when amylopectin, amylose, or mixtures of the two fractions were substituted for granular starch.

Wilson and Donelson (1963) obtained further information concerning ingredient interrelationships when they varied the level of water in white layer cakes made from different cake flours. A standard formula and Kissell's (1959) lean formula were used. With both formulas an optimal amount of water resulted in maximum volume, a rounded contour, and a satisfactory, although not optimal, crumb structure; a slightly higher level of water was required for optimal crumb structure. Low levels of water resulted in sunken centers; rather than collapsing, the batters failed to rise in the center. Excessive levels of water resulted in peaked cakes; the peaks developed through attainment of a large volume, followed by peripheral collapse. The effect of low levels of water on crumb structure was dryness and an open, irregular grain; the effect of excessive levels was moistness and compactness. With low levels of water, the starch apparently could not compete with sugar and protein for the water and thus was inadequately gelatinized; with excessive levels there was sufficient water to satisfy the demands of the hydrophilic constituents and also gelatinize starch excessively, resulting in a gellike crumb.

Cakes of the standard formula required more water for optimal results than did those of the Kissell formula, containing no milk or egg, indicating that water-binding by milk solids and egg protein made some of the water unavailable to other ingredients. Of the two formulas, the Kissell formula showed greater sensitivity to differences due to the flours; whereas the Kissell formula, therefore, might be preferred for experimental work, the margin of safety apparently conferred by milk and eggs is undoubtedly useful in product formulation.

Additional Considerations Regarding Baking

The internal temperature attained by baked products is limited by their aqueous nature. Regardless of the oven temperature used, the interior of a baking cake can get no hotter than the boiling point of the sugar solution present and usually does not get quite as hot. Raising the oven temperature simply shortens the time required to reach the maximum internal temperature. Just as the boiling point of water or a solution in an open container decreases with decreasing atmospheric pressure, so also does the boiling point of the solution within a batter. Thus relatively low internal temperatures are reached at high altitudes. Crusts dry out sufficiently to attain higher temperatures, probably not exceeding 150° C (302° F), according to Barackman and Bell (1938).

The elevated temperature attained at the surface makes possible the development of brown color, mainly through carbonyl-amine reactions. Browning reactions were discussed in Chapter 1. As has been indicated previously, crust browning is favored by a relatively high pH and by the presence of milk solids, including dried whey, and of honey or other sources of reducing sugars. Even when milk solids and reducing sugars as such are not added, flour provides a source of both reducing sugars and amino groups. A relatively low oven temperature may be needed to compensate for a formula that particularly favors carbonyl-amine browning, such as one containing honey.

Optimal baking temperature varies somewhat with cake formula, as has been implied in the previous discussion. With a given cake batter, too hot an oven produces humping and sometimes cracking of the crust and tunnel formation in the crumb; too cool an oven results in low volume and a crumb with heavy cell walls. Jooste and Mackey (1952) baked high-sugar batters at 149, 163, 191, and 218° C (300, 325, 375, and 425° F). Batters were made with butter and with hydrogenated vegetable shortening, each with and without monoglyceride. Except for the batters containing butter without monoglyceride, cake volume and overall quality increased with increasing oven temperature. Regardless of the oven temperature used, the time-temperature relationship is important.

Charley (1950, 1952) studied the effects of size, shape, and material of baking pans. Cakes baked in shallow pans were superior to those baked in deeper pans of the same capacity or in deeper pans of greater capacity. Rapid, relatively uniform heat penetration was probably the key factor. With pans having dark and/or dull surfaces and thus permitting relatively rapid baking, cakes superior in volume and overall crumb quality were produced; with pans having bright, shiny surfaces and thus causing slower baking, cakes tended to be less humped in shape but were inferior in other respects. Because different baking times were required for cakes in the different pans, another study (Charley, 1956) was carried out in which oven temperatures were adjusted in order to permit equal baking times. The cakes baked in the "faster-baking pan" still had a finer grain, more velvety texture, and higher ratings for overall crumb quality than did those baked in the "slower-baking pan."

Cake Problems

Faults of Freshly Baked Cakes

Matz (1960) lists the following common problems with possible causes: (1) low volume, due to insufficient leavening agent, undermixing (resulting in inadequate aeration), high oven temperature, or prolonged holding of batter; (2) toughness and dryness, due to too little water, overmixing, overbaking, insufficient sugar or fat, or too strong flour; (3) too open grain, due to low oven temperature or improper amount of mixing; (4) too fine grain, due to overmixing; (5) spotted crust, due to undermixing; (6) pale crust, due to low oven or too little batter in pan; (7) dark crust, due to high oven or too much reducing sugar (such as honey); and (8) "burst" crust, due to overmixing, high oven, or too much or too strong flour. Additional problems—for example a fallen cake—can result from an imbalance of ingredients.

Firming of Crumb

Cake crumb is subject to firming during storage, as is bread crumb. However, Pence and Standridge (1958) reported that the firming rate of layer cakes decreased as the freezing point was approached, in contrast to the behavior of bread, in which the rate of firming increases as the freezing point is approached and then becomes very slow at the freezing point. The relatively large amounts of sugar, shortening, and egg in cakes are apparently responsible for the difference in behavior. The significance of the difference is that rate of freezing and thawing and the temperature of freezer storage are not very critical for cakes, whereas they are very important with respect to maximum retention of softness of bread crumb.

Quickbreads

The ingredients in chemically leavened quickbreads serve the same functions in these products as have been discussed in relation to other products. As in other products, qualitative variations in ingredients affect physical properties; and interactions exist between concentrations of ingredients and manipulation, baking conditions, and other factors.

Quickbreads differ from one another because of differences in proportions of ingredients and differences in manipulation. Biscuits are shaped differently from muffins because biscuit dough contains a little less liquid and no sugar and because it receives more manipulation than does muffin batter. Biscuits usually have a crisper, more tender crust than muffins because of a higher concentration of fat. Biscuits frequently have a layered crumb due to the cutting in of fat and to a type of kneading that involves folding. Muffins, containing sugar, are greatly affected by the sugar concentration; their grain varies from open and breadlike with the low sugar concentration of a basic muffin to fine and more cakelike with the relatively high sugar concentrations used in commercial mixes. In both biscuits and muffins, overdevelopment of gluten resulting from overmanipulation results in decreased tenderness and an effect on crumb and on shape. In biscuits the crumb becomes dry and the shape unsymmetrical with overdevelopment of gluten. In muffins the interior becomes tunneled due to delayed, slow movement of gas toward the top center after the outer portion is rather well crusted; the crust becomes abnormally smooth and the center peaked. A potential problem of muffins but not of biscuits is the development of a waxy crumb. This occurs when the milk and egg are not thoroughly blended prior to addition of liquids to the dry ingredients.

OTHER BATTER AND DOUGH PRODUCTS

Foam Cakes

Even in cakes that contain no chemical leavening agent, air actually contributes relatively little to the total leavening. Either air or carbon dioxide has the potential of expanding only $\frac{1}{273}$ of its volume per degree centigrade rise in temperature, whereas one volume of water can form 1600 volumes of steam. In angel food cake, with its large amount of occluded air, steam is responsible for two to three times as much expansion as is the air. As in chemically leavened products, however, incorporated air is extremely important to foam cakes. Similarly to the diffusion of carbon dioxide into air cells in chemically leavened products, water in foam products evaporates into the air cells, which then expand, in part because of air and in part because of steam.

Borders (1968) states two principles for the formulation of angel food cake: (1) the weight of liquid egg white should be equal to or slightly greater than weight of sugar and (2) the flour weight should be about one third the weight of egg white.

In an angel food cake the egg albumin is important to structure, but its mechanical strength is not adequate to provide total support. Some wheat protein helps during baking, and gelatinized starch makes considerable contribution to support of the final structure.

Foam cakes are discussed more extensively in Chapter 9.

Unleavened or Steam-Leavened Products

Pastry

Pastry is tender because of its high fat concentration and crisp because of the combination of high fat and low water. Flakiness, seen as a horizontal layering effect, depends on incomplete blending of fat and flour. Factors that contribute to flakiness, therefore, are the cutting in of cold, solid fat, the use of cold water, and the chilling of dough before rolling. If the mixing procedure favors the development of flakiness, then increasing the water content tends to enhance flakiness because additional steam is available to separate the horizontal strata.

The quality of tenderness is independent of that of flakiness, although both qualities may be achieved to a high degree in the same pastry. All combinations of flakiness and tenderness are possible. Tenderness depends on the extent of gluten development. Increased flour strength, increased manipulation, increased water level, and decreased level of shortening increase gluten development; therefore, they result in decreased tenderness of pastry.

Tenderness of pastry is probably affected more by shortening than by any other factor. In fact, over the years, the breaking strength of pastry wafers has served as the most common criterion of shortening power of different fats. Extensive comparisons of different shortenings have been made under a variety of experimental conditions, and efforts have been made to relate shortening power to chemical and physical properties of the fats. In one of the more recent of such studies, Matthews and Dawson (1963) compared a series of oils and solid fats. Tenderness of pastry seemed to be related to relatively high specific gravity of the fat. Other studies have shown other relationships, and probably the interactions are so great that findings can be expected to vary with the experimental conditions. Pastry is discussed in more detail in Chapter 5.

Popovers and Cream Puffs

Popovers and cream puffs have both similarities and differences. Both have a high proportion of liquid, which provides the steam for leavening; both are baked at a high temperature in order to provide a great deal of steam and early crust formation. In neither mixture is gluten structure important; in a popover batter the gluten particles are too widely dispersed to adhere to one another, and in a cream-puff batter both gelatinized starch and a high fat concentration interfere with gluten development. In both mixtures a high concentration of egg is essential for structure. In a cream-puff mixture, additional egg is needed for emulsification of the large amount of fat.

Neither popovers nor cream puffs are made from a sweet mixture, and the high fat level of cream puffs makes the difference between the "bready" nature of popovers and the dessertlike nature of the cream puffs. In fact, the fat concentration is so high in cream puffs that excessive loss of water can result in a broken emulsion, evidenced as oozing of fat from the puffs during baking. The peculiar method of mixing cream puffs provides an opportunity for evaporation. The effect may not be apparent until the baking period, and may include not only a broken emulsion but also low volume because of insufficient steam for leavening.

Although popovers and cream puffs are similar in flour:liquid ratios, popover batter has an extremely low viscosity, whereas cream puffs have the consistency of soft dough when placed in the oven. In the popover batter, gelatinization of starch occurs during baking; in the cream-puff mixture, gelatinization of starch occurs in the heating step that is a part of the mixing process. Both products have relatively large central cavities because of the rapid production of steam and the relatively large increase in volume.

EVALUATION OF PRODUCTS

Sensory evaluation of food quality is discussed in Chapter 15. Physical measurements of flour mixtures are included in Chapter 16.

References

YEAST-LEAVENED PRODUCTS

American Home Economics Association. 1971. *Handbook of Food Preparation*, pp. 16, 17. American Home Economics Association. Washington, D.C.

Audidier, Y. 1968. Effects of thermal kinetics and weight loss kinetics on biochemical reactions in dough. *Baker's Digest 42 (5)*: 36.

Beaverson, R. M. 1966. Role of ingredients and fermentation in the shelf-life of white bread. *Baker's Digest 40 (4)*: 82.

Bechtel, W. G., D. F. Meisner, and W. B. Bradley. 1953. The effect of crust on the staling of bread. *Cereal Chem. 30*: 160.

Bohn, R. T. 1959. How sugar functions in high-sugar yeast doughs. *Cereal Sci. Today 4*: 174.

Bohn, R. T., and W. R. Junk. 1960. Sugars. In *Bakery Technology and Engineering*, S. A. Matz, ed. Chap. 6. The Avi Publishing Co., Westport, Conn.

Bushuk, W. 1966. Distribution of water in dough and bread. *Baker's Digest 40 (5)*: 38.

Coffman, J. R. 1967a. Bread flavor. In *Chemistry and Physiology of Flavors*, H. W. Schultz, E. A. Day, and L. M. Libbey, eds. Chap. 8. The Avi Publishing Co., Westport, Conn.

Coffman, J. R. 1967b. Bread flavor and aroma—a review. *Baker's Digest 41 (1)*: 50.

Cooper, E. J., and G. Reed. 1968. Yeast fermentation—effects of temperature, pH, ethanol, sugars, salt, and osmotic pressure. *Baker's Digest 42 (6)*: 22.

deRuiter, D. 1968. Some observations on the effects of different breadmaking systems. *Baker's Digest 42 (5)*: 24.

Elton, G. A. H. 1969. Some quantitative aspects of bread staling. *Baker's Digest 43 (3)*: 24.

Herz, K. O. 1965. Staling of bread—a review. *Food Technol. 19*: 1828.

Jackel, S. S. 1967. Flour usage in commercial bread manufacture. *Baker's Digest 41 (1)*: 30.

Jongh, G. 1961. The formation of dough and bread structures. I. The ability of starch to form structures, and the improving effect of glyceryl monostearate. *Cereal Chem. 38*: 140.

Kline, L., and T. F. Sugihara. 1968a. Factors affecting the stability of frozen bread doughs. I. Prepared by the straight dough method. *Baker's Digest 42 (5)*: 44.

Kline, L., and T. F. Sugihara. 1968b. Factors affecting the stability of frozen bread doughs. II. Prepared by the sponge and dough method. *Baker's Digest 42 (5)*: 51.

Kline, L., T. F. Sugihara, and L. B. McCready. 1970. Nature of the San Francisco sour dough French bread process. I. Mechanics of the process. *Baker's Digest 44 (2)*: 48.

MacDonald, I. A. 1968. The functional properties of various surface-active agents. *Baker's Digest 42 (2)*: 24.

Martin, W. 1966. Dough tests and breadmaking. In *The Practice of Flour Milling*, D. Povey, ed. Vol. 2, Chap. 24. The Northern Publishing Co. Ltd., Liverpool, Eng.

Maselli, J. A. 1960. Water. In *Bakery Technology and Engineering*, S. A. Matz, ed. Chap. 3. The Avi Publishing Co., Westport, Conn.

Matz, S. A. 1960. Formulations and procedures for yeast-leavened bakery foods. In *Bakery Technology and Engineering*, S. A. Matz, ed. Chap. 9. The Avi Publishing Co., Westport, Conn.

Mykleby, R. W. 1960. Milk and milk derivatives. In *Bakery Technology and Engineering*, S. A. Matz, ed. Chap. 4. The Avi Publishing Co., Westport, Conn.

Pence, J. W. 1967. Factors affecting bread flavor. *Baker's Digest 41 (2)*: 34.

Pence, J. W., and N. N. Standridge. 1955. Effects of storage temperature and freezing on the firming of a commercial bread. *Cereal Chem. 32*: 519.

Pence, J. W., N. N. Standridge, D. R. Black, and F. T. Jones. 1958. White rings in frozen bread. *Cereal Chem. 35*: 15.

Pomeranz, Y., G. L. Rubenthaler, R. D. Daftary, and K. F. Finney. 1966. Effects of lipids on bread baked from flours varying widely in breadmaking potentialities. *Food Technol. 20*: 1225.

Pomper, Seymour. 1969. Biochemistry of yeast fermentation. *Baker's Digest 43 (2)*: 32.

Salem, A., L. W. Rooney, and J. A. Johnson. 1967. Studies of the carbonyl compounds produced by sugar-amino acid reactions. II. In bread systems. *Cereal Chem. 44*: 576.

Schoch, T. J. 1965. Starch in bakery products. *Baker's Digest 39 (2)*: 48.

Sugihara, T. F., L. Kline, and L. B. McCready. 1970. Nature of the San Francisco sour dough French bread process. II. Microbiological aspects. *Baker's Digest 44 (2)*: 51.

Swortfiguer, M. J. 1968. Dough absorption and moisture retention in bread. *Baker's Digest 42 (4)*: 42.

Waldt, L. 1968. The problem of staling—its possible solution. *Baker's Digest 42 (5)*: 64.

Yasunaga, T., W. Bushuk, and G. N. Irvine. 1968. Gelatinization of starch during bread-baking. *Cereal Chem. 45*: 269.

PRODUCTS CONTAINING CHEMICAL LEAVENING AGENTS

American Home Economics Association. 1971. *Handbook of Food Preparation*, pp. 12, 66. American Home Economics Association, Washington, D.C.

Bailey, L. H. 1940. Development and use of baking powder and baking chemicals. United States Department of Agriculture Circular no. 138.

Barackman, R. A. 1931. Chemical leavening agents and their characteristic action in doughs. *Cereal Chem. 8*: 423.

Barackman, R. A. 1954. Chemical leavening agents. *Trans. Am. Assoc. Cereal Chemists 12*: 43.

Barackman, R. A., and R. N. Bell. 1938. Temperatures attained in baking products. *Cereal Chem. 15*: 841.

Bennion, E. B., J. Stewart, and G. S. T. Bamford. 1966. Chemical aeration. In *Cake Making*. Chap. 7. Leonard Hill Books, London.

Carlin, G. T. 1944. A microscopic study of the behavior of fats in cake batters. *Cereal Chem. 21*: 189.

Charley, H. 1950. Effect of baking pan material on heat penetration during baking and on quality of cakes made with fat. *Food Research 15*: 155.

Charley, H. 1952. Effects of the size and shape of the baking pan on the quality of shortened cakes. *J. Home Econ. 44*: 115.

Charley, H. 1956. Characteristics of shortened cake baked in a fast- and in a slow-baking pan at different oven temperatures. *Food Research 21*: 302.

Conn, J. F. 1965. Baking powders. *Baker's Digest 39 (2)*: 66.

deGoumois, J., and F. Hanning. 1953. Effects of dried whey and various sugars on the quality of yellow cakes containing 100% sucrose. *Cereal Chem. 30*: 258.

Dyar, E., and E. Cassel. 1950. Mile-high cakes. Recipes for high altitudes. Colo. Ext. Service and Agr. Exp. Sta. Technical Bulletin No. 40.

Feldberg, C. 1959. Glucono-delta-lactone. *Cer. Sci. Today 4*: 96.

Handleman, A. R., J. F. Conn, and J. W. Lyons. 1961. Bubble mechanics in thick foams and their effects on cake quality. *Cereal Chem. 38*: 294.

Howard, N. B., D. H. Hughes, and R. G. K. Strobel. 1968. Function of the starch granule in the formation of layer cake structure. *Cereal Chem. 45*: 329.

Hunter, M. B., A. M. Briant, and C. J. Personius. 1950. Cake quality and batter structure. Cornell University Agr. Exp. Sta. Bulletin 860.

Jooste, M. E., and A. O. Mackey. 1952. Cake structure and palatability as affected by emulsifying agents and baking temperatures. *Food Research 17*: 185.

Kissell, L. T. 1959. A lean-formula cake method for varietal evaluation and research. *Cereal Chem. 36*: 168.

MacDonald. I. A. 1968. The functional properties of various surface-active agents. *Baker's Digest 42 (2)*: 24.

Matz, S. A. 1960. Formulating and processing chemically leavened goods. In *Bakery Technology and Engineering*. Chap. 10. Avi Publishing Co., Inc., Westport, Conn.

Miller, B. S., and H. B. Trimbo. 1965. Gelatinization of starch and white layer cake quality. *Food Technol. 19*: 640.

Pence, J. W., and N. N. Standridge. 1958. Effects of storage temperature on firming of cake crumb. *Cereal Chem. 35*: 57.

Pohl, P. H., A. C. Mackey, and B. L. Cornelia. 1968. Freeze-drying cake batter for microscopic study. *J. Food Sci. 33*: 318.

Trimbo, H. B., Shao-mu Ma, and B. S. Miller. 1966. Batter flow and ring formation in cake baking. *Baker's Digest 40 (1)*: 40.

Wilson, J. T., and D. H. Donelson. 1963. Studies on the dynamics of cake-baking. I. The role of water in formation of layer cake structure. *Cereal Chem. 40*: 466.

Wootton, J. C., N. B. Howard, J. B. Martin, D. E. McOsker, and J. Holme. 1967. The role of emulsifiers in the incorporation of air into layer cake batter systems. *Cereal Chem. 44*: 333.

OTHER BATTER AND DOUGH PRODUCTS

Borders, J. H. 1968. A look at foam cakes. *Baker's Digest 42 (4)*: 53.

Matthews, R. H., and E. H. Dawson. 1963. Performance of fats and oils in pastry and biscuits. *Cereal Chem. 40*: 291.

CHAPTER 13

Prepared and Precooked Frozen Foods

HELEN H. PALMER

The attraction of prepared and precooked frozen foods is largely based on convenience and on retention of the quality of freshly prepared foods. Some of these foods, however, are unstable in texture or flavor when preserved by freezing. Recent research in this field has dealt with the effects of composition, processing, or storage conditions on quality of foods that are commonly frozen and with improvement in the stability of specific foods that are particularly sensitive to freezing. This chapter concerns those prepared and precooked frozen foods in which the preparation, formulation, or cooking methods are of significant importance in determining the quality or stability of the final product. For information on packaging, marketing, and freezing of all types of prepared frozen foods, the reader is referred to the detailed discussion in "The Freezing Preservation of Foods," Volume IV, *Freezing of Precooked and Prepared Foods* (Tressler et al., eds., 1968).

Problems of maintaining the texture or structure of precooked or prepared foods after freezing and storage occur primarily in starch- or egg-thickened foods and in those having emulsion, foam, or gel structures. In some cases, changes are apparent in foods thawed immediately after freezing; in others, they develop or increase in severity during frozen storage and are affected by storage temperatures. Research on foods with structural instability has been designed to determine the constituents responsible and the conditions under which adverse changes occur, and to devise means of preventing or reducing them.

FLOUR- and STARCH-THICKENED FOODS

Sauces and gravies thickened with the common cereal flours and starches look curdled when thawed immediately after freezing; frozen storage increases the severity of the problem. The change is especially noticeable in thawed foods observed at ambient or refrigerator temperature before they are heated to serving temperature. The separation decreases if the products are heated, particularly if they can be stirred. The starch fraction of the thickening agent is of major importance in the stability of these products (Hanson et al., 1951; Osman and Cummisford, 1959). (See also Chapter 4 of this volume.) Sauces and gravies prepared from the "waxy" varieties of cereals are considerably more stable to freezing than are those prepared from the common cereals. The difference between common and waxy cereals is primarily a difference in the starch fraction. Starches in common cereals contain approximately 17 to 30 percent by weight of amylose, the linear polysaccharide (Schoch, 1962), while those in waxy cereals contain less than 1 percent of these unbranched chains. The remaining component in each case is amylopectin, the branched fraction. Solutions of the common starches or flours retrograde or aggregate more rapidly during frozen storage than waxy cereal starches or flours (Kerr, 1950). All waxy cereal thickening agents do not produce equal stability in frozen sauces. Those containing waxy rice can be stored for longer periods without liquid separation than can those containing waxy corn or waxy sorghum (Hanson et al., 1951; Schoch, 1966). This difference may be related to the higher degree of branching and smaller particle size in the waxy rice starch (Bates et al., 1943; Meyer and Fuld, 1941). Mixtures of waxy and common cereal thickening agents produce stability between that of the two types. Products thickened with the waxy rice *flour* have a "short" consistency similar to that of products thickened with wheat flour; products thickened with waxy rice *starch* have a long, somewhat stringy consistency similar to that obtained with tapioca starch.

The separation and curdled appearance of thawed sauces does not occur for about a year at $-18°$ C with waxy rice flour as the thickening agent. Sauces thickened with waxy rice flour, however, separate when thawed after storage for about two months at a higher temperature ($-12°$ C). The addition of stabilizers such as citrus pectin and gum tragacanth increases stability to a year at $-12°$ C (Hanson et al., 1957). Products stored at a constant temperature of $-18°$ C are stable for two to six times longer than those stored at temperatures fluctuating uniformly from -12 to $-25°$ C in a 24-hour sine wave cycle. Storage of products at -12, -18, and $-25°$ C shows that the stability defect has a high temperature coefficient, and whether temperature fluctuation has a specific effect independent of the effect expected with such a temperature coefficient has not been determined.

Heating and stirring of sauces thickened with the *common* cereals partially eliminates separation and partially restores smoothness. However, heating of sauces thickened with *waxy* cereals without stirring restores their original smoothness even if adverse storage conditions cause over 50 percent liquid separation from thawed sauces. Since the association between branched chains with splitting out of water is more readily reversible than the association between linear chains in the starch molecule, these thickening agents are particularly useful in products that cannot be stirred during heating, for example, foods frozen and heated in plastic bags.

A solution to the problem of freezing thickened foods has been the development of "freeze-resistant" starches. These are usually chemically modified waxy corn or maize starches. Cross-bonding of the molecules and the addition of ester groups reduces the stringy consistency of cooked starch pastes and improves their stability to freezing (Schoch, 1968). Blends of natural and "freeze-resistant" starches are often used to obtain the specific consistency and stability desired in a variety of prepared foods (Palmer, 1968).

GEL STRUCTURES

Products with gel structures containing a high concentration of cooked egg white show serious texture changes after freezing and storage. The white of hard cooked eggs becomes rubbery, granular, watery, and separates into small clumps or layers (Woodroof, 1946). Cooked egg yolks, on the other hand, can be frozen and stored at −18° C for at least a year without significant texture changes. Studies of Davis et al. (1952) indicate that the damage caused by freezing is due to the mechanical effects of ice crystal formation. During freezing, the gel structure contracts as water migrates from within the gel to form ice crystals. Liquid-filled spaces within the gel after thawing indicate that the contraction is largely irreversible. The damage is reduced by conditions promoting supercooling and small crystal formation. A blend of egg white and yolk, mixed under specified conditions before cooking, could be used to incorporate hard cooked egg into frozen foods. Bengtsson (1967) reported that freezing in a conventional blast freezer at −35° C did not produce acceptable cooked egg white, but that ultrafast freezing with liquid nitrogen produces a product approaching the quality of unfrozen cooked white.

Maintenance of a gel structure in custards, puddings, and fillings that depend on egg or starch for their structural characteristics has long been a problem (Tressler and Evers, 1957). Substitution of waxy rice flour for part or all of the usual thickening agents reduces separation and curdled appearance in some of these products (Hanson et al., 1953). Although the frozen-storage stability of cornstarch pudding and soft-custard types of desserts can be improved in this manner, no solution has been found that permits successful freezing of a typical baked custard. As expected, the use of egg yolk in place of whole egg increases stability of soft-custard-type desserts. Substitution of waxy rice flour for a starchy thickening agent that gels on cooling improves stability, but an additive such as gelatin is required to provide the desired stiffness. Puddings containing waxy rice flour and gelatin are stable for 6 to 9 months at $-18°$ C but for less than a month at $-12°$ C. Stabilizers such as citrus pectin or gum tragacanth improve the stability of soft custards and puddings at $-12°$ C (Hanson et al., 1957). "Freeze-resistant" starches and stabilizers such as carrageenin improve stability in cream pies that are to be frozen (Palmer, 1968).

COATINGS

The problem of peeling of batter coatings on cooked meats and poultry is accentuated in precooked frozen products. Failure of the coatings to adhere after reheating results in a nonuniform appearance and complicates serving and handling. Cooking the poultry before application of the batter reduces the peeling tendency of coating on frozen fried chicken (Hanson and Fletcher, 1963). The usefulness of the method was also shown by tests on pork chops. Batter coatings applied in the usual way form a loose-fitting covering on the meat, since the covering sets before the meat shrinks during cooking. If the meat is cooked before application of the coating, the coating forms a close fit over the meat. It resists peeling and also has less tendency to stick to the container in which it is frozen. Variations in the formulas of the coatings influence their adhesive quality, thickness, appearance, and consistency. Peeling tendency increases with increasing thickness of the coating. Waxy cereal thickening agents produce more elastic coatings than do the common cereals, and inclusion of waxy or common cornstarch improves adhesive qualities more than do other cereals. The egg yolk content of the coating influences color but has little effect on adhesion. Mixtures of thickening agents may be used to obtain the particular attributes desired.

EMULSIONS

Since freezing of emulsions generally causes the dispersed phase to coalesce, salad dressings with a structure dependent on a stable emulsion were not used until recently in frozen salads and sandwiches.

Oil separates from mayonnaise that is thawed after freezing, and also usually separates from salad dressings of the type containing an emulsion and a cooked starch paste under such conditions. However, two methods have been reported by which salad dressings can be successfully frozen and stored. One such method involves selection or treatment of the oil for the storage temperatures involved (Hanson and Fletcher, 1961). Crystallization of oil fractions at refrigerator temperature (4 to 7° C) has long been known to have a detrimental effect on salad dressing or mayonnaise. Elimination or reduction of these fractions is the basis of the "winterization" of cottonseed oil used in salad dressings. "Winterization" involves fractional crystallization of the oil at about 4° C. Other frequently used oils, such as corn or soybean, do not contain sufficient fractions solidifying at refrigerator temperature to require winterization. Principles applied to the selection of oils for emulsion stability at above-freezing temperatures also apply at below-freezing temperatures. Solidification of the oil fractions in crystalline form is the main cause of increasing oil separation as storage temperature is lowered. The oils used successfully in the freezing of salad dressing either do not solidify in crystalline form, solidify to only a limited extent, or solidify slowly at the storage temperature selected. Of six vegetable oils tested, safflower oil alone does not solidify at −7° C. At −12° C safflower oil requires winterizing to prevent oil separation. The oil fractions that crystallize at −12° C must then be removed before the oil is used. Safflower oil cannot be winterized for use at −18° C or lower, since too high a proportion of the oil solidifies at that temperature. Although peanut oil solidifies to some extent at −7° C and lower, selection of optimum thickening and emulsifying agents makes peanut oil salad dressing stable for 3 months at temperatures from −34° to −7° C; only at −18° C was there significant separation after 6 months. The stability of peanut oil salad dressings, in spite of a high degree of oil solidification at the lower temperatures, may be attributed to the gelatinous character of solidified peanut oil. The protective emulsifying film around the dispersed oil droplets is not destroyed and the oil droplets do not coalesce. Probably for a similar reason salad dressings prepared with other oils, such as cottonseed, can be stored indefinitely without oil separation at temperatures low enough to cause almost complete oil solidification. At −34 to −46° C the oils solidify in an amorphous rather than a crystalline form. The product temperature must be lowered through the critical crystallization range rapidly enough so that crystallization does not occur.

Ingredients other than oil, particularly thickening and emulsifying agents, influence the stability of frozen salad dressings. The rate at which thickening agents retrograde during frozen storage is important. Retrogradation proceeds more rapidly in unbranched than in branched starch chains. Waxy rice flour, containing almost entirely branched starch chains, is superior to others tested because of its slower rate of retrogradation. The advantage of this type of thickening agent in retarding oil separation is most obvious under conditions in which the oil does not solidify, solidifies slowly or to a small extent, or solidifies in an amorphous form. The water separation typical of starch retrogradation is not apparent if large amounts of oil crystallize and separate on thawing because the water is masked by the oil.

The conditions under which the emulsifying agent, egg yolk, is held prior to use in the salad dressings influence the stability of the dressings. The use of unfrozen egg yolks generally results in the greatest stability. Frozen salted yolks, generally used in commercial salad-dressing manufacture, have reduced emulsifying power. The lower the storage temperature for the salted yolks, in the range of -7 to $-34°$ C, the less stable are the salad dressings prepared from them. As expected, increasing the amount of emulsifying agent improves salad-dressing stability.

Other factors influencing stability are the salt concentration and the emulsion-starch paste ratio. In the 0 to 1.2 percent range, an increase in salt concentration increases stability. With a high ratio of emulsion to starch paste, oil separation occurs under some storage conditions; with a high ratio of starch paste to emulsion, water separation occurs (Hanson and Fletcher, 1961).

Another method of preparing salad dressings stable to freezing and at least limited frozen storage involves the use of hard fats that were previously considered detrimental to emulsion stability (Partyka, 1963; Krett and Gennuso, 1963). Winterizable components need not be removed from oils in the method described by these patents. The oils should cloud in less than 5.5 hours in ice water under conditions of the cold test of the American Oil Chemists' Society, and the iodine value of the oil should be higher than 75. Not less than 8 percent of emulsifying egg yolk and use of freeze-resistant starch are required. Salad dressings are stable for a week or more at -23 and $-40°$ C. Development of the method was based on the observation that butter and margarine, which also contain hard fat, can be frozen without separation.

FOAMS AND SPONGES

The foam or sponge structure of soft pie meringues and souffles may be damaged by freezing and frozen storage. The stability of such products can be influenced by their composition and concentration of their ingredients. It is directly related to their sugar concentration. Soft pie meringues and baked egg white dessert souffles containing 46 percent sugar, an amount comparable to that in a soft pie meringue, are more stable than those containing less sugar (Cimino et al., 1967). Egg white souffles are equally stable at temperatures ranging from -18 to $-34°$ C. Sweetened whole-egg dessert souffles can be stored at -18 to $-23°$ C for 6 months with less than 10 percent loss in height if the flour concentration is increased. The maximum permissible flour concentration is about 8 percent because of the difficulty in combining the very thick white sauce with the egg white foam. Variations in yolk or salt concentration have little effect on stability of these souffles. Sweetened whole-egg souffles must be stored in the range of -18 to $-23°$ C. At higher temperatures off-flavors develop; at lower temperatures volume and texture decline.

Height loss is more rapid in unsweetened than in sweetened souffles. In unsweetened whole-egg souffles, an increase in flour concentration and the addition of cheese or methyl cellulose retard height loss. These improvements are probably related to an increase in solids content (cheese) and structural improvement (cellulose). Unbaked souffles lose their characteristic structure more rapidly than do baked souffles during frozen storage; unbaked cheese souffles develop off-flavors at the usual frozen-storage temperatures within one month (Cimino et al., 1967).

VEGETABLES

Texture problems in precooked frozen vegetables may result from overcooking before freezing, long reheating, or changes occurring in the starchy component during storage. Overcooking or prolonged reheating of vegetables such as peas, lima beans, and broccoli cause them to develop a mushy texture and lose their desirable color (Woodroof, 1946; Hanson et al., 1950). Careful control of heating conditions is necessary to assure desirable texture in such vegetables. A few vegetables, such as Chinese water chestnuts, corn, and snap beans, show little or no change in color or texture with heating times beyond optimum (Hanson et al., 1950). The use of such vegetables is indicated when heating conditions cannot be adequately controlled.

Cooked sweet potatoes and rice can be frozen and stored satisfactorily at $-18°$ C or lower (Mountjoy and Kirkpatrick, 1951; Woodroof and Atkinson, 1944; and Boggs et al., 1951). However, adverse texture changes occur during the storage of cooked frozen white potatoes (Woodroof, 1946; Longree, 1950; and Dawson et al., 1952). Longree reported a "cottony" texture associated with a microscopically visible change in cell structure in thawed potatoes after storage. The most severe storage condition tested was two months at $-18°$ C. Heating to $56°$ C eliminated these changes in potatoes held frozen for three days. Whether the changes were also reversible on heating after longer storage was not determined. Dawson et al. (1952), however, reported a decrease in tenderness and the development of a harder, drier texture in frozen French-fried potatoes stored longer than two months at $-18°$ C.

Stale flavors have been encountered following frozen storage of cooked vegetables; cooked frozen vegetables do not have flavor stability equal to that of blanched frozen vegetables (Woodroof et al., 1946; Hanson et al., 1950; and Paul et al., 1952). The use of a "solid" pack reduces oxidative off-flavor development. Little or no flavor difference is found between cooked frozen peas stored in a sauce and peas blanched before freezing, then cooked and added to the sauce at the end of storage periods ranging from 2 to 12 months at $-18°$ C (Hanson et al., 1950). Packing in the cooking liquid reduces but does not eliminate stale flavor development in asparagus, carrots, green beans, broccoli, and cauliflower (Paul et al., 1952). Since the texture and color of the cooked vegetables were also adversely affected in the latter study, it is possible that a shorter cooking time would give a more flavorable result.

FLAVOR STABILITY OF COOKED MEAT

Rentention of freshly cooked flavor and prevention of stale and rancid flavor development are critical problems in precooked frozen meats. Flavor stability is influenced by stability differences inherent in different meats, by the cooking methods used, by the package atmosphere, and by storage conditions. Although most of the illustrations of flavor-stability problems are drawn from poultry research, the methods developed to overcome the problems apply as well to red meats as to poultry.

Stability differences inherent in the meat can be illustrated by comparisons of chicken and turkey. Chicken becomes rancid less rapidly than turkey because chickens are more efficient than turkeys in depositing tocopherol, a natural antioxidant, in the fat (Mecchi et al., 1956).

Flavor changes and rancidity develop more rapidly in cooked than in raw frozen meat because the cooking process accelerates development of fat rancidity (Watts et al., 1948). The cooking method influences the rate of flavor change. Greater rancidity develops in roasted turkeys, because they are exposed to the air in the oven, than in simmered or pressure-cooked turkeys, which are in a steam or water environment (Hanson et al., 1950). However, even when turkeys are simmered, rancidity develops in some lots. Rancidity may occur in turkey gravy if turkey fat is used to prepare the gravy. However, since gravy increases the storage life of the cooked meat by excluding air from the package, preparation of gravy with a more stable fat is recommended.

Antioxidants added to the water in which turkey is cooked retard rancidity development in the fat and thus increase the stability of frozen meat covered with a sauce or gravy prepared with the fat (Lineweaver et al., 1952). However, the use of antioxidants has not been specifically approved for turkey products by the Food and Drug Administration. Antioxidants did not improve flavor stability of Swiss steaks or stews during storage. However, the conditions were such that no deterioration occurred in the samples without antioxidants. Storage temperatures were low (-18 to $-29°$ C) and air was adequately excluded from the package (Harrison et al., 1953).

The atmosphere within the package is important to storage stability of frozen cooked meat. Air (oxygen) should be excluded as much as possible by using a tight-fitting vapor-proof package, by packing with sauce or gravy, or by replacing air with an inert atmosphere such as nitrogen. Foods such as chicken a la king, turkey dinners, turkey pies, sliced goose meat with gravy, and vegetables with sauces retain an acceptable flavor for about a year at $-18°$ C. These products are surrounded by dressing, sauce, or gravy that protects them from the air (Hanson et al., 1950; Hanson and Fletcher, 1958; and Bean and Hanson, 1962). In contrast, frozen fried chicken has a shorter storage life because air is not easily excluded from the package. After four to six months at $-18°$ C, fried chicken develops a stale or "warmed over" flavor, and rancidity can be detected after approximately nine months' storage (Hanson et al., 1959). Rancidity that is detectable in frozen fried chicken after two months' storage at $-7°$ C in commercial containers is not detectable after 12 months in nitrogen-packed samples at the same temperature. Nitrogen packing preserves flavor so well in precooked frozen products that it may one day be adopted as a practical method of preventing rancidity in high-cost food with an otherwise limited storage life (Bean and Hanson, 1962; Hanson et al., 1959).

Storage temperature and time are more important in maintaining the flavor of some precooked foods than of others. Products in an air atmosphere are more sensitive to elevated temperatures than are products in a solid pack or an inert atmosphere. For example, rancidity is detectable in commercial samples of frozen fried chicken in two months at $-7°$ C, in six months at $-12°$ C, and in nine months at $-18°$ C (Hanson et al., 1959; Carlin et al., 1959). Cooked sliced goose meat develops off-flavors more rapidly at $-18°$ C than at lower temperatures (Bean and Hanson, 1962).

References

Bates, F. L., D. French, and R. E. Rundle. 1943. Amylose and amylopectin content of starches determined by their iodine complex formation. *J. Am. Chem. Soc. 65*: 142.

Bean, M. L., and H. L. Hanson. 1962. Utilization of geese. 2. Precooked frozen foods. *Poultry Sci. 41*: 243.

Bengtsson, N. 1967. Ultrafast freezing of cooked egg white. *Food Technol. 21*: 1259.

Boggs, M. M., C. E. Sinnott, O. R. Vasak, and E. B. Kester. 1951. Frozen cooked rice. *Food Technol. 5*: 230.

Carlin, A. F., R. M. V. Pangborn, O. J. Cotterill, and P. G. Homeyer. 1959. Effect of pretreatment and type of packaging material on quality of frozen fried chicken. *Food Technol. 13*: 557.

Cimino, S. L., L. F. Elliott, and H. H. Palmer. 1967. The stability of souffles and meringues subjected to frozen storage. *Food Technol. 21*: 97.

Davis, J. G., H. L. Hanson, and H. Lineweaver. 1952. Characterization of the effect of freezing on cooked egg white. *Food Res. 17*: 393.

Dawson, E. H., O. A. Hammerle, and P. Trimble. 1952. Home-frozen French-fried potatoes. *J. Home Econ. 44*: 36.

Hanson, H. L., A. Campbell, and H. Lineweaver. 1951. Preparation of stable frozen sauces and gravies. *Food Technol. 5*: 432.

Hanson, H. L., and L. R. Fletcher. 1958. Time-temperature tolerance of frozen foods. XII. Turkey dinners and turkey pies. *Food Technol. 12*: 40.

Hanson, H. L., and L. R. Fletcher. 1961. Salad dressings stable to frozen storage. *Food Technol. 15*: 256.

Hanson, H. L., and L. R. Fletcher. 1963. Adhesion of coatings on frozen fried chicken. *Food Technol. 7*: 115.

Hanson, H. L., L. R. Fletcher, and A. A. Campbell. 1957. The time-temperature tolerance of frozen foods. V. Texture stability of thickened pre-cooked frozen foods as influenced by composition and storage conditions. *Food Technol. 11*: 339.

Hanson, H. L., L. R. Fletcher, and H. Lineweaver. 1959. Time-temperature tolerance of frozen foods. XVII. Frozen fried chicken. *Food Technol. 13*: 221.

Hanson, H. L., K. D. Nishita, and H. Lineweaver. 1953. Preparation of stable frozen puddings. *Food Technol. 7*: 462.

Hanson, H. L., H. M. Winegarden, M. B. Horton, and H. Lineweaver. 1950. Preparation and storage of frozen cooked poultry and vegetables. *Food Technol. 4*: 430.

Harrison, D. L., G. Vail, and J. Kalen. 1953. Precooked frozen stews and Swiss steak. *Food Technol. 7*: 139.

Kerr, R. W. 1950. *Chemistry and Industry of Starch*. Academic Press, New York.

Krett, O. J., and S. L. Gennuso. 1963. Salad dressing. U.S. Patent 3,093,486, June 11.

Lineweaver, H., J. D. Anderson, and H. L. Hanson. 1952. Effect of antioxidant on rancidity development in frozen creamed turkey. *Food Technol.* 6: 1.

Longree, K. 1950. Quality problems in cooked, frozen potatoes. *Food Technol.* 4: 98.

Mecchi, E. P., M. F. Pool, M. Nonaka, A. A. Klose, S. J. Marsden, and R. J. Lillie. 1956. Further studies on tocopherol content and stability of carcass fat of chickens and turkeys. *Poultry Sci.* 35: 1246.

Meyer, K. F., and M. Fuld. 1941. Recherches sur l'amidon. XVII. L'amidon du riz collant. *Helv. Chim. Acta 24*: 1404.

Mountjoy, B. M., and M. E. Kirkpatrick. 1951. Freezing sweet potatoes. *Food Packer 32 (11)*: 23.

Osman, E. M., and P. D. Cummisford. 1959. Some factors affecting the stability of frozen white sauces. *Food Res. 24*: 595.

Palmer, H. H. 1968. Sauces and gravies; thickened desserts and fillings; whipped toppings; salad dressings and souffles. In *The Freezing Preservation of Foods*, D. K. Tressler, W. B. Van Arsdel, and M. J. Copley, eds., Vol. 4, Ch. 14, p. 314.

Partyka, A. 1963. Salad dressings. U.S. Patent 3,093,485, June 11.

Paul, P. C., B. I. Cole, and J. C. Friend. 1952. Precooked frozen vegetables. *J. Home Econ. 44*: 199.

Schoch, T. J. 1962. Recent developments in starch chemistry. *Brewers Digest 37 (2)*: 41.

Schoch, T. J. 1966. Properties and uses of rice starch. In *Starch: Chemistry and Technology*, Whistler, R. L., and E. F. Paschall, eds., Vol. 2, p. 79.

Schoch, T. J. 1968. Effects of freezing and cold-storage on pasted starches. In *The Freezing Preservation of Foods*, Tressler, D. K., W. B. Van Arsdel, and M. J. Copley, eds., Vol. 4, p. 44.

Tressler, D. K., and C. F. Evers. 1957. *The Freezing Preservation of Foods*, 3rd ed., Vol. II. Avi Publishing Co., Westport, Conn., p. 18.

Tressler, D. K., W. B. Van Arsdel, and M. J. Copley, eds. 1968. *The Freezing Preservation of Foods*. Vol. 4, *Freezing of Precooked and Prepared Foods*. Avi Publ. Co., Westport, Conn.

Watts, B. M., D. H. Peng, and E. A. Kline. 1948. Precooking pork for freezing storage. *J. Home Econ. 40*: 579.

Woodroof, J. G. 1946. Problems in freezing cooked foods. *Quick Frozen Foods 8 (9)*: 90.

Woodroof, J. G., and I. S. Atkinson. 1944. Preserving sweet potatoes by freezing. *Georgia Exp. Station Bull. 232*.

CHAPTER 14

Planning and Conducting Experiments

DOROTHY L. HARRISON

INTRODUCTION

Research is a scientific method to obtain answers to current problems, or to extend the bounds of knowledge with no immediate plan for using the findings. Research is expensive in the time and effort of scientists and in money. It is desirable to obtain as much information as possible from each experiment that is conducted. However, a frequent error is to try to get too much information from one experiment. A "hodge-podge" of data results from which no sound conclusions can be drawn. The scope of the work must be limited so that a thorough rather than a superficial study is conducted.

Too much work often is planned, because of the available materials, or because of interesting questions that arise as a project develops. Good planning avoids such a situation. The overall plan should be reevaluated as each unit of work is completed.

Some characteristics of a good research problem are:

1. It should interest the investigator. Research is not routine, but requires originality and creative thought. An uninterested worker is likely to produce few new ideas.

2. The problem may be entirely new or in an untouched field. Today such problems are hard to find, but some new theory, experimental method, or apparatus occasionally makes it possible to enter a new domain.

3. Treatments (variables) selected for study should improve understanding of a whole subject.

4. Facilities and personnel for conducting the research should be adequate, or arrangements for obtaining them should be possible.

5. The problem should be capable of accurate evaluation. In food research it is desirable to use both objective (chemical, physical, microbiological, and histological) and subjective (sensory) measurements.

6. The experiment or series of experiments should be capable of definite results within the limit of available time and money.

Some characteristics of an effective investigator are:

1. He understands clearly what he wants to do. He should have new ideas about the problem before undertaking it. An old problem may be solved because some new tool has become available or an available tool is used in a new way. For example, the early methods for estimating the collagen content of muscle were considered laborious, and were often unreliable. Hartley and Hall (1949) used a blender and centrifuge to separate the connective tissue from the muscle fibers. Labor and time were saved, but the blender-centrifuge method did not always give clear-cut results. Next, Adams et al. (1960) used enzymes to separate the two types of tissue. Their work did not solve all of the difficulties in measuring the collagen content of muscle, but some progress was made by attacking an old problem with new ideas.

2. The investigator needs knowledge and must be able to see relationships among facts.

3. The investigator must have some skill in the application of knowledge. Development of skill requires practice. No amount of instruction without practice makes an outstanding athlete or musician. Likewise, investigators with knowledge must become skillful in applying that knowledge. This requires persistence and courage.

THE SCIENTIFIC APPROACH

Solution of problems requires experiments with concise, clearly defined objectives; appropriate techniques for conducting the experiment, from selecting the sample to collecting the data; and proper analyses of results. Efficient research procedure includes three steps commonly referred to as the *scientific method*: (1) setting up a hypothesis, (2) testing the hypothesis by a well-planned experiment, and (3) presenting and interpreting the results. The scientific method seeks to establish truth in an objective manner. In food research, emphasis is placed on *why* specific changes occur in a food during production, processing, storage, and preparation for serving.

PLANNING THE WORK

The Cooperative and Interdisciplinary Approach

Efficient research often requires extensive cooperation among specialists, including scholars well trained in one or more disciplines specifically related to the problem, and a statistician. The experimental food scientist is not the lonely worker who designs and completes his own experiments. Problems in food science research are complicated and broad. Their solution may require methods of the biological, physical, and social sciences. Interdisciplinary research is increasing. Cox (1944) pointed out that the mastery of more than one science is possible for only a few; most scientists must advance by cooperation, which should be of advantage to all. For example, she stated that investigators need the help of statisticians, and research statisticians require the stimulus of practical needs. As investigators use new designs and methods of sampling, statisticians have an opportunity to examine the efficiency of the methodology they have suggested.

To obtain the most useful information possible, *all* cooperators on a project should participate in the total planning and design of the experiment(s), whereas data may be collected by a part of the team. For example, a study of the effect of processing and marketing conditions on the acceptability of frozen meat on the retail market would benefit from the knowledge and experience of:

1. Meat scientists, including animal scientists in the areas of livestock production and processing and home economists from foods and nutrition.
2. Research engineers familiar with refrigeration systems.
3. Economists with an academic and practical background in livestock marketing and food marketing at both the wholesale and retail levels.
4. Biochemists interested in the application of the knowledge of the biochemistry of muscle to the use of muscle as a food.
5. Physical chemists interested in cryogenics and heat transfer in heterogeneous systems.
6. Statisticians with some understanding of agricultural and food problems.

At its best, interdisciplinary research is complicated and difficult, but the effort invested by each member of a research team pays dividends in proportion to the input.

The Written Plan

A well-written plan summarizing the ideas of leaders of the research team saves time and effort of all workers and reduces costs. The plan must be flexible enough to permit beneficial changes as the work progresses, but should provide definite guidelines for meeting the objectives of the study. The essentials of a project outline (Harrison, 1967a) include:

1. *Title.* The title should be brief but definite. It should characterize the concrete, limited unit of work to be undertaken. Avoid phrases such as "A study of ———" or "Investigations on ———." If a specific unit of work is a part of a larger unit, a double title is permissible. The title of the larger unit is followed by the title of the smaller unit. For example, "Effect of preslaughter environmental temperature and postmortem treatment on selected characteristics of ovine muscle. I. Shortening and pH or II. Cooking losses and palatability factors."

Jacks (1967) discussed the importance of the title and summary or abstract of publications in the scientific literature. His ideas also are applicable to the title of a research proposal. He pointed out that the "literature explosion," that is, the increased quantity of scientific literature, has been more than enough to create an emphatic buyers' (readers') market for such publications. To get a paper read he recommends that the title (a) be informative, (b) not distract the reader with useless words and phrases, and (c) begin with the most important phrase.

2. *Justification.* The justification should convince the reader that the proposed study is important. Include a brief statement concerning the nature of the problem, the reason(s) why the problem is worthy of study, and a review of *selected* literature related to the problem. The review of literature is the basis for presenting the need of the proposed study. It should indicate available information related to the problem and point out limitations of previous work. Make some transition from the justification to objectives. The objectives may be included in the justification, and this section used as the part called "Introduction" in the published paper.

3. *Objectives.* The plan includes one or more *definite* objectives possible of attainment within the scope of the work. If an objective includes the terminology "to determine," be sure that it will be possible to determine the factor named in the objective. Usually such terminology as "to investigate," "to study," or "to compare" is preferable to "to determine."

4. *Procedure.* The procedure is an outline of the important steps and/or methods of collecting data. Minute details are unnecessary, but

there should be sufficient details to point out the suitability of the proposed methods for accomplishing the objectives. Attaching forms to be used or diagrams of sampling plans is an efficient method of explaining procedures. Certain procedures may need to be selected or developed through preliminary work. This should be indicated.

5. *References.* References cited in the justification and/or procedure should be listed.

The project outline may include plans for reporting the results of the work. Large projects may be divided into several phases and the results of each phase reported separately, or those of two or more related phases presented in one report.

DESIGN OF THE EXPERIMENT AND ANALYSIS OF DATA

Fundamentals of Designing Experiments

To obtain the correct answers to problems and the most information for the time, effort, and money invested, it is necessary to be systematic in planning research and in summarizing and interpreting data. Using statistical methods is the most efficient way to do so. Statistical methods involve mathematics and mathematical symbols, whose meanings are agreed on, and are organized into a usable system to communicate information. The symbols are a shorthand that reduces mass data to forms readily understood and interpreted by persons familiar with the symbols. Information thus communicated facilitates comparisons with other data.

Statistical methods are organized mathematical operations, and all mathematical operations are based on assumptions of some kind. Hence, statistical analyses cannot be applied to any data with the idea of thereby adding efficiency, objectivity, and precision. Experiments should be designed with analysis of the data in mind; that is, the analysis is set up *before* any data are collected. Cox (1944) stated that by applying statistical methods to the design of an experiment and to the interpretation of the data, the value of an experiment may be increased 3 to 10 times. She also pointed out that (1) analysis of data calls for clear thinking, (2) routine application of statistical procedures may lead to misinterpretation of data, and (3) statistical tools cannot increase the validity of data.

The statistician can help design the experiment so that the measurements taken will fit a statistical model, thus making it possible to analyze the data and draw conclusions from the analysis. Experimental observations are recorded in numerical form, because such measurements are objective and relatively precise.

The research worker must be able to give the statistician definite information such as (1) the foremost question to be answered, (2) related questions to be answered, (3) measurements to be made, (4) the inherent variability of the material to be studied, and (5) physical limitations. Under physical limitations, the statistician must know the population available for sampling and the work that can be managed in one day or one experimental period.

The population available for sampling and the work that can be managed will influence the number of variables that are planned. The quantity of work that can be managed in one period will depend in part on the available equipment and laboratory space and on the degree of precision and accuracy of the technicians.

For analysis of data, the statistician will supervise the mathematical operations necessary. The actual operations are routine, and technical staff can be trained to carry them out. The research worker should know something about the steps involved in the analysis so that he may understand and check the results of the analysis.

The research worker and statistician should study the results of the analysis independently. Then they should discuss them together to be sure of correct interpretation of results and of drawing correct conclusions. If conclusions seem illogical, can the occurrence be explained? New research problems may develop from such situations. If the research worker can plan with the same statistician each time he designs an experiment, communication between the two specialists becomes progressively easier.

Examples of Experimental Designs

Federer (1963) discussed the applications, advantages, and disadvantages of specific types of experimental designs. Some commonly used experimental designs with examples of problems in food research were described by Cox (1944). Additional examples of experimental designs used in the author's laboratory follow. These designs may be used for studies with all types of food products.

Randomized Complete Block

In this type of design the experimental units are arranged in groups (blocks), each of which contains enough material for one replication of each treatment.

A randomized complete block design utilizing 48 loin steaks was employed to evaluate the effects of marination in 0.03 M sodium hexametaphosphate solution (Miller and Harrison, 1965). There were 12 blocks of four steaks each; one steak in each block was untreated, and the remaining three steaks were marinated 1, 2, or 6 hours prior to cooking (see Table 1).

TABLE 1.   Randomized Complete Block Design

Blocks (Cooking Periods)	Treatments			
		Marinating Time (Hours)		
	Untreated	1	2	6
	Steak Code Numbers[a]			
1	15c	16a	03b	12c
2	15a	06f	07b	06c
3	06b	14a	15d	11d
4	16c	12a	10b	15e
5	15b	01a	07a	10d
6	09a	08c	13b	11c
7	03c	12b	14b	16b
8	02b	04b	06d	10c
9	08a	09c	05c	05f
10	06a	13a	10e	06d
11	04a	09b	05b	05d
12	12d	08b	13c	02a

[a] Arabic numbers refer to loins; letters refer to position of steaks within a loin.

The analysis of variance (AOV) was:

Source of Variation	D/F
Treatments	3
Remainder	44
Total	47

Incomplete Block

A design in which only a part of the treatments is evaluated at one time, and each treatment is compared with every other treatment an equal number of times, is an *incomplete block*. When each block contains the same number of experimental units and every pair of treatments occurs together in the same block the same number of times, the design is a *balanced incomplete block*. The term "balanced" is used, because all pairs of treatments are compared with about the same precision, although differences among blocks may be large (Amerine et al., 1965).

The effects of endpoint temperature in unheated muscle and in muscle heated to five endpoint temperatures were investigated (Rogers et al., 1967). Thirty turkeys were cut into left and right breast and thigh-leg pieces. An incomplete block design (Cochran and Cox, 1950) was used to assign endpoint temperatures to breast (Experiment I) and thigh-leg pieces (Experiment II). There were 30 blocks (heating periods) for breasts and 30 for thigh-legs, with left and right sides from one turkey composing one block and 10 replications of each of six endpoint temperatures, each endpoint temperature occurring with each other twice (Table 2).

TABLE 2. Incomplete Block Design for Assigning Endpoint Temperatures, °C, to Breast and Thigh-Leg Pieces of Turkey[a]

Block[b] (Heating Period)	Endpoint Temperature		Block[b] (Heating Period)	Endpoint Temperature	
1	45L	55R	16	25L	45R
2	10R	45L	17	35R	55L
3	55L	65R	18	35L	45R
4	10R	55L	19	45L	65R
5	25R	55L	20	10R	35L
6	10R	65L	21	25R	45L
7	10R	55L	22	35L	45R
8	25L	55R	23	10R	35L
9	10L	65R	24	25R	35L
10	25L	65R	25	10R	25L
11	25R	65L	26	35L	65R
12	45L	65R	27	45L	55R
13	55L	65R	28	35L	55R
14	10R	45L	29	25L	35R
15	10R	25L	30	35R	65L

[a] Cochran and Cox (1950).
[b] Left (L) and right (R) pairs from one turkey equal one block.

AOV:

Source of Variation	D/F
Temperature (unadjusted)	5
Blocks (adjusted)	29
Intrablock error	25
Total	59

"Adjusted" means for each endpoint, temperature and approximate least significant differences (LSD, $P < 0.05$) were calculated to study the effect of heating on a specific measurement. AOV for a completely randomized design was used for data where there were no values for unheated (10° C) pieces.

In another experiment, an incomplete block design was used to study the effects of degree of doneness (endpoint temperatures of 55, 70, and 85° C) on roasts from three beef muscles (Visser et al., 1960). An incomplete block consisted of six roasts (three from the left and three from the right side of the animal) from a given muscle, and that muscle from one animal was one replication (Table 3).

TABLE 3.   Incomplete Block Design for Assigning Endpoint Temperatures to Roasts From Three Beef Muscles

Muscle	Animal Number	Roast Code Numbers[a] and Endpoint Temperatures, °C					
		Jl	Jr	Kl	Kr	Ll	Lr
Semitendinosus	II	70	55	85	55	70	85
(ST)	IV	85	70	55	85	70	55
	V	55	70	85	70	55	85
		Ml	Mr	Nl	Nr	Ol	Or
Longissimus dorsi,	II	85	55	70	55	85	70
(LD, loin section)	IV	70	85	55	85	55	70
	V	85	55	55	70	70	85
		Tl	Tr	Ul	Ur	Vl	Vr
Longissimus dorsi,	II	55	70	85	55	70	85
(LD, rib section)	IV	85	55	70	85	70	55
	V	85	55	55	70	85	70

[a] J (proximal end), K (middle), L (distal end) of ST.
 M (anterior), N (middle), O (posterior) of LD, loin.
 T (anterior), U (middle), V (posterior) of LD, rib.
 l, left side of animal.
 r, right side of animal.

AOV:

Source of Variation	D/F
Animals	8
Endpoint temperature	2
Error	7
Total	17

Split Plot

A design in which the experimental units are distributed among several levels or phases of one treatment (whole plots), and within each level or phase of that treatment each experimental unit receives a second treatment (sub-plots), is called a *split plot*. This type of design provides for studying the effect of two or more levels of the second treatment on each level or phase of the first treatment. Federer (1963) pointed out that the split-plot design is an incomplete block design.

The effect of breed and three ante-mortem and two post-mortem treatments on the development of brown color in porcine muscle from 24 barrows (12 Poland China and 12 Duroc) were investigated. The experimental design was a split plot (whole-plot, breed, and ante-mortem treatment; subplot, post-mortem treatment) with four replications of each treatment combination (Bowers et al., 1968). Eight barrows, four from each breed, were subjected to each ante-mortem treatment. Carcasses were split in half, and each half randomly assigned to the two post-mortem treatments (Table 4).

TABLE 4.   Design for Assigning 24 Barrows to the Ante- and Post-Mortem Treatments[a]

| Replication | Poland China | | | Duroc | | |
	UT	SF	E	UT	SF	E
I	4	1	5	3	6	2
II	8	9	12	7	10	11
III	14	15	18	13	16	17
IV	23	20	21	24	19	22

[a] Ante-mortem treatment:
   UT, untreated.
   SF, sugar fed.
   E, exercised.

Post-mortem treatment:

30° F ⎰ Randomly assigned to
42° F ⎱ the left or right side of each carcass.

AOV:

Source of Variation	D/F
Whole plot:	
Breed (B)	1
Ante-mortem treatment (AT)	2
B × AT	2
Animals: B × AT (error a)	18
Subplot:	
Post-mortem treatment (PMT)	1
PMT × B	1
PMT × AT	2
PMT × B × AT	2
Error b	18
Total	47

A *modified split-plot* design (Goulden, 1952) with four replications was used to compare selected characteristics of untreated steaks and steaks injected with three levels of 0.03 M sodium hexametaphosphate solution that were cooked to four degrees of doneness (Rust, 1963). A whole plot consisted of one specific degree of doneness for untreated and treated (three levels of phosphate solution) steaks. A subplot consisted of one level of phosphate solution. Each of the four replications contained four whole plots and 16 subplots. Subplots were randomized within whole plots, whole plots within replications, and replications within the experiment (Table 5).

TABLE 5.   Randomized Split-Plot Design for Untreated and Treated Steaks Cooked to Four Degrees of Doneness

Replication	Whole Plots — Degree of Doneness (° C)	Subplots — Sodium Hexametaphosphate (Percent)			
I	70	10	5	15	0
	90	5	15	0	10
	80	0	10	5	15
	60	10	0	15	5
II	90	5	10	0	15
	70	5	0	10	15
	80	5	0	10	15
	60	10	15	0	5
III	70	15	5	10	0
	60	15	10	5	0
	90	5	15	0	10
	80	5	10	0	15
IV	60	15	10	0	5
	70	10	0	5	15
	80	15	10	0	5
	90	0	5	15	10

AOV:

Source of Variation	D/F
Replications (R)	$3 (R - 1)$
Degree of doneness (W)	$3 (W - 1)$
Error A (R $\times$ W)	$9 (R - 1)(W - 1)$
Treatments (S)	$3 (S - 1)$
Degree of doneness $\times$ Treatments	$9 (W - 1)(S - 1)$
Error B (W $\times$ S $\times$ R)	$36 R (W - 1)(S - 1)$
Total (N)	$63 (N - 1)$

Food Theory and Applications

Latin Square

For the latin-square design, treatments are grouped into replications in two ways, that is, in rows and in columns. Every treatment appears once in each row and once in each column.

A 3 × 3 latin square with four replications was followed to roast anterior, middle, and posterior sections (A,B,C) of 12 pork loins to three endpoint temperatures (65, 75 and 85° C) (Pengilly and Harrison, 1966). The specific design is presented in Table 6.

TABLE 6. A 3 × 3 Latin Square With Four Replications[a]

Replication (Square)	Evaluation Period	Loin Number	Endpoint Temperature (° C) and Section of Loin		
			65	75	85
I	1	121	C	B	A
	2	127	B	A	C
	3	129	A	C	B
II	4	122	A	B	C
	5	131	B	C	A
	6	125	C	A	B
III	7	130	C	B	A
	8	123	B	A	C
	9	126	A	C	B
IV	10	128	B	A	C
	11	124	A	C	B
	12	120	C	B	A

[a] A, anterior; B, middle; C, posterior.

AOV:

Source of Variation	D/F
Replications (Squares)	3
Sections (A, B, C)	2
Endpoint temperatures	2
Pooled loins	8
Remainder	20
Total	35

A 4 × 4 latin square with six replications was used to study the effect of four post-mortem aging periods and four positions in 24 loins from three breeds of pigs (Harrison et al., 1970). The specific design is presented in Table 7.

TABLE 7. A 4 × 4 Latin Square With Six Replications

Replication (Square)	Evaluation Period	Breed and Animal Number		Position on Loin[a] and Aging Period[b]			
				A	B	C	D
I	1	Duroc	I	8	1	4	12
	2		II	12	4	1	8
	3		III	4	8	12	1
	4		IV	1	12	8	4
II	5	Duroc	V	1	4	12	8
	6		VI	8	12	4	1
	7		VII	4	8	1	12
	8		VIII	12	1	8	4
III	9	York-	IX	1	8	4	12
	10	shire	X	12	4	8	1
	11		XI	4	1	12	8
	12		XII	8	12	1	4
IV	13	York-	XIII	12	4	1	8
	14	shire	XIV	8	4	1	12
	15		XV	4	12	8	1
	16		XVI	1	8	12	4
V	17	Hamp-	XVII	4	1	12	8
	18	shire	XVIII	1	12	8	4
	19		XIX	12	8	4	1
	20		XX	8	4	1	12
VI	21	Hamp-	XXI	4	12	1	8
	22	shire	XXII	12	8	4	1
	23		XXIII	8	1	12	4
	24		XXIV	1	4	8	12

[a] Position on loin: A, B, C, D → anterior to posterior.
[b] Aging period, days (1, 4, 8, 12).

AOV:

Source of Variation	D/F
Squares	5
Animals within squares	18
Position within squares	18
Aging periods	3
Aging × squares	15
Error	36
Total	95

Experimental designs for studies involving sensory evaluation of food are discussed by Amerine et al. (1965). Those authors also illustrate the AOV for the various types of designs presented.

CONDUCTING THE EXPERIMENT

Throughout the period of collecting data extreme care should be exercised to (a) follow the experimental design, (b) make accurate measurements, and (c) prepare an adequate and accurate record of all data.

Controlling Conditions of the Experiment

With repetition of most experiments, the observed effects of the treatments, that is, differences among or between variables, vary from trial to trial. Such variation is referred to as experimental error, which can cause an experiment to have little value. Practices used to reduce experimental error include the following:

1. *Selection of an efficient experimental design and plan for analysis of the data.* Appropriate experimental designs allow for replication and randomization of treatments. Replication decreases random errors associated with the average effects of any treatment and increases the precision of the experiment. Randomization protects against favoring any one treatment in any replicate more than in another, and insures every treatment an equal chance of being assigned to a favorable or unfavorable set of units. After treatments have been assigned to experimental units, none should be protected or handicapped by circumstances related to the collection of data.

An efficient experimental design requires an appropriate sample. Data collected are no better than the *sample,* a small collection of a larger aggregate, the *population,* about which information is desired. Usually data cannot be collected on an entire population, so sampling should truly represent the population. Optimum sample size depends on the desired accuracy of the results, the variability of the experimental material, and the time and money available for the study (Harrison, 1967b).

2. *Selection of experimental material.* Foods are heterogeneous systems whose properties are dependent on their history, and the experimental material for any research with food must be selected accordingly. For example, when biological materials (plant and animal) are involved, the units are selected to reflect similarity of managemen'. during production, maturity, and processing procedures. For problems in food preparation such as those with batters and doughs, all staple supplies to be used in the entire experiment are secured from one source.

3. *Standardization of technique, laboratory equipment, and instruments.* Good technique is the responsibility of the person doing the experiment. It should be both accurate and precise. Cox (1944) listed some objectives of good technique as (a) to secure uniformity in the application of treatments, (b) to control external influences so that every treatment produces its effects under comparable and desired conditions, (c) to use suitable measurements of the effects of treatments, and (d) to prevent gross errors.

Work is simplified and controlled by the development of efficient habits, such as weighing one item for several variables or replications at the same time.

The same laboratory equipment and instruments are used throughout the experiment. Following exactly the instructions for the use of instruments and an understanding of the principles of their operation are of paramount importance.

Refinement of technique is accomplished by practice. "Preliminary" work may require more time and effort than collecting data for the designed experiment.

4. *Miscellaneous conditions.* The list of conditions to consider in controlling experiments with food could become endless. Some conditions not mentioned previously are (a) shelf life of certain foods under specific conditions of temperature and humidity; (b) time limitation for refrigerator or frozen storage of samples, when those conditions are not a part of the experimental design; and (c) proper handling of an unplanned variable that may develop in the course of collecting data. An unexpected variable may change the direction of the work if it suggests a new approach to the problem. However, changes that would make it impossible to use data already collected should be avoided.

Recording Data

Data should be recorded in a bound notebook as measurements are made. Such a practice prevents loss of data by the misplacing of loose papers and avoids error from recopying values.

Laboratory workers should develop forms easy to use in recording data and understandable to other workers reasonably familiar with the type of data to be collected. Some workers use forms that fit on one page or on facing pages in the notebook and provide space to record all measurements made in one experimental unit or period of work. Other workers prefer to record all data for a specific measurement, such as pH, for the entire experiment in one area of the notebook. The former method eliminates turning of pages in the notebook during a given experimental period, whereas the latter method may facilitate summarizing data and computing mean values for a specific measurement. For some experiments, a data book set up with a combination of the two methods may be desirable. The number of measurements made on any one unit of experimental material within a given period will influence the form(s) used to record data.

Organization and Presentation of Data

After data have been recorded, they must be organized for interpretation by the research worker and for presentation to others. Masses of data must be reduced to a usable form. Tables and graphs (often referred to as figures) are commonly used for presenting data and communicating the results of an experiment. The same data should not be presented in both a table and a graph.

A table or graph should be constructed so that it "stands alone" and presents the data in an understandable form. All tables and graphs should have numbers and clear, concise titles. The exact style of the table or graph varies with the medium of communication. If the table or graph is part of a written manuscript, it should be understood without reference to the text. If used for oral presentation of data, it should be understandable to the observer in a short span of time.

General guides for presenting data and constructing tables and graphs were given by Griswold (1962) and Hall (1967). Research workers will also find it helpful to study tables and graphs published by others.

Interpretation of Data

Many scientists find the most interest and satisfaction in interpreting data and drawing conclusions. Success is associated with meeting the objectives of the experiment and obtaining answers to the original question(s). Additional questions raised may stimulate further work.

Cox (1944) pointed out that in an attempt to draw reasonable conclusions, the investigator and statistician use the theory of probability to determine how much confidence to place in the results of an experiment and what sense can be made of the data. Common sense aids in interpreting experimental results. Variability of the experimental material and the magnitude of the differences measured must be considered. When the experimental material is heterogeneous, which is the situation with most food systems, differences between treatment means must be large to be significant, unless an unusually large sample was used. For example, Norris (1968) studied the effect of maturity and marbling of the beef carcass on the palatability of rib steaks. Analysis of variance of palatability scores indicated no significant differences attributable to treatments (maturity and marbling levels). Variation among treatment means for four palatability factors ranged from 0 to 0.6 point on a 7-point scale. However, when panel scores for each palatability factor were subjected to Bartlett's test for homogeneity, there was a high degree of variation among the steaks. This may be attributable to variation in scores assigned by individual panel members and/or to variation among the steaks themselves. Heterogeneity of panel scores might account for the nonsignificant differences, attributable to treatment, in the palatability of the steaks. Thus, maturity and marbling of the beef carcass may affect palatability of the meat more than is indicated by the data from this study.

Conclusions are the investigator's interpretation of the results of an experiment. The line of demarcation should be clear between the conclusions validated by the data and legitimate implications drawn by the investigator.

SAMPLING IN FOOD RESEARCH

Cox (1944) and Cochran (1962) discussed the principles of sampling and pointed out the importance of random sampling.

Sampling procedures such as those reported for the following experiments with vegetables are adaptable to many experiments with foods. Tinklin and Harrison (1959) studied the cost and quality of fresh, frozen, and canned green beans purchased at intervals throughout a three-year period. Before sampling, fresh beans used for one experimental unit were sorted, tipped, snapped, and *tossed together,* and two packages of frozen beans were *broken apart* and *tossed together.* Aliquots from the *combined lot* of two cans of the same brand and grade of canned beans were used for one experimental unit.

When canned and frozen asparagus were compared for certain quality factors, three cases, *enough for the entire experiment,* of each product (10-ounce packages of frozen asparagus and No. 2 cans of canned asparagus) were purchased approximately three months after the peak of the processing season. At each experimental period, a sufficient number of packages and cans were opened to allow for measurements of palatability and ascorbic acid. (Tinklin et al., 1961).

In a third study, six two-pound packages from one lot of U.S. Grade A fancy individual frozen peas were used to compare two methods of analysis for reduced ascorbic acid (Stowell et al., 1962). The peas in each two-pound package were *mixed thoroughly.* Samples of peas were weighed into polyethylene bags that were labeled to indicate the number of the two-pound package, the number of the sample, the method date, and the time (morning or afternoon) of analysis. The analysis of variance to which the data were subjected provided for a study of *differences among packages* and between methods.

In addition to selecting the sample of experimental material to represent the population, it is often necessary to sample within a single unit. In experiments with meat and poultry, specific areas within a retail cut or muscle may be selected arbitrarily for making such measurements as palatability scores, shear-force values, press-fluid yields, collagen nitrogen values, and histological evaluation. Figures 1 and 2 illustrate plans for arbitrary sampling within the longissimus dorsi muscle.

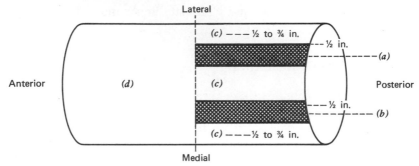

FIGURE 1. Sampling porcine longissimus dorsi muscle. (*a*) Lateral shear core and water-holding capacity, (*b*) medial shear core and water-holding capacity, (*c*) press fluid, pH, total moisture, and color, and (*d*) palatability samples cut from cores ½ in. in diameter and ½ in. long. (Pengilly and Harrison, 1966.)

When a specific area of a retail cut or muscle is selected arbitrarily for a certain measurement, the question arises as to how much variation there is within the single unit. Data on variation in shear values within one muscle from lamb carcasses and another from pork carcasses are presented in Table 8.

The limited data in Table 8 indicate that there may be greater variation within the porcine semimembranosus muscle than within the longissimus dorsi muscle of lamb. This suggests that a given measurement should not always be made on a sample from the same area in each piece of meat used in a study. Harrison et al. (1967) published more extensive data from studies with porcine longissimus dorsi that support this idea.

Adams et al. (1960) selected, at random, areas within slices of beef semimembranosus muscle used for palatability and shear measurements. A grid, prepared from acetate sketching paper to conform to the shape of the muscle slices, was divided into 1-inch squares (Figure 3). The

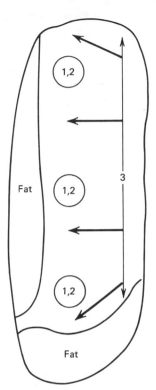

FIGURE 2. Sampling the longissimus dorsi in beef loin steaks. A diagram of the surface of a steak. 1 = cores ($\frac{1}{2}$ inch) for shear values; 2 = water-holding capacity (0.3 g from the center of each core); and 3 = cubes ($\frac{1}{2}$ inch) for palatability samples were cut from area 3. Total moisture and pH were determined on samples of ground meat prepared from that remaining after the cubes for palatability evaluation were removed. (Miller and Harrison, 1965.)

squares were numbered, and a table of random numbers was used to select the numbers on the grid that represented the positions in each slice used for the two measurements. Specific sampling areas were cut out of the sketching paper grids prepared for individual slices of muscle, and the grid was placed over the meat as a guide for removing samples.

The Committee on Preparation Factors, National Cooperative Meat Investigations (1942), stated that each member of a palatability panel should be given a sample from the same location in each cut of the same kind. For some time this was the accepted practice. However, other sampling techniques have been reported. Fenton et al. (1956) used every second or third slice from the portion of roasts designated for palatability

TABLE 8.   Average Shear Values, in Pounds, for $\frac{1}{2}$-Inch Cores Taken From Three Positions in the Longissimus Dorsi of Lamb and the Semimembranosus of Pork

	Position[a]		
Muscle	A	B	C
Longissimus dorsi, lamb, $n = 19$	6.0	5.0	5.5
Semimembranosus, pork, $n = 24$	8.7	9.3	7.0

[a] Lamb:
    A = anterior.
    B = middle.
    C = posterior.
  Pork:
    A = 1 inch from center of muscle, distal end.
    B = 1 inch from center of muscle.
    C = 1 inch from center of muscle, proximal end.

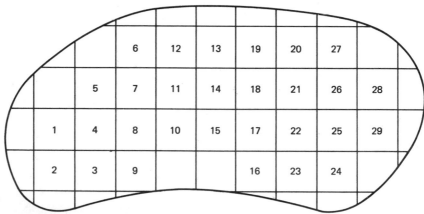

FIGURE 3.   Diagram of the numbered grid composed of 1-inch squares used to select portions of a muscle slice used for palatability and shearing tests.

measurements. The slices were numbered and the assignment of slice numbers to the judges was randomized.

Pengilly and Harrison (1966) cut cores of muscle ($\frac{1}{4}$ inch in diameter) into $\frac{1}{2}$-inch pieces that were selected at random by members of their palatability panel, whereas Miller and Harrison (1965) provided $\frac{1}{2}$-inch cubes of muscle for random selection by panel members. The technique for cutting uniform cubes of muscle is illustrated in Figure 4. Cores of

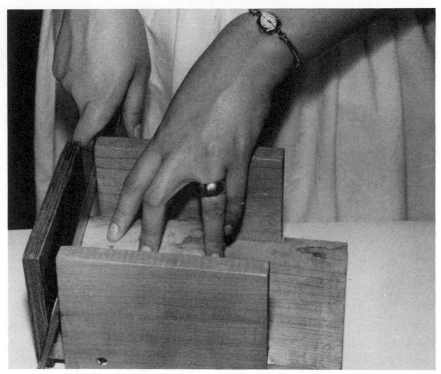

FIGURE 4. Cutting ½-inch cubes of muscle for the palatability panel using a mitre box and a sharp, long blade knife.

muscle (½-inch in diameter) that may be used for shear measurements and/or palatability samples and ½-inch cubes for palatability samples are shown in Figure 5.

REPORTING RESULTS

Importance of Publication

No research is completed until the results are published. Publication is accepted as the first and traditional step in spreading the news of any new discovery or development. Other publicity media such as radio, television, and films are regarded only as satellites of the printed word. Publication is necessary before the knowledge gained through research can be applied generally to practical problems. Publication should be a part of the overall plan for all research projects and entire research programs.

Research findings, whether they confirm or negate the hypothesis that

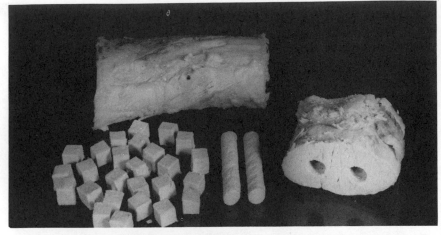

FIGURE 5. Cubes (½ inch) and cores (½ inch in diameter) removed from the lateral and medial positions of porcine longissimus dorsi.

the scientist investigated, are important. Publication informs other scientists of work done in a certain area and often provides information to enhance the meaning or understanding of the work of other researchers.

Findings from a single study may appear to have little value by themselves. However, when those findings are added to the total knowledge in the problem area, they increase in value. That is the philosophy behind interdisciplinary research. The benefits of pooling the "know-how" and research facilities available within or between laboratories pay large dividends for the time, effort, and money invested.

Basic, pure, or fundamental research findings, that is, those resulting from studies planned with no immediate application in mind, are recorded in the literature by publication in scientific journals. Kettering (1938) suggested that basic research data are equivalent to money deposited in a checking account. The data may be "checked out" at a later date to help solve a specific problem. Findings from basic food research reach other investigators in food science through publication in one of several scientific journals published for food scientists and scientists in disciplines related to food science.

Applied research is that designed to obtain knowledge that will provide a basis for solving a specific problem. The term "developmental research" refers to work on the improvement of existing products or the creation of new products. Results of applied and developmental research are published in the technical and trade journals. In this way new information becomes available to the entire food industry. Such findings may not be put to work immediately, because often costly and time-consuming changes in processing equipment and/or marketing may be involved.

The Written Report

Many publications are available on writing scientific journal papers and technical reports. Harrison (1967a) outlined and described the steps in preparing a research manuscript and in submitting the manuscript for publication. Editors of most scientific and technical journals will furnish prospective authors with information about the style required for publication in the journal. The Institute of Food Technologists (1970) published a style guide for their Journal of Food Science. Similar style guides are available for other journals.

The Oral Report

Results of research may be reported at a professional meeting before publication in a scientific or technical journal. Usually the speaker is required to present findings from one or more years of work in 15 to 20 minutes. He must thus be brief and to the point. Only a *brief* justification for the study, highlights of methods, and significant data can be given effectively. It may be helpful to the audience if the speaker makes his main point at the beginning of the talk. A short summary statement may be made to emphasize the "punch line."

Talking from an outline with notes is more interesting and effective than reading a manuscript. The speech should be rehearsed; the speaker should know his material and should make it sound extemporaneous rather than memorized. Rehearsing the speech allows the speaker to adjust his material so that he stays within his time limit. He should allow himself a margin of one to two minutes.

Slides used to present data or explain methods should be few and simple. Tables should contain selected data, and should be designed especially for the oral presentation. Abbreviations may be used and explained by the speaker. Graphs may be preferred to tables for presenting data. Well-designed graphs make it easy for the audience to grasp in a short time the trends of the data.

SUMMARY

Characteristics of high-quality research are careful advanced planning and an experimental design that gives a secure basis for obtaining new knowledge. High-quality research comes from teamwork of investigators, representing the various disciplines related to the problem, and statisticians in planning and conducting the experiment or series of experiments, in summarizing and interpreting the data, and in drawing conclusions. In planning, it is necessary to consider the number of replications of each treatment, proper sampling techniques, methods for controlling the conditions of the experiment(s), and methods for recording and analyzing the data.

Publication of research findings is extremely important. Research is not completed until the results are published.

References

Adams, R., D. L. Harrison, and J. L. Hall. 1960. Comparison of enzyme and Waring Blendor methods for determination of collagen in beef. *J. Agr. Food Chem.* 8: 229–232.

Amerine, M. A., R. M. Pangborn, and E. B. Roessler. 1965. *Principles of Sensory Evaluation of Food.* John Wiley & Sons, Inc., New York, pp. 459–472.

Bowers, J. A., D. L. Harrison, and D. H. Kropf. 1968. Browning and associated properties of porcine muscle. *J. Food Sci.* 33: 147–151.

Cochran, W. G. 1962. Design and analysis of sampling. In *Statistical Methods,* 5th ed., G. W. Snedecor. Chapter 17. Iowa State University Press, Ames, Iowa.

Cochran, W. G., and G. M. Cox. 1950. *Experimental Designs,* p. 446. John Wiley & Sons, Inc., New York.

Committee on Preparation Factors, National Cooperative Meat Investigations. 1942. *Meat and Meat Cookery,* p. 225. National Live Stock and Meat Board, Chicago, Ill.

Cox, G. M. 1944. Statistics as a tool for research. *J. Home Economics* 36: 575–580.

Federer, W. T. 1963. *Experimental Design, Theory and Application.* Chapters 4, 5, 6, 8, 10, 11. The Macmillan Company, New York.

Fenton, F., I. T. Flight, D. S. Robson, K. C. Beamer, and J. S. How. 1956. *Study of Three Cuts of Lower and Higher Grade Beef, Unfrozen and Frozen, Using Two Methods of Thawing and Two Methods of Braising.* Memoir 341, Cornell University, Agr. Exp't Sta., Ithaca, N.Y.

Goulden, C. H. 1952. *Methods of Statistical Analysis,* pp. 222–229. John Wiley & Sons, Inc., New York.

Griswold, R. M. 1962. *The Experimental Study of Foods,* pp. 553–555. Houghton Mifflin Company, Boston.

Hall, O. A. 1967. *Research Handbook for Home Economics Education,* 2nd ed., pp. 135–147. Burgess Publishing Company, Minneapolis, Minn.

Harrison, D. L. 1967a. *Preparing a Research Manuscript.* Kansas Agr. Exp't

Sta. Circular 396. Kansas State University of Agriculture and Applied Science, Manhattan, Kansas.

Harrison, D. L. 1967b. *The Language of Statistics.* Kansas Agr. Exp't Sta., Kansas State University, Manhattan, Kansas.

Harrison, D. L., L. L. Anderson, J. Baird, C. I. Pengilly, R. A. Merkel, D. H. Kropf, and D. L. Mackintosh. 1967. Variation of selected factors from the anterior to the posterior of pork loin. *J. Food Sci. 32,* 336–339.

Harrison, D. L., J. A. Bowers, L. L. Anderson, H. J. Tuma, and D. H. Kropf. 1970. Effects of post-mortem aging on porcine muscle. *J. Food Sci. 35:* 292–294.

Hartley, L. M., J. L. Hall. 1949. Rapid determination of collagen in beef by Waring blendor and centrifuge technique. *Food Research 14:* 195–202.

Institute of Food Technologists. 1970. Style guide for research papers. Journal of Food Science. Institute of Food Technologists, Chicago, Illinois.

Jacks, S. V. 1967. A buyer's market, the importance of title and summary. *Experimental Agriculture 3:* 257–261.

Kettering, C. F. 1938. More music please, composers! *Saturday Evening Post 211:* 32.

Miller, E. M., and D. L. Harrison. 1965. Effect of marination in sodium hexametaphosphate solution on the palatability of loin steaks. *Food Technol. 19:* 94–97.

Norris, H. L. 1968. Effect of maturity and marbling level of the beef carcass on histological characteristics, tenderness, and juiciness of longissimus dorsi. M.S. thesis, Farrell Library, Kansas State University, Manhattan, Kansas.

Pengilly, C. I., and D. L. Harrison. 1966. Effect of heat treatment on the acceptability of pork. *Food Technol. 20:* 98–101.

Rogers, P. J., G. E. Goertz, and D. L. Harrison. 1967. Heat induced changes of moisture in turkey muscles. *J. Food Sci. 32:* 298–304.

Rust, M. E. 1963. The effect of injected sodium hexametaphosphate solution on the palatability of fresh beef. Ph.D. Dissertation, Farrell Library, Kansas State University, Manhattan, Kansas.

Stowell, M. L., G. L. Tinklin, and D. L. Harrison. 1962. A comparison of two colorimetric methods for determining reduced ascorbic acid in frozen peas. *J. Food Sci. 27:* 347–349.

Tinklin, G. L., and D. L. Harrison. 1959. Cost and quality of fresh, frozen, and canned green beans. *J. Amer. Diet. Assoc. 35:* 1270–1274.

Tinklin, G. L., D. L. Harrison, and J. S. Beck. 1961. Frozen and canned all-green asparagus spears. *J. Amer. Diet. Assoc. 39:* 473–475.

Visser, R. Y., D. L. Harrison, G. E. Goertz, M. Bunyon, M. M. Skelton, and D. L. Mackintosh. 1960. The effect of the degree of doneness on the tenderness and juiciness of beef cooked in the oven and in deep fat. *Food Technol. 14:* 193–198.

CHAPTER 15

Sensory Methods in Food-Quality Assessment

HELEN H. PALMER

Food quality is evaluated by sensory, chemical, and physical methods. Sensory methods are used to determine whether foods differ in such qualities as taste, odor, juiciness, tenderness, or texture, and the extent and direction of the differences. They are also used to determine consumer preferences among foods and whether a certain food is acceptable to a specific consumer group. The two general types of sensory tests are *difference* tests to determine quality differences and *consumer* tests to determine preference or acceptability. They differ in such important ways that selection of the appropriate method and use of suitable conditions are essential for proper interpretation of research results (Harries, 1953). Because of the time and expense involved, consumer studies are used only after significant differences in one or more important qualities have been determined by small laboratory panels. Since only the commercial application of food research requires consumer tests, the discussion in this chapter will be confined to analytical sensory tests of differences in foods.

Chemical and physical methods for testing of food (Chapter 16) are often useful in conjunction with sensory methods to elucidate the reasons for differences detected by sensory methods. They can replace sensory methods after correlation with sensory tests has been established as, for example, shear resistance measurements and sensory tenderness evaluation (Palmer et al., 1965). Physical and chemical methods are usually more readily reproducible and less time-consuming than sensory tests and often are more economical, but they are limited to areas in which they have been shown to measure the quality apparent to the senses.

The terminology used in sensory testing has been subject to considerable discussion in the past. The following definitions of commonly used terms were compiled primarily from *Webster's Third New International Dictionary*.

Flavor: The blend of taste and smell sensations evoked by a substance in the mouth.

Taste: The sweet, sour, bitter, or salty quality of a dissolved substance as perceived by the sense of taste.

Odor: A quality of a substance that affects the sense of smell.

Texture: The characteristic consistency; the overall structure; includes hardness, cohesiveness, viscosity, elasticity.

Tender: Having a soft or yielding texture; easily broken.

Tough: Having the quality of being strong or firm in texture but flexible and not brittle; yielding to force without breaking; capable of resisting great strain without coming apart; not easily chewed or masticated.

There are at least four basic tastes that can be distinguished: salt, typified by sodium chloride; sweet, typified by sucrose; sour, typified by tartaric acid; and bitter, typified by quinine or caffeine. Receptors on the tongue are used to distinguish these tastes; they are most readily apparent in different areas of the tongue. Salt and sweet are most apparent at the tip of the tongue, bitter at the back, and sour along the edges. Studies with sodium chloride, sucrose, tartaric acid, and quinine sulfate have shown that there are concentrations at which each of these substances elicits pleasantness and unpleasantness. Mixtures of sucrose and sodium chloride have been used to demonstrate contrast effects; a sucrose solution on one side of the tongue will enhance recognition of sodium chloride on the other, and vice versa (Amerine et al., 1965). Foods usually contain two, three, or more individual tastes in varying concentrations; the interaction of tastes and of odors complicates the sensory evaluation of food flavors. (See also Chapter 16.)

Although odors are of considerable importance in the enjoyment of foods, little is known about the mechanism of olfaction. The present state of our knowledge has been reviewed by Amerine et al. (1965). Odorous substances must be volatile; they are perceived when they are transmitted in air passing into the nose to a small olfactory area deep within the nasal cavity. Many odor-testing techniques have been devised, including special containers for the product and rooms designed for introducing odorants; but sniffing remains the simplest, most inexpensive, and most popular method (Sullivan, 1958; Amerine et al., 1965). Breathing in short, quick inhalations aids detection of odors by increasing the air flow to the olfactory region. A major problem of odor testing is fatigue or adaptation; after only a few observations an odor is no longer perceived. Recovery from fatigue occurs at a slower rate than its development. There are many osmophoric groups, the chemical entities that confer odor on compounds; they include sulfur, esters, amines, imines, and double-bond structures. The three primary elements of odor are considered to be intensity, type, and variety. Odors have been classified by many systems, but all of them commonly include some of the following terms: fragrant, acid, burned, caprylic, ethereal, putrid, spicy, resinous, musty, rancid, nutty, mint, and fruity.

A classification of texture nomenclature has been developed by Szczesniak (1963a). She considers texture as "the composite of the structural elements of food and the manner in which it registers with the physiological senses." Textural characteristics are classified in this system as mechanical (reaction of food to stress), geometrical (related to size and shape of particles and orientation), and other (mainly moisture and fat content). A method for describing the texture characteristics of food products by means of a texture profile has been developed by Brandt et al. (1963). A series of rating scales for components of texture have been developed with points on the scale represented by well-known food products (Szczesniak et al., 1963b). The hardness scale includes cream cheese, hard-cooked egg, carrots, and rock candy. The brittleness scale includes graham crackers and peanut brittle. The cohesiveness includes rye bread and gum drops. Gumminess is typified by various concentrations of flour paste. The adhesiveness scale includes cream cheese and marshmallow topping. Viscosity differences are illustrated by water, cream, syrup, and condensed milk. This texture-profile concept advanced by the above authors has been critically examined and modified by Sherman (1969) to place it on a more basic rheological foundation. Primary characteristics include analytical characteristics, particle size, and air content; secondary characteristics include elasticity, viscosity, and adhesion; and tertiary characteristics include mechanical properties (hard, brittle, smooth, creamy, and sticky) and disintegration (greasy, gummy, stringy, and melting down on palate).

The analytical sensory methods for determining quality are similar for most foods. In general, they are used to determine whether differences among foods can be detected, the magnitude of the differences, and the direction of the difference (which product has more or less of a particular quality). Ideally they are applied to foods differing in a single quality such as taste or tenderness. Since the usual test methods have been thoroughly described in the literature, brief descriptions of the essential features of the methods will be supplemented by pertinent references.

A general text covering all aspects of sensory testing has been published recently (Amerine et al., 1965). Although the value of sensory testing is well documented in numerous articles in the technical literature, the pitfalls of these tests are often overlooked. A recent publication, "Looking Askance at Statistical Sensory Testing," (Byer, 1964), should be given serious consideration by anyone concerned about possible biased testing situations, slanted questions, and unjustified inferences.

DESIGN AND ANALYSIS OF TESTS

Several well-known tests are available for determining whether foods are significantly different in one or more qualities. Variations of the methods can be used to estimate the magnitude of the difference and determine its direction. No matter what method is used, comparison with standards of known composition aids in interpretation of magnitude and importance of differences. Simple methods for statistical analysis of results are readily available. It should be emphasized, however, that even the smallest difference is statistically significant if replicated a sufficient number of times, and trained panels can detect exceedingly small differences. There is a real danger in the assumption that a statistically significant difference is an *important* difference. A difference that is readily detectable when two samples are compared directly may not even be detectable when samples are presented singly with a different food tasted between samples, as is usual in food consumption during a meal (Hanson et al., 1960). Thus, the conduct and interpretation of sensory difference tests cannot be done routinely but requires continual questioning of methods, supervision of the operation, and judgment and common sense in interpretation of results.

The method most frequently used for determining the existence of a detectable difference between two products is the triangle test, described by Helm and Trolle (1946), Peryam and Swarz (1950), and Peryam (1958). Three samples, two of which have had the same treatment, are presented to judges. The judges select the sample that differs from the other two. The position of the samples is randomized to prevent possible bias due to order of presentation, and the test is replicated for statistical analysis. The probability of selecting the different or odd sample by chance is 1 in 3. The probability that the number who select the different sample is no greater than might occur by chance may be calculated by the chi-square analysis (Boggs and Hanson, 1946; Bengtsson, 1953). Tables of the number of correct selections necessary to establish statistical significance at various probability levels for given numbers of replicates have been prepared to eliminate the need for calculations (Bengtsson, 1953; Helm and Troll, 1946; and Roessler et al., 1948). The degree of difference between samples is not determined by such analyses, but the relative frequency of odd-sample identification may be used to estimate degrees of difference (Gray et al., 1947). The greater the difference between the odd sample and the duplicates, the greater is the probability of identifying it.

Variations of the triangle test are used to obtain additional information. Judges may be asked to select the odd sample and also to indicate the basis for their selection. Such information is useful if samples are expected to differ in several respects. The results of a simple triangle test might be erroneously interpreted as indicating a flavor difference, for example, but the additional information obtained on the basis for selection might show that selection was based primarily on tenderness or juiciness. The triangle-intensity test may be used to obtain additional information if samples are known to differ only in a single quality (Davis and Hanson, 1954). The judges indicate whether the intensity of the particular quality is stronger in the odd sample or in the duplicates. The probability of selecting both the odd sample and the direction of the difference by chance is one sixth. Utilization of the partially as well as the completely correct judgments increases efficiency of the test by reducing the number of trials necessary to detect a difference at a given level of significance (Davis and Hanson, 1954).

Differences between samples are also determined by use of the duo-trio test. A known control sample is presented, followed by two coded samples, one of which is a duplicate of the control (Peryam and Swarz, 1950; Peryam, 1958). The order of presenting the two unknowns is randomized, and the judges are asked to decide which sample differs from the control. With most products, two such tests may be conducted at the same session without affecting the precision of the results. The probability of selecting the correct sample by chance is one half. Statistical significance of the results can be calculated by such methods as the chi-square analysis. Also, tables showing the number of correct responses required for significance for different numbers of replicates are available (Harrison and Elder, 1950). The dual-standards test, used to a limited extent, is similar to the duo-trio test except that two samples are presented and identified, and the problem is to identify coded unknowns. In the multiple-standards test, the standard or control sample is not homogeneous. Several coded standards or controls are presented with a coded unknown, and the problem is to select the sample most different from the group (Peryam, 1958).

The paired-comparison test is also used to determine whether a detectable difference exists between two samples. The chance probability of correctly identifying the samples according to the criterion specified is one half. A disadvantage of the test is that failure of the results to show a statistically significant difference can be interpreted in more than one way. A difference may not be detectable; or, if a difference is detectable, the panel may not agree on the sample to be selected according to the criterion specified. A slight flavor difference between foods, for example, is often detectable before the flavors are sufficiently distinctive to be identified and described.

Flavor intensity of homogeneous foods can be evaluated by a dilution test, a variation of a threshold test. Control samples are compared with mixtures of controls and treated samples to determine the amount of treated sample needed to cause a detectable difference from the control. The relative difference between samples can be estimated by comparison of amounts of treated sample that must be added to be detectable (Bohren and Jordan, 1953). If the controls can be maintained without change, the test is useful in storage studies in which direct comparisons between samples stored for different time intervals are not possible. The large amounts of time and materials required for this test limit its use.

Flavor intensity has also been evaluated by tests consisting of pairs of samples of known and unknown concentration (Sinsheimer, 1959). Judges are asked to select the sample of the pair having the higher intensity or to indicate equal intensity.

Ranking and scoring methods of evaluating qualities of foods are used in some situations. Samples may be ranked in order of the intensity of an attribute such as flavor or tenderness, or they may be scored on a numerical scale. These methods are usually used when a large number of samples must be evaluated or when differences in quality are readily detectable. The methods are fast, since multiple samples may be evaluated at the same time. The use of known control samples aids in interpretation of results. The ranking method, however, lacks precision and may give inconsistent results if the differences among samples are small (Anderson, 1958). Scoring has had its greatest use in commercial grading, a situation that often requires an overall judgment of quality. Among prerequisites mentioned for use of scoring by Anderson (1958) are a realistic scorecard with proper weighting of the various factors, judges thoroughly familiar with all aspects of the problem, a scale such that differences in scores will reflect detectable differences in factors being scored, and agreement among judges concerning standards of perfection so that the entire scoring scale may be utilized. Even if the above conditions are met, there are other limitations of the method. These include the tendency to be too arbitrary, a false sense of exactness, and the tendency to try to obtain too much information from too many samples at one time. Hanson et al. (1951) noted the tendency for samples of intermediate quality to be given a high score when judged with low-quality samples and a low score when judged with high-quality samples. Samples of turkey meat seem more tender when they are judged following a tough sample than when they follow a tender sample (White et al., 1964). This contrast effect is a common reaction and was described by Fernberger (1920) in relation to judgments of lifted weights. Unless objective standards are available, products are apt to be graded too critically when average quality is high and too leniently when average quality is low (Kramer, 1955). Because professional graders make absolute judgments of quality on a rating scale with only a memory standard for reference, studies have been made of the consistency of graders operating under such conditions. These studies were reviewed by Sheppard (1954) who also conducted self-consistency tests under laboratory conditions. He found that the judges were not rated very consistent by any of the tests.

The methods for detecting differences have been compared by various criteria such as sensitivity, efficiency, simplicity, appropriateness, and frequency of usage (Byer and Abrams, 1953; Filipello, 1956; and Peryam, 1958). Probably because of the many bases for comparison, the results of such comparisons have not been conclusive in the sense that one method can be regarded as clearly superior to others. The requirements or limitations of the test situation will ultimately determine which method is used. In one situation it may be important to detect the smallest possible difference; in another it may be to use the simplest test to eliminate possible errors by panel members or to obtain the most information with a minimum of time and product.

THE PANEL MEMBERS

In addition to selecting the test most suitable for the problem, considerable attention should be given to other aspects of the test situation. These include selection and training of panel members and consideration of physiological and psychological factors that influence the judges. These factors and others that influence the accuracy of the tests have been reviewed (Boggs and Hanson, 1949; Amerine et al., 1965).

Selection of judges is usually made on the basis of their acuity and consistency in detecting differences of the type expected in the product being studied. Such selection reduces experimental error and increases the probability of detection of small differences between samples. Potential judges are usually first made familiar with the product and the range of differences to be expected in it, as well as with the general test situation. Rapid improvement in performance is generally noted with such preliminary training. Selection on the basis of sensitivity to sweet, sour, salt, or bitter tastes or on the basis of low thresholds for various substances in foods has not been of much value in predicting the performance of judges in a more complicated test situation (Boggs and Hanson, 1949; Amerine et al., 1965). Therefore, selection of judges is usually made on the basis of performance in a situation and with products that correspond as closely as possible to those in the actual test. Sawyer et al. (1962) compared test methods for selecting panel members on the basis of repeatability estimates. Two, three, and nine samples per test were compared at sessions of varying length using reconstituted dry milk solids with added vanillin as the test material. Two-sample tests were somewhat more sensitive than the other test designs, and the study indicated that sessions of extended length with paired comparisons may have advantages.

Psychological and physiological factors that influence judges are important. In many cases, well-known psychological and physiological principles that have been studied in other types of sensory evaluation apply and have been demonstrated (Guilford, 1954; Beidler, 1958). Test performance is affected by the general attitude of the judges. This involves bias, motivation and interest, knowledge of results, fatigue, adaptation and practice, the environment, and the quality of the food. The conflicting forces of fatigue, adaptation, warm-up, learning, interest, and motivation may vary with the number of samples tested. Whether detection of differences will be impaired by an increase in number of judgments also depends to some extent on the quality of the samples, the intensity of flavor, and the "carry-over" effect found in the testing of some foods. Sensory-difference tests are usually worthwhile only on foods of relatively high quality. Quality differences are less readily detected in low-quality samples, probably partly because of the judges' dislike for the products, and consequent lack of application to the task, and partly because of the greater difficulty in distinguishing differences as flavor intensity increases. Pfaffman (1954) reported on the basis of 75 separate tastings of an orange drink and brown bread that fatigue or adaptation are not necessarily to be expected. Parts of the work curve that may differ in prolonged and continuous performance are the "warm-up period," a high level of efficiency at the beginning, followed by loss of efficiency, and an "end-spurt" or increase in efficiency, classed as an incentive, if the subject is aware of the approaching end of the tests (Murchison, 1934). For some products known to have a "carry-over" effect, such as sulfited foods, the number of samples must be restricted (Boggs and Ward, 1950).

Motivation or interest of the judges is improved by informing them of the results of tests whenever this can be done without the danger of biasing the results of subsequent tests. This is possible if the products can be distinguished only on the basis of a single variable such as flavor. If other variables are not adequately masked, knowledge of results of the first replicates may aid the judges in distinguishing between subsequent samples on the basis of such differences, and the results then could not be interpreted to show a flavor difference. Giving information about results has a strong, persistent effect with both naive and experienced observers and with easy or difficult discriminations (Pfaffman, 1954). Raffensperger and Pilgrim (1956) studied the relative effectiveness of seven types of instructions giving information about the variable in a triangle test compared with tests in which no information was given. They found that information using either physical or psychological terms was equally effective. Individuals tend to become indifferent or discouraged if they cannot distinguish differences in samples, and they react by finding a difference where none exists. The situation can be avoided by adequate experiment design and sample selection to assure that a detectable difference exists occasionally.

Bias may be introduced into a test by the positional arrangement of samples. There is a tendency to choose the central sample in a series (Harries, 1956; Harrison and Elder, 1950). Methods used to overcome this bias include placing samples in a circle or presenting each sample in each position for an equal number of replicates. Harries (1956) recommends the former method, particularly when results are close to the accepted levels of significance, since the increase in precision achieved is important in such cases. Possible "first-sample bias," a tendency to judge the flavor of the first sample to be more intense than that of subsequent samples, has been overcome by using a "warm-up" sample, not a part of the test series, or by systematic randomization to assure that each sample is in the first position an equal number of times.

Because of possible masking of flavors of primary interest, seasonings are usually omitted or reduced to the minimum necessary to make foods reasonably palatable. In judging flavor, differences in other qualities of the foods, such as tenderness or juiciness, should be eliminated to assure that any difference detected is actually based on flavor. Methods used for masking differences in texture, tenderness, juiciness, color, and the like include pureeing or preparing broths to eliminate texture or tenderness differences in such foods as vegetables or meats. Cooking-time differences that might influence juiciness or tenderness are eliminated by preparing products of the same size so that they will require equal cooking time. Colored lights, sodium-vapor lights, colored containers, or blindfolds are used to mask color or other differences in appearance.

Various media are useful for evaluating the flavor of spices and other flavoring materials (Swaine, 1957; Sair, 1963). These include water, simple sirup, broth, sugar patties, custards, mashed potato, and ground meat. Criteria cited for selecting these simplified experimental test materials include ease of preparation, stability, reproducibility, and correlation between results obtained with the test material and the final product. Techniques found useful for particular foods are discussed in greater detail in the sections of this book dealing with those foods.

THE ENVIRONMENT

Sensory analysis of foods should be conducted in an environment that prevents distraction of the judges and collaboration among them. Individual booths provide desirable isolation. Air conditioning, temperature and humidity control, adequate lighting, and a neutral gray background have been recommended (Boggs and Hanson, 1949; Jones, 1958). Mitchell (1957) presented evidence of the detrimental effect of distraction on sensitivity during a taste-difference test. The sensitivity of a single subject testing alone was decreased when one or more other subjects were tested at the same time; and a further decrease in sensitivity resulted if noise or other distraction occurred during the testing.

Evidence concerning the most desirable time of day for testing is contradictory (Jones, 1958; Mitchell, 1957). The possible influence of time of day can be removed by testing at the same time each day. Although the study of Mitchell (1957) showed a better performance at some times than at others with continuous testing every 15 minutes, the applicability of these results to other timing sequences was not tested.

References

Amerine, M. A., R. M. Pangborn, and E. B. Roessler. 1965. *Principles of Sensory Evaluation of Food.* Academic Press, New York.

Anderson, E. E. 1958. Scoring and ranking. In *Flavor Research and Food Acceptance,* Arthur D. Little Symposium. New York, Reinhold Publication Corp., 75.

Bengtsson, K. 1943. Provsmakning som analysmetod. Statistisk behandling av resultaten. *Svenska Bryggareföreningens Månadsblad 58:* 59. Reprinted in English, 1953. Taste testing as an analytical method. Statistical treatment of the data. *Wallerstein Lab. Communication 16:* 231.

Biedler, L. M. 1958. The physiological basis of flavor. In *Flavor Research and Food Acceptance*, Arthur D. Little Symposium. New York, Reinhold Publ. Corp., *3*.

Boggs, M. M., and H. L. Hanson. 1949. Analysis of foods by sensory difference tests. *Advances in Food Research 2*: 219.

Boggs, M. M., and A. C. Ward. 1950. Serving techniques for sulfited foods. *Food Technol. 4*: 282.

Bohren, B. B., and R. Jordan. 1953. A technique for detecting flavor changes in stored dried eggs. *Food Res. 18*: 583.

Brandt, M. A., E. Z. Skinner, and J. A. Coleman. 1963. Texture profile method. *J. Food Sci. 28*: 404.

Byer, A. J. 1964. Looking askance at statistical sensory testing. *Food Technol. 18*: 1717.

Byer, A. J., and D. Abrams. 1953. A comparison of the triangular and 2-sample taste test methods. *Food Technol. 7*: 185.

Davis, J. G., and H. L. Hanson. 1954. Sensory test methods 1. The triangle intensity (T-I) and related test systems for sensory analysis. *Food Technol. 8*: 335.

Fernberger, S. W. 1920. Interdependence of judgments within the series for the method of constant stimuli. *J. Exp. Psychol. 3*: 126.

Filipello, F. 1956. A critical comparison of the two-sample and triangular binomial designs. *Food Res. 21*: 235.

Gray, P. P., I. Stone, and L. Atkin. 1947. Systematic study of the influence of oxidation on beer flavor. *Wallerstein Lab. Communication 10*: 183.

Guilford, J. P. 1954. *Psychometric Methods*, 2nd ed. McGraw-Hill, New York.

Hanson, H. L., L. Kline, and H. Lineweaver. 1951. Application of balanced incomplete block design to scoring of ten dried egg samples. *Food Technol. 5*: 9.

Hanson, H. L., M. J. Brushway, and H. Lineweaver. 1960. Monosodium glutamate studies. I. Factors affecting detection of and preference for added glutamate in foods. *Food Technol. 14*: 320.

Harries, J. M. 1953. Sensory tests and consumer acceptance. *J. Sci. Food and Agri. 4*: 477.

Harries, J. M. 1956. Positional bias in sensory assessments. *Food Technol. 10*: 86.

Harrison, S., and L. W. Elder. 1950. Some applications of statistics to laboratory taste testing. *Food Technol. 4*: 434.

Helm, E., and Trolle, B. 1946. Selection of a taste panel. *Wallerstein Lab. Communication 9*: 181.

Jones, F. N. 1958. Prerequisites for test environment. In *Flavor Research and Food Acceptance*, Arthur D. Little Symposium. Reinhold Pub. Corp., New York: 107.

Kramer, A. 1955. Food quality and quality control. In *Handbook of Food and Agriculture*, F. C. Blanck, ed. Reinhold, New York.

Mitchell, J. W. 1957. Problems in taste difference testing. I. Test environment. II. Subject variability due to time of day and day of week. *Food Technol.* 11: 476.

Murchison, C., ed. 1934. *A Handbook of General Experimental Psychology.* Clark Univ. Press, Worcester, Massachusetts.

Palmer, H. H., A. A. Klose, S. Smith, and A. A. Campbell. 1965. Evaluation of toughness differences in chickens in terms of consumer reaction. *J. Food Sci. 30:* 898.

Peryam, D., and V. Swartz. 1950. Measurement of sensory differences. *Food Technol. 4:* 390.

Peryam, D. R. 1958. Sensory difference tests. *Food Technol. 12:* 231.

Pfaffman, C. 1954. Variables affecting difference tests. In *Food Acceptance Testing Methodology, A Symposium,* D. R. Peryam, F. J. Pilgrim, and M. S. Peterson, eds. Natl. Acad. Sci., Natl. Res. Council, Washington, D.C.: 4.

Raffensperger, E. L., and F. J. Pilgrim. 1956. Knowledge of the stimulus variable as an aid in discrimination tests. *Food Technol. 10:* 254.

Roessler, E. B., J. Warren, and J. F. Guymon. 1948. Significance in triangular taste tests. *Food Res. 13:* 503.

Sair, L. 1963. Food flavor—art or science. *Food Manuf. 38* (1): 32.

Sawyer, F. M., H. Stone, H. Aplanalp, and G. F. Stewart. 1962. "Repeatability" estimates in sensory-panel selection. *J. Food Sci. 27:* 386.

Sheppard, D. 1954. An experimental comparison of self-consistency tests, I, II. *Laboratory Practice 3:* 53, 101.

Sherman, P. 1969. A texture profile of foodstuffs based upon well-defined rheological properties. *J. Food Sci. 34:* 458.

Sinsheimer, J. E. 1959. An intensity-response method for measurement of flavor intensity. *Food Res. 24:* 445.

Sullivan, F. 1958. Presentation of odor samples. In *Flavor Research and Food Acceptance,* Arthur D. Little Symposium. Reinhold, New York: 100.

Swaine, R. L. 1957. Experimental media for evaluating flavor. *Coffee and Tea Inds. 80* (6): 93.

Szczesniak, A. S. 1963a. Classification of textural characteristics. *J. Food Sci. 28:* 385.

Szczesniak, A. S., M. A. Brandt, and H. H. Friedman. 1963b. Development of standard rating scales for mechanical parameters of texture and correlation between the objective and the sensory methods of texture evaluation. *J. Food Sci. 28:* 397.

White, E. D., H. L. Hanson, A. A. Klose, and H. Lineweaver. 1964. Evaluation of toughness differences in turkeys. *J. Food Sci. 29:* 673.

CHAPTER 16

Physical and Chemical Tests of Food Quality

MARION JACOBSON

Quality will be considered as the relative excellence of a food based on sensory estimates of color, texture, and flavor. These attributes make food desirable to consumers. However, quality, considered broadly, also encompasses wholesomeness (microbial or chemical safety and nutritive content), economy and convenience (cost, quantity, prepreparation, and packaging), and market appearance (size, shape, and absence of defects); these are not within the scope of the present discussion.

Since food is for people, sensory attributes of quality can be best tested by trained, discriminating people responding under controlled conditions. (See the discussion of sensory evaluation in Chapter 15.) Because such sensory appraisal is often unavailable or impractical, adequate substitutes for the ideal method are sought. So-called "objective" tests can partially replace human appraisal.

The search for accurate and precise tests of quality is a continuous one. New instruments and methods are being devised and improved. The degree to which an instrumental or laboratory technique measures the intended quality attribute is evidence of the *accuracy* of the test (Kramer and Twigg, 1962). High correlations with sensory panels will prove accuracy. How reproducible the results are on identical samples is evidence of *precision*. Calculations of deviations among measurement data will indicate the relative precision of a test.

People respond strongly to color, texture, and flavor in foods. Often, specific characteristics within these general attributes will be selected for measurement, because color, texture, and flavor are each too complex for estimation as a whole. Color, for instance, has elements of reflection, absorption, and transmission, together with the effects of gloss. Texture includes such mechanical parameters as hardness, cohesiveness, viscosity, and elasticity as well as particle size, shape, and structural detail. Flavor involves the effects of volatile and soluble compounds almost without number. An introduction to the nature and measurement of the quality attributes follows.

MEASUREMENT OF COLOR

Perception of color depends on both physical and psychological factors. The physical nature of the light reflected or transmitted by a food can be measured. What the eye and brain add by way of interpretation of these variations in radiant energy is difficult to assess; however, what the nervous system adds to vision is important to a student of foods (Gregory, 1966). Perhaps the future will bring techniques of measuring neural response. Objective testing of color at present is a measurement of light.

The radiant energy that stimulates vision is a small part of the electromagnetic spectrum. Table 1 shows only the central portion of the *spectrum*, that which has been applied in food study. Of this, the visible region for the normal eye is only within wavelengths of about 780 and 380 mμ. Interestingly, it is reported that after surgical removal of the lens, an eye can "see" blue down to 330 or 320 mμ (Mackinney and Little, 1962). Color, then, is limited by the capacity of the eye to receive light.

The apparent color of a food depends on (1) the wavelengths (frequencies) of the incident light, (2) the wavelengths (frequencies) reflected or transmitted by the food (resulting from its selective absorption of light), (3) the background conditions, and, as previously mentioned, (4) eye and brain functions.

Since the color of an object derives from the light that strikes it, any appraisal of color requires knowledge of the nature of the *incident light*. Both its intensity and its spectral composition (proportion of various wavelengths) are important. For precise measurements three standard illuminants have been established; these are "A" (incandescent lamp), "B" (light similar to noon sunlight), and "C" (cloudy daylight or north light). Of these, illuminant C emits the most uniform radiant energy at the wavelengths critical for direct observation of color (Brice, 1954). Incident light is carefully controlled for tests of food color.

Components of the light striking the food will be reflected, absorbed, or transmitted. If white light strikes an opaque substance (like bread) and all wavelengths (frequencies) are *reflected* equally, it appears

TABLE 1. Approximate Wavelength and Frequency Ranges of the Electromagnetic Spectrum Used in Food Study

Region	Application	Wavelength (Millimicrons, mμ)[a]	Frequency[b]
Microwaves	Electronic cookery	—[c]	915 mHz[d] or 2450 mHz
Infrared	Heating and structural analysis	750 to 10^4	10^{12} to 10^{14} Hz
VISIBLE	Red	620 to 750	Within 10^{14} to 10^{15} Hz
	Orange	590 to 620	
	Yellow	570 to 590	
	Green	500 to 570	
	Blue	450 to 500	
	Violet	400 to 450	
Ultraviolet	Sterilization of surfaces Activation of sterols to form vitamin D Analysis by fluorescence	100 to 380	10^{15} to 10^{17} Hz

[a] 1 mμ = 1×10^{-6} mm or .000001 mm.

[b] 1 Hertz = 1 cycle/sec.

[c] At 915 mHz the wavelength is 3.3×10^8 mμ (.33 meters); at 2450 mHz the wavelength is 1.2×10^8 mμ (.12 meters).

[d] 915 mHz = 915 megacycles = 915,000 kilocycles per second = 9.15×10^8 cycles per second.

white. If little light of any frequency is reflected, a sample appears dark gray or black. Spinach appears green under white light because the red and blue parts of the spectrum are absorbed and the wavelengths that give the green stimulus are reflected. Under green light, both bread and spinach will appear green.

The physical structure of the food, as well as the chemical nature of its components, affects reflectance. If light falls on a transparent or translucent food (liquid, gel, or solid), a portion of that light passes through. Some of it may be transmitted directly; the remainder will be refracted to various degrees. The food may also absorb light in certain wavelengths. Hence, *transmitted light* will not be the same, in spectral composition or intensity, as light reflected from the surface of a food.

The reflected or transmitted light coming from the food is the visual stimulus. It is the light that tests are designed to measure by various systems.

The attributes of spectral color, saturation, and brightness have been designated by different terms. Two widely accepted systems of characterizing color are that of the C.I.E. (Commission Internationale de L'Eclairage, formerly called International Commission on Illumination) and the Munsell system.

	Spectral Color	Degree of Saturation	Brightness
C.I.E.	Dominant wavelength (x)	Purity (y)	Lightness (Y)
Munsell	Hue	Chroma	Value

Spectral color (hue) is the attribute sensed as redness, greenness, blueness, or intermediates among them. Saturation (purity or chroma) is the strength of hue, or freedom from mixture with white. Brightness (lightness or value) is associated with the luminous energy transmitted or reflected by the substance. Spectral color and saturation together describe "chromaticity"; with brightness these attributes describe the color.

The C.I.E. system defines perceived color by computations relating percent reflectance readings on the test substance to the reflectance values for three primary filters that simulate the response of a "standard" observer. The primary filters are X (amber), Y (green), Z (blue). By the procedure, spectrophotometer readings of reflectance are made on a test food from 380 to 770 mμ at 10 mμ intervals. The percent reflectance at each wavelength interval is multiplied by published conversion factors to obtain values for X, as well as for Y and Z. Conversion factors vary with the illuminant used (Kramer and Twigg, 1962). The products obtained for all wavelengths are totaled and then used to calculate x and y as follows:

$$x = (X)/(X + Y + Z)$$

and

$$y = (Y)/(X + Y + Z)$$

When the coordinates x and y are plotted on a chromaticity diagram, the color of the test food can be located in "color space." With Y (lightness), the color is further defined. A chromaticity diagram is shown in Figure 1.

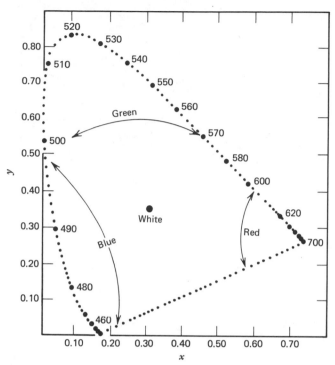

FIGURE 1. C.I.E. chromaticity diagram.

This method of color definition is precise, but it is time-consuming unless a spectrophotometer equipped to yield x and y is available. Such instrumentation is costly and often unavailable to students of food quality. Other color systems use different terminology and instrumentation for tristimulus measurements, but values equivalent to the C.I.E. system can be calculated from values in other systems.

Spectrophotometers allow extensive and precise analysis of certain properties of a food substance. As will be discussed later, this class of instruments allows measurement of transmission through, absorption by, or emission from a sample, as well as reflectance. Determination of color by reflectance is only a part of the broad capabilities of spectrophotometers.

A spectrophotometer employs monochromatic light (a narrow band of wavelengths). This is produced by light from a lamp being first focused, by mirrors or lenses, and slits into a beam. The beam strikes a prism (or a diffraction grating), which separates it into a spectrum. By instrument controls on the prism, specific wavelengths can be

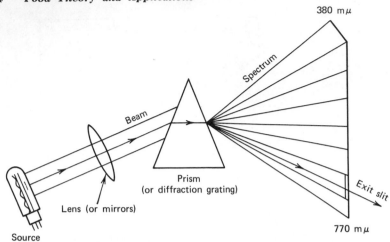

FIGURE 2. Selection of monochromatic light for spectrophotometric analysis.

directed against the exit slit. Hence, monochromatic light can be obtained at specific wavelengths (Figure 2).

To measure *reflectance with a spectrophotometer*, monochromatic light is directed against the surface of a sample. With attachments, the sample is positioned over the opening to an integrating sphere (Figure 3). Reflected light from the sample exits through a shutter opening at

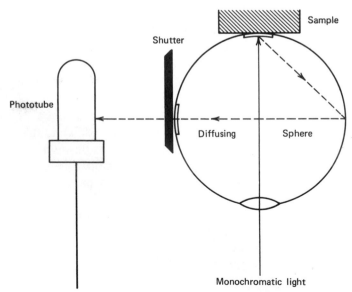

FIGURE 3. Measurement of reflectance by one type of spectrophotometer.

another position in the sphere. This light strikes a phototube, which responds with varying current dependent on the reflectance. Other spectrophotometers employ a diffusing plate instead of the integrating sphere; angles at which the incident light is caused to strike the sample also vary with different instruments (Little et al., 1958).

Wavelength bands from 380 mμ to 770 mμ can be used successively to scan the full range of the sample reflectance. From these observations a reflectance curve can be plotted; or, as previously explained, the C.I.E. chromaticity coordinates *x* and *y*, and the luminance (*Y*) factor, can be calculated.

A study of changes in pigments of beef involved use of reflectance spectrophotometry (Greene, 1966).

The *Munsell system of color notation* uses terminology and symbols different from the C.I.E. designations to describe color. Hue, value, and chroma are each expressed on a numerical scale (Figure 4). For example,

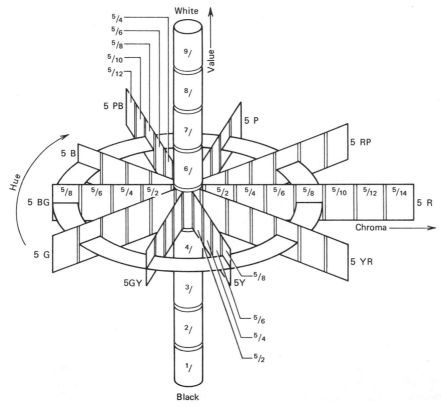

FIGURE 4. Munsell color space. (Published with permission of Munsell Color Co.)

a green apple could have a Munsell notation of 5GY8/4. This denotes a yellow-green hue (5GY) that is light in value (8/) and moderately weak (/4) in chroma. Or, a wine-red apple may be 9RP3/6, by which is indicated that it is reddish purple in hue (9RP), dark in value (3/), and moderate in chroma (/6). The system is psychophysical in that human visual response is fundamental to it. The color notations have been made available as precisely prepared papers, standard color plates for photometric measurements, and tables of spectrophotometric values. Munsell numbers can be readily converted to the C.I.E. tristimulus specifications (X,Y,Z) by reference to published tables.

The history of the Munsell system is an interesting one (Nickerson, 1940). Its development is traced from an initial observation in 1879, through the publication of *The Munsell Book of Color* in 1929 and to correlation with the C.I.E. system. To preserve their identity, a master set of Munsell papers has been stored with the U.S. Bureau of Standards. In 1964 the Japan Color Research Institute prepared papers for a *Munsell Renotation Color Book* and distributed it privately to researchers.

Color measurement by the Munsell system is facilitated by use of an instrument that allows a combination of three or four discs, the blended light from which is matched against the sample food. Discs are selected and overlapped to produce the hue, chroma, and value to be matched (Judd, 1952). Either the discs themselves or the viewing lens (Nickerson, 1946) spin rapidly to blend the reflected light into a composite. Incident light is controlled as to intensity and spectral composition. Food-research observations have been aided by this method—for example, those by Noble (1958).

The *Hunter color and color-difference* meter, widely used in food studies, employs yet another set of symbols for color. Rd or L measuring circuits may be selected. Rd (luminous reflectance) is related to the C.I.E. system and L (visual lightness) to the Munsell system. Associated with each circuit are switches that can be positioned "$+a$" (red) or "$-a$" (blue) and "$+b$" (yellow) or "$-b$" (blue). Light reflected from the sample thus can be read in four selected wavelength segments.

Comparison of readings for a standard red plate made on both scales indicates that numerical values will vary with the circuit selected:

Rd color scale:	Rd 7.3	a +61.5	b +20.6
L color scale:	L 27.0	a_1 +48.8	b_1 +16.4

In the operation of this meter, a light of controlled intensity is focused against a sample positioned over an aperture. Light that is reflected perpendicularly from the sample is diffused within a white-coated enclosure. This reflected light is measured as "Rd" or "L." Openings covered by color filters are located around the enclosure. Photocells in back of the filters allow "a" and "b" readings. Before samples are tested, a standard plate is placed over the aperture and the instrument is adjusted to the Rd (or L), a, and b values of the plate. Accuracy of readings requires the use of a standard plate having color dimensions close to those of the sample to be measured.

When testing a sample, the food is placed over the aperture and readings of Rd (or L), a, and b are made manually or automatically. These values may be reported just as observed, as relative values (for example, a/b), as converted into C.I.E. or Munsell designations, or by comparison with a previous reading to indicate "color difference."

Measurements made by use of the color and color-difference meter have shown good agreement with judges' estimates, as in the study by Borchgrevink and Charley (1966) on carrots. In another study the Rd (reflectance) reading alone served to measure browning in pork (Bowers et al., 1968).

Other instruments have been developed for color measurement, several of which have been described by Mackinney and Little (1962) and included in a review of color problems in foods (Mackinney and Chichester, 1954).

Certain cautions need to be considered in using the various techniques of reflectance colorimetry. First, *sample preparation and presentation* will affect color readings obtained by any instrumental method. Surface texture, surface moisture, and thickness of sample, as well as degree of uniformity of color in various parts of sample, need to be considered. Exposure of the surface to light or air, initial sample temperature, and heat from the instrument may affect color. For certain studies, mixing or homogenization of the food may be effective in obtaining uniform measurements. Alternately, mechanical devices for spinning the sample will produce an "average" reading for nonhomogeneous materials. It must be recognized, however, that in removing variability, one may misrepresent the visually observed color.

The *importance of gloss* to the visual appearance of foods has been explained by Mackinney et al. (1966). This factor of "sheen" or "sparkle" of surfaces results from directional reflectance. The angle of the incident light and the viewing angle affect the glossiness observed. Satisfactory techniques for measuring gloss have not been perfected but, with recognition of the importance of this factor in color evaluations, methods will be developed.

Also, it may be noted that colorimeters and spectrophotometers will not yield absolute color values, and error may be incurred in converting observations from one set of instrumental measurements to another system (Little et al., 1958).

Transmitted light, as well as reflected light, can be used to measure food color. Transparent juices, color extracts from food obtained with water or other solvents, and translucent sirups or gels will transmit measurable light. The amount of light transmitted (or absorbed) at various wavelengths will indicate the concentration of pigments, as well as colored substances produced by natural or laboratory-induced changes.

In a filter photometer, light from a standard source is reduced to a limited band of wavelengths by a suitable glass filter. The beam through the filter is directed against a sample cell that contains the food or extract (Figure 5). Transmitted light received by a photo cell is mea-

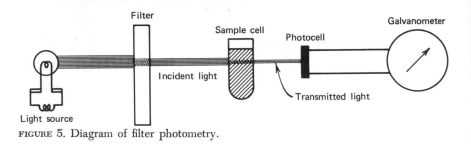

FIGURE 5. Diagram of filter photometry.

sured by a galvanometer or other electronic means. Measurement may be in terms of percent transmission or absorbance and will be indicated by the instrument used.

$$\text{Transmittance } (T) = \frac{\text{Transmitted radiant power}}{\text{Incident radiant power}} \text{ or } P/P_0$$

$$\text{Absorbance } (A) = \log_{10} P_0/P$$

When the test is made with a spectrophotometer, wavelength selection is made by prism or grating as previously described. A scan of the spectrum is then possible. When plotted graphically, scanned transmittance values will reveal a curve. This can be used for comparison with that of a standard material. Or, the response at a specific wavelength can be used as a quantitative measure of saturation of color in the food.

Worthington (1961) compared percent transmission with other techniques for measuring the color of a canned fruit. The method was among three that showed high correlation between photometric readings and consumer acceptability of the color.

When instruments for measuring color are unavailable or impractical, standardized colored objects, plates, chips, or papers can be *matched visually* against a food to arrive at a relatively exact estimate of the color quality of the product. In this way, food-color guides are used by government inspectors for grading such products as butter, vegetables, or fruit. Such plates, discs, or food forms have surfaces that are permanent in color and durable in use; these are available (Magnuson Engineers; Munsell Co.).

Less durable than the food-color guides are such *printed color plates* as those of Maerz and Paul (1930) or those in the *Munsell Book of Color* (1929). The Maerz and Paul book consists of 56 pages of colored squares organized into seven main groups according to the spectrum, from red through purple. Within each group, pages are arranged from full purity of a color through degrees of gray to nearly black. Munsell colors are arranged by hue, value, and chroma. Books of color plates are perishable, owing to the effects of light and air, so a match may have no accurate meaning. But to aid objectivity in judgment, students have found such printed representations useful in description of food colors. The effects of incident light on plate and sample, product surface or shape, and surrounding colors should be recognized when colors are matched.

Original techniques for color comparison are developed for food studies. Dried or frozen samples have served as color "standards" for judging experimental products. In one study (Zolber, 1962), a series of *photographs* representing degrees of browning of peaches made the visual estimation of color change more precise (repeatable). Extracts, juices, and artificially colored fluids are other color "standards" that can aid evaluation.

If a person imagines a meal eaten in absolute darkness he will appreciate the emotional response created by pronounced or subtle color differences in food. Color is often the first index people use in predicting food quality. Its measurement, though not simple, can be challenging.

MEASUREMENT OF TEXTURE

What people sense as "texture" in foods derives from the physical characteristics of these materials. One needs only to think of the hardness of nutmeats, the softness of tender jellies, the chewiness of steak, the thickness of sauces, the elasticity of bread, the sticky surface of caramel, the roughness of salt crystals or celery fibers, or the effects

of wetness and oiliness of mayonnaise to realize how many characteristics provide textural stimuli in foods.

From the great variety in kind and degree, classification of characteristics has been sought. Grouping by types of food texture—such as
liquids, gels, fibers, cell aggregates, unctuous foods, friable foods, glassy
structure, foams, and sponges—was made by Matz (1962). This classification aids description of types of textures and is useful in developing
techniques of sensory evaluation.

For the purposes of measurement, however, classification in terms of
physical properties has been proposed by Szczesniak (1963). This system groups characteristics as *mechanical* (hardness, cohesiveness, viscosity, elasticity, and adhesiveness), *geometrical* (particle size and
shape or particle shape and orientation), and *"other"* (moisture content
and fat content). Meanings and terminology applied to the various
attributes approximate those used by engineers when making measurements on materials other than foods.

The following definitions are based on Szczesniak (1963) and
Friedman et al. (1963). Hardness, cohesiveness, viscosity, elasticity, and
adhesiveness are mechanical characteristics described in physical terms.

Hardness is defined as the force necessary to affect a given deformation. When judged by human senses, it is the force required to penetrate
a food with molar teeth. Solids and some semisolids have this property.
Cream cheese is low in hardness, rock candy very high.

Cohesiveness derives from the strength of internal bonds holding the
body of a substance together. Brittleness (the force necessary to fracture
a material), chewiness (the energy needed to masticate a solid food), and
gumminess (the energy required to disintegrate a semisolid food prior
to swallowing) are related to cohesiveness. *Brittleness* is judged by the
taster as the ease with which the food can be cracked, then shattered or
crumbled; both hardness and overall cohesiveness are involved. For
example, a muffin is low in brittleness; peanut brittle, of course, is high.
Chewiness can be rated organoleptically as to the time necessary to
masticate a food for swallowing when the rate of chewing is specified.
Engineers caution that to make this definition comparable with the one
above (in terms of energy), the assumption must be made that the force
applied and the distance traveled by the jaws are controlled by the
taster. Hardness and elasticity, as well as overall cohesiveness, are parameters of the chewiness property. Fresh bread crumb is low in chewiness; caramels are high. *Gumminess* can be understood to include the
resistance offered by the food when teeth or tongue are withdrawn
after first penetrating the food. This assumption will allow reference to
measurement of energy. Gumminess as a characteristic is not well de-

fined and seems inadequately described by reference to flour pastes of varying composition.

Viscosity is measured as the rate of flow per unit force. The resistance of liquids to flowing is readily observed and is usually conveniently measured. In the mouth it is sensed as "body" or "thickness" by small variations of resistance against the sensitive touch receptors of lips, cheeks, palate, and tongue. It is suggested that, organoleptically, viscosity might be estimated as the force required to draw a liquid from a spoon over the tongue. Water is of course low in viscosity; whipping cream is high. See Chapter 1 for further discussion of viscosity.

Elasticity is defined as the rate at which a deformed material goes back to its original shape. Elasticity is difficult to measure independently of other parameters; it is a part of chewiness.

Adhesiveness is measured as the work necessary to overcome the attractive forces between the surface of the material and other surfaces that contact it. In eating, this property is sensed between the food surfaces and mouth or throat tissues. Oil allows little adhesion, peanut butter much.

The characteristics defined above, as a working basis for food researchers, are explained in greater detail in physics textbooks or handbooks. Instruments that measure these properties are now discussed.

Measuring Penetration to Assess the Mechanical Characteristics of Foods

A penetrometer consists, essentially of a probe attached to a measuring system. The probe may be a sharp or blunt needle, a knifelike wedge, or a cone—and it can be of varying sizes. The measuring system may estimate distance traveled by a probe when subjected to a given force, or the force required to penetrate a stated distance into the food. Force may be determined by weights, by a mechanical spring device, or by a transducer that can activate an electronic recorder.

A sturdy and convenient instrument of this sort is the universal penetrometer (Precision Scientific Company) illustrated in Figure 6. The method of operation is relatively simple. With the instrument leveled and the penetrating cone raised to its highest position on the mechanism head, the mechanism head is lowered so that the tip of the probe is at the surface of the food positioned below it. A trigger is pressed to release the probe and allow it to penetrate the food during a designated time. At the completion of the test, a depth gauge is lowered to measure the distance of penetration. Readings are made on a circular dial calibrated in millimeters, with 0.1 mm subdivisions.

In a strict sense, resistance to penetration is measured by use of a

FIGURE 6. Precision universal penetrometer. (Published with permission of Precision Scientific Co., Chicago, Illinois.)

needlelike probe. An early apparatus of this type was that of Hawkins and Sando (1920). When larger probes are used, compression as well as shear will be part of the measurement. More recently, penetrometer equipment has been used to measure compressibility and even elasticity (Deethardt et al., 1965).

Very recently, a recording micropenetrometer has been devised and tested on small fruits and specific tissues. In this system, a fine probe penetrates a small area to a controlled distance, the resistance being measured as grams of force required to make the penetration (Jacobson and Armbruster, 1968). The motor-driven probe is attached by a lever arm to a transducer (variable transformer type). The electrical output of the transducer is recorded. The micropenetrometer is illustrated in Figure 7. This instrument has been used successfully on strawberries, raspberries, blueberries, cranberries, and canned peas.

FIGURE 7. Recording micropenetrometer. (Photo from Washington State University.)

Measuring Compression to Assess the Mechanical Characteristics of Foods

A compressimeter measures the relative hardness of a food by a technique different from that of the penetrometers just described. Compression can be observed by applying a force on the total surface of a food sample that has a porous structure like foam or sponge products.

One commercially built compressimeter has been described by Platt and Powers (1940) and is illustrated in Figure 8. This compressimeter is used primarily for measuring initial, or changes in, firmness of bakery goods. Its lever system permits a direct reading of the applied force and the resulting deformation of the test sample. Although either fixed force or deformation can be used as the stopping point for the test, the

FIGURE 8. Baker compressimeter. (Published with permission of Wallace and Tiernan.)

manufacturer's instructions suggest that a fixed deformation is more reliable.

In using this instrument, a round or square plunger is attached at any of three locations to a lever arm, the place chosen being dependent on the mechanical advantage needed. The string attached to the lever is first unrolled from the motor drum so that the system is free. A counterweight can be moved to balance the system; this brings the pointer to zero on the deformation (mm) scale. A screw adjustment is employed to position the pointer attached to the string at zero on the force (g) scale. With the lever system in balance, a test sample is placed under the plunger. The sample is cut to such a thickness that the plunger rests freely on the test piece. If only compressibility is to be measured, the test piece must be cut somewhat smaller in circumference than the plunger. If the sample is larger than the plunger, shear force as well as compression will be measured in the reading.

In operation, the motor is started and, as the drum turns, the string gradually applies a force until a specific deformation of the sample is attained (for example, 2.5 mm on the deformation scale). The force in grams is indicated simultaneously on the force scale. The reading in grams is multiplied by the mechanical advantage due to the plunger position. For more specific measurements, the effective plunger area can be taken into consideration.

Compressimeters varying in details of construction, but essentially the same in principle, have been used in research studies like that of Pomeranz et al. (1966).

Measuring Shear Force to Assess the Mechanical Characteristics of Foods

Measurement of the force required to shear a food can give an estimate not only of its hardness but also of the cohesiveness of the material. Often the tissue structures of natural foods cause chewiness, a type of cohesiveness. A number of testing devices measure shear force directly or as a secondary component of the resistance.

Shearing is defined as the action of a force to separate a substance into two or more parts, with one part sliding beyond another part. Shearing has been shown diagrammatically in Figure 9a.

The shear press (Kramer and Aamlid, 1953) makes a combined measurement of the force needed to compress and the force needed to shear a food sample. In the recording model of the instrument, force is measured by compression of a proving-ring dynamometer within which a transducer is positioned to convert the force into an electrical output that is recorded (Figure 10).

One of the test cells (Figure 9b) consists of a sample box that holds the food and a device of parallel steel blades that enters the food through slots in the cover of the sample box and forces the food out slots in the bottom. This test cell exerts force on the proving-ring transducer system. A hydraulic drive system moves the blade device downward into the box at a controlled rate of travel.

Through the use of other test cells, shear and compression measurements can be made independently, or the instrument can act as a succulometer that presses liquids from food of high water content.

Initially developed for testing peas and corn, the shear press has been used with some modifications for testing such diverse foods as peaches (Kanujoso et al., 1967), broccoli (Lebermann et al., 1968), grapefruit sections (Mannheim et al., 1968), parfried potatoes (Reeve et al., 1968), and pork (Tuomy and Helmer, 1967). These are only a few of recent applications of the shear press.

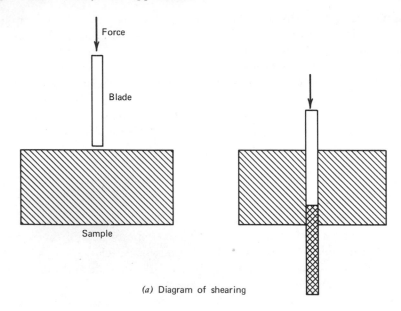

Force

Blade

Sample

(*a*) Diagram of shearing

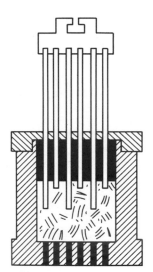

(*b*) Shear compression cell

FIGURE 9. Shear measurement of texture.

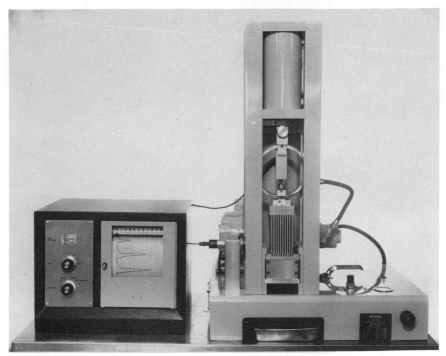

FIGURE 10. Shear press. (Published with permission of Food Technology Corporation, Reston, Virginia.)

A Universal testing machine (Figure 11), which consists of a drive mechanism and a load-sensing and recording system, has been adapted to be used with many texture-measuring devices (Bourne et al., 1966). Maximum force, slope, area under curve, plateau height, and recovery shown by the recorded force-distance curves may be correlated with certain sensory characteristics under study.

The Warner-Bratzler shear apparatus has been used successfully for many years to measure the relative shear resistance of meat (Black et al., 1931). High correlations of shear-force readings with sensory-panel judgments of meat tenderness (or the number of chews required to masticate a sample) have often been reported. Figure 12 is a photograph of the shear apparatus.

Narrowly spaced cutting bars are attached to an arm extending from the testing head which can move on a vertical post. When the testing head is raised manually, pressing the two lugs on the testing head engages it to the drive mechanism. A motor lowers the testing head with the attached arm.

FIGURE 11. Universal testing machine. (Published with permission of Instron, Canton, Massachusetts.)

A metal plate slips between the cutting bars. The plate is attached to a spring scale mounted above. A triangular opening in the plate receives the sample. When the motor is started, the cutting bars are forced against the meat, finally shearing it into two parts against the edge of the plate opening. The force required to shear is indicated by the scale in grams or pounds; a "dead hand" stops at the maximum reading. Continuous photographic records, or intermittent readings, during the shearing process have been used to study the probable effects of the various tissue layers within a single sample.

As with other instrumental measurements, sample preparation may affect the data obtained for meat tenderness. Smith et al. (1968) state, on the basis of a series of studies on lamb, that differences in cooking methods may be as important as handling, storage, quality, or heritability in determining cooked-meat tenderness. Cookery, sample temperature, and sample cutting should be controlled for any test. Temperature of sample, identification of muscle, position within muscle, orientation along fibers, and even manner of pressing the corer to obtain the sample, may be critical if meaningful tests are to be made.

One modification of the apparatus involves substitution of a recording system for the spring scale with an increase in sensitivity and provision for a continuous record (Spencer et al., 1961). In this modification, the

FIGURE 12. Warner-Bratzler meat-shear apparatus. (Published with permission of the GR Electric Manufacturing Co., Manhattan, Kansas.)

mechanism is mounted horizontally and the plate attached to a cantilever beam equipped with strain gauges. The force of cutting on the sample is transferred to the plate, hence to the beam, causing a conversion to an electrical output, which is recorded.

A review of the history of mechanical methods of measuring shear resistance in meat, from Lehman's shear device in 1907 and including the Warner-Bratzler apparatus, Tressler penetrometer, Volodkevich's device with wedges, motorized grinders, a denture tenderometer, the shear press, and other instruments has been prepared by Pearson (1963).

Measuring Viscosity to Assess the Mechanical Characteristics of Foods

Viscosity, as previously indicated, is a resistance to flow and can be considered as the rate of flow per unit force. Cohesive forces between molecules (or particles) of a fluid cause the resistance to a change of form when a force is operative. Only homogeneous fluids have true viscosity; for some foods, like sauces, dressings, purees, melted substances, or batters, "consistency" may be a better term.

The unit of viscosity is the "poise." It is defined as a force of one dyne per square centimeter to produce a one centimeter per second difference in velocity between two planes separated by one centimeter of fluid. A centipoise is, of course, one hundredth of a poise.

Uniform fluids of relatively low viscosity can be measured by timed flow through a capillary tube. The Baker jelmeter is a simple form of such a viscosimeter. Extracts strained from cooked fruits that have more pectin are more viscous. If sufficiently acid, high-pectin juices will form good-quality fruit jellies with proportionately larger amounts of sugar. In use, the jelmeter is filled with juice and then allowed to drain exactly one minute. The lower end is closed at the end of this time and the level of the remaining liquid is read. The number, ranging from $\frac{1}{2}$ to over $1\frac{1}{4}$, indicates how many cups of sugar that each cup of juice will support in jell formation.

A viscosimeter that operates on the same flow principle was used recently to measure the viscosity of egg whites (Baldwin et al., 1967).

Estimates of products with greater viscosity (consistency) have also been made by observing the elapsed time of travel when a heavy sphere falls through a specified depth of the food material.

One type of viscosimeter measures the torque on a rotating spindle by means of a calibrated spring. The Brookfield Viscometer is an instrument of this type. Readings are made from the 0–100 scale on the dial. Calculation of viscosity (centipoises) is made conveniently by multiplication by factors that are dependent on instrument model, size of spindle, and speed of rotation. Models of the instrument are available with up to 7 spindles and 8 speeds, giving 56 ranges encompassing 0 to 8 million centipoises. Exact control of sample temperature is essential for meaningful readings of viscosity. For this disc-spindle viscosimeter, a modified sample holder has been devised that serves to stabilize readings on products that tend to separate (McCollum, 1967). Also, Figure 13 shows the instrument fitted with a special bar-type spindle and mounted on a helipath stand that will lower the spindle slowly through the test material. These adaptations make possible consistency measurements on products like batters and mashed potatoes.

Another instrument often used for measuring viscosities is the MacMichael viscosimeter (Figure 14). In it a plunger of known dimensions is suspended by a torsion wire of fixed length into a cup that is turned at constant speed (9 to 40 rpm) on a plate that can be heated.

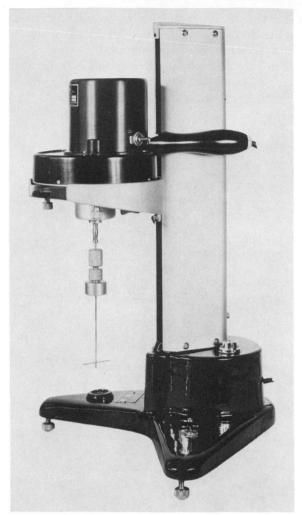

FIGURE 13. Brookfield viscometer adapted for consistency measurements. (Published with permission of Brookfield Engineering Laboratories, Stoughton, Massachusetts.)

The sample cup is filled accurately to control the depth of immersion of the plunger. As the sample turns, the resistance between sample and plunger causes a torsion on the wire. Readings are made on a scale attached to the plunger shaft. Scale units are arbitrary, "degrees M," each of which is $\frac{1}{300}$ of a circle. By standardizing the instrument against solutions of known viscosity, the readings can be converted to centipoises. A thermostat allows control of sample temperatures up to

300° F. The advantage of temperature control for measurement of viscosity in sauces, gravies, and other liquid or semiliquid foods at serving temperature can easily be recognized.

The consistency of semisolid food materials like batters and purees can be given a quantitative estimate by observing the spread of a controlled amount of product in a specified time period. The spread can

FIGURE 14. The MacMichael viscosimeter. (Published with permission of Fisher Scientific, Pittsburgh, Pennsylvania.)

be measured in one direction in a troughlike device (Bostwick Consistometer) or in all directions on a metal plate marked with concentric circles (Adams Consistometer).

Advanced students of consistency of fluids are referred to the mathematical analysis made by Charm (1962). Such fundamental explorations caution against oversimplification when relating an instrumental reading to specific characteristics. The complex nature of this group of properties requires that a high degree of correlation between physical methods and sensory evaluation be observed before measurements are considered valid.

Measurements of Elasticity and Adhesion

It is difficult to measure elasticity as an independent property of a food. Baked products with an open or foamlike structure will recover from a compression; however, when tensile force is applied to such products, breaking strength, not elasticity, is measured. Animal muscle fibers can be stretched and their recovery measured. Instrumentation designed to measure the tensile strength of fabrics can be applied to the fibers in vegetables, but their elastic recovery has not been measured. A standardized method of making measurement of dimensions after recovery may supply useful information.

Recent studies have included a measurement of Young's modulus of elasticity as an indication of the firmness of fruit and vegetable tissues. Sonic vibrations are passed through the product, and a curve showing amplitude versus frequency of vibration is recorded. From this the ratio of stress to strain within the food is obtained and interpreted as relative firmness (Finney et al., 1967).

Adhesiveness ("stickiness") of the surface is readily sensed by the fingers or in the mouth, but few physical methods have been suggested for making direct measurements of this characteristic. Indirectly, of course, the property contributes to shear measurements and is responsible for part of the resistance observed in withdrawing penetrating, compressing, or shearing devices from the samples tested.

One device designed to measure adhesion was developed by Heiss (1959) to test surface stickiness of candies. In this apparatus two moveable plates are attached horizontally from an upright beam marked with a graduated scale. The upper plate has a rubber lower surface and is attached to a calibrated spring mounted above. The lower plate holds a flat sample of the material to be tested. First, the upper plate is pressed on the sample with a constant weight and for a specified time (10 seconds). Then, the bottom plate is moved downward at a constant rate until the food and upper plate separate. The distance traveled before release is read from the graduated beam and serves to estimate the surface stickiness.

Using Microscopy, Photography, and Surface Printing to Reveal the Geometrical Characteristics of Texture

The size, shape, and orientation of particles or structures within foods give rise to certain textural characteristics that have been called "geometrical." Crystals, cells, fibers, spaces, or layers observed may indicate the sensory effects to be expected when the food is eaten. Some structural variation can be seen with the unaided eye, although normal vision is limited to details no smaller than about 0.1 mm. Even a hand lens extends this range considerably.

Through photography or ink printing, permanent records of structure can be made. Measurement of dimensions of large cells and thick cell walls is also possible from such reproductions.

Photography, with black-and-white or color conventional or rapid-development film, reveals structural detail that can be compared with verbal description of structure. Professional experience in photography is essential for best results, but a patient amateur can frequently obtain useful reproductions. If complete records of lens type, distance of focus, lens opening, exposure time, film type and speed, and lighting are made, the accumulated experience will be useful in later trials.

Microscopy is so frequently studied in biological-science courses that a description of instruments and techniques is probably unnecessary here. Microscopy combined with photography adds new dimensions to observation of food. Photomicrography has a practical limit of about $200\times$ magnification, dependent on lenses and film. Sample preparation and magnification should be specifically noted.

A new method of preparation of cake batters for microscopic study has been described by Pohl et al. (1968). By this technique, batters are first freeze-dried, then fixed and stained, subjected to infiltration with paraffin, and finally sectioned.

In advanced studies of structure, electron microscopy can extend the limits of observation to $100,000\times$ that of unaided vision. Future findings regarding the relationship of textural components may develop from subcellular studies.

Investigators of quality in baked products have developed a simple and inexpensive technique of recording grain, cell-wall structure, and general contour of foods. It is called "ink printing." Ink prints are made by pressing a cut surface of the food against an ink pad and then imprinting the inked surface against absorbent uncoated paper, like mimeograph or newsprint stock. The method was probably first described by Child and Purdy (1926). A regular stamp pad can be used, but for larger specimens a pad can be constructed. Blotting paper or several layers of an absorbent fabric (like washed flannel) can be attached to a piece of soft wood or cardboard; then a thin covering of muslin or linen is secured tightly over the pad by stapling. The pad is moistened by brushing on mimeograph or stamp-pad ink.

A variation of the technique has been reported (Barnard, 1966) by which foam-backed table padding is glued to cardboard or Masonite to form the pad. Tempera color diluted to the thickness of the cream is applied evenly to the foam surface. Separate pads are made for various colors.

Techniques of cutting samples without damage, of pressing specimens against the pad without distortion, and of maintaining the pad surface are quickly mastered. Permanent and informative records are made this way with little cost.

MEASUREMENT OF FLAVOR

The distinguishing characteristics of flavor are odors (aroma) rather than tastes. As one sniffs a food, movement of air over the olfactory epithelium, located in the upper part of the nasal cavity, initiates sensations. Compounds present in air in dilutions as low as several parts-per-billion (ppb) can induce odor response. Receptor cells in the epithelium of the sensory area have olfactory rods (hairs) that extend into the surface mucus. These receptors produce minute electrical discharges that are transmitted along the olfactory nerve to the olfactory bulb, where synapse occurs. The pulse then follows the olfactory tract to the olfactory area at the base of the frontal lobe of the brain (Amerine, 1965). Interpretation, of course, occurs at this point.

Several theories have been proposed to explain how the receptor structures can function to detect highly complex odors. It is difficult to understand how a limited number of receptor sites can yield aroma sensations of almost limitless subtlety. Explanations are based on intramolecular vibrations owing to bonding, or on molecular interactions affecting properties (like solubility), or possibly on the size and shape of molecules. Clarification of the physiological aspects of aroma detection may lead to methods for direct and objective measurement of flavor quality based on neural response. Meanwhile, flavor-inducing components are being actively investigated through chemical and physical analyses.

Taste differs from smell in that its sensations are produced by substances in solution rather than by compounds volatilized in air (Amerine, 1965). On the tongue one can see four kinds of papillae. Some of these contain many taste buds that act as receptors of chemical stimulation from sweet, sour, salty, or bitter substances. Nerves lead from taste buds via the seventh or ninth cranial nerve to the medulla, on to the thalamus, and finally to rather nonspecific parts of the cerebral cortex. The taste buds vary in the way they respond. Their physiological and biochemical nature is not fully understood.

The entire flavor response includes not only aroma and taste, but also pressure, temperature effects, and pain. These tactile sensations modify the effects of other stimuli. When one also considers the influences of psychological effects of surroundings and experience, it is not surprising that "flavor" is a complex phenomenon. Therein lies its unique challenge.

Objective Tests that Relate to Tastes

Sweetness of sirups, juices, or water extractions from foods that contain sugars can be estimated by measurement of refraction of light. A refractometer is an instrument used to measure soluble components. This method is specific for pure solutions of sucrose but is widely employed to obtain approximate values for solutions containing invert sugar and soluble nonsugar compounds.

For certain models of refractometers, the following method applies. The principle applies with some changes to other models. A drop of the sample is introduced between a refracting prism and another prism against which light is directed. As observed through the eyepiece, the border line image (total reflection) is brought to the crossbars of the lighted circle by the movement of a handwheel. The border line is made achromatic by adjusting the compensator dial and is then repositioned accurately. In some refractometers a second eyepiece allows reading percent soluble solids and index numbers on a transparent glass plate. The soluble solids scale is based on the International Sucrose Tables; it can be read to 0.5 percent and estimated to 0.1 percent. Refractive indices can be read to the fourth decimal. The refractive index is the ratio of the sine of the angle of incidence to the sine of the angle of refraction. In making this measurement values are adjusted if the temperature is above or below 28° centigrade.

Tests of sirups used in canning fruits illustrate the influence of percent sugar (degrees Brix) on taste acceptance. High sugar concentration (50° or 55° Brix) was preferred with the acid flavor of raspberries, and lower sugar concentration was preferred for less-acid strawberries (40° to 50° Brix) in a study by Board et al. (1966). A refractometer was used to test the sirups.

Acidity is measured conveniently by means of a pH meter. The most common form of this instrument makes use of a glass electrode that consists of a bulb of special glass filled with an electrolyte in contact with a metallic electrode. When the bulb is placed in a liquid or moist food, potential difference develops between the inner electrolyte and the liquid of the food. This potential is measured by combining the glass electrode with a standard calomel electrode and determining the voltage of the system. Recently, the functions of the two electrodes have been combined into a single device that contains two Ag-AgCl half cells. Voltage developed from the system is amplified and then measured potentiometrically on a 0–14 log scale.

Sometimes it is useful to know, not only the activity of the H^+ ions, but also the percent of total acids. All the acid-forming molecules may not be ionized until the equilibrium is shifted during neutralization. Titration with a standardized base to a pH near 7 (or to a color change of a standard indicator) will allow calculation of the amount of acid. The content is expressed as grams of anhydrous acid (example, citric) per 100 g of the product.

Flavor balance of a fruit is indicated by its soluble-solids/acid ratio. This ratio is determined by dividing the percent of soluble solids (degrees Brix) by the percent of citric acid in the sample. An illustration of the use of this relationship is its application to evaluation of strawberry flavor (Wolford et al., 1961).

Saltiness is the response of taste receptors to compounds that contain certain cations (ammonium, sodium, potassium, calcium, magnesium, or lithium) associated with anions like SO_4, Cl, Br, I, HCO_3, or NO_3. Since any one receptor in the taste bud may respond to more than one of the four basic tastes (Amerine, 1965), the intensity of "saltiness" depends on other taste stimuli being sensed at the same time. It is difficult, therefore, to find an objective measurement that will give evidence of the saltiness of a food as perceived in the mouth.

Since sodium chloride and other sodium salts are used liberally in food preparation or preservation, analysis for the Na^+ ion becomes an indication of the saltiness to be expected.

Flame photometric methods for determination of sodium and/or potassium are recognized as official (A.O.A.C., 1970). Dilute solutions are first prepared from ashed samples of the food. Then these solutions are atomized in a flame and the altered composition of the light analyzed by a spectrophotometer. Concentrations of the element in a food are calculated by comparison with measurements on standard solutions of pure compounds tested by the same flame-photometric technique.

The availability of a new type of electrode (Rechnitz, 1967) makes it possible to measure specific ions, like Na^+, electrometrically. A special electrode selecting specific ions and a calomel reference electrode can be used with several models of pH meters. A calibration curve is established relating the concentration of a salt to electrode potential in millivolts. The electrodes are placed in a representative sample of the food, or a dilution of it, the instrument read, and the ion content calculated from the calibration curve. Recent experience indicates that certain substances in food mixtures, like fats, may interfere with the response of electrodes; also the water content of the food is important. Improved techniques are being sought for application of the electrometric method to foods.

Bitterness, like the other taste sensations, is not stimulated by a single compound. However, when the major compound causing bitterness in any particular food is known, direct chemical analysis may establish the probable level of bitterness in the product.

Tannins occur in foods, producing both bitterness and astringency. Vegetables, juices, beverages (wines, beer, tea, and coffee), essential oils, and fruit preserves are among the foods that have an appreciable but variable tannin content. The tannins in foods are considered to be catechins, leucoanthocyanins, and similar compounds (Meyer, 1960). In one method of chemical analysis of tannin compounds, a water extract of the food is reacted with a Folin-Denis solution (phosphomolybdic acid with sodium tungstate) to develop a blue color, the absorbance of which is read at 725 mμ with a spectrophotometer (Swain and Hillis, 1959).

Investigation of Volatiles Causing Aroma in Foods

The human olfactory system is so sensitive to minor components in aroma that chemical analysis to disclose the causative substances requires instrumentation and technical skill of a high order. An introduction to this frontier of food study may be found in recent journal summaries (Hornstein and Teranishi, 1967) and reports of symposia (American Chemical Society, 1966; Oregon State University, 1967).

To detect minute concentrations of substances that have odor, micro-analytical methods are employed. Aroma substances can be obtained from a food by such methods as freeze-condensation of volatiles, precipitation of the chemically active compounds of the vapor, or solvent extraction followed by solvent removal. Then separation of the many components may be carried out by chromatographic techniques in their several forms (paper, column, or gas-liquid partition chromatography). Some evidence as to the identity of the individual compounds is obtained from sensory and instrumental observations during the separation procedures, but confirmation of the presence of specific compounds requires additional analyses. Infrared spectroscopy and mass spectroscopy are among the techniques that may identify specific components.

As an example of the application of these methods, a recent study of the volatile components of pineapple (Creveling et al., 1968) can be cited. Gas chromatographic retention times, infrared-spectrographic analysis, and mass and nuclear magnetic resonance spectroscopy yielded complementary data that together confirmed the compounds present. Such techniques are revealing the nature of complex flavor-stimulating mixtures that have been a mystery during all preceding time.

Once established, the compounds found present in aroma fractions must be shown to have importance in the flavor. This is done by correlation with controlled organoleptic tests. If the constituents are important to flavor, quantitative procedures for measuring those compounds can be developed. Recently, a method of correlating gas-chromatographic data with flavor, through a stepwise discriminant analysis for classifying samples, was developed that involved the use of a computer (Powers and Keith, 1968). These advanced techniques are usually not available to students of experimental foods, but hold interest for advanced study.

Not only natural components but also those developed in cookery, preservation, or storage are studied. With each passing year, more food is processed for storage for indefinite lengths of time and often under conditions of varying temperature. Also, the composition of foods is changing; for example, unsaturated fats are used in increased amounts. The factors of time and temperature affect the stability of the stored fats. Rancidity has become a troublesome flavor defect. A method (Tarladgis et al., 1964) can be recommended to measure the presence of malonaldehyde, which is a substance associated with oxidative rancidity. When this off-flavor is tested in stored foods, chemical analysis can support the organoleptic evaluations.

Apparatus in Aroma Assessment

Food aroma studies may in the future be assisted by an "artificial electrical nose." Dravnieks (1961) has developed an instrument based on the assumption that absorption is one link in the physiological process of odor perception. The instrument measures the contact-potential changes caused by a vapor passing over rotating plates coated with solids of differing chemical reactivity. Just as in the olfactory mechanism, an electrical impulse is the signal indicating reception of a stimulating volatile.

Another approach to quantifying odor has been through modification of the Elsberg olfactometer. The idea for the olfactometer originated with a neurosurgeon by that name. He used the device for detection of brain tumors on the olfactory nerve tract by asking patients to sniff odor samples of known strengths. The odor gas was passed by pressure within a sample bottle into a glass nosepiece inserted in a nostril. The olfactometer has been modified to include a motor-driven syringe plunger that delivers the gaseous sample to the subject's nose. Volatiles from packaged foods can be confined and delivered for detection by this method.

Selection of the Best Test

Although many tests have been described in the foregoing chapter, many others have been omitted. Entire books could be written on quality evaluation of a single class of food or individual quality characteristic. What has been included is an organized summary of typical "objective" methods. Almost every investigator adapts established techniques to the conditions of the experiment or originates totally new methods of measuring characteristics. A test will serve its purpose only if evidence can be established that the property being measured is related to a characteristic important to human response. High correlation between the data from an objective test with judgment by controlled sensory panels can establish the accuracy of the procedure. Availability of apparatus or materials, knowledge of and skill in performing laboratory tests, and creative analysis of the experiment will suggest the choice of objective method. The rewards of such a choice in terms of precision, extent of observations, and economy in the use of time can be appreciable.

References

COLOR

Borchgrevink, N. C., and H. Charley. 1966. Color of cooked carrots related to carotene content. *J. Am. Dietet. Assoc. 49*, 116.

Bowers, J. A., D. L. Harrison, and D. H. Kropf. 1968. Browning and associated properties of porcine muscle. *J. Food Sci. 33*, 147.

Brice, B. A. 1954. The measurement and specification of color. *Color in Foods— A Symposium,* Quartermaster Research and Development, National Academy of Science, National Research Council, Washington, D.C.

Greene, B. E. 1966. Lipid oxidation and pigment changes in fresh and irradiated beef. Ph.D. dissertation, Florida State University Library, Tallahassee, Florida.

Gregory, R. L. 1966. *Eye and Brain, The Psychology of Seeing.* World University Library, McGraw-Hill Book Co., New York.

Judd, D. B. 1952. *Color in Business, Science, and Industry.* John Wiley and Sons, New York.

Kramer, A., and B. A. Twigg. 1962. *Fundamentals of Quality Control for the Food Industry*. Avi Publ. Co., Westport, Conn.

Little, A. C., C. O. Chichester, and G. Mackinney. 1958. On color measurements of foods. *Food Technol. 12*, 403.

Mackinney, G., and C. O. Chichester. 1954. The color problem in foods. *Advances in Food Research 5*, 301.

Mackinney, G., and A. C. Little. 1962. *Color of Foods*. Avi Publ. Co., Westport, Conn.

Mackinney, G., A. Little, and L. Brinner. 1966. Visual appearance of foods. *Food Technol. 20*, 1300.

Maerz, A., and M. R. Paul. 1930. *A Dictionary of Color*. McGraw-Hill Publ. Co., New York.

Magnuson Engineers, Inc., San Jose, California.

Munsell Color Co., Baltimore, Maryland.

Nickerson, D. 1940. History of the Munsell color system and its scientific application. *J. Optical Soc. Am. 30*, 575.

Nickerson, D. 1946. Color measurement and its application to the grading of agricultural products. *U.S. Dept. Agr. Misc. Publ. No. 580*.

Noble, I. T. 1958. Effect of holding temperature on ascorbic acid and color in frozen and cooked asparagus. *J. Home Econ. 50*, 780.

Worthington, O. J. 1961. The correlation of color measurements on canned purple plums with consumer acceptability. *Food Technol. 15*, 283.

Zolber, K. K., and M. Jacobson. 1962. Quality of Redhaven and Earlihale peaches frozen by four methods. *J. Home Econ. 54*, 387.

TEXTURE

Baldwin, R. E., J. C. Mather, R. Upchurch, and D. M. Breidenstein. 1967. Effects of microwaves on egg white. 1. Characteristics of coagulation. *J. Food Sci. 32*, 305.

Barnard, K. M. 1966. New materials and comparisons of volume, texture, and contour of baked products. *J. Home Econ. 58*, 479.

Black, W. H., K. F. Warner, and C. V. Wilson. 1931. Beef production as affected by grade of steer and feeding of grain supplement on grass. *U.S. D.A. Tech. Bull. 217*.

Bourne, M. C., J. C. Moyer, and D. B. Hand. 1966. Measurement of food texture by a universal testing machine. *Food Technol. 20*, 522.

Charm, S. E. 1962. The nature and role of fluid consistency in food engineering applications. *Adv. in Food Res. 11*, 355.

Child, A. M., and D. I. Purdy. 1926. Method for a graphic record of texture, volume, and contour of cakes. *Cereal Chem. 3*, 57.

Deethardt, D. E., L. M. Burrill, and C. W. Carlson. 1965. Relationships of egg yolk color to the quality of sponge cake. *Food Technol. 19*, 73.

Finney, E. E. Jr., I. Ben Gera, and D. R. Massie. 1967. An objective evaluation of changes in firmness of ripening bananas using a sonic technique. *J. Food Sci. 32*, 642.

Friedman, H. H., J. E. Whitney, and A. S. Szczesniak. 1963. The texturometer —A new instrument for objective texture measurement. *J. Food Sci. 28*, 390.

Hawkins, L., and C. E. Sando. 1920. Effect of temperature on the resistance to wounding of certain small fruits and cherries. *U.S.D.A. Bull. 830.*

Heiss, R. 1959. Prevention of stickiness and graining in stored hard candies. *Food Technol. 13*, 433.

Hodgman, C. D., ed. 1962. *Handbook of Chemistry and Physics.* 44th ed., p. 3201. Chemical Rubber Publ. Co., Cleveland, Ohio.

Jacobson, M., and G. Armbruster. 1968. A recording micro-penetrometer, design and application. *Food Technol. 22*, 1007.

Kamujoso, B. W. T., and B. S. Luh. 1967. Texture, pectin and syrup viscosity of canned cling peaches. *Food Technol. 21*, 457.

Kramer, A., and K. Aamlid. 1953. The shear-press, an instrument for measuring quality of foods. III. Application to peas. *Proc. Am. Soc. Hort. Sci. 61*, 417.

Lebermann, K. W., A. I. Nelson, and M. P. Steinberg. 1968. Post-Harvest changes of broccoli stored in modified atmospheres. 2. Acidity and its influence on texture and chlorophyll retention of the stalks. *Food Technol. 22*, 490.

Mannheim, N. C., and A. Bakal. 1968. An instument for evaluating firmness of grapefruit segments. *Food Technol. 22*, 331.

Matz, S. A. 1962. *Food Texture.* Avi. Publ. Co., Westport, Conn.

McCollum, J. P., and Y. H. Foda. 1967. A modified sample holder for determining viscosity of a diphasic fluid. *J. Food Sci. 32*, 562.

Pearson, A. M. 1963. Objective and subjective measurements for meat tenderness. *Proceedings, Meat Tenderness Symposium.* Campbell Soup Co., Camden, N.J.

Platt, W., and R. Powers. 1940. Compressibility of bread crumb. *Cereal Chem. 17*, 60.

Pohl, P. H., A. C. Mackey, and B. L. Cornelia. 1968. Freeze-drying cake batter for microscopic study. *J. Food Sci. 33*, 318.

Pomeranz, Y., G. L. Rubenthaler, R. D. Daftary, and K. F. Finney. 1966. Effects of lipids on bread baked from flours varying widely in bread-making potentialities. *Food Technol. 20*, 1225.

Reeve, R. M., B. Feinberg, F. P. Boyle, and G. K. Notter. 1968. Deterioration of frozen par-fried potatoes upon holding after thawing. 2. Composition, histology and objective measurements of texture. *Food Technol. 22*, 208.

Smith, G. C., C. W. Spaeth, Z. I. Carpenter, G. T. King, and K. E. Hoke. 1968.

The effects of freezing, frozen storage conditions and degree of doneness on lamb palatability characteristics. *J. Food Sci. 33*, 19.

Spencer, J. V., M. Jacobson, and J. T. Kimbrell. 1961. A research note—recording strain-gage shear apparatus. *Food Technol. 16*, 113.

Tuomy, J. M., and R. L. Helmer. 1967. The effect of freeze-drying on the longissimus dorsi muscle of pork. *Food Technol. 21*, 653.

FLAVOR

American Chemical Society. 1966. *Flavor Chemistry, A Symposium*. Adv. in Chemistry Series 56. Am. Chem. Soc. Publ., Washington, D.C.

Amerine, M. A., R. M. Pangborn, and E. B. Roessler. 1965. *Principles of Sensory Evaluation of Food*. Academic Press, New York.

Association of Official Analytical Chemists. 1970. *Official Methods of Analysis*, p. 22. A.O.A.C., Washington, D.C.

Board, P. W., R. A. Gallop, and W. M. Sykes. 1966. Quality of canned berry fruits. 1. The influence of sucrose concentration and of low-methoxyl pectin added to the syrup. *Food Technol. 20*, 1203.

Creveling, R. K., R. M. Silverstein, and W. G. Jennings. 1968. Volatile components of pineapple. *J. Food Sci. 33*, 284.

Crocker, E. C. 1945. *Flavor*. McGraw-Hill Book Co., New York.

Crocker, E. C., and L. F. Henderson. 1927. Odor directory. American Perfumer *22*, 325.

Dravnieks, A. 1961. ARF lays groundwork for synthetic nose. *Chem. and Eng. News 39* (14), 56.

Hornstein, I., and R. Teranishi. 1967. The chemistry of flavor. *Chem. and Eng. News 45* (14), 92.

Meyer, Lillian H. 1960. *Food Chemistry*, p. 250. Reinhold Publ. Co., New York.

Oregon State University. 1967. *Symposium on Foods: The Chemistry and Physiology of Flavors*. Avi Publ. Co., Westport, Conn.

Powers, J. J., and E. S. Keith. 1968. Stepwise discriminant analysis of gas chromatographic data as an aid in classifying the flavor quality of foods. *J. Food Sci. 33*, 207.

Rechnitz, G. A. 1967. Ion-selective electrodes. *Chem. and Eng. News 45* (24), 146.

Swain, T., and W. E. Hillis. 1959. The phenolic constituents of Prunus domestica. 1. The quantitative analysis of phenolic constituents. *J. Sci. Food Agr. 10*, 63.

Tarladgis, B. G, A. M. Pearson, and L. R. Dugan. 1964. Chemistry of the 2-thiobarbituric acid test for determination of oxidative rancidity in foods. 11. Formation of the TBA-malonaldehyde complex without acid-heat treatment. *J. Sci. Food Agr. 15*, 602.

Wolford, E. R., J. A. Sacklin, and C. D. Schwartze. 1961. Evaluation of new strawberry varieties for freezing and preserving. *Food Technol. 15*, 152.

RECENT DOCTORAL RESEARCH STUDIES ON FOODS IN WHICH OBJECTIVE MEA-
SUREMENTS WERE APPLIED. FROM DISSERTATION ABSTRACTS B (SCIENCES AND
ENGINEERING) VOL. 26, 27, 28 AND 29 (1966–1969)

Armbruster, Gertrude   Washington State University   1965
*Microscopic, Physical, and Sensory Measurements of Characteristics of Texture
of Fresh and Frozen Strawberries.*
    Microscopic observations of stained sections; shear press; micropenetro-
    meter designed.

Badenhop, A. F.   The Ohio State University   1966
*A Quantitative and Qualitative Study of Some of the Volatile Components in
Processed Tomato Juice.*
    Infrared absorption spectrophometry; mass spectrometry; nuclear mag-
    netic resonance analysis.

Buck, E. M.   University of Massachusetts   1966
*The Effect of Stretch-Tension During Rigor on Fiber Diameter, Fiber Extensi-
bility, and Tenderness of Bovine Longissimus Dorsi Muscle.*
    Shear press; histological preparation; photomicrographs.

Burgheimer, Yvonne F.   University of Illinois   1968
Antioxidant Activity of Aquaeous Extracts of Several Edible Plant Materials.
    Oxygen absorption; peroxide and TBA values; flavor scores.

Chaudhry, Mohammad S.   Kansas State University   1968
Preparation and Evaluation of Attas and Chapatis from U.S. Wheats.
    Farinograph and extensigraph values; organoleptic evaluation.

Clydesdale, F. M.   University of Massachusetts   1966
*Chlorophyllase Activity in Green Vegetables with Reference to Pigment Sta-
bility in Thermal Processing.*
    Differential colorimeter used.

Collins, J. L.   University of Maryland   1965
*Effect of Calcium Ion-Structural Polysaccharide Interaction on Texture of Pro-
cessed Apple Slices.*
    Shear measurements on slices; chromatograms; calcium measured photo-
    metrically and autoradiogramed.

Darivingas, G. V.   Oregon State University   1966
Thermal and Enzymatic Degradation of Raspberry Anthocyanins.
    Paper chromatographic method; spectrophotometric techniques.

Davis, C. O.   Cornell University   1967
Some Factors Influencing Translucency in Frozen Cream of Potato Soup.
    Starch-iodine colorimeter measurement; amylograph measurements of
    viscosity.

Deck, R. E.   Rutgers—The State University   1968
The Chemistry of Potato Chip Flavor.
    Gas chromatography; infrared and mass spectroscopy.

Everson, T. C.   The University of Wisconsin   1968
Utilization of Acoustical Measurements for the Estimation of a Gross Composition of Condensed Skimmilk and for the Determination of Rennet Coagulation Time in Milk.
Ultrasonic measurements; chemical analysis.

Fox, J. D.   Louisiana State University and   1968
Agricultural and Mechanical College
Quantitation and Characterization of Acid Mucopolysaccharides of Bovine Muscle and Their Relationship to Certain Quality Attributes.
Water binding; shear values.

Fuleki, T.   University of Massachusetts   1967
Development of Quantitative Methods for Individual Anthocyanins in Cranberry and Cranberry Products.
Chemical precipitation; paper chromatography; densitometer; planimeter measurements.

Greene, Barbara E.   Florida State University   1966
Lipid Oxidation and Pigment Changes in Fresh and Irradiated Beef.
TBA analysis; absorbance spectra; reflectance spectrophometry of pigments.

Harvey, Mary Ann   University of Tennessee   1965
Effect of Re-Use of Frying Fat from Selected Food Service Establishments and on the Lipid Components of Fried Shrimp.
Viscosity; silicic acid column fractionation; phospholipid analysis; thin-layer and gas liquid chromatography.

Herz, Karl O.   Rutgers—The State University   1968
A Study of the Nature of Boiled Beef Flavor.
Gas chromatography, infrared and mass spectrometry.

Hirano, Yoshio   The Florida State University   1968
Antioxidants in Brassica Rapa.
Polarographic oxygen analysis.

Hudspeth, J. P.   University of Georgia   1968
A Study of the Emulsifying Capacity of the Salt Soluble Proteins of Poultry Meat.
Viscosity; electrophoresis.

Lindsay, R. A.   Oregon State University   1965
Flavor Chemistry of Butter Culture.
Gas chromatography, mass spectrometry.

Liska, B. J.   Purdue University   1965
The Effect of Ration and Cooking Treatment on the Retention of Chlorinated Insecticides in Edible Chicken Tissue.
Gas chromatography; moisture determination; infrared analyses.

Macy, R. L.   University of Missouri   1966
Acid-Extractable Flavor and Aroma Constituents of Beef, Lamb and Pork.

Chemical tests of nucleotides, creatine and creatinine, nitrogen, carbohydrate; moisture determined.

Meyer, Dorothy M.   Purdue University   1966
Hypoxanthine-Uric Acid and Apparent Inosinic Acid Content and Sensory Evaluation of Selected Beef Muscles.

Moisture, pH; inosinic acid and hypoxanthine-uric acid determined.

Motawi, Kamal El-Din H.   Michigan State University   1966
Enzymatic Systems and Substrates Involved in Freestone Peach Browning.

Phenolic content analyzed; paper chromatography; spectrophotometric techniques.

Pankey, R. D.   Purdue University   1967
The Effect of Dietary Fats on Some Chemical and Functional Properties of Eggs and on Some Chemical Properties of Lipids of Liver, Blood, and Depot Fat of the Hen.

Emulsification capacity; cake volumes measured.

Parliment, T. H.   University of Massachusetts   1965
An investigation on the Origin and Occurrence of Delta-Lactones in Heated Milk Fat.

Gas chromatography; infrared and mass spectroscopy; polystyrene gel filtration; silica gel chromatography; thin layer chromatography.

Peng, Chung-Yen   Michigan State University   1965
Some Studies on the Composition and Structure of Phospholipids in Chicken Muscle.

Silicic acid column chromatography; thin-layer chromatography; gas-liquid chromatography; infrared spectral analysis.

Rao, A. V.   Oregon State University   1967
The Effect of Freezing and Freeze-Drying on the Physico-Chemical Changes in Northwest Strawberries.

Soluble solids, pH, titratable acidity, pectins, cellulose, ash determined.

Reinke, W. C.   Cornell University   1967
Investigations on Egg Yolk Gelation.

Column chromatography; paper and disc electrophoresis; phase contrast microscopy; chemical analyses.

Rhee, Ki Soon (Choi)   Florida State University   1965
Lipoxidase and Lipid Oxidation in Vegetables.

Polarographic method for measuring enzyme activity developed; TBA test adapted.

Rogers, Patricia J. B.   Kansas State University   1966
Heat Induced Changes in Turkey Muscle as Related to Moisture Retention.

Moisture determinations (total, centrifuged, expressed); pH; Warner-Bratzler shear values.

Selby, Anne E.   University of Illinois   1967
A Comparison of Changes Occurring in Starch Pastes During Retrogradation.

X-ray diffraction; transmittance and reflectance of light; iodine affinity; enzyme susceptibility; photomicrography.

Sharon, Hilbert D.   Texas A & M University   1965
Organoleptic, Chemical, Biochemical and Physical Studies on the Quality of Spanish-Type Peanuts.

Optical density and refractive index of oil; kernel specific gravity and kernel size.

Smith, Gary C.   Texas A & M University   1968
Effects of Maturational, Physical and Chemical Changes on Ovine Carcass Composition, Quality and Palatability.

Chemical Analyses; histological; organoleptic tests.

Taki, Ghazi H.   University of Florida   1965
Physical and Chemical Changes Occurring in Beef, Post-Mortem, as Related to Tenderness and Other Quality Characteristics.

Warner-Bratzler shear used; starch gel electrophoresis.

Turkki, Pirkko Reetta   University of Tennessee   1965
Relation of Phospholipids to Other Tissue Components in Two Beef Muscles.

Analysis of total lipid, phospholipid, DNA, and total nitrogen; thin-layer chromatography.

Wells, Gordon H.   Michigan State University   1966
Tenderness of Freeze-Dried Chicken with Emphasis on Enzyme Treatments.

Warner-Bratzler shear test; shear press measurements.

Index